Until recently the Isma'ilis, a major Shi'i Muslim community, were studied and judged almost exclusively on the basis of the hostile accounts of their Muslim enemies and the fanciful tales of the Crusaders and other occidental sources. As a result, numerous misconceptions and legends were disseminated about the teachings and practices of the Isma'ilis, made famous in European tradition as the Assassins. In the 1930s, however, authentic Isma'ili texts began to be recovered on a large scale from private collections in the Yemen, Syria, Iran, Central Asia and India which threw new light on mediaeval Isma'ili history and thought. This collective volume, the first major effort of its kind in this branch of Islamic studies, brings together some of the original results of modern scholarship in the area, written by leading contemporary authorities as well as some distinguished Islamists.

The chapters in the book, covering selected themes and developments related to the pre-Fatimid, Fatimid and Nizārī phases of Isma'ili history, deal with a wide variety of topics ranging from the Qarmaṭīs of Baḥrayn and their relations with the Fatimids, the earliest cosmological doctrine of the Isma'ilis, the traditions of learning and the development of jurisprudence under the Fatimids, to the Isma'ili perceptions of the 'other', the origins of the Nizārī Isma'ili movement, Saljuq perspectives on the early Nizārīs, a new perspective on Naṣīr al-Dīn al-Ṭūsī's religious affiliations, and the ginanic literary tradition of the Isma'ili Khojas of the Indian subcontinent. As a significant contribution to modern Isma'ili studies, this book serves to underline the richness of the Isma'ilis' literary heritage and the diversity of their religio-political experience and intellectual traditions.

MEDIAEVAL ISMA'ILI
HISTORY AND THOUGHT

MEDIAEVAL ISMAʿILI HISTORY AND THOUGHT

EDITED BY

FARHAD DAFTARY

CAMBRIDGE
UNIVERSITY PRESS

Published by the Press Syndicate of the University of Cambridge
The Pitt Building, Trumpington Street, Cambridge CB2 1RP
40 West 20th Street, New York, NY 10011-4211, USA
10 Stamford Road, Oakleigh, Melbourne 3166, Australia

First published 1996

Printed in Great Britain at the University Press, Cambridge

A catalogue record for this book is available from the British Library

Library of Congress cataloguing in publication data

Mediaeval Isma'ili history and thought / edited by Farhad Daftary.
p. cm.
Includes bibliographical references and index.
ISBN 0 521 45140 X
1. Ismailites – History. I. Daftary, Farhad.
BP195.I8M43 1996
297'.822'0902 – dc20 95-21159 CIP

ISBN 0 521 45140 X hardback

VN

To the memory of Wladimir Ivanow (1886–1970),
a pioneer in modern Isma'ili studies

Contents

Preface

INITIATED IN the 1930s, the modern progress in Isma'ili studies has continued at an astonishingly swift pace during the last few decades. As a result, many aspects of Isma'ili history and thought are no longer shrouded in mystery; and the ground has been effectively prepared for the long-overdue dispelling of the major mediaeval myths of the Isma'ilis. I have been convinced for several years now of the value of collecting in one volume some of the scattered results of modern scholarship in Isma'ili studies, dealing especially with selective subjects which had not previously received sufficient treatment in scholarly literature. Such a collection could serve to show the richness of the literary heritage of the Isma'ilis and the diversity of their religio-political experience and intellectual traditions, and, hopefully, make possible a better understanding of Isma'ilism.

With these aims in mind, the present project was conceived in 1992 and invitations were sent out to some of the leading scholars of Isma'ili studies to write original essays for a collective volume, offering the results of many decades of research and expertise in the field. Professor W. Madelung, in addition to contributing a new article, also kindly agreed to the inclusion in this volume of a somewhat updated English version of his classic study of the Qarmaṭīs of Baḥrayn and their relations with the Fatimids. Invitations for contributions were extended also to a number of other distinguished scholars who, though not particularly active in Isma'ili studies, could shed light on specific issues of Isma'ili history drawing on their own specialized knowledge of Islamic and Iranian studies. The results of this collaborative effort of Isma'ili and non-Isma'ili scholars, of both Eastern and Western origins, are now offered in this volume. Needless to add that none of the individual contributors would necessarily subscribe to all the views or interpretations expressed in this book. Indeed, responsibility for the contents of each chapter rests solely with the author of that chapter.

I would like to extend my sincerest gratitude to all the eminent scholars who participated in this joint project. I would also like to thank Azizeh Azodi who in accordance with her own high standards of scholarship translated three of the essays contributed by Professors W. Madelung and H. Halm from German into English. I owe special debts of gratitude to Dr Patricia Crone who read an earlier draft of the book and made many valuable suggestions for its improvement, and to Farhad Hakimzadeh who searched for the cover illustration. Finally, it remains to record my thanks to Gill Thomas who assisted in the initiation of this volume and to Marigold Acland who ensured its orderly completion. May this volume prove to represent yet another step forward in the modern progress in Isma'ili studies, and may it be a source of satisfaction to all those involved in its production.

F. D.

Note on transliteration and abbreviations

THE SYSTEM of transliteration used in this book for the Arabic and Persian scripts is essentially the same as that adopted in the new edition of *The Encyclopaedia of Islam*, with a few modifications, namely *ch* for *č*, *j* for *dj*, and *q* for *ḳ*. Furthermore, an attempt has been made to reproduce the more elaborate vowel system of Turkish and Mongol names, thus Hülegü and not Hūlāgū. Diacritical marks are dispensed with, except those for *ʿayn* and *hamza*, for some of the dynastic and community names which occur frequently in the book.

BIFAO	*Bulletin de l'Institut Français d'Archéologie Orientale*
BSO(A)S	*Bulletin of the School of Oriental (and African) Studies*
EI	*The Encyclopaedia of Islam*, lst edition
EI2	*The Encyclopaedia of Islam*, New edition
EIR	*Encyclopaedia Iranica*
IJMES	*International Journal of Middle East Studies*
JAOS	*Journal of the American Oriental Society*
JBBRAS	*Journal of the Bombay Branch of the Royal Asiatic Society*
JRAS	*Journal of the Royal Asiatic Society*
NS	New Series
SEI	*Shorter Encyclopaedia of Islam*
WO	*Die Welt des Orients*
ZDMG	*Zeitschrift der Deutschen Morgenländischen Gesellschaft*

Notes on the contributors

ABBAS AMANAT is Professor of History at Yale University, and Editor of *Iranian Studies*, published by the Society for Iranian Studies. He is also a Consulting Editor of *Encyclopaedia Iranica*, to which he has been a regular contributor. A specialist in Persian history and religious movements, his books include *Cities and Trade: Consul Abbott on the Economy and Society of Iran, 1847–1866* (London, 1983), *Resurrection and Renewal: The Making of the Babi Movement in Iran* (Ithaca, 1989), and *The Pivot of the Universe: Monarchy under Nasir al-Din Shah Qajar of Iran* (Berkeley, 1996). His shorter studies have been published in the learned journals.

ALI S. ASANI is Professor of the Practice of Indo-Muslim Languages and Cultures at Harvard University. A specialist in Isma'ili literary traditions of the Indian subcontinent, he is the author of *The Būjh Nirañjan: An Ismaili Mystical Poem* (Cambridge, Mass., 1991) and numerous shorter studies on the ginanic literature of the Nizārī Isma'ilis. He has recently published his catalogue of *The Harvard Collection of Ismaili Literature in Indic Languages* (Boston, 1992), a pioneering survey of some 1,350 texts and manuscripts in the regional languages of South Asia.

C. EDMUND BOSWORTH, a leading British Islamist and (Emeritus) Professor of Arabic Studies at the University of Manchester, is Co-editor of the *Encyclopaedia of Islam* and a Consulting Editor of *Encyclopaedia Iranica*, and has contributed extensively to both of these encyclopaedias. He is also Co-editor of *Iran* (Journal of the British Institute of Persian Studies). Professor Bosworth was on the Editorial Board of *The Cambridge History of Iran*, and contributed several chapters to Volumes III, IV and V of that work, as well as to *The*

Cambridge History of Arabic Literature. He is the author of numerous books, including *The Ghaznavids* (Edinburgh, 1963), *The Islamic Dynasties*, Islamic Surveys (Edinburgh, 1967), *Sīstān under the Arabs* (Rome, 1968), *The Later Ghaznavids* (Edinburgh, 1977), and *The History of the Saffarids of Sistan and the Maliks of Nimruz* (Costa Mesa, Calif., and New York, 1994). He has recently translated into English three volumes of *The History of al-Ṭabarī*, for the Bibliotheca Persica series; and two volumes of his numerous scholarly articles on Islamic and Iranian history have already appeared in the Variorum Collected Studies series.

HAMID DABASHI is Associate Professor of Persian Studies at Columbia University. He is the author of *Authority in Islam* (New Brunswick, 1989), which in 1989 won the Association of American Publishers' Award for the most outstanding publication in philosophy and religion, and *Theology of Discontent: The Ideological Foundations of the Islamic Revolution in Iran* (New York, 1993). His numerous shorter studies on Islamic philosophy as well as Persian history and literature have appeared in a number of collective volumes and learned journals.

FARHAD DAFTARY is Head of the Department of Academic Research and Publications at the Institute of Ismaili Studies, London. A specialist in Isma'ili studies, he is the author of *The Ismā'īlīs: Their History and Doctrines* (Cambridge, 1990), *The Assassin Legends: Myths of the Isma'ilis* (London, 1994), and *A Short History of the Isma'ilis*, Islamic Surveys (Edinburgh, forthcoming). He has contributed articles to *Encyclopaedia Iranica*, and the *Encyclopaedia of Islam*; and his shorter studies have appeared in a number of collective volumes and in learned journals.

HEINZ HALM is Professor of Islamic History at the University of Tübingen. A leading German Islamist and a specialist in Isma'ili studies, he is also Editor of *Die Welt des Orients*. Professor Halm is the author of numerous books on Islam, Shi'ism, and Isma'ilism, including *Kosmologie und Heilslehre der frühen Ismā'īlīya* (Wiesbaden, 1978), *Die islamische Gnosis* (Zürich–Munich, 1982), and *Das Reich des Mahdi: Der Aufstieg der Fatimiden* (Munich, 1991); his *Die Schia* (Darmstadt, 1988) has been published in English as *Shiism* in Islamic Surveys (Edinburgh, 1991). His shorter studies have appeared in *Encyclopaedia Iranica*, the *Encyclopaedia of Islam*, and in the learned journals.

ABBAS HAMDANI is Professor of Middle Eastern History at the University of Wisconsin, Milwaukee. Belonging to a prominent

Isma'ili Bohra family from Surat, India, Professor Hamdani is an Isma'ili specialist and is in possession of a valuable collection of Isma'ili manuscripts, which he has used extensively in his original Isma'ili studies. His family collection, used by eminent scholars such as P. Kraus, L. Massignon, W. Ivanow, A. A. A. Fyzee, S. M. Stern and many others, has played a significant role in opening up the field of Fatimid studies to western scholarship. He is also a leading authority on the famous Brethren of Purity and their *Epistles*, about which he has written several major articles in the learned journals. Professor Hamdani's other Isma'ili publications include *The Beginnings of the Isamā'īlī Da'wa in Northern India* (Cairo, 1956), *The Fatimids* (Karachi, 1962), and several studies on Yemenite Isma'ilism published in different volumes of the *Arabian Studies* (Cambridge) and elsewhere. Recently, his 'Faṭimid History and Historians', appeared in *The Cambridge History of Arabic Literature* (Cambridge, 1990).

CAROLE HILLENBRAND is Reader in Arabic and Islamic Studies at the University of Edinburgh and General Editor of the Islamic Surveys series published by Edinburgh University Press. A specialist in Islamic history, she has contributed numerous articles to the *Encyclopaedia of Islam* and the learned journals. Author of *A Muslim Principality in Crusader Times: The Early Artuqid State* (Istanbul, 1990), and Co-editor of *Qajar Iran* (Edinburgh, 1983), she has also translated a number of works, including Volume XXVI of *The History of al-Ṭabarī* (Albany, N.Y., 1989), and G. Endress' *Einführung in die islamische Geschichte*, which appeared in a revised English form as *An Introduction to Islam*, Islamic Surveys (Edinburgh, 1988).

WILFERD MADELUNG is Laudian Professor of Arabic at the University of Oxford. He is a leading contemporay Islamist and an authority on mediaeval Islamic communities and movements. Professor Madelung has made significant contributions to modern scholarship in Isma'ili studies, especially in connection with early Isma'ilism. A Consulting Editor of *Encyclopaedia Iranica*, he has contributed extensively on Isma'ilism and Shi'ism to that encyclopaedia and to the *Encyclopaedia of Islam*. He has edited several volumes of Zaydī texts from Iran and the Yemen, and his other books include *Der Imam al-Qāsim ibn Ibrāhīm und die Glaubenslehre der Zaiditen* (Berlin, 1965), and *Religious Trends in Early Islamic Iran* (Albany, N.Y., 1988). He has contributed to Volume IV of *The Cambridge History of Iran* and to numerous *Festschrift*s and learned journals. So far two volumes of Professor Madelung's many articles on religious schools, sects and movements in Islam have appeared in the Variorum Collected Studies series.

CHARLES MELVILLE is Lecturer in Islamic Studies at the University of Cambridge, and a Fellow of Pembroke College, Cambridge. Co-editor of Volume VII of *The Cambridge History of Iran* (Cambridge, 1991), and Co-author of *Christians and Moors in Spain* (Warminster, 1992), he is also Editor of the *Pembroke Persian Papers*, published for the Centre of Middle Eastern Studies, Cambridge. He has contributed several articles on the Īlkhānid Mongols to *Encyclopaedia Iranica* and to a number of collective volumes and learned journals.

AZIM A. NANJI is Professor and Chairman of the Department of Religion at the University of Florida. His research on Ismaʿilism is set within the broader context of the study of pluralism and diversity in Islamic intellectual and cultural history. He is the author of *The Nizārī Ismāʿīlī Tradition in the Indo-Pakistan Subcontinent* (Delmar, N.Y., 1978), and editor of *The Muslim Almanac* (Michigan, 1995); he has published numerous shorter studies, including 'Ismāʿīlism', in *Islamic Spirituality: Foundations*, ed. S. H. Nasr (London, 1987). Professor Nanji has also produced several important studies on the modern conditions of the Nizārī Ismaʿili community and has contributed to the *Encyclopaedia of Islam*, the *Encyclopedia of Religion*, and the new *Oxford Encyclopedia of the Modern Islamic World* (Oxford, 1995).

ISMAIL K. POONAWALA is Professor of Arabic and Islamic Studies at the University of California, Los Angeles. A specialist in Ismaʿili studies, he is the author of the monumental *Biobibliography of Ismāʿīlī Literature* (Malibu, California, 1977), a comprehensive survey of Ismaʿili writings and manuscript collections. He is the editor of several Ismaʿili texts, including *al-Urjūza al-mukhtāra* of al-Qāḍī al-Nuʿmān, about whom he has published several important studies; he has also translated into English Volume IX of *The History of al-Ṭabarī* (Albany, N.Y., 1990). Professor Poonawala is a regular contributor to *Encyclopaedia Iranica* and the *Encyclopaedia of Islam*.

PAUL E. WALKER is currently Visiting Professor of Islamic Studies at the University of Michigan; he has also taught at the Institute of Islamic Studies at McGill University. A specialist in Ismaʿili studies, he is the author of *Early Philosophical Shiism: The Ismaili Neoplatonism of Abū Yaʿqūb al-Sijistānī* (Cambridge, 1993), the first major examination of Ismaʿili Neoplatonism as it is presented in the extant works of its chief proponent, and *The Wellsprings of Wisdom: A Study of Abū Yaʿqūb al-Sijistānī's Kitāb al-Yanābīʿ* (Salt Lake City, 1994). He is also the author of numerous shorter studies on aspects of Isma'ili thought and Fatimid history, including most recently 'The Ismaili Da'wa in the Reign of the Fatimid Caliph al-Ḥākim', *Journal of the American Research Center in Egypt*, 30 (1993).

ONE

Introduction: Isma'ilis and Isma'ili studies

FARHAD DAFTARY

A MAJOR Shi'i Muslim community, the Isma'ilis appeared on the historical stage on the death of the Imam Ja'far al-Ṣādiq in the year 148/765. This 'Alid imam, in whose time the 'Abbasids overthrew the Umayyads and installed their own dynasty to the caliphate, had succeeded in consolidating Shi'ism on a quiescent basis and according a distinctive identity to its Imāmī branch, the common heritage of the Isma'ili and the Ithnā'asharī or Twelver Shi'is. The Imam al-Ṣādiq's succession was however disputed among his progeny and as a result, his Imāmī Shi'i following subdivided into a number of separate groups, including those comprising the earliest Isma'ilis.

The early Isma'ilis laid the foundations for a distinctive Isma'ili movement and community. However, early Isma'ilism, stretching until the establishment of the Fatimid caliphate, remains an obscure subject, because only a handful of authentic Isma'ili texts have survived from that formative pre-Fatimid period in Isma'ili history while non-Isma'ili sources have in general remained hostile towards the Isma'ilis. Nevertheless, our understanding of early Isma'ilism has been greatly enhanced during the last few decades by the results of modern scholarship in the field, especially the studies of S. M. Stern (1920–1969) and W. Madelung.

It is now generally agreed by Isma'ili scholars that a line of central leaders, descendants of Ja'far al-Ṣādiq, worked secretly during that obscure early period from different headquarters to organize a revolutionary Shi'i movement against the 'Abbasids who, in the eyes of the Shi'a, had usurped the legitimate rights of the 'Alid family to the leadership of the Muslim community. This movement, designated as *al-da'wa* (the mission) or *al-da'wa al-hādiya* (the rightly guiding mission) by the early Isma'ilis themselves, began to be particularly successful from around the middle of the 3rd/9th century, when a multitude of Isma'ili *dā'īs*, religio-political missionaries or propagandists, started their activities in Iraq, Persia, eastern Arabia, and the Yemen. These *dā'īs* summoned the Muslims to the allegiance of the Isma'ili Imam-Mahdi who was to deliver them from the injustices of the established regime. His rule would also herald the restoration of the caliphate to the dispossessed 'Alids, the rightful leaders belonging to the Prophet's family, the *ahl al-bayt*.

The success of early Isma'ilism was crowned in 297/909 by the establishment of the Fatimid caliphate in Ifrīqiya in North Africa, where the Isma'ili imam was now installed to a new, and the first Shi'i, caliphate. Only a decade earlier, in 286/899, the then unified Isma'ili movement had split into two rival factions, the Fatimid Isma'ilis and the Qarmaṭīs, over the all-important issue of the imamate. The dissident Qarmaṭīs, who did not acknowledge 'Abd Allāh ('Ubayd Allāh) al-Mahdī (d. 322/934) and his successors in the Fatimid dynasty as their imams, founded a state of their own in Baḥrayn, eastern Arabia, and menaced the Muslim world for almost two centuries. The pillaging activities of the Qarmaṭīs of Baḥrayn culminated in their sacking of Mecca in 317/930 during the pilgrimage season. The Sunni establishment, always ready to defame the Isma'ilis, capitalized on the ravaging acts of the Qarmaṭīs of Baḥrayn to discredit the entire Isma'ili movement, also alleging that the Qarmaṭī leaders received their orders secretly from the Fatimid caliph-imams. Open warfare, in fact, broke out between the Qarmaṭīs and the Fatimids in the aftermath of the Fatimid conquest of Egypt in 358/969.

The early Isma'ilis also laid the foundations of Isma'ili intellectual traditions which were further elaborated during the Fatimid period. They made a fundamental distinction between the exoteric (*ẓāhir*) and the esoteric (*bāṭin*) aspects of the sacred scriptures and religious commandments, holding that every literal meaning implied an inner, hidden reality (*ḥaqīqa*). These immutable truths, the common and eternal truths of the religions recognized in the Qur'an, were in fact developed in terms of a gnostic system of thought by the early Isma'ilis. This system represented an esoteric world of spiritual reality, a reality common to the great monotheistic religions of the Abrahamic tradition. The early Isma'ilis further maintained that the religious laws enunciated by prophets, or speaker-prophets (*nuṭaqā'*), would undergo periodical changes while the *ḥaqā'iq* would remain eternal. It was the function of the prophets' successors, the *awṣiyā'* and the imams, to explain in every era (*dawr*) the hidden meanings of the revelations through *ta'wīl* or esoteric exegesis. The gnostic system of the early Isma'ilis was thus comprised of a cyclical view of the religious history of mankind; it also contained a cosmological doctrine. Their system was thoroughly Islamic and Shi'i however, as the prophets of its cyclical history were those recognized in the Qur'an and the Shi'i doctrine of the imamate was superimposed on it; and this Shi'i doctrine continued to occupy a central position in the complex metaphysical systems of thought developed by the Isma'ili theologian-philosophers of the Fatimid times.

The Isma'ili *da'wa* of the 3rd/9th century, as noted, led to the foundation of the Fatimid *dawla* or state, initiating a new phase in Isma'ili history. The Fatimids made important contributions to Islamic civilization. It was in recognition of these contributions that the 4th/10th century was designated by Louis Massignon as the 'Isma'ili century' of Islam.[1] It was also during this century, coinciding with the first century of Fatimid rule, that the famous *Rasā'il Ikhwān al-Ṣafā'* (*The Epistles of the Brethren of Purity*) were compiled by a group of authors with strong Isma'ili affiliations. The Isma'ilis had now come to possess their own state, in rivalry with the 'Abbasids, and the Fatimid caliphs were acknowledged as the rightful imams by Isma'ilis not only within the Fatimid dominions but also in many other Muslim lands. It is worth noting that the Fatimids did not abandon their *da'wa* activities in the aftermath of their victory in North Africa, as they aspired to extending their rule over the entire Muslim community. As a result, the Fatimids also developed an elaborate *da'wa* organization for the activities of their *dā'īs* throughout the Muslim world, also paying particular attention to the training of the Isma'ili *dā'īs*, especially after transferring the seat of their state to Egypt. Important institutions such as the Dār al-Ḥikma and al-Azhar were established for this purpose. These institutions as well as special quarters in the Fatimid palace compound in Cairo were also used for the dissemination of Isma'ili teachings to broader audiences.

The Fatimid period, especially until the time of al-Mustanṣir bi'llāh (427–487/1036–1094), was indeed the 'golden age' of Isma'ilism. It was during this part of the classical phase in Isma'ili history that Isma'ili thought and literature attained their summit, while the Isma'ili Fatimid caliph-imams ruled over a vast empire stretching from North Africa and Sicily to Syria and Palestine. The Fatimids developed elaborate administrative and financial systems, also paying considerable attention to the Islamic sciences and other cultural as well as commercial activities.

The newly founded Fatimid capital, Cairo, rivalled ʿAbbasid Baghdad as the international metropolis of the Islamic world. It was during this same period that the classical works of Ismaʿili literature dealing with theology, philosophy and other esoteric as well as exoteric subjects were produced by many learned *dāʿī*s and authors such as Abū Yaʿqūb al-Sijistānī, Ḥamīd al-Dīn al-Kirmānī, al-Mu'ayyad fi'l-Dīn al-Shīrāzī, and Nāṣir-i Khusraw, who flourished during the 4th/10th and 5th/11th centuries, while Ismaʿili law was codified by al-Qāḍī al-Nuʿmān (d. 363/974), the foremost jurist of the period and the founder of a distinguished family of Fatimid *qāḍī*s or judges. At the same time, a distinctive intellectual tradition, designated as philosophical Ismaʿilism by Paul Walker,[2] was elaborated by the *dāʿī*s of the Iranian lands, starting with Muḥammad b. Aḥmad al-Nasafī (d. 332/943), who is actually credited with introducing philosophy into Ismaʿili thought, and Abū Ḥātim al-Rāzī (d. 322/934). These *dāʿī*s and their successors, who starting with al-Sijistānī preached the *daʿwa* in the name of the Fatimid caliph-imams, amalgamated in a highly original manner their Ismaʿili theology with a form of Neoplatonic philosophy then current in Persia and Transoxania.

In 487/1094 the Ismaʿilis were permanently split into two rival communities, the Nizāriyya and the Mustaʿliyya, over al-Mustanṣir's succession. The all-powerful Fatimid vizier al-Afḍal succeeded in installing al-Mustanṣir's youngest son to the Fatimid caliphate with the title of al-Mustaʿlī bi'llāh (487–495/1094–1101), depriving al-Mustanṣir's eldest son and heir-designate Nizār of his succession rights. The Ismaʿilis of Egypt and the regions dependent on the Fatimid regime now recognized al-Mustaʿlī also as their new imam after al-Mustanṣir; they became known as the Mustaʿliyya. By contrast, the Ismaʿilis of the Saljuq lands, then under the leadership of Ḥasan-i Ṣabbāḥ who was already following an independent revolutionary policy, upheld the succession rights of Nizār (d. 488/1095) and severed their relations with the Fatimid regime and the *daʿwa* headquarters in Cairo, which were now working in al-Mustaʿlī's name. The Ismaʿilis of Persia and other eastern lands came to be known as the Nizāriyya.

The Mustaʿlian Ismaʿilis themselves were soon split into Ṭayyibī and Ḥāfiẓī wings on the death of al-Mustaʿlī's son and successor al-Āmir (495–524/1101–1130). The Ḥāfiẓī Ismaʿilis recognized the later Fatimid caliphs as their imams, but Ḥāfiẓī Ismaʿilism did not survive the downfall of the Fatimid dynasty in 567/1171. The Ṭayyibī Ismaʿilis, who have not had a manifest imam after al-Āmir, soon found their permanent stronghold in the Yemen where their community flourished under the leadership of their chief *dāʿīs*, designated as *al-dāʿī al-muṭlaq* or the *dāʿī* with absolute authority. By the end of the 10th/16th century, the Ṭayyibī Ismaʿilis were split into Dāʾūdī and Sulaymānī factions over the issue of the rightful succession to the office of the *dāʿī*. By that time, the Indian Ṭayyibīs, known locally as Bohras, had greatly outnumbered the Ṭayyibī community of the Yemen. The Dāʾūdī and Sulaymānī Ismaʿilis have since followed different lines of *dāʿīs*. The Ṭayyibī Ismaʿilis have also played an important role both in the Yemen and India by preserving numerous Ismaʿili texts of the Fatimid period; the Ṭayyibī *dāʿīs* of the Yemen themselves engaged in literary activities and produced a voluminous literature.

In the meantime, it was mainly through the efforts of Ḥasan-i Ṣabbāḥ (d. 518/1124) that the independent Nizārī Ismaʿili *daʿwa* was founded in the East. By the time of the Nizārī–Mustaʿlī schism of 487/1094, Ḥasan had already launched from his headquarters at Alamūt his anti-Saljuq revolt with much success in northern Persia as well as in Quhistān, in southeastern Khurāsān. In fact, Ḥasan's seizure of the mountain fortress of Alamūt in 483/1090 marked what was to become the Nizārī Ismaʿili state of Persia with a later subsidiary in Syria. This state lasted for some 166 years until it, too, collapsed under the onslaught of the Mongol hordes in 654/1256. The Nizārī state went through numerous vicissitudes. Initially, it was led by *dāʿīs*, but later the Nizārī imams emerged at Alamūt taking charge of the affairs of their community and state. The Nizārī Ismaʿilis did not succeed in overthrowing the Saljuq Turks, whose rule was intensely detested in Persia, nor did the Saljuqs succeed in uprooting the Nizārīs, despite their much more superior military power. Eventually the Saljuq–Ismaʿili relations developed into what Marshall Hodgson has termed a 'stalemate'; and the Nizārī state with its scattered territories found its own place among the principalities of the Muslim world.

The Nizārī Ismaʿilis of the Alamūt period devoted much of their time and energies to their struggle and survival tactics in the midst of an extremely hostile milieu. Therefore, instead of producing learned *dāʿīs* as in Fatimid times, they came to possess capable military commanders and strategists suited to their aims. These commanders were often placed in charge of the major fortresses, and they were at the same time *dāʿīs* preaching on behalf of the Nizārī Ismaʿili imam. Nevertheless, the Nizārī Ismaʿilis, comprised mainly of mountain dwellers and villagers and with only scattered support among urban groups, did maintain a sophisticated outlook and literary tradition. Ḥasan-i Ṣabbāḥ himself was a learned theologian, and he was largely responsible for reformulating the old Shiʿi doctrine of *taʿlīm*, or the necessity of authoritative teaching by the imam.

At any rate, the doctrine of *taʿlīm*, emphasizing the teaching authority of each imam independently of his predecessors, laid the foundation for all the subsequent Nizārī teachings of the Alamūt period, including the declaration of the *qiyāma* or resurrection in 559/1164. This declaration, in fact, heralded the spiritual independence of the Nizārī Ismaʿili community at large. However, resurrection was interpreted spiritually on the basis of Ismaʿili *taʾwīl* to mean the recognition of the unveiled truth in the spiritual reality of the rightful imam of the time who was none other than the Nizārī Ismaʿili imam. It was through the recognition of the spiritual reality of this imam that Paradise would be actualized for the faithful, his community of followers. At the time of the declaration of the *qiyāma*, the Syrian Nizārīs were under the leadership of their most famous leader, Rāshid al-Dīn Sinān (d. 589/1193), who through an intricate network of alliances with his Sunni neighbours and the Crusaders ensured the survival of his community in difficult times. Later, Jalāl al-Dīn Ḥasan III (607–618/1210–1221), the sixth lord of Alamūt, attempted a daring rapprochement with the Sunni establishment, giving the Nizārī community a much needed respite. As a rare instance of Ismaʿili historiography, the Nizārī Ismaʿilis, like the Fatimids before them, also commissioned the compilation of official chronicles, recording the events of their state in Persia according to the reigns of the successive lords of Alamūt. Ḥasan-i Ṣabbāḥ also founded an important library at Alamūt, whose collections of Ismaʿili and non-Ismaʿili books had grown impressively by the time the Mongols consigned it to fire. In Quhistān and Syria, too, the Nizārīs had established libraries, containing not only books written on different religious subjects, but also archival documents and scientific tracts and equipment.

It was under such circumstances that, despite the military entanglements of the Nizārīs with outsiders, many Muslim scholars, including Sunni and Twelver Shiʿi ones as well as Jewish scientists, availed themselves of the Nizārī libraries and patronage of learning. Some of these outside scholars even converted to Ismaʿilism, at least while they were amongst the Nizārī Ismaʿilis. The most prominent member of this select group was the celebrated philosopher, theologian and astronomer Naṣīr al-Dīn al-Ṭūsī (597–672/1201–1274), who spent some three decades among the Nizārīs of Khurāsān and northern Persia and was with the last lord of

Alamūt, Rukn al-Dīn Khurshāh (653–655/1255–1257), when the Nizārīs finally surrendered to the Mongols. The bulk of the meagre literature produced by the Nizārī Ismaʿilis during the Alamūt period was either destroyed by the Mongols or perished soon afterwards in Īlkhānid Persia. The Persian Nizārīs, unlike the Mustaʿlians of the Yemen, did not play a major role in preserving the Ismaʿili literature of the Fatimid period. In this connection it is important to note that Ḥasan-i Ṣabbāḥ, as an expression of his 'Iranian' sentiments, had adopted the Persian language as the religious language of the Persian Ismaʿili community. As a result, the Persian Ismaʿilis of the Alamūt period did not find ready access to the Ismaʿili writings of the Fatimid period, although such works were evidently available in the collections of Alamūt Library and elsewhere in the community. However, the Syrian Nizārī Ismaʿilis who used Arabic did preserve a certain number of the Fatimid Ismaʿili texts, also producing a literary tradition of their own.

In Persia, the Nizārī Ismaʿilis survived the Mongol destruction of their mountain fortresses and state in 654/1256, while many of them sought refuge in the adjacent regions in Afghanistan and Badakhshān in Central Asia as well as in the Indian subcontinent. The Syrian Nizārīs, who had been spared the Mongol catastrophe, were subdued by the end of the 7th/13th century by the Mamlūks who had checked the westward advances of the Mongols and had extended their own hegemony over Egypt and Syria in succession to the Ayyūbids. In the meantime, the Nizārī imamate had been handed down in the progeny of Rukn al-Dīn Khurshāh, the last lord of Alamūt who was murdered by the Mongols in 655/1257. The early post-Alamūt centuries represent the most obscure phase in the history of the Nizārī Ismaʿili community, when the Nizārīs lived clandestinely in different regions under the local leadership of their *dāʿī*s. The Nizārī imams, too, were now living secretly in Persia without direct contacts with their followers. It was during these early post-Alamūt centuries that the Nizārī Ismaʿili imams and their followers began to disguise themselves under the mantle of Sufism, another Muslim esoteric tradition then flourishing in Persia in the form of diverse orders or *ṭarīqa*s. By the end of the 9th/15th century when the Nizārī imams emerged at Anjudān, in central Persia, strong ties had been forged between Nizārī Ismaʿilism and Sufism. The Ismaʿili imam now appeared to the outside world as a Sufi *pīr* or *murshid* and his followers were his *murīd*s, making it possible for the Persian Ismaʿilis to escape persecution in a hostile milieu.

The mediaeval period in the history of Nizārī Ismaʿilism came to an end with what W. Ivanow has termed the Anjudān revival,[3] a renaissance of Nizārī *daʿwa* and literary activities. During this period, lasting about two centuries until the 11th/17th century, the Nizārī imams succeeded in asserting their central leadership over the various Nizārī communities. The literary and proselytizing activities of the Nizārī *daʿwa* were also revived during this period. The Nizārī *daʿwa* now achieved particular success on the Indian subcontinent, where large numbers of Hindus from the Lohāṇā caste converted to Ismaʿilism, especially in Sind and Gujarāt, and they became locally known mainly as Khojas. The Indian Nizārī Ismaʿilis developed their own indigenous literary tradition in the form of devotional hymns known as *ginān*s, representing an interfacing of Ismaʿili and Hindu elements. Originally transmitted orally, the *ginān*s were in time collected and recorded in writing in different Indic languages, mostly in the Khojkī script which is unique to the Ismaʿili Khojas. In modern times, the Nizārī Ismaʿilis have benefited from the progressive policies and the network of institutions of their imams, who have acquired international fame under their hereditary title of Aga Khan. The Nizārī Ismaʿilis are currently scattered in more than twenty-five countries of Asia, Africa, Europe and North America. Representing diverse ethnic, linguistic and literary traditions, the Nizārī Ismaʿilis have remained united as a *jamāʿat* or religious community in their devotion to their spiritual leader or current imam (*ḥāḍir imām*).

Most of what is now known about the history and doctrines of the Ismaʿilis of the mediaeval times was not known until a few decades ago. This is simply because the Ismaʿilis had been studied almost exclusively on the basis of sources and accounts produced by non-Ismaʿilis who were generally hostile towards them. In particular, Sunni polemicists, starting with Ibn Rizām who flourished in the first half of the 4th/10th century, began to fabricate evidence that would lend support to the refutation of the Ismaʿilis on specific doctrinal grounds. The ʿAbbasids themselves continued to encourage the compilation of such anti-Ismaʿili tracts, culminating in the writings of al-Ghazālī (d. 505/1111) who addressed his polemics particularly to the Nizārī Ismaʿilis. In his *al-Mustaẓhirī*, written in refutation of the Ismaʿilis at the request of the ʿAbbasid caliph al-Mustaẓhir (487–512/1094–1118), al-Ghazālī presented his own elaborate Ismaʿili system of graded initiation and indoctrination leading to an ultimate stage of unbelief. The anti-Ismaʿili authors also produced a number of travestied accounts in which they readily attributed all sorts of heretical beliefs to the Ismaʿilis. These forgeries circulated as genuine Isma'ili works and were used as source materials by subsequent generations of heresiographers and polemicists. As a result, they contributed significantly to shaping the anti-Isma'ili opinions of the Muslims at large.

In sum, by the 4th/10th century, a widespread anti-Isma'ili literary campaign had come into existence in the Muslim world. This campaign, led by heresiographers and polemicists, aimed to discredit the entire Isma'ili movement from its very beginnings. Concerted efforts were now persistently made by these anti-Isma'ili sources to attribute all sorts of sinister objectives, heretical beliefs and immoral practices to the Isma'ilis, while the 'Abbasids themselves sponsored carefully designed campaigns to refute the 'Alid ancestry of the Isma'ili imams. There soon came into being a 'black legend' which portrayed Isma'ilism as the arch-heresy (*ilḥād*) *par excellence* in Islam, conceived by some non-'Alid imposters, perhaps even a Jewish magician, to destroy Islam from within. In time, this 'black legend', with forgotten origins, came to be accepted as an accurate description of Isma'ili motives, beliefs and practices, leading to more anti-Isma'ili polemical writings and contributing further to the anti-Isma'ili stances of other Muslims.

The Europeans of the Crusader and later times added their own fanciful tales to the anti-Isma'ili travesties and polemics produced by the Muslims. Mediaeval Europeans remained almost completely ignorant of Islam and its internal divisions, including Shi'ism, even though the Crusaders had come into contact with a number of Muslim communities in the Near East. In fact, the Nizārī Isma'ilis of Syria were the first Shi'i community with whom the Crusaders had diverse encounters from the opening decades of the 6th/12th century. However, it was some half a century later, in the time of Rāshid al-Dīn Sinān, the original 'Old Man of the Mountain' of the Crusaders, that occidental travellers and Crusader chroniclers began to collect some fragmentary information on the Nizārī Isma'ilis of Syria. They were particularly impressed by the self-sacrificing behaviour of the Nizārī *fidā'ī*s, or devotees, who were sent on dangerous missions to eliminate the prominent enemies of their community, especially since almost any assassination then taking place in the central Islamic lands was attributed to the daggers of the Nizārī *fidā'ī*s.

However, proximity to the Syrian Nizārīs, who were soon made famous in Europe as the Assassins, did not motivate the Europeans to gather more accurate information on the teachings and practices of this oriental community. Instead, the Crusaders and their occidental observers now resorted to their imagination in order to explain to their own satisfaction the reasons behind the devotion of the *fidāʾīs*. By the middle of the 7th/13th century, a number of Crusader chroniclers and other European sources claimed to possess reliable information on the secret practices of the Nizārī Ismaʿilis and their leader, the Old Man of the Mountain, especially regarding the recruitment and training of the *fidāʾīs*. These so-called Assassin legends developed gradually and in stages, and they culminated in the version popularized by Marco Polo (1254–1324) who synthesized a number of such legends with his own contribution in the form of a 'secret garden of paradise'. The Venetian traveller whose tales were treated as eyewitness reports in mediaeval Europe, explained in great detail how the *fidāʾīs* were motivated for carrying out their missions by their deceitful chief who procured bodily pleasures for them in his secret garden of paradise into which they would be temporarily admitted under the influence of hashish or some such intoxicating potion. Henceforth, the Nizārī Ismaʿilis were readily reduced in mediaeval European sources to a sinister order of drugged assassins, bent on senseless murder and mischief. The anti-Ismaʿili 'black legend' of the Muslim authors, rooted in hostility, had now found its companion in the 'Assassin legends' of the mediaeval Europeans, rooted in ignorance and imaginative fantasies. And both sets of myths continued to circulate for centuries as accurate descriptions of the Ismaʿili teachings and practices in their respective eastern and western milieux.

The orientalists of the nineteenth century, led by Silvestre de Sacy (1758–1838), began their more scholarly study of Islam on the basis of the Islamic manuscripts which were written mainly by Sunni authors. As a result, the orientalists studied Islam according to the Sunni viewpoint, treating Shiʿism as the 'heterodox' version of Islam. The orientalists did identify the Ismaʿilis correctly as a Shiʿi Muslim community, but they were obliged to study the Ismaʿilis exclusively on the basis of the hostile Sunni sources and the fictitious occidental accounts of the Crusader times. Orientalism, too, had now lent its own seal of approval to the myths of the Ismaʿilis. In his 'Memoir on the Dynasty of the Assassins', de Sacy summarized all the information on the Nizārīs of the Alamūt period that he was then able to extract from Islamic sources and a number of Crusader chronicles. It is, therefore, not surprising that he endorsed, at least partially, some of the Assassin legends.[4] Later, in the long introduction to his major work on the Druzes,[5] de Sacy also reaffirmed the 'black legend' of the Sunni polemicists regarding the origins of Ismaʿilism. De Sacy's distorted evaluation of the Ismaʿilis set the frame within which other orientalists of the nineteenth century studied the mediaeval history of the Isma'ilis. At the same time, misconceptions, negative biases, misinformation and plain fiction came to permeate another widely read book, the first of its kind based on oriental sources and devoted to the Nizārīs of the Alamūt period, written by Joseph von Hammer-Purgstall (1774–1856);[6] and the Isma'ilis continued to be misrepresented and misjudged to various degrees in the studies of later orientalists such as Charles François Defrémery (1822–1883) and Michael Jan de Goeje (1836–1909). The myths of the Isma'ilis had indeed found a new lease on life by Orientalism; and the deplorable state of the Isma'ili studies remained essentially unchanged until the 1930s.

In the meantime, the recovery and study of genuine Isma'ili sources was establishing a scholarly basis for Isma'ili studies, a development that led to the initiation of nothing less than a revolution in this field of Islamic learning. These manuscript sources had begun to surface on a limited scale already during the nineteenth century. However, it was not until the opening decades of the twentieth century that more of such sources, hitherto guarded secretly in many private Isma'ili collections, began to become more systematically available to public libraries and scholars from diverse provenances such as the Yemen and Central Asia. By the early 1920s, the number of Isma'ili works known to orientalists was still relatively meagre.[7]

Subsequently, this crucial breakthrough for Isma'ili studies acquired a new momentum through the efforts of a handful of scholars based in Bombay. The leading member of this group was Wladimir Ivanow (1886–1970), who played a key role in the modern progress in Isma'ili studies.[8] He succeeded through his network of Isma'ili friends in India and elsewhere to identify a large number of Isma'ili sources which he described for the first time in an annotated catalogue published in 1933.[9] The initiation of modern scholarship in Isma'ili studies may in fact be traced to the publication of this very catalogue, which attested to the hitherto unknown richness of the literary heritage of the Isma'ilis. In the same year, Ivanow was instrumental in founding the Islamic Research Association in Bombay which produced a series of publications devoted mainly to Isma'ili works. Ivanow's systematic efforts towards identifying, recovering, and studying Isma'ili manuscripts led to the creation of the Ismaili Society of Bombay in 1946, under the patronage of Sir Sulṭān Muḥammad Shāh, Aga Khan III (1877–1957), the forty-eighth imam of the Nizārī Isma'ilis. Ivanow acquired a large number of manuscripts for the Ismaili Society's Library, also publishing numerous Isma'ili texts and monographs in the Society's series of publications. By 1963, when Ivanow published a second revised edition of his Isma'ili bibliography, many more manuscript sources had become known.[10]

In the meantime, besides Ivanow, several Isma'ili scholars, notably Zāhid 'Alī (1888–1958), Ḥusayn F. al-Hamdānī (1901–1962), and Asaf A. A. Fyzee (1899–1981), belonging to the Isma'ili Bohra community, had started to produce important studies based on their own private collections of Isma'ili manuscripts. These manuscripts were now made readily available also to non-Isma'ili scholars, who produced valuable studies and critical editions. In this connection, particular mention must be made of the Fatimid texts edited by the Egyptian scholar Muḥammad Kāmil Ḥusayn (1901–1961) in his Silsilat Makhṭūṭāt al-Fāṭimiyyīn published in Cairo, and the Isma'ili works of the Fatimid and later times edited with elaborate contextualizing introductions and textual analysis by Henry Corbin (1903–1978) and included in his renowned Bibliothèque Iranienne series published simultaneously in Paris and Tehran. By the mid-1950s progress in the field had already enabled Marshall Hodgson (1922–1968) to produce the first scholarly study of the Nizārī Isma'ilis of the Alamūt period,[11] a long overdue replacement for von Hammer's hostile and distorted tract on the subject. The modern progress in Isma'ili studies was now truly proceeding at a remarkable pace. By 1977, some 1,300 titles attributable to more than 200 Isma'ili authors had been identified in the monumental bibliography of Ismail Poonawala.[12] Many of these texts have now been published in critical editions, while numerous secondary studies of Isma'ili history and thought have been produced by three successive generations of Isma'ili scholars, including some of the contributors to this collective volume.

Modern scholarship in Isma'ili studies promises to continue unabated as the Isma'ilis themselves are becoming interested in studying their literary heritage and as the Institute of Ismaili Studies founded in London under the patronage of H. H. Prince Karim Aga Khan IV, the forty-ninth present imam of the Nizārī Isma'ilis, is preparing to make its own contribution to the field through its diverse programmes of research and publications, including its Ismaili Heritage Series. It is also noteworthy that the Institute's collection of some 1,000 Isma'ili manuscripts in Arabic,[13] Persian and Khojkī, including the bulk of the collections formerly in the possession of the Ismaili Society of Bombay and the Ismailia Association of Pakistan, representing the largest collection of its kind in the West, is readily accessible to both Isma'ili and non-Isma'ili scholars and researchers.

This volume aims to make available to students, scholars, and Isma'ilis themselves, some of the scattered results of modern scholarship in Isma'ili studies on aspects of mediaeval Isma'ili history and thought, especially on those themes or topics which have not received sufficient attention in contemporary scholarly literature. The leading chapter in Part I, devoted to the pre-Fatimid and the classical Fatimid periods in Isma'ili history, was originally published in German in 1959. Here Professor Wilferd Madelung offers a somewhat updated English version of his earlier article, a landmark in modern Isma'ili studies and a major contribution to our understanding of early Isma'ilism in general and the relations between the Qarmaṭīs of Baḥrayn and the Fatimids in particular. The Sunni heresiographers, polemicists, and historians had propagated the idea that the Qarmaṭīs of Baḥrayn, notorious for their pillaging and anti-Islamic activities, were in collusion with the Fatimids, an idea that was reaffirmed by de Goeje and other scholars in modern times. In this classical study, which is still also the best modern survey of the relevant sources, Madelung shows that the leaders of the Qarmaṭī state of Baḥrayn could not have acted under orders from the Fatimids. The important findings of this study, published some thirty-five years ago, attest to the meticulous scholarship of Professor Madelung. In his second contribution, contained in chapter 4, Professor Madelung briefly deals with the more technical topic of the Intellect (*al-'aql*) in Isma'ili thought on the basis of a major work by al-Sijistānī. In particular, he shows how the defective conditions of some Isma'ili manuscripts could lead to erroneous interpretations of their subject matter.

More than any other modern scholar, Professor Heinz Halm has studied the earliest cosmological doctrine of the Isma'ilis. He has in fact reconstructed this doctrine on the basis of fragmentary evidence preserved in later sources, devoting an entire monograph in German to the subject. In chapter 3, Professor Halm presents for the first time in the English language a summary of his study of this particular cosmology, which was later superseded by an Isma'ili Neoplatonic one. In chapter 5, Halm takes up an entirely new field of investigation. Initiation into Isma'ilism was a favourite subject matter for anti-Isma'ili authors who produced imaginative travesties showing how the neophyte would be led by Isma'ili *dā'īs* through several stages of initiation until he reached the final stage of unbelief and atheism. In this chapter, the first scholarly treatment of the subject, Professor Halm investigates the actual initiation process of the Isma'ili adepts, using a variety of Isma'ili and non-Isma'ili sources. He also presents the evidence for the more advanced education programmes of the Isma'ilis in Fatimid times, especially the Isma'ili lectures known as the 'sessions of wisdom'.

In chapter 6, Professor Ismail K. Poonawala takes up the subject of Isma'ili legal thought and explains how Isma'ili law became codified almost exclusively through the efforts of al-Qāḍī al-Nu'mān, the foremost jurist of the early Fatimid times. He discusses the chronological sequence of al-Nu'mān's legal compendia, published and unpublished, and examines both the main sources of Isma'ili law and its agreements and disagreements with other schools of jurisprudence.

Much controversy has surrounded the questions of the authorship and the date of composition of the *Rasā'il Ikhwān al-Ṣafā'*, frequently translated as the *Epistles of the Brethren of Purity*. The French orientalist Paul Casanova (1861–1926), who produced some valuable studies on the Isma'ilis, was the first western scholar to have recognized, in 1898, the Isma'ili origin of the *Epistles*. Using an astrological prediction contained in the *Epistles*, Casanova also tried to date this encyclopaedic work, concluding that it was compiled shortly before 439/1047. In chapter 7, Professor Abbas Hamdani, who has published several important articles on the subject, refutes Casanova's dating on the basis of internal evidence contained in the *Epistles* and other relevant information.

Chapters 8 and 9 investigate how the Isma'ilis perceived the 'other' during the early Fatimid times. The Isma'ilis, in line with their cyclical view of the sacred history of mankind, in fact, made interesting attempts to accommodate the major religions known to them, such as Judaism, Christianity, Zoroastrianism and Manichaeism, in their gnostic system of thought. Professor Azim Nanji presents selected evidence, drawn particularly from the *Rasā'il Ikhwān al-Ṣafā'* and the writings of certain Isma'ili thinkers, which would define an Isma'ili perspective on the history of religions, reflecting above all the pluralistic and non-dogmatic approaches of the Isma'ilis towards other religions. Dr Paul Walker, in a complementary study, introduces the only known Isma'ili heresiography on Muslim sects, which has been discovered only recently. This work, called *Kitāb al-shajara*, was produced by an obscure Khurāsānī *dā'ī*, Abū Tammām, who flourished in the first half of the 4th/10th century. As a follower of the *dā'ī* al-Nasafī, Abū Tammām probably belonged to the dissident branch of Isma'ilism. In contrast with other Muslim heresiographers, Abū Tammām seems to have been more concerned with understanding and explaining sectarian differences than with refuting and condemning the 'other'; his descriptions of several sects are, in fact, unique. As a result, his book promises to be highly valuable for the study of Muslim 'sects' and the heresiographical tradition about them.

The mediaeval phase of Nizārī Isma'ili history, especially its Alamūt period, provides the focus of Part II, which opens with a study of the origins of Nizārī Isma'ilism. Adopting a somewhat novel approach to this subject, and instead of treating the Nizārī Isma'ili movement merely as a schismatic movement, chapter 10 investigates the complex circumstances leading to the anti-Saljuq revolt of the Persian Isma'ilis under the leadership of Ḥasan-i Ṣabbāḥ, who played a key role also in the establishment of the independent Nizārī *da'wa* and state. In particular, an attempt is made to identify the 'Isma'ili' and the 'Iranian' roots of this revolt, also tracing these roots to earlier religio-political and social traditions of protest. This chapter also looks at certain political and doctrinal developments during the initial decades of the Nizārī history which proved crucial for the survival of the Nizārī community and state under highly adverse circumstances of the early Alamūt period. In a complementary study in chapter 11, Dr Carole Hillenbrand looks at the Saljuq's attitudes and conduct towards the Isma'ilis of Alamūt during the same period of Ḥasan-i Ṣabbāḥ's leadership. Examining closely the relevant historiographical evidence, including especially the reports of the general chroniclers such as Ibn al-Athīr and Ibn al-Jawzī, she also draws attention to some hitherto unknown anti-Isma'ili biases of these sources in connection with their reporting of particular Saljuq-Isma'ili encounters.

Quhistān (Persian, Kūhistān) in southeastern Khurāsān, was the second most important territory, after Rūdbār in Daylam, of the Nizārī Isma'ili state in Persia during the Alamūt period. The Nizārīs of Quhistān possessed the authority of a local chief, called *muḥtasham*, who was appointed from Alamūt but enjoyed a great deal of local initiative in managing the affairs of the community there. From early on, these *muḥtasham*s were confronted with the hostile reactions of the Saljuqs and other rulers of Khurāsān and adjacent regions, who could not tolerate the success of the Nizārī Isma'ilis in their midst. Drawing on his vast knowledge of Khurāsān and Sīstān or Nīmrūz in eastern Persia, and their regional Persian chronicles, Professor Edmund Bosworth presents in chapter 12 an overview of the encounters between the Quhistānī Nizārīs and their ruling neighbours to the south, the Naṣrid Maliks of Sīstān and their successors, during the Alamūt period.

Naṣīr al-Dīn al-Ṭūsī's religious affiliation and the circumstances of his long stay in the Nizārī Isma'ili strongholds of Persia have been subjects of different interpretations throughout centuries. The same issues have been debated in the contemporary writings on this controversial Muslim philosopher, theologian, and astronomer. While al-Ṭūsī's modern Ithnāʿasharī biographers generally contend that he was kept amongst the Ismaʿilis against his will, others reject this view and further argue that in fact he converted to Ismaʿilism voluntarily during that same period. In chapter 13, Professor Hamid Dabashi takes a fresh look at these issues. Arguing that too much emphasis on the 'sectarian' affiliations of major intellectual and political figures of mediaeval times only distorts the complexity of their characters, he examines al-Ṭūsī's character and his Ismaʿili connection from the perspective of a philosopher/vizier, simultaneously concerned with matters of knowledge/power or philosophy/politics, and as such representing an important mode in Persian political culture.

In chapter 14, Dr Charles Melville examines the curious reports of the Sunni chroniclers concerning the Mamlūk employment of *fidāʾī*s or *fidāwī*s in the wider context of Mamlūk–Mongol relations during the early decades of the 8th/14th century. More specifically, he analyzes the detailed reports on how the Mamlūk sultan on numerous occasions despatched *fidāwī*s to Mongol Persia for the assassination of a Mamlūk defector there. Doubtless, assassins, and probably professional ones, were sent on these missions. However, the term *fidāwī*, linked so closely with the Nizārīs of earlier times, seems to have been used rather loosely in the Mamlūk sources in the sense of a 'murderer', rather than an 'Ismaʿili *fidāwī*'. By that time, the Syrian Nizārīs no longer had any *fidāwī*s, and the Mamlūk sultan could have recruited such *fidāwī*s from anywhere. It is also possible, however, that the Syrian Nizārīs were forced on occasion to supply individuals for the missions in question. That the chroniclers evidently identify the Syrian Nizārī Ismaʿili community of the Mamlūk times as the sole source of supply for the sultan's would-be 'assassins' clearly attests to the durability of the legends and hostile rumours regarding the practices of the Nizārī Ismaʿilis of the Alamūt period.

In chapter 15, Professor Ali Asani re-examines the traditional views on the 'authorship' of the *ginān*s, the devotional poems that enjoy a 'sacred' status within the Nizārī Ismaʿili Khoja community. The *ginān*s, as it is well-known, contain instructions on a range of themes and topics related to religious obligations, moral issues, and the spiritual quest of the soul. The authorships of the *ginān*s, which were initially transmitted orally for several centuries, are attributed by the Khoja tradition to a few early missionaries or *pīr*s who converted the Hindus to Isma'ili Islam on the Indian subcontinent. In this thought-provoking essay, Professor Asani discusses the complex issues stemming from the traditional interpretation of the 'authorship' of the *ginān*s, including the significance of their *bhaṇitā*s or signature-verses, and demonstrates that a better understanding of this subject requires a new approach that would allow for a clear distinction between 'authority', in the sense of invoking someone's seal of approval for a work, and 'authorship', his actual authoring of that work in the modern sense of the term.

The final chapter 16, contributed by Professor Abbas Amanat, stands apart from other studies in this volume. It deals with the Nuqṭawiyya, an obscure esoteric sect that emerged as a significant religio-political movement in Ṣafawid Persia and, later, briefly enjoyed some eminence in Mughal India. The Nuqṭawiyya, as well as their parent sect of the Ḥurūfiyya, cannot be regarded as part of the spectrum of Isma'ili communities. Maḥmūd Pisīkhānī (or Pasīkhānī), the founder of the Nuqṭawī sect who died around 831/1427–1428, in fact claimed to have founded a new religion. However, the Ḥurūfīs and the Nuqṭawīs did belong to those esoteric and mystic movements of post-Mongol Persia which were influenced by Isma'ilism. Indeed, Ivanow cited the Nuqṭawiyya among the post-Mongol sectarian movements influenced by Isma'ilism.[14] But the matter has been barely investigated by modern scholars, mainly because Nuqṭawī writings have not survived. As the first scholarly attempt of its kind, Professor Amanat has pieced together in this chapter a good deal of information on the ideas propagated by Maḥmūd Pisīkhānī. His study demonstrates that the central Nuqṭawī doctrines, such as its materialist type of metempsychosis, were fundamentally at variance with Isma'ili teachings. There is also the crucial matter of Maḥmūd's 'un-Islamic' claim to prophethood, not to mention the fact that the Nuqṭawīs did not uphold the Shi'i doctrine of the imamate so central to Isma'ilism. However, Isma'ili antecedents may be detected in the Nuqṭawī cyclical view of time and hierohistory. The Nuqṭawīs also relied heavily on esoteric (*bāṭinī*) exegesis which had found its fullest elaboration among the Isma'ilis.

NOTES

1 L. Massignon, 'Mutanabbi, devant le siècle Ismaélien de l'Islam', in *Al Mutanabbi: Recueil publié à l'occasion de son millénaire* (Beirut, 1936), p. 1.

2 Paul E. Walker, *Early Philosophical Shiism: The Ismaili Neoplatonism of Abū Ya'qūb al-Sijistānī* (Cambridge, 1993), pp. 13 ff., 30 ff., 61, 147 ff.

3 W. Ivanow, *Brief Survey of the Evolution of Ismailism* (Leiden, 1952), p. 29.

4 Silvestre de Sacy, 'Mémoire sur la dynastie des Assassins, et sur l'étymologie de leur Nom', *Mémoires de l'Institut Royal de France*, 4 (1818), pp. 1–84; English trans., 'Memoir on the Dynasty of the Assassins, and on the Etymology of their Name', in F. Daftary, *The Assassin Legends* (London, 1994), pp. 136–188.

5 Silvestre de Sacy, *Exposé de la religion des Druzes* (Paris, 1838), vol. 1, introduction pp. 1–246.

6 Joseph von Hammer, *Die Geschichte der Assassinen* (Stuttgart–Tübingen, 1818); French trans., *Histoire de l'ordre des Assassins*, tr. J. J. Hellert and P. A. de la Nourais (Paris, 1833; reprinted, Paris, 1961); English trans., *The History of the Assassins*, tr. O. C. Wood (London, 1835; reprinted, New York, 1968).

7 See, for instance, V. A. Ivanov, 'Ismailitskiya rukopisi Aziatskago Muzeya', *Bulletin de l'Académie des Sciences de Russie*, 6 série, 11 (1917), pp. 359–386; English summary in E. Denison Ross, 'W. Ivanow, Ismaili MSS in the Asiatic Museum', JRAS (1919), pp. 429–435, and L. Massignon, 'Esquisse d'une bibliographie Qarmaṭe', in *A Volume of Oriental Studies Presented to Edward G. Browne*, ed. T. W. Arnold and R. A. Nicholson (Cambridge, 1922), pp. 329–338.

8 See F. Daftary, 'W. Ivanow: A Biographical Notice', *Middle Eastern Studies*, 8 (1972), pp. 241–244; also his 'Bibliography of the Publications of the late W. Ivanow', *Islamic Culture*, 45 (1971), pp. 56–67, and 56 (1982), pp. 239–240, and 'Anǰoman-e Esmāʿīlī', EIR, vol. 2, p. 84.

9 W. Ivanow, *A Guide to Ismaili Literature* (London, 1933). See also P. Kraus, 'La Bibliographie Ismaëlienne de W. Ivanow', *Revue d'Etudes Islamiques*, 6 (1932), pp. 483–490.

10 See W. Ivanow, *Ismaili Literature: A Bibliographical Survey* (Tehran, 1963).

11 M. G. S. Hodgson, *The Order of Assassins: The Struggle of the Early Nizārī Ismāʿīlīs against the Islamic World* (The Hague, 1955).

12 I. K. Poonawala, *Biobibliography of Ismāʿīlī Literature* (Malibu, Calif., 1977).

13 See A. Gacek, *Catalogue of Arabic Manuscripts in the Library of the Institute of Ismaili Studies* (London, 1984). Catalogues of the Institute's collections of Persian Ismaʿili manuscripts and the *ginān*s have not been published yet. The Institute also holds photocopies of the Ismaʿili manuscripts donated by Fyzee to the Bombay University Library; see M. Goriawala, *A Descriptive Catalogue of the Fyzee Collection of Ismaili Manuscripts* (Bombay, 1965).

14 See Ivanow, *Ismaili Literature*, pp. 12–13, 188–190; now also see H. Algar, 'Nuḳtawiyya', EI2, vol. 8, pp. 114–117.

PART I

The classical phase

TWO

The Fatimids and the Qarmaṭīs of Baḥrayn

WILFERD MADELUNG

INTRODUCTORY NOTE

THE PRESENT article is a slightly revised translation of my 'Fatimiden und Baḥrainqarmaṭen' published in the journal *Der Islam*, XXXIV (1959), pp. 34–88. It substantially reflects the state of research at that time. In a few instances references to more recent studies have been added in the notes. It has not been the intention, however, to bring the article systematically up to date. My thanks are due to Madam Azizeh Azodi, Paris, for translating the main text of the article.

Among the rebellious movements of the 3rd/9th and 4th/10th centuries characterized by the Arab chronicles as 'Qarmaṭī', the one in Baḥrayn assumes a special position. Here alone the rebels succeeded in founding a powerful state which enjoyed unlimited power over a wide area. They easily managed to repel the attacks on their independence to which they were exposed at the beginning. In the following decades, they disposed of the most effective and redoubted fighting forces in the Islamic world. They became a true scourge for the caliphate of Baghdad. Plundering and assassinating, they penetrated into southern Mesopotamia in ever renewed incursions, and attacked the pilgrim caravans on their way to or from Mecca. The armies of the caliph, though often far outnumbering them, could not hold out against them. In 316/928, it was as by miracle that Baghdad escaped being conquered. A year later, they occupied Mecca, wrought a terrible massacre among the inhabitants and pilgrims, and robbed the Kaʿba of its Black Stone, a sacrilege that is unparalleled in the history of Islam. The caliph was incapable of even raising a finger to recover the relic by force. It was not until twenty-two years later that the stone was brought back to its place voluntarily, against payment of a high ransom.

The Qarmaṭīs justified their rebellion against the existing order by proclaiming the sovereignty of the Mahdi, the rightly-guided imam from the house of the Prophet who would rule over the world and establish justice and order. Two decades after the establishment of the Qarmaṭī state in Baḥrayn, another rebel, who claimed to be the expected imam of the Prophet's lineage, founded a Fatimid counter-caliphate in Raqqāda near Qayrawān. Repeated attempts at conquering Egypt and intensive anti-ʿAbbasid propaganda showed the seriousness of the claim.

The importance of the question about the relationship between the Qarmaṭī state and the rising Fatimid empire in North Africa for a proper understanding of the political history of the period is obvious. Yet to the opponents of the Fatimids, this question was interesting in another sense. For in the history of the Qarmaṭīs of Baḥrayn they believed they had found for the first time a clear confirmation of the accusations of unbelief and libertinism which they had quite generally levelled against the Bāṭinīs. Had not the Qarmaṭīs murdered thousands of defenceless pilgrims, had they not burned Qur'ans, defiled the holy city and openly blasphemed against the Lord of the Kaʿba? Did not these deeds reveal the true face of the Ismaʿili heresy, which was normally concealed under the cloak of devotion to the family of the Prophet, in order to recruit proselytes and to escape persecution at the hands of the faithful? 'Externally they feign the Shiʿi faith, internally they hide pure unbelief', was the judgement, for example, of the Qāḍī Abū Bakr al-Bāqillānī,[1] alluding to their doctrine that behind the outward text of the Qur'an and the laws of Islam, lie concealed the inner, esoteric truths of religion.

The most detailed study of the history of the Qarmaṭīs in Baḥrayn is that of M. J. de Goeje, who directed particular attention to their relations with the Fatimids. Relying on a wealth of source material, he arrived at the following conclusions: Qarmaṭīs and Fatimids had sprung from one and the same movement. Despite the secession of Ḥamdān Qarmaṭ, after whom the sect was named, and that of his brother-in-law ʿAbdān, the master of the missionary propaganda, Abū Saʿīd al-Jannābī, the head of the Qarmaṭīs of Baḥrayn, kept his allegiance to the Fatimid imams even after the establishment of their sovereignty in North Africa.[2] Under Abū Saʿīd's son Abū Ṭāhir, the collaboration between the Qarmaṭīs and their lords grew particularly close. In all important enterprises they acted on the direct command of ʿUbayd Allāh, the Fatimid caliph.[3] But the Fatimids did not dare acknowledge them publicly as allies.[4] With ʿUbayd Allāh's death, their close co-operation ended, but the Qarmaṭīs still continued acknowledging his successors as imams. The breach occurred when al-Ḥasan al-Aʿṣam gained control in Baḥrayn in 358/969. He entered the service of the ʿAbbasids and led the Qarmaṭīs to fight against the Fatimids. After the year 375/985, however, they once again returned under the sway of the Fatimids.[5]

A more recent investigation has been presented by B. Lewis.[6] For the early history of the Qarmaṭīs of Baḥrayn, he uses contradictory source material and leaves the question open whether they originally adhered to an Ismaʿili or a Ḥanafī[7] succession of imams.[8] In any case they formed a group of their own. Around the beginning of the 4th/10th century, they were won over to the Fatimid doctrine. Later they paid homage, for a short time, to a false prophet, seceded from the Fatimids and published all the secrets of the doctrine. But still later, they returned under the sway of the Fatimids until the secession of al-Aʿṣam.

W. Ivanow, on the other hand, upholds the Ismaʿili origin of the Qarmaṭīs.[9] He says that they may have issued from the defection of Aḥmad b. al-Kayyāl from the Imam ʿAbd Allāh b. Muḥammad b. Ismāʿīl, which is mentioned in the *ʿUyūn al-akhbār*, the historical work of the Ismaʿili *dāʿī* Idrīs b. al-Ḥasan.[10] Ibn al-Kayyāl may be identical with Aḥmad, the son of ʿAbd Allāh b. Maymūn al-Qaddāḥ, whom the anti-Ismaʿili historiographers consider as the founder of the Bāṭinī heresy.[11] Later, the relations of the Qarmaṭīs with the Fatimids were determined by the fact that they did not recognize the Fatimid imamate, but anticipated the return of the Imam Muḥammad b. Ismāʿīl. Whenever they were disappointed in their expectation, which was to be fulfilled on specific dates, they might turn to the Fatimids again.[12] The arguments which de Goeje had presented for the continuation of the close association between the Qarmaṭīs of Baḥrayn and the Fatimids, however, were not refuted by Ivanow.

Ḥ. I. Ḥasan and Ṭ. A. Sharaf represent the view, in their biography of the Fatimid ʿUbayd Allāh,[13] that a group of Ḥanafī Kaysānīs[14] under Ḥamdān Qarmaṭ were converted to the Ismaʿili doctrine by the ancestors of the Fatimids.[15] Later, however, Ḥamdān Qarmaṭ seceded.[16] He or a descendant of Maymūn al-Qaddāḥ, who resided in Ṭāliqān,[17] sent Abū Saʿīd al-Jannābī to Baḥrayn. Abū Saʿīd founded the Qarmaṭī state there and himself stood in opposition to the Fatimids.[18] Elsewhere the authors assume, however, that Abū Saʿīd was opposed to Ḥamdān Qarmaṭ and at first supported the Fatimids.[19] Encouraged by his success, he took more and more of a fancy to his independence. Nevertheless, he continued to recognize the Fatimid imamate nominally. Perhaps ʿUbayd Allāh, weary of Abū Saʿīd's dubious politics, had a hand in his assassination.[20] The description of the later history of the Qarmaṭīs and their relations with the Fatimids essentially follows that of de Goeje.

Here it is proposed to re-examine these very different conclusions. The general history of the Qarmaṭī movement will be discussed only as far as the context requires. On that subject the reader may still be referred to de Goeje's work.[21]

The oldest tangible event in the sources is the conversion of Ḥamdān Qarmaṭ by a missionary.[22] What Ḥamdān's earlier confession was is not stated in the reports. The new doctrine which he now adopted, and to the propagation of which he was soon to contribute considerably as a high-ranking missionary, was no doubt the one spread from Salamiyya in Syria through the ancestors of the Fatimids. Admittedly, al-Ṭabarī only mentions that after winning numerous adherents for his doctrine, the foreign missionary went to Syria, where he was never heard of again.[23] But reliable information is given in definite statements by Ibn Rizām,[24] Akhū Muḥsin,[25] and Ibn Ḥawqal.[26] Even in later times, works of ʿAbdān, Ḥamdān's brother-in-law and companion in the propagation of the doctrine, were current among the Ismaʿilis.[27]

Ḥamdān Qarmaṭ and ʿAbdān eventually quarrelled with their lord at Salamiyya and broke off the propaganda conducted in his name. In retaliation for this defection ʿAbdān was assassinated by the followers of the missionary Zikrawayh. But Ḥamdān Qarmaṭ disappeared,[28] as is reported in detail by Akhū Muḥsin.[29] De Goeje has expressed serious doubts about the accuracy of certain details of the account, but not about the fact of the defection itself.[30] In this connection the question about the date is of primary interest. Akhū Muḥsin places the events in the year 286/899.[31] But de Goeje establishes a connection with the defection of Abū ʿAbd Allāh al-Shīʿī, who had paved the way for ʿUbayd Allāh in North Africa, and of his brother. He thinks that Ḥamdān Qarmaṭ and ʿAbdān, too, had seceded after ʿUbayd Allāh had gained supremacy and proclaimed himself the expected Mahdi.[32] This view is contradicted by two sources which could hardly have been influenced by Akhū Muḥsin. The Ismaʿili work *Istitār al-imām* of Aḥmad b. Muḥammad al-Nīsābūrī, written during the caliphate of the Fatimid al-ʿAzīz (365–386/975–996), reports that the sons of Abū Muḥammad – i.e., Zikrawayh – had killed their brother-in-law, whom they accused of being a hypocrite and disobedient to the imam.[33] This is cited, in conformity with Akhū Muḥsin's account, among the events which took place between the succession of ʿUbayd Allāh and the rebellions of Zikrawayh's sons in Syria. It is highly probable, as suggested by Ivanow,[34] that the murdered person was ʿAbdān. Ibn Ḥawqal also mentions the assassination of ʿAbdān without giving a definite date. It led, however, to the assassination of Abū Zakariyyāʾ al-Ṭamāmī by Abū Saʿīd, which, according to all reports,[35] happened at the beginning of the latter's rule in Baḥrayn.[36]

Abū Saʿīd al-Jannābī was entrusted by Ḥamdān Qarmaṭ and ʿAbdān with the propagation of the doctrine in Baḥrayn. This is unanimously reported by such different sources as the pro-Fatimid Ibn Ḥawqal,[37] the anti-Fatimid Akhū Muḥsin,[38] and ʿAbd al-Jabbār.[39] But how did Abū Saʿīd comport himself at the defection of his teachers? De Goeje still believed that he did not let himself be influenced in his attitude towards the Fatimids and that he remained faithful to them.[40] This is contradicted by the text of the new edition of Ibn Ḥawqal, which says:[41] 'He [Abū Saʿīd] then espoused the doctrine of the one residing in the Maghrib,[42] until his master ʿAbdān was killed. Then he defected from what he had believed and killed Abū Zakariyyāʾ al-Ṭamāmī, a missionary who had represented the lords of the Maghrib before him.' The assassination of Abū Zakariyyāʾ is also mentioned in other sources,[43] although without the motivation mentioned here.

The thesis about the Ḥanafī origin of the Qarmaṭīs is based on two sources. Al-Ṭabarī describes their creed in a manner which poses several problems.[44] He does not name his informant, but begins with the statement: 'Of those Qarmaṭīs it is said,[45] among other things with respect to their doctrine, that they bring a book in which it is written . . .' There now follows a word-by-word quotation. A certain al-Faraj b. ʿUthmān from a village called Naṣrāna, 'the missionary of the Messiah, who is Jesus, who is the Word, who is the Mahdi, who is Aḥmad b. Muḥammad b. al-Ḥanafiyya, who is Gabriel' declares that the Messiah has appeared to him in human shape and has said to him: 'You are the envoy, you are the evidence (*ḥujja*), you are the she-camel (*nāqa*),[46] you are the beast (*dābba*),[47] you are the Holy Spirit, you are John, son of Zachariah.' Thereupon, he had explained to him the prayer and other prescriptions of the law. In the call to prayer, seven prophets are attested: Adam, Noah, Abraham, Moses, Jesus, Mohammed and Aḥmad b. Muḥammad b. al-Ḥanafiyya. In the prayer itself, the opening (*al-istiftāḥ*) is recited from the revelation of the seventh prophet. Al-Ṭabarī quotes this *sūra* verbatim, a primitive imitation of the Qur'an with a *bāṭinī* exegesis.[48] The law is based on the model of the Islamic *sharīʿa*, but considerably alters and simplifies the individual prescriptions.

Paul Casanova says about this report that it turns the Qarmaṭīs into a sect which is quite alien to Isma'ilism, since they acknowledged a son of Muḥammad b. al-Ḥanafiyya as the imam.[49] But this judgement must be modified to a large extent.

1. The doctrine undoubtedly shows *bāṭinī* characteristics. But it was not only the Isma'ilis who were searching for the inner meaning of the laws at the time. On the other hand, early Isma'ili doctrine seems to know nothing of a revelation by the seventh emissary of God. It was not expected until his return and was to consist, according to the doctrine of the esoterics, of the proclamation of the inner meaning. Laws and ritual prescriptions such as those described here reveal no similarity with the laws of the Fatimids, which only differed slightly from those of the Twelver Shi'is.

2. Nothing is known of a son of Muḥammad b. al-Ḥanafiyya by the name of Aḥmad.[50] This means that we are not dealing with evidence of a sect formed in a succession dispute after the death of Muḥammad b. al-Ḥanafiyya. Rather, the name and the person are freely invented in order to legitimize the mission of al-Faraj b. 'Uthmān. But then the question arises as to how the choice of this name for the seventh prophet is to be explained. Aḥmad is the prophet whose coming Jesus had prophesied according to the Qur'an.[51] This is evidently applied to the seventh prophet here. But why is he made a son of Muḥammad b. al-Ḥanafiyya? It cannot be construed as reliable evidence that the members of the sect addressed by al-Faraj had already earlier professed to a Ḥanafī succession of imams. The names and the number of the other prophets mentioned conform precisely with Isma'ili doctrine. This suggests that the Isma'ili system was altered for some reason here.[52] The reversion to a son of Muḥammad b. al-Ḥanafiyya is perhaps to be understood as a challenge to the 'Abbasid house, which traced back its own claim to the imamate to the bequest of one of his sons.

3. Al-Ṭabarī gives no information about the person of al-Faraj b. 'Uthmān. Neither the Qarmaṭī nor the Fatimid traditions know him, despite the high rank he is given in the text. Only Ibn Khaldūn explains that al-Faraj b. 'Uthmān al-Qāshānī was another name of Zikrawayh b. Mahdawayh.[53] Is he basing himself on information from an earlier source, or is this simply an attempt to explain al-Ṭabarī's account, which he quotes at length? Ibn Khaldūn's working method speaks for the second alternative.[54] The Isma'ili character of the rebellions of Zikrawayh's sons is well-known.[55] They traced their genealogy to Muḥammad b. Ismā'īl. If Ibn Khaldūn's identification were nonetheless true, it would

have to be assumed that Zikrawayh himself had brought this strange book to his followers at his last appearance. But for this conjecture there is no support.

To sum up, it seems certain that the doctrine described by al-Ṭabarī is merely evidence of a fractional sect, not that of 'the Qarmaṭīs' in general. It can further be assumed, with some likelihood, that it represents an Isma'ili heresy. But about its originator and followers nothing definite can be said. Quite unjustified is the conclusion, based on al-Ṭabarī's account, that Ḥamdān Qarmaṭ and his followers had been Ḥanafīs before their conversion to Isma'ilism.[56]

As a second source for the Ḥanafī origin of the Qarmaṭīs, B. Lewis referred to a statement by the Qāḍī 'Abd al-Jabbār b. Aḥmad.[57] According to the latter, Abū Sa'īd al-Jannābī had said of himself as early as the eighties of the third Islamic century (893–902 AD) that he was the envoy of the Imam Muḥammad b. 'Abd Allāh b. Muḥammad b. al-Ḥanafiyya, who lived somewhere in the mountains. He was the Mahdi and would appear in the year 300/912–913.

Here, too, the name and the person of the Imam-Mahdi are invented. History reports nothing about a son of 'Abd Allāh b. Muḥammad b. al-Ḥanafiyya. The anti-'Abbasid tendency, however, is quite evident. For Abū Hāshim 'Abd Allāh was widely known to have bequeathed his right to the imamate to the 'Abbasid Muḥammad b. 'Alī before he died.[58] The name of the son is also well-founded. An old tradition had it that the Mahdi would have the same name as the Prophet, Muḥammad b. 'Abd Allāh.

'Abd al-Jabbār names Abū Sa'īd as the originator of this doctrine. In this statement B. Lewis sees confirmation of Casanova's hypothesis that the Qarmaṭīs were originally Ḥanafīs.[59] But 'Abd al-Jabbār himself is among the sources that connect Abū Sa'īd with Ḥamdān Qarmaṭ.[60] Abū Sa'īd is said to have made the assertion several years after 280/893. 'Abd al-Jabbār reports it in connection with Abū Sa'īd's return after his flight and the assassination of Abū Zakariyyā' al-Ṭamāmī, which was, according to Ibn Ḥawqal, a result of his secession from the Fatimids. So, were one to trust 'Abd al-Jabbār, who is quite an unreliable source to be used with caution, one would have to consider the new doctrine too, as a result of the secession from the Fatimids.

The conflict between Ḥamdān Qarmaṭ and his masters had broken out over the question of the imamate. Ḥamdān and 'Abdān had been instructed to teach that the Imam Muḥammad b. Ismā'īl was alive and that his return as the Mahdi was imminent. Now 'Ubayd Allāh claimed the imamate for himself and denied the return of Muḥammad b. Ismāʿīl. Ḥamdān and ʿAbdān considered themselves cheated and broke off the propagation of the doctrine. All this is reported in detail by Akhū Muḥsin.[61] After the disappearance of Ḥamdān and the assassination of ʿAbdān their followers found themselves without a leader and in an ideological crisis. Even Zikrawayh and his sons, who at first pretended to remain faithful to ʿUbayd Allāh, were seized by a confidence crisis. It soon turned out that they were merely working for their own advantage.[62] For Abū Saʿīd this must have seemed a favourable opportunity to make himself completely independent. He had been appointed to his office by Ḥamdān Qarmaṭ and ʿAbdān, and he must have shared the ideological crisis with his teachers. He may very well have tried to solve it by designating another Imam-Mahdi and giving himself out to be his emissary.

Quite similar motives may have been at the origin of the doctrine of al-Faraj b. ʿUthmān. There is no reason, however, to relate them, on the basis of ʿAbd al-Jabbār's statements, to the Qarmaṭīs of Baḥrayn. For one thing, the difference in the names of the Mahdi in the two texts goes against their being connected. For another, one would have to identify al-Faraj with Abū Saʿīd, which is hardly possible.

Equally untenable is the opinion espoused by Ivanow that the Qarmaṭī movement issued from the defection of Aḥmad b. al-Kayyāl. Ivanow starts out with al-Nawbakhtī's statement that the Qarmaṭīs belonged to the followers of Muḥammad b. Ismāʿīl,[63] but subsequently let the imamate end with him and expected his return as the Mahdi.[64] He connects this statement with the report of the Ismaʿili *dāʿī* Idrīs b. al-Ḥasan about the defection of Ibn al-Kayyāl from the Imam ʿAbd Allāh b. Muḥammad b. Ismāʿīl, and says that this defection is probably identical with the break between Qarmaṭīs and Ismaʿilis,[65] i.e., the later Fatimids.

If Idrīs' report is to be trusted,[66] this defection must have occurred soon after the death of Muḥammad b. Ismāʿīl. It cannot, therefore, be identical with the secession of the Qarmaṭīs from the Fatimids. The Qarmaṭī tradition confirms the view that its leader, Ḥamdān Qarmaṭ,[67] was first converted by the Fatimids.

According to al-Shahrastānī, Ibn al-Kayyāl had also claimed the imamate for himself and asserted that he was the Qāʾim.[68] We hear nothing of this from the Qarmaṭīs. Ibn al-Kayyāl's whole doctrine has little in common with theirs.[69] Finally, Ivanow's basic assumption that the secession of the Qarmaṭīs was due to the fact that, contrary to the

Fatimids, they had the imamate end with Muḥammad b. Ismāʿīl, is debatable. To all appearances, this had long been the doctrine of the fathers of the Fatimids as well. It was only the later Fatimid theory about the imamate which elevated ʿUbayd Allāh's ancestors to the rank of imams.

Let us go back to Abū Saʿīd. Apart from Ibn Ḥawqal, the secession of Abū Saʿīd is also explicitly mentioned by Muḥammad b. Mālik al-Yamānī, a contemporary of the Fatimid caliph al-Mustanṣir (427–487/1036–1094), who had ostensibly gone over to the Bāṭinīs in order to discover their secrets.[70] According to him, the Qarmaṭī ʿAlī b. al-Faḍl who carried the mission to the Yemen together with Ibn Ḥawshab, had explained his apostasy from ʿUbayd b. Maymūn (meaning ʿUbayd Allāh) to his associate by saying that he had a precedent in Abū Saʿīd al-Jannābī. The latter had given up Maymūn and his son and carried on the mission in his own name.[71]

De Goeje, who did not know all these reports and who assumed that Abū Saʿīd had remained loyal to ʿUbayd Allāh, found it astonishing that the Qarmaṭīs of Baḥrayn had remained completely passive during the rebellions of Zikrawayh's sons. He saw an explanation in the fact that the latter gave themselves out as the awaited imam one after the other.[72] But that does not explain why no attempt was made to support ʿUbayd Allāh, the real imam, who was now in utmost danger both from the pretenders and the ʿAbbasids. Nor does it explain why ʿUbayd Allāh, if in fact offered such a nearby and secure refuge in the solidly established Qarmaṭī state, should set off on the dangerous road to an unknown future in the west, only to turn his eyes eastward again immediately after his triumph.

De Goeje found confirmation of his view in an invasion by the Qarmaṭīs of the Baṣra area in the year 300/912–913.[73] Since the Fatimids began their first eastern campaign in that year, one could assume the Qarmaṭī invasion to have been incited by ʿUbayd Allāh in his view. But an examination of the reports about the two campaigns yields the following results: Only ʿArīb b. Saʿd,[74] Ibn Miskawayh,[75] al-Hamadhānī,[76] and Ibn al-Athīr[77] mention the Qarmaṭī raid. It was evidently a very small enterprise, since Ibn Miskawayh, al-Hamadhānī and Ibn al-Athīr speak of a unit of thirty men. Abū Saʿīd certainly did not take part in it. For a dating, the end of the year 299/July – August 912, according to the accounts of Ibn Miskawayh and Ibn al-Athīr, is to be preferred, because Ibn Miskawayh reports that the governor of Baṣra had written to Ibn al-Furāt, who was vizier at the time. In the month of Dhu'l-Ḥijja/19 July–17 August, Ibn al-Furāt fell out of favour and was thrown into prison.[78] ʿArīb's mention of it among the events of the following year is perhaps to be explained by the fact that the news did not become generally known in Baghdad until then.[79] As the date for the assassination of Abū Saʿīd, the very well-informed al-Masʿūdī mentions Dhu'l-Qaʿda 300/9 June–8 July 913.[80]

The Fatimid campaign against Egypt, however, did not begin until the year 301/913–914. Admittedly, Abu'l-Qāsim, ʿUbayd Allāh's son, was sent against the rebellious city of Tripoli, which had successfully resisted a Fatimid army for several months in the year 300/912–913.[81] But after conquering the city he returned to Raqqāda.[82] In the following year Ḥubāsa b. Yūsuf set off east with further aims. He conquered Surt and Ajdābiyya. On 7 Rajab 301/6 February 914 he entered Barqa.[83] On Thursday 14 Dhu'l-Ḥijja/7 July 914 Abu'l-Qāsim followed him from Raqqāda with a large army.[84] Against his order, Ḥubāsa, without waiting for his arrival, pushed further east and invaded Alexandria on 2 Ṣafar 302/27 August 914.[85] Abu'l-Qāsim arrived there on Friday 14 Rabīʿ II/4 November 914.[86] In view of the weakness of the Qarmaṭī enterprise and the interval between the two campaigns – if the Qarmaṭī raid can be thus designated – there can evidently be no question of a joint strategy.[87]

It is precisely this argument which has so far been used as a significant basis to prove a specially close bond of the Qarmaṭīs under Abū Saʿīd's son Abū Ṭāhir with the Fatimid imams. The question of military co-operation is, indeed, particularly important in this respect. For no matter how painstaking the effort to conceal the secret connection between the various branches of the Ismaʿili movement, the overthrow of the ʿAbbasids – the supreme aim of the rebels – required that all available forces be combined and subjected to a unified strategy. How could the imams of North Africa have desisted from harnessing those formidable fighting forces so near the heart of the ʿAbbasid empire to further their own aims, using them to tie up the hostile armies so that they themselves might force their way east by way of Egypt? Thus Ibn Khaldūn reports:[88] 'In the year 306[89] (918–919), Abu'l-Qāsim reached Egypt, summoned Abū Ṭāhir, the Qarmaṭī, and waited for him. But Mu'nis al-Khādim stole a march on him. He set off [for Egypt] on behalf of al-Muqtadir and defeated him. [Abu'l-Qāsim] returned to Mahdiyya. Thereupon, Abū Ṭāhir marched against Baṣra, overran it and withdrew. Baghdad was terror-stricken, and al-Muqtadir ordered that the defects of the city walls be repaired.'

This is the account on which de Goeje,[90] and Ḥasan and Sharaf,[91] base their assumption of a unified strategy between the Fatimid and Qarmaṭī armies in the second campaign against Egypt. But a closer examination proves it to be untenable.

Abu'l-Qāsim's renewed invasion of Egypt must be viewed in connection with the constant pressure exercised by the Fatimid armies on the eastern borders since Ḥubāsa's campaign, from 301/913–914 to the end of the year 311/beginning of 924. At his withdrawal from Egypt towards the end of the year 302/spring 915, Abu'l-Qāsim had left a garrison in Barqa. After his departure, however, it had been overpowered and killed by the population. Thereupon ʿUbayd Allāh had sent an army against the city under Abū Madyan b. Farrūkh al-Lahīṣī at the beginning of 303/autumn 915.[92] He was only able to conquer it after an eighteen-month siege.[93] In the month of Shawwāl 304/April 917 fugitives from Lūbiya and Marāqiya, the area east of Barqa, arrived in Alexandria. Dhukā, the governor of Egypt, transferred troops to Alexandria.[94] Under the Aghlabids, Barqa had belonged to the governorship of Egypt. It was the gateway to Egypt, and the Fatimids did not relinquish it again.[95] Its fall was the prerequisite for Abu'l-Qāsim's new campaign. For the year 305/917–918 there is only a report of Maṣāla b. Ḥabūs' activity in the service of ʿUbayd Allāh in the western part of the country. Then, strong contingents of Berbers and Arabs were concentrated in Raqqāda.

Abu'l-Qāsim set off eastward on Monday 1 Dhu'l-Qaʿda 306/5 April 919.[96] On Friday 8 Ṣafar 307/9 July 919 the vanguard of the army arrived in Alexandria.[97] In the month of Jumādā 11/29 October–26 November news reached Baghdad of a battle, in which each side had lost about 4,000 men. Thereupon the caliph al-Muqtadir commissioned the eunuch Mu'nis to march on Egypt for the second time. But it was not until Ramaḍān 307/February 920 that the latter left Baghdad.[98] Nor did he give any signs of hurry on the way. He only arrived in Fusṭāṭ on Thursday 4 Muḥarram 308/26 May 920,[99] and camped in Jīza. Meanwhile, Abu'l-Qāsim had marched south, settled in Ushmūnayn and collected the land tax in the area of Fayyūm.[100] For a year the fighting went on, more by means of defamatory poetry than with the sword.[101] Only after Thamil al-Khādim had succeeded in driving out the Fatimid armies from Alexandria and joining up with Mu'nis did the joint armies of Fusṭāṭ advance and capture the city of Fayyūm on Thursday 18 Ṣafar 309/28 June 921.[102] Abu'l-Qāsim had no choice but to retreat, and arrived in Mahdiyya on Saturday 1 Rajab 309/13 November 921.[103]

During this entire period the Qarmaṭīs of Baḥrayn were entirely quiet.

For the attack recorded by Ibn Khaldūn evidently did not take place. None of the early chroniclers, such as ʿArīb, Ibn Miskawayh, nor even Ibn al-Athīr, report any activity on the part of the Qarmaṭīs in those years.[104] Al-Masʿūdī,[105] Akhū Muḥsin,[106] and ʿAbd al-Jabbār,[107] who describe the history of the Qarmaṭīs consecutively, even emphasize the fact that after the death of Abū Saʿīd they remained peaceful until Abū Ṭāhir's capture of Baṣra in the year 311/923.[108] During the invasion of that year the inhabitants of Baṣra did not even suspect that the assailants were Qarmaṭīs. They first took them for ordinary Arabs.[109] This would hardly have been possible if the Qarmaṭīs had already overrun the city four years earlier. The Qarmaṭīs, moreover, are reported to have declared to the inhabitants of the city that the removal of ʿAlī b. ʿĪsā by the caliph had motivated their campaign.[110] Yet ʿAlī b. ʿĪsā had already been in office in the year 307/919.

The first source to mention the earlier invasion is apparently Ibn al-Jawzī. He reports under the year 307/919–920 that: 'In this year the Qarmaṭīs penetrated into Baṣra. Ḥāmid was dismissed from his office as vizier, and Abu'l-Ḥasan Ibn al-Furāt took charge [of it] for the third time.'[111] The second statement evidently offers a clue to the riddle, for the removal of Ḥāmid b. al-ʿAbbās and the new tenure of Ibn al-Furāt certainly occurred in 311/923.[112] Presumably, then, the notice of the Qarmaṭī incursion also refers to that year.

The details given by Ibn Khaldūn are not very convincing either. Nowhere is there any mention of an agitation in Baghdad on account of the Qarmaṭīs before the year 311/923,[113] or of a restoration of the city walls. On the contrary, after the disaster of that year Ibn al-Furāt criticized ʿAlī b. ʿĪsā for having neglected to pay the people entrusted with the maintenance of the walls of Baṣra and for thus having attracted the Qarmaṭīs.[114] Abu'l-Maḥāsin, who mentions the invasion of the year 307/919–920 after Ibn Khaldūn, reports no more than this: 'In this year the Qarmaṭīs penetrated into Baṣra, plundered the city, murdered and robbed.'[115]

It is obvious, then, that Ibn Khaldūn's account in this passage is based on a late, faulty source, rather than on a particularly well-informed report, as one might have expected considering his precise knowledge of the relations between Fatimids and Qarmaṭīs. But even if there had really been a Qarmaṭī invasion in the year 307/919–920, his report could easily have been recognized as an unacceptable historical reconstruction. The Qarmaṭīs made no attempt to follow the alleged command of Abu'l-Qāsim to march towards Egypt. Mu'nis did not forestall them by driving the

Fatimids out of Egypt. In fact, after Mu'nis finally reached Egypt in May 920 the armies stood facing each other for over a year, while the Qarmaṭīs did not stir.[116]

In the year 310/922–923, a battle is reported between a Fatimid detachment under Falāḥ b. Qamūn and Egyptian troops near Dhāt al-Ḥumām, 38 miles west of Alexandria.[117]

A further attack by Fatimid troops on Egyptian soil took place in the year 311/April 923–March 924. Masrūr b. Sulaymān b. Kāfī raided two oasis forts in upper Egypt and defeated their governor. He occupied the place, but the outbreak of an epidemic among his soldiers forced him to retreat to Barqa. Ibn ʿIdhārī, the only source to report this event, gives no precise date for it.[118] But since news of the victory was read out publicly in Qayrawān only on Thursday 22 Muḥarram 312/29 April 924,[119] it may be assumed that the raid took place not earlier than towards the end of the year 311 AH, i.e., hardly earlier than February 924. De Goeje connects this enterprise with the invasion of Baṣra by Abū Ṭāhir.[120] But that event took place more than six months earlier, at the end of Rabīʿ I 311/beginning of July 923. If one were to compare the movements of the two 'partners' closely, it would be more appropriate to bring up Abū Ṭāhir's attack on the pilgrim caravan returning from Mecca to Iraq in Muḥarram 312/April 924. Yet, Masrūr's campaign was obviously an enterprise with limited means and limited aims. Abū Ṭāhir, on the other hand, made no signs of marching towards Egypt, although he was certainly in a position to do so.

The following decade saw the greatest activity of the Qarmaṭīs of Baḥrayn. Almost every year Abū Ṭāhir led a raid into Mesopotamia or attacked the pilgrim caravans. The end of the ʿAbbasid reign seemed imminent. Meanwhile ʿUbayd Allāh was keeping his troops busy subduing northwestern Africa. The eastern border suddenly grew quiet.[121] The favourable opportunity to seize further parts of the impotent ʿAbbasid empire or to wipe it out altogether in collaboration with the Qarmaṭīs slipped by unused. For many a contemporary who saw in the two rebellious powers in Baḥrayn and North Africa simply two arms of the same Shiʿi movement, this must have been as incomprehensible as it is for the later observer who presupposes a general imamate of ʿUbayd Allāh over all Ismaʿilis. Thus ʿAbd al-Jabbār reports about the year 316/928, when Abū Ṭāhir was threatening Baghdad itself: 'Some people thought he [Abū Ṭāhir] was waiting for the arrival of the Maghribī Qarmaṭīs, according to an arrangement between them. But when no one came, he returned to al-Aḥsā.'[122]

The next eastern advance of the Fatimids did not occur until after the impetus of the Qarmaṭī incursions had died down. It is a misunderstanding of Ḥ. I. Ḥasan and Ṭ. A. Sharaf to assume, on the basis of al-Kindī's account,[123] that already in the year 321/933 troops from the Maghrib sent by ʿUbayd Allāh were stationed in Egypt.[124] These Maghribīs under the leadership of Ḥabashī b. Aḥmad were in fact part of the Egyptian army which the powerful Muḥammad b. ʿAlī al-Mādharāʾī had contrived to use for his private purposes. They first fought against the governor Muḥammad b. Tekin, then against Muḥammad b. Ṭughj al-Ikhshīd after his nomination by the caliph.[125] Muḥammad b. Ṭughj, however, gained the upper hand, and the rebellious Maghribīs decided to retreat to Barqa at the end of the year 323/October–November 935. At the same time they wrote to Abu'l-Qāsim, who had meanwhile succeeded ʿUbayd Allāh under his regnal name al-Qāʾim bi-Amr Allāh, asking him for permission to enter his domain and calling upon him to send an army with them to Egypt, since they knew the way and were familiar with the ins and outs of warfare. Thereupon, al-Qāʾim sent an army.[126] In the month of Rabīʿ II 324/March 936 the vanguard arrived in Alexandria. But Muḥammad b. Ṭughj sent his brother al-Ḥasan with an army to meet the aggressors. He defeated them on 5 Jumādā I 324/31 March 936, reconquered Alexandria, and the remnants of the Fatimid army fled to Barqa.[127] For this year there are no reports of activities by the Qarmaṭīs.[128]

Equally unconvincing is de Goeje's view that the raids of the Qarmaṭīs of Baḥrayn on Syria at the time of the Fatimid al-Muʿizz were carried out on the latter's instructions.[129] It is well-known that after the years of their most intensive activity the Qarmaṭīs freely negotiated and concluded agreements with the ʿAbbasid viziers, Būyids and Ḥamdānids, who granted them certain tributes and rights, above all that of taxing the pilgrims to Mecca as a reward for guarding them.[130] In the year 353/964 they exacted a consignment of iron from the Ḥamdānid Sayf al-Dawla. The latter showed such zeal in fulfilling their wish that he had the gates of Raqqa pulled down and the weights of merchants and tradesmen confiscated.[131] In the same year there is a report from Egypt about a general agitation because of a Qarmaṭī march on Syria.[132] Was it perhaps a detachment sent to watch over the transportation of the iron?

At the end of the year 354/965 Arabs of the Banū Sulaym tribe attacked and robbed the pilgrims from Egypt and Syria.[133] But the plundered goods were brought back to Kāfūr, the ruler of Egypt, by the Qarmaṭīs.[134] After Kāfūr's death on Tuesday 21 Jumādā I 357/21 April 968,[135] the Qarmaṭīs again attacked Syria under the leadership of al-Ḥasan al-Aʿṣam. They conquered Damascus and defeated the governor of Syria, al-Ḥasan b. ʿUbayd Allāh b. Ṭughj, on 2 Dhu'l-Ḥijja 357/28 October 968 before Ramla. Al-Ḥasan b. ʿUbayd Allāh fled to Egypt. The Qarmaṭīs entered Ramla and plundered the town for two days. Finally, the inhabitants ransomed themselves from the plague with the sum of 125,000 Egyptian dinars, and the Qarmaṭīs left.[136] Al-Ḥasan set out from Egypt on the 1st of Rabīʿ II/22 February 969 to return to his province.[137]

Two weeks earlier, on 14 Rabīʿ I 358/5 February 969, the Fatimid army under Jawhar had set off to conquer Egypt.[138] In the letter of safety he issued for the inhabitants of Fusṭāṭ, at the beginning of Shaʿbān 358/end of June 969, Jawhar promised in the name of his suzerain to reopen and protect the routes for the Mecca pilgrims, whose life and property had been threatened by the repeated attacks.[139] This signified an open declaration of war against the Qarmaṭīs.[140] At the first Friday worship which Jawhar attended in Fusṭāṭ on 20 Shaʿbān/9 July, the preacher read out at the end of his sermon the affirmation that al-Muʿizz had sent his armies for a holy war against the infidels (Byzantium) and those who prevented the pilgrimage.[141] That same month Jawhar also wrote a general letter of safety for the inhabitants of the country and of upper Egypt, explicitly naming and cursing the Qarmaṭīs.[142]

Al-Ḥasan b. ʿUbayd Allāh, having heard of the conquest of Egypt by Jawhar, had left Damascus in Ramaḍān 358/July–August 969 and gone to Ramla, where he was preparing for a defence against the Fatimid army. Here the Qarmaṭīs again attacked and defeated him. But he was able to conclude peace with them, and also established marriage ties with them (*ṣāharahum*) in Dhu'l-Ḥijja/16 October–13 November.[143] After the Qarmaṭīs had camped near the city for thirty days, they withdrew. A detachment evidently remained, however, for the contemporary Ibn Zūlāq reports that Jaʿfar b. Falāḥ, the Fatimid general, fought and defeated the Qarmaṭīs early in the year 359/970,[144] in a battle near Ramla in which al-Ḥasan b. ʿUbayd Allāh was taken prisoner.[145] Among the prisoners whom Jawhar sent to his suzerain on 17 Jumādā II 359/27 April 970, there was, besides al-Ḥasan, a certain Ibn Ghazwān, chief of the Qarmaṭīs.[146]

It was probably at the peace treaty between al-Ḥasan and the Qarmaṭīs that the former had bound himself to an annual tribute of 300,000 dinars.[147] The loss of this tribute with the conquest of Syria by Jaʿfar b. Falāḥ is given by most sources as the cause for the Qarmaṭī attack on the Fatimid army in the following year. De Goeje's opinion that this reason is too insignificant seems tenable only if it is assumed that the Baḥrayn

Qarmaṭīs had hitherto been loyal followers of the Fatimids.[148] But it is already clear that this was by no means the case. The true motive of the Qarmaṭīs for their raids in Syria lay in their desire for booty and tribute, which had determined the policies of their, by nature, very poor state of Baḥrayn since the thirties of the 10th century AD. To the Syrians and Egyptians who had duly paid their pilgrimage taxes they were prepared to secure the return of robbed properties, as they had to do in order to preserve their good reputation as protectors of the pilgrim caravans. But the confusion which ensued in Egypt after Kāfūr's death offered them a good opportunity to gain booty. As soon as this aim was reached, they withdrew without making any attempt to introduce the Shiʿi doctrine in the conquered areas or to subject them to Fatimid reign, as might have been expected if these campaigns had been carried out on the order of al-Muʿizz. When the advance of the Fatimid army cut off their new source of income, and Jawhar openly announced his intention to deprive the Qarmaṭīs of their right to pose as guardians of the pilgrim caravans, there was no alternative left to them but war.

Among the accounts of the Arab historians on which the argument for a close co-operation between Qarmaṭīs of Baḥrayn and Fatimids during the reign of al-Muʿizz is normally based, special mention must be made of Ibn Khaldūn. In a closely-written three-page report[149] he describes how the Fatimid caliphs again and again interfered from North Africa in the internal affairs of the Qarmaṭīs, until al-Ḥasan rebelled against his distant masters in the year 360/971. He does not mention his sources, but he seems to have had at his disposal an account which is no longer available to us, for he reports a series of events that are not mentioned in our other sources. On the whole, however, he gives the impression of having dealt very freely with his sources.

De Goeje has already found evidence of numerous errors in this report.[150] Nevertheless, Ibn Khaldūn is his most valuable witness in his demonstration of an understanding between the Qarmaṭī and Fatimid movements. It may, therefore, be useful to juxtapose the reports suggesting a subordination of that kind on the part of the Qarmaṭīs with the oldest available accounts.

Ibn Khaldūn writes about the events leading from Abū Saʿīd's assassination to Abū Ṭāhir's succession: 'Abū Saʿīd had destined his eldest son, Saʿīd, for the succession . . . (gap in text) . . . But his youngest brother Abū Ṭāhir[151] Sulaymān rebelled against him, killed him, and assumed the rule over them. The ʿIqdāniyya[152] swore allegiance to him, and he received ʿUbayd Allāh's letter with the investiture.'[153]

It is known that Abu'l-Qāsim Saʿīd was not killed at the time, but rather died in the year 361/972.[154] The Baghdad chronicles, which were generally copied by later historical works,[155] confirm that Abū Saʿīd had appointed his eldest son as his successor, and that Abū Ṭāhir had then forced his way to power. In addition there is another tradition which no doubt has its origin in the Qarmaṭī history by the anti-Ismaʿili polemical writer Abū ʿAbd Allāh Muḥammad b. ʿAlī b. Rizām al-Ṭāʾī of Kūfa.[156] According to this tradition, Abū Saʿīd had provided that after his death his eldest son, Saʿīd, should first assume the succession. When Abū Ṭāhir had grown up, however, he should turn over the rule to him. Following this direction, Saʿīd had surrendered the command to his brother in the year 305/June 917–July 918.[157] Abū Ṭāhir, to be sure, must have been only ten years old at the time.[158] Similarly, Ibn Ḥawqal reports that Abū Saʿīd had instructed his elder sons to submit and be obedient to the youngest when he came of age 'for a reason which he communicated to his survivors'.[159] An intervention by ʿUbayd Allāh is nowhere mentioned.

The untenability of Ibn Khaldūn's report about the Qarmaṭī attack on Baṣra in the year 307/919–920 has already been shown. After describing the pillage of Mecca, the massacre of the pilgrims, and the seizure of the Black Stone of the Kaʿba, he writes: "ʿUbayd Allāh al-Mahdī wrote to him [Abū Ṭāhir] from Qayrawān, reproved, and warned, him about it. So he wrote to him that he was incapable of restoring the [killed] people and promised the return of the Black Stone.'[160] ʿUbayd Allāh's letter is known from the report of Thābit b. Sinān, who quotes a passage from it verbatim.[161] But this letter should not be interpreted as proof of the unity of the Qarmaṭīs and the Fatimids, or of the continuation of this unity. For the Black Stone was not returned until years after Abū Ṭāhir's death. De Goeje is therefore forced to assume a secret order on the part of ʿUbayd Allāh which ran counter to the public letter.[162] But it has already been shown that the way the Qarmaṭīs acted around this time by no means gives grounds for the assumption that they acted on secret orders from the Fatimids. It is certainly possible that the motive for ʿUbayd Allāh's letter was to wash himself clean of any suspicions of his complicity in the outrage.[163] For during those very years there had evidently been a widespread suspicion that the two Shiʿi movements in North Africa and Baḥrayn were acting hand in glove with each other.[164]

Ibn Khaldūn goes on: 'Then he gave it [the Black Stone] back in the year 339 (951), after al-Manṣūr Ismāʿīl of Qayrawān had approached him regarding its return.'[165] If de Goeje relies on this passage to substantiate his opinion that the Qarmaṭīs had returned the Black Stone on al-Manṣūr's order,[166] then Quṭb al-Dīn's statement, which he also interprets in his favour, suggests the contrary. For the latter reports that al-Manṣūr had written to Aḥmad b. Abī Saʿīd and offered him 50,000 dinars for the return of the stone, but he had refused.[167] This version of the correspondence seems the only one which is consistent with the accounts in the other sources. For as de Goeje himself explains, the return was negotiated with the ʿAbbasid government and probably paid with a large tribute.[168] The account of Ibn ʿIdhārī, the third of de Goeje's sources, is totally useless. According to him, al-Manṣūr had set out for the orient (*bilād al-mashriq*) in the year 339/950–951 and had brought back the Black Stone to its place in its corner of the Kaʿba.[169] Al-Manṣūr actually never left his empire.

Ibn Khaldūn then reports: 'So they brought it back. Bajkam,[170] the usurper of the power in Baghdad in the days of al-Mustakfī,[171] had offered them 50,000 gold [dinars] to restore it. But they had refused and maintained that they had taken it away by the order of their imam, ʿUbayd Allāh, and would only restore it by his order or that of his successor.' This seems to be a typical result of Ibn Khaldūn's working method. For the Qarmaṭīs' claim that they had been ordered to take the stone away and would restore it only by order actually recurs in numerous sources,[172] but a name is nowhere mentioned. This omission cannot be accidental, for if the Qarmaṭīs had really said they had acted on ʿUbayd Allāh's order, this would certainly have been handed down by the earliest chroniclers, who mostly had anti-Fatimid attitudes.

The Qarmaṭīs' motive in maintaining that they were acting on order evidently was not meant to shift the responsibility for these actions to someone else. At the root of it lay one of their essential convictions, namely, that everything that happened was precisely predestined to happen, and they alone, as the true believers, possessed the knowledge of this predestination. Through this knowledge they were infallible and invincible in their actions.[173] Al-Dhahabī clearly understood this when he explained their words by saying what they meant was predestination (*al-qadar*).[174]

About the events following Abū Ṭāhir's death in 332/944, Ibn Khaldūn reports as follows:[175] At first his brother Aḥmad assumed the power. The ʿIqdāniyya council, however, was inclined towards Sābūr, the son of Abū Ṭāhir, and wrote to the Fatimid al-Qāʾim on this matter. The latter invested Aḥmad and appointed Sābūr as his successor. So Aḥmad continued ruling. It was he who restored the Black Stone.[176] In the year 358/969, Sābūr imprisoned his uncle by arrangement with his brothers. But Aḥmad's brother rebelled and freed him. Sābūr was killed, and his brothers and followers were banished to the island of Uwāl. In the year 359/970, Abū Manṣūr Aḥmad died, allegedly poisoned by Sābūr's followers. Then his son al-Ḥasan al-Aʿṣam took over the reign.

This description of the succession deviates considerably from the accounts in other sources. Aḥmad b. Abī Saʿīd is mentioned by Quṭb al-Dīn as the partner of the ineffectual correspondence with the Fatimid al-Manṣūr about the return of the Black Stone.[177] As successors of Abū Ṭāhir, however, three of his brothers are usually named: Abu'l-Qāsim Saʿīd, who was apparently the most influential, the ailing Abu'l-ʿAbbās al-Faḍl and Abū Yaʿqūb Yūsuf, who was addicted to drink.[178] Already in Abū Ṭāhir's time it can be assumed that nominally power lay jointly in the hands of Abū Saʿīd's sons, although the personality of Abū Ṭāhir secured him the decision.[179] This system came into full force after his death. The letter announcing the return of the Black Stone was written jointly by Abū Ṭāhir's brothers.[180] This exactly corresponds with the picture of the structure of the Qarmaṭī state presented by Ibn Ḥawqal.[181] It was only for warfare that a leader was agreed on. Even when al-Ḥasan al-Aʿṣam acted as the constant commander of the Qarmaṭī army during the fights against the Fatimids, the supreme power remained in the hands of Abū Saʿīd's sons. Thus Ibn al-Jawzī reports under the year 361/972:[182] 'In Jumādā II, Abu'l-Qāsim Saʿīd b. Abī Saʿīd al-Jannābī died in Hajar. After him his brother Abū Yaʿqūb Yūsuf ruled. Except for him, none of the sons of Abū Saʿīd al-Jannābī remained alive. After Abū Yaʿqūb,[183] the Qarmaṭīs transferred the authority to six of their sons jointly.'[184]

By further developing Ibn Khaldūn's account, de Goeje has tried to elucidate the background for Sābūr's rebellion which led to his imprisonment and death in the middle of Ramaḍān 358/beginning of August 969. He believed that al-Muʿizz had nominated Sābūr as successor to his father Abū Ṭāhir since he could not expect any effective support for the conquest of Egypt from Sābūr's uncle Aḥmad[185] who had contented himself with an annual tribute after his victory over al-Ḥasan b. ʿUbayd Allāh in 357/968. This hypothesis is untenable. According to Ibn Ḥawqal, Aḥmad's son al-Ḥasan al-Aʿṣam, who had led the invasion of Syria, was suspected after his return of having embezzled booty.[186] This has nothing to do with Sābūr's revolt. Nor was he immediately rehabilitated after Sābūr's death. In the second Syrian campaign, which followed two months later, two of his cousins obtained the command over the army in his place.[187]

Although the scanty sources for the history of the Qarmaṭī state in this period allow us no insight into the details of the developments, the overall balance of power leading to Sābūr's revolt appears to be quite clear. After the death of Abū Ṭāhir, who had practically ruled as an autocrat, his brothers divided the authority among themselves. The seven sons of Abū Ṭāhir enjoyed high esteem and honour, but they were excluded from power.[188] Sābūr, the eldest and most esteemed among them, was not satisfied with the situation. He demanded the rule and the command of the army on the grounds that his father had designated him as his successor.[189] Thereupon he was thrown into prison by his uncles and died. There is no reason whatsoever to assume an intervention by the Fatimids.

Ibn Khaldūn describes the events leading to the 'secession' of the Qarmaṭīs as follows: After the conquest of Damascus by Jaʿfar b. Falāḥ, al-Ḥasan al-Aʿṣam demanded the tribute levied from the city, but this was refused. Al-Muʿizz wrote him a rude letter and engaged in intrigues on behalf of the followers and sons of Abū Ṭāhir, who had been exiled to the island of Uwāl after Sābūr's revolt. When al-Ḥasan heard of this, he renounced his allegiance to al-Muʿizz and marched towards Damascus. In the year 361/972, al-Muʿizz once again wrote to him, severely rebuked him, and deposed him.

By the second letter which Ibn Khaldūn mentions here, the letter preserved by Akhū Muḥsin must be meant.[190] In fact, al-Muʿizz wrote it only after his arrival in Cairo,[191] that is not before Ramaḍān 362/June 973. From its contents one is inclined to conclude that it was the first letter he sent to al-Ḥasan. There is no mention of a dismissal in it. On the other hand, Ibn Ḥawqal also refers to the continuation of political rivalries among the Qarmaṭīs of Baḥrayn after Sābūr's death, but without giving any definite reasons.[192]

The defectiveness of the continuation of Ibn Khaldūn's report has been sufficiently pointed out by de Goeje.[193] Yet he believed that he could follow him in supposing that the Qarmaṭīs returned to the allegiance of the Fatimids because around the year 378/988 al-Muqaddasī mentions a treasury of the Mahdi (*khizānat al-Mahdī*) in al-Aḥsā.[194] This must indeed seem surprising, because only ten years earlier the Fatimid al-ʿAzīz had promised the Qarmaṭīs an annual tribute to restrain them from further attacks on Syria.[195] Is de Goeje perhaps wrong here in equating the Mahdi with the Fatimids? This becomes almost a certainty when one considers Ibn Ḥawqal's report for the year 367/977 that a fifth of the revenues of the Qarmaṭī state was set aside for the 'Lord of the Time'.[196]

On the basis of de Goeje's investigations and the examples mentioned here, Ibn Khaldūn's report proves to be a late historical construction which is worthless for a critical assessment of the question regarding the connection between Qarmaṭīs and Fatimids. Here only a strict examination of the earliest sources can lead us further.[197]

Al-Masʿūdī's report in his *Kitāb al-tanbīh waʾl-ishrāf*, written in 345/956, is only a short synopsis of his earlier, lost accounts to which he frequently refers. This is all the more unfortunate since he was exceptionally knowledgeable in Qarmaṭī affairs. He mentions that he had talked to many of their envoys and scholars.[198] He briefly points out the ideological union of the movements in Baḥrayn, the Yemen, and North Africa which he had described at length elsewhere.[199]

A consecutive history of the Qarmaṭīs was written by Thābit b. Sinān, who continued it until the year of his death, 365/976. His work was extensively used by Ibn al-Athīr.[200] He only reports definite events which he evidently considered well-authenticated and never directly deals with the connection between the Qarmaṭīs and the Fatimids. But several passages which have been pointed out by B. Lewis,[201] imply a union of this kind. An inhabitant of Baghdad who had immigrated from Shīrāz was accused of treasonable correspondence with Abū Ṭāhir and declared at his trial that his imam was the Fatimid one in North Africa.[202] The secretary of Yūsuf b. Abi'l-Sāj, who was commissioned by the caliph to fight against the Qarmaṭīs of Baḥrayn, accused his master of having secretly revealed to him that he believed in the imamate of the ʿAlid in North Africa whom Abū Ṭāhir also followed.

These reports, both recorded under the year 315/927, are of great interest as regards the mental atmosphere in Baghdad at the time. Hitherto they had evidently had no suspicion of a relationship between the two Shiʿi movements.[203] So the statements of the Ismaʿili must have made them prick up their ears. This is perhaps the reason why the otherwise insignificant episode was recorded by the chronicler. It does not offer any certain proof for the political bonds between Baḥrayn and Qayrawān. A follower of the Fatimid imams in Baghdad might well supply Abū Ṭāhir with information in order to support him in fighting the common enemy, whether or not he knew if the latter directly served his master. He himself said that he did not know Abū Ṭāhir personally. The secretary's accusation of Yūsuf b. Abi'l-Sāj, which can easily be assumed to be a calumny,[204] springs from a similar reflection: Two Shiʿi rebellions were threatening the ʿAbbasid empire. What was more natural than to see a single conspiracy behind them?

Finally, Thābit mentions the letter of al-Muʿizz to al-Ḥasan al-Aʿṣam in which he reminded him 'that the doctrine is one, and that the Qarmaṭīs had summoned to allegiance to him and his fathers'.[205]

The pro-Fatimid attitude is represented by Ibn Ḥawqal in his *Kitāb ṣūrat al-arḍ*, written around the year 367/978. He also had connections with high-ranking personalities among the Qarmaṭīs. In 361/972 he had spoken to Abu'l-Ḥusayn ʿAlī al-Jazarī in Sicily, who had told him about the events leading to the alliance between the Qarmaṭīs and the ʿAbbasids.[206] From him stems the information that Abū Saʿīd was originally a follower of the Fatimids but had defected after the assassination of ʿAbdān and killed the missionary Abū Zakariyyā' al-Ṭamāmī. He curses Abū Saʿīd and Abū Ṭāhir for their atrocities for which reason de Goeje calls him a hypocrite.[207] Elsewhere he speaks in connection with Abū Zakariyyā' al-Ṭamāmī of the 'first doctrine and old rule' of the Qarmaṭīs.[208] He characterizes their doctrine at his time by the fact that they let the imamate come to an end.[209] With Shiʿi sects this normally meant that they were expecting the return of the last imam as the Mahdi. Unfortunately, he does not name the latter.

Shortly after the year 372/983, the Sharīf Akhū Muḥsin from Damascus, himself a descendant of the same Muḥammad b. Ismāʿīl to whom the Fatimids traced back their genealogy, wrote one of those polemical works intended to reveal the secrets of the Ismaʿilis and refute their doctrine from a Sunni point of view.[210] In the historical section of his work he presents a detailed history of the Qarmaṭī movement which relies on Ibn Rizām for its passages on the earlier history. He reports at great length about the secession of Ḥamdān Qarmaṭ and ʿAbdān, though without saying anything about the attitude of the Qarmaṭīs of Baḥrayn. Only in his explanation of the threatening letter which al-Muʿizz wrote to al-Ḥasan al-Aʿṣam, he reports, following al-Nuwayrī: After his arrival in Egypt, al-Muʿizz decided to write to al-Ḥasan b. Aḥmad to let him know that they belonged to the same confession, and that the Qarmaṭīs had received their doctrine from the Ismaʿilis, who were their masters in this respect. From al-Ḥasan's reply to his threats he hoped to learn what he had up his sleeve, and whether the news of his arrival in Egypt would frighten him. 'Al-Ḥasan knew full well that the two sects were one and the same, for it was not unknown to him that the one and the other confessed to the exoteric and the esoteric doctrine. In fact, both agreed on teaching atheism and total anarchy regarding men and property, and on denying the prophetic mission. But even if agreement on the doctrine prevails, as soon as the adherents of one party have the advantage over those of another, they consider it permissible to kill them, and grant them no mercy.'[211]

Here a union of Qarmaṭīs and Isma'ilis, i.e., followers of the Fatimids, is shown not on the basis of definite political relations, but on the grounds of an ideological conformity of the most general kind. Despite this conformity they form two parties. The same Akhū Muḥsin writes at the end of that section of his book where he describes the doctrine of the Bāṭinīs: 'This original doctrine went through a few changes in the course of time, and the community split up into different branches after its dissemination in the Maghrib, Egypt and Syria. In particular, there was a change of opinion about Muḥammad b. Ismā'īl, for whom they first demanded recognition as the imam and who was then replaced by a descendant of 'Abd Allāh b. Maymūn al-Qaddāḥ, whose progeny ruled in the Maghrib, Egypt and Syria.'[212]

In Akhū Muḥsin's work we also first come across an allegedly Isma'ili writing which was to excite the minds of pious people for a long time to come. For the heresiographers and polemicists it became one of the main sources from which they drew their knowledge about the secret doctrine of the Bāṭinīs. They found in it all the atheism, libertinism and blasphemy they could have wished for to demonstrate the infamy of these heretics. It even radiated its effect towards the Christian Occident. According to L. Massignon, it is to be regarded as the first version of the legend 'de tribus impostoribus', which circulated two centuries later in the West and was finally credited to Frederic II Hohenstaufen.[213]

Akhū Muḥsin knew the work under the title *Kitāb al-siyāsa*. He states that he had read it himself and quotes two fragments from it.[214] This 'book of methodology' consists of instructions for the missionaries about the procedure of catching souls. The author speaks of seven steps of attainment (*balāgh*) through which the neophyte is gradually initiated into the atheistic doctrine.[215] Only a few years later Ibn al-Nadīm (writing in 377/987) mentions these seven degrees. The book of the first degree is destined for the general public, that of the second for the somewhat advanced, that of the third for people converted in the second year, etc. Of the 'book of the seventh attainment' (*Kitāb al-balāgh al-sābi'*) he says that he has read it himself and has found in it a great deal of libertinism and mockery of the prophets.[216] This description is characteristic and shows that it was a supplement to the 'book of methodology'. 'Abd al-Qāhir al-Baghdādī (d. 429/1038) knows the book under the title of *Kitāb al-siyāsa wa'l-balāgh al-akīd wa'l-nāmūs al-a'ẓam*, and his quotations from it bear out Ibn al-Nadīm's verdict.[217] While Akhū Muḥsin and Ibn al-Nadīm name neither the author nor a definite addressee,[218] he claims that ʿUbayd Allāh had sent the work to Abū Ṭāhir. The Qāḍī Abū Bakr al-Bāqillānī (d. 403/1013) refuted it in his lost *Kitāb hatk al-astār wa-kashf al-asrār* and seems to have named a Fatimid *qāḍī* as its author.[219] ʿAbd al-Jabbār (wrote around 400/1010) reports, however, that the Fatimid Abu'l-Qāsim had sent it to Abū Ṭāhir while his father was still alive. For ʿUbayd Allāh had first described him as an orphan from the house of ʿAlī, descending from Ismāʿīl b. Jaʿfar (al-Ṣādiq).[220] Niẓām al-Mulk (wrote in 485/1092) suggests that Abū Ṭāhir had requested it from the missionaries.[221] Abu'l-Qāsim al-Qayrawānī is also mentioned by the Yemenite Muḥammad b. al-Ḥasan al-Daylamī (wrote in 707/1308) as the author of the work, from which he quotes at length under the title of *al-Balāgh al-akbar*.[222] The Zaydī Imam Ibn al-Murtaḍā (d. 840/1437) says that Abu'l-Qāsim al-Qayrawānī had sent it to a certain Waṣīf al-Muḥammadī.[223]

Abu'l-Muẓaffar ʿImād al-Dīn Ṭāhir al-Isfarā'inī (d. 471/1078) mentions the work without naming its title, probably following al-Baghdādī.[224] Ibn al-Jawzī (d. 597/1200) quotes an excerpt, without naming the title of the book, as an instruction to the missionaries.[225] The theologian Sayf al-Dīn ʿAlī al-Āmidī (d. 631/1233) knows at least the title.[226] Ibn Taymiyya (d. 728/1328) mentions it in his legal opinion about the Nuṣayrīs.[227] The later historian ʿImād al-Dīn b. Kathīr knows it from al-Bāqillānī's refutation and tries to identify the Fatimid *qāḍī* who is alleged to have written it. He believes it was the Qāḍī ʿAbd al-ʿAzīz, the son-in-law of Jawhar, the conqueror of Egypt.[228] He means ʿAbd al-ʿAzīz b. Muḥammad b. al-Nuʿmān, the grandson of the well-known *qāḍī* under the Fatimids al-Manṣūr and al-Muʿizz and author of the most important Ismaʿili law book. But ʿAbd al-ʿAzīz was only born in the year 355/966, and Ibn Ḥajar al-ʿAsqalānī tries to correct Ibn Kathīr. The book, he says, was written by ʿAlī, the uncle of ʿAbd al-ʿAzīz, and by al-Nuʿmān, his grandfather.[229]

The Ismaʿili tradition, however, seems to know this work merely from the polemics of its opponents. Ḥamīd al-Dīn al-Kirmānī, an important author and teacher of the Fatimid Ismaʿilis (d. around 411/1020), at any rate denies, in his letter *al-Risāla al-kāfiya fi'l-radd ʿalā'l-Hārūnī al-Ḥasanī*, that it belongs to the literature of his community. His opponent, the Daylamī Zaydī Imam Abu'l-Ḥusayn al-Mu'ayyad bi'llāh Aḥmad b. al-Ḥusayn b. Hārūn al-Buṭḥānī (d. 411/1020), who had substantiated his accusations against the Ismaʿilis on the strength of the *al-Balāgh al-akbar*, is advised by him to read reliable and well-known Ismaʿili works.[230]

Already C. H. Becker saw a malevolent forgery in the work as quoted by Akhū Muḥsin,[231] and the details given by al-Daylamī and al-Baghdādī fully confirm this. It hardly seems likely that the preaching of a religion should be based on such cynicisms; and the doctrine ascribed to the Isma'ilis here is an intentional distortion, though based on considerable knowledge, as are repeated attempts to prove that they belonged to the Dahriyya, the Naturalists, who considered the material world to be uncreated.[232]

Al-Maqrīzī, who often used Akhū Muḥsin, though usually without acknowledging his source, does not quote his commentary to the threatening letter of al-Mu'izz.[233] Instead, he adds to his account of the Qarmaṭī attack on Egypt the following quotation from a contemporary, probably the well-known man of letters and *qāḍī* Abū 'Alī al-Muḥassin al-Tanūkhī (d. 384/994):[234] 'All this after the Qarmaṭīs had first bragged about the Mahdi and made people believe that he was the lord of the Maghrib, and that their propaganda was for him. They had exchanged letters with the Imam al-Manṣūr Ismā'īl b. Muḥammad al-Qā'im b. 'Ubayd Allāh al-Mahdī and revealed to their greatest friends that they belonged to his following.[235] Until their lie became obvious through the war led against them by the general Jawhar . . .'

This judgement must be understood against the background of the external situation. The Qarmaṭīs, who had hitherto given themselves out to be the followers of the Mahdi, now all of a sudden publicly embraced the cause of the 'Abbasid caliphate. They formed the only effective fighting force which offered resistance to the further eastern advance of the Fatimids. They cursed the latter from the pulpit, although the Fatimids had claimed to represent the Mahdi.[236] From their speeches about the Mahdi, some people had taken them for vassals of the Fatimids. Now the observer concludes from their volte-face that they had formerly lied in order to lead the world astray.[237] As a proof for this, however, he can only mention an exchange of letters with al-Manṣūr,[238] of which he unfortunately does not give the content, and vague rumours.

The real difficulty in assessing the Qarmaṭī movement in Baḥrayn lies in the scarcity of sources bearing witness to their creed. While the religious literature of the Fatimids has been preserved in rich abundance through the survival of the community of their adherents, the historian has to rely in respect of Qarmaṭī views almost exclusively on the statements of their Sunni opponents. The latter, however, treated all Bāṭinīs as a unit and rarely took the trouble, in their polemic zeal, to distinguish between spatially and temporally limited phenomena. This approach was intensified by the strict secrecy in which the Bāṭinīs themselves enveloped part of their doctrine, as well as their early history. Thus, there are only very few occasional reports which definitely refer to the creed of the Qarmaṭīs of Baḥrayn. These reports indicate that the expectation of the imminent coming of the Mahdi played a significant part in their doctrine, and also that this expectation was not fulfilled by the appearance of the Fatimids.

In the year 316/928, a young Persian from Iṣfahān, ostensibly a descendant of the Persian kings, joined the Qarmaṭīs in Baḥrayn.[239] In Ramaḍān 319/September–October 931, Abū Ṭāhir surrendered the government to him. For a short time he disposed of absolute power, ordered the most senseless atrocities, and had a number of influential people killed.[240] De Goeje has translated and commented various reports about these events.[241] His explanation that the false prophet had attained his power by claiming to be an emissary of ʿUbayd Allāh[242] is unacceptable and has been rejected in more recent investigations.[243] Nor is it consistent with al-Masʿūdī's report that the Iṣfahānī had already lived with the Qarmaṭīs for years.

Remarkable, however, is the explanation in one of the reports that Ibn Sanbar had initiated the Iṣfahānī into some secrets which Abū Ṭāhir had confided to him alone and had instructed him: 'Go to Abū Ṭāhir and tell him that you are the man to whose allegiance his father and he himself have summoned the people. If he then asks you for signs and proofs, reveal these secrets to him.' Abū Ṭāhir had no doubts about the authenticity of these signs and proclaimed to his adherents: 'This is the man I have summoned you to follow, and to him belongs the command.'[244]

Particularly interesting, in spite of certain hardly credible details, is the eyewitness report of the physician Ibn Ḥamdān which Ibn Rizām added to his description of the episode. Here, too, there is a mention of a sign by which the Iṣfahānī was able to delude Abū Ṭāhir and his brothers into believing that he was the expected one.[245] Abū Ṭāhir now proclaimed to his adherents that they had all been asses so far. God in his goodness had now sent them the young Persian, who was Abū Ṭāhir's own and their Lord and God, and they were his servants. To him belonged the sovereignty, and he possessed them all. Then they picked up earth and strewed it on their heads. Thereupon, Abū Ṭāhir declared: 'Know then, community of men, that the religion has henceforth appeared. It is the religion of our father Adam, and all the belief we had was false. All the things the missionaries made you hear, their talk about Moses, Jesus and Mohammed, was falsehood and deceit. The [true] religion is in fact the original religion of Adam,[246] and those are all wily deceivers (*dajjālūn*); so curse them.' Then the people cursed them, including Abraham, Mohammed, even ʿAlī and his descendants.[247]

Here the antinomian tendency which had from the beginning more or less latently characterized a major part of the Ismaʿili movement evidently led to a drastic turn. The lawgivers, the prophets, are unequivocally condemned. The true religion is the lawless religion of Adam which is now revived by the expected one turned God. For the reform of the Iṣfahānī consisted of the abrogation of religious laws. Thus far Ibn Ḥamdān's statements can certainly be trusted.

On the basis of this report the account of ʿAbd al-Jabbār seems to require certain corrections.[248] According to him, Abū Ṭāhir had explained to his followers that the doctrines dished out to them about Muḥammad, then ʿAlī, then Ismāʿīl b. Jaʿfar, then Muḥammad b. Ismāʿīl and the Mahdi were nonsense. This was a secret which he and his predecessors had kept for sixty years and were now making public. Abū Ṭāhir ordered them to curse the 'liars', namely, the prophets, including Adam, and ordered the missionaries to reveal their secrets. So they reported the machinations of ʿAbd Allāh b. Maymūn and Muḥammad b. al-Ḥusayn,[249] as they were mentioned in the books of Ibn Rizām, a certain ʿAṭiyya, and other scholars.

From this account, taken by itself, it would be possible to deduce with B. Lewis[250] a secession from the Fatimids who were pilloried as the descendants of that very ʿAbd Allāh b. Maymūn. Yet ʿAbd al-Jabbār is too much of a secondary polemical source to be trusted without reservation as is clear from a comparison of his statements with those of Ibn Ḥamdān, one of his sources by way of Ibn Rizām.[251] Whether it was exactly at that time that 'the machinations of ʿAbd Allāh b. Maymūn and Muḥammad b. al-Ḥusayn' were made public for the first time is uncertain.[252] What is more important is the fact that the Iṣfahānī owed his success to the expectation of the Mahdi which the Qarmaṭīs of Baḥrayn had already held long before his appearance despite the Fatimids' claim to the title.

Here another aspect of the episode may briefly be discussed. The false Mahdi was a Persian and, according to al-Masʿūdī, a descendant of the Persian kings. It is a favourite theme of anti-Ismaʿili polemics that the motive of the founders of the Ismaʿili movement was a plot against Islam and the reign of the Arabs in order to re-establish the reign of the Persians and their faith. The polemicists refer above all to Muḥammad b. al-Ḥusayn Dindān, who is described as a fanatical Shuʿūbī and hater of

Arabs. According to Ibn Rizām,[253] he claimed to have discovered in the stars that the hegemony of Islam would be replaced by that of the Persians and their religion in the eighth conjunction, because of (or after) the transition of the triplicity of Scorpio, the sign of Islam, to Sagittarius, the sign of the Persian religion. A similar prediction is mentioned by al-Bīrūnī and al-Baghdādī in connection with the Qarmaṭī creed. It was predicted that the Persians would recover their hegemony in the 18th conjunction after the birth of Muḥammad.[254]

These polemic accusations are not particularly credible as regards the Ismaʿili movement in general. In the Fatimid doctrine there are no reverberations of Shuʿūbī tendencies, and this is also true of the doctrine of Ḥamdān Qarmaṭ and ʿAbdān, as far as we know. So here the Qarmaṭīs of Baḥrayn went their own way.[255]

The expectation of the Mahdi is also reflected in a poem, by Abū Ṭāhir, of which fragments are extant.[256] In it he warns the inhabitants of Iraq against false hopes because of his retreat to Hajar. He will return, he will inflict defeat after defeat on them and slaughter them without mercy. Then he designates himself as the one who summons to obey the Mahdi. Does he mean ʿUbayd Allāh, as Ṭ. A. Sharaf and Ḥ. I. Ḥasan assume?[257] Characteristically, they do not quote another verse where Abū Ṭāhir declares that he will live until the coming of Jesus, son of Mary. There can hardly be any doubt that he means the appearance of the expected Mahdi.[258]

De Goeje has cautiously dated the poem in 319/931, after Abū Ṭāhir's voluntary retreat from Kūfa. The verse with the astrological content, which he analyzed in detail and which prompted him to carry out a valuable investigation of the significance of astrological predictions for the Fatimids and Qarmaṭīs, is unfortunately handed down in variants and cannot be interpreted unequivocally.[259] But from the fragments of the poem transmitted by al-Dhahabī it may be inferred that Abū Ṭāhir meant his retreat after the fighting of the year 316, beginning of Shaʿbān/end of September 928. In four lines[260] he mentions details of his campaigns in that year, the capture of al-Anbār, and the advance to ʿAqarqūf,[261] only four hours away from Baghdad. The context in which the poem is handed down by al-Bīrūnī and al-Baghdādī points to the same conclusion.

It was around this time, at any rate, that the expectation of the Mahdi consolidated itself into the firm conviction that his appearance was imminent. Thus al-Bīrūnī writes: 'Before the appearance of this boy [the Iṣfahānī], the Qarmaṭīs . . . had promised each other the arrival of the expected one in the seventh conjunction of the fiery triplicity.'[262] As evidence he then quotes Abū Ṭāhir's poem. The conjunction referred to occurred in the year 316/928.[263] The same is reported by al-Baghdādī, who adds that Abū Ṭāhir had set out from al-Aḥsā with this assertion, had waylaid the pilgrims, and finally overrun Mecca.[264] His statement that Abū Ṭāhir had sent the poem to the Muslims after a defeat can only refer then to the retreat of 316/928, not to the peaceful surrender of Kūfa in 319/931. Finally, ʿAbd al-Jabbār[265] adds to his description of the pillage of Baṣra and Kūfa in the years 311/923 and 312/925:[266] 'The Shiʿis . . . said: Abū Ṭāhir b. Abī Saʿīd is the friend of God, the proof of God (*walī Allāh wa-ḥūjjat Allāh*) and the deputy (*khalīfa*) of the Mahdi, who will soon appear, in Baḥrayn. Abū Ṭāhir is his deputy, who conquers the earth for him, and his [the Mahdi's] reign will be in Baḥrayn. Then a large crowd of the inhabitants of Kūfa and surroundings set out, and saying: let us emigrate to the land of the Mahdi before he appears, brought their goods and chattels and their families [to Baḥrayn].'

In his *al-Tanbīh*, al-Masʿūdī hints that there were certain reasons, evidently of a special kind, for Abū Ṭāhir's retreat in 316/928, and that he had mentioned them elsewhere.[267] Unfortunately, this passage is not extant. But it is not unlikely that these reasons were precisely the fact that the Mahdi was now to appear in Baḥrayn. Ibn al-Jawzī's report[268] is significant in this respect: 'After Abū Ṭāhir al-Qarmaṭī had returned to his country, he built an abode (*dār*), which he called "abode of emigration",[269] and summoned to the Mahdi.[270] His affair was taking on serious forms, the number of his adherents increased, and he felt tempted to attack Kūfa. The tax-collectors of the government in the cultivated land (*sawād*) fled, and his followers raided the villages, murdered and plundered.' As can be gathered from subsequent statements, what is meant by the followers is the group of Qarmaṭīs in the surroundings of Kūfa whom the chroniclers know under the name of Baqliyya.[271] They had so far remained quiet. While Abū Ṭāhir was in Syria[272] they had assembled in their 'abode of emigration' and summoned the whole population to follow them.[273] It is reported of them, too, that they summoned to the Mahdi.[274] The revolt was, however, quickly suppressed by troops of the caliph.

Since de Goeje considers these Qarmaṭīs of the Kūfa area, the former arena of Ḥamdān Qarmaṭ and ʿAbdān, as followers of ʿUbayd Allāh,[275] we may briefly go into the rather sparse reports about the Ismaʿili movement in Iraq after the death of Zikrawayh. Akhū Muḥsin reports that after the disappearance of Abū Ḥātim al-Zuṭṭī, a group of Qarmaṭīs maintained that Zikrawayh was still alive. But another group said: 'God's proof (*ḥujja*) is Muḥammad b. Ismāʿīl.'[276] Of the followers of Zikrawayh there are no reports later on. From the year 312/925 we learn, however, that near Kūfa a man appeared who pretended to be Muḥammad b. Ismāʿīl. He was able to gather around him a large number of Arabs and inhabitants of the cultivated land (*sawād*). When the matter took on a threatening aspect in Shawwāl 312/January 925, an army was sent against him from Baghdad. He was defeated, and many of his adherents were killed.[277]

In Baghdad around this time the vizier Abu'l-Qāsim al-Khāqānī tracked down those inhabitants of the town who were accused of corresponding with Abū Ṭāhir and being followers of the Ismaʿili religion. He learned of a missionary of the Qarmaṭī doctrine called al-Kaʿkī. He himself managed to avoid being arrested, but in his house they found his deputy and a few pupils. Al-Muqtadir learned that the Shiʿis usually assembled in the mosque of Barāthā,[278] and cursed the 'Companions of the Prophet'. In Ṣafar 313/May 925, thirty men were caught there at the Friday prayer, who declared their dissociation from those who recognized al-Muqtadir as their imam. They were arrested. When they were inspected, white[279] clay seals were found that had been stamped for them by al-Kaʿkī with the inscription: Muḥammad ibn Ismāʿīl, the Mahdi-Imam, the friend of God. Al-Khāqānī had the jurists issue a warrant that the mosque was a shelter for mischief, infidelity and discord among the Muslims. He testified that, unless it were destroyed, it would be a sanctuary for the missionaries and Qarmaṭīs. Then al-Muqtadir ordered its destruction.[280]

This report only mentions connections with Abū Ṭāhir, not with the Fatimids. As their imam and Mahdi the rebels named Muḥammad b. Ismāʿīl, not ʿUbayd Allāh. Two years later it caused a stir when a follower of the Fatimids was found as well. Everything thus indicates that the majority of the Ismaʿilis in Iraq co-operated closely with the Qarmaṭīs of Baḥrayn and rejected the Fatimid imamate.

After the defeat of the rebellious Baqliyya some of them joined Abū Ṭāhir on his retreat from Hīt to Baḥrayn. They were known in his army as the Ajamiyyūn.[281] At the beginning of the reign of the false Mahdi they were still in Baḥrayn.[282] The course of events and the disastrous end subsequently led to their departure. Many of the Qarmaṭī leaders defected.[283] Among them was Abu'l-Ghayth b. ʿAbda of the tribe of ʿIjl,[284] who is said to have had 30,000 men under his command and to have taken part in the Baqliyya rising.[285] In the following decades,

Qarmaṭīs are often mentioned as being in the service of Sunni rulers and generals. ʿArīb, who emphasizes the disastrous consequences of the episode with the Persian for the affairs of the Qarmaṭīs of Baḥrayn,[286] refers for the first time, evidently as an oddity, to seventy Qarmaṭīs of rank in the service of Mu'nis in 320/932.[287] Later, it was no longer considered unusual. About the origin of these Qarmaṭīs nothing is mentioned anywhere. It seems likely, however, that they were members of the Qarmaṭī Arab tribes from Iraq who, after their heavy defeats and their ideological crisis, hired themselves out to Sunni masters.

Abu'l-Qāsim ʿĪsā b. Mūsā, the nephew of ʿAbdān, was one of the leaders of the Baqliyya rising and was imprisoned. During the disturbances towards the end of al-Muqtadir's reign (320/932) he escaped. He stayed in Baghdad and won followers for his doctrine. As he is said to have ascribed books to his uncle,[288] it may be assumed that he continued teaching the imamate of Muḥammad b. Ismāʿīl. He was now an opponent both of the Fatimids and of the Qarmaṭīs of Baḥrayn. According to ʿAbd al-Jabbār, his son Abū Ṭālib 'and the likes of him' cursed Abū Ṭāhir bitterly whenever they mentioned his lapse.[289] ʿĪsā's school still existed at the time when Akhū Muḥsin was writing.[290]

After the short interlude with the Iṣfahānī, the Qarmaṭīs of Baḥrayn reverted to their old doctrine about the future advent of the Mahdi. For it is no doubt to the expected one, rather than to the Fatimids, that the reports about their later history relate, where the Mahdi is mentioned. ʿAbd al-Jabbār reports that Abū Ṭāhir now tried to collect some of his soldiers' booty for the Mahdi, as he had done before, but that they only answered him with insults.[291] As noted, according to Ibn Ḥawqal, one fifth was set aside for the 'Lord of the Time', and al-Muqaddasī mentions a treasury of the Mahdi in al-Aḥsā. There are also reports that after the death of Kāfūr, the ʿAlid ʿAbd Allāh b. ʿUbayd Allāh b. Ṭāhir, known as Akhū Muslim, sought recognition for himself as the Mahdi among the ʿAlids. When he failed to succeed, he joined the Qarmaṭīs and took part in their war against al-Muʿizz.[292] But apparently they would not acknowledge him either. A century later, Nāṣir-i Khusraw reports that the Qarmaṭīs of Baḥrayn were expecting the return of the Sharīf Abū Saʿīd which he himself had promised them.[293] Did he really understand all this correctly?

There is yet an important document to be discussed in which de Goeje rightly saw the most obvious evidence for his theory that the Qarmaṭīs remained loyal to the Fatimids until the year 358/969,[294] the letter al-Muʿizz wrote to al-Ḥasan al-Aʿṣam after his arrival in Cairo in

Ramaḍān 362/June 973. Its authenticity can hardly be questioned.[295] Formally it agrees with other letters by al-Muʿizz. The doctrines that are expounded in it fall within the framework of what is known from other Fatimid writings.

The letter was evidently made public by the recipient for propaganda purposes shortly after it had arrived. Thus ʿAbd al-Jabbār reports: 'Al-Ḥasan . . . read out his [al-Muʿizz's] letter to the people and thereby showed up his false doctrine and lies.'[296] That is why Thābit b. Sinān knew and reported it already in 363/974.[297] A few years later, Akhū Muḥsin recorded it fully in his history of the Qarmaṭīs where it has been preserved in its most complete form.[298]

Al-Muʿizz begins with a long introduction about the nature of the prophets and their deputies, the imams. God has created us as spirits before the creation of the world and has equipped us with power.[299] All the things of the world, from the heavenly spheres to the innermost souls, are ours and for our sake and point to us.[300] No prophet has been sent, no executor (*waṣī*) has appeared without pointing to us.[301] 'We are the everlasting words of God, His perfect names, His shining lights, His illuminated signposts, His clear chandeliers, His created miracles, His dazzling signs and active destinies. Nothing is without relation to us (*lā yakhruju minnā amr*), no age is empty of us.'[302] Al-Muʿizz has come to Egypt at a predestined time: 'We do not lift our foot or set it down without a firm knowledge, a universally valid decision, a predestined term, a prior command and a realized destination.'[303]

Then al-Muʿizz turns to al-Ḥasan. He calls him a perjured traitor and reproaches him for apostasy from the faith of his fathers and for kindling the flame of rebellion. But his case has not remained hidden from al-Muʿizz. 'We have learned what views you have made your own (*ʿalā ayyi raʾyin aṣalt*), what paths you are treading. Do you not have an example in your grandfather Abū Saʿīd, a model in the actions of Abū Ṭāhir? Have you not seen their writings and their history, have you not read their enactments and their poems? Were you absent from their houses, is nothing known to you of their deeds (*mā kāna min āthārihim*)? Do you not know[304] that they were servants of ours, of great bravery, firm will, of righteousness and praiseworthy actions, toward whom our substance flowed and over whom our blessing spread? So they overcame the provinces, all the princes and governors served them, and they obtained the title of 'lords' (*al-sāda*) and ruled, as a favour from us.'[305] They spread terror everywhere, fear among the sons of ʿAbbās, they defeated army upon army, 'and our eyes followed them, our support was allotted them, as God the exalted has said: Verily, We support our messengers and those who have faith in the present life . . . [306]This remained their attitude,[307] while God's eye looked upon them, until he chose, in accord with their own choice, to lead them from the realm of transitoriness to the realm of eternity, from transitory joy to lasting joy. They were praised in life and mourned when departing for peace and life in the gardens of bliss. Joy is theirs and a good end.'[308] Al-Muʿizz continues by addressing reproaches, warnings and threats to al-Ḥasan.

The letter as a whole clearly displays its essentially political purpose. It does not reveal any secrets, but rather the opponent is to be frightened with arguments that are to make the strongest impressions on him. The whole doctrine of the Qarmaṭīs was dominated by the idea of the Mahdi who commands the world, so al-Muʿizz describes his omnipotence and that of his fathers in glittering colours.[309] Abū Saʿīd and Abū Ṭāhir enjoyed the highest honour as founders of the Qarmaṭī state and of its powerful position, that is why al-Muʿizz tries to impress al-Ḥasan with the reproach that he has betrayed the faith of his fathers. The latter, however, owed their success exclusively to the favour of the Fatimids, and dire punishment was in store for al-Ḥasan.

If Abū Saʿīd and Abū Ṭāhir had really been such loyal followers of the Fatimids, why does al-Muʿizz try to prove this in so many vague words? He surely cannot suppose that al-Ḥasan does not know of their deeds, writings and poems, his questions here are quite rhetorical. On the other hand, the reference to their works clearly implies that they contained clear proof of Abū Saʿīd's and Abū Ṭāhir's loyalty. But the ancient chroniclers and polemicists who were sometimes quite well informed about the internal affairs of the Qarmaṭīs, had no concrete information to offer on this subject,[310] whereas they mention the expected Mahdi time and again in their reports. So it seems that al-Muʿizz was doing what many observers before and after him were tempted to do. He applied Abū Saʿīd's and his son's speeches and prophecies about the Mahdi to the Fatimids. Only, he was no doubt aware of his falsifying strategy.

This move is not so nonsensical as it might appear at first sight. The Qarmaṭī doctrine had insisted from its beginning that the coming of the expected one was imminent. It was even believed that the exact date for it could be read in the stars. This conviction was so firm that it had led to the fiasco with the Iṣfahānī which had shaken the order of the state in Baḥrayn to its foundations. Even now the hope of the Qarmaṭīs must have been directed towards the fulfilment of their expectations. Why not win them over to the Fatimid claim? For al-Muʿizz this would have meant an enormous increase in power, which would have brought him near the realization of his most ardent desire, the overthrow of the ʿAbbasid caliphate.[311]

In order to win over the Qarmaṭīs, al-Muʿizz had to avoid giving the lie to their most respected teachers and the founders of their power. So he tried to prove that they had in fact acted in the service of the Fatimids. The course of events shows that he failed.

NOTES

1 Ibn Kathīr, *al-Bidāya wa'l-nihāya* (Cairo, 1932–1939), vol. 11, p. 346: *yuẓhirūna'l-rafḍ wa-yubṭinūna'l-kufra'l-maḥḍ*. In this or a similar form the sentence was later frequently quoted as a standing phrase. See, for instance, Ibn al-Jawzī, *al-Muntaẓam* (Hyderabad, 1357–1362/1938–1943), vol. 5, p. 115, and al-Qazwīnī, *Mufīd al-ʿulūm* (Cairo, 1310/1892), p. 37.

2 M. J. de Goeje, *Mémoire sur les Carmathes du Bahraïn et les Fatimides* (2nd edn, Leiden, 1886), p. 69; henceforth quoted as *Carmathes*.

3 *Carmathes*, pp. 82–83.

4 Ibid., p. 185.

5 Ibid., pp. 194–195.

6 B. Lewis, *The Origins of Ismāʿīlism* (Cambridge, 1940), pp. 76 ff.

7 Thus termed after Muḥammad, a son of ʿAlī, called Ibn al-Ḥanafiyya after his mother.

8 The view that the Qarmaṭīs adhered to a Ḥanafī line of imams and were not Ismaʿilis at all had been proposed by P. Casanova, 'La doctrine secrète des Fatimides d'Egypte', BIFAO, 18 (1921), pp. 121–165.

9 W. Ivanow, 'Ismailis and Qarmatians', JBBRAS, NS, 16 (1940), pp. 43–85.

10 Ibid., p. 81.

11 Ibid., p. 83. This identification had already been suggested by de Goeje, *Carmathes*, p. 21. He considered Aḥmad b. al-Kayyāl, however, as an ancestor of the Fatimids.

12 *Carmathes*, pp. 82–83. In his *Brief Survey of the Evolution of Ismailism*, (Leiden, 1952), p. 10, Ivanow suggested, however, that the Qarmaṭīs who expected the return of Muḥammad b. Ismāʿīl perhaps honoured the Fatimids as his direct and genuine descendants. Perhaps they wished, Ivanow conjectured, to give them a special place in their own sect, but the repudiation of this undesired honour by the Fatimids offended the Qarmaṭīs and called forth their enmity and revenge.

13 Ḥasan Ibrāhīm Ḥasan and Ṭāhā Aḥmad Sharaf, *ʿUbayd Allāh al-Mahdī* (Cairo, 1947).

14 Kaysāniyya was the name given to the followers of Muḥammad b. al-Ḥanafiyya after one of their leaders in Kūfa.

15 Ḥasan and Sharaf, *ʿUbayd Allāh*, p. 26.

16 Ibid., pp. 93 ff.

17 The *Ṣāḥib al-Nāqa* in the presentation of L. Massignon, *La Passion d'al-Hosayn-Ibn-Mansour al-Hallaj* (Paris, 1922), vol. 2, pp. 734–735, and his 'Ḳarmaṭians', EI, vol. 2, pp. 767–772. He may be identical with Abū Muḥammad, brother of the caliph al-Mahdī, as suggested by H. Halm, 'Die Söhne Zikrawaihs und das erste fatimidische Kalifat (290/903)', WO, 10 (1979), pp. 32, 36, and his *Das Reich des Mahdi: Der Aufstieg der Fatimiden* (Munich, 1991), pp. 70, 76.

18 Ḥasan and Sharaf, *'Ubayd Allāh*, pp. 110–111.

19 Ibid., pp. 210 ff.

20 Ibid., p. 214. See also B. Carra de Vaux, 'al-Djannābī', EI, vol. 1, p. 1016.

21 For a new study of their history, valuable material would be available in al-Maqrīzī's *Itti'āẓ*, al-Mas'ūdī's *Tanbīh*, and in al-Nuwayrī's account which had been only partly translated by de Sacy.

22 The two available accounts go back to al-Ṭabarī and Akhū Muḥsin, who is probably using Ibn Rizām here as his source. See *Carmathes*, pp. 16–17.

23 Al-Ṭabarī, *Ta'rīkh al-rusul wa'l-mulūk*, ed. M. J. de Goeje et al. (Leiden, 1879–1901), III, p. 2128.

24 Ibn al-Nadīm, *Kitāb al-fihrist* (Cairo, 1348/1929–1930), p. 265. The date of the conversion is given there as the year 261/874–875.

25 Al-Maqrīzī, *Itti'āẓ al-ḥunafā'*, ed. H. Bunz (Leipzig, 1909), pp. 13, 114.

26 Ibn Ḥawqal, *Kitāb ṣūrat al-arḍ*, ed. J. H. Kramers (2nd edn, Leiden, 1938–1939), p. 295.

27 See S. M. Stern, ''Abdān', EI2, vol. 1, pp. 95–96. The Fatimid Isma'ili author Ja'far b. Manṣūr al-Yaman discusses his doctrine; see Zāhid 'Alī, *Ta'rīkh-i Fāṭimiyyīn-i Miṣr* (Hyderabad, 1367/1948), p. 436 n. 3. Al-Qāḍī al-Nu'mān quotes with approval from a book of 'Abdān entitled *al-Ibtidā'* in his *al-Risāla al-mudhhiba*, in *Khams rasā'il Ismā'īliyya*, ed. 'Ā. Tāmir (Salamiyya, 1956), p. 41. Zāhid 'Alī quotes in his *Hamārē Ismā'īlī madhhab kī ḥaqīqat awr us kā niẓām* (Hyderabad, 1373/1954), pp. 548 and 615, a *Kitāb al-rusūm wa'l-izdiwāj* in his possession, which is ascribed to Abū Muḥammad 'Abdān. Ibn al-Nadīm does not name it among 'Abdān's works. A heresiographer of the 6th/12th century, however, enumerates a *Kitāb al-izdiwāj*, without mentioning its author, among the Isma'ili books read by himself; see *Kitāb al-kashf*, ed. R. Strothmann (London, etc., 1952), introduction p. *Ḥā'*. The Syrian Nizārī Isma'ili Shihāb al-Dīn Abū Firās (d. 937/1530) mentions in his *Risālat maṭāli' al-shumūs*, in *Arba' rasā'il Ismā'īliyya*, ed. 'Ā. Tāmir (Salamiyya, 1952), p. 52, 'Abdān's *Kitāb al-mīzān* among his sources. This work may be identical with the *Kitāb al-mīdān* mentioned by Ibn al-Nadīm, *al-Fihrist*, p. 267, where the title should probably be read *Kitāb al-mīzān*. Most of the books attributed to 'Abdān, however, were, as stated by Ibn al-Nadīm himself, later forgeries. His nephew 'Īsā b. Mūsā in particular is said to have been active in this regard. He composed numerous works and ascribed them to 'Abdān in order to create the impression that he was a scholar in all branches of philosophy and other sciences and was endowed with the gift of predicting future events. See Akhū Muḥsin in al-Nuwayrī, *Nihāyat al-arab*, vol. 25, ed. M. J. 'A. al-Ḥīnī and 'A. al-Ahwānī (Cairo, 1984), pp. 295–296, and al-Maqrīzī, *Itti'āẓ*, p. 130.

28 According to Ibn Mālik, *Kashf asrār al-Bāṭiniyya wa-akhbār al-Qarāmiṭa* (Cairo, 1357/1939), p. 18, he was killed in Baghdad. Ibn Mālik does not mention a date. According to Ibn Ḥawqal (p. 96), however, Ḥamdān Qarmaṭ survived and was later known under the *kunya* Abū 'Alī. This would imply that after initially defecting together with 'Abdān, he rejoined the Fatimid camp and was moved to Fusṭāṭ in Egypt from where he maintained the links between the headquarters of the movement in Salamiyya and the Isma'ili missionaries in the Yemen and the Maghrib. His son Abu'l-Ḥasan later became chief of the Fatimid treasury in the Maghrib. Ibn Ḥawqal knew Abu'l-Ḥasan personally. His information may well be reliable.

29 Silvestre de Sacy, *Exposé de la religion des Druzes* (Paris, 1838), vol. 1, introduction pp. 193 ff., and al-Maqrīzī, *Itti'āẓ*, pp. 114 ff.

30 *Carmathes*, p. 59.

31 This date refers directly only to the assassination of ʿAbdān. The account does not suggest, however, that a long time had passed since the defection. This is confirmed by the statement of Ibn Ḥawqal quoted below that Abū Saʿīd still served the Fatimids at the beginning of his career in Baḥrayn (not before 281/894; *Carmathes*, p. 34). The suggestion of Zāhid ʿAlī, *Ta'rīkh*, p. 436, that Ḥamdān since 268/August 881–July 882 was spreading a new doctrine, is thus hardly justified.

32 *Carmathes*, p. 67. By contrast, see Stern, 'ʿAbdān', in EI2.

33 *Istitār al-imām*, ed. W. Ivanow, in *Majallat Kulliyyat al-Ādāb*, 4 (1936), p. 96.

34 W. Ivanow, *Ismaili Tradition Concerning the Rise of the Fatimids* (London, etc., 1942), p. 78.

35 Lewis, *Origins*, pp. 77–78.

36 Ibn Ḥawqal, p. 295. That Ibn Ḥawqal here calls the Fatimid 'the one residing in the Maghrib' (*al-muqīm bi'l-Maghrib*) is an anticipation without significance.

37 Ibn Ḥawqal, p. 295.

38 Al-Maqrīzī, *Ittiʿāẓ*, p. 107.

39 Cited in Lewis, *Origins*, p. 78. Abū Saʿīd had been converted to the doctrine at an earlier date. The contradictory information about the beginnings of his career is summed up by Lewis. See further the article 'Abū Saʿīd Jannābī' in EIR, vol. 1, pp. 380–381.

40 *Carmathes*, p. 69.

41 Ibn Ḥawqal, p. 295.

42 See note 36 above.

43 Listed in Lewis, *Origins*, pp. 77–78; see also al-Masʿūdī, *Kitāb al-tanbīh wa'l-ishrāf*, ed. M. J. de Goeje (Leiden, 1894), pp. 384, 392.

44 Al-Ṭabarī, III, pp. 2128–2129.

45 *Wa-kāna fīmā ḥakaw ʿan hā'ulā'i'l-Qarāmiṭa*. Casanova, 'La doctrine secrète', p. 151, considered this report as part of the statements made by the brother-in-law of Zikrawayh captured in 294/906. These statements were transmitted to al-Ṭabarī by a companion (*baʿḍ aṣḥābinā*) who is mentioned as his informant on pp. 2127 and 2130. The present text, however, belongs to a different tradition as is evident from the indefinite plural. It may refer back to the anonymous Kūfans mentioned on p. 2127.

46 The camel of the prophet Ṣāliḥ, Qur'an, VII:73–79, is meant. See de Sacy, *Exposé*, vol. 1, introduction p. 177 n. 1.

47 The beast which God will send forth from the earth at the end of time according to the Qur'an, XXVII:82, is meant here. See de Sacy, ibid.

48 Say: The new moons are fixed times for mankind (see Qur'an, II:189). Their exterior is that the number of years may be recognized, the calculation, the months, and the days. Their inner meaning is My helpers who guide My servants on My path.

49 Casanova, 'La doctrine secrète', p. 151.

50 See C. van Arendonk, 'Kaisānīya', EI, vol. 2, pp. 658–659.

51 In Qur'an, LXI:6, Muḥammad is meant.

52 There does not seem to be evidence of any group fixing the number of prophets at seven before the Ismaʿilis, certainly not with the same names. The speculations about the number seven presumably started in respect to the imamate, the central idea of the Shiʿis. Ismāʿīl b. Jaʿfar, or his son, Muḥammad b. Ismāʿīl, was the seventh imam and thus entitled to the highest rank. A son of Muḥammad b. al-Ḥanafiyya could not claim that for himself.

53 Ibn Khaldūn, *Kitāb al-ʿibar* (Cairo, 1289/1872), vol. 4, p. 84, vol. 3, p. 336. See G. Weil, *Geschichte der Chalifen* (Mannheim, 1846–1862), vol. 2, p. 495 n. 4. The statement of Ibn al-ʿIbrī in his Syriac chronicle that the first missionary of the Qarmaṭīs in Kūfa was the author of the book (ibid.; de Sacy, *Exposé*, vol. 1, introduction p. 177 n.1) is obviously worthless.

54 This seems all the more likely since Zikrawayh is also identical with the founder of the Qarmaṭī sect in Iraq in his account. Here the first missionary, who converted Ḥamdān Qarmaṭ, Qarmaṭ himself, and Zikrawayh are all fused as a single person. The explanation that Zikrawayh was meant in the book of the Qarmaṭīs was then quite natural since al-Ṭabarī before and afterwards named Zikrawayh's brother-in-law as the source of his information about the Qarmaṭīs. But where did Ibn Khaldūn find the name al-Qāshānī? According to his account (*al-ʿIbar*, vol. 2, p. 336), this al-Faraj b. Yaḥyā, i.e., Zikrawayh, was also the one who negotiated with the *Ṣāḥib al-Zanj*. Al-Ṭabarī (III, p. 2130) rather names Ḥamdān Qarmaṭ. The brother-in-law of Zikrawayh was merely the transmitter. According to Akhū Muḥsin, however, it was the father of Zikrawayh who conducted these negotiations. He is said to have already proclaimed doctrines of his own; see al-Maqrīzī, *Ittiʿāẓ*, p. 107.

55 Lewis, *Origins*, pp. 73–74; Ivanow, *Rise*, pp. 87 ff.; Ḥasan and Sharaf, *ʿUbayd Allāh*, pp. 98 ff. See now further Halm, 'Die Söhne Zikrawaihs', pp. 30–53, who suggests that the sons of Zikrawayh did not claim descent from Muḥammad b. Ismāʿīl for themselves but were in fact proclaiming ʿUbayd Allāh as the Mahdi.

56 Thus Ḥasan and Sharaf, *ʿUbayd Allāh*, p. 26.

57 Lewis, *Origins*, p. 78; ʿAbd al-Jabbār, *Tathbīt dalāʾil al-nubuwwa*, ed. ʿAbd al-Karīm ʿUthmān (Beirut, 1966–1968), p. 379.

58 See S. Moscati, 'Il testamento di Abū Hāšim', *Rivista degli Studi Orientali*, 27 (1952), pp. 28 ff.

59 Lewis, *Origins*, p. 79.

60 ʿAbd al-Jabbār, *Tathbīt*, p. 379, and Lewis, *Origins*, p. 78.

61 Al-Maqrīzī, *Ittiʿāẓ*, pp. 106, 114.

62 This statement should now be modified in the light of the discussion of Halm, 'Die Söhne Zikrawaihs'.

63 Al-Nawbakhtī, *Firaq al-Shīʿa*, ed. H. Ritter (Istanbul, 1931), p. 61.

64 Ivanow, 'Ismailis and Qarmatians', p. 79.

65 Ibid., p. 81.

66 Ivanow evidently does not do so since he ('Ismailis and Qarmatians', p. 84) considers it possible that Idrīs simply took the name of the apostate from al-Shahrastānī. In reality, he suggests, perhaps ʿAbd Allāh b. Maymūn al-Qaddāḥ was meant.

67 He is presumably identical with the Qarmaṭawayh (Qarmaṭōē) mentioned by al-Nawbakhtī.

68 Al-Shahrastānī, *al-Milal waʾl-niḥal*, in the margin of Ibn Ḥazm, *al-Fiṣal* (Cairo, 1317–1321/1899–1903), vol. 2, p. 17.

69 Ibid., vol. 2, pp. 17–21.

70 So at least he himself claimed. He may be the brother of the Ismaʿili chief missionary and *qāḍī* in the Yemen, Lamak b. Mālik, as suggested by Fuʾād Sayyid; see al-Jaʿdī, *Ṭabaqāt fuqahāʾ al-Yaman*, ed. Fuʾād Sayyid (Cairo, 1957), p. 234 n. 3.

71 Ibn Mālik, *Kashf*, p. 33; see also p. 20: Abū Saʿīd asserted that he was the Mahdi who acts in accordance with the religion of God (*al-Mahdī al-qāʾim bi-dīn Allāh*). See

al-Jawbarī in *Carmathes*, p. 208: *iddaʿāʾl-nubuwwa*.

72 *Carmathes*, pp. 57–58.

73 Ibid., p. 69.

74 ʿArīb b. Saʿd, *Ṣilat taʾrīkh al-Ṭabarī*, ed. M. J. de Goeje (Leiden, 1897), p. 38.

75 Ibn Miskawayh, *Tajārib al-umam* (Cairo, 1914–1916), vol. 1, pp. 33–34.

76 Al-Hamadhānī, *Takmilat taʾrīkh al-Ṭabarī*, ed. A. Y. Kanʿān, in *al-Mashriq*, 51 (1955), p. 41.

77 Ibn al-Athīr, *al-Kāmil fīʾl-taʾrīkh*, ed. C. J. Tornberg (Leiden, 1851–1876), vol. 8, p. 49.

78 Al-Ṭabarī, *III*, p. 2287.

79 Al-Hamadhānī reports the event only under the year 301/913–914.

80 Al-Masʿūdī, *al-Tanbīh*, p. 394. Al-Jawbarī (in *Carmathes*, p. 208) and ʿAbd al-Jabbār (*Tathbīt*, p. 397) also give the date as the year 300, and other sources mention 301 AH. The fact that the news reached Baghdad only at the end of the year 301/middle of 914 speaks against the early date (see *Carmathes*, p. 70). Perhaps the death was at first kept secret by the Qarmaṭīs. According to al-Masʿūdī, Abū Saʿīd was assassinated by two slaves whom he had captured in war against Badr al-Maḥallī and taken into his service. According to Akhū Muḥsin (in al-Maqrīzī, *Ittiʿāẓ*, p. 112) and ʿAbd al-Jabbār, the murderer had once been a servant of Abuʾl-Faḍl al-Ghanawī. All this information does not speak for the assumption that ʿUbayd Allāh had a hand in the matter.

81 According to Ibn ʿIdhārī, *al-Bayān al-mughrib*, ed. G. S. Colin and E. Lévi-Provençal (New edn, Leiden, 1948–1951), vol. 1, p. 169, Abuʾl-Qāsim left Raqqāda on Sunday 2 Jumādā I 300/13 December 912. The conversion of the Hijra dates will be based on the tables of Wüstenfeld-Mahler. Wherever the day of the week is mentioned, the dates of the Christian era have been, when necessary, adjusted. Usually the Hijra date was one or two, and occasionally up to four, days earlier than indicated by the tables. It is, thus, likely that the Christian dates in the cases where the day of the week is not specified should frequently also be moved back one or two days.

82 Ibn ʿIdhārī, *al-Bayān*, vol. 1, p. 169. The identity of the leader about whose defeat the ʿAbbasid governor of Barqa sent a report to Baghdad in this year (al-Ṭabarī, III, p. 2288) is unknown. The governor was, no doubt, Abuʾl-Nimr Aḥmad b. Ṣāliḥ who had been sent by Tekin, the governor of Egypt, to Barqa with a strong army and reached Surt further west; see al-Kindī, *Kitāb al-wulāt wa-kitāb al-quḍāt*, ed. R. Guest (Leiden–London, 1912), p. 268. Perhaps the Fatimid contingent moved, after the conquest of Tripoli, further east. It was, however, hardly an attempt to reach Egypt.

83 Idrīs ʿImād al-Dīn, *Taʾrīkh al-khulafāʾ al-Fāṭimiyyīn biʾl-Maghrib* (= *ʿUyūn al-akhbār*, vol. 5 and part of vol. 6), ed. M. al-Yaʿlāwī (Beirut, 1985), p. 193.

84 Idrīs, *Taʾrīkh*, p. 194.

85 Idrīs, *Taʾrīkh*, p. 195. According to al-Kindī, *Wulāt*, p. 269, Alexandria was taken already on Saturday 8 Muḥarram 302/31 July 914.

86 Idrīs, *Taʾrīkh*, p. 195.

87 Ibn Kathīr, *al-Bidāya*, vol. 11, p. 122, reports that the Mecca pilgrims of the year 302/915 were attacked and pillaged by Arabs and a group of Qarmaṭīs. According to Ibn al-Jawzī, *al-Muntaẓam*, vol. 6, p. 128, whose report is probably Ibn Kathīr's source, and ʿArīb (p. 54) the rebels were an ʿAlid and the sons of Ṣāliḥ b. Mudrik of the tribe of Ṭayyiʾ. The Qarmaṭīs of Baḥrayn were certainly not involved; see de Goeje, *Carmathes*, p. 76. Ṣāliḥ b. Mudrik had in Muḥarram 286/February 899 pillaged

the caravan of pilgrims returning from Mecca. At the end of the same year, January 900, he was captured during a new attack on the pilgrim caravan and was killed (al-Ṭabarī, *III,* pp. 2191–2192).

88 Ibn Khaldūn, *al-ʿIbar*, vol. 4, p. 89.

89 For *thamānīn* read *thalāthmiʾa.*

90 *Carmathes*, p. 78. De Goeje expressed some reservations since Abū Ṭāhir did not attempt to move to Egypt and since Muʾnis, according to ʿArīb, left Baghdad only in Ramaḍān 307/February 920.

91 Ḥasan and Sharaf, *ʿUbayd Allāh*, pp. 186 ff.

92 Ibn ʿIdhārī, *al-Bayān*, vol. 1, p. 173.

93 Ibid., vol. 1, p. 175.

94 Al-Kindī, *Wulāt*, p. 274.

95 After the defection of al-Muʿizz b. Bādīs under the Fatimid al-Mustanṣir, Jabbāra b. Mukhtār al-ʿArabī, governor of Barqa, submitted to the former in the year 443/1051–1052 and had the Fatimids cursed (Ibn ʿIdhārī, *al-Bayān*, vol. 1, p. 288).

96 Ibn ʿIdhārī, *al-Bayān*, vol. 1, p. 181.

97 Al-Kindī, *Wulāt*, p. 275, and al-Maqrīzī, *al-Khiṭaṭ* (Būlāq, 1270/1853–1854), vol. 1, p. 328. According to Ibn al-Athīr (vol. 8, p. 83), Abu'l-Qāsim arrived in Alexandria in Rabīʿ II 307/September 919. F. Wüstenfeld, *Die Statthalter von Ägypten zur Zeit der Chalifen* (Göttingen, 1875–1876), vol. 4, p. 14, is to be corrected here.

98 ʿArīb, *Ṣila*, p. 79.

99 ʿArīb, *Ṣila*, p. 80, but al-Kindī, *Wulāt*, p. 277, gives 5 Muḥarram, likewise as a Thursday.

100 Ibn ʿIdhārī, *al-Bayān*, vol. 1, p. 182; ʿArīb, *Ṣila*, p. 80, and al-Kindī, *Wulāt*, p. 277.

101 ʿArīb, *Ṣila*, p. 80.

102 Al-Kindī, *Wulāt*, p. 278.

103 Ibn ʿIdhārī, *al-Bayān*, vol. 1, p. 185.

104 This has been pointed out already by H. Bowen, *The Life and Times of ʿAlī Ibn ʿĪsā* (Cambridge, 1928), p. 205.

105 Al-Masʿūdī, *al-Tanbīh*, pp. 380, 391.

106 Cited in al-Maqrīzī, *Ittiʿāẓ*, p. 124.

107 ʿAbd al-Jabbār, *Tathbīt*, p. 381.

108 Al-Maqrīzī, *Ittiʿāẓ*, p. 124, erroneously mentions 310/922.

109 Ibn Miskawayh, *Tajārib*, vol. 1, p. 109.

110 See de Goeje, *Carmathes*, p. 79; and, similarly, ʿAbd al-Jabbār, *Tathbīt*, p. 381. According to him the Shiʿis wrote to the sons of Abū Saʿīd from Baghdad and asked them to make war on the caliph. They answered, however, that ʿAlī b. ʿĪsā was a good man and that they did not want to stand up against him. When al-Muqtadir deposed ʿAlī b. ʿĪsā, the Shiʿis sent the news with carrier pigeons to Baḥrayn. Bowen, *ʿAlī Ibn ʿĪsā*, p. 206, rightly points out, however, that any connection between the dismissal of ʿAlī b. ʿĪsā and the attack of the Qarmaṭīs on Baṣra is highly unlikely because of the shortness of the interval.

111 Ibn al-Jawzī, *al-Muntaẓam*, vol. 6, p. 153. Bowen, *ʿAlī Ibn ʿĪsā*, p. 205, mentions Sibṭ Ibn al-Jawzī. The latter presumably took the report from his grandfather's work.

112 ʿArīb, *Ṣila*, p. 110, and Ibn Miskawayh, *Tajārib*, vol. 1, p. 85. Ibn al-Jawzī himself mentions the events in this year once more (*al-Muntaẓam*, vol. 6, p. 173).

113 ʿArīb, *Ṣila*, p. 110.

114 Ibn Miskawayh, *Tajārib*, vol. 1, p. 109, and Ibn al-Athīr, vol. 8, p. 105.

115 Abū'l-Maḥāsin b. Taghrībirdī, *al-Nujūm al-zāhira*, ed. T. G. J. Juynboll and B. F. Matthes (Leiden, 1855–1861), vol. 2, p. 207. He probably took the report from al-Dhahabī, *Ta'rīkh al-Islām*, one of his main sources. Al-Dhahabī on his part is dependent on Ibn al-Jawzī. Ibn Kathīr, *al-Bidāya*, vol. 11, p. 130, quoted the report together with the information about the dismissal of Ḥāmid and the third vizierate of Ibn al-Furāt from Ibn al-Jawzī.

116 It is also uncertain whether Abū Ṭāhir was at that time already the leader of the Qarmaṭīs. Al-Mas'ūdī, *al-Tanbīh*, p. 391, mentions as his birth date Ramaḍān 294/June–July 907. This agrees with the common statement in the sources (de Goeje, *Carmathes*, pp. 73–74) that Abū Ṭāhir was seventeen years old at the time of his attack on the pilgrim caravan returning from Mecca at the beginning of the year 312/April 924. Al-Mas'ūdī goes on to state that Abū Ṭāhir took over the command of the army in Ramaḍān 310/23 December 922–21 January 923. Akhū Muḥsin, in contrast, reports, as cited in al-Maqrīzī, *Itti'āẓ*, p. 112, that Abū Ṭāhir acceded to the rule in the year 305/June 917–June 918.

117 Ibn 'Idhārī, *al-Bayān*, vol. 1, p. 187.

118 Ibid., vol. 1, p. 188.

119 Ibid., vol. 1, p. 190.

120 De Goeje, *Carmathes*, p. 78.

121 In the year 316/928, while Abu'l-Qāsim was occupied with his troops in the west, the Fatimid governor of Barqa, Faḥl b. Nūḥ al-Lahīṣī, moved to Dhāt al-Ḥumām and defeated the Egyptians under Abu'l-Nimr Aḥmad b. Ṣāliḥ. He withdrew, however, immediately; see Idrīs 'Imād al-Dīn, *'Uyūn al-akhbār*, ed. M. Ghālib (Beirut, 1973–1984), vol. 5, p. 150.

122 'Abd al-Jabbār, *Tathbīt*, p. 383.

123 Al-Kindī, *Wulāt*, pp. 281 ff.

124 Ḥasan and Sharaf, *'Ubayd Allāh*, pp. 181 ff. The authors infer from this that the unsuccessful incursion of the Qarmaṭīs in southwestern Persia in the year 321/933 was carried out at the order of 'Ubayd Allāh.

125 For details, see H. Gottschalk, *Die Mādarā'ijjūn* (Berlin–Leipzig, 1931), pp. 93 ff.

126 Al-Kindī, *Wulāt*, p. 287; Ibn Sa'īd, *al-Mughrib fī ḥula'l-Maghrib*, ed. K. C. Tallquist (Leiden, 1899), p. 14.

127 Al-Kindī, *Wulāt*, p. 288.

128 De Goeje, *Carmathes*, p. 139.

129 Ibid., p. 182.

130 *Carmathes*, pp. 138 ff., and Ḥ. I. Ḥasan and Ṭ. A. Sharaf, *al-Mu'izz li-Dīn Allāh* (Cairo, 1367/1948), p. 100.

131 Ibn Miskawayh, *Tajārib*, vol. 2, p. 203; Ibn al-Jawzī, *al-Muntaẓam*, vol. 7, p. 19, and de Goeje, *Carmathes*, p. 180.

132 Al-Maqrīzī, *al-Khiṭaṭ*, vol. 1, p. 329, and de Goeje, *Carmathes*, p. 182. According to the anonymous continuator of Eutychius, *Eutychii Patriarchae Alexandrini Annales*, ed. L. Cheikho et al. (Paris, 1909), vol. 2, p. 293, there was a Qarmaṭī revenge attack on the 'Uqaylid Mulhim (read *li-ṭalab tha'rihi min Mulhim b. Dīnār*) in Ṭabariyya on 15 Rabī' II 353/1 May 964. In the same month, a rising of the Berbers of Alexandria took place. Abu'l-Maḥāsin, *al-Nujūm*, vol. 2, p. 355, reports the same events, probably erroneously, under the year 352/963 and claims that the Berbers were sent by al-Mu'izz. This seems quite unlikely. The Berber rebellion, according to Abu'l-

Maḥāsin, prevented the Egyptians from repelling the Qarmaṭī attack.

133 Ibn Miskawayh, *Tajārib*, vol. 2, p. 215; Ibn al-Athīr, vol. 8, p. 424, and anonymous continuator of Eutychius, *Eutychii Annales*, vol. 2, p. 294. The latter source (vol. 2, p. 295) also mentions an attack of a Fatimid commander (*Ṣāḥib Abī Tamīm Maʿadd*) on the oases of upper Egypt in Ṣafar 355/February 966. This attack is probably the one mentioned also by al-Maqrīzī, *al-Khiṭaṭ*, vol. 2, p. 27, according to whom Kāfūr sent an army which expelled the Maghribīs.

134 Al-Kindī, *Wulāt*, p. 297.

135 Ibn Ẓāfir, in F. Wüstenfeld, *Statthalter*, vol. 4, p. 59, and al-Maqrīzī, *al-Khiṭaṭ*, vol. 2, p. 27.

136 Yaḥyā b. Saʿīd al-Anṭākī, *Kitāb al-dhayl*, ed. I. Kratchkovsky and A. Vasiliev (Paris, 1924–1932), p. 119.

137 Ibn Khallikān, *Wafayāt al-aʿyān* (Cairo, 1310/1892), vol. 2, p. 42.

138 Al-Maqrīzī, *Ittiʿāẓ*, p. 62.

139 Ibid., p. 68.

140 See M. Jamāl al-Dīn Surūr, *al-Nufūdh al-Fāṭimī fī bilād al-Shām waʾl-ʿIrāq* (Cairo, 1957), p. 17.

141 Al-Maqrīzī, *Ittiʿāẓ*, pp. 75–76.

142 Ibn Ḥammād, *Akhbār mulūk Banī ʿUbayd*, ed. M. Vonderheyden (Algiers–Paris, 1927), p. 42.

143 Al-Maqrīzī, *Ittiʿāẓ*, pp. 80, 131; *Eutychii Annales*, vol. 2, p. 295; Idrīs, *Taʾrīkh*, p. 694 (presumably based on Ibn Zūlāq's *Sīrat Jawhar*), and Ibn al-Dawādārī, *Kanz al-durar*, vol. 6, ed. Ṣ. al-Munajjid (Cairo, 1961) p. 122. De Goeje was unaware of this renewed invasion of the Qarmaṭīs. It has also been ignored in the more recent studies. The divergence of circumstances and the testimony of the contemporary chronicler Ibn Zūlāq (cited in al-Maqrīzī, *Ittiʿāẓ*, p. 77 l.6 and p. 78 l.12; Idrīs, *Taʾrīkh*, pp. 694–695) show that there is no confusion with the invasion of 357/968. The account of the campaign of Jaʿfar b. Falāḥ inserted by al-Maqrīzī into his report appears to have been taken from an early Syrian chronicle which is quoted again on p. 131. Since these passages do not quite agree with the account of Ibn Zūlāq and Akhū Muḥsin, respectively, they were most likely added by al-Maqrīzī.

The new campaign of the Qarmaṭīs was under the command of Kisrā b. Abiʾl-Qāsim (Saʿīd) and Ṣakhr b. Abī Isḥāq (Ibrāhīm), cousins of al-Ḥasan al-Aʿṣam, since the latter was accused of having withheld some of the booty gained during the previous campaign; see Ibn Ḥawqal, p. 26. De Goeje (*Carmathes*, p. 182) identified the two invasions of Syria mentioned by Ibn Ḥawqal with those of 353/964 and 357/968. This is not tenable, since according to the account of Ibn Ẓāfir (in Wüstenfeld, *Statthalter*, vol. 4, p. 61) the campaign of 357/968 was led by al-Aʿṣam. Ibn ʿAsākir likewise states that al-Aʿṣam overcame Syria in the year 357/968 and then returned to Damascus in the year 360/971; see Ibn Manẓūr, *Mukhtaṣar taʾrīkh Dimashq* (Damascus, 1984–1990), vol. 6. p. 133.

144 Jaʿfar set out from Cairo on 18 Muḥarram 359/1 December 969 (al-Maqrīzī, *Ittiʿāẓ*, p. 78). News of the battle reached Jawhar in Egypt in Rabīʿ II/February–March 970 (Idrīs, *Taʾrīkh*, p. 695). Th. Bianquis, *Damas et la Syrie sous la domination Fatimide, 359–468/969–1076* (Damascus, 1986–1989), vol. 1, p. 40, gives the date of the battle as 7 Rabīʿ II/17 February 970 without mentioning a source. The date mentioned by al-Maqrīzī's Syrian source (*Ittiʿāẓ*, p. 81; similarly by Ibn Ẓāfir, in Wüstenfeld,

Statthalter, vol. 4, p. 62, and by Ibn al-Dawādārī, *Kanz*, vol. 6, p. 123), namely middle of Rajab 359/end of May 970, is too late.

145 Al-Maqrīzī, *Itti'āz*, p. 78, and Idrīs, *Ta'rīkh*, p. 695.

146 *Ṣāḥib al-Qarāmiṭa*; see al-Maqrīzī, *Itti'āz*, p. 79, and Idrīs, *Ta'rīkh*, p. 695 (Abū Ghazwān).

147 F. Wüstenfeld, *Geschichte der Faṭimiden-Chalifen* (Göttingen, 1881), p. 112, states that al-Ḥasan b. 'Ubayd Allāh after his return to Syria made peace with al-A'ṣam and committed himself to an annual tribute of 100,000 dinars in return for the undisturbed possession of his province. This is hardly correct in this form. Both Hilāl al-Ṣābi' (in Ibn al-Qalānisī, *Dhayl ta'rīkh Dimashq*, ed. H. F. Amedroz, Leiden, 1908, p. 1) and Ibn al-Athīr (vol. 8, p. 452), however, confirm that it was Ibn Ṭughj, i.e., al-Ḥasan b. 'Ubayd Allāh, who committed himself to the tribute. According to Akhū Muḥsin (in al-Maqrīzī, *Itti'āz*, p. 131) it was rather a tribute of the Ikhshīdids which had been paid from Egypt for many years. This version seems less likely in the course of the events.

148 *Carmathes*, p. 187. De Goeje's doubts based on chronological considerations are not cogent. Even if the Qarmaṭīs entered into negotiations with the 'Abbasid government already before the conquest of Damascus by Ja'far b. Falāḥ (end of 359/autumn 970), the situation was clear after the capture of al-Ḥasan b. 'Ubayd Allāh at the latest.

149 Ibn Khaldūn, *al-'Ibar*, vol. 4, pp. 88–91.

150 *Carmathes*, pp. 74, 78, 142, 144, 151, 194.

151 Read Abū Ṭāhir for *wa'l-ẓāhir*.

152 A high council which made the most important political decisions. See de Goeje, *Carmathes*, p. 74.

153 Ibn Khaldūn, *al-'Ibar*, vol. 4, p. 88.

154 *Carmathes*, p. 74, and Ibn al-Jawzī, *al-Muntaẓam*, vol. 7, p. 57.

155 Listed in *Carmathes*, p. 74.

156 'Abd al-Jabbār, for whom he is an important source, seems to have known two works by him, *al-Marātib al-khams*, and *al-Kitāb al-kabīr* (*Tathbīt*, p. 393, the text is ambiguous). Two extracts of several pages' length from his work, without any mention of a title, are extant in Ibn al-Nadīm, *al-Fihrist*, pp. 264–267 and al-Dhahabī, *Ta'rīkh al-Islām*, printed in Ibn Miskawayh, *Tajārib*, vol. 2, pp. 57–60 where he names as his informant a physician called Ibn Ḥamdān who had lived among the Qarmaṭīs in Baḥrayn. For a proper assessment of his work it is essential to recognize that his informants came from the Qarmaṭī circles of Iraq. This is evident from his statements and is only natural since he lived in Kūfa in the centre of the Iraqī Qarmaṭī movement. 'Abd al-Jabbār does in fact report (*Tathbīt*, pp. 392–393) that he mentioned a number of Qarmaṭī leaders who defected from the movement apparently after the disaster with the false prophet of the Qarmaṭīs of Baḥrayn. Among them, there was Abu'l-Ghayt al-'Ijlī who now wrote a book in which he explained that 'their (the Qarmaṭīs') matter had been unclear to him, and he had believed them to be Shi'is and followers of the Mahdi'. On the basis of these quotations it is evident that the common dating of the work of Ibn Rizām to the beginning of the 4th/10th century (I. Goldziher, *Streitschrift des Ġazālī gegen die Bāṭinijja-Sekte*, Leiden, 1916, p. 15; S. M. Stern, "Abd Allāh b. Maymūn', EI2, vol. 1, p. 48) is too early. In the extract of Ibn al-Nadīm he evidently continues his

account to the death of the Fatimid al-Manṣūr (29 Shawwāl 341/18 March 953). The dates of the later Fatimids were presumably added by Ibn al-Nadīm. Al-Masʿūdī knew Ibn Rizām's refutation of the Qarmaṭīs in the year 345/956 (*al-Tanbīh*, p. 396, also without any mention of a title). L. Massignon's suggestion, in his 'Esquisse d'une bibliographie Qarmaṭe', in *A Volume of Oriental Studies Presented to Edward G. Browne*, ed. T. W. Arnold and R. A. Nicholson (Cambridge, 1922), p. 344, that he is identical with the *nāẓir al-maẓālim* in Baghdad in the year 329/941 mentioned by Hilāl al-Ṣābi', in *Kitāb al-wuzarā'*, ed. H. F. Amedroz (Leiden, 1904), p. 317, is probably erroneous. The *nāẓir al-maẓālim* here is most likely Aḥmad b. ʿAlī al-Kūfī. Ibn Rizām's work was extensively used by the Damascene Sharīf Akhū Muḥsin Muḥammad b. ʿAlī (d. 398/1008) who had met Ibn Rizām personally; see Ibn al-Dawādārī, *Kanz*, vol. 6, p. 55. Large parts of Akhū Muḥsin's work are preserved by al-Nuwayrī, Ibn al-Dawādārī, and al-Maqrīzī. He mentions the death of ʿAḍud al-Dawla in 372/983 (in al-Maqrīzī, *Ittiʿāẓ*, p. 15). But he deviates substantially from Ibn Rizām's account on some points; for instance, in respect to the genealogy of the Fatimids. His account is independant of that of Thābit b. Sinān, Ibn al-Athīr's source, even for the later history not covered by Ibn Rizām.

157 Al-Maqrīzī, *Ittiʿāẓ*, p. 112; Ibn al-Dawādārī, *Kanz*, vol. 6, p. 62; al-Dhahabī, *Ta'rīkh*, quoted in Ibn Miskawayh, *Tajārib*, vol. 2, p. 57 n. 1. The express quote from Ibn Rizām begins in the text of al-Dhahabī only afterwards. The partly literal agreement of the passage preceding it is evidence, however, that it is taken from the same source.

158 See note 116 above.

159 Ibn Ḥawqal, p. 296.

160 Ibn Khaldūn, *al-ʿIbar*, vol. 4, p. 89.

161 Translated by Lewis, *Origins*, p. 81. Contrary to Lewis' suggestion, Ibn Rizām and Akhū Muḥsin apparently knew nothing of the letter. Al-Nuwayrī's quotation is from Ibn al-Athīr.

162 De Goeje, *Carmathes*, p. 83.

163 Ibid.

164 A different account of the events is provided by Quṭb al-Dīn al-Nahrawālī, *Die Chroniken der Stadt Mekka*, ed. F. Wüstenfeld (Leipzig, 1857), vol. 3, p. 165. According to him, Abū Ṭāhir gave orders for ʿUbayd Allāh to be mentioned in Mecca in the Friday prayer. When the latter heard this he cursed Abū Ṭāhir in a letter. Abū Ṭāhir then renounced his allegiance to him. This account, whose source is unknown, is less credible than that of Thābit, especially since the naming of ʿUbayd Allāh in the Friday sermon is not mentioned in any of the reports about the Qarmaṭī sacking of Mecca. A fact of such significance would surely have attracted more attention. A defection of Abū Ṭāhir at this time is quite unlikely, as will be seen. No reliability can be attributed to the report of Niẓām al-Mulk, *Siyāsat-nāma*, ed. ʿA. Iqbāl (Tehran, 1320/1941), p. 279, according to whom Abū Ṭāhir sent presents to ʿUbayd Allāh after the conquest of Mecca.

165 Abū Ṭāhir is meant here. This is obviously an error for which Ibn Khaldūn, however, had a precedent in Ibn al-Athīr, vol. 8, p. 158. Abū Ṭāhir had died in Ramaḍān 322/May 944.

166 *Carmathes*, p. 145.

167 Al-Nahrawālī, *Chroniken*, vol. 3, p. 166.

168 *Carmathes*, p. 146. Here it would again be necessary to assume a secret order of the

Fatimids which the Qarmaṭīs did not carry out until they had extorted money from the ʿAbbasids. De Goeje rather suggests that al-Manṣūr wanted to win the hearts of the Muslims for himself and his dynasty by his order for the return of the Black Stone.

169 Ibn ʿIdhārī, *al-Bayān*, vol. 1, p. 220. This is presumably how de Goeje understood the passage, and E. Fagnan, *Histoire de l'Afrique et de l'Espagne intitulée: Al-Bayano'l-Mogrib* (Algiers, 1901), vol. 1, p. 320, translated it accordingly. Perhaps *rudda*, the Black Stone was returned, should be read instead of *radda*. The departure of al-Manṣūr would then refer to some campaign to the east. There is, however, no other information about such a campaign.

170 Read thus for *al-ḥkm*. See Ibn Miskawayh, *Tajārib*, vol. 2, p. 126.

171 In reality Bajkam was no longer alive at the time of the accession of al-Mustakfī; see Ibn Miskawayh, *Tajārib*, vol. 2, p. 9.

172 See, for instance, Ibn Miskawayh, *Tajārib*, vol. 2, p. 127; Ibn al-Jawzī, *al-Muntaẓam*, vol.6, p. 367; Ibn al-Athīr, vol. 8, p. 339, and al-Nahrawālī, *Chroniken*, vol. 3, p. 166.

173 This conviction is severely censured above all by ʿAbd al-Jabbār. The 'shameful scandals' (*faḍāʾiḥ*) of the Bāṭiniyya, including the Fatimids, which he constantly uncovers consisted mostly in their grandiose predictions which turned out to be nothing but lies and fraud. They had, however, a disarming answer ready: 'Whenever they were unmasked or their lying became manifest they said: There is a hidden meaning to this (*li-hādhā bāṭin*)'; see ʿAbd al-Jabbār, *Tathbīt*, p. 396.

174 Al-Dhahabī added that they were lying here since according to the Qur'an, VII:27, God does not order abomination (*Taʾrīkh al-Islām*, Ms. Paris 1581, fol. 163r, quoted by Abu'l-Maḥāsin, *al-Nujūm*, vol. 2, p. 238). When Sanbar b. al-Ḥasan b. Sanbar returned the Black Stone to Mecca he is supposed to have said: 'We took it with God's power and we brought it back with God's will.' See al-Maqrīzī, *Ittiʿāẓ*, p. 129, probably Akhū Muḥsin, and similarly al-Musabbiḥī quoted by al-Dhahabī in the footnote to Ibn Miskawayh, *Tajārib*, vol. 2, p. 137.

175 Ibn Khaldūn, *al-ʿIbar*, vol. 4, p. 90.

176 If Ibn Khaldūn meant by this that Aḥmad returned it personally, it is erroneous. That was done by Sanbar b. al-Ḥasan b. Sanbar (al-Maqrīzī, *Ittiʿāẓ*, p. 129), the head of the family which occupied the highest rank in the social order of the Qarmaṭī state after the descendants of Abū Saʿīd al-Jannābī (Ibn Ḥawqal, pp. 25–26).

177 Al-Nahrawālī, *Chroniken*, vol. 3, p. 166. Al-Maqrīzī states in his *al-Muqaffā* (in *Akhbār al-Qarāmiṭa*, ed. Suhayl Zakkār, Damascus, 1400/1980, p. 402) that Abū Ṭāhir was succeeded by his two brothers Abu'l-Qāsim Saʿīd and Abu'l-ʿAbbās (*sic*) Aḥmad.

178 De Goeje, *Carmathes*, pp. 143–144, and Ibn al-Jawzī, *al-Muntaẓam*, vol. 6, p. 336. The reports are not uniform.

179 Ibn al-Athīr, in de Goeje, *Carmathes*, p. 143.

180 Ibn Miskawayh, *Tajārib*, vol. 2, p. 127.

181 Ibn Ḥawqal, pp. 25–26.

182 Ibn al-Jawzī, *al-Muntaẓam*, vol. 7, p. 57.

183 Abū Yaʿqūb died in 366/977 (de Goeje, *Carmathes*, p. 191).

184 On the coins minted at the order of al-Ḥasan al-Aʿṣam in Ramla and Damascus in 361/972 the caliph al-Muṭīʿ and al-Ḥasan himself are named on one side and the 'reigning lords' (*al-sāda al-ruʾasāʾ*), namely, the sons of Abū Saʿīd, on the other. In the following year, the title properly appears in the singular (*al-sayyid al-raʾis*). See

Stanley Lane-Poole, 'Unpublished Arabic Coins from the Collection of the Rev. T. Calvert', *Numismatic Chronicle*, NS, 19 (1879), pp. 74 ff. On a dirham minted in Damascus, al-Ḥasan is also called *al-sayyid*, but this is perhaps an arrogation; see H. Porter, 'Unpublished Coins of the Caliphate', *Numismatic Chronicle*, 5th series, 1 (1921), p. 331.

185 De Goeje, *Carmathes*, p. 186.

186 Ibn Ḥawqal, p. 26; see note 143 above. Whether Aḥmad was still alive seems doubtful.

187 Ibn Ḥawqal, p. 26.

188 Ibid., p. 25.

189 Ibn al-Athīr, vol. 8, p. 443.

190 Al-Maqrīzī, *Itti'āẓ*, pp. 133 ff.

191 Ibid., pp. 133, 138.

192 Ibn Ḥawqal, p. 26.

193 *Carmathes*, p. 194.

194 Al-Muqaddasī, *Aḥsan al-taqāsīm*, ed. M. J. de Goeje (2nd edn, Leiden, 1906), p. 94.

195 De Goeje, *Carmathes*, pp. 192, 194. Ibn al-Qalānisī, *Dhayl*, p. 20, mentions the amount as 30,000 dinars. The leader of the Qarmaṭīs was, however, Ja'far b. Aḥmad b. Abī Sa'īd, not his brother al-Ḥasan al-A'ṣam, as Ibn al-Qalānisī and Ibn al-Athīr (vol. 8, p. 487) state. Al-Ḥasan had died on 23 Rajab 366/17 March 977 in Ramla during the siege of Jawhar (al-Maqrīzī, *al-Muqaffā*, in *Akhbār al-Qarāmiṭa*, p. 405). The tribute is said to have been paid until the death of Ja'far (or al-'Azīz?, the passage is ambiguous; Ibn al-Qalānisī, *Dhayl*, p. 21).

196 Ibn Ḥawqal, pp. 25, 27. De Goeje, *Carmathes*, p. 173, and Lewis, *Origins*, p. 89, also took Ibn Ḥawqal to mean that this amount was sent as tribute to the Fatimid imams. But in this year there was war between the Qarmaṭīs and the Fatimids. To be sure, Ibn Ḥawqal primarily knew and described the situation before the outbreak of the war and the alliance of the Qarmaṭīs with the 'Abbasid caliphate. But the uninhibitedness with which he reports on the use of the fifth suggests that he did not think that anything had changed. De Goeje, however, took this to mean that he was trying to conceal the allegiance of the Qarmaṭīs to the Fatimids. 'Lord of the Time' (*ṣāḥib al-zamān*) was a term mostly used for the expected Mahdi and sometimes more generally for the imam of the age.

197 Concerning the gradual growth of knowledge among Sunni historians of the unity of the Bāṭinī movement, see C. H. Becker, 'Zur Geschichtsschreibung unter den Fatimiden', in *Beiträge zur Geschichte Ägyptens unter dem Islam* (Strassburg, 1902–1903), vol. 1, pp. 3 ff, and Lewis, *Origins*, pp. 3 ff.

198 Al-Mas'ūdī, *al-Tanbīh*, p. 384.

199 Al-Mas'ūdī, *al-Tanbīh*, p. 392. His mention here (l. 10) of 'their expectation', no doubt of the Mahdi, perhaps indicates that he meant their original unity, since at least for the followers of the Fatimids this expectation had for the time being been fulfilled with the 'appearance' of 'Ubayd Allāh.

200 Lewis, *Origins*, p. 5. Ibn Miskawayh is independent of Thābit. For the early history, he evidently used the same source as the latter, but usually quoted it more fully. See the juxtaposition in Lewis, *Origins*, pp. 80–81.

201 Lewis, *Origins*, pp. 80–81.

202 In the parallel report of Ibn Miskawayh, *Tajārib*, vol. 1, p. 181, there is no mention that the imam was 'the one residing in the Maghrib' (*al-muqīm bi'l-Maghrib*) as

specified by Thābit.

203 See de Goeje, *Carmathes*, p. 71.

204 Against de Goeje, *Carmathes*, p. 93, see Bowen, *'Alī Ibn 'Īsā*, p. 263. New light is shed on the campaign of Ibn Abi'l-Sāj by the account of Akhū Muḥsin, in al-Maqrīzī, *Itti'āẓ*, p. 126, who is using here a Kūfan source, presumably Ibn Rizām, as is evident from the exact dates for the conquests of Kūfa. He reports that Ibn Abi'l-Sāj was worried about marching through the desert to Baḥrayn with his large army. He therefore relied on a ruse and wrote to Abū Ṭāhir that their aims were the same and that he, Ibn Abi'l-Sāj, would assist him in the conquest of Baghdad. Abū Ṭāhir was deceived by this and set out with all his followers, even women and children. Al-Maqrīzī, on the other hand, reported in his *al-Muqaffā* that Yūsuf b. Abi'l-Sāj sent money to 'Ubayd Allāh and offered him military assistance. 'Ubayd Allāh advised him, however, to exercise restraint for the time being. See Ḥ. I. Ḥasan, *Ta'rīkh al-dawla al-Fāṭimiyya* (Cairo, 1958), p. 70. If this report is reliable, as Ḥ. I. Ḥasan assumes, one would have to conclude from the murder of Ibn Abi'l-Sāj by Abū Ṭāhir that the latter stood in sharp opposition to 'Ubayd Allāh at that time.

205 Lewis, *Origins*, pp. 81–82, and Ibn al-Athīr, vol. 8, p. 469.

206 Ibn Ḥawqal, p. 26.

207 *Carmathes*, p. 81.

208 Ibn Ḥawqal, p. 27.

209 This is presumably how the sentence *wa-umūruhum ka'l-wāqifa fīmā baynahum* is to be understood. *Fīmā baynahum*, among themselves, that is in contrast to the official recognition of the caliphate of the 'Abbasids, whose names were mentioned in the Friday sermons in the towns conquered by them at that time. This placed the Qarmaṭīs obviously also in ideological conflict with the followers of the Fatimids.

210 Against Becker's view (*Beiträge*, vol. 1, p. 5), he is certainly the 'pious Sharīf al-Ḥasanī of Damascus' mentioned by Ibn Ẓāfir (in Wüstenfeld, *Faṭimiden*, p. 3), as is evident from the description of his book. Al-Ḥasanī is to be corrected to al-Ḥusaynī.

211 Translated from the French rendering of de Sacy, *Exposé*, vol. 1, introduction pp. 228–229.

212 Translated from the French of de Sacy, *Exposé*, vol. 1, introduction pp. 137–138.

213 Massignon, 'Esquisse', p. 336, and his 'La legende "de tribus impostoribus" et ses origines Islamiques', *Revue de l'Histoire des Religions*, 82 (1920). See now further S. M. Stern, 'The Book of the Highest Initiation and other anti-Ismā'īlī Travesties', in his *Studies in Early Ismā'īlism* (Jerusalem–Leiden, 1983), pp. 56–83.

214 De Sacy, *Exposé*, vol. 1, introduction pp. 148–164.

215 De Sacy (*Exposé*, vol. 1, introduction p. 153 n. 2) sought to identify these steps with the degrees of initiation related from Akhū Muḥsin previously (in *Exposé*, vol. 1, introduction pp. 74–137). They are, however, different. De Sacy's proposal to read *nine degrees* instead of *seven* (*Exposé*, vol. 1, introduction p. 160) is mistaken.

216 Ibn al-Nadīm, *al-Fihrist*, p. 268.

217 Al-Baghdādī, *al-Farq bayn al-firaq*, ed. M. Z. al-Kawtharī (Cairo, 1948), pp. 177 ff. Whether books of the first six degrees actually existed seems doubtful. There are apparently no quotations from them. Ibn al-Nadīm may have deduced their existence merely from allusions to them in the work itself. The nine degrees named and described by al-Baghdādī differ from those of Akhū Muḥsin and are independent of the *Kitāb al-balāgh*. It is evident even from their names that they are

also fictitious. They were, however, the second major source of the heresiographers. Even al-Ghazālī relied on them in his refutation of the Bāṭiniyya (see Goldziher, *Streitschrift*, introduction pp. 40–41), while he does not mention the *Kitāb al-balāgh*. Nothing is known about the *Kitāb al-dars al-shāfī li'l-nafs* mentioned by Akhū Muḥsin (cited in de Sacy, *Exposé*, vol. 1, introduction p. 159).

218 Massignon erroneously states (in his 'Esquisse', p. 331 and 'Ḳarmaṭians', EI) that Ibn al-Nadīm ascribes the book to ʿAbdān.

219 See Ibn Kathīr, *al-Bidāya*, vol. 11, p. 62. Here as many as sixteen degrees are mentioned, and the title is given as *al-Balāgh al-aʿẓam wa'l-nāmūs al-akbar*. Later (vol. 11, p. 311), the title is, probably more correctly, quoted as *al-Balāgh al-akbar wa'l-nāmūs al-aʿẓam*. Al-Bāqillānī's *Kitāb fī madhāhib al-Qarāmiṭa*, quoted by Ibn Ḥazm, *al-Fiṣal*, vol. 4, p. 22, is presumably identical with his *Kitāb hatk al-astār*, as suggested by M. al-Khuḍayrī and M. Abū Rīda in their edition of al-Bāqillānī's *al-Tamhīd fi'l-radd ʿalā'l-mulḥida* (Cairo, 1947), p. 259 n. 3.

220 ʿAbd al-Jabbār, *Tathbīt*, pp. 359 and 601, where the title is given as *al-Balāgh al-sābiʿ wa'l-nāmūs al-akbar*.

221 Niẓām al-Mulk, *Siyāsat-nāma*, p. 277.

222 Al-Daylamī, *Bayān madhhab al-Bāṭiniyya wa-buṭlānih*, ed. R. Strothmann (Istanbul, 1939), see index.

223 Ibn al-Murtaḍā, *al-Munya wa'l-amal fī sharḥ kitāb al-milal wa'l-niḥal*, ed. M. J. Mashkūr (Beirut, 1399/1979). Ibn al-Murtaḍā's source is al-Ḥākim al-Jushamī (Abū Saʿīd al-Bayhaqī), *Sharḥ ʿuyūn al-masā'il*; see Stern, *Studies*, pp. 63–64.

224 Al-Isfarā'inī, *al-Tabṣīr fī'l-dīn*, ed. M. Z. al-Kawtharī (Cairo–Baghdad, 1955), p. 126. Al-Isfarā'inī evidently did not know who was meant by the alleged author ʿUbayd Allāh b. al-Ḥasan al-Qayrawānī.

225 Ibn al-Jawzī, *al-Muntaẓam*, vol. 5, pp. 114–115. The passage was recognized by J. de Somogyi, 'A Treatise on the Qarmaṭians in the Kitāb al-Muntaẓam of Ibn al-Jauzī', *Rivista degli Studi Orientali*, 13 (1932), p. 252 n. 2, as an abridged version of a section of the *Kitāb al-siyāsa*. He erroneously named Akhū Muḥsin as its author.

226 Al-Āmidī, *Abkār al-afkār*, Ms. Berlin Pet. I 233, fol. 280r. After describing the eighth degree and the allegorical exegesis he adds: *wa-hādhā huwa'l-nāmūs al-aʿẓam wa'l-balāgh al-akbar al-ladhī ʿalayhi madār iʿtiqādihim*.

227 S. Guyard, 'Le Fetwa d'Ibn Taimiyyah sur les Nosairis', *Journal Asiatique*, 6 série, 18 (1871), text pp. 171–172, translation p. 191: *nihāyat al-balāgh al-akbar wa'l-nāmūs al-aʿẓam*.

228 Ibn Kathīr, *al-Bidāya*, vol. 11, p. 311; while on p. 331 he speaks of Muḥammad b. al-Nuʿmān (d. 389/999), who is made out to be the brother of ʿAbd al-ʿAzīz. Muḥammad composed the *Balāgh* in which he tried to refute al-Bāqillānī. Is the passage corrupt or did such a refutation really exist?

229 Al-Kindī, *Wulāt*, p. 603.

230 Ivanow, *Rise*, p. 142; see also his *A Guide to Ismaili Literature* (London, 1933), pp. 41, 78. The refuted book of al-Buṭḥānī, however, is not his *Siyāsat al-murtaddīn* as suggested by Ivanow, *The Alleged Founder of Ismailism* (Bombay, 1946), p. 3 n. 3. This is rather a short treatise of mystical and paraenetic contents. The correct title is *Siyāsat al-murīdīn*. At the beginning of his *Kitāb ithbāt nubuwwat al-nabī*, al-Buṭḥānī sharply attacks the Bāṭiniyya denouncing them as the most dangerous critics of the miracles of the Prophet and states that he had elsewhere described the contents of their treatise *al-Balāgh al-sābiʿ* or *al-Balāgh al-akbar wa'l-nāmūs al-aʿẓam*; see al-Mu'ayyad

bi'llāh, *Ithbāt nubuwwat al-nabī*, ed. Kh. A. Ibrāhīm al-Ḥājj (Beirut, 1980), p. 13.

231 Becker, *Beiträge*, vol. 1, p. 7; and similarly, Massignon, 'Esquisse', p. 332.

232 See, for instance, al-Baghdādī, *al-Farq*, p. 177, and al-Daylamī, *Bayān*, p. 72.

233 Al-Maqrīzī, *Ittiʿāẓ*, p. 133. As a defender of the authenticity of the genealogy of the Fatimids, al-Maqrīzī omitted many of the polemical statements of Akhū Muḥsin about them and about the doctrine of the Bāṭiniyya.

234 Cited in al-Maqrīzī, *Ittiʿāẓ*, p. 133. Ibn al-Jawzī, *al-Muntaẓam*, vol. 6, p. 224, quotes the passage in a longer text which he attributes to al-Tanūkhī. Whether al-Maqrīzī quotes from Ibn al-Jawzī or from another source cannot definitely be established. The small additions in his text may be al-Maqrīzī's own, although he was generally more inclined to abridge his sources. The marginal note earlier in the text (*wa-aqāma . . . al-khalīfa al-ʿAbbāsī*) is taken from the same source. Al-Tanūkhī was generally conscientious in mentioning his informants. It thus seems likely that these were his own reflections.

235 *Yukhrijūna ilā akābir aṣḥābihim annahum min aṣḥābih*, missing in Ibn al-Jawzī.

236 Abu'l-Maḥāsin, *al-Nujūm*, vol. 2, p. 445.

237 The whole text is a commentary on the heinous crimes of the Qarmaṭīs at their sacking of Mecca. Al-Tanūkhī wants to prove that they were not really Shiʿis but rather infidels (*zanādiqa*). Just before the passage quoted by al-Maqrīzī, he mentions as an argument for this thesis that Abū Ṭāhir had been in Kūfa several times but had never visited the grave of ʿAlī and that he had passed by Karbalā' without paying a visit to the tomb of al-Ḥusayn. Al-Tanūkhī displayed some sympathies for the Shiʿis in his works; see Rouchdi Fakkar, *At-Tanūḫi et son livre: La délivrance après l'angoisse* (Cairo, 1955), pp. 19, 109, and also for the Fatimids. But only infidel heretics could commit acts like those of the Qarmaṭīs. Their claim to represent the Mahdi, by which they compromised honest Shiʿis like the Fatimids, seemed an outrageous lie to the cosmopolitan Sunni al-Tanūkhī.

238 A reference to the exchange about the return of the Black Stone mentioned in other sources?

239 According to ʿArīb, *Ṣila*, pp. 162–163, who calls him a Khurāsānī, he was among the prisoners which the Qarmaṭīs carried away on their raid of Qaṣr Ibn Hubayra in 318/931. H. Halm (*Das Reich des Mahdi*, p. 414) suggests that the reference is to the raid of Qaṣr Ibn Hubayra by Ibn Sanbar in 316/928, as reported by Ibn Miskawayh, *Tajārib*, vol. 1, p. 183.

240 Al-Masʿūdī, *al-Tanbīh*, pp. 391–392.

241 *Carmathes*, pp. 129 ff.

242 *Carmathes*, p. 136. That the Yaḥyā b. al-Mahdī mentioned here is a different person was later recognized by de Goeje himself; see al-Masʿūdī, *al-Tanbīh*, p. 384 n. u, and de Goeje, 'La fin de l'empire des Carmathes du Bahraïn', *Journal Asiatique*, 9 série, 5 (1895), p. 27.

243 Massignon, 'Ḳarmaṭians', EI, and Lewis, *Origins*, pp. 87 ff. They interpreted the episode as a temporary defection from the Fatimids.

244 Ibn Miskawayh, *Tajārib*, vol. 2, pp. 55–56, and de Goeje quoting *Kitāb al-ʿuyūn* in his *Carmathes*, pp. 131 ff. It is evident from the detail of these passages that the account is older than the book of Thābit b. Sinān. The latter abridged it and erroneously placed it in the year 326/938. Ibn al-Athīr, vol. 8, pp. 263–264, followed him in this error. For this reason the dating of the episode by de Goeje is still valid against

Bowen, *ʿAlī Ibn ʿĪsā*, p. 358, and the doubts of Lewis, *Origins*, p. 88.

245 When he recognized that his fraud had been uncovered, he is reported to have begged that he be not immediately killed. He said that he would tend their riding animals until his father would appear, from whom he had stolen the sign, and who should judge him. In order to justify the murder of the Iṣfahānī, Ibn Sanbar then told the Qarmaṭīs: 'This young man has come with a lie which he stole from a source of truth (*maʿdin ḥaqq*) and with a sign which he used fraudulently. Because of this we believed him.' (Ibn Miskawayh, *Tajārib*, vol. 2, p. 59).

246 Or: The religion of the first Adam (*dīn Ādam al-awwal*). An adamology in which several persons bear that name is not necessarily implied.

247 Ibn Miskawayh, *Tajārib*, vol. 2, p. 57.

248 ʿAbd al-Jabbār, *Tathbīt*, p. 386, summarized in Lewis, *Origins*, p. 88.

249 Dindān; see Lewis, *Origins*, pp. 69 ff.

250 Lewis, *Origins*, pp. 87–88.

251 ʿAbd al-Jabbār asserts, on the one hand, that Abū Ṭāhir received his instructions from the Fatimid Abu'l-Qāsim and, on the other, that his followers were predicting the advent of the Mahdi in Baḥrayn. Apart from this inconsistency, nothing in his account points to an allegiance of the Qarmaṭīs of Baḥrayn towards the Fatimid imams.

252 The relevant information, however, certainly came from Qarmaṭī circles. Ibn Rizām merely adapted it to his own polemical purposes; see also S. M. Stern, 'Heterodox Ismāʿīlism at the time of al-Muʿizz', BSOAS, 17 (1955), pp. 20–21. Ivanow's suggestion that the Qarmaṭīs wanted to accord the Fatimids, as descendants of Muḥammad b. Ismāʿīl, a special rank in their sect, but these gave them the cold shoulder, is quite mistaken. In fact the reverse was the case. The Fatimids could only regret the defection of their former adherents, and al-Muʿizz made every effort to regain their allegiance. They, however, accused the Fatimids of having forged their genealogy.

253 Cited in Ibn al-Nadīm, *al-Fihrist*, p. 267. Contrary to the assumption of Lewis, *Origins*, p. 56, the passage is almost certainly quoted from Ibn Rizām.

254 Al-Bīrūnī, *al-Āthār al-bāqiya*, ed. C.E. Sachau (Leipzig, 1878), p. 213, and al-Baghdādī, *al-Farq*, p. 172. According to his own statement (pp. 211, 213), al-Bīrūnī reported on the Qarmaṭīs in an earlier work entitled *Fī akhbār al-Mubayyiḍa wa'l-Qarāmiṭa*. This work was evidently used by al-Baghdādī who usually does not name his sources. Al-Baghdādī's information about al-Muqannaʿ and the Mubayyiḍa of Transoxania is probably also taken from there. Al-Bīrūnī was not particularly well informed about the history of the Qarmaṭīs. Thus he erroneously names the Iṣfahānī as Ibn Abī Zakariyyā' al-Ṭamāmī (*Āthār*, p. 213, and al-Baghdādī, *al-Farq*, p. 172). The 18th conjunction of Jupiter and Saturn occurred in the year 296/908. P. Casanova connects the prediction of Dindān with this one and proposes to read 'in the 18th conjunction' there too (*al-thāmin ʿashar* instead of *al-thāmin*); see his 'Une date astronomique dans les Epîtres des Ikhwān as-Ṣafā', *Journal Asiatique*, 11 série, 5 (1915), p. 10. Casanova rightly rejects the emendations proposed by O. Loth and de Goeje.

255 Since when did this Shuʿūbī tendency have a decisive influence on their doctrine? Abū Saʿīd al-Ḥasan b. Bahrām was of Persian origin (al-Maqrīzī, *Ittiʿāẓ*, p. 107). During his mission in southwest Persia he is said to have expressed strongly anti-Arab sentiments (see de Goeje, *Carmathes*, p. 33). The settled population of

Baḥrayn, formerly a province of the Persian empire, consisted largely of Persians and Jews (*Carmathes*, p. 36). Some of Abū Saʿīd's grandsons bore the names of Persian kings: Sābūr b. Abī Ṭāhir and Kisrā b. Abi'l-Qāsim (Ibn Ḥawqal, p. 26). In spite of this, it is unlikely that Abū Saʿīd and Abū Ṭāhir preached the transfer of the reign to the Persians from the beginning. From the outset of their career they relied on the support of Arab tribes and many of the leading men were of Arab descent (see *Carmathes*, p. 161). Abū Ṭāhir, moreover, could hardly have won the backing of the Qarmaṭī Arab tribes from Iraq for an extreme Shuʿūbī programme. The question rather arises as to what extent some of the relevant statements of the heresiographers are influenced by their endeavour to explain the surprising action of Abū Ṭāhir and to discover his spiritual ancestors for it. This endeavour is quite clear in the case of al-Bīrūnī. He emphasizes that the Qarmaṭīs before the advent of the Iṣfahānī espoused a Bāṭinī doctrine and were counted among the Shiʿa. He refers to an alleged ancient Persian prophecy that 1,500 years after Zoroaster the reign of the Magians would be restored. This corresponded to the end of the year 1242 of the era of Alexander (Ramaḍān 319/September 931). Al-Bīrūnī adds that the Qarmaṭīs hit on the right time, yet the reign was not transferred to the Magians. The Shuʿūbī with his astrological prediction had been equally mistaken. Al-Bīrūnī does not put him directly in connection with the Qarmaṭīs. Al-Baghdādī's vague description of him as 'a man of the Bāṭiniyya' is probably a personal elaboration.

256 Translated by de Goeje, *Carmathes*, pp. 113 ff; see also al-Baghdādī, *al-Farq*, p. 173.

257 Ḥasan and Sharaf, *'Ubayd Allāh*, p. 230. The authors also see (p. 221) in the letter of Abū Ṭāhir quoted by Ibn Mālik, *Kashf*, pp. 34–35, which they date to around 313/925, an open declaration of his allegiance to ʿUbayd Allāh. Ibn Mālik unfortunately does not mention the source from which he took the letter. He first calls the author of the letter Saʿīd and then Abū Saʿīd, while in the letter itself the author is called Abu'l-Ḥasan (read Ibn al-Ḥasan?). Abū Ṭāhir would seem to be the most likely author. The pun on p. 351 l.10 definitely identifies the addressee as the caliph al-Muqtadir (295–320/908–932). There is, however, no good reason to assume that the vague words 'the expected imam has arisen against you like a lion' refer to ʿUbayd Allāh. The Shuʿūbī tendency in the remark that the imam has no need of the help of the Arabs could rather point to the Iṣfahānī. The year 313/925 seems to be only the earliest possible date of the letter, and it could have been written years later. The extremely insolent tenor rather speaks for a later date, whereas in 312/924 Abū Ṭāhir was still negotiating with the ʿAbbasid government about a surrender of Baṣra and Ahwāz to him (see de Goeje, *Carmathes*, p. 86). But the letter may also have been written before the advent of the Iṣfahānī without any necessity to identify the expected imam with ʿUbayd Allāh. For the Mahdi was imagined to be actually present even if not apparent. The Qarmaṭīs always claimed that they were acting on his order.

258 In another line of the poem, Abū Ṭāhir refers to himself as the one announced in the *sūra al-Zumar* (Qur'an, XXXIX:37, *'wa-man yahdi Allāhu famā lahū min muḍill'*). This should evidently not be interpreted as a claim to be the Mahdi.

259 De Goeje, *Carmathes*, p. 129.

260 Al-Dhahabī, *Ta'rīkh al-Islām*, fol. 56v. Abu'l-Maḥāsin, *al-Nujūm*, vol. 2, p. 239, quoted al-Dhahabī, but omitted these four lines.

261 See *Carmathes*, p. 97, and al-Masʿūdī, *al-Tanbīh*, p. 382.

262 Al-Bīrūnī, *al-Āthār*, p. 213.

263 *Carmathes*, p. 122. Al-Baghdādī, *al-Farq*, p. 173, states explicitly that Jupiter and Saturn were meant by the 'two stars' mentioned in the poem. This would exclude the interpretation of de Goeje, *Carmathes*, p. 123, that Jupiter and the moon were meant. The problem remains how Mars, according to al-Baghdādī's variants rejected by de Goeje as unreasonable, is to enter into conjunction with the two stars. It is evident, however, that al-Bīrūnī saw the line as alluding to the conjunction of the year 316/928.

264 Al-Baghdādī, *al-Farq*, p. 173.

265 'Abd al-Jabbār, *Tathbīt*, pp. 381–382.

266 This is no doubt the correct date of the conquest of Kūfa contrary to the view of Bowen, *'Alī Ibn 'Īsā*, pp. 249 and 250 n. 1. In al-Mas'ūdī, *al-Tanbīh*, p. 281, l.1, the date has to be read twice as 312.

267 Al-Mas'ūdī, *al-Tanbīh*, p. 385.

268 Ibn al-Jawzī, *al-Muntaẓam*, vol. 6, p. 216. Al-Dhahabī (in Ibn Miskawayh, *Tajārib*, vol. 1, p. 183), Abu'l-Maḥāsin, *al-Nujūm*, vol. 2, p. 232, and Ibn Kathīr, *al-Bidāya*, vol. 11, p. 157, are probably all dependent on him.

269 *Dār al-hijra*. De Goeje, *Carmathes*, p. 130, ignored the religious significance in suggesting that the term signified for the Qarmaṭīs merely the residence of the missionary and in arguing on that basis that the report about Abū Ṭāhir building a *dār al-hijra* as late as 316/928 must be mistaken. Medina, the *dār al-hijra* of Muḥammad, was the place of foundation of Islam. Similarly, for the Isma'ilis the *dār al-hijra* was the residence of the Mahdi and the place of foundation of his religion. The Isma'ilis attributed great significance to the well-known *ḥadīth* which Shi'is attributed to the Imam Ja'far: 'Islam began as a stranger (*gharīban*, meaning in Medina), it will return as a stranger as it began. Good tidings therefore to the strangers.' According to al-Nawbakhtī, *Firaq al-Shī'a*, pp. 62–63, the Qarmaṭīs founded their thesis of the abrogation of Islam by the religion of the Mahdi on this. The abrogation of Islam was the background of the removal of the Black Stone a year later.

270 *Da'ā ila'l-mahdī*. Abu'l-Maḥāsin: *al-mahdi'l-'Alawī*. De Goeje, *Carmathes*, p. 82 n. 2, interpreted this as referring to 'Ubayd Allāh (similarly, Weil, *Geschichte der Chalifen*, vol. 2, p. 611). Ibn Kathīr, who quotes Ibn al-Jawzī almost literally, adds as an explanation: 'who was in the Maghrib in the town of al-Mahdiyya'. Time and again the later historiographers sought to identify the Mahdi of the Qarmaṭīs in this manner. Another example is evidently Abu'l-Maḥāsin's statement, *al-Nujūm*, vol. 2, p. 238: 'Abū Ṭāhir . . . claimed that he was the missionary of the Mahdi 'Ubayd Allāh.' Yet the contemporary chroniclers and polemicists would certainly have given prominence to any public confession of Abū Ṭāhir that he was a follower of the Fatimids.

271 Thus the name in al-Mas'ūdī, *al-Tanbīh*, p. 391, and in 'Abd al-Jabbār, *Tathbīt*, p. 383. Al-Nafaliyya and al-Naqaliyya in the other sources (*Carmathes*, p. 99) must be corrected. Al-Mas'ūdī stresses that it was a religious name. The origin of the name is explained by Akhū Muḥsin (see 'Baḳliyya', in EI2). He reports that in 295/908 a certain Abū Ḥātim al-Zuṭṭī visited the followers of al-Būrānī, a missionary of 'Abdān in Ṭassūj al-Tustar (al-Maqrīzī, *Itti'āẓ*, p. 104), and taught them things 'which are accepted only by an idiot'. He forbade them to eat garlic, onions, leeks

and radishes, and to shed the blood of any animal. They were called Baqliyya (al-Maqrīzī, *Itti'āẓ*, p. 124; de Sacy, *Exposé*, vol. 1, introduction p. 210). Akhū Muḥsin adds that Abū Ḥātim stayed only one year with them. Thereafter, discord prevailed among them. It is thus uncertain whether the rebels of the year 316/928 still held on to his teaching. Perhaps only the name remained.

272 See al-Maqrīzī, *Itti'āẓ*, p. 130, and al-Mas'ūdī, *al-Tanbīh*, p. 391. The chronology of the report and of de Goeje, *Carmathes*, p. 99, must be corrected on this basis.

273 Al-Maqrīzī, *Itti'āẓ*, p. 130, and Ibn al-Athīr, vol. 8, p. 136. The eschatological character of the movement is reflected in the statement of 'Abd al-Jabbār, *Tathbīt*, p. 383: 'They said: The truth has appeared, the Mahdi has risen, the reign of the 'Abbasids, the scholars of the law, the readers of the Qur'an, and the traditionists has come to an end . . . Nothing remains to be expected, and we have not come to establish a reign, but to abolish a law.'

274 Ibn al-Athīr, vol. 8, p. 136: *wa-kānū yad'ūna ilā'l-mahdī*. De Goeje supplies 'Ubayd Allāh (*Carmathes*, p. 99). Similarly, Ibn Kathīr, *al-Bidāya*, vol. 11, p. 158, quoting the passage from Ibn al-Athīr, adds: 'who appeared in the Maghrib, the ancestor of the Fatimids'.

275 *Carmathes*, p. 99, and, likewise, Weil, *Geschichte*, vol. 2, p. 611. Since 'Īsā b. Mūsā, 'Abdān's nephew, was among the rebels, de Goeje suggested that the defection of 'Abdān was a personal affair.

276 Al-Maqrīzī, *Itti'āẓ*, p. 124.

277 Ibn al-Athīr, vol. 8, p. 115.

278 A quarter of Baghdad inhabited mainly by Shi'is. See 'Barāthā', in EI2.

279 The colour of the Isma'ilis in contrast to the black colour of the 'Abbasids. See *Carmathes*, pp. 179–180.

280 Ibn al-Jawzī, *al-Muntaẓam*, vol. 6, p. 195.

281 Al-Mas'ūdī, *al-Tanbīh*, p. 391, where the name is explained.

282 'Abd al-Jabbār, *Tathbīt*, p. 386.

283 See note 156 above.

284 The 'Ijl lived in the environs of Kūfa and had previously participated in Shi'i rebellions. In the edition of 'Abd al-Jabbār, *Tathbīt*, the name of Abu'l-Ghayth's father is given as 'Ubayda. In the manuscript, however, it appears as 'Abda.

285 'Abd al-Jabbār, *Tathbīt*, pp. 383, 392.

286 'Arīb, *Ṣila*, p. 163.

287 'Arīb, *Ṣila*, p. 168. See *Carmathes*, pp. 136–137.

288 See note 27 above.

289 'Abd al-Jabbār, *Tathbīt*, p. 392.

290 Al-Nuwayrī, *Nihāyat al-arab*, vol. 25, p. 296, and al-Maqrīzī, *Itti'āẓ*, p. 130.

291 'Abd al-Jabbār, *Tathbīt*, p. 388.

292 E. M. Quatremère, 'Vie du khalife Fatimite Möezz-li-din-Allah', *Journal Asiatique*, 3 série, 3 (1837), p. 182, and Wüstenfeld, *Faṭimiden*, p. 122. See now Th. Bianquis, 'La prise du pouvoir par les Fatimides en Egypte (357–363/968–974)', *Annales Islamologiques*, 11 (1972), pp. 63–64.

293 Nāṣir-i Khusraw, *Safar-nāma* (Berlin, 1922), p. 123.

294 *Carmathes*, p. 190.

295 Lewis, *Origins*, p. 82, and Zāhid 'Alī, *Ta'rīkh*, p. 147.

296 'Abd al-Jabbār, *Tathbīt*, p. 607.

297 See Lewis, *Origins*, p. 81.
298 Cited in al-Maqrīzī, *Itti'āẓ*, pp. 133 ff.
299 Ibid., p. 134.
300 Ibid.
301 Ibid., p. 136.
302 Ibid., pp. 137–138.
303 Ibid., p. 138.
304 Read *ta'lam* for *ta'mal*, as in al-Maqrīzī, *Itti'āẓ*, ed. Jamāl al-Dīn al-Shayyāl (Cairo, 1367/1948), p. 259.
305 Al-Maqrīzī, *Itti'āẓ*, ed. Bunz, p. 139.
306 Qur'an, XL:51.
307 Read *da'buhum* for *dānuhum*, as in al-Maqrīzī, *Itti'āẓ*, ed. al-Shayyāl, p. 260.
308 Al-Maqrīzī, *Itti'āẓ*, p. 139, read *ma'āb* for *ma'āt*, as in *Itti'āẓ*, ed. al-Shayyāl, p. 260.
309 See also al-Maqrīzī, *Itti'āẓ*, p. 134: *minnā wa-min ābā'inā'l-rāshidīna'l-mahdiyyīna'l-muntakhabīn*.
310 Characteristic is Akhū Muḥsin's commentary on the letter mentioned above. Rather than seeing in it a confirmation of the unity of the Fatimids and Qarmaṭīs, he finds it necessary to explain the motives of al-Mu'izz. They all originated, to be sure, in the same heresy, yet they form two parties.
311 See al-Maqrīzī, *Itti'āẓ*, p. 141: 'Don't you know that al-Muṭī' is the last of the sons of al-'Abbās and the last to arrogate the reign over mankind to himself?'

THREE

The cosmology of the pre-Fatimid Ismāʿīliyya

HEINZ HALM

UNTIL WELL into the twentieth century, the religious ideas and doctrines of the Ismaʿilis were obscured by misunderstandings, speculations and wilful calumnies on the part of the sect's Muslim opponents. Even modern research has long let itself be misled by hostile propaganda, the more so since the original literature of the Ismaʿilis was for the most part inaccessible.

The pendulum swung in the other direction when Stanislas Guyard published his *Fragments relatifs à la doctrine des Ismaélîs* in 1874. Recognizing the Neoplatonic character of some of the texts he had published, Guyard drew the conclusion that the doctrines of the Ismaʿilis were based on Greek philosophy. He considered the alleged founder of the Ismāʿīliyya, ʿAbd Allāh b. Maymūn al-Qaddāḥ, as the person responsible for acquainting the Shiʿi sect with Greek thought. Guyard sought to corroborate his theory by referring to an early witness. In his well-known verdict (*fatwā*) against the Nuṣayrī sect, the orthodox Sunni theologian Ibn Taymiyya (d. 728/1328) had already maintained that the doctrine of the Ismaʿilis was identical with that of the 'Brethren of Purity' (Ikhwān al-Ṣafāʾ) of Baṣra, who had indeed drawn on the philosophy of late classical antiquity to elaborate the treatises of their great encyclopaedia (*Rasāʾil*). When in 1898, Paul Casanova proved in the light of a manuscript from Maṣyāf in Syria that the *Rasāʾil* had in fact been highly esteemed by the Ismaʿili 'Assassins', who quoted them in their own writings, Ibn Taymiyya's statements appeared to be confirmed.

Later editions of Ismaʿili texts pointed to the same direction. The theological treatises of the Ṭayyibī Ismaʿilis of the Yemen contain ample quotations from the *Rasāʾil Ikhwān al-Ṣafāʾ*, and in the *ʿUyūn al-akhbār* by the Yemenite *dāʿī* Idrīs ʿImād al-Dīn (d. 872/1468), Aḥmad b. ʿAbd Allāh b. Muḥammad b. Ismāʿīl b. Jaʿfar al-Ṣādiq, the ninth imam and the second of the leaders of the Ismaʿili *daʿwa* residing in Salamiyya, is explicitly named as the author of the *Rasāʾil*.[1] Certain passages in the *Rasāʾil* – at least in some critical editions of the text – are indeed highly reminiscent of Ismaʿili doctrines. As late as 1933, Wladimir Ivanow still presented the *Rasāʾil* as an Ismaʿili work in his *A Guide to Ismaili Literature*, though assuming that they were 'most probably . . . produced some time near the end of the fourth/tenth century (after the seizure of Egypt), under the patronage of the early Fatimides.'[2] So it is understandable that even today, scholars like Yves Marquet still believe that the doctrines of the 'Brethren of Purity' represent the original, unadulterated teachings of the Ismāʿīliyya.

Doubts about this opinion were, however, soon expressed by Ivanow himself, who was the first European to gain access to original Ismaʿili literature in India. He found out that the work of Ḥamīd al-Dīn al-Kirmānī, the most important theologian of the early Fatimid period, did not mention a word about the *Rasāʾil* or even make any recognizable allusions to them. Yet the Neoplatonic character of numerous works of the Fatimid period grew more and more obvious in the course of Ivanow's research. It soon became apparent, however, that Neoplatonic philosophy was not the root of the Ismaʿili doctrine, but a secondary stage in its evolution. In his *Alleged Founder of Ismailism*, Ivanow states that neither the earliest known treatises of the Ismaʿilis from the time prior to the establishment of the Fatimid caliphate, nor the works of the Qāḍī al-Nuʿmān (d. 363/974) contain any trace of Neoplatonic influence.[3] Ivanow, therefore, arrived at the conclusion that Neoplatonism was merely a later, secondary layer of the dogmatic development of the sect.

What, then, had there been before? Though the earlier writings, such as the *Kitāb al-ʿālim waʾl-ghulām*, the *Kitāb al-rushd waʾl-hidāya* or the six treatises of the *Kitāb al-kashf*, admittedly offer insights into the imamate doctrine, the mission practices and the technique of the *taʾwīl*, they do not provide any systematic picture of the entire doctrinal framework of the early Ismāʿīliyya.

Some intriguing information by non-Ismaʿili authors led the scholars to the right track. A Yemenite poet, al-Tamīmī, a contemporary of the earliest Ismaʿili mission in the Yemen, refers to the Ismaʿilis in three separately transmitted verses and says:

'They make Qadar a god, and Kūnī its creator, who provided subsistence and then veiled himself';

They consider as gods Qadar and Kūnī, together with al-Jadd which is joined to al-Khayāl and al-Istiftāḥ . . . What an abberation!

The Zaydī historian al-Hamdānī (4th/10th century), who handed down these curious verses, makes the following comments about them:

> There are seven gods (*āliha*), one in each heaven. The first and highest one, who dwells in the seventh and highest heaven, is called Kūnī. Kūnī created Qadar, who dwells in the second heaven. Qadar created the gods who are beneath him, viz., al-Jadd, al-Istiftāḥ, and al-Khayāl, and the other creatures . . . But they now call that which they used to call Kūnī 'the preceding one' (*al-sābiq*), and they now call Qadar 'the following one' (*al-tālī*) . . . They also call these two 'the first two principles', and they say that they are the intellect (*al-ʿaql*) and the soul (*al-nafs*), and that al-Jadd, al-Fatḥ and al-Khayāl have, as it were, emanated from them (*ka'l-inbiʿāthāt*).[4]

Al-Hamdānī's commentary on al-Tamīmī's verses already reflects the later development of the Ismaʿili doctrine: what was previously called Kūnī and Qadar is now called 'intellect' and 'soul', and these do not 'create' al-Jadd, al-Fatḥ and al-Khayāl, but the latter three 'emanate' from the two 'principles'. The 'Neoplatonization' of the earlier doctrine is carried out simply in a few words.

The fact that al-Tamīmī's three verses indeed reveal the central dogmas of the earliest Ismāʿīliyya could easily be proved in the light of original Ismaʿili literature of later times, for even such Neoplatonic authors as al-Sijistānī (d. between 386/996 and 393/1003) and al-Kirmānī (d. after 411/1020) often mention the names Kūnī, Qadar, al-Jadd, al-Fatḥ and al-Khayāl, and 'Neoplatonize' them in exactly the same way as al-Hamdānī does in his commentary. However, the part they played in the original system of the earliest Ismāʿīliyya could not be discovered from these isolated references.

The puzzle was successfully solved by Samuel Miklos Stern, who had already identified the authors of the *Rasā'il Ikhwān al-Ṣafā'* in 1946. In a manuscript of some Ismaʿili writings which the Indian Ismaʿili scholar, Professor Asaf A. A. Fyzee, had placed at his disposal from his private library, Stern accidentally discovered a treatise which used the same names and terminology as the Yemenite poet and his commentator, but this time in an original Ismaʿili text of some length (the treatise consists of sixteen manuscript pages). Stern's edition of the text appeared posthumously, together with a partial translation and a commentary, under the title *The Earliest Cosmological Doctrines of Ismāʿīlism*.[5]

The original author of the treatise is named right at the beginning as the Fatimid caliph al-Muʿizz, who had settled in Egypt in 362/973 and died in Cairo in 365/975; the transmitter is mentioned as a certain Shaykh Abū ʿĪsā al-Murshid, whom Stern was able to identify. The Fatimid conqueror of Egypt, Jawhar, had during his four years as viceroy of Egypt (358–362/969–973) delegated to this very Abū ʿĪsā, his deputy, the jurisdiction of 'grievances' (*maẓālim*), and the Qāḍī al-Nuʿmān, the 'chief ideologue' of the Fatimids, who died in Cairo in 363/974, had addressed a letter to this man, the '*dāʿī* of Miṣr' (i.e., of Fusṭāṭ or Old Cairo).

Thus, there are three chronological grounds for dating the cosmogonical treatise of Abū ʿĪsā al-Murshid to the earliest period of Fatimid rule in Egypt. In addition, it is proved to be a product of official Ismaʿili propaganda (*daʿwa*): it stems from a missionary who was active in the old Sunni city of Cairo (Miṣr cannot be interpreted as 'Egypt' here, it definitely means Fusṭāṭ), and invokes the authority of the imam-caliph al-Muʿizz. In other words, it reflects the official doctrine of that period. Making the imam-caliph himself appear as the original author is in line with Fatimid practice; all statements regarding the doctrine had to proceed from the imam, and the person who committed them to writing was no more than the 'transmitter' (*rāwī*). In his own writings, the Qāḍī al-Nuʿmān several times confirms that the teachings presented in the doctrinal sessions (*majālis al-ḥikma*) had to be personally authorized by the imam before the *dāʿī* could convey them to the adepts.

According to the untitled treatise of Abū ʿĪsā al-Murshid, there existed before all space and before all time nothing but God alone. His will calls creation into being, and creation emerges from light, which emanates from God himself. To this light God calls out the creative command *kun*!: 'Be!' or 'Become!'

Through God's calling and naming, this word *kun* acquires an existence of its own, it is the first creature, and through it God creates all other creatures. However, it does not exist under the name *kun*, but under the feminine form of the Arabic imperative, *kūnī*. This transformation of the masculine imperative into the feminine form has a special meaning, which will be discussed later.

At this point we must insert a passage which, in Abū ʿĪsā al-Murshid's rather unsystematically structured treatise, is slipped in towards the end of the text. It reads:

> Know . . . that when the First (Kūnī) was created . . . , he saw no other beings besides him. Thus, he conceived a proud thought that there is nobody but himself. Upon this, six dignitaries (*ḥudūd*) immediately emanated from him through God's power, in order to teach him that

> there is an omnipotent being above him from Whom he derives his power and upon Whose will all his actions depend . . . When the First saw that this happened neither through his own power nor according to his own will, he was convinced that there was something above him and acknowledged his Creator; it was then that he said: 'There is no god but God' – i.e., 'I am not a god'.

God's first creature, Kūnī, thus succumbs to the error of considering himself as God. This leads us to the conclusion that God the Creator is invisible and concealed to him. So God has to remind His creature of Himself, and He does so by having six other creatures arise from Kūnī. Perplexity about the unexpected appearance of these new creatures makes Kūnī realize that he is not alone, and that there must be an invisible Creator ruling over him. Kūnī relinquishes his pride and acknowledges his Creator. This passage is of crucial significance for the study of Ismaʿili cosmology and cosmogony; we shall come back to it later.

Then God orders Kūnī:

> Create for yourself out of your own light a creature to act for you as a vizier and helper and to carry out Our command.

Kūnī thereupon creates a second creature, to whom he gives the name Qadar. This is a well-known concept of Ismaʿili theology. It signifies God's power of determination or predestination. God now uses these two entities to call into being all the rest of creation:

> Through Kūnī God brought to being (*kawwana*) all things, and through Qadar He determined (*qaddara*) them.

How this happens is not detailed in our text. It merely says:

> Kūnī consists of four letters, Qadar of three, which makes seven letters.

The meaning of this enigmatic sentence is only clarified by referring to another early Ismaʿili text: the second treatise of the *Kitāb al-kashf*, which the Ismaʿili tradition attributes to Jaʿfar b. Manṣūr al-Yaman, who ended his life at the Fatimid court in Manṣūriyya near Qayrawān in North Africa. However, the *Kitāb al-kashf* ascribed to him, consisting of a collection of six very old and evidently pre-Fatimid texts, was probably only redacted by him; and he had presumably taken the collection with him to North Africa from his home in the Yemen. In the second treatise of this collection,[6] the Arabic alphabet, which consists of twenty-eight consonant signs, is divided into four groups of seven letters each, and thus into four heptads, from the combinations of which all words – and with them the very things they signify – come into being. There must be a very similar idea, reminiscent of the Jewish Cabbala, behind the statement in the treatise of Abū ʿĪsā al-Murshid that Kūnī and Qadar are composed of seven characters: they form the original heptad out of which all other names emerge.

The creative activity of Kūnī and his 'vizier' Qadar first brings forth the beings of the spiritual world: from the light of Kūnī there emerge the seven Cherubs (*karūbiyya*), who later – after the creation of the material world – rule the seven heavenly spheres, while Qadar creates the twelve Spiritual Beings (*rūḥāniyya*), who subsequently control the signs of the zodiac. The text also provides a list of their names: it starts with al-Jadd (good fortune), al-Fatḥ (conquest or triumph) and al-Khayāl (imagination or fantasy), and it also contains several well-known names of angels of the Islamic tradition, such as Riḍwān (the guardian of Paradise), Mālik (the angel of Hell) and the two funerary angels Munkar and Nakīr. In other Ismaʿili texts, al-Jadd, al-Fatḥ and al-Khayāl are identified with the angels Jibrāʾīl, Mīkāʾīl and Isrāfīl.

As indicated above, the error of the first creature, Kūnī, who regarded himself as God, is of special significance to the Ismaʿili cosmogony. Kūnī's error, his presumption and hubris, causes God the Creator to intervene; this is what sets in motion the process of creation.

Time and again the text quotes several verses from the Qurʾan in order to 'prove' that the latter contains cryptic allusions to the processes illustrated, and although the names Kūnī and Qadar can themselves be derived from the Qurʾan, it is apparent, not only from the names of some of the Cherubs and Spiritual Beings but from the entire narrative as such, that we are dealing here also with ideas and motifs borrowed from a foreign realm. This would hardly upset a faithful Ismaʿili, for according to his conviction, the Islamic revelation was in fact the last manifestation of an age-old eternal truth.

The cosmogony of Abū ʿĪsā's treatise represents a type that is familiar to us from the Gnosis of late antiquity. This spiritual movement, which penetrated not only the ancient mystery cults, but also Judaism and Christianity, and even gave rise to the world religion of Manichaeism, had its apogee between the 1st and 4th centuries AD, but its after-effect lasted much longer. Manichaeism did not disappear until the 11th century AD, and the Gnostic Baptist sect of the Mandaeans has survived to this day in southern Iraq. With the Manichaeans and Mandaeans we already have two Gnostic religions that arose in Iraq, which is precisely where the Ismaʿili mission (*daʿwa*) also appeared in the middle of the 3rd/9th century. But while we are quite well informed about the numerous Gnostic sects of Egypt and their literature through the manuscripts discovered at Nag Hammadi, we are completely in the dark about the Gnostic milieu of pre-Islamic Mesopotamia and know next to nothing about the sources that inspired the Islamic Gnosis in general or the Ismaʿili Gnosis in particular. The source could not have been Manichaeism, however, for there is no evidence of any specific Manichaean ideas and concepts in Ismaʿili teachings.

Nor is there any need to associate the Ismāʿīliyya with a particular pre-Islamic Gnostic sect. If we qualify the cosmogonical myth of the Ismaʿilis, as handed down to us in the treatise of Abū ʿĪsā al-Murshid, as 'gnostic', we merely have in mind certain fundamental characteristics which we encounter repeatedly in a similar form in the cosmogonies of very different Gnostics of late antiquity – Ophites and Valentinians, Barbelo-Gnostics and Manichaeans. The most striking characteristic here is the belief that the creation of the universe is the result of a Fall, not the Fall of a terrestrial man, but that of the non-material first creature. This first creature is deluded into believing that it is God, since it does not recognize its hidden Creator. This Fall is the cause of the emergence of the cosmos, consisting at first of a 'higher' spiritual world with its multiple degrees – which the Gnostics of late antiquity called 'fullness' (*pleroma*) – and later of the material cosmos with its seven heavenly spheres and the sublunar, terrestrial world. As a result, man, who appears at the end of this process, is far from his origin; he is literally worlds apart from his Creator. The sense of Gnostic religiosity is to explain man's distance from God and to show a way to abolish this distance, and this way is precisely the 'knowledge' (Greek, *gnōsis*) which man is not capable of acquiring on his own, but which has to be communicated to him from above. When man has come to recognize his origin and the causes for his distance from God, he will also have achieved salvation. Cosmology and soteriology are, therefore, closely connected in this system.[7]

The cosmology of Abū ʿĪsā's treatise contains all these essential Gnostic characteristics. In the system of the ancient Gnostics, the first of God's creatures who rebels and succumbs to hubris is usually of the female sex (*sophia*). The Ismaʿili myth preserves a reflection of this idea by transforming the Qur'anic creation command *kun* into the feminine form of the imperative, *kūnī*. The progressive development first of the non-material, and then of the material world, man's distance from God, his illumination and salvation through knowledge (*ʿilm* or *ḥikma* = *gnōsis*), which is communicated to him by messengers sent by God – all these separate characteristics justify qualifying the Ismaʿili doctrine as 'gnostic'.

Since the Ismaʿili mission (*daʿwa*) started in southern Mesopotamia in the middle of the 3rd/9th century, we may assume that the Gnostic pattern which provides its basis is of Mesopotamian origin. More cannot be said, however, since we only know the Mesopotamian Gnosis in its Manichaean and Mandaean forms. We must, nevertheless, assume that there were a great number of Gnostic sects and circles in pre-Islamic Iraq – as there were in Egypt, Syria and Asia Minor – which never appeared in the public eye and did not leave the slightest trace. Like Judaism, Christianity and Zoroastrianism, Islam was affected by this important spiritual movement.

The pre-Fatimid Ismaʿili cosmogony is not the only Gnostic myth in Islamic garb known to us. About a century older is the *Umm al-kitāb*, the 'Original Book', an apocalypse initially written in Arabic which is now extant only in a (subsequently enlarged) Persian translation handed down by Ismaʿili communities in the Pamir and Karakorum regions, and which has nothing to do with the doctrines of the Ismāʿīliyya.[8] This curious book is apparently traceable to the Iraqī sectarians belonging to the circle of the Shiʿi heresiarch Abu'l-Khaṭṭāb.[9] Here, creation is set in motion through the hubris of an angelic being called ʿAzāzi'īl. Closely akin to the cosmogony of the *Umm al-kitāb* is that of another apocalypse belonging to the same tradition, the 'Book of Shadows' (*Kitāb al-aẓilla*).[10] This book, in its turn, forms the basis of the cosmogonical myth of the Syrian sect of the Nuṣayrīs or ʿAlawīs, known to us mainly by the written disclosures of the Nuṣayrī renegade Sulaymān Effendi al-Adhanī in the year 1864.[11]

The closely related cosmogonies of the *Umm al-kitāb*, the *Kitāb al-aẓilla* and the Nuṣayrīs are distinctly different from the cosmogony of the early Ismaʿilis. We are dealing with two totally different religions. Although they are based on a similar Gnostic pattern, they have nothing to do with one another. They represent two completely independent, autonomous traditions. The former is the tradition of the so-called 'exaggerators' (*ghulāt*), which had its roots in Madā'in (Ctesiphon) and Kūfa and which can be traced back to the dawn of Shiʿism; the Ismaʿili doctrine, on the other hand, is a more recent, independent product of the 3rd/9th century. Its inventor was presumably the founder of the Ismaʿili *daʿwa*, ʿAbd Allāh the Elder (*al-Akbar*), the ancestor of the Fatimids, who started his activity in his native town of ʿAskar Mukram in Khūzistān, and then in Baṣra, and who subsequently settled in Salamiyya in Syria. If this assumption is true, ʿAbd Allāh al-Akbar was the founder of a gnostic tradition on a par with the well-known creators of earlier Gnostic systems such as Simon Magus, Valentinian, or Mani.

NOTES

The editor would like to express his gratitude to Madam Azizeh Azodi for her masterful translation of this chapter from German into English.

1 Idrīs ʿImād al-Dīn, *ʿUyūn al-akhbār wa-funūn al-āthār*, vol. 4, ed. M. Ghālib (Beirut, 1973), pp. 367 ff.
2 W. Ivanow, *A Guide to Ismaili Literature* (London, 1933), pp. 30 ff.
3 W. Ivanow, *The Alleged Founder of Ismailism* (Bombay, 1946), pp. 145 ff.
4 Quoted from C. van Arendonk, *Les débuts de l'Imāmat Zaidite au Yémen*, tr. J. Ryckmans (Leiden, 1960), p. 333; see also S. M. Stern, *Studies in Early Ismāʿīlism* (Jerusalem–Leiden, 1983), pp. 3 ff.
5 Included in Stern's *Studies in Early Ismāʿīlism*, pp. 3–29.
6 Jaʿfar b. Manṣūr al-Yaman, *Kitāb al-kashf*, ed. R. Strothmann (London, etc., 1952), pp. 48 ff.; ed. M. Ghālib (Beirut, 1984), pp. 54 ff. For the German translation of the passage in question, see H. Halm, *Kosmologie und Heilslehre der frühen Ismāʿīlīya: Eine Studie zur islamischen Gnosis* (Wiesbaden, 1978), pp. 39–42.
7 See Halm, *Kosmologie und Heilslehre der frühen Ismāʿīlīya.*
8 *Umm al-kitāb*, ed. W. Ivanow, in *Der Islam*, 23 (1936), pp. 1–132; Italian translation, *Ummu'l-Kitāb*, tr. P. Filippani-Ronconi (Naples, 1966).
9 See H. Halm, *Die islamische Gnosis: Die extreme Schia und die ʿAlawiten* (Zürich–Munich, 1982), pp. 113 ff; also containing a partial German translation of the *Umm al-kitāb.*
10 Ibid., pp. 240 ff.
11 Ibid., pp. 298 ff.

FOUR

Abū Yaʿqūb al-Sijistānī and the seven faculties of the Intellect

WILFERD MADELUNG

IN THE sixteenth chapter of his *Book of Wellsprings* (*Kitāb al-yanābīʿ*), the Ismaʿili *dāʿī* Abū Yaʿqūb al-Sijistānī describes the seven faculties (*quwā*) which were, he says, originated together with the Universal Intellect all at once, and which necessarily accompany it.[1] The first among them is Eternal Time (*dahr*).[2] The proof for its coextension with the Universal Intellect is that the individual intellect, when it becomes acquisitive (*muktasib*) through the perception of an intelligible, will be permanently accompanied by that intelligible. Thus it becomes known that the absolute Eternal Time extends with the Preceder (*sābiq* = Universal Intellect) at the origination (*ibdāʿ*) and ever thereafter.

The second faculty of the Intellect is Truth (*ḥaqq*). For the truth of any intelligible coextends with the acquisitive intellect. The supposition that it could be removed from it is false, since its contrary would annihilate the intellect.[3] Thus it becomes known that absolute Truth extends with the Intellect at the origination and thereafter.

The third faculty is Joy (*surūr*). For joy is present in the acquisitive intellect whenever it comprehends an intelligible. Thus it becomes known that absolute Joy extends with the Intellect at the origination and thereafter.

The fourth faculty is Demonstration (*burhān*). For demonstration does not lag behind the acquisitive intellect when it comprehends an intelligible. Thus is becomes known that Demonstration is coextensive with the Intellect at the origination and thereafter.

The fifth faculty is Life (*ḥayāt*). Life exists with the intellect when it is set in motion by the perception of intelligibles. Thus it becomes known that absolute Life extends with the Preceder at the origination and thereafter without a delay.

The sixth faculty is Perfection (*kamāl*). Perfection does not lack behind the partial acquisitive intellect whenever it comprehends an intelligible, for in comprehension it does not imagine the intelligible in deficiency but in perfection. Thus it becomes known that Perfection extends with the Preceder at the origination and thereafter.

The identity of the seventh, and highest, faculty of the Intellect has caused some confusion among the later Isma'ili transmitters of texts and among modern scholars. In his edition of the *Kitāb al-yanābī'*, H. Corbin preserved the reading *ghayba*, absence or occultation, which he found in his manuscripts. He pointed out, however, that Nāṣir-i Khusraw in his Persian paraphrase of the text in his *Khwān al-ikhwān* rendered it by *bī-niyāzī*, needlessness or self-sufficiency, which clearly presupposed the reading *ghunya* in Arabic.[4] While admitting the plausibility of the reading *ghunya*, Corbin preferred the reading *ghayba* as the original one, noting that in both Nāṣir-i Khusraw's *Jāmi' al-ḥikmatayn* and in the Commentary to the Isma'ili *Qaṣīda* of Abu'l-Haytham al-Jurjānī, attributed to Muḥammad b. Surkh al-Nīsābūrī, the word equally appears as *ghaybat*. He argued, further, that *ghunya* does not add anything significant to the meaning of *kamāl*, perfection, the two words being a mere doublet. The reading *ghunya* would, thus, banalize the sense and deprive it of its profoundness and originality. *Ghayba*, in contrast, was a term loaded with significance in Shi'i theology,[5] as well as in Sufism. In the present context, it meant 'occultation, the hidden state, ecstatic absence from the visible world, presence in the invisible world, and as such the invisible, suprasensible dimension of a being'.[6]

A close reading of the relevant texts, however, reveals clearly that *ghunya*, self-sufficiency, rather than *ghayba*, must have originally been intended in all of them. In *Jāmi' al-ḥikmatayn*, Nāṣir-i Khusraw gives an esoteric interpretation of six of the seven terms mentioned in the *Qaṣīda* of Abu'l-Haytham.[7] Concerning *kamāl*, he explains that the human soul reaches perfection when it completely accepts the emanation (*ifāḍat*) of the Universal Intellect. The six major prophets, Adam, Noah, Abraham, Moses, Jesus and Mohammed, have over a period of nearly 7,000 years established their rule over a part of mankind by conveying the emanation of the Intellect to them. The fact, however, that they have not been able to establish their rule over all of mankind is proof that no one has yet completely accepted the Intellect. Thus the day when, according to the Qur'an (LXXXII:19), 'the Order will belong to God', has not yet come.

The sentence opening the next paragraph in the edition of the *Jāmi' al-ḥikmatayn* reads: *wa-ʿināyat-i nafs-i kullī az iḥtiyāj-i khwīsh bi-dān shakhṣ bāshad ki ifāḍat-i ʿaql-i kullī rā tamām ū padhīrad wa bar khalq bi-jumlagī ū sālār shawad.*[8] This is quite incomprehensible. The expression *az iḥtiyāj-i khwīsh* requires the reading *ghunyat-i* or, graphically more likely, the equivalent *ghanā-yi*, instead of *ʿināyat-i*. 'The self-sufficiency of the Universal Soul [of which the individual souls are parts] from the neediness of its own self will occur through that person who accepts the emanation of the Universal Intellect completely and who will become ruler over all of creation.' Nāṣir-i Khusraw goes on to explain that this person will be the last of these rulers with whom the cycle will be closed. Some people call him the Messiah, who will return, others call him the Mahdi, and still others the Qā'im. God thus says: 'About what do they question each other? About the great announcement concerning which they differ' (Qur'an, LXXVIII:1–3). It is evident, then, that Nāṣir-i Khusraw must also have read *ghunyat*, rather than *ghaybat*, in the poem of Abu'l-Haytham.[9]

The commentator of the *Qaṣīda* of Abu'l-Haytham says about the seven faculties, described as lights in the poem, that they are called 'divine emanation' (*ifāḍat-i ilāhī*). They exist with the Intellect and are concealed from the Soul. Every soul accepts them to the extent of its nobility, disposition, subtleness, and effort. Thus, it may accept one, two, or three, and the souls of prophets accept all seven.[10] The commentator describes the last, and most noble, of these emanations of the Intellect which shine upon the soul thus: 'Everyone upon whom this emanation shines becomes independent[11] of the two worlds. Self-sufficiency (reading *ghunyat* instead of *ghaybat*) consists in independence from the humiliation of posing questions, of the pain of reading, writing, and learning. He reaches a station about which God says: 'In it is what the souls long for and the eyes delight in' (Qur'an, XLIII:71). For every longing that may emerge from the soul, a means to deal with it arises from that emanation, and a response comes to him from his intellect. The soul has no longer a need of anything else.'[12] Translating this passage, Corbin commented that the *ghaybat* thus defined a privileged relationship between the individual soul and the Intellect, of which *ghunya* is merely the result.[13] Much more likely, the self-sufficiency of the soul is itself described here as the highest state it can reach. A state of ecstatic absence, as Corbin interpreted the term *ghaybat*, is not described or implied in any of the texts.

Abū Yaʿqūb's description of the seventh faculty of the Intellect can on this basis be translated thus: 'The seventh is Self-sufficiency. For self-sufficiency is in the partial acquisitive intellect, when it comprehends any intelligibles, an existent entity (*ʿayn mawjūd*). Thus it becomes known that Self-sufficiency extends with the Preceder at the origination and thereafter. Among the faculties of the Intellect which were originated together with it, Self-sufficiency is certainly the most excellent and noble one. When the Preceder emanates self-sufficiency of its faculties upon anyone, this emanation is the most excellent and highest emanation.'[14]

Abū Yaʿqūb goes on to explain that the lowest emanation of the Intellect is Eternal Time, even though in relation to physical matters it is of the utmost nobility because of its permanence and because God has made it the custodian of the movements of time. Each of the seven faculties branches out into countless and unlimited branches. Above them there are things which cannot be described by reason or imagined, since the Preceder alone possesses them. We do not know when he will emanate them on his effects (the human souls), so that the effects will be able to imagine, express, and establish them. They will manifest themselves in the aeons (*akwār*) and cycles (*adwār*), of which only he has knowledge. At present, they are all retained by him and are gathered in a point which is the centre of the universe (*al-ʿālamīn*).[15]

Abū Yaʿqūb's concept of the faculties of the Intellect is thus less mystical than Corbin had thought. It is, rather, grounded in the philosophical tradition. Some of the faculties were mentioned as attributes of the Intellect in earlier Neoplatonic texts.[16] Their confinement to seven basic qualities is probably Abū Yaʿqūb's own Ismaʿili contribution. There is so far no evidence suggesting that his teacher, the Transoxanian *dāʿī* Muḥammad b. Aḥmad al-Nasafī (d. 332/943), had envisaged this heptad.

The prevalence of the misreading *ghayba(t)* in all the relevant texts illustrates the deplorable current state of the Ismaʿili manuscript tradition. While the correct reading was still fully available in the 5th/11th century, it was evidently later forgotten in the course of centuries of persecution and decline of learning among the Ismaʿilis. *Ghunyat* is, as Corbin pointed out,[17] hardly used in Persian and was, therefore, easily replaced by *ghaybat*. But in the Arabic text of Abū Yaʿqūb's *al-Yanābīʿ*, too, the faulty variant now established itself. Without Nāṣir-i Khusraw's Persian rendering of it as *bī-niyāzī*, it would have been difficult to recover Abū Yaʿqūb al-Sijistānī's original concept of the seventh faculty of the Intellect.[18] The poor condition of the modern Ismaʿili manuscript tradition must be taken into account in editing and studying these and other Ismaʿili texts.

NOTES

1 Abū Ya'qūb al-Sijistānī, *Kitāb al-yanābī'*, ed. and tr. H. Corbin in his *Trilogie Ismaélienne* (Tehran–Paris, 1961), Arabic text pp. 41–43.

2 The variant reading *dhihn* in the editions of Nāṣir-i Khusraw's *Khwān al-ikhwān*, containing the Persian paraphrase of Abū Ya'qūb's chapter, has been rightly rejected by Corbin (*Trilogie*, translation p. 60) as an atrocious misreading of a copyist.

3 Reading *wa-buṭlānuhu 'anhu tawahhumun bāṭilun li-anna khilāfahu mubṭilun lahu.*

4 Corbin, *Trilogie*, translation pp. 62–63.

5 See *Commentaire de la Qasida Ismaélienne d'Abu'l-Haitham Jorjani attribué à Mohammad ibn Sorkh de Nishapour*, ed. H. Corbin and M. Mu'īn (Tehran–Paris, 1955), French introduction p. 52.

6 Corbin, *Trilogie*, translation p. 62.

7 Nāṣir-i Khusraw, *Jāmi' al-ḥikmatayn*, ed. H. Corbin and M. Mu'īn (Tehran–Paris, 1953), Persian text pp. 112–122. Nāṣir-i Khusraw omits the term *burhān* taking it as part of the context. He is able to do so by separating the previous line of the poem, which speaks of seven shining lights from which every being accepts fire to the extent of its subtleness.

8 Nāṣir-i Khusraw, *Jāmi'*, Persian text p. 121 l.18 – p. 122 l.1.

9 Ibid., Persian text p. 112 l.9. Read also *ghunyat* in place of *ghaybat* in lines 6 and 14.

10 *Commentaire*, Persian text p. 19.

11 *Chāra*, glossed by Corbin in his translation (*Trilogie*, p. 63) as *bī-niyāz*. Note that the term occurs in this sense in the last line of the section of the *Qaṣīda* dealing with the seven lights (*Commentaire*, Persian text p. 19 l.13): Independence comes only to a place where there are four (*chār*); evidently the last four lights, Demonstration, permanent Life, Perfection, and Self-sufficiency. In the version of Nāṣir-i Khusraw's *Jāmi' al-ḥikmatayn*, p. 112 l.10, the text of the line differs and is probably corrupt: Independence is in the place where four do not come. This reading is consistent with Nāṣir-i Khusraw's omission of Demonstration from his list of mystical terms.

12 *Commentaire*, Persian text pp. 21–22.

13 Corbin, *Trilogie*, translation p. 63.

14 Abū Ya'qūb al-Sijistānī, *al-Yanābī'*, in *Trilogie*, Arabic text pp. 42–43.

15 Ibid., Arabic text p. 43.

16 See P. Walker, *Early Philosophical Shiism: The Ismaili Neoplatonism of Abū Ya'qūb al-Sijistānī* (Cambridge, 1993), pp. 91 and 179 n. 20.

17 Corbin, *Trilogie*, translation p. 62.

18 Another passage in Corbin's edition of the Arabic text of *al-Yanābī'* which Nāṣir-i Khusraw's Persian paraphrase helps to correct relates to the reading *shaṭriyya* on p. 71 l.17, and p. 72 l.1 and l.10. In his translation Corbin used Nāṣir's Persian text which has *dandāna*, meaning here the tooth, or bit, of a key (*Trilogie*, pp. 93 and 95 n. 185). The word in Arabic must, therefore, be read *shaẓiyya*; it is correctly preserved on p. 73 l.1 of the Arabic text.

FIVE

The Isma'ili oath of allegiance (*'ahd*) and the 'sessions of wisdom' (*majālis al-ḥikma*) in Fatimid times

HEINZ HALM

LIKE ITS contents, the external forms of the Isma'ili *da'wa* were long wrapped in mystery and embroidered with all sorts of speculations by non-initiates. The opponents of the Isma'ilis did not shrink from malevolent defamations and falsifications. An ostensible book of instructions for the initiation of adepts entitled 'The Book of the Highest Initiation' (*Kitāb al-balāgh al-akbar*) was circulated by anti-Isma'ili pamphleteers and already widely distributed in the 4th/10th century; it described how the neophyte could be led through nine stages to the highest degree of initiation, that of absolute unbelief and atheism. It was only quite recently that this text was unmasked as a propagandist travesty.[1]

From the authentic literature of the Isma'ilis we know that initiates were pledged to observe the secrecy of the 'inner meaning' (*bāṭin*), and that they were sworn to such secrecy prior to their initiation by taking an oath, called a *mīthāq* or *'ahd*; apart from these two nouns, our sources also often contain the verbal phrase *akhadha 'alayhi* 'he pledged him', and the initiate is accordingly called *al-ma'khudhu 'alayhi*.

I

In stories about conversions by the earliest *dā'īs*, the act of the pledge or promise is briefly mentioned as a matter of course, without being described in detail. Thus the *dā'ī* al-Ḥusayn al-Ahwāzī made the carter Ḥamdān Qarmaṭ pledge with the following words, after having made him perform his ablutions in a canal: 'I administer to you the same oath and promise that God administered to his prophets and envoys' (*ākhudhu 'alayka 'ahdan wa-mīthāqan akhadhahu'llāhu 'alā'l-nabiyyīna wa'l-mursalīn*).[2] The *dā'ī* Ibn Ḥawshab Manṣūr al-Yaman describes in his autobiography how his mentor administered the oath to him (*akhadha ʿalayyaʾl-ʿahda*);[3] later he himself administered it to the Kutāma Berbers he had converted, and non-initiates speculated about the secret (*amr maktūm*) that was kept from them: 'Had it been a good thing, they would not have concealed it; it must certainly be directed against the religion of Islam!'[4]

One of the earliest Ismaʿili texts to provide us with information about forms of initiation is the 'Book of the Teacher and the Pupil' (*Kitāb al-ʿālim waʾl-ghulām*), which Ismaʿili tradition ascribes to Ibn Ḥawshab Manṣūr al-Yaman or to his son Jaʿfar. This initiation romance describes in an idealized way how a young man is taken into the confidence of an itinerant *dāʿī*, who eventually initiates him. The climax of the text is a description of the preparations leading to the revelation of the secrets. Here, too, the *ʿahd* forms the beginning of the instruction. The master says to the young man:[5] 'For religion there is a key which grants or forbids access to it, like the difference between whoring and marriage.'

The pupil: 'The key of which you speak must be a great thing with God, if it actually distinguishes between what is allowed and what is forbidden, between truth and falsehood! What is it?'

The master: 'It is God's *ʿahd*, which confirms his truths and contains our duties towards him. It is Paradise for his followers (*awliyāʾ*), God's rope on earth and a guarantee of safety (*amān*) among his servants. I will say it to you and pledge you to it!'

The pupil: 'Yes, pledge me to what you will; I shall not reject your opinion nor act against your custom!'[6]

The text continues: 'Then the master began to read the *ʿahd* to the pupil, reciting it in a chant (*fa-aqbalaʾl-ʿālimu yatluʾl-ʿahda ʿalāʾl-ghulāmi wa-yurattiluhū lahu*) and pledging him to it (*yaʿqiduhū ʿalayhi*). But the pupil was quite beside himself with fear, and in view of the forceful warning (*shiddat al-ʿibra*), tears poured out of his eyes, until [the master] came to the end of the *ʿahd* with him; then he praised and glorified God and thanked him for what he had allotted to him, and became aware that he now belonged to the party of God (*ḥizb Allāh*) and to the party of the saints (*awliyāʾ*), because he had accepted their *ʿahd* (*bi-qubūli ʿahdihim*); then he ended his praise. The teacher, however, began to explain and clarify, and his explanations and clarifications regarding the foundations of external things (*al-ẓāhira*) and their initial creation started with God's having created all things and called them into existence from nothing.'

Although the story of the teacher and pupil is fictitious, we may assume that the details of the process described correspond to the usual practice of Ismaʿili missionaries. The wording of the *ʿahd* is not known to us, but it appears from the context that it must have been a fairly long text, which was recited to the initiate in a chant, and perhaps repeated by him sentence by sentence and finally sworn to. It is only then that the instruction begins, and it does so *ab ovo*: with the creation of the world.

II

The second authentic Isma'ili source containing a detailed description of the *'ahd* is the *Risāla al-mūjaza al-kāfiya fī ādāb al-du'āt* of Aḥmad al-Nīsābūrī, who was active under the reign of the Fatimids al-'Azīz and al-Ḥākim.[7] The text of this *Risāla*, an instruction for missionaries, is preserved in the second volume of al-Bharūchī's *Kitāb al-azhār* and it has been edited in facsimile by Verena Klemm.[8] Here, the *dā'ī* is told that he must first of all break the adept's former faith, 'so that he will be left without an argument'.[9] The text then continues:

'Once he has broken it and wants to administer the *'ahd* to him, the custom (*sunna*) is to administer it to him after [the initiate] has fasted for three days. Both the *dā'ī* and the adept have to be ritually pure: both have to pray two *rak'as* to complete their purification. Then [the *dā'ī*] starts by praising and glorifying God, his envoy and the pure imams, and administers to him the *'ahd* of God, of his angels, his envoys, the authorized representatives (*awṣiyā'*) and imams – peace be with them – as well as the *'ahd* and homage (*bay'a*) to the imam of the time (*imām zamānihī*), as prescribed to him in the form of the *'ahd* (*kitāb al-'ahd*). [The *dā'ī* pledges him] to believe in God, in his angels, in his pure imams – from the *waṣī* down to the present imam – to adhere to the exoteric (*ẓāhir*) as well as the esoteric (*bāṭin*), to stand up for the imam and not betray him, not to divulge the secrets of the religion to an unauthorized person or one who has not taken the *'ahd*; not to betray any of the brothers who have taken the *'ahd* with him; to be a friend to the friends of the imams and an enemy to their enemies; to disassociate himself from their enemies; to be true to God and his friends; and should he break his vow, may his lot be that of the faithless and treacherous. [The *dā'ī*] then summons [the adept] to the imam of his time;[10] to him [alone] he attributes knowledge (*'ilm*) without ascribing a single letter of it to himself. Once the initiate has taken the *'ahd* and paid his homage, he will be nourished (*rubbiya*) with knowledge, and the principles (*uṣūl*) will be confided to him one by one, but at the beginning of his knowledge, he ought not to be burdened with too much, lest he should mix up everything, just as a child is ruined if he is given too much food at the beginning of his existence. So [the *dāʿī*] feeds him with light knowledge that he can absorb, and first teaches him the unity [of God, *tawḥīd*], faith and obedience to God, to his envoy and his imam,[11] as God has said: Obey God and the envoy and those among you who are meant to command.'[12]

Al-Nīsābūrī's instructions confirm what we have gathered from the *Kitāb al-ʿālim waʾl-ghulām*. Here, there is an explicit reference to a written form of the *ʿahd* (*kitāb al-ʿahd*). Al-Nīsābūrī does not quote this text *verbatim* or *in extenso*, but paraphrases it, so that we learn what the initiate is pledged to do. It appears that at the end, the name and identity of the 'present imam' – i.e., the currently ruling Fatimid caliph – is revealed to him, so that he may pay homage (*bayʿa*) to him. The pledge to secrecy is explicitly mentioned. Only then does the instruction begin with the explanation of the *tawḥīd* and the belief in God, the Creator.

III

No authentic form of the oath has been handed down to us in any of the original Ismaʿili books. The forms we know come from non-Ismaʿili sources and should, therefore, be treated with a certain amount of caution.

The earliest text of this type stems from the lost anti-Fatimid treatise of the Damascene Sharīf Akhū Muḥsin Muḥammad b. ʿAlī, which was written after the year 372/983.[13] In this treatise Akhū Muḥsin, who was himself a direct descendant of Muḥammad b. Ismāʿīl b. Jaʿfar al-Ṣādiq, contests the Fatimid caliph's claim to descent from that lineage. His book was used as a source by several later Sunni Egyptian authors, so that numerous comparatively long passages of it have been preserved, the longest being those in al-Nuwayrī's *Nihāyat al-arab* and Ibn al-Dawādārī's *Kanz al-durar*, as well as in al-Maqrīzī's *al-Khiṭaṭ* and in his Fatimid history *Ittiʿāẓ al-ḥunafāʾ*.

Al-Nuwayrī[14] and al-Maqrīzī[15] fully quote the form of the *ʿahd*, which reads as follows:

'The *dāʿī* shall say to the person to whom he administers the *ʿahd*: You impose on yourself God's oath (*ʿahd*), compact (*mīthāq*) and obligation (*dhimma*), as well as the obligation of God's envoy, of his prophets, angels, books[16] and envoys, the same pledge, contract and obligation which he entered into with his [earlier] prophets: that you will keep secret (*annaka tasturu*) what you will hear and what you have already heard, what you know and what you will learn, what knowledge you have and what knowledge you will yet acquire concerning myself and the one [*dā'ī* or *ḥujja*] who dwells in this city as representative of the Lord of Truth, the imam for whom – as you know – I declare myself, and to whose committed adherents I openly and honestly belong; [that you shall further keep secret] the concerns of his brothers (*ikhwān*), his adherents and descendants, his family, so far as they follow him in this religion and are sincerely devoted to him, men and women, young and old. Thus you must[17] reveal nothing of it, neither little or much, nor in allusions, except those things about which I myself or the person responsible (*ṣāḥib al-amr*) dwelling in this city explicitly allow you to speak, so that in this matter you must only act according to our command, which you must not contravene and to which you must add nothing.

'Before and after the oath, you must observe the following in word and deed: you must attest that there is no divinity but God alone, and that he has no equal; you must attest that Muḥammad is his servant and his envoy, that Paradise and Hell really exist, that death and resurrection truly are, that the hour [of the Last Judgement] will unquestionably come and that God will awaken the dead from their graves; you must perform the *ṣalāt* at the prescribed time and take the *zakāt* to him who has a rightful claim on it,[18] fast in the month of Ramaḍān, carry out the *ḥajj* to the holy shrine and conduct the *jihād* in the way of God according to regulations, as God has commanded to his envoy. You must be friendly to the friends of God and hostile to his enemies and observe God's duties and customs (*sunan*)[19] as well as the customs of his prophet, in the exoteric and in the esoteric sense (*ẓāhiran wa-bāṭinan*), both openly and in secret. All this is confirmed by this oath, rather than being invalidated by it; it is corroborated rather than cancelled by it, brought closer rather than removed, strengthened rather than weakened, imposed as a duty rather than repealed, clarified rather than obscured. This is equally true of the exoteric and the esoteric, and of all that the prophets have revealed of their lord,[20] according to the manifest conditions contained in this oath. – If you pledge to observe all this, then say: 'yes'. Thereupon, the summoned one (*al-mad'ūw*)[21] says: 'Yes'.

'Then the *dā'ī* says to him: The security and warrant for it are that you will not reveal any of the things which you have pledged by this oath, neither in our lifetime nor after our death, neither in anger nor in a contented mood, neither from desire nor from fear, neither in distress nor when at ease, neither out of greed nor out of need – may God assume the protection and guarantee for it! – according to the manifest conditions contained in this oath! You impose on yourself God's oath, contract and obligation and the obligation of his envoy to defend me and all those whom I shall name to you and commend to you together with myself, against all things against which you will defend yourself, and to be honest to us and to your friend – the friend of God (*walī Allāh*) in the exoteric and in the esoteric sense. So never betray either God or his friend, either us or one of our brothers and friends or anyone of whom you know that he belongs to us, whether for family reasons or for money, or else because of an opinion, an oath or an agreement which you might interpret as invalidating[22] [this oath].

'If you do anything of the kind, although you know that in so doing you violate [the oath], which you remember exactly, then you renounce God, the Creator of heaven and earth, who has superbly created you and has put you together and shown you blessings in your religion, in this world and in the next. You renounce his earlier and later envoys, his angels who are close to him, the Cherubs (*al-karūbiyyīn*) and the Spiritual Beings (*al-rūḥāniyyīn*), the perfect words, the seven tales and the mighty Qur'an (*sūra* XV:87). You renounce the Torah, the Gospel, the Psalter and the Wise Admonition [Qur'an, III:58 and elsewhere], every religion sanctioned by God in the approaches of the world to come, and every servant who is pleasing to God. You leave the party of God and his saints, to God's unconcealed disappointment, but he will soon bring retribution and punishment on you, and you will walk into the fire of Jahannam [Hell], in which there is no mercy. You renounce the power and strength of God and rely on your own power and strength – so may there be on you the same curse of God with which he cursed the Iblīs, which barred Paradise to him and assigned the fire to him forever!

'If you violate any part of all this, you will some day appear before an angry God. God will demand of you [as atonement] that you carry out the *ḥajj* to his holy shrine thirty times as a necessary vow, and that you do so barefoot; God will accept from you only the fulfilment of this [atonement]. And if you violate it, then everything you have acquired during the time of your violation shall be given as *ṣadaqa* to poor and miserable people who are not related to you by blood. This will bring you no reward from God, and no advantage will arise to you from it. If you violate any part of it, all your slaves (*mamlūk*), male or female, who are in your possession and whom you will take into your service[23] until the hour of your death will be free before God's countenance; all your wives, including those whom you will marry until the hour of your death, will be divorced definitively by a triple divorce – a divorce [as expiation] for a sin (*ṭalāq al-ḥaraj*);[24] you shall have no reward[25] for this, no right of cancellation,[26] no revision and no free decision. Everything you own as regards family, property and the like, is denied (*ḥarām*) to you; however, the *ẓihār* is obligatory for you.[27]

'I am the one who has you swear to your imam and your *ḥujja*,[28] and you are the one who swears to them. If you now intend or plan or contemplate anything that runs counter to what I have enjoined on you and what I have had you swear, then this oath lies bindingly established for you[29] from the first to the last word; God will accept nothing but its complete fulfilment and the compliance with what you have covenanted with me. Say: Yes! – And he says: Yes!'

This pledge to follow the commands of the *sharī'a* is – so our source maintains – nothing but a trick to gain the confidence of the deceived person (*ta'nīs al-makhdū'*). To prove this allegation, a fairly long passage of the *Kitāb al-siyāsa* (or *Kitāb al-balāgh al-akbar*) is added, according to which the novice is then supposedly led to atheism by way of nine stages of initiation. However, while the *Kitāb al-siyāsa* is an anti-Isma'ili travesty, as S. M. Stern has shown, the text of the *'ahd* seems to be genuine; at any rate, it does not contain a single detail that might raise doubts about its authenticity.

The text is quoted from the Sharīf Akhū Muḥsin. Al-Nuwayrī introduces the quotation with the words: *qāla'l-sharīf*. However, Akhū Muḥsin himself had used an earlier source, namely the lost anti-Isma'ili pamphlet of Abū 'Abd Allāh Muḥammad b. 'Alī b. Rizām al-Ṭā'ī al-Kūfī, which was based on information stemming from anti-Fatimid circles of Qarmaṭīs from Iraq,[30] and which was also used by other authors such as al-Mas'ūdī, Ibn al-Nadīm, Ibn Ḥawqal, al-Qāḍī 'Abd al-Jabbār, al-Baghdādī, Niẓām al-Mulk and al-Dhahabī. Akhū Muḥsin may have taken the form of the *'ahd* from Ibn Rizām al-Kūfī, in which case it would have been the form originally used in Iraq. But it is also possible that Akhū Muḥsin had copied a form used by the Fatimids at the time – i.e., under the caliphs al-'Azīz and al-Ḥākim – during their mission in Syria.

IV

Another form of the *'ahd* is quoted by Ibn Faḍl Allāh al-'Umarī (d. 749/1349).[31] Al-Qalqashandī in his turn quotes it from al-'Umarī. Bernard Lewis has translated the text.[32] This text takes into account not only the Nizārī schism of 487/1094, but also the overthrow of the Fatimid caliphate by Saladin in 567/1171. As 'Alā' al-Dīn Muḥammad III is referred to as the Grand Master of Alamūt, the form must date from his reign, between 618/1221 and 653/1255.

The form is probably incomplete; the impression it produces is that it is merely an appendix or an addition to a form (not quoted by al-ʿUmarī) whose purpose it is to differentiate between the two confessions that had meanwhile emerged. The Nizārī addition is probably the original one, while the anti-Nizārī addition is simply a reaction to it. The reference to the 'Old Man of the Mountain' Rāshid al-Dīn Sinān points to Syria as the form's country of origin, and the anti-Nizārī Ismaʿilis referred to may also have lived in Syria; there can be no other explanation for the similarity of the two forms.

We may, therefore, assume that the passages quoted by al-ʿUmarī and al-Qalqashandī were preceded by a longer text, perhaps of the kind quoted by al-Nuwayrī and al-Maqrīzī, or perhaps even identical with it. At any rate, the text handed down by al-Nuwayrī and al-Maqrīzī, which goes back to Akhū Muḥsin's treatise, appears to be the only complete authentic form of the *ʿahd* that has come down to us from the Fatimid period.

V

Wladimir Ivanow discovered that the *ʿahd* quoted by al-Nuwayrī after Akhū Muḥsin (which he in fact only knew from Silvestre de Sacy's translation)[33] corresponds almost word for word to the one the Indian Mustaʿlian Ismaʿilis (Bohras) swear even today to their hidden imam year after year.[34] He also pointed out similar passages in the *Daʿāʾim al-Islām* of al-Qāḍī al-Nuʿmān. This oath, which the Bohras call *ʿahd Allāh, ʿahd al-awliyāʾ* or simply *ʿahd-nāma*, has been translated into English by Mian Bhai Mulla Abdul Husain.[35]

The close correspondence between the *ʿahd* of the Fatimid period and the one used today by the Bohras serves as further evidence for the assumption that the form of the oath has remained essentially the same throughout the centuries, and that there existed only *one* form, which the *dāʿīs* used all over the world. The Bohras as the heirs of the Fatimid tradition and literature have preserved this form. However, the additions quoted by al-ʿUmarī and al-Qalqashandī must merely reflect a post-Fatimid, regional (Syrian) variant.

VI

The taking of the oath (*ʿahd*) is the prerequisite for the neophyte's initiation into the secrets of the Ismaʿili doctrine, which are called 'wisdom' (*ḥikma*). Instruction is provided in sessions (*majālis*) which the initiate attends either individually (as in the *Kitāb al-ʿālim waʾl-ghulām*) or together with others. The ultimate source of the *ḥikma* is looked upon as the divine revelation communicated to the faithful (*mu'minūn*), i.e., the Isma'ilis, through the imams. The *dā'ī* who holds the sessions is thus merely the mouthpiece through which the imam speaks to the faithful. This representation of the imam by the *dā'ī* poses a few practical problems, which we shall discuss later.

We owe the earliest information about the *majālis al-ḥikma* to the *Kitāb iftitāḥ al-da'wa* of al-Qāḍī al-Nu'mān, whose source was a biography (*sīra*) of the *dā'ī* Abū 'Abd Allāh al-Shī'ī – probably even his autobiography. It contains several passages describing how this *dā'ī* used to hold the *Majālis* among the Kutāma Berbers. At first, 'he would hold sessions for them (*kāna yajlisu lahum*) and tell them the external (*ẓāhir*) virtues of 'Alī b. Abī Ṭālib and the imams among his descendants. When he saw how one after the other learned from him and felt that he had [the novice] where he wanted him, he would give away one little piece after another, as long as he acquiesced, and would finally administer the oath to him (*fa-ya'khudhu 'alayhi*).'[36] Exclusive sessions were then organized for the initiates: the clan of the Banū Saktān, who offered the missionary their hospitality, were the first to enjoy this privilege: 'He summoned (*da'ā*) some of the Banū Saktān; thereupon they reserved him a session to hear him (*fa-akhlaw lahu majlisan li'l-samā'*).'[37] The *dā'ī* himself assumed this task: 'again and again he addressed admonishments (*mawā'iẓ*) to them and taught them wisdom (*ḥikma*); to this end he assembled them and sat for them (*yajlisu lahum*) most of the day';[38] 'every day he would sit for the faithful, talk to them and explain, and he ordered the *dā'īs* to do the same'.[39] The women, too, 'used to participate in the sessions and hear the wisdom'.[40]

VII

After the fall of the Aghlabid emirate and the entry of the *dā'ī* Abū 'Abd Allāh into the royal city of Raqqāda on 25 March 909/1 Rajab 296, the Isma'ili *da'wa* was begun in Qayrawān as well: 'Abū 'Abd Allāh let the chiefs of the Kutāma carry on their mission among the people to promote their doctrines, i.e., for the preference of 'Alī and the renunciation of all the others [Companions of the Prophet]. Many people joined them in this.'[41] On 4 January 910, the caliph-imam al-Mahdī himself made his entry into Raqqāda, and on the following day, a Friday, the *khuṭba* was for the first time read in his name in the Great Mosque of Qayrawān. Only a year later, on 18 February 911, al-Mahdī had the *dāʿī* Abū ʿAbd Allāh and his brother Abu'l-ʿAbbās killed in Raqqāda. It may be assumed that until that time, the *daʿwa* had continued to be under the leadership of Abū ʿAbd Allāh.

The successor of Abū ʿAbd Allāh al-Shīʿī as supreme leader of the Ismaʿili mission was one of his pupils, the distinguished Kutāma Berber Aflaḥ b. Hārūn of the Malūsa tribe. He had rapidly been won over for the *daʿwa* by Abū ʿAbd Allāh, and had subsequently acted as a *dāʿī* in his own tribe; hence his sobriquet 'the *dāʿī* of Malūsa'. After the establishment of the Fatimid caliphate he became *qāḍī* of Tripoli in Libya, and later *qāḍī* of Raqqāda and Mahdiyya, i.e., the highest judge of the empire.[42] Throughout the North African period of the Fatimid caliphate, the chief *qāḍī* was simultaneously the leader of the *daʿwa*, i.e., the supreme *dāʿī*, even if this title does not appear to have been used at the time: *ẓāhir* and *bāṭin* were thus still united in the same hand; not until much later, in Egypt, were the two functions separated, and even then only for short periods.

About Aflaḥ's activities we have a very interesting account. It stems from the *Sīrat al-Imām al-Mahdī*, which is only preserved in fragments, and which must have been written by the *dāʿī* Abū ʿAbd Allāh b. al-Aswad b. al-Haytham.[43] The author knew Aflaḥ personally, of course, since he was his highest superior; on the occasion of Aflaḥ's death (before 311/923), which he records in his chronicle, Ibn al-Haytham reminisces about his methods of teaching in the *majālis al-ḥikma*:[44]

'I listened to him while he was performing his missionary function among women and using allusions for them in his sermon that their intelligence could grasp and that impressed themselves upon them, for he used to say: God disposes of the appropriate argument [Qur'an, VI:149]; it is the one with which he addresses the knowing person according to his knowledge and the unknowing person only within the limits of his understanding! He had the habit, when talking to women, of choosing as examples finery or the finger-ring, the earring and diadem, necklace, anklet or bracelet, dress or scarf, spinning and weaving, hairstyle, wardrobe and other things with which women adorn themselves; to the artisan he spoke about his respective trade; to the tailor, for instance, about needle and thread, eyelet and scissors, to the shepherd about his staff and wrap, and the flock and the shepherd's pouch.'

We have no other testimony of the early Fatimid period that might better illustrate the ways in which the *dāʿī*s practised popular instruction. When Aflaḥ b. Hārūn al-Malūsī died before 311/923, his successor was probably Abū ʿAbd Allāh b. al-Aswad b. al-Haytham, to whom we owe the obituary we have just quoted. We have no further information about his activities as supreme *dāʿī*.

In the year 336/948, when the caliph al-Manṣūr returned to his new residence, Manṣūriyya, near Qayrawān, as victor over the Khārijī rebel Abū Yazīd, he appointed al-Nuʿmān b. Muḥammad, who was until then the judge of Tripoli, as supreme *qāḍī* and supreme *dāʿī*. Al-Qāḍī al-Nuʿmān's writings contain several accounts about his teachings, both of the *ẓāhir* and of the *bāṭin*.

The teaching sessions of the *ẓāhir*, i.e. the Ismaʿili jurisprudence (*fiqh*), were public and accessible to everybody. Al-Qāḍī al-Nuʿmān held them every Friday following the Friday prayer, that is between the midday prayer (*ẓuhr*) and the afternoon prayer (*ʿaṣr*), at first – to the displeasure of the Mālikī *fuqahāʾ*[45] – in the Great Mosque of Qayrawān, and later in the mosque of Manṣūriyya, which bore the name al-Azhar.[46]

The *majālis al-ḥikma*, however, were only accessible to the initiates. To control them better, they were held inside the palace of the caliph-imam in Manṣūriyya, where a special room (*majlis*) was reserved for the purpose. The indefatigable al-Nuʿmān held these sessions himself as well, evidently also on Fridays, and that after the *ʿaṣr*, following the public *ẓāhir* lessons in the mosque.[47] All his lectures were first personally authorized by the imams al-Manṣūr and al-Muʿizz.[48] About this activity, too, al-Nuʿmān himself reports:

'When al-Muʿizz li-Dīn Allāh opened the door of compassion to the faithful and turned to them his face full of grace and benevolence, he sent me books with secret knowledge (*ʿilm al-bāṭin*) and ordered me to read them every Friday in a room (*majlis*) of his palace, as long as he lived. There was a great throng; the room was overcrowded; more people came than could participate. They filled the room he had destined for the assembly, and even a part of the palace's courtyard, so that my voice no longer reached the ones at the very back. This was reported to the imam and he was informed that among the followers of the *daʿwa*, there were also people who were new and hardly capable of understanding the explanations; these would benefit more if they were separated and assigned a room of their own in which they would be given lectures that they could grasp and understand.' The imam intimated to the *qāḍī* – who must have been himself the author of the proposal – that he should continue acting as before; each person would comprehend the wisdom according to his own mental capacity, 'just as a pot you put in the rain will catch as much water as will fall into its opening'.[49]

VIII

After the Fatimid conquest of Egypt and the founding of Cairo in 358/969, there can hardly have been any major changes in the practices of the *daʿwa*. On 7 Ramaḍān 362/10 June 973, al-Qāḍī al-Nuʿmān entered Cairo side by side with the caliph al-Muʿizz. As he was already in his eighties, he did not assume the office of *qāḍī* of Egypt; it was Abū Ṭāhir al-Dhuhlī, to whom this function had already been entrusted by Jawhar, who was confirmed in it. Al-Nuʿmān was assigned 'the judicial office in the army camp of al-Muʿizz' (*qaḍāʾ fī ʿaskar al-Muʿizz*),[50] that is, he only had jurisdiction over the Ismaʿili courtiers, officials and soldiers. We may safely assume that at the same time he also maintained the supreme leadership of the *daʿwa*.

When al-Nuʿmān died at the end of Jumādā II 363/27 March 974, he was succeeded by his son ʿAlī, who first shared his function with the Qāḍī Abū Ṭāhir; it was not until Ṣafar 366/September 976, when the latter was partially paralyzed by a stroke, that ʿAlī b. al-Nuʿmān took over the office of *qāḍī*.[51] After his premature death – he died in 374/984 at the age of 44 – his brother Muḥammad (born 345/956) succeeded him as *qāḍī*.[52]

Both of al-Nuʿmān's sons had evidently also inherited the leadership of the *daʿwa* from their father, for they held the *majālis al-ḥikma* by turns in the Fatimid palace in Cairo. Our source is al-Musabbiḥī, the court chronicler of the caliphs al-Ḥākim and al-Ẓāhir, from whose lost chronicle *Akhbār Miṣr* numerous later authors, including Ibn Ḥajar al-ʿAsqalānī and al-Maqrīzī, have quoted.

'In Rabīʿ I of the year 385/April–May 995, the Qāḍī Muḥammad b. al-Nuʿmān was sitting on a seat in the palace, about to read out the sciences of the house of the Prophet (*ʿulūm āl al-bayt*), as he and his brother had already been doing in Egypt and his father in the Maghrib. In the crush eleven people were killed; al-ʿAzīz biʾllāh had them wrapped in shrouds [at his own expense].'[53]

It is equally to the chronicler al-Musabbiḥī that we owe some detailed information about the way the *majālis* were conducted in his days:[54]

'The *dāʿī* used to hold continuous sessions in the palace to read what was read to the saintly [*al-awliyāʾ* = the initiates] and [collect] the duties connected with it.[55] [The *dāʿī*] would hold a separate session for the *awliyāʾ*; another for the courtiers (*al-khāṣṣa*) and high officials as well as all those attached to the palaces as lackeys or in other capacities; a further session for the simple people and strangers in the city; a separate session for women in the mosque of Qāhira called al-Azhar; and a session for the wives (*ḥurum*, *scil.* of the caliph) and the noble women of the palaces. He wrote the *majālis* at home and then sent them to the person in charge of serving the state. For these *majālis* he used books, of which fair copies were made (*yubayyiḍūnahā*) after they were submitted to the caliph. At each of these sessions he collected the *najwā* which was taken in gold and silver from all – men and women – who paid a part of it, and he noted the names of those who had paid; he equally noted, on the feast of breaking the fast (*fiṭr*), how much *fiṭra* had been paid. This amounted to a handsome sum which he each time delivered to the state purse (*bayt al-māl*). The sessions of the mission were called Sessions of Wisdom.'

This important text contains much interesting information. To begin with, we learn that there were now in Cairo – unlike earlier in Ifrīqiya – separate sessions for different groups of people. Some of these *majālis* must have been of a merely propagandist and introductory character. It is hard to imagine any esoteric subjects being discussed in the sessions for the common people (*'awāmm al-nās*) and for strangers who happened to be in town (*al-ṭāriʾūn 'alāʾl-balad*); these sessions could not have had the *'ahd* as a prerequisite. Women and men were separately instructed, the noble women in the palace, the others in the al-Azhar Mosque, which is here only once mentioned as a place for holding the *majālis*; these normally took place in the palace, as is several times confirmed in the sources. The al-Azhar Mosque was *not* used to spread the secret Isma'ili doctrine.

Interesting are al-Musabbiḥī's explanations about the writing of the *majālis*, which are here already conceived as texts. The *dā'ī* made a rough draft at home, which was handed to a high official (*man yakhtaṣṣu bi-khidmat al-dawla*) – hence probably the vizier (*wāsiṭa*). The caliph-imam had to endorse the text; after his glosses and corrections, a fair copy (*mubayyaḍa*) was made, which was then read at the session. This is probably how the *majālis* collections of various authors were produced, as we shall discuss below.

The sessions, however, were not merely devoted to the readings, they also served for collecting the duties that had to be paid by the initiates. This is what was meant by the phrase *al-da'āwā al-muttaṣila* at the beginning of the text. Such duties had been customary from the time of the earliest Isma'ili *da'wa*; already in the first community in Iraq, 'Abdān, the brother-in-law of Ḥamdān Qarmaṭ, had introduced these duties, which bore the names *fiṭra* (1 dirham), *hijra* (1 dinar), *bulgha*, *khums* and *ulfa*.[56] In Ifrīqiya, the *dā'ī* Abū 'Abd Allāh al-Shī'ī had also levied the *dirham al-fiṭra* and the *dīnār al-hijra*.[57] Al-Musabbiḥī mentions *fiṭra* and *najwā*. The name of the latter, which apparently replaced the old *hijra* tax, evidently refers to the Qur'an (LVIII:12): 'Ye faithful! If you have something confidential to discuss (*nājaytum*) with the envoy, then prior to your confidential discussion (*najwākum*) pay some alms (*ṣadaqa*) in anticipation.' So the *najwā* is a charge that the faithful have to pay for being introduced into the secret doctrine. Following the passage quoted above, al-Musabbiḥī reports that in the year 400/1009–1010, the caliph al-Ḥākim abolished all special Isma'ili duties – *khums*, *zakāt*, *fiṭra* and *najwā* – by means of a *sijill*. We shall return to this subject below.

Al-Musabbiḥī's text may be compared with an undated document (*sijill*) about the appointment of a *dāʿī*, which al-Qalqashandī quotes as a model.[58] In it, the nominee is assigned the following task: 'Read the *majālis al-ḥikam*, which were handed to you at the court [*fi'l-ḥaḍra*, *scil.* of the imam], to the faithful, male and female, and to the novices, male and female, in the brilliant palaces of the caliphs and in the Friday mosque in al-Muʿizziyya al-Qāhira! But keep the secrets of the *ḥikam* from the unauthorized, and distribute them only to those who are entitled to them! Do not reveal to the weak what they are unable to grasp, but at the same time, do not look upon their understanding as too poor to absorb it!'[59] In this document, the *dāʿī* is authorized to appoint a *kātib al-daʿwa*, for whose choice, to be sure, the strictest standards had to be applied.[60] But we are not told what exactly his tasks consisted of.

IX

Throughout the reigns of al-Muʿizz and al-ʿAzīz and in the first years of al-Ḥākim's reign, al-Nuʿmān and his sons and grandsons always singlehandedly held both the office of supreme *qāḍī* and that of supreme *dāʿī*. But later the two functions began to be differentiated, and this happened by way of the institution of deputyship. As in judgeship, so also in the leadership of the *daʿwa*, the supreme *qāḍī* could have himself represented by a *khalīfa* or a *nā'ib*.[61]

Al-Ḥusayn b. ʿAlī b. al-Nuʿmān, who held office during 389–394 AH, from February 999 until his removal in June 1004,[62] 'also led the *daʿwa*; he was supreme *qāḍī* and supreme *dāʿī*.'[63] However, his successor, his cousin ʿAbd al-ʿAzīz b. Muḥammad b. al-Nuʿmān, was the first to have himself represented in both functions: 'as his deputy in judgeship he appointed Abu'l-Ḥasan Mālik b. Saʿīd al-Fāriqī . . . As his secretary (*kātib*) he nominated Abū Yūsuf Yinal,[64] who was present at his hearings and prepared his rescripts (*tawqīʿāt*). Then he issued a *sijill* for him, authorizing him to collect the *fiṭra* and the *najwā*, to appear in the session room (*majlis*) in the palace, to initiate people,[65] and to lecture to those who had joined the *daʿwa*. Thus, he appeared on Thursday the 12th [Ramaḍān 394/July 1004], held the usual lecture in the palace and collected the *najwā* and the *fiṭra*.'[66]

This *kātib* or deputy supreme *dāʿī* Yinãl is perhaps identical with the Turk Yinãl al-Ṭawīl, whom al-Ḥākim sent out to fight the rebel Abū Rakwa in the following year, 395/1004–1005, and who died in the process.[67] Among al-Ḥākim's *dāʿī*s there were several Turks who had evidently joined the army or the court of his father al-ʿAzīz as young *mamlūk*s and had been brought up in the Ismaʿili faith; al-ʿAzīz was the first Fatimid caliph to import Turks in relatively large numbers.[68] Like this Yinãl, who bore a Turkish name, the Turk Khuttakīn (Turkish, Qut Tegin = 'Lucky Prince'), whom we shall discuss later, was also employed both for military tasks and for the *daʿwa*. Judging by his name, the eponym of the Druze sect, Anūshtegin al-Darzī, was also a Turk.

In Rajab 398/March 1008, the supreme *qāḍī* ʿAbd al-ʿAzīz b. Muḥammad b. al-Nuʿmān was removed from office; his successor was Mālik b. Saʿīd al-Fāriqī, who had been his deputy until then, and who remained in office until his overthrow in Rabīʿ II 405/October 1014.[69] Among his numerous functions, the *daʿwa* is explicitly mentioned.[70]

The *majālis* of the two supreme *qāḍī*s ʿAbd al-ʿAzīz and Mālik b. Saʿīd are often quoted in the writings of the Druze canon, so they must have been published as books.[71]

x

An as yet unsolved problem is the repeated interruptions of the *majālis al-ḥikma* during the reign of al-Ḥākim. We cannot simply attribute them to his alleged 'fickleness'; the rumours and insinuations circulating on this subject in the ʿAbbasid-Sunni sources ought to be taken with a grain of salt. Of course, al-Ḥākim's wavering religious policy cannot be examined here, and the interested reader will have to refer to the specialized literature.[72]

Al-Ḥākim's eccentric measures began with a *sijill* of Muḥarram 395/October–November 1004, forbidding the eating of various vegetables. Later, in Dhu'l-Qaʿda or Dhu'l-Ḥijja 396/August–September 1006, the *majālis* were closed:

'The people who usually appeared in the palace to listen to the readings from the books of the missionary sessions (*majālis al-daʿwa*) would assemble, but they were beaten and nothing was read to them.'[73]

However, a proper edict (*sijill*) was not issued until four years later, in Dhu'l-Qa'da 400/June–July 1010: 'An edict was read out announcing that the *majālis al-ḥikma* which used to be read to the saintly people (*awliyā'*) on Thursdays and Fridays were cancelled.'[74] As shown at the end of al-Musabbiḥī's text quoted in Section VIII above, this was connected with a series of other measures which altogether boiled down to a suspension of the entire Isma'ili *da'wa*: 'In the year 400 al-Ḥākim bi-Amr Allāh issued an edict cancelling the *khums*, the *zakāt*, the *fiṭra* and the *najwā* with which [the initiates] had been burdened, through which favours were acquired and which remained in the hands of the *qāḍī*s. Through another edict the *majālis al-ḥikma* which were read to the *awliyā'* on Thursdays and Fridays were cancelled.'[75]

But already in Rabī' II 401/November or December 1010, this edict – together with the other pro-Sunni measures – was cancelled: 'In all the mosques, an edict was read out forbidding disobedience of the imam's provisions and ordering that all senseless discussion be stopped. The [Isma'ili] call to prayer "Up for the best of deeds" was to be renewed and the formula "Prayer is better than sleep" was to be omitted again from the call to the early morning prayer; the late morning prayer (*ṣalāt al-ḍuḥā*) and the *tarāwīḥ* [additional prayers in the nights of Ramaḍān] were forbidden; the mission (*da'wa*) and the *majālis* were to be continued as usual. Between their ban and their renewed resumption, only five months had elapsed.'[76]

The following passage refers to the same edict: 'A decree was issued following which the *majālis al-ḥikma* were to be held again, and the *najwā* was to be levied anew.'[77]

The first suspension of the *majālis* was thus clearly connected with measures through which al-Ḥākim wanted to accommodate the Sunnis; five months later – perhaps under pressure from the Isma'ili 'establishment' – these measures had to be rescinded.

Three years later, the *majālis* were again interrupted: 'On Thursday the 28th [Rajab 404/2 February 1014], the *awliyā'* and others assembled in the palace to listen to the readings of the *qāḍī* from the books of the *majālis al-ḥikam*, but they were prevented from doing so.'[78] Unfortunately, we are not told what the reasons were.

The *majālis* were interrupted for the third time at the end of the year 405/1015, after the nomination of Aḥmad b. Muḥammad b. al-'Awāmm as supreme *qāḍī*.[79] This is testified by the Druze Ḥamza in one of his writings in the Druze canon.[80] It is confirmed by Yaḥyā al-Anṭākī, who reports for the same year: 'Al-Ḥākim locked the door to the room (*majlis*) in which they administered the oath (*bay'a*) to his followers (*shī'a*) and read to them each week from his sciences (*'ulūm*); it remained locked for some time.'[81] Here, too, we fail to learn precisely what the reasons were, but this closure seems to be connected with the Druze troubles, which began about this time; the earliest testimony of the activity of the Druze agitators is al-Kirmānī's *al-Risāla al-wā'iẓa*, dated 408/1017, which is directed against the heretic al-Ḥasan b. Ḥaydara al-Akhram; it implies earlier activities on the part of this earliest 'Druze'.

It is difficult to explain this closure of the *majālis*. Did al-Ḥākim want to end the Isma'ili *da'wa* as patron of the Druze doctrine? Or, on the contrary, was the Isma'ili 'establishment' trying to ward off heresy with the closure of the *majālis*? According to Yaḥyā al-Anṭākī, it was al-Ḥākim himself who had the session room (*majlis*) locked, and Yaḥyā continues: 'He [al-Ḥākim] bestowed the title of supreme *dā'ī* on Khuttakīn al-Ḍayf and entrusted him with the control of the room, so that it was used for the customary proceedings; later he also granted him the title of *al-ṣādiq al-amīn*.'[82] This Khuttakīn (Qut Tegin) subsequently proved to be the most embittered opponent of the Druzes. When the followers of Ḥamza and those of Khuttakīn met, they cursed each other.[83] So it is quite possible that al-Ḥākim had the *majālis* closed either in agreement with the Isma'ili *dā'ī*s or yielding to their pressure, in order to forestall the appearance of the Druze dissidents among them.

XI

We have no information about the *majālis* during the last years of al-Ḥākim's reign. But it was evidently his son and successor al-Ẓāhir who reintroduced the *da'wa* in its entirety and reopened the *majālis* after his accession in Shawwāl 411/February 1021. 'He conferred the office of judge and the mission in the palace of the caliphs (*bāb al-khilāfa*) to the Qāḍī Qāsim b. 'Abd al-'Azīz b. [Muḥammad b.] al-Nu'mān and ordered him to take care of the mission (*da'wa*) and the proper guidance (*hidāya*), of the readings of the *majālis al-ḥikma* and the spread of the science of *ta'wīl* among the followers (*ahl al-walāya*); he was to reinstate those principles of the 'Alid–Fatimid mission that had been abolished (*indarasa*); he was to wipe out all traces of the criminals (*ulu'l-baghy*) and clearly point out what had been cancelled. He sent an edict to this effect to all his followers (*ahl da'watihi*) and he ordered all his *dā'ī*s to read it out to the faithful [i.e. the Isma'ilis] in their respective districts.'[84]

By 'criminals' he meant the Druzes, against whom al-Ẓāhir's reformatory measures were primarily directed. His edict of 5 Shaʿbān 417/21 September 1026 has been preserved in its original wording.[85] Here it is explicitly stated that 'the gate of wisdom was open . . . until our lord al-Ḥākim bi-Amr Allāh thought it right to close it because of the prevailing circumstances and on political grounds (*bi-siyāsatiʾl-jumhūr*)'.[86] But now, continues the edict, the conditions that had then led to its closure no longer apply, and so the new Commander of the Faithful has ordered 'the highest *dāʿī* . . . Qāsim b. ʿAbd al-ʿAzīz [b.] Muḥammad b. al-Nuʿmān to open the gate of wisdom to those who long for it, and to read the *majālis* again in the palaces of the caliphs as had been customary there before'.[87]

Samuel M. Stern has published a letter found in the Geniza of the synagogue in Fusṭāṭ, in which a *dāʿī* addresses congratulations to a supreme *qāḍī*; this letter explicitly mentions the *majālis*.[88] Stern assumes that the caliph referred to in the letter, whose name is no longer legible, is al-Ẓāhir, and that consequently the supreme *qāḍī* in question is Qāsim b. ʿAbd al-ʿAzīz. The letter, however, merely discusses a lecture from the *Daʿāʾim al-Islām* by al-Qāḍī al-Nuʿmān, which is an exoteric work accessible to the general public; this corresponds with the writer's remark that he introduced the innovation of holding a session every Friday after the Friday prayer, which would take place in turn in the three principal mosques (ʿAmr, al-Azhar, al-Ḥākim). So what is meant here is by no means the *majālis al-ḥikma* properly speaking, but the public Friday readings about Ismaʿili law, which had been introduced by al-Qāḍī al-Nuʿmān and which continued to be part of the functions of the supreme *qāḍī*.

XII

There is very little information about the *majālis* during the long reign of caliph al-Mustanṣir (427–487/1036–1094). Apparently, the leadership of the *daʿwa* was at first assumed by the supreme *qāḍī*, in accordance with the original custom. This was, to begin with, the *qāḍī* appointed by al-Ẓāhir in 419/1028, namely ʿAbd al-Ḥākim b. Saʿīd al-Fāriqī, the brother of the previous supreme *qāḍī* and supreme *dāʿī* Mālik al-Fāriqī.[89] He was succeeded in 427/1036 by Qāsim b. ʿAbd al-ʿAzīz b. Muḥammad b. al-Nuʿmān, who had already been supreme *qāḍī* under al-Ẓāhir. Among his titles, the leadership of the *daʿwa* is explicitly stated;[90] he performed the 'service of the *majālis*' (*khidmat al-majālis*) every Thursday.[91] The well-known *dāʿī* and author al-Muʾayyad fiʾl-Dīn al-Shīrāzī has enthusiastically sung the praises of Thursday morning as the 'feast for the faithful' in a poem of his *Dīwān*: '*Yā ṣabāḥa'l-Khamīsi ahlan wa-sahlā . . . anta 'īdun li'l-m'minīna 'atīdun.*'[92] Together with the information mentioned above, these data confirm our assumption that the actual *majālis al-ḥikma* for the initiates were only held on Thursdays in the palace, while the public legal readings open to everybody and based on the *Da'ā'im* of al-Qāḍī al-Nu'mān took place in the Great Mosques on Fridays after the Friday prayer.

When Qāsim was removed from office on Monday 2 Muḥarram 441/5 June 1049, the function of supreme *qāḍī* was conferred on the Palestinian upstart al-Ḥasan b. 'Alī al-Yāzūrī. How close the traditional connection was between the leadership of the *da'wa* and the office of supreme *qāḍī* is shown by the fact that al-Yāzūrī, a Ḥanafī Sunni, also bore the title of supreme *dā'ī*. When a year later, on 7 Muḥarram 442/1 June 1050, the caliph appointed him to be vizier as well, the *sijill* of investiture expressly mentioned his title *dā'ī al-du'āt*.[93]

It may be imagined that the nomination of a Sunni as leader of the *da'wa* was considered a scandal by the Isma'ili *dā'ī*s. The *dā'ī* al-Mu'ayyad fi'l-Dīn al-Shīrāzī cannot have been alone in calling this appointment 'something unprecedented and unheard-of'.[94] Al-Mu'ayyad himself had hoped to be appointed supreme *dā'ī*, were it only as deputy of the all-powerful al-Yāzūrī: 'when it was seen that the office [of vizier] which he had taken over would not allow him to appear personally in the assemblies (*andiya*) to read the *majālis al-da'wa*, everybody thought that he would not deny me this function and would designate no one else but me for it'. But al-Mu'ayyad was disappointed in this hope. Al-Yāzūrī entrusted the *majālis* to his predecessor, the aged Qāsim. Al-Mu'ayyad protested, but in vain; al-Yāzūrī pleaded that 'the reason for the appointment of [Qāsim] Ibn al-Nu'mān were old women of the palace from the families of al-Ḥākim and al-'Azīz; these considered that al-Nu'mān had founded this [the *da'wa*], and therefore his sons and descendants had the greatest legal claim to his post'.[95]

It was not until 450/1058, when al-Yāzūrī was overthrown and executed, that al-Mu'ayyad's time came; now at last he was assigned the post of *dā'ī al-du'āt*.[96] He may have held it until his death in 470/1077, at all events with a brief interruption during his banishment to Syria. As he is buried in the building of al-Ḥākim's former Dār al-'Ilm,[97] it may be assumed that he had lived and worked there. The former academy was evidently no longer needed for scientific purposes, and as we shall see below, it was actually used for the *da'wa* in the late Fatimid period.

However, the Thursday sessions probably continued to be held in the palace.

It is well known that the supreme *qāḍī* maintained the nominal leadership of the *da'wa* and the title *dā'ī al-du'āt*. Only thus can it be explained that, for example, 'Abd al-Ḥākim al-Malījī, the successor of al-Yāzūrī in the office of supreme *qāḍī*, who occupied the function of supreme judge no less than seven times between 450/1058 and 460/1068, is considered the author of the *Majālis al-Mustanṣiriyya*.[98] Each of the descendants of 'Abd al-Ḥākim b. Sa'īd al-Fāriqī – his sons 'Abd al-Karīm and Aḥmad and his grandson Aḥmad b. 'Abd al-Karīm – simultaneously bore the title of vizier, supreme *qāḍī* and supreme *dā'ī*.[99] The vizier Ibn Abī Kudayna, who also functioned as supreme *qāḍī* seven times, was called the leader of the *da'wa*,[100] and bore the title *dā'ī al-du'āt*.[101] So it appears that the *qāḍī al-quḍāt* of the day was the official leader of the *da'wa*, while it was in fact al-Mu'ayyad who held the *majālis al-ḥikma*.

XIII

The passage quoted in Section VIII above from al-Musabbiḥī's chronicle refers to the *majālis al-ḥikma* as 'books' written by the *dā'ī*, then authorized by the caliph-imam and finally published in a fair copy (*mubayyaḍa*). Collections of such *majālis* are often mentioned and quoted in Isma'ili and Druze literature; some of them have even been preserved.

The *majālis* of al-Qāḍī al-Nu'mān are collected in his *Ta'wīl al-da'ā'im*, which is divided into twelve parts, each containing ten *majālis*.[102] The *Majālis al-'Azīz bi'llāh* and the *Majālis al-ḥikma al-Ḥākimiyya* are only known from later quotations.[103] The *Majālis al-Mustanṣiriyya* are attributed either to al-Mu'ayyad or to the Armenian vizier and military dictator Badr al-Jamālī.[104] Its editor, Muḥammad Kāmil Ḥusayn, dates them – on the basis of internal evidence – to the period between 446/1054 and 455/1063 and, therefore, concludes that they must have been written by Muḥammad b. al-Qāsim b. 'Abd al-'Azīz b. Muḥammad b. al-Nu'mān. S. M. Stern has shown, however, that the titles (*alqāb*) mentioned in the work itself point to the supreme *qāḍī* al-Malījī as the official author.[105]

In addition to these collections, which are classed under different imams – that is, they were written in their time and in their names and authorized by them – there also exist collections of the *majālis* of specific *dā'īs*; the best-known of these is the *Majālis al-Mu'ayyadiyya*.[106] It consists of eight volumes containing 100 *majālis* each; some of them have been published.[107] It goes without saying that the missionaries working outside the Fatimid empire also held *majālis*; Ḥamīd al-Dīn al-Kirmānī himself on one occasion mentions his *Majālis al-Baṣriyya waʾl-Baghdādiyya*, which, however, have not survived.[108]

XIV

The lack of detailed sources for the late Fatimid period – as far as the *majālis al-ḥikma* are concerned – is partially made up for by a fairly long passage from the work of the chronicler Ibn al-Ṭuwayr (524–617/1130–1220), who is quoted by al-Maqrīzī; the text speaks for itself and needs no commentary.[109]

'The *dāʿī al-duʿāt* immediately follows the *qāḍī al-quḍāt* in rank and wears the same attire and other [insignia]. He has to know the entire jurisprudence of the Holy Family (*madhāhib ahl al-bayt*) and hold lectures about it; he must administer the oath (*ʿahd*) to anyone converting from his own *madhhab* to their *madhhab*. He has twelve stewards (*nuqabāʾ*) of the faithful [i.e. the Ismaʿilis] under his command; in addition, he has deputies (*nuwwāb*) in all cities like deputy judges. The jurists of the dynasty (*fuqahāʾ al-dawla*) appear before him; they have a place called Dār al-ʿIlm, and some of them receive substantial salaries because of their superior positions[110] in it. The jurists among them usually administer the *fatwā* on the strength of a booklet (*daftar*) called *majlis al-ḥikma*, which is read out every Monday and Thursday. It is presented to the supreme *dāʿī* in a fair copy; he hands it to them and takes it back from them. On the two days referred to, he brings it to the caliph and reads it to him, if possible, and receives his signature (*ʿalāma*) on the back of it. He holds sessions in the palace to read it out to the faithful [i.e. the Ismaʿilis], and he does this at two different places: for the men on the pulpit of the mission (*kursī al-daʿwa*) in the great hall (*al-īwān al-kabīr*), and for the women in the room (*majlis*) of the *dāʿī*, one of the largest and most spacious buildings [in the palace].

'When he has finished the reading in front of the faithful, men and women, they walk up to him and kiss his hands, and he touches their heads with the place of the signature, that is the monogram (*khaṭṭ*) of the caliph. He also collects the *najwā* from the faithful of Cairo, Miṣr [= Fusṭāṭ] and the provinces belonging to it, especially upper Egypt; it amounts [per head] to three and a third dirhams. This adds up to a considerable sum; he presents this to the caliph and hands it to him in private (*baynahū wa-baynahū*), whereby only God alone is the guarantor [for the completeness of the sum]. Thereupon the caliph determines a certain amount for him and his stewards. There are some well-to-do Ismaʿilis who pay thirty-three and two-third dinars as *najwā*; together with it, they deliver a piece of paper on which their name is written; this is separated from the petitions and then given back to them with a note written in the caliph's own hand: God bless you, your fortune, your descendants and your faith. This [autograph] is proudly kept [by the contributor]. This service was handed down from father to son in a family called Banū ʿAbd al-Qawī, whose last member was al-Jalīs. Al-Afḍal, the son of the *amīr al-juyūsh* had exiled them into the Maghrib, so that al-Jalīs was born and bred there and inclined towards the *madhhab* of the Sunnis. [Later, in Egypt] he assumed the office of the *qāḍī* and the *daʿwa*. Asad al-Dīn Shīrkūh still lived to see him, highly esteemed him and made him a *wāsiṭa* with the caliph al-ʿĀḍid [555–567/1160–1171]. He blocked the access to al-ʿĀḍid; otherwise there would have remained nothing in the treasuries because of his generosity – as though he knew that he would be the last caliph.'

NOTES

The editor would like to express his gratitude to Madam Azizeh Azodi for her masterful translation of this chapter from German into English.

1 S. M. Stern, 'The Book of the Highest Initiation and other anti-Ismāʿīlī Travesties', in his *Studies in Early Ismāʿīlism* (Jerusalem–Leiden, 1983), pp. 56 ff.

2 Ibn al-Dawādārī, *Kanz al-durar*, vol. 6, ed. Ṣ. al-Munajjid (Cairo, 1961), p. 45.

3 Al-Qāḍī al-Nuʿmān, *Iftitāḥ al-daʿwa*, ed. W. al-Qāḍī (Beirut, 1970), p. 37; ed. F. al-Dashrāwī (Tunis, 1975), p. 8; hereafter cited as *Iftitāḥ*.

4 *Iftitāḥ*, ed. al-Qāḍī, p. 76; ed. al-Dashrāwī, pp. 52 ff.

5 *Kitāb al-ʿālim waʾl-ghulām*, ed. M. Ghālib in his *Arbaʿ kutub ḥaqqāniyya* (Beirut, 1983), p. 23. See also W. Ivanow, *Studies in Early Persian Ismailism* (2nd edn, Bombay, 1955), pp. 66 ff.; H. Corbin, 'L'initiation Ismaélienne ou l'ésotérisme et le Verbe', *Eranos Jahrbuch*, 39 (1970), p. 62, and H. Halm, *Das Reich des Mahdi* (Munich, 1991), pp. 49 ff.

6 The text of Ghālib is incorrect here; read: *lā akrahu raʾyataka wa-lā ataʿaddā sunnataka*.

7 See I. K. Poonawala, *Biobibliography of Ismāʿīlī Literature* (Malibu, Calif., 1977), pp. 91 ff.

8 V. Klemm, *Die Mission des fāṭimidischen Agenten al-Muʾayyad fī d-dīn in Šīrāz* (Frankfurt, etc., 1989), pp. 205 ff. This edition is based on Ms. 292.822 B141KA of the American University in Beirut.

9 Ibid., pp. 200–202; Arabic text pp. 232 ff. (=46 ff.).

10 Read: *yadʿūhu ilā imāmi zamānihī*.

11 Read: *waʾl-īmāna biʾl-imāmi wa-ṭāʿatahū*.

12 Qur'an, IV:59.

13 He still mentions the death of the Būyid ʿAḍud al-Dawla in that year; see W. Madelung, 'Fatimiden und Baḥrainqarmaṭen', *Der Islam*, 34 (1959), p. 59 n. 1 and pp. 68 ff.

14 Al-Nuwayrī, *Nihāyat al-arab*, vol. 25, ed. M. J. ʿA. al-Ḥīnī and ʿA. al-Ahwānī (Cairo, 1984), pp. 217–220.

15 Al-Maqrīzī, *al-Khiṭaṭ* (Būlāq, 1270/1853–1854), vol. 1, pp. 396–397; hereafter cited as

al-Khiṭaṭ. This Būlāq press version is altogether better than the al-Nuwayrī edition.
16 *wa-kutubihī* is missing in al-Nuwayrī.
17 Read: *fa-lā tuẓhir (al-Khiṭaṭ)*.
18 Read: *li-ḥaqqihā (al-Khiṭaṭ)*.
19 Read: *wa-taqūma bi- (al-Khiṭaṭ)*.
20 Read: *min rabbihim (al-Khiṭaṭ)*.
21 Thus in al-Maqrīzī's *al-Khiṭaṭ*; al-Nuwayrī has 'the deluded one' (*al-maghrūr*) instead.
22 Read: *tata'awwalu 'alayhi bi-mā yubṭiluhū (al-Khiṭaṭ)*.
23 Al-Maqrīzī, *al-Khiṭaṭ*: *tastafīduhū*; al-Nuwayrī: *tasta'biduhū*.
24 Thus in *al-Khiṭaṭ*; al-Nuwayrī has: *ṭalāq al-ḥaraj wa'l-sunna*.
25 Read: *lā mathwabata (al-Khiṭaṭ)*.
26 Read: *lā khiyāra (al-Khiṭaṭ)*.
27 In the ancient Arabic divorce of *ẓihār*, the formula: *anti 'alayya ka-ẓahri ummī*, 'you are to me like the back of my mother' is applied.
28 Read: *anā'l-mustaḥlif (al-Khiṭaṭ)*.
29 *Al-Khiṭaṭ*: *mujaddada 'alayka*; al-Nuwayrī: *muḥaddada 'alayka*.
30 See Madelung, 'Fatimiden', p. 59 n. 1 and p. 68.
31 Al-'Umarī, *Ta'rīf bi'l-muṣṭalaḥ al-sharīf* (Cairo, 1312/1894–1895), p. 157.
32 Aḥmad b. 'Alī al-Qalqashandī, *Ṣubḥ al-a'shā* (Cairo, 1331–1338/1913–1920), vol. 13, pp. 246 ff.; English translation in B. Lewis, 'Ismā'īlī Notes', BSOAS, 12 (1947–1948), pp. 597 ff.
33 Silvestre de Sacy, *Exposé de la religion des Druzes* (Paris, 1838), vol. 1, introduction pp. 136–147.
34 W. Ivanow, *A Creed of the Fatimids* (Bombay, 1936), pp. 13–17.
35 See Mulla Abdul Husain, *Gulzare Daudi for the Bohras of India* (Ahmadabad, 1920), pp. 125–138.
36 *Iftitāḥ*, ed. al-Qāḍī, p. 73; ed. al-Dashrāwī, p. 49.
37 Thus in *Iftitāḥ*, ed al-Dashrāwī, p. 53; see al-Qāḍī's edition, p. 76.
38 *Iftitāḥ*, ed. al-Qāḍī, p. 130; ed. al-Dashrāwī, p. 128.
39 *Iftitāḥ*, ed. al-Qāḍī, p. 140; ed. al-Dashrāwī, p. 146.
40 *Iftitāḥ*, ed. al-Qāḍī, p. 133; ed. al-Dashrāwī, p. 132.
41 Ibn 'Idhārī, *al-Bayān al-mughrib*, ed. G. S. Colin and E. Lévi-Provençal (New edn, Leiden, 1948–1951), p. 152.
42 Idrīs 'Imād al-Dīn, *'Uyūn al-akhbār*, vol. 5, ed. M. Ghālib (Beirut, 1975), pp. 125, 137 ff., and Ibn 'Idhārī, *al-Bayān*, p. 159.
43 The fragments of the *Sīrat al-Mahdī* are handed down in Idrīs 'Imād al-Dīn's *'Uyūn al-akhbār*, vol. 5. See H. Halm, 'Zwei fatimidische Quellen aus der Zeit des Kalifen al-Mahdī (909–934)', WO, 19 (1988), pp. 102–117.
44 Idrīs, *'Uyūn*, vol. 5, p. 137 (= Stern, *Studies in Early Ismā'īlism*, pp. 102 ff.).
45 Abū Bakr al-Mālikī, *Riyādh al-nufūs*, ed. B. al-Bakkūsh (Beirut, 1981–1983), vol. 2, pp. 475 ff.
46 Al-Nu'mān, *al-Majālis wa'l-musāyarāt*, ed. al-Ḥ. al-Faqī et al. (Tunis, 1978), pp. 348, 434, 487, 546.
47 Ibid., p. 487.
48 Ibid., the *Majālis* 57, 77–79, 156, 158, 185, 208–210, 227, 241, 281.
49 Ibid., pp. 386–388 (*Majlis* 201). The *majālis al-ḥikma* are also mentioned in the *Majālis* on pp. 224 l.11, 467 l.7, and 487 l.6 (*samā' al-ḥikma*).

50 Ibn Ḥajar, *Raf*ʿ, in al-Kindī, *Kitāb al-wulāt wa-kitāb al-quḍāt*, ed. R. Guest (Leiden–London, 1912), p. 586 l.17, probably after Ibn Zūlāq.

51 Ibn Ḥajar, *Raf*ʿ, pp. 585, 587, 589–591.

52 Ibid., pp. 592–595.

53 Al-Musabbiḥī, quoted in *al-Khiṭaṭ*, vol. 1, p. 391; see also al-Maqrīzī, *Ittiʿāẓ al-ḥunafāʾ*, ed. Jamāl al-Dīn al-Shayyāl and M. Ḥ. M. Aḥmad (Cairo, 1967–1973), vol. 1, p. 285 l.6; hereafter cited as *Ittiʿāẓ*; and Silvestre de Sacy, *Chrestomathie Arabe* (2nd edn, Paris, 1826–1827), vol. 1, pp. 140, 141, 142.

54 *Al-Khiṭaṭ*, vol. 1, p. 391, and de Sacy, *Chrestomathie*, vol. 1, pp. 141, 143 ff.

55 I read: *wa-liʾl-daʿāwā al-muttaṣilati*. The Būlāq printed version: *waʾl-daʿāwā al-muttaṣila* makes no sense; de Sacy's version: *mā yuqraʾu ʿalāʾl-awliyāʾi waʾl-duʿāti waʾl-muttaṣilati* and his translation of *al-muttaṣila* as 'ceux qui venoient se faire initier' – meaning, say, adepts or neophytes – is not convincing.

56 Akhū Muḥsin, quoted in al-Nuwayrī, *Nihāya*, vol. 25, pp. 193 ff., and in Ibn al-Dawādārī, *Kanz*, vol. 6, pp. 48 ff.

57 *Iftitāḥ*, ed. al-Qāḍī, p. 172; ed. al-Dashrāwī, p. 189.

58 Al-Qalqashandī, *Ṣubḥ*, vol. 10, pp. 434 ff.; S. M. Stern, 'Cairo as the Centre of the Ismāʿīlī Movement', in his *Studies in Early Ismāʿīlism*, p. 242; hereafter cited as 'Cairo'.

59 Al-Qalqashandī, *Ṣubḥ*, vol. 10, p. 37.

60 Ibid., vol. 10, p. 438.

61 Stern, 'Cairo', pp. 236 ff.

62 Al-Kindī, *Kitāb al-wulāt*, pp. 596–599.

63 *Ittiʿāẓ*, vol. 2, pp. 24 l.2, 40 l.16, 50 l.1.

64 Printed: M.nāl.

65 Printed: *wa-akhdh al-daʿwa ʿalāʾl-nās*. Perhaps it should be read: *wa-akhdh al-ʿahd ʿalāʾl-nās*.

66 *Ittiʿāẓ*, vol. 2, p. 50 lines 9–15.

67 Ibid., vol. 2, p. 61; Yaḥyā b. Saʿīd al-Anṭākī, *Taʾrīkh*, ed. I. Kratchkovsky and A. A. Vasiliev, in *Patrologia Orientalis*, 23 (1932), p. 473, and Ibn Ẓāfir, *Akhbār al-duwal al-munqaṭiʿa*, ed. A. Ferré (Cairo, 1972), p. 45.

68 Y. Lev, *State and Society in Fatimid Egypt* (Leiden, 1991), pp. 90 ff.

69 Al-Kindī, *Kitāb al-wulāt*, pp. 602, 603; *Ittiʿāẓ*, vol. 2, p. 106.

70 *Ittiʿāẓ*, vol. 2, pp. 72 l.3, 106 l.10.

71 Those of ʿAbd al-ʿAzīz in treatises Nos. 72 and 76, those of Mālik in treatise No. 42; see Stern, 'Cairo', p. 239.

72 See the divergent interpretations of Burkhard May, 'Die Religionspolitik der ägyptischen Fāṭimiden 969–1171' (Thesis, University of Hamburg, 1975); Josef van Ess, *Chiliastische Erwartungen und die Versuchung der Göttlichkeit. Der Kalif al-Ḥākim* (Heidelberg, 1977), and H. Halm, 'Der Treuhänder Gottes: Die Edikte des Kalifen al-Ḥākim', *Der Islam*, 63 (1986), pp. 11–72.

73 *Ittiʿāẓ*, vol. 2, p. 73 l.2 ff., and p. 106 l.10.

74 Ibid., vol. 2, p. 82.

75 *Al-Khiṭaṭ*, vol.1, p. 391; de Sacy, *Chrestomathie*, vol. 1, p. 141.

76 *Ittiʿāẓ*, vol. 2, p. 86.

77 Ibid., vol. 2, p. 85 l.9. Read: *bi-iʿādati majālisiʾl-ḥikmati wa-akhdhiʾl-najwā*, instead of: *wa-ukhidha al-naḥwī*; note 2 of this edition is superfluous.

78 Ibid., vol. 2, p. 103.

79 His nomination took place, according to al-Maqrīzī, *Ittiʿāẓ*, vol. 2, p. 108, on 21

Sha'bān 405/14 February 1015; and according to Yaḥyā b. Sa'īd al-Anṭākī, *Ta'rīkh*, ed. L. Cheikho et al. (Paris–Beirut, 1909), p. 209, in Shawwāl/March–April of the same year.

80 D. Bryer, 'The Origins of the Druze Religion', *Der Islam*, 52 (1975), p. 63, and 53 (1976), p. 25.

81 Al-Anṭākī, ed. Cheikho, pp. 209, 221.

82 Ibid., p. 209.

83 Ibid., p. 224; see also pp. 222, 223.

84 Idrīs, *'Uyūn al-akhbār*, vol. 6, ed. M. Ghālib (Beirut, 1984), p. 311.

85 Ibid., pp. 311–317.

86 Ibid., p. 314.

87 Ibid., p. 315.

88 Stern, 'Cairo', pp. 243–245.

89 Al-Kindī, *Kitāb al-wulāt*, pp. 613 ff.

90 Ibid.

91 *Itti'āẓ*, vol. 2, p. 205 l.1.

92 *Dīwān*, ed. M. Kāmil Ḥusayn (Cairo, 1949), p. 314; Stern, 'Cairo', in his *Studies*, p. 241.

93 *Itti'āẓ*, vol. 1, p. 212.

94 Al-Mu'ayyad fi'l-Dīn al-Shīrāzī, *Sīra*, ed. M. Kāmil Ḥusayn (Cairo, 1949), p. 88.

95 Ibid., p. 91. About the entire process, see also Stern, 'Cairo', pp. 240 ff., and Klemm, *Die Mission*, pp. 56–58.

96 *Itti'āẓ*, vol. 2, p. 251.

97 *Al-Khiṭaṭ*, vol. 1, p. 460, after Ibn 'Abd al-Ẓāhir.

98 Stern, 'Cairo', pp. 239 ff.

99 Ibn al-Ṣayrafī, *al-Ishāra ilā man nāla'l-wizāra*, ed. 'A. Mukhliṣ (Cairo, 1925), pp. 48–50.

100 *Itti'āẓ*, vol. 2, p. 307.

101 Ibn al-Ṣayrafī, p. 51.

102 Poonawala, *Biobibliography*, p. 64. The two volumes are edited by M. Ḥ. al-A'ẓamī (Cairo, 1968–1972); volume one also edited by 'Ādil al-'Awwā, in his *Muntakhabāt Ismā'īliyya* (Damascus, 1958). See Stern, 'Cairo', p. 238.

103 Poonawala, *Biobibliography*, pp. 82, 319.

104 Ibid., p. 319.

105 Stern, 'Cairo', pp. 239 ff.

106 Poonawala, *Biobibliography*, p. 106.

107 Al-Mu'ayyad fi'l-Dīn al-Shīrāzī, *al-Majālis al-Mu'ayyadiyya*, vols. 1 and 3, ed. M. Ghālib (Beirut, 1974–1984).

108 Al-Kirmānī, *Kitāb al-riyāḍ*, ed. 'Ārif Tāmir (Beirut, 1960), p. 108, and Poonawala, *Biobibliography*, p. 102.

109 Al-Maqrīzī, *al-Khiṭaṭ*, vol. 1, p. 391; Ibn al-Ṭuwayr, *Nuzhat al-muqlatayn fī akhbār al-dawlatayn*, ed. A. Fu'ād Sayyid (Beirut, 1992), pp. 110–112, and Stern, 'Cairo', pp. 242 ff.

110 A. Fu'ād Sayyid here reads: *al-taṣaddur* instead of *al-taṣdīr* (Būlāq).

SIX

Al-Qāḍī al-Nuʿmān and Ismaʿili jurisprudence

ISMAIL K. POONAWALA

A CLOSE scrutiny of early Ismaʿili literature reveals that there did not exist a distinct Ismaʿili law before the establishment of the Fatimid dynasty.[1] In fact, the Ismaʿili community and the activities of the *daʿwa* were widely diffused throughout the ʿAbbasid empire and there seems to be some evidence to suggest that the early Ismaʿilis followed the law of the land wherever they had settled.[2]

With the foundation of the Fatimid caliphate the situation changed drastically as Ismaʿili law started taking definite shape with the backing of the caliphs. Before the works of al-Qāḍī al-Nuʿmān (hereafter cited as Nuʿmān) were embraced officially by the Fatimid caliphs, our information about the state of Ismaʿili law is derived chiefly from the Sunni historians. Ibn ʿIdhārī (d. after 712/1312) reports that after his triumphant entry into Qayrawān, Abū ʿAbd Allāh al-Shīʿī, the founder of the Fatimid caliphate, introduced the addition of '*ḥayya ʿalā khayr al-ʿamal*' (come to the best of work) in the call to prayer (*adhān*) and ordered the omission of '*al-ṣalāt khayr min al-nawm*' (prayer is better than sleep) from the morning call to prayer. In the Friday sermon he added the blessings (*ṣalāt*) on ʿAlī, Fāṭima, al-Ḥasan and al-Ḥusayn after the blessings on the Prophet, and prohibited the recitation of *tarāwīḥ* prayers during the month of Ramaḍān. It is further reported that Muḥammad b. ʿUmar b. Yaḥyā al-Marwazī (d. 303/915–916), the first Fatimid *qāḍī* (judge) appointed by Abū ʿAbd Allāh al-Shīʿī and confirmed in his position by the first Fatimid caliph al-Mahdī, issued an order which forbade jurists (*fuqahāʾ*) to give legal opinions except according to the Jaʿfarī (i.e., the Shiʿi) *madhhab* (rite of jurisprudence), declared *ṭalāq al-batta* (irrevocable divorce) invalid, and upheld the right of a daughter to inherit the whole of her father's property, to the exclusion of *ʿaṣāba* (agnates), in the absence of a son.[3] We have the testimony of Nuʿmān in this respect which states that al-Mahdī disapproved of the jurists' exclusion of the uterine heirs (*dhawū al-arḥām*) from inheritance.[4]

While dealing with the reign of al-Muʿizz, Ibn ʿIdhārī further reports that in the year 349/960 the caliph dispatched a *qāḍī* to the imams and muezzins of the mosques ordering that the call to prayer should not be given without reciting *ḥayya ʿalā khayr al-ʿamal*, that the *basmala* should be recited [loudly] at the beginning of every *sūra* [in the obligatory prayers], that they should pronounce the two-fold final salutations (*yusallimu taslīmatayn*) [at the end of each prayer], and the five-fold *takbīr* in funeral prayers. They were further ordered not to delay the *ʿaṣr* prayers and not to recite the *ʿishāʾ* prayers early. Women were forbidden to wail while accompanying the funeral procession, and except during the actual interment, the blind were forbidden to recite [the Qurʾan] over graves.[5]

In addition to the above changes, Ibn Ḥammād (d. 628/1231), a Berber *qāḍī* and historian, reports the introduction of *qunūt* (invocation) in Friday prayers,[6] while al-Maqrīzī (d. 845/1442) reports that after his conquest of Egypt, the Fatimid general Jawhar discarded sighting of the moon as the criterion for determining the beginning of Ramaḍān and introduced a fixed calendar based on astronomical calculation.[7] The exact date when a fixed calendar was introduced is not known; however, the following comments by Nuʿmān are revealing and indicate that it might have been instituted by al-Muʿizz with the adoption of the *Daʿāʾim* as the official Fatimid code. In the *Iqtiṣār*, composed before the *Daʿāʾim*, Nuʿmān states that one should not begin fasting for the month of Ramaḍān until he sees the new moon and should not end fasting until he sees it, or [if he fails to see it] he should complete thirty days. But in the *Daʿāʾim* he states that he who lives in the presence of the imam, or is in communication with him, should fast with the fasting of the imam and break [his fast] with the breaking of the imam, because the imam takes care of religious matters.[8]

Al-Khushanī (d. 371/981), the Mālikī *faqīh* (jurist) from Khushan, near Qayrawān, who left his homeland around 311/923 because he was unable to come to terms with Shiʿism, records four persons who succeeded Muḥammad b. ʿUmar al-Marwazī in the judgeship of Qayrawān but does not give any information about their writings on *fiqh* (jurisprudence, law).[9] Aflaḥ b. Hārūn al-Malūsī, who was al-Mahdī's *qāḍī* in Raqqāda and Mahdiyya, is reported by the Ismaʿili historian Idrīs ʿImād al-Dīn (d. 872/1468) on the authority of Abū ʿAbd Allāh Jaʿfar b.

Muḥammad b. al-Haytham (a companion of Abū ʿAbd Allāh al-Shīʿī)[10] to have composed some works on *fiqh*, but they did not survive.[11] One can surmise that some of those *fuqahāʾ* and judges were engaged with legal compositions hoping that their works would be recognized officially; however, as will be seen below, after the official recognition of Nuʿmān as the Fatimid law-giver, the works of his Maghribī contemporaries probably fell into disuse and were lost.

Now we turn to Nuʿmān's elder contemporaries in the East. Both Abū Ḥātim Aḥmad b. Ḥamdān al-Rāzī (d. 322/934) and Abu'l-Ḥasan Muḥammad al-Nasafī (d. 332/943) apparently attempted to create and develop an independent Ismaʿili legal system, since Ibn al-Nadīm, who compiled his *Fihrist* in 377/987, reports that they composed significant works on *fiqh*.[12] But, there is no confirmation of this from the extant Ismaʿili sources.[13] In his extant *Kitāb al-zīna*,[14] al-Rāzī covers many aspects of ritual, such as purity, prayers, fasting, pilgrimage, and also aspects of law dealing with marriage, divorce and inheritance. However, as the author's primary objective is the etymology of Islamic nomenclature, he does not dwell on the points of law.[15]

The first three Fatimid caliphs encountered numerous problems while consolidating their power. Al-Mahdī was faced with several rebellions and internal dissensions resulting from his disposing of Abū ʿAbd Allāh al-Shīʿī. Both al-Qāʾim and al-Manṣūr were preoccupied with the Khārijī revolt of Abū Yazīd, with whom the hostile Sunni-Mālikī population of Qayrawān had made common cause, which almost brought the nascent state to the brink of collapse. It was during the reign of the fourth caliph al-Muʿizz that the state achieved sufficient stability and internal security to embark on a policy of conquest and territorial expansion.

The establishment of Fatimid rule required some modifications to the revolutionary objectives and policies of the *daʿwa* as dictated by the needs of the state and the realities of the North African Sunni milieu where the Mālikī *madhhab* was firmly entrenched. The doctrinal reform undertaken by al-Mahdī with this aim thus became more pronounced during the reign of al-Muʿizz[16] and the time was ripe to promulgate a state *madhhab* and a legal code. Nuʿmān, who had faithfully served all the first four caliphs and composed massive legal works with their explicit approval, was finally commissioned by the fourth caliph al-Muʿizz to compile his *Daʿāʾim al-Islām* (*The Pillars of Islam*), which was given official recognition. Hence, we now turn to him.

According to his own statement, Nuʿmān served the first Fatimid caliph al-Mahdī for nine years, some months and some days before the latter's death, and thereafter he served the second caliph, al-Qā'im, for the whole of his reign.[17] Unfortunately, he does not describe the exact nature of his office except that his duty was to report news of the royal entourage to the caliph daily. In this assignment he seems to have enjoyed the confidence of both al-Mahdī and al-Qā'im. In addition, he also served the grandson of al-Mahdī, the young prince al-Manṣūr, who later became the third caliph, by collecting and transcribing books for him for some time in the reign of al-Mahdī and throughout the reign of al-Qā'im.

Shortly after his accession to the caliphate (in 334/946) and before officially announcing the death of al-Qā'im (i.e., in 336/947 after suppressing the Khārijī revolt), al-Manṣūr appointed Nuʿmān to the judgeship of Tripoli.[18] In 337/948 when the caliph moved his capital to the new city of Manṣūriyya, he promoted Nuʿmān from modest provincial *qāḍī* to supreme *qāḍī* by conferring on him the judgeship of the capital as well as that of Mahdiyya and Qayrawān with a right to appoint other judges in the Fatimid domain.[19] Nuʿmān's elevation to the highest judicial office in the government thus coincided with the consolidation of the state after the crushing defeat of the Khārijī revolt and the enfeeblement of the Sunni-Mālikī opposition.

Al-Muʿizz (341–365/953–975), with whom Nuʿmān was on intimate terms even before his accession to the caliphate,[20] not only confirmed him in his high position, but in 343/954 issued a royal decree entrusting him with the *maẓālim* proceedings throughout the Fatimid realm.[21] The edict clearly states that Nuʿmān was given wide authority and his jurisdiction extended to every case wherein the *maẓālim* matters were brought to him directly, or as an appeal from any corner of the domain. No other judge could entertain matters related to the royal entourage, or the various classes of the caliph's bondsmen, or the soldiery stationed in the capital. In all these matters Nuʿmān was granted absolute judicial powers. He was thus elevated by al-Muʿizz to the most eminent judicial position in the Fatimid government. In addition to this he was also authorized by the caliph to hold the *majālis al-ḥikma* (sessions of wisdom) every Friday, following the noon prayers, in the royal palace to instruct the congregation in the religious sciences of the *daʿwa*, especially the *bāṭinī* (esoteric) sciences.[22]

Nuʿmān's rise to such a lofty position was not an accident. He was very close to the third and the fourth caliphs and had won their confidence. While holding his office as supreme *qāḍī* he must have given an exemplary image of both competence and high moral qualities. But, above all, he had distinguished himself as a most prolific author and the founder of a juridical system not only accessible to the masses but conformable to the universalist concept of the Fatimid imamate. Hence, we turn to Nuʿmān's works on jurisprudence.[23]

His first work entitled *Kitāb al-īḍāḥ*, according to Idrīs ʿImād al-Dīn, was undertaken while he was still serving al-Mahdī, at the latter's suggestion.[24] Referring to it, Nuʿmān states in the introduction of his *Kitāb al-iqtiṣār* that he embarked on the collection of a vast number of legal *ḥadīth*s (traditions) transmitted from the family of the Prophet by scrutinizing various sources accessible to him. He further states that out of a huge mass he selected only the well-known *ḥadīth*s (*mashhūr, maʿrūf, maʾthūr*), irrespective of the agreement or discord of the narrators. Out of this material he compiled the *Īḍāḥ*, indicating the points on which the narrators agreed and disagreed and explaining what was firmly established doctrine in them with evidence and proofs. It was a voluminous composition comprised of some 3,000 folios (*waraqa*).[25] In it, Nuʿmān fully quotes the chain of transmission (*isnād*) for each *ḥadīth*, and cites several *ḥadīth*s on each legal matter. As for the cases of apparent conflict, he resolves them either by harmonizing the alternatives or by explaining why one side should be preferred over the other.[26]

Unfortunately, except for a small fragment from the chapter, called *kitāb* (book), on ritual prayer (*ṣalāt*), the entire work seems to be lost.[27] Wilferd Madelung who examined this extant portion and analyzed the sources listed by Nuʿmān concludes by stating:

> Ismaʿili law thus appears in the *K. al-īḍāḥ*, both materially and theoretically, as a compromise between Imāmī and Zaydī law. Materially, it is based on sources accepted as authoritative in Imāmī *fiqh* as well as those accepted as authoritative in Zaydī *fiqh*. Theoretically, al-Nuʿmān recognizes, in agreement with the Zaydīs, the authority of the *ahl al-bayt* in general, not merely that of the imams. But he makes a concession to the Imāmī position in granting the imams superior authority to that of the other ʿAlids. In particular, the importance of Imam Jaʿfar, whose role is quite limited in Zaydī law but paramount in Imāmī law, is evident in the fragment of the *K. al-īḍāḥ*.[28]

The sources of the *Īḍāḥ* thus seem to be widely spread. This work also suggests that due to the absence of Ismaʿili law, Nuʿmān was attempting to lay the foundation on which Ismaʿili law could then be built. Hence, his first efforts were directed to the collection and classification of legal *ḥadīth*s from the family of the Prophet from all the available sources. Nuʿmān continued his work on jurisprudence by making several abridgments of the *Īḍāḥ*. Unfortunately, we do not have the sources to attempt an exact chronology and dating of his works. However, on the basis of internal evidence, cross references in his own works, and prefatory remarks in some of his works, we can attempt to date a large number of his works. Moreover, with regard to his works on jurisprudence, beginning with the *Īḍāḥ* and culminating in the *Daʿāʾim*, we can also discern certain developments in his thought and doctrine. Based on this information, it seems that the *Kitāb al-akhbār* (or *al-Ikhbār*) was the next. It is an abridgment of the first in 300 folios.[29] In it, Nuʿmān reports both the generally accepted and the conflicting doctrines on a given point of law and then gives his own preference for what he regards as reliable. Although the *ḥadīth*s are cited without *isnād*s they are graded roughly into the following scale: *aṣaḥḥ* (most authentic), *athbat* (most confirmed), *aslam* (with sound *isnād*s), *ashhar* and *akthar* (widely related), *shādhdh* (rare), *afsar* (interpretive) and *mujmal* (concise). It is all done, in the words of Lokhandwalla, in the manner of a *muḥaddith* (traditionist).[30] As the conflicting viewpoints are put together, it seems that at this stage there is some hesitation on Nuʿmān's part for the selection of a particular doctrine, hence he tries to eliminate the conflict by explanation.

Next to follow was another abridgment entitled *Mukhtaṣar al-īḍāḥ*.[31] Though no longer extant, it seems to have contained the *ḥadīth*s accepted as firmly established (*thābit*). This was the next step taken by Nuʿmān in consolidating the legal practices and moving towards codification of Ismaʿili jurisprudence. *Al-Urjūza al-muntakhaba* (or *al-Muntakhaba*) was another summary in verse form. Nuʿmān states in the introduction that he versified it to make it easy for the students to memorize it.[32] The *Kitāb al-iqtiṣār* was yet another abridgment containing mainly the firmly established doctrine of the *ahl al-bayt*. In it, the *isnād* is omitted and instead all the chapters begin with 'it has been narrated to us on the authority of the family of the Prophet'. The *Muntakhaba*, which was composed during the reign of al-Qāʾim (as stated in the introduction), refers to the *Īḍāḥ* and alludes to earlier abridgments. In the same way in the preface to his *Kitāb al-iqtiṣār*, Nuʿmān refers to the *Īḍāḥ*, *Akhbār*, and the *Muntakhaba*. All the aforecited legal compendia were semi-official, therefore in each of his later works Nuʿmān refers to his earlier compositions.

Thus it is clear that already at the time of his appointment to the highest judicial office, Nuʿmān had several legal compendia to his credit, in addition to a comprehensive work on Ismaʿili jurisprudence. Moreover, we have the testimony of al-Ustādh Jawdhar, a high ranking official and a confidant of the first four Fatimid caliphs, that the *Īḍāḥ* was one of the most highly treasured books of al-Manṣūr and that the caliph had asked Jawdhar for its safe keeping with other precious books. Al-Manṣūr even advised the latter that he should transcribe a copy for his own benefit and use.[33]

Next came the *Kitāb al-ikhtiṣār li-ṣaḥīḥ al-āthār ʿan al-aʾimmat al-aṭhār* (or *Mukhtaṣar al-āthār* or *Ikhtiṣār al-āthār*), composed before 348/959 during the reign of al-Muʿizz, which enjoys more or less equal respect with the *Daʿāʾim* as an authoritative work on Ismaʿili law. Nuʿmān explains the reason for its composition by stating that he was asked by the *qāḍī*s, governors, and students to compile a concise work, neither too comprehensive nor too condensed, easy to handle and memorize, on jurisprudence based on the authority of the family of the Prophet. He states that not only did he consult the caliph regularly while composing this work but the caliph himself also scrutinized the whole book, made several corrections and suggested its title.[34] Al-Muʿizz then permitted him to relate the whole book on his authority and that of his forefathers. In it the *ḥadīth*s are generally reported without the *isnād*s. The *Ikhtiṣār* was thus a step forward in the propagation and promulgation of the Ismaʿili law.[35]

Before proceeding further, it is appropriate to cite an example to illustrate that Nuʿmān, from the time he embarked on his ambitious *Īḍāḥ*, was gradually moving closer to the codification of Ismaʿili law. For instance, on the subject of ritual purity (*ṭahāra*) one outstanding disagreement between the Sunni schools of jurisprudence and the Shiʿa is whether the feet are to be washed (*ghasl*) or to be slightly rubbed with water by the fingers (*masḥ*).[36] The Sunni schools, with the exception of the Ẓāhirī school, opted for *ghasl* on the strength of some *ḥadīth*s from the Prophet and by giving the relevant verse of the Qur'an a slightly different reading.[37] The Shiʿis, on the other hand, stuck to the logical reading of the Qur'anic verse, and with support from the *ḥadīth*s from the Prophet and the imams chose *masḥ*. In the *Akhbār*, Nuʿmān relates both the Sunni and Shiʿi views and approves of both. In a conciliatory tone he even states that *masḥ* may be performed, but that washing is better.[38] In the *Muntakhaba* he states that *masḥ* is obligatory but *ghasl* is *jāmiʿ* (agreed upon). In the *Iqtiṣār*, he is still not certain, because he states that the feet should be wiped, but it is better to wash them [afterwards].[39] In the *Ikhtiṣār*, which was given official recognition by al-Muʿizz, in contrast to his earlier works, a definite stand is taken by Nuʿmān. It doctrinally supports *masḥ* with supporting evidences from the Qur'an (V:6) and *ḥadīth*.[40]

Another major change relates to the fact that all the previous works commence with the chapter on ritual purity, but the *Ikhtiṣār* starts with a chapter on *ʿilm* (knowledge) and its authoritative source.[41] Thus it becomes clear that law and theology should be taken from the rightful imams from the family of the Prophet. The theory of the imamate, as will be seen below, is the key for understanding all the Shiʿi religious formulations. The importance of this work could be judged from the fact that three successive caliphs, al-Muʿizz, al-ʿAzīz and al-Ḥākim permitted Nuʿmān's son ʿAlī and his grandson al-Ḥusayn b. ʿAlī to read and dictate it to those who came to them for religious instruction. The extant text is in the recension of Nuʿmān's grandson al-Ḥusayn b. ʿAlī, who obtained the *ijāza* (permission to teach and transmit) from his father ʿAlī, who in turn had read it with his father Nuʿmān in 348/959, who then permitted him to relate it on his authority.[42] It is rightfully considered by the Ismaʿilis as the second most reliable work on Ismaʿili law after the *Daʿāʾim*.[43]

In addition to his legal texts Nuʿmān composed several works refuting the views of the Sunni schools and their founders, especially Mālik, Abū Ḥanīfa, and Shāfiʿī, and defending his own views.[44] Unfortunately, none of these works, with the exception of the *Risāla dhāt al-bayān fiʾl-radd ʿalā Ibn Qutayba* and the *Kitāb ikhtilāf uṣūl al-madhāhib*, dealing with the principles of Islamic law, have survived.[45] Ibn Ḥajar states that the latter was taught by Nuʿmān's grandson ʿAbd al-ʿAzīz b. Muḥammad in the Jāmiʿ Mosque with the permission of al-Ḥākim, and copies of it have come down to us in the recension of this grandson of Nuʿmān. As it is an important work, pertinent to the subject and composed before the *Daʿāʾim*,[46] a brief review of it would be useful.

According to the *Ikhtilāf*, the principles of jurisprudence (or the authorities) are: the Qurʾan, the *sunna* of the Prophet, the decisions of the imams from the family of the Prophet, and the ruling imam.[47] In his *Iqtiṣār* and *Ikhtiṣār* Nuʿmān proposed a similar theory and advised the judges not to base their decisions on *raʾy* (individual judgement), *qiyās* (analogical deduction), or *istiḥsān* (discretionary preferences). He states that the judge should decide according to the Book of God, and if he does not find it in the Book, he should then seek it in the firmly established practices (*al-thābit*, i.e., the *sunna*) of the Prophet and the imams from his progeny. If he fails to find the matter in the preceding sources, then he should refer it to the imam.[48] It seems that in matters of substantive law, the authorities were confined to Jaʿfar al-Ṣādiq and his predecessors, but for the day-to-day running of the state and other matters, the ultimate authority was the ruling imam. For this reason earlier imams are not mentioned as authorities.

Ismaʿili law evolved at a time when other schools were attaining maturity. With the rising tide of the *muḥaddithūn* after Shāfiʿī, the emphasis on the Qur'an mounted and the concept of *sunna*, which was hitherto used to indicate the practice of the community, was gradually steered towards the concept of the *sunna* of the Prophet, and in the absence of the latter to the *sunna* of the Prophet's Companions. Out of the notions of the agreed practice of the local communities of the ancient schools of law in Medina and Kūfa and the consensus (*ijmāʿ*) of their scholars, there were attempts to promote the consensus of the whole community and that of all the *fuqahā'*. Hence, when Nuʿmān was writing, the general theory of Islamic jurisprudence was in the process of veering around the well-defined four sources of law, viz., the Qur'an, the *sunna* of the Prophet, *ijmāʿ* and *qiyās*/*ijtihād* (the method of reasoning by analogy).[49] This development had put a check on the growth of law. It not only curtailed but even prohibited the use of *ra'y*, so widely employed in the ancient schools of Kūfa and Medina, which led to the development of new concepts, such as *istidlāl*,[50] *naẓar* or *ʿaql*,[51] *istiḥsān* and *istiṣlāḥ*.[52]

It was at this time that the Shiʿi schools grew. Parallel to the Shiʿi doctrine of the imamate, the Sunni version of the *sunna* of the rightly guided caliphs and the Companions of the Prophet emerged. The Zaydīs, being the most moderate of the Shiʿa, preserved tendencies and characteristics of both the Sunni and Shiʿi schools. Thus, maintaining the pre-eminence of the imamate in the family of the Prophet, most of the Zaydīs except the Jārūdiyya also accepted the first three rightly guided caliphs as legitimate rulers and adopted all four sources of Islamic jurisprudence.[53] As for the Imāmīs, because of the occultation (*ghayba*) of their twelfth imam, the imam ceased to be the active source of law. I have argued elsewhere that even before the *ghayba*, the *de facto* authority of the *ʿulamā'*/*fuqahā'* had already emerged among the Imāmīs.[54] During the pre-*ghayba* period, the use of *ra'y, qiyās*, and *ijtihād* was prohibited; however, later, as the imam had gone into occultation and had ceased to contribute towards the growth of law, they had to accept the Sunni theory with certain Shiʿi modifications. For this reason, *ijmāʿ* and *ijtihād* crept into the Imāmī theory as sources of law.[55]

The Ismaʿilis, on the other hand, when their legal theories evolved, were in a more convenient and accommodating position. With the establishment of the Fatimid caliphate in North Africa, the doctrine of the imamate was transformed into a living organism, hence the theory of law had to be approached differently.[56] For this reason, the *ijmāʿ* and *ijtihād*,[57] and its substitutes, such as *istidlāl*, *naẓar* or *ʿaql*, *istiḥsān* and *istiṣlāḥ*, were rejected as sources of law. The authority of the infallible and divinely guided imam, therefore, became, after the Qur'an and the *sunna*, the third and decisive source. In effect, as it will be seen below, the authority of the imam was a projection of the *sunna* of the Prophet. In theory, the imam's authority was unlimited, but in practice his authority was circumscribed by the social conventions of the time. For this reason the theory remained a theory, and the Ismaʿili substantive law, especially the *muʿāmalāt* (worldly affairs or bilateral contracts), developed on its own under unavoidable socio-economic pressures.

The officially promulgated Fatimid code, however, came through the composition of the *Daʿāʾim*, which was commissioned by al-Muʿizz. Hence, Nuʿmān neither mentions its author nor refers to his previous works in it, as he does in his earlier works.[58] It was the culmination of Nuʿmān's efforts after more than thirty years. Describing the circumstances under which Nuʿmān was asked to compose it, Idrīs states that once at the court there was a large gathering of the *dāʿī*s when the conversation turned to the fabrication of *ḥadīth* and differences of opinions among the Muslims which had led to the division of Islam into various sects. Al-Muʿizz remembered the *ḥadīth* of the Prophet which stated that his community would be divided and will follow the footsteps of the previous communities. The caliph then recalled another *ḥadīth* wherein the Prophet is stated to have said that when harmful innovations multiply in my community, it was incumbent upon the *ʿālim* (learned person) to manifest his learning. Al-Muʿizz then turning to Nuʿmān said: 'You, O Nuʿmān, are the one meant by it in these times.' The caliph then expounded the principles (*aṣṣala lahu uṣūlahu*), deduced the branches (*farraʿa lahu furūʿahu*), related to him the authentic *ḥadīth*s of the Prophet on the authority of his forefathers, and commissioned its composition. It is further stated that it was revised by al-Muʿizz, chapter by chapter and section by section, confirming what was firmly established and authentic, polishing its rough edges, and filling the gaps.[59]

Although there is no internal evidence for determining the exact date of the *Daʿāʾim*'s composition, I am inclined to assume that it was composed around 349/960, because of Ibn ʿIdhārī's earlier report that the caliph al-Muʿizz promulgated important instructions to the imams and muezzins of the mosques in the same year.[60] Ibn ʿIdhārī had already reported major changes introduced by al-Shīʿī, hence the issuance of a royal decree by al-Muʿizz, reiterating Shiʿi Ismaʿili rites, was a clear indication of a major change in the state's policy. Perhaps the Sunni historians did not realize the full import of this event of proclaiming the *Daʿāʾim* as the official code of the Fatimid state. All the changes reported by Ibn ʿIdhārī are ascertained by the *Daʿāʾim*.[61] Nuʿmān himself states that al-Muʿizz urged people to read, copy and study the *Daʿāʾim*. He further reports that it was read in the weekly gatherings of the *majālis al-ḥikma* in the palace.[62]

Al-Muʿizz further told Nuʿmān on the authority of Jaʿfar al-Ṣādiq that Islam was founded on seven pillars, viz., *walāya* (devotion to the imam), *ṭahāra*, *ṣalāt*, *zakāt* (alms giving, welfare tax), *ṣawm* (fasting in the month of Ramaḍān), *ḥajj* (pilgrimage to Mecca) and *jihād* (holy war). Nuʿmān thus added two more pillars to the generally accepted five: the *walāya* and *ṭahāra*. The *Ikhtiṣār* had prepared the ground for the introduction of the corner-stone of the Ismaʿili faith, *al-walāya*, elaborated in the *Daʿāʾim*, which became an inseparable part of the faith. It embodies the doctrine of the imamate which lies at the basis of Shiʿism and was transformed into a dynamic principle after the establishment of the Fatimid caliphate. It is regarded as the highest and the noblest of the seven pillars, without which no human acts of devotion and worship are acceptable to God. It is worth noting that unlike with the Ismaʿilis, the doctrine of the imamate did not become part of the Imāmī legal textbooks.[63] The *Daʿāʾim* was the first juristic text to give a legalistic place to *al-walāya*. For the Fatimids, it was not merely a religious belief but the basis of their claim to the political leadership of the Muslim community (*umma*). This chapter along with that on the *jihād*, which includes the *ʿahd* dealing with the ruler's conduct with his subjects and the good qualities and practices that he should observe, ascribed to ʿAlī,[64] represents the Ismaʿili theory of the state. For this reason Wadād al-Qāḍī rightly states that the *Daʿāʾim* represents not only the paramount divine constitution of the Fatimid state but also its civil constitution.[65] For the Imāmīs, the doctrine of the imamate had no practical value, as their imam had gone into occultation, but to the Fatimids it was of the utmost importance, since their philosophical and esoteric doctrines revolved around it. The Sunni political theory of the caliphate was not yet formulated, and when it was, it never formed a part of their legal code. *Ṭahāra*, which implies both physical and spiritual purification, a necessary prelude and condition for the valid performance of prayers and certain other acts, was raised to the status of a pillar.

In the *Daʿāʾim*, Nuʿmān confines himself to the firmly established doctrine of the imams from the family of the Prophet as related to him by al-Muʿizz. The only authoritative sources of the law (*uṣūl al-fiqh*), accordingly, are the Qurʾan, the *sunna* of the Prophet, and the teachings of the imams. This change of attitude was evidently influenced by al-Muʿizz. Yet on the substantive level, the legal doctrine of the *Daʿāʾim* appears identical with the positions worked out in his *Īḍāḥ*. In the *Daʿāʾim*, he quotes a few *ḥadīth*s not found in the latter, but mostly in support of the same views. Only occasionally his doctrine seems to differ on minor points of detail. In spite of his promise to present only the doctrine of the imams, Nuʿmān does in a few places quote the views of the Zaydī ʿAlids as the basis of law in the *Daʿāʾim*.[66] The share of legal doctrine derived from Zaydī sources in the latter, according to Madelung, is much larger, but the bulk of the Zaydī material is hidden by the omission of the Zaydī *isnād*s for the *ḥadīth*s of the Prophet, ʿAlī, and other imams.[67] Madelung concludes his aforecited study by stating that the description of the legal doctrine of the *Īḍāḥ* as a compromise between Imāmī and Zaydī law is thus applicable to Ismaʿili *fiqh* in general.[68] It should also be noted that in spite of a strong Mālikī tinge of the Ismaʿili law in the *Daʿāʾim*, there are significant differences where the Ismaʿilis could not, for reasons of invalidating their political claims, agree with the Mālikī system.[69]

In a major point of difference with Imāmī law, the prohibition of temporary marriage (*mutʿa*) is admitted by Nuʿmān, and for it he relies on the *ḥadīth*s from the Imams ʿAlī and al-Ṣādiq, used also by the Zaydīs.[70] The authorities in the *Daʿāʾim* are confined to al-Ṣādiq for the simple reason that the latter and the preceding imams were accepted by the Sunnis as well as the Imāmīs as trustworthy authorities for *ḥadīth*. Besides, the Ismaʿili imams after al-Ṣādiq lived in a period of concealment, hence *ḥadīth*s from them did not exist. Al-Muqaddasī, who wrote his work around 375/985 and had perused the *Daʿāʾim*, states that in most of the *uṣūl* it agrees with the position of the Muʿtazila. He then divides the distinguishing features of the Fatimid *madhhab* into three categories: (i) practices about which the founders of the Sunni schools differ among themselves, such as the *qunūt* in the morning prayer, the pronouncement of the *basmala* loudly, and the *witr* prayer consisting of one *rakʿa*, (ii) revival of early Islamic practices, such as repeating the wording of the *iqāma* (the Umayyads intended it to be recited singly), and wearing of white clothes (the ʿAbbasids changed them to black); and (iii) practices which are uniquely Fatimid but not contrary to the founding imams, such as the *ḥayya ʿalā* in the *adhān*, determining the beginning of the month when the new moon could be sighted, the eclipse prayer consisting of five *rakaʿāt*, and two prostrations in every *rakʿa*.[71] The major differences between the *Daʿāʾim* and other schools of law have been pointed out by Fyzee, Strothmann and Brunschvig.[72]

It is fair to state that the juridical and legal system constructed in the *Daʿāʾim*, both for the use of the state and the Ismaʿili community, was oriented towards reconciliation of the Shiʿi Ismaʿili doctrine with that of the Sunni Mālikī *madhhab* of North Africa. The points of doctrinal differences between the two, leaving aside the first chapter on the *walāya*, are therefore not very flagrant. Compared to other *bāṭinī* (esoteric) works, the theory of the imamate presented in the *Daʿāʾim*, without its philosophical and esoteric embellishments, is very judicious, logical, and scrupulously constructed from Qurʾanic verses and Prophetic *ḥadīth*, with compelling interpretations and edifying reports of the imams.[73] With the compilation of the *Daʿāʾim*, Nuʿmān completed his task as the official *faqīh* by formulating a juridical and doctrinal system adaptable to the universalist claims of the Fatimids. It also explains why al-Muʿizz took such a keen interest in the works of Nuʿmān. It is, therefore, not surprising that the *Daʿāʾim* is considered by the Mustaʿlī-Ṭayyibīs as the greatest authority on Ismaʿili law and has until today remained a source of supreme authority in legal matters.

Our study of Nuʿmān would be incomplete without a few words as to how he conceives of the Qurʾan and the *sunna* as theoretical sources of law. Although the historical development of Islamic law was not totally dependent on the Qurʾan and it did include much of the Arab customary law,[74] with the rising tide of Islamicization the importance of both the Qurʾan and the *sunna* were accentuated. This led to the differences of opinion as to the relative importance of each, and the superiority of one over the other. Some refused to accept the *ḥadīth* of the Prophet on grounds of both the absolute authority of the Qurʾan and uncertainty in the reliability of the *ḥadīth*. This group recognized the sole authority of the Qurʾan with the right of interpretation.[75] Nuʿmān, building on those foundations, takes certain verses together and argues that the Qurʾan contains guidance for everything, but at the same time it needs correct interpretation.[76] The Qurʾan (IV:59, 83; XVI:43) also commands the Muslims to obey and refer their [disputes] to 'those who hold the authority' (*uliʾl-amr*) and if they fail to understand they are commanded to ask 'those who possess the message' (*ahl al-dhikr*). With additional evidence from the *ḥadīth*, which puts the imams from the progeny of the Prophet on a par with the Qurʾan,[77] Nuʿmān identifies the *uliʾl-amr* and the *ahl al-dhikr* as the imams. It is thus the right to the interpretation of the Qur'an which is reserved for the imams. In Fatimid times this prerogative could have been used by the imams to modify the laws, but it was difficult to use it for various reasons, and the interpretation of the Qur'an was confined to validating their right to rule the Muslim community, and the emphasis was placed on Qur'anic evidence for the imamate.[78]

Since al-Shāfiʿī provided Qur'anic sanctions for the acceptance of the Prophet's *sunna* with its three-fold definition,[79] by the time of Ibn Ḥanbal the *sunna* came to occupy an equal status with the Qur'an; to some, it could even abrogate the Qur'an. When Nuʿmān was writing Ismaʿili law books, the *muḥaddithūn* held the field, although all the problems connected with the reliability of *ḥadīth* and standards of its acceptance had not been finally settled.[80] Thus, we find Nuʿmān's law books taking the shape of works on *ḥadīth*, like al-Kulaynī's *al-Kāfī*. Hence every chapter of the *Daʿāʾim* opens with the relevant verse of the Qur'an, followed by what the Prophet said or did in the matter under discussion, and the decisions of the imams to Jaʿfar al-Ṣādiq. The *Daʿāʾim* contains approximately five hundred *ḥadīth*s from the Prophet, a very small number compared to Sunni works. In the *Daʿāʾim*, the *sunna* is generally assigned an interpretative and explanatory role with reference to the Qur'an.[81] At times, Nuʿmān exhorts the faithful to follow the *sunna* of the Prophet, mostly where there is a difference of opinion between the Sunnis and the Ismaʿilis. The *sunna* thus, in the *Daʿāʾim*, becomes the *sunna* accepted by the Ismaʿilis. In some cases, Nuʿmān uses the *sunna* of the Prophet to put a stamp of final authority on disputed doctrines, such as wiping one's feet in the ritual purity and *qunūt* during the Friday prayers.

For Nuʿmān the criterion for the acceptance of the *sunna* of the Prophet in matters of difference was its emanation from the imams. When there were agreements, the *ḥadīth*s of the Sunnis came in handy as complementary evidence for their own doctrine. This attitude of the Ismaʿilis towards the *sunna* of the Prophet spared them the laborious task of *ḥadīth* collection and the methods of determining the credibility of the narrators, etc., as the Sunnis and other Shiʿi schools had done. The analysis of the *isnād*s used by Nuʿmān cuts across the factional confinements, and the Sunni, Imāmī, and Zaydī *isnād*s were used for their own purposes. Of course, the Imāmī sources were more advantageous and effective in matters of dogma and belief, hence it is incorrect to characterize Ismaʿili law simply as a compromise between Imāmī and Zaydī law.

After the conquest of Egypt and the transfer of the seat of the Fatimid state from Manṣūriyya in North Africa to Cairo, Nuʿmān, who was then probably in his seventies, accompanied the caliph in his capacity as the chief judicial official (*kāna yatawallā qaḍāʾ al-jaysh*). As Jawhar had confirmed Abū Ṭāhir al-Dhuhlī in his office as the chief judge of Egypt at the time of its conquest, al-Muʿizz honoured that agreement but asked Abū Ṭāhir to consult Nuʿmān before giving his legal opinion. Nuʿmān was therefore appointed to look into the *maẓālim* cases. He died at the end of Jumādā II (i.e., on the 29th according to the Ismaʿili calendar based on fixed astronomical calculation) in 363/27 March 974, and the funeral prayers were led by the caliph al-Muʿizz.[82]

After Nuʿmān, there was no significant development in Ismaʿili law. Although his sons and grandsons held the office of chief judge of the Fatimid empire in Cairo for approximately half a century, there is no information about their legal writings except that they taught Nuʿmān's works.[83] Ibn Killis (d. 380/991), who was appointed by al-ʿAzīz as his vizier in 367/977 and had his own entourage of scholars, jurists, and poets, wrote a legal treatise based on the pronouncements of al-Muʿizz and al-ʿAzīz.[84] It is known by various titles: *Muṣannaf al-wazīr*, *Mukhtaṣar al-muṣannaf*, *Mukhtaṣar al-wazīr* and *al-Risāla al-wazīriyya*. Idrīs states that it begins with *ṭahāra* followed by the rest of the chapters of *fiqh* wherein Ibn Killis walked in the steps of Nuʿmān. Al-Maqrīzī reports that it was used as a source for giving decisions and that in 416/1025 when the caliph al-Ẓāhir expelled the Mālikī *fuqahāʾ* from Egypt, he ordered that whoever memorized the *Daʿāʾim* and the *Mukhtaṣar al-wazīr* would be rewarded.[85] Idrīs, on the other end, warns that only those matters which agree with the *Daʿāʾim* are to be relied upon, but in matters of disagreement with the *Daʿāʾim* the latter and the *Mukhtaṣar al-āthār* are to be given preference over the *Mukhtaṣar al-wazīr*.[86]

From the Yemenite period among the Mustaʿlī-Ṭayyibī Ismaʿilis, who inherited the Fatimid legacy, there is hardly a book worth mentioning on law.[87] But in India the works of Nuʿmān were glossed, especially by the eminent jurist Amīnjī b. Jalāl (d. 1010/1602).[88] His works deserve to be critically edited because they contain extensive excerpts from the works of Nuʿmān and Ibn Killis' *Muṣannaf al-wazīr* which is now considered lost. Moreover, Amīnjī poses some questions directly related to socio-economic life of the community in western India. His books are highly esteemed by the Dāʾūdī Bohras and are ranked next to Nuʿmān's works in authority. During the nineteenth century, the last representative of Ismaʿili legal tradition was Ibrāhīm al-Sayfī. His *Kitāb al-najāḥ fī maʿrifat aḥkām al-nikāḥ*, dealing with socio-economic, moral, and legal aspects of marriage, is the most comprehensive work on the subject based on the works of Nuʿmān.[89]

The Mustaʿlī-Ṭayyibī community of the Yemen and India had a precarious existence, living most of the time under Sunni persecution, and hence the *Daʿāʾim* served their basic needs. This small Ṭayyibī community was time and again further subdivided on the question of succession. Moreover, they live in the period of concealment (*dawr al-satr*) of their imams and the *dāʿī*, who heads the *daʿwa* and leads the community, does not have the wide-ranging authority of the imam. Too much emphasis on the *bāṭinī* (esoteric) sciences, as opposed to the *ẓāhirī* (exoteric, especially the Qurʾan and the *sharīʿa*) sciences, also contributed its share to the neglect of law. For these reasons even today the *Daʿāʾim* reigns supreme in the community and is applied by the courts in the Indo-Pakistan subcontinent in personal and family matters as the Ismaʿili law manual.[90] During the last century, in most of the Muslim countries a vast number of modifications and reforms have been introduced even in those spheres of life where the *sharīʿa* officially prevails. Many educated and progressive members of the community are themselves conscious of the need for certain reforms, but unfortunately the Bohra religious establishment, for its own selfish motives, remains adamant to the changing needs of the society. Thus we can conclude that Ismaʿili law began with Nuʿmān and ended with him. Before him, there was no independent Ismaʿili law and what came after him was nothing but repetition and restatement.

NOTES

I would like to thank my student Megan Reid and my colleague Michael Morony for their comments on the final draft of this essay.

1 See F. Daftary, *The Ismāʿīlīs: Their History and Doctrines* (Cambridge, 1990), pp. 136–143; and his 'The Earliest Ismāʿīlīs', *Arabica*, 38 (1991), pp. 242–245, and H. Halm, *Kosmologie und Heilslehre der frühen Ismāʿīlīya* (Wiesbaden, 1978); older sources are listed therein.

2 In the *Kitāb al-ḥawāshī* (Ms. Mullā Qurbān Ḥusayn Godhrawala Collection, vols. 1–2), ascribed to Amīnjī b. Jalāl who died in 1010/1602 (see Poonawala, *Biobibliography of Ismāʿīlī Literature*, Malibu, Calif., 1977, p. 185; hereafter cited as Poonawala), two opinions of Jaʿfar b. Manṣūr al-Yaman differing from those expressed by al-Qāḍī al-Nuʿmān in his *Daʿāʾim al-Islām*, ed. A. A. A. Fyzee (3rd edn, Cairo, 1969), vol. 1, and (2nd edn, Cairo, 1965), vol. 2, are cited:

i. The number of *rakaʿāt* for the *sunna* prayers, set forth by Jaʿfar, are in agreement with those of the Ḥanafī school and in contrast with those adopted by Nuʿmān.

The author of the *Kitāb al-ḥawāshī* writes that it is stated in the *Kitāb al-shawāhid wa'l-bayān* [by Jaʿfar b. Manṣūr al-Yaman, see Poonawala, p. 71] that one should offer ten *rakaʿāt* for the *ẓuhr*, eight *rakaʿāt* for the *ʿaṣr*, five *rakaʿāt* for the *maghrib*, and ten *rakaʿāt* for the *ʿishāʾ* prayers. The question is then posed as to which authority one should follow. The answer provided by the then *dāʿī* is that what is stated in the *Daʿāʾim* should be relied upon. I was unable to locate this reference in the *Kitāb al-shawāhid*, Ms. Fyzee Collection, no. 24; see M. Goriawala, *A Descriptive Catalogue of the Fyzee Collection of Ismaili Manuscripts* (Bombay, 1965), p. 16. See Nuʿmān, *Daʿāʾim*, vol. 1, pp. 211–212 and his *Kitāb al-iqtiṣār*, ed. M. W. Mirza (Damascus, 1957), p. 35, wherein the *sunna* prayers are specified and listed as thirty-four *rakaʿāt*, twice the number of the *farīḍa* prayers.

ii. The author of the *Kitāb al-ḥawāshī* writes that it is stated by Jaʿfar in his book entitled *Kitāb al-rushd wa'l-hidāya* that if a Muslim contracts over four marriages, it invalidates not only the fifth but also all the previous four marriages. This view is repudiated in the answer given by the then *dāʿī* stating that it invalidates only the fifth. See *Daʿāʾim*, vol. 2, p. 235 n. 4, citing the aforecited passage from the *Kitāb al-rushd*. It should be noted that this book, also ascribed to Jaʿfar's father Manṣūr al-Yaman (Poonawala, p. 34), belonged to the early period and its extant fragments are edited by M. Kāmil Ḥusayn under the title of *Fragments of the Kitābu'r-rushd wa'l-hidāyat*, in *Collectanea*: Vol. 1 (Leiden, 1948), pp. 185–213. The above passage is not found in the edited fragments, which implies that the greater portion of the book was extant and available to Amīnjī. It is quite possible that a complete copy still exists in the private collections of the community, especially that of the head of the Bohra community. It is reported that the autograph copy of the *Muntakhaba* was extant in the Yemen until the beginning of the 9th/15th century; see Poonawala, p. 53.

These differences, although minor, indicate that Ismaʿili law was not formulated before the establishment of the Fatimid dynasty. S. T. Lokhandwalla, 'The Origins of Ismāʿīlī Law' (D. Phil. thesis, Oxford University, 1951), p. 21, after citing the above examples, but without going into further details, states that both Abū Ḥātim al-Rāzī and Jaʿfar b. Manṣūr al-Yaman betray the eastern influences of the Ḥanafī school.

3 Ibn ʿIdhārī, *al-Bayān al-mughrib*, ed. G. S. Colin and E. Lévi-Provençal (New edn, Leiden, 1948–1951), vol. 1, pp. 151, 159, 173. The Mālikī historian ʿAbd Allāh b. Muḥammad al-Mālikī (d. ca. 438/1046–1047), *Riyāḍ al-nufūs fī ṭabaqāt ʿulamāʾ al-Qayrawān wa-Ifrīqiya*, ed. Bashīr al-Bakkūsh (Beirut, 1983), vol. 2, pp. 41, 55–56, 60–62, also reports that the above changes were introduced by al-Marwazī after assuming the office of *qaḍāʾ Ifrīqiya*. He further states that al-Marwazī was known for his Shiʿi proclivity and had embraced the call of Abū ʿAbd Allāh al-Shīʿī and was attached to him. He also reports a long debate between al-Marwazī and the Mālikī jurists about the *tarāwīḥ* prayers. Al-Qāḍī al-Nuʿmān (*Iftitāḥ al-daʿwa*, ed. F. al-Dashrāwī, Tunis, 1975, p. 247), refers to al-Marwazī as a man 'with long Shiʿi standing and with insight in the jurisprudence related on the authority of the imams'. Al-Marwazī's son Abū Jaʿfar Aḥmad served al-Qāʾim and al-Manṣūr as a *qāḍī*; see al-Jawdharī, *Sīrat al-ustādh Jawdhar*, ed. M. K. Ḥusayn and M. ʿA. Shaʿīra (Cairo, 1954), p. 53; al-Maqrīzī, *Ittiʿāẓ al-ḥunafāʾ*, ed. Jamāl al-Dīn al-Shayyāl (Cairo, 1967), vol. 1, pp. 88–89, and Ibn Khallikān, *Wafayāt al-aʿyān*, ed. Iḥsān ʿAbbās (Beirut, 1968),

vol. 1, p. 234. Al-Maqrīzī (*al-Khiṭaṭ*, Būlāq, 1270/1853–1854, vol. 2, pp. 270, 340; *Ittiʿāẓ*, vol. 1, pp. 117, 120, 230), reports that after his conquest of Egypt, Jawhar introduced the same changes.

The addition of *ḥayya ʿalā khayr al-ʿamal* in the *adhān*, and invoking blessings on ʿAlī, Fāṭima, al-Ḥasan and al-Ḥusayn in the Friday sermon is reported by Nuʿmān, *Iftitāḥ al-daʿwa*, pp. 249, 250, 293, and Idrīs ʿImād al-Dīn, *ʿUyūn al-akhbār*, vol. 5, ed. M. Ghālib (Beirut, 1975), pp. 87, 109. For the Sunni practices on the aforecited issues, see ʿAbd al-Raḥmān al-Jazīrī, *Kitāb al-fiqh ʿalā al-madhāhib al-arbaʿa*, (2nd edn, Cairo, [1964]), vol. 1, pp. 250, 257, 312, 340, 394, and Th. Juynboll, 'Adhān', EI2, vol. 1, pp. 187–188.

4 Al-Qāḍī al-Nuʿmān, *Kitāb al-majālis waʾl-musāyarāt*, ed. al-Ḥabīb al-Faqī et al. (Tunis, 1978), p. 97.

5 Ibn ʿIdhārī, *al-Bayān*, vol. 1, p. 223.

6 Ibn Ḥammād, *Akhbār mulūk Banī ʿUbayd*, ed. and tr. M. Vonderheyden (Algiers–Paris, 1927) text pp. 15–16, translation pp. 29–30. Most of the aforecited Shiʿi features are to be found in the earliest Shiʿi works on law ascribed to Zayd b. ʿAlī (*Musnad al-Imām Zayd*, Beirut, 1966) and ʿAlī al-Riḍā (*al-Fiqh al-mansūb liʾl-Imām al-Riḍā*, or *Fiqh al-Riḍā*, Beirut, 1990). J. Schacht (*The Origins of Muhammadan Jurisprudence*, Oxford, 1950, pp. 262 ff.), however, is of the opinion that those works are spurious and that authentic legal Shiʿi literature began only towards the end of the third century *AH*. He further states that Shiʿi law became distinguished from that of the Sunni schools by a limited number of differences, such as *qunūt*, *masḥ ʿalā ʾl-khuffayn*, *umm al-walad*, and *mutʿa*, which in themselves were not necessarily either Sunni or Shiʿi.

7 Al-Maqrīzī, *Ittiʿāẓ*, vol. 1, pp. 119, 120, 121, 138, 146, and *al-Khiṭaṭ*, vol. 1, p. 451 and vol. 2, p. 270. Ibn Ḥajar al-ʿAsqalānī (*Rafʿ al-iṣr ʿan quḍāt Miṣr*, ed. R. Guest in *The Governors and Judges of Egypt*, Leiden, 1912, p. 584), states that after his conquest of Egypt, Jawhar reinstated Abū Ṭāhir al-Dhuhlī in his position as *qāḍī al-quḍāt* on the condition that he should decide the cases of inheritance and divorce according to the *madhhab* of the *ahl al-bayt*. Idrīs (*ʿUyūn al-akhbār*, vol. 6, ed. M. Ghālib, 2nd edn, Beirut, 1984, pp. 162–166, 170), reports that most of the changes were implemented a few months after the conquest. The fixed calendar was likewise not imposed on the people but it was gradually adopted by them.

8 See the following works by Nuʿmān: *al-Iqtiṣār*, p. 46; *Muntakhaba* (Ms. Mullā Qurbān Ḥusayn Godhrawala Collection) in *bāb al-dukhūl fiʾl-ṣawm*; *Mukhtaṣar al-āthār*, (Ms. Mullā Qurbān Ḥusayn Godhrawala Collection) in *dhikr ibtidāʾ al-ṣawm*, and his *Daʿāʾim*, vol. 1, pp. 278–279. For the Sunni point of view see al-Jazīrī, *Kitāb al-fiqh*, vol. 1, pp. 548 ff.

9 Muḥammad b. Ḥārith al-Khushanī, *Kitāb ṭabaqāt ʿulamāʾ Ifrīqiya*, ed. M. Ben Cheneb [with *Kitāb ṭabaqāt ʿulamāʾ Ifrīqiya* of Abu'l-ʿArab], (Paris, 1915–1920), vol. 1, pp. 239–240. He reports that al-Marwazī was from Qayrawān. It should be noted that all the names of the Fatimid judges of Qayrawān appear to be Maghribī. Although the Mālikī *madhhab* was dominant in the Maghrib, especially in Qayrawān, Shiʿism was not unknown there before the rise of Abū ʿAbd Allāh al-Shīʿī to power. See, for instance, W. Madelung, 'Some Notes on Non-Ismāʿīlī Shiism in the Maghrib', *Studia Islamica*, 44 (1976), pp. 87–97. Al-Khushanī, (*Kitāb ṭabaqāt*, pp. 223–226), himself lists seventeen scholars from Qayrawān (six Mālikīs and eleven Ḥanafīs, most of the latter served as judges) who had embraced Ismaʿilism. R. Brunschvig, 'Un aspect de la

littérature historico-géographique de l'Islam', in *Mélanges Gaudefroy-Demombynes* (Cairo, 1935–1945), vol. 1, pp. 150–151, states that although al-Khushanī gives interesting information on the Fatimids, he is far from being impartial and paints a gloomy picture of the *ʿulamāʾ* who remained behind in Qayrawān. Another Mālikī author, ʿAbd al-Raḥmān al-Dabbāgh, *Maʿālim al-īmān fī maʿrifat ahl al-Qayrawān* (Tunis, 1320/1902) vol. 3, pp. 6, 25, 53, 55, 60, reports that several Ḥanafī and Mālikī *fuqahāʾ* accepted to be judges during the early years of Fatimid rule.

10 Poonawala, pp. 34–35.

11 He was also a *dāʿī*, an eloquent speaker, and was in charge of instructing women (*ʿindahu daʿwat al-nisāʾ*) on Ismaʿili doctrines, see Idrīs, *ʿUyūn*, vol. 5, pp. 137–138; Ibn Ḥammād, *Akhbār*, p. 17; Ismāʿīl b. ʿAbd al-Rasūl al-Majdūʿ, *Fihrist*, ed. ʿA. N. Munzavī (Tehran, 1966), p. 74. Al-Khushanī, *Kitāb ṭabaqāt*, vol. 1, p. 241, states that Aflaḥ b. Hārūn, a Kutāmī *shaykh*, was appointed *qāḍī* of Raqqāda by al-Shīʿī after his entry into Qayrawān and was later moved to Mahdiyya by al-Mahdī. Wadād al-Qāḍī, 'An Early Fāṭimid Political Document', *Studia Islamica*, 48 (1978), pp. 105 ff., speculates that al-Malūsī was the author of the *ʿahd* ascribed to ʿAlī in the *kitāb al-jihād* of Nuʿmān's *Daʿāʾim*.

12 Ibn al-Nadīm, *Kitāb al-fihrist*, ed. M. R. Tajaddud (Tehran, 1971), p. 240; English trans., *The Fihrist of al-Nadīm*, tr. B. Dodge (New York, 1970), vol. 1, p. 472. See also Poonawala, pp. 36–39, 40–43.

13 The silence of Ismaʿili sources could partly be explained by the fact that both al-Rāzī and al-Nasafī belonged to the dissident Qarāmiṭa group. However, their works on law, especially that of al-Rāzī, raise another question as to the nature of their relations with the Qarāmiṭa who believed in the doctrine of *taʿṭīl al-sharīʿa* (suspension of the religious obligations). For the split in the Ismaʿili movement, see F. Daftary, 'A Major Schism in the Early Ismāʿīlī Movement', *Studia Islamica*, 77 (1993), pp. 123–139.

14 Only a small portion of it was edited by Ḥusayn F. al-Hamdānī in two parts before he died; see al-Rāzī, *Kitāb al-zīna* (Cairo, 1956–1958). The section dealing with the Islamic sects is edited by ʿAbd Allāh Sallūm al-Sāmarrāʾī from a manuscript in the Iraqī Museum in Baghdad as the third part of the *Kitāb al-zīna* in his *al-Ghuluww waʾl-firaq al-ghāliya* (Baghdad, 1972), pp. 227–312. It should be noted that al-Rāzī's approach to the classification of the Islamic sects differs from other heresiographers and he also provides some new information. Unfortunately, he it totally silent about the Qarāmiṭa but speaks about *al-Ismāʿīliyya* as if he belonged to them.

15 It should be noted that al-Rāzī also rejects *mutʿa* marriage, stating that it was permitted in the beginning of Islam but was later prohibited by the Prophet. Unlike Nuʿmān in his *Daʿāʾim*, vol. 2, pp. 226, al-Rāzī elaborates the arguments of those (i.e., the Imāmīs) who consider it valid and refutes them linguistically.

16 Nuʿmān's role in the reform of the doctrine of the *imāma* by al-Muʿizz, especially the older teaching about Muḥammad b. Ismāʿīl and its esoteric implication, is beyond the scope of this essay. However, in the opinion of the present writer both the reform and Nuʿmān's role are overstated and taken out of their contexts by W. Madelung, 'Das Imamat in der frühen ismailitischen Lehre', *Der Islam*, 37 (1961), pp. 86 ff. See also Daftary, *The Ismāʿīlīs*, pp. 177 ff.

17 Nuʿmān, *Kitāb al-majālis*, p. 79, and Idrīs, *ʿUyūn*, vol. 5, p. 346. The above statement (*khadamtu al-Mahdī . . .*) implies that before exclusively serving the caliph from about the year 312/924, Nuʿmān must have entered into the service of the new state a

few years earlier, and after having won the caliph's confidence he must have been chosen to serve him.

I have pointed out elsewhere, 'A Reconsideration of al-Qāḍī al-Nuʿmān's *Madhhab*', BSOAS, 37 (1974), pp. 572–579 (see also F. Dachraoui, 'al-Nuʿmān', EI2, vol. 8, pp. 117–118) that most probably Nuʿmān was raised and educated as an Ismaʿili. The following two additional pieces of evidence corroborate my earlier contention. First, in his *Kitāb al-himma*, ed. M. K. Ḥusayn (Cairo, n.d.), p. 102, while discussing the question of intention and good works, Nuʿmān states: 'In my youth, when I was busy with the collection and transcription of books, I was admonished by an old man whose religious belief I did not share and whose assertion I did not accept.' The context in which this statement is made, clearly implies that the old man belonged to the Sunni persuasion while Nuʿmān was a Shiʿi Ismaʿili. See also al-Nuʿmān's, *Kitāb ikhtilāf uṣūl al-madhāhib*, ed. S. T. Lokhandwalla (Simla, 1972), English introduction p. 5; hereafter cited as Lokhandwalla and all the references are to his introduction unless stated otherwise.

Secondly, in the introduction to his *al-Iqtiṣār*, p. 9, Nuʿmān states: '[For compiling the *Kitāb al-īḍāḥ*] I scrutinized the books [of *ḥadīth*] narrated on the authority of the *ahl al-bayt* which were [accessible] to me by way of *simāʿ* (oral transmission), *aw munāwala, aw akhadhtuhu bi-ijāzatin, aw ṣaḥīfatin*.' This clearly suggests that he had received a formal Shiʿi education. W. Madelung's contention in his 'The Sources of Ismāʿīlī Law', *Journal of Near Eastern Studies*, 35 (1976), p. 30, that Nuʿmān probably was originally a Sunni and apparently never received formal training in Shiʿi *ḥadīth* and *fiqh* seems incorrect. Nuʿmān used the Imāmī and Zaydī sources for the obvious reason that Ismaʿili law had not yet developed and they did not have the *ḥadīth* collections of their own.

18 Nuʿmān, *Kitāb al-majālis*, pp. 80–81, and Idrīs, *ʿUyūn*, vol. 5, p. 346.

19 Nuʿmān, *Kitāb al-majālis*, pp. 51, 57, 69, 75, and Idrīs, *ʿUyūn*, vol. 5, p. 331. According to Idrīs, Nuʿmān was also entrusted with the *daʿwa* by al-Manṣūr (*wa-qalladahu amra quḍātihi wa-daʿwatihi*), which means that he became the chief *dāʿī* directing the affairs of the powerful religious organization within and without the Fatimid domain. However, at another place Idrīs (*ʿUyūn*, vol. 6, p. 39), states that al-Muʿizz appointed Nuʿmān as the chief *qāḍī* and also assigned the affairs of the *daʿwa* to him (*jaʿalahu qāḍī al-quḍāt wa-aḍāfa ilayhi al-daʿwa*). This discrepancy, as to whether or not Nuʿmān headed the *daʿwa*, either during the reign of al-Manṣūr or al-Muʿizz, does not affect the following discussion. Unfortunately, the present editions of the *ʿUyūn* are replete with errors and cannot be relied upon. There are numerous good manuscripts of this important work which deserves a critical edition. Ibn Ḥawqal, *Kitāb ṣūrat al-arḍ* (Beirut, 1979), p. 74, states that al-Manṣūr moved to the new capital on Tuesday 28 Shawwāl 337 AH.

20 Nuʿmān states that during the reign of al-Manṣūr, the heir-apparent al-Muʿizz was his intermediary to the caliph. Throughout his *Kitāb al-majālis*, Nuʿmān takes pride in his being very close and having free access to both of them.

21 The royal decree dated 28 Rabīʿ I 343/30 September 954 is recorded by Nuʿmān in his *Kitāb ikhtilāf uṣūl al-madhāhib*; see Lokhandwalla, text pp. 19–22, translation pp. 52–58. Al-Muʿizz's letter of investiture is also an important document outlining the principles of Ismaʿili jurisprudence. For the jurisdiction of the *maẓālim*, see J. Nielsen, 'Maẓālim', EI2, vol. 6, pp. 933–935.

22 Nuʿmān, *Kitāb al-majālis*, pp. 386, 435, 487, 546.

23 Our discussion will be confined to his works on jurisprudence. For a complete list of his works see Poonawala, pp. 51–68. The *Kitāb al-yanbūʿ* (Ms. Mullā Qurbān Ḥusayn Godhrawala Collection), ascribed to Nuʿmān by Idrīs (*ʿUyūn*, vol. 6, p. 42; *Kitāb al-buyūʿ* in the edited text is an error) and al-Majdūʿ (*Fihrist*, p. 35), is omitted from the discussion. The extant second volume deals with the *muʿāmalāt* and does not give *isnād*s, but at several places quotes al-Manṣūr's opinions. A. A. A. Fyzee, *Compendium of Fatimid Law* (Simla, 1969), p. xxviii (the diagram on the next page illustrating the mutual relationship of Nuʿmān's works is incorrect) is of the opinion that it is of much later date than the *Daʿāʾim*; however, he is unable to explain why al-Manṣūr's authority is cited. The present writer concurs with Lokhandwalla (Lokhandwalla, pp. 33–37) that the author of the *Yanbūʿ* was probably a contemporary of Nuʿmān who was trying to put the Fatimid theory of substantive law into practice.

Another work omitted from the following discussion is the *Kitāb al-ṭahāra* or *Kitāb al-ṭahārāt*. Although it is an authentic work of Nuʿmān, unlike his other works, it is not comprehensive, but an abridgment of certain chapters from the *Īḍāḥ*. As the latter is lost, this book is an important source for reconstructing the contents of the *Īḍāḥ*. Moreover, it supports my contention that Nuʿmān in the *Daʿāʾim* was moving towards a moderate and reconciliatory position compared to his earlier views. For example, the following three reports found in the *Kitāb al-ṭahāra* (Ms. Mullā Qurbān Ḥusayn Godhrawala Collection) are omitted both from the *Ikhtiṣār* and the *Daʿāʾim*: (1) A *ḥadīth* from the Prophet stating that no one except a bastard would harbour rancour against ʿAlī (section on *ḥayḍ*); (2) A disparaging report about Abū Bakr and ʿUthmān (sections on *masājid* and *imāma*); (3) A full version of the Shiʿi *adhān* with the additions of *ashhadu anna ʿAliyyan walī Allāh* and *Muḥammadun wa-ʿAliyyun khayr al-bashar wa-ʿitratuhumā khayr al-ʿitar* (section on *adhān* and *iqāma*).

24 Idrīs, *ʿUyūn*, vol. 6, p. 42.

25 Nuʿmān, *al-Iqtiṣār*, pp. 9–10. Although it is presumed to be lost, its contents and arrangements could be surmised from his later extant works, because Nuʿmān's division of his works into books and sections, and the arrangement of materials therein, remained rather uniform in all his works.

26 This is in contrast to his practice in the *Daʿāʾim*, where he cites only a single *ḥadīth* on any question in support of the actual doctrine or simply formulates the position himself.

27 In the *Muwaṭṭaʾ* of Mālik b. Anas (*riwāya* of Yaḥyā al-Laythī, ed. A. ʿArmūsh, 2nd edn, Beirut, 1977), the oldest extant work on *ḥadīth*, the chapters, arranged according to the categories of religious law, are called *kitāb*s. Both volumes of the *Kitāb al-ḥawāshī*, as the title indicates, served as glosses to the *Daʿāʾim* and follow the latter in its arrangement. The *Kitāb al-ḥawāshī* contains extensive quotes from the *Kitāb al-īḍāḥ*. The last citation from the latter comes from the *kitāb al-diyāt* (see the sixteenth book/chapter in the *Daʿāʾim*, vol. 2, p. 399). This implies that almost the whole book was still available to the author of the *Kitāb al-ḥawāshī*. Al-Majdūʿ (*Fihrist*, p. 33), who died around 1183/1769, however states that except for a small portion from the beginning of the chapter on ritual prayer, the whole book is not to be found in the *daʿwa* collection.

28 Madelung, 'The Sources', p. 32.

29 Nuʿmān, *al-Iqtiṣār*, p. 10. Āghā Buzurg al-Ṭihrānī's statement in his *al-Dharīʿa ilā taṣānīf al-Shīʿa* (Najaf–Tehran, 1355-/1976-), vol. 1, pp. 310, 363, that the *Iqtiṣār* is an

abridgment of the *Daʿāʾim* is incorrect.

30 Lokhandwalla, pp. 17, 23. Only the first part of it dealing with the *ʿibādāt* (i.e., *ṭahāra, ṣalāt, janāʾiz, zakāt, ṣawm, ḥajj* and *jihād*) is preserved.

31 It is more frequently quoted in the *Kitāb al-ḥawāshī* than is the *Īḍāḥ*. This implies that it was available to the author of the *Kitāb al-ḥawāshī*. Although I have not found any manuscripts of it in the private collections accessible to me, I am tempted to believe that it might still exist in some private collection.

32 It is extant and in two volumes as is the case with his other works on jurisprudence. The first deals with the *ʿibādāt* (acts of devotion, or laws of rituals) and the second with the *muʿāmalāt* (worldly affairs, or bilateral contracts). Probably it was the first versified version of *fiqh* and might have served as a precedent for the later Sunni works.

33 Al-Jawdharī, *Sīrat al-ustādh Jawdhar*, p. 53.

34 Nuʿmān had entitled it *Kitāb al-dīnār*, with the hope that it would be transcribed for a *dīnār* or less, see his *Kitāb al-majālis*, pp. 359–360.

35 I agree with Lokhandwalla, pp. 22–25, as he has argued convincingly that it was composed before the *Daʿāʾim*, and was not an abridgment of the latter as stated by Idrīs, *ʿUyūn*, vol. 6, p. 44. In this study I have given some additional arguments and dates to support the above view. H. F. Hamdani ('Some Unknown Ismāʿīlī Authors and their Works', JRAS, 1933, p. 369) and A. A. A. Fyzee ('Qadi an-Nuʿmān: The Fatimid Jurist and Author', JRAS, 1934, p. 25; and his *Compendium*, p. xxxi) were also misled by Idrīs. Fyzee's statement in the introduction to the *Daʿāʾim* (English p. 4, Arabic p. 12) that the *Mukhtaṣar*, and *Iqtiṣār*, and the *Muntakhaba* were all abridgments of the *Daʿāʾim* is incorrect.

36 It is one of the four essential elements of ablution and should not be confused with *masḥ ʿalāʾl-khuffayn*, see Poonawala, 'Ablution, Islamic', EIR, vol. 1, pp. 224–225.

37 The verse in question is V:6; for the Sunni point of view see, for instance, al-Jazīrī, *Kitāb al-fiqh*, vol. 1, pp. 54–62.

38 Nuʿmān, *Akhbār*, vol. 1, in *dhikr ṣifāt al-wuḍūʾ*, Ms. Mullā Qurbān Ḥusayn Godhrawala Collection.

39 Nuʿmān, *al-Iqtiṣār*, p. 15.

40 Nuʿmān, *Mukhtaṣar al-āthār*, vol. 1, fol. 9a.

41 He first cites the Qur'anic verses LVIII:11, XXXIX:9, XXIX:49 and then gives the *ḥadīth*s, especially the *ḥadīth* of the Prophet which states: 'Acquire knowledge from the *ʿālim* of my family, because one who acquires knowledge from the *ʿālim* of my family saves himself from the hellfire'; Nuʿmān, *Mukhtaṣar al-āthār*, fols. 2b–3a.

Of all the virtues possessed by the imam in the Shiʿi doctrine of the imamate, his possession of *ʿilm* is the most significant and is given the central position since his task is the guidance of mankind. The paramount status of his knowledge is also reflected in the fact that he is often described as the *ʿālim par excellence*, and the word *ʿālim* is frequently used interchangeably with the word *imām* in the Imāmī sources. Although Muḥammad b. Yaʿqūb al-Kulaynī (d. 329/940) begins his *al-Uṣūl min al-Kāfī*, ed. ʿAlī Akbar al-Ghaffārī (Tehran, 1388/1968), vol. 1, pp. 30–71, which is the earliest of the Four Books on Imāmī *ḥadīth*/*fiqh*, with a chapter on *ʿilm* he does not explicitly state from whom it should be accepted. Nuʿmān's chapter on *ʿilm* compared to al-Kulaynī's is very brief, but it is pertinent to the point and forceful in advocating the cause.

42 Nuʿmān, *Mukhtaṣar al-āthār*, vol. 1, fol. 1b; see also Fyzee, *Compendium*, pp. xxix–xxx.

Al-Maqrīzī, *al-Khiṭaṭ*, vol. 2, p. 341, states that in the year 365/975 Nuʿmān's son ʿAlī sat in the al-Azhar Mosque dictating the *Mukhtaṣar* to a large audience, but he incorrectly identifies it with the *Iqtiṣār*. This error is repeated in A. A. Harīdī, *Fihrist khiṭaṭ Miṣr* (Cairo, 1983), vol. 2, p. 70.

43 Idrīs, *ʿUyūn*, vol. 6, p. 232, and Fyzee, *Compendium*, pp. xxix–xxxii.

44 It should be noted that Nuʿmān does not mention Ibn Ḥanbal in any of his works, probably because the latter was recognized more as a *muḥaddith* than a *faqīh*.

45 Noteworthy in this respect are the following works: *Kitāb al-ittifāq waʾl-iftirāq* (wherein Nuʿmān gave all the legal doctrines indicating where the Sunni schools agreed with the Ismaʿilis and where they disagreed, which implies that it must have been composed after the Ismaʿili doctrines were established); *Kitāb al-muqtaṣar* (an abridgment of the former); *al-Risāla al-Miṣriyya fiʾl-radd ʿalā al-Shāfiʿī* (refutation of al-Shāfiʿī, probably composed shortly before or after the conquest of Egypt where this school was consolidating); *al-Radd ʿalā Aḥmad b. Surayj al-Baghdādī* (refutation of Ibn Surayj, who was an elder contemporary of Nuʿmān and a leading Shāfiʿī jurist); *Dāmigh al-mūjaz fiʾl-radd ʿalā al-ʿUtbī* (refutation of al-ʿUtbī, whose full name was Muḥammad b. Aḥmad al-ʿUtbī, an influential Mālikī jurist of North Africa); *Risāla dhāt al-bayān fiʾl-radd ʿalā Ibn Qutayba* (refutation of the famous literary figure Ibn Qutayba and his son Aḥmad b. ʿAbd Allāh, who was a jurist and a *qāḍī* in Egypt). The first half of the latter has survived (Poonawala, p. 63), but the other works are lost. However, the essence of Nuʿmān's refutations against them could be gleaned from his arguments against them in the *Daʿāʾim* and the *Ikhtilāf*.

46 The *Ikhtilāf* was composed after 343/954, as Nuʿmān records al-Muʿizz's decree appointing him to the *maẓālim* in that year. For its contents, see A. A. A. Fyzee, 'Shīʿī Legal Theories', in *Law in the Middle East*: Vol. 1, *Origins and Development of Islamic Law*, ed. M. Khadduri and H. Liebesny (Washington D.C., 1955), pp. 125–127.

47 The decrees issued by the Fatimid caliphs, especially al-Manṣūr and al-Muʿizz, appointing Nuʿmān to the judicial posts, advised him about the foundations upon which he should base his legal decisions. The decree of al-Muʿizz preserved in the *Ikhtilāf* states: 'In your decisions and judgements, you should follow the Book of God . . . If you neither find in the Book any text [concerning a problem] nor any [decision] in the *sunna* of the forefather of *amīr al-muʾminīn*, Muḥammad, the Messenger of God, . . . then seek it in the *madhāhib* of the imams from the progeny of the Prophet . . . If a matter seems dubious and baffling to you [i.e., you do not know the ways therein], refer it to the *amīr al-muʾminīn* [i.e., us, the imams] and he will guide you to the proper decision.' Lokhandwalla, p. 55, Arabic text p. 22.

48 Nuʿmān, *Mukhtaṣar al-āthār*, vol. 2, section on *ādāb al-quḍāt*, and his *al-Iqtiṣār*, p. 167. Compare this passage with the *Daʿāʾim*, vol. 2, pp. 535–536. The words *wa-lam yajidhu radda dhālika ilā imāmihi wa-saʾalahu ʿanhu* (if he does not find it [in the Book and the *sunna*], he should refer it to the imam) are dropped from the latter; instead Nuʿmān reports a *ḥadīth* on the authority of Jaʿfar al-Ṣādiq which states that the *qāḍī* should decide according to the Book and the *sunna*. When the imam was asked if it was not in the Book and the *sunna*, what should he do, the imam replied: 'everything relating to the religion of Allāh is in the Book and the *sunna*, for Allāh has perfected his religion'. The Qurʾanic verse 'Today I have perfected my religion' [V:3] is then cited. Thus, it is clear that the authority of the ruling imam is dropped from the *Daʿāʾim*. This development in Nuʿmān's thought clearly indicates that the *Daʿāʾim* was composed

later than the *Ikhtilāf*. It also suggests that gradually the Fatimid caliphs, in theory at least, gave up interfering in legal matters, hence the legal authorities were confined to al-Ṣādiq and his predecessors, who were accepted both by the Sunnis and the Shiʿis.

49 For al-Shāfiʿī *qiyās* and *ijtihād* were two terms with the same meaning; for details, see Muḥammad b. Idrīs al-Shāfiʿī, *al-Risāla*, ed. Aḥmad M. Shākir (Cairo, 1940), pp. 476–503; English trans., *al-Shāfiʿī's Risāla*, tr. Majid Khadduri (2nd edn, Cambridge, 1987), pp. 288–303; Schacht, *Origins*, pp. 98, 127, and his 'The Schools of Law and Later Developments of Jurisprudence', *in Law in the Middle East*, vol. 1, pp. 57–84, and Wael Hallaq, 'Was al-Shāfiʿī the Master Architect of Islamic Jurisprudence?', IJMES, 25 (1993), pp. 587–605. With the growing influence of the *muḥaddithūn* after al-Shāfiʿī, the use of *ra'y* (i.e., the unrestrained use of one's discretion) fell into disfavour as it was severely criticized while *qiyās* was confined to the use of one's reasoning restricted by analogical deduction based on some parallel decision drawn from the Qur'an, or the *sunna*, or the *ijmāʿ*.

50 This means proof by circumstantial evidence. This concept was developed by the Ẓāhirī school, which stressed the sufficiency of the Qur'an and the *sunna* and insisted upon the apparent literal interpretations to seek for a *dalīl* from the Qur'an and the *sunna* for any new situation.

51 These concepts originated with the speculative theologians and were accepted as one of the *uṣūl al-fiqh* by the Muʿtazila and the Shiʿa; see Hossein Modarressi Tabātabā'i, *An Introduction to Shīʿī Law: A Bibliographical Study* (London, 1984), pp. 32 ff.

52 These were the two methods of reasoning in connection with the doctrine of *qiyās*. They were the attempts on the part of the ancient schools of Kūfa and Medina to validate decisions which were not based on the Qur'an and the *sunna* and had departed from *qiyās*.

53 Al-Nawbakhtī, *Firaq al-Shīʿa*, ed. H. Ritter (Istanbul, 1931), pp. 18–19, 50–51; al-Ashʿarī, *Maqālāt al-Islāmiyyīn*, ed. H. Ritter (Wiesbaden, 1963), pp. 65–74, and al-Shahrastānī, *al-Milal wa'l-niḥal*, ed. ʿAbd al-ʿAzīz M. al-Wakīl (Cairo, 1968), vol. 1, pp. 154–162.

54 Ismail K. Poonawala, 'The Imām's Authority during the Pre-*ghayba* period: Theoretical and Practical Considerations', in *Shīʿī Islam: Faith, Experience and Worldview*, ed. M. Ayoub et al. (forthcoming).

55 Modarressi Tabātabā'i, *Introduction*, pp. 32–48.

56 For its full implication, see Fyzee, 'Shīʿī Legal Theories', pp. 113 ff.

57 *Ijtihād* was acceptable to the *muḥaddithūn* if it were limited to mere finding of the sanctions from the Qur'an and the *sunna*, and Nuʿmān quotes one of the views of al-Shāfiʿī wherein he limits the use of *ijtihād* to seeking the relevant verse of the Qur'an or searching for the binding *ḥadīth*. Nuʿmān accepts this viewpoint.

58 It is referred to in his later esoteric works such as the *Asās al-ta'wīl*, ed. ʿĀ. Tāmir (Beirut, 1960), pp. 23, 26, 27, and his *Ta'wīl al-daʿā'im*, ed. M. Ḥ. al-Aʿẓamī (Cairo, 1967–1972), *passim*.

59 Idrīs, *ʿUyūn*, vol. 6, pp. 42–43; Fyzee, *Compendium*, pp. xxii–xxiii, and Lokhandwalla, pp. 28–29. Al-Majdūʿ (*Fihrist* p. 34) also states that the *Daʿā'im* was the last work of Nuʿmān on jurisprudence, hence it is the most authoritative.

60 See note 5 above. Al-Qāḍī, 'An Early Fāṭimid', p. 71, dates the *Daʿā'im* to around 347/957 in accordance with W. Ivanow's *A Creed of the Fatimids* (Bombay, 1936), p. 6; however, Ivanow does not explain how he arrived at that dating. He states that the

Kitāb al-zīna was composed in the beginning of the 4th/10th century and submitted to the second Fatimid caliph al-Qā'im (322–334/934–946) soon after his accession. Then he adds that the *Daʿā'im al-Islām* was probably composed some twenty-five years or so after the preceding work. It seems that Ivanow misread Idrīs' *ʿUyūn*, vol. 5, pp. 168–169. The latter does not give any date as to when al-Qā'im received a copy of the *Kitāb al-zīna*. Ivanow was probably trying to connect together two events which occurred in the same year: al-Rāzī's death and al-Qā'im's accession to the caliphate. Ivanow's dating of the *Daʿā'im* is, therefore, pure conjecture.

61 Nuʿmān, *Daʿā'im*, vol. 1, pp. 139, 140, 143, 162, 167, 186, 210, 225–231, 238, 240.

62 Nuʿmān, *Kitāb al-majālis*, pp. 306–307.

63 Al-Kulaynī, *al-Uṣūl*, vol. 1, pp. 168–548, has a long chapter entitled '*kitāb al-ḥujja*' containing an elaborate exposition of the doctrine of the imamate, and it is significantly placed under the *uṣūl* immediately following the '*kitāb al-tawḥīd*', and preceding the '*kitāb al-īmān wa'l-kufr*' while the *furūʿ* begins with the *ṭahāra*. It should be noted that al-Kulaynī (*al-Uṣūl*, vol. 2, p. 18) enumerates *walāya* as one of the five pillars of Islam in the '*kitāb al-īmān wa'l-kufr*'.

64 Nuʿmān, *Daʿā'im*, vol. 1, pp. 359 ff. This *ʿahd* is found neither in the *Iqtiṣār* nor in the *Mukhtaṣar al-āthār*. It is translated by G. Salinger, 'A Muslim Mirror for Princes', *Muslim World*, 46 (1956), pp. 24–39.

65 Al-Qāḍī, 'An Early Fāṭimid', p. 104.

66 See, for example, *Daʿā'im*, vol. 1, pp. 131, 352. Unfortunately, the first reference to Muḥammad b. ʿAbd Allāh, known as al-Nafs al-Zakiyya, in the *isnād*, in the first edition of the *Daʿā'im* (Cairo, 1951), vol. 1, p. 102, is omitted from the third edition; see *Daʿā'im* (Cairo, 1969), vol. 1, p. 83. See also R. Strothmann, 'Recht der Ismailiten', *Der Islam*, 31 (1954), p. 134.

67 Madelung, 'Sources', p. 32 n. 22.

68 Ibid., p. 33.

69 For example, in both the laws of marriage and sale there is a close resemblance between Ismaʿili and Mālikī law; see Lokhandwalla, 'Origins'. Mālikī influence on Ismaʿili law needs further investigation.

70 See Schacht, *Origins*, pp. 266–267, and note 15 above.

71 Muḥammad b. Aḥmad al-Muqaddasī, *Aḥsan al-taqāsīm fī maʿrifat al-aqālīm*, ed. M. J. de Goeje (2nd edn, Leiden, 1906), pp. 237–238; R. Brunschvig, 'Fiqh Fatimide et histoire de l'Ifriqiya', in *Mélanges d'histoire et d'archéologie de l'occident Musulman, Hommages à G. Marçais* (Algiers, 1957), vol. 2, p. 15.

72 A. A. A. Fyzee, 'Aspects of Fatimid Law', *Studia Islamica*, 31 (1970), pp. 81–91, and his *Compendium*, pp. xxxv–xxxviii; Strothmann, 'Recht der Ismailiten', pp. 142–146, and Brunschvig, 'Fiqh Fatimide', pp. 13–20.

73 The chapter on *walāya* is translated by A. A. A. Fyzee under the title of *The Book of Faith* (Bombay, 1974); for its analysis, see Azim Nanji, 'An Ismāʿīlī Theory of *Walāyah* in the *Daʿā'im al-Islām* of Qāḍī al-Nuʿmān', in *Essays on Islamic Civilization Presented to Niyazi Berkes*, ed. D. P. Little (Leiden, 1976), pp. 260–273.

74 The Qur'an is a revealed book of guidance and not a code of law. Out of approximately 6,000 verses in the Qur'an, only 600 deal with legal obligations; again the majority of them deal with religious obligations, such as prayers, fasting, pilgrimage, etc. Only eighty verses deal with legal topics in the strict sense of the word, the bulk of which refer to women, marriage, and inheritance, since

fundamental changes were introduced by the Prophet in family law. See J. Schacht, *An Introduction to Islamic Law* (Oxford, 1966), pp. 10 ff., and David Pearl, *A Textbook on Muslim Law* (London, 1979), pp. 1 ff.

75 They were the Muʿtazila, see Schacht, *Origins*, pp. 128, 258.

76 For example: 'We have not neglected anything in the Book (VI:38)'; 'We have revealed the Book to you explaining everything (XVI:89)'; 'Today I have perfected your religion for you (V:3).'

77 The *ḥadīth al-thaqalayn* is well known among the Shiʿa. Its Sunni version reads 'the Qur'an and the *sunna*', while in the Shiʿi version, the *sunna* is replaced by *ʿitra* (the Prophet's family).

78 Islamic law developed without the collaboration of the state, and many times state interference was resisted, since law was regarded as sacred and part of religion. For the Fatimids who were not accepted by the Sunni masses as their politico-religious leaders, it was very difficult to assert their authority in law. It is interesting to note that al-Muʿizz had instructed Nuʿmān (*Kitāb al-majālis*, pp. 393–394) to the effect that all the bondsmen of the imams, who had embraced Ismaʿili faith but were not manumitted, were to be regarded as freemen and Ismaʿili laws of inheritance and testimony would apply to them.

79 A-Shāfiʿī, *al-Risāla*, pp. 91–92; tr. Khadduri, *al-Shāfiʿī's Risāla*, pp. 119–120.

80 There is no reference to any of the six Sunni canonical *ḥadīth* collections in Nuʿmān's works. Even Muslim, whose *Ṣaḥīḥ* later achieved precedence in North Africa is not referred to. This implies that probably by this time the six collections had not yet claimed a large scale acceptance and currency. It should be noted that all the collectors of *ḥadīth* had a special chapter in their collections urging the Muslims to accept *ḥadīth*. Many *ḥadīth*s were also quoted from the Prophet himself to give his *sunna* a due place. For example, see Muḥammad b. Ismāʿīl al-Bukhārī, *Bukhārī bi-ḥāshīyat al-Sindī* (Beirut, 1978), vol. 4, p. 256 (*bāb al-iqtidāʾ bi-sunan rasūl Allāh*), and Muḥammad b. ʿAbd Allāh al-Tabrīzī, *Mishkāt al-maṣābīḥ*, ed. M. N. al-Albānī (Damascus, 1961), vol. 1, pp. 51–69 (*bāb al-iʿtiṣām biʾl-kitāb waʾl-sunna*); English trans., *Mishkat al-Masabih*, tr. J. Robson (Lahore, 1975), vol. 1, pp. 39–49. Moreover, the comments of Nuʿmān indicate that the rules of criticism were neither standardized nor were universally agreed upon.

81 For example, see *Daʿāʾim*, vol. 1, pp. 14–15; Nuʿmān cites a *ḥadīth* on the authority of al-Bāqir.

82 Idrīs, *ʿUyūn*, vol. 6, p. 200; Ibn Muyassar, *Akhbār Miṣr*, ed. A. F. Sayyid (Cairo, 1981), p. 165; the report stating that Nuʿmān died on the 1st of Rajab is taken from Ibn Zūlāq's *Sīrat al-Imām al-Muʿizz*; while Ibn Khallikān, *Wafayāt*, vol. 5, p. 416, gives both dates.

83 Muḥammad b. ʿUbayd Allāh al-Musabbiḥī, *Akhbār Miṣr*, ed. A. F. Sayyid et al. (Cairo, 1978–1984), part 1, pp. 71, 81, 105, 111, and part 2, pp. 10, 19; Ibn Muyassar, *Akhbār*, pp. 9, 57, 166, 167 (the last two reports are taken from Ibn Zūlāq), 173, 175, 176, 178, 179 (taken from al-Musabbiḥī); Ibn Khallikān, *Wafayāt*, vol. 5, pp. 417–423; Ibn Ḥajar, *Rafʿ al-iṣr*, pp. 589–591, 592–595, 596–603, 613; Ibn Ḥajar states that Ibn Killis was very jealous of Nuʿmān's sons because of their close relations with al-ʿAzīz. *Al-Balāgh al-akbar* ascribed to Nuʿmān and his sons is a forgery; see Poonawala, p. 56.

84 See Poonawala, pp. 78–79, where older sources are indicated.

85 Al-Maqrīzī, *al-Khiṭaṭ*, vol. 1, p. 355, and vol. 2, p. 7.

86 Idrīs, *ʿUyūn*, vol. 6, p. 232; see also al-Majdūʿ, *Fihrist*, p. 34. It would be interesting to know what the disagreements, even if minor, were. The *Kitāb al-ḥawāshī* contains numerous excerpts from it. An anonymous manuscript entitled *Mansak al-ḥajj* (Ms. Zāhid ʿAlī Collection) contains excerpts from the *Muṣannaf al-wazīr*. I have not seen any manuscripts of it, but the late Zāhid ʿAlī (*Taʾrīkh-i Fāṭimiyyīn-i Miṣr*, Hyderabad, 1948, p. 399) states that it is extant.

87 Shamʿūn al-Ghūrī's *Kitāb al-suʾāl waʾl-jawāb*, or *al-Masāʾil al-Shamʿūniyya*, seems to be in the form of glosses over the *Daʿāʾim*; see Poonawala, p. 177.

88 Poonawala, pp. 185–186.

89 Poonawala, pp. 214–215.

90 A. A. A. Fyzee, *Outlines of Muhammadan Law* (4th edn, Delhi, 1974), pp. 41, 446; and his *Compendium*, pp. xxi ff. For the situation in the Indian subcontinent, see D. Pearl, *A Textbook on Muslim Personal Law* (2nd edn, London, 1987), pp. 21 ff., and J. N. Anderson, *Law Reform in the Muslim World* (London, 1976), pp. 19–25.

SEVEN

A critique of Paul Casanova's dating of the *Rasāʾil Ikhwān al-Ṣafāʾ*

ABBAS HAMDANI

THE PRESENT study[1] pertains to an astrological prediction contained in the mediaeval Islamic encyclopaedia, *Rasāʾil Ikhwān al-Ṣafāʾ*,[2] which P. Casanova had used in the dating of the work.[3] The purpose of this study is not to analyze the astronomical thought of the Brethren of Purity but only to determine the time of the composition of their work. The proper understanding of the above-mentioned prediction is only a means toward an end which remains chronological. The question of the dating and authorship of the *Rasāʾil* is further involved with the religious persuasion of the Brethren.

The seventeenth-century historian of Spain and North Africa, al-Maqarrī, in his voluminous work, *Nafḥ al-ṭīb*, reports that the great mathematician of Spain, Abu'l-Ḥākim ʿUmar b. ʿAbd al-Raḥmān al-Kirmānī (d. 462/1070) visited the Sabaean city of Ḥarrān and from there brought back with him copies of the *Rasāʾil* to Spain. Al-Maqarrī's translator, P. de Gayangos,[4] says that it was actually Maslama b. Aḥmad al-Majrīṭī (d. 395/1005) who introduced the *Rasāʾil* in Spain, basing his conclusion on Ḥājjī Khalīfa who records under the year 395 AH that the *Rasāʾil* were written by al-Majrīṭī. This was also echoed by A. Nicoll, J. Uri and M. Casiri, cataloguers of the Arabic manuscripts at Oxford and Escorial. However, Ḥājjī Khalīfa's statement was soon to be rejected by all serious studies such as those undertaken by Flügel[5] and Dieterici,[6] who had accepted the story related by Abū Ḥayyān al-Tawḥīdī (ca. 320–414/932–1023) in his *Kitāb al-imtāʿ waʾl-muʾānasa* that the encyclopaedia had been composed around 373–375/983–985 by a few contemporaries whom he named. In addition, they considered the work as Muʿtazilī.[7] This view continues to be defended and we find it expressed as late as 1948 in the work of ʿĀdil ʿAwwā.[8]

The first scholar to notice the Isma'ili tendency of the Brethren was S. Guyard.[9] P. Casanova confirmed this in 1898 by his discovery of *al-Risāla al-Jāmiʿa*, which is explicitly Ismaʿili in character, and by establishing the connection between *al-Jāmiʿa* and the main corpus of the *Rasāʾil*.[10] In another article published in 1915,[11] Casanova acknowledged that he was aware of Abū Ḥayyān's story of the composition of the *Rasāʾil* in the 4th/10th century; yet he did not accept it. Casanova also mentioned that he used the printed edition of the *Rasāʾil*, which in his time was the Bombay one, in the full knowledge that it might not have represented the earliest form of the text. However, using an astrological prediction contained in it, he arrived at the period just preceding the year 439/1047 as the time of the *Rasāʾil*'s composition. We shall return to this dating of Casanova later.

Husayn Hamdani observed for the first time in 1932 that the encyclopaedia had been accepted by the Ṭayyibī Ismaʿili *daʿwa* as an Ismaʿili work for centuries, also pointing to sufficient internal evidence to show the Ismaʿili nature of the Brethren's ideas.[12] This tradition did not accept Abū Ḥayyān's story and assigned the *Rasāʾil* to the pre-Fatimid period of *satr* or concealment in Ismaʿili history. In two articles published in 1946 and 1964, S. M. Stern revived Abū Ḥayyān while at the same time accepting the Ismaʿili character of the *Rasāʾil*.[13]

Yves Marquet, who has devoted a lifetime to the *Rasāʾil* studies, while accepting the Ismaʿili nature of the encyclopaedia, puts the time of its writing from around 290/902 to 370/980, thus reviving Dieterici's theory of a long and staggered period for the encyclopaedia's composition.[14]

In several studies, I have endeavoured to establish the Ismaʿili character of the *Rasāʾil* from internal and external evidence, to reject Abū Ḥayyān's story and to assign the *Rasāʾil*'s composition to the period between 260/873 and 297/909.[15]

There are other theories advanced by A. L. Tibawi and S. H. Nasr about the *Rasāʾil*'s Shiʿi character; by Susanne Diwald and A. Bausani about the work being Sunni-Sufi; by Zāhid ʿAlī and W. Madelung, who consider it as Qarmaṭī; and lastly by I. R. Netton and L. E. Goodman, who consider it just Neoplatonic. They have not addressed themselves to the time of the *Rasāʾil*'s composition.[16]

Let us now return to the prediction mentioned earlier. The 48th *Epistle* of the *Rasāʾil*, entitled *Fī kayfiyyat al-daʿwa ila Allāh*,[17] is the most explicitly Shiʿi or Ismaʿili *Risāla* of the work. It is couched in the form of an address of the imam himself to his followers. It describes several groups of the Shi'a in various degrees of closeness to the imam. To the most favoured, a *bashāra* (good tidings) is given in the following words: 'From among the special of our excellent brethren are those who are knowledgeable about the religions; who are aware of the secrets of the prophethoods [and] who are trained in philosophical disciplines. If you meet one of them and are comforted by his straightforwardness then give him the good tidings which will delight him. Remind him of the emergence of the period of *kashf* (uncovering) and awakening and of the removal of grief from the devotees when the conjunction of the sign of the triplicity of Fire passes into the sign of the triplicity of Earth (literally, plants and animals), in the tenth cycle corresponding to the house of sovereignty (*sulṭān*) and the appearance of the dignitaries (*a'lām*).'[18]

It is principally on the basis of this passage that Casanova has built his argument about the dating of the *Rasā'il*.[19] He explains the conjunctions according to the *Muqaddima* of Ibn Khaldūn, while we have the explanation of the Brethren themselves given at another place in the *Rasā'il*. In a *Risāla* on astronomy (the 3rd *Epistle*), the Brethren state that the astronomers describe several conjunctions of planets. The most important are the ones that occur every thousand years and indicate the birth of new religions and states; then there are those that occur every 240 years and result in the change of nations, kingdoms and dynasties; again there are those that occur every twenty years and correspond to events such as wars and civil strife.[20]

All these conjunctions relate to the superior planets Saturn and Jupiter. The world year concept was familiar to the Brethren.[21] The 240 years conjunctions or the triplicities of Fire and Earth mentioned by the Brethren were probably based on the work of Abū Ma'shar al-Balkhī (d. after 246/860), who is mentioned by name in the *Rasā'il*.[22] There is also a reference to an anonymous Persian astronomer in the encyclopaedia.[23] In their recent studies, E. S. Kennedy and David Pingree have examined early mediaeval sources which relate to the Brethren's thinking.[24] Casanova used the tables of conjunctions prepared by the competent Dutch astronomer H. G. van de Sande Bakhuyzen and appended to de Goeje's book on the Qarmaṭīs.[25] We now have the works of Stahlman and Gingerich, and Tuckerman;[26] they all bear out Casanova's calculations.

According to these calculations, a triplicity occurred on 28 August 571 when Saturn and Jupiter were in Scorpio. This was the triplicity of Water and it corresponded to the birth of the Prophet Muḥammad. On 3 October 809, Saturn and Jupiter were in conjunction in Sagittarius. This represented the triplicity of Fire which is referred to in the passage quoted above. Again, the prediction of a great event was in connection with the passage to the triplicity of Earth, when Saturn and Jupiter would be in conjunction in Capricorn. This would occur on 19 November 1047.

Casanova's argument was that the Brethren composed their *Rasā'il* a few years before the passage to the Earth triplicity, and that they could correctly compute and predict the relevant conjunction of 439/1047.[27] Furthermore, they were expecting a great event which actually occurred in 450/1059, the Fatimid sponsored conquest of Baghdad by al-Basāsīrī. Before Casanova made this supposition, however, he went into a long digression about the expectation of the fall of the rule of the Arabs and the impending rule of the Persians, for which the Isma'ili movement was supposed to play an instrumental role. He weaved the correlation between the activities of Maymūn al-Qaddāḥ, his son 'Abd Allāh and grandson Aḥmad, and also of Dindān or Zaydān, with the various conjunctions as mentioned in the *Fihrist* of Ibn al-Nadīm and in the works of 'Abd al-Qāhir al-Baghdādī and al-Bīrūnī. In fact, Casanova made good scientific calculations, only to vitiate them by bad historical speculation.

One thing is certain. Although the Brethren were not themselves astronomers, they were drawing on people, such as Abū Ma'shar al-Balkhī, who had expertise in the matter. They knew that their own time was after the triplicity of Fire and before the triplicity of Earth. It is also certain that they were expecting the imam to establish his new state. In order to give a stamp of authority to their expectations, the talk of the passage from one triplicity to another was useful, but in no way was this evidence that they themselves lived in the proximity of the date predicted. If they used Abū Ma'shar's work, then they would surely be writing after around the year 246/860.[28] The twelfth Ithnā'asharī imam disappeared in 260/873. The period following it was one of great messianic expectations among the Shi'a in general, and was certainly exploited by the Isma'ili movement for the establishment of their Fatimid caliphate in 297/909. It is quite likely that the Brethren were preparing their readers for that event.

This brings us to another supposition made by Casanova. In the same section of the *Rasā'il* in which the prediction is made, the imam is addressing the Shi'a and says: 'And from them are those who hold that the expected imam (*al-imām al-muntaẓar*) is hidden out of the fear of the opponents; nay he is apparent in their midst (*ẓāhirun bayn ẓahrānīhim*). He knows them; yet they deny him.'[29] Casanova cited this passage and interpreted it as having reference to the Fatimid caliph al-Ẓāhir's rule (411–427/1021–1036). By focusing on the period of al-Ẓāhir's rule subsequent to the conjunction of 418/1027, Casanova narrowed down the time of the composition of the *Rasāʾil* to the period between the years 418/1027 and 427/1036. Of course, the passage to the Earth triplicity was still to occur in 439/1047, and the great but very brief event of the conquest of Baghdad lay still beyond, occurring eventually in 450/1059. The passage cited above can hardly be interpreted as having any reference to the caliph al-Ẓāhir. Rather, the message is to urge the Shiʿa to give up waiting for the *imām al-muntaẓar* and to begin working for the imam who is manifest (*ẓāhir*) and in their midst (*bayn ẓahrānīhim*). There is an air of imminence about the passage. The imam is there, and he is about to declare his mission and establish his state. In fact, I consider this as evidence that the *Rasāʾil* were written shortly before 297/909, the date of the establishment of the Fatimid caliphate.

Casanova's dating is further proved to be wrong by the fact that already around 373/983 Abū Ḥayyān al-Tawḥīdī and his mentor, Abū Sulaymān al-Manṭiqī, were reading the *Rasāʾil* in their complete form.[30] This was about forty years before the time of composition suggested by Casanova.

There is a minor matter that remains to be understood in the Brethren's prediction passage used by Casanova. Speaking of the passage to the Earth triplicity, they say it would happen 'in the tenth cycle (*dawr*) corresponding to the house of sovereignty (*bayt al-sulṭān*)'. This line is not clear. In their 52nd and last *Risāla*, in a section on the twelve zodiacal houses,[31] the tenth house is, indeed, stated to be the 'house of sovereignty', but then what could be the tenth cycle (*dawr*) corresponding to the house of sovereignty? Probably the tenth cycle refers to the tenth sign (*burj*) which is Capricorn and is relevant here, as the conjunction of the Earth triplicity is in Capricorn. Interestingly, the *Rasāʾil* use the Indian term *nawbharat* for the zodiacal signs.[32] The use of the term *dawr* is thus loose. The emphasis is on sovereignty, predicting the establishment of a new power. This idea is fortified by the words immediately following: '*wa ẓuhūr al-aʿlām*' (and the appearance of the dignitaries).

In conclusion, in rejecting Casanova's dating of the *Rasāʾil*, one should bear in mind that he was one of the first scholars to recognize the Ismaʿili character of the ideas propounded by the Brethren of Purity and also one of the first who did *not* believe the dubious story of Abū Ḥayyān al-Tawḥīdī about the authorship of the *Rasā'il*. He was, however, quite out of focus on his reference to the time of the Fatimid caliph al-Ẓāhir and on his dating of the *Rasā'il*. I would rather interpret the astrological passage in the 48th *Risāla*, cited by Casanova, in the following manner: The time of the authors of the *Rasā'il* was within the triplicity of Fire, starting in 194/809, but after the death of Abū Maʿshar al-Balkhī in 246/860 and the beginning of the messianic expectations in 260/873, when the twelfth Ithnāʿasharī imam disappeared. It was, however, before the establishment of the Fatimid caliphate in 297/909, when the Fatimid imam was present (*ẓāhir*) in the midst of his followers (*bayn ẓahrānīhim*) but had not yet publicly declared his mission. The great event predicted was this event of the unfolding of the Fatimid caliphate. It would happen anytime before the conjunction of Saturn and Jupiter in Capricorn and the passage from the triplicity of Fire to that of Earth in 439/1047. No one could predict with certainty the exact date of this dynastic event; hence the date of the *next* triplicity (of Earth) was indicated. This event could happen sooner or later within that terminus. In fact, it happened sooner, in 297/909 when the Fatimid caliphate was declared. There was an actual conjunction of Jupiter and Saturn in 296/908, much before the transit to the triplicity of Earth.[33] The date of the *Rasā'il* was, I think, just prior to the establishment of the Fatimid caliphate.

NOTES

1 This article is a revised version of a paper presented at the 194th Annual Meeting of the American Oriental Society, in Seattle, on Monday 26 March 1984. I am grateful to my friends, George Saliba, Professor of Islamic Philosophy and Science at Columbia University, and David King, Professor of the History of Islamic Science at the University of Frankfurt, for helping me understand the astrological material contained here, for providing me with several references and for sharpening my argument. I dedicate this article to the memory of my dear friend and colleague, John McGovern, Professor of Medieval History at the University of Wisconsin, Milwaukee, who died on 24 September 1987 and whose kindness and advice I sorely miss. I thank Ms. Antoinette Newell for carefully preparing the typescript of this article.

2 *Kitāb Ikhwān al-Ṣafā'*, ed. Wilāyat Ḥusayn (Bombay, 1305–1306/1887–1889), 4 vols.; *Rasā'il Ikhwān al-Ṣafā'*, ed. Khayr al-Dīn al-Zirkilī (Cairo, 1928), 4 vols., with two separate introductions by Ṭāhā Ḥusayn and Aḥmad Zakī Pāshā; *Rasā'il Ikhwān al-Ṣafā'* (Beirut, 1957), 4 vols.; hereafter references are to the Beirut edition.

3 P. Casanova, 'Une date astronomique dans les Epîtres des Ikhwān aṣ-Ṣafā', *Journal Asiatique*, 11 série, 5 (1915), pp. 5–17.

4 P. de Gayangos, *Muhammadan Dynasties in Spain* (London, 1840–1843), vol. 1, pp. 427–429.

5 G. Flügel, 'Über Inhalt und Verfasser der arabischen Encyclopädie *Rasā'il Iḫwān*

al-Ṣafā' wa-Ḫullān al-Wafā', d.i. die Abhandlungen der aufrichtigen Brüder und treuen Freunde', ZDMG, 13 (1859), pp. 22–24.

6 F. Dieterici, *Die Philosophie der Araber in X Jahrhundert N. Chr. aus den schriften der Lautern Brüder* (Leipzig, 1858–1872), 8 vols.

7 See my article, 'Abū Ḥayyān al-Tawḥīdī and the Brethren of Purity', IJMES, 9 (1978), pp. 345–352.

8 'Ā. 'Awwā, *L'Esprit critique des Frères de la Pureté: Encyclopédistes Arabes du IVe/Xe siècle* (Beirut, 1948).

9 S. Guyard, *Fragments relatifs à la doctrine des Ismaélîs* (Paris, 1874), p. 253.

10 P. Casanova, 'Notice sur un manuscrit de la secte des Assassins', *Journal Asiatique*, 9 série, 11 (1898), pp. 151–159.

11 See note 3 above.

12 H. F. al-Hamdānī, 'Rasā'il Ikhwān aṣ-Ṣafā in the Literature of the Ismā'īlī Ṭaiyibī Da'wat', *Der Islam*, 20 (1932), pp. 281–300, and his *Baḥth ta'rīkhī fī Rasā'il Ikhwān al-Ṣafā' wa-'aqā'id al-Ismā'īliyya fīhā* (Bombay, 1935).

13 S. M. Stern, 'The Authorship of the Epistles of the Ikhwān-aṣ-Ṣafā', *Islamic Culture*, 20 (1946), pp. 367–372; 'Additional Notes to . . .', *Islamic Culture*, 21 (1947), pp. 403–404, and his 'New Information about the Authors of the Epistles of the Sincere Brethren', *Islamic Studies*, 3 (1964), pp. 405–428.

14 Y. Marquet, 'Ikhwān al-Ṣafā'', EI2, vol. 3, pp. 1071–1076; *La Philosophie des Iḫwān al-Ṣafā'* (Algiers, 1973); 'Iḫwān al-Ṣafā', Ismaïliens et Qarmaṭes', *Arabica*, 24 (1977), pp. 233–257, and '910 en Ifrīqiya: Un épître des *Iḫwān aṣ-Ṣafā'*', *Bulletin des Etudes Orientales*, 30 (1978), pp. 61–73.

15 See note 7 above and my following articles: 'An Early Fāṭimid Source on the Time and Authorship of the *Rasā'il Iḫwān al-Ṣafā'*', *Arabica*, 26 (1979), pp. 62–75; 'Shades of Shī'ism in the Tracts of the Brethren of Purity', in *Traditions in Contact and Change*, ed. P. Slater and D. Wiebe (Waterloo, Ont., 1983), pp. 447–460, 726–728, and 'The Arrangement of the *Rasā'il Ikhwān al-Ṣafā'* and the Problem of Interpolations', *Journal of Semitic Studies*, 29 (1984), pp. 97–110.

16 See A. L. Tibawi, 'Ikhwān al-Ṣafā and their *Rasā'il*: A Critical Review of a Century and a half of Research', *Islamic Quarterly*, 2 (1955), pp. 28–46; S. H. Nasr, *An Introduction to Islamic Cosmological Doctrines* (2nd edn, Albany, N.Y., 1993); Susanne Diwald, *Arabische Philosophie und Wissenschaft in der Enzyklopädie Kitāb Iḫwān aṣ-Ṣafā' (III)* (Wiesbaden, 1975); A. Bausani, 'Scientific Elements in Ismā'īlī Thought: The Epistles of the Brethren of Purity', in *Ismā'īlī Contributions to Islamic Culture*, ed. S. H. Nasr (Tehran, 1977), pp. 123–140; Zāhid 'Alī, *Ta'rīkh-i Fāṭimiyyīn-i Miṣr* (Hyderabad, 1948); W. Madelung, 'Ḳarmaṭī', EI2, vol. 4, pp. 660–665; Ian R. Netton, *Muslim Neoplatonists: An Introduction to the Thought of the Brethren of Purity* (London, 1982), and Lenn E. Goodman, *The Case of the Animals versus Man Before the King of the Jinn* (Boston, 1978).

17 *Rasā'il*, vol. 4, pp. 145–197.

18 Ibid., vol. 4, p. 146.

19 See note 3 above; Casanova translates *a'lām* as 'banners'.

20 *Rasā'il*, vol. 1, p. 154.

21 Ibid., vol. 4, p. 362.

22 Ibid., vol. 4, p. 288.

23 Ibid., vol. 3, pp. 111–112.

24 E. S. Kennedy and B. L. Van der Waerden, 'The World Year of the Persians', JAOS, 83 (1963), pp. 315–327; E. S. Kennedy, 'Ramifications of the World Year Concept in Islamic Astrology', *Ithaca*, 1 (1964), pp. 23–43; David Pingree, *The Thousands of Abū Maʿshar* (London, 1968), and E. S. Kennedy and D. Pingree, *The Astrological History of Māsha Allāh* (Cambridge, Mass., 1971).

25 M. J. de Goeje, *Mémoire sur les Carmathes du Bahraïn et les Fatimides* (2nd edn, Leiden, 1886), pp. 229–232.

26 William D. Stahlman and Owen J. Gingerich, *Solar and Planetary Longitudes for Years −2500 to +2000 by 10-day Intervals* (Madison, Wisconsin, 1963), and B. Tuckerman, *Planetary, Lunar and Solar Positions* (Philadelphia, 1962–1964), 2 vols.

27 George Saliba in a letter written to me, dated 19 January 1972, says: 'Now there remains the problem of whether the Ikhwān knew of the 1047 conjunction beforehand or not. All the medieval tables that I could find simply list the conjunctions up to the year 928 A.D.; hence including the 809 conjunction . . . I contend that any medieval competent astrologer of the 9th or 10th century could easily compute the conjunction of 1047 A.D., and know the shift from Fire to Earth triplicity. Now whether the Ikhwān did that themselves or whether they copied it from a table is hard to tell.' See also the sources mentioned in note 24 above.

28 According to Pingree, *Thousands*, pp. 19–20, Abū Maʿshar's *Kitāb al-ulūf* was composed sometime between 840 and 860 AD.

29 *Rasāʾil*, vol. 4, p. 148.

30 See note 7 above.

31 *Rasāʾil*, vol. 4, pp. 354–358.

32 Ibid., vol. 4, pp. 350–351.

33 The conjunction of 296/908 is identified by Māsha Allāh with 'the prosperity of the people of prophecy and science'; see Kennedy, 'Ramifications', p. 34. This conjunction, however, has nothing to do with the 'house of sovereignty' or the transit to the Earth triplicity.

EIGHT

Portraits of self and others: Isma'ili perspectives on the history of religions

AZIM A. NANJI

THE EMERGENCE and development of Islam marked two types of intellectual beginnings in the study of Muslim perceptions of other religions. The first was a major transition from an ethnic culture bound primarily by pre-Islamic Arab oral tradition to that set in a more universalizing framework grounded in a revealed text, recorded and preserved in writing. Literacy and logocentrism thus displaced mythic orality, initiating an alternative form of historical self-consciousness. Muslim self-definition therefore, in its Qur'anic context, sought to project 'Islam' as a 'religion' (*dīn*) negating pre-Islamic (*jāhilī*) religious and cultural assumptions, and representing itself as a scripturally based continuation of the monotheistic imperative embodied in previous revelations. It is worth noting that the nascent Muslim community was in the minority. The teachings of the Qur'an revised radically the relationship between the new 'Muslim' identity and the opposite *jāhilī* status of pre-Islamic Arabs. Simultaneously, it reconstructed the relationship between the new community and Jews and Christians, who as members of the *ahl al-kitāb* (People of the Book) became part of a privileged (albeit on a sliding scale) relationship as fellow-monotheists.

The second beginning is marked by Muslim contact, conversation with and conversion of peoples in the conquered territories. At the same time, Muslims began a process of selective study and appropriation of other traditions of culture, learning and administrative practice. In addition to Jews and Christians, there were now others among the *ahl al-dhimma* (Protected Peoples): Sabaeans, Zoroastrians, Indians, and others, some of whom included in their world-views residual philosophical and intellectual traditions of classical antiquity. The process of exchange and reflexivity generated by the confluence became a major factor in encouraging the interest of Muslim scholars in other religious and intellectual traditions. It has been acknowledged that Muslims may indeed have initiated the first steps in developing a mediaeval history of religions. The stance taken by Muslims during this stage of expansion in their history was determined by their role as a dominant and majority tradition, in which Islam's perceived pre-eminence was clearly established within the *dār al-Islām*. The study of both Islam and other religions, came also to be set within the broader context of developing human and administrative sciences in the Muslim world of the early centuries, as well as by the necessity of explaining, justifying and encompassing other religious communities within the Qur'anic history of religions.

Most existing studies on the Muslim understanding of the other are based on heresiographical literature. This genre, which flourished in the 4th/10th and 5th/11th centuries, represents the dialogical attempt to define and classify the Muslim self in all its growing diversity: Khārijī, Muʿtazilī, Sunni, or Shiʿi, and to create a normative pattern of belief and practice against which 'heresy' and difference could be measured.[1] It can be argued that Muslim heresiography alters the way in which we perceive Muslim 'history of religions' to have been constructed, primarily because it locks us into the legal and theological language of heresiography that had developed as an intellectual practice by that time. Such descriptive texts which were also theological and juristic attempts to portray subdivisions within Islam, attained normative status within each of the Muslim schools of thought, and are primary scholarly resources for a Muslim history of religions as well as sectarianism. They employed a discourse in which identities and differences are constructed negatively, as illustrated by terms such as *bidʿa*, *ghulāt*, and *mulḥid*.[2] The polemical conventions of that legal and theological discourse, based on essentialist interpretations of Islam and on binary oppositions that seek clear and precise distinctions of identity, have prevented sufficient attention from being paid to the other areas of mediation and exchange between Muslims and others and, consequently, distorted their representation in the totality of Muslim discourse. In defining an Ismaʿili perspective on the history of religions, this essay attempts to outline alternative perspectives that emerged within various traditional heresiographical accounts.

The notion of 'Ismaʿili perspectives' calls for some explanation and qualification. There had emerged in the late 3rd/9th and 4th/10th centuries a matrix of theological and intellectual concerns that received subsequent articulation in philosophical, Muʿtazilī as well as Shiʿi/Ismaʿili contexts.[3] Such a discursive process in the theological and philosophical fields paralleled that in the area of jurisprudence.[4] The formative periods of all these intellectual disciplines and concerns were defined by an increasingly cross-cultural and pluralistic milieu. Community formation and definition emerged as part of a broader cultural discourse. The Isma'ili perspectives that emerge in this milieu endeavour to bring the universalistic conceptions of Islam by discovering resonances with other traditions through a reading of their own primary texts in relation to the texts of others. They do not in all instances suggest a fully formulated or agreed upon 'Isma'ili' view. The writers however reflect affiliation, a pattern of approaching issues in a similar vein and of addressing difference in a non-dogmatic way. This methodological stance and non-polemical approach indicates that at this stage of development the Isma'ili writers were more concerned with mediation through intellectual as well as institutional and social organizations.

In considering the sources used here, it is worth pointing out that while in many preceding and succeeding attempts at definition and self-definition, theological and political issues seem to be primarily at stake,[5] the portraits represented in our sources provide testimony that conceptions of peoples could also be emancipated from a mere focus on differentiation and mutual castigation.

THE IKHWĀN AL-ṢAFĀ'

'We were sleepers in the Cave of Adam, our Father' (*Rasā'il Ikhwān al-Ṣafā'*).[6]

In his study on the Ikhwān al-Ṣafā', Ian Netton suggests that it would be more worthwhile to show what *kind* of philosophy is reflected by the group, 'rather than to say *who* they were individually'.[7] This emphasis on the elusiveness of their identity, self-consciously concealed by their choice of a symbolic group name, illustrates the Ikhwān's interest in identifying with ideas, rather than movements, of conversation between traditions rather than their differential character.

Their starting position towards others is indicated at the outset of the *Rasā'il*. They affirm the validity of all the sciences and wisdoms produced by divine inspiration and human reflection. The theory of knowledge adopted by them is not superficially 'encyclopaedic', viz., a compendium of the then existing systems, but an attempt to present a synthesized world-view that is not exclusive to any one tradition. It is this approach that allows the Ikhwān to present, analyze and draw conclusions from the ancient wisdom of all those peoples whose heritage was part of the milieu of the 3rd/9th to the 4th/10th-century Muslim life. As Muslims, the Ikhwān considered knowledge from the past, 'revealed' or 'philosophical', to belong to the wider purview of Islam which was an inclusive and all-encompassing faith. Their sources included revealed books and writings, the books of 'Nature', the philosophical and scientific works of the ancient philosophers and sages and the inspired ideas intuited by pure individuals.[8]

Netton also indicates that any revealed religion faces enormous problems in attempting to reconcile 'pagan philosophy' with its own dogmatic theology.[9] The non-dogmatic posture of the Ikhwān al-Ṣafā' is less arbitrary and it envisages a genuine pluralism in which it may be possible to learn from any tradition. They were committed to the view that there are multiple modes of knowing, which may create parallel discourses, all driving towards the same set of goals. In particular, like other philosophically minded Muslims, the Ikhwān were inclined to take a more inclusive view of the heritage of antiquity, some of whose wisdom they considered to have a status as valid in its essence and expressions of truth as those based on revelation. Indeed, the great prophets such as Abraham, Moses, Joseph and Muḥammad, in their view, were accompanied at the highest rank of the hierarchy of the 'pure brethren' by Pythagoras and Socrates.[10] In considering the *Rasā'il*'s approach to others, it seems evident that they do not locate the notion of barbarism – the *jāhiliyya* – on an axis of salvation, where believers are saved and pagans doomed. The damned are those who have rendered society impervious by their own self-centred opaqueness and the depths of their ignorance.

In the section dealing with the *qiyāma* (Resurrection), there is in the *Rasā'il* a dialogue between the saved (*al-nājī*) and the damned (*al-hālik*). It is worth quoting it in full:[11]

al-nājī: How art thou?
al-hālik: I am in the grace of God; I help the Religion and fight against the enemies of God!
al-nājī: And who are the enemies of God!
al-hālik: Those who do not share my right beliefs!
al-nājī: Even if they are monotheists?
al-hālik: Yes!
al-nājī: And if thou capturest them, how dost thou treat them?
al-hālik: I invite them to accept my ideology (*madhhab*), my belief (*iʿtiqād*), my opinion (*ra'y*)!
al-nājī: And if they do not obey?

al-hālik: I fight against them, I spill their blood, I confiscate their belongings and enslave their offspring.

al-nājī: And if thou dost not succeed in overcoming them?

al-hālik: Then I curse them night and day in my prayers, in order to come nearer to God!

al-nājī: And dost thou know whether these prayers have an effect?

al-hālik: No, I do not know, but I know that in doing so my heart is full of satisfaction. I feel happy!

al-nājī: And dost thou know why?

al-hālik: No, tell me why!

al-nājī: Because thy soul is sick, thy heart is tormented, thy spirit is tortured; because pleasure is nothing but relief of pain. Thou art prisoner in one of the deepest layers of Hell, in the *Ḥuṭama* [Qur'an, CIV: 4–5] till you are saved from it and your soul is delivered from its torment!

al-hālik: Tell me now of thy opinion (*ra'y*), thine ideology (*madhhab*) and of how thou art!

al-nājī: I think I have entered the grace of God. He is so generous with me that I do not succeed in repaying His generosity. I am content with what God gives me, and I am patient at His orders. I do not hate any creature and hurt no one; my soul is at peace, my heart is free, no creature needs to fear anything from me. I commit my religion (*dīn*) and my ideology (*madhhab*) to God alone: I am of the Religion of Abraham!

ABŪ ḤĀTIM AL-RĀZĪ AND ABŪ YA'QŪB AL-SIJISTĀNĪ

Both Abū Ḥātim al-Rāzī (d. 322/934) and Abū Ya'qūb al-Sijistānī (d. after 361/971) belong to the period of the Isma'ili *da'wa* that preceded the full emergence to political power of the Fatimid Isma'ili caliphate.[12] Abū Ḥātim and al-Sijistānī were important participants in establishing the intellectual foundations of what was to develop into a specifically Isma'ili articulation of the theological and philosophical issues debated by Muslims in the 4th/10th century.[13]

Abū Ḥātim al-Rāzī is well-known for his famous debate with the physician-philosopher and his namesake Rhazes, Abū Bakr al-Rāzī. In his work *A'lām al-nubuwwa*, Abū Ḥātim summarizes his arguments in the debate but also extends the discussion to ideas attributed to past sages and prophet-like figures not part of a normatively conceived chain of prophets. His defence of the institution of 'prophecy' develops into a broader treatment of the role of foundational figures in the history of past religions and communities of interpretation, and a reconciliation of revealed religion and rationality.[14]

Abū Ḥātim, and after him al-Sijistānī, created an inclusive framework for a history of religions, in which they tried to place figures such as Zoroaster and communities such as the Sabaeans (mentioned in the Qur'an). Abū Ḥātim relates a tradition from the Imam Jaʿfar al-Ṣādiq that the name *Zardust* (Zoroaster) meant 'the reliable elder', a prophet who gave laws to his people.[15] What is quite significant here is that the writers of the early period of the Ismaʿili *daʿwa* actually debated the issue of the historical placement of Zoroastrianism. Setting aside for the time being the relevance and overall context of Ismaʿili meta-history within which these discussions are set, it is noteworthy that these writers were laying claims to historical knowledge about 'founding' figures at the same time as they were trying to situate them within a cyclical framework of the 'sacred history' of humankind, which included a diversity of religions and philosophical traditions.

In contesting Abū Bakr al-Rāzī's theory of knowledge, which had no place for prophecy or divinely inspired messengers, Abū Ḥātim asserts a parallel between some philosophical discourse and revelation, where there is a congruence of ultimate meaning and moral purpose. In fact, he regarded Plato and the later Neoplatonists, such as Democritus and Proclus, as philosophers whose teachings had characteristics common to the key elements of the revealed truth.[16] Moreover, their views reflected a belief in *tawḥīd*, the unity of God. Although it is certain that Neoplatonic thought as received by Muslim intellectuals played a very influential role for Ismaʿili as well as other Muslim thinkers, one must note, as Stephen Gersh has pointed out, that the indirect traditions spawned by Platonism were part of a complex and developing process.[17] We should be careful not to think of Neoplatonism as a monolithic legacy uncritically appropriated by Muslims.[18]

As more detailed studies of the evolution of Neoplatonism become available, we may be in a better position to understand more fully the channels of its transmission to the Muslim world and the manner of the Muslim appropriations of and responses to this complex and evolving heritage. As the discussion in this essay shows, neither Neoplatonism nor Ismaʿilism admit of determinate definitions in their respective contacts and histories. For our two thinkers, true philosophers and sages offered an opportunity to link diverse moments in the intellectual, religious and moral life of communities.

The history of religions and of wisdoms according to these two thinkers, comes to be enacted in communities in a linear manner across time and across space, but it also unfolds cyclically, because each pattern is an enactment of the process of recovering a beginning. In each pattern, the messengers who bring a revelation or a message enunciate a *sharīʿa*, a legal system which encodes the boundaries that regulate community and daily life and make it possible for faith to operate in society. Those are the boundaries that enable a community to define itself, within the framework of a juridically and ethically conceived way of being religious. This accounts for the historical differences among communities and also suggests why distortions and deviations from original teachings could intrude at later stages of the development of various religious communities, as disputes arose over authority and interpretation of foundational texts.

While recognizing that historical contingency and social contexts influenced the formation of traditions, the above perspectives from Isma'ilism suggest that it is possible to develop mediating categories by which to define a common purpose and goal for human history and its meaning across the spectrum of all societies and traditions.

NOTES

Some of the ideas expressed here were presented at two conferences, one on 'Muslim perceptions of Others' held in Lausanne, Switzerland, and another on 'Muslim–Jewish relations', in Portland, Oregon. I am grateful to Professors Jacques Waardenburg and Stephen Wasserstrom for inviting me to participate and to various other colleagues at these meetings for their helpful comments and suggestions.

1 For an analysis of this process, see W. M. Watt, *Early Islam* (Edinburgh, 1990), pp. 173–184, and Bernard Lewis, *Islam in History* (Chicago, 1993), pp. 275–294. Both are collections of earlier articles.

2 In addition to an historical analysis of these terms as used in heresiographical literature, see the following articles: J. Robson 'Bid'a', EI2, vol. 1, p. 1199; M. G. S. Hodgson, 'Ghulāt', EI2, vol. 2, pp. 1093–1095, and W. Madelung, 'Mulḥid', EI2, vol. 7, p. 546.

3 For an analysis of the context against which Isma'ili ideas developed, see Paul E. Walker, *Early Philosophical Shiism: The Ismaili Neoplatonism of Abū Yaqʿūb al-Sijistānī* (Cambridge, 1993), pp. 3–63.

4 Norman Calder's recent study, *Studies in Early Muslim Jurisprudence* (Oxford, 1993), traces this parallel process for jurisprudence, but links it also to the wider discursive processes in theology.

5 This was particularly so in the case of the 'Abbasid dynasty; see J. Lassner, *Islamic Revolution and Historical Memory: An Inquiry into the Art of ʿAbbāsid Apologetics* (New Haven, 1986).

6 *Rasā'il Ikhwān al-Ṣafā'* (Beirut, 1957), vol. 4, p. 18. For the Qura'nic reference, see the Qur'an, XVIII.

7 I. R. Netton, *Muslim Neoplatonists: An Introduction to the Thought of the Brethren of Purity (Ikhwān al-Ṣafā')* (London, 1982), p. 8; he also provides an extensive bibliography. For a summary analysis of the Isma'ili affiliations of the work, see Farhad Daftary, *The Ismā'īlīs: Their History and Doctrines* (Cambridge, 1990), pp. 246–248.

8 See Seyyed Hossein Nasr, *An Introduction to Islamic Cosmological Doctrines* (2dn edn, Albany, N.Y., 1993), p. 39.

9 Netton, *Muslim Neoplatonists*, p. 33.

10 The hierarchy is developed in the *Rasā'il*, vol. 4, p. 36. See also Nasr, *Islamic Cosmological Doctrines*, pp. 31–32.

11 *Rasā'il Ikhwān al-Ṣafā'*, vol. 3, pp. 312–313; the condensed translation cited here appeared originally in *Ismā'īlī Contributions to Islamic Culture*, ed. S. H. Nasr (Tehran, 1977), p. 136, where it was part of an article by A. Bausani, 'Scientific Elements in Ismā'īlī Thought: The Epistles of the Brethren of Purity', pp. 121–140.

12 Walker, *Early Philosophical Shiism*, pp. 13–24, 51–55; Daftary, *The Ismā'īlīs*, pp. 165–168; and for their respective writings, see I. K. Poonawala, *Biobibliography of Ismā'īlī Literature* (Malibu, Calif., 1977), pp. 82–89.

13 For an overview of the historical and intellectual contexts, see Daftary, *The Ismā'īlīs*, chapters 3 and 4.

14 Abū Ḥātim al-Rāzī, *A'lām al-nubuwwa*, ed. Ṣ. al-Ṣāwī and G. R. A'vānī (Tehran, 1977). For sections and background related to the debate, see P. Kraus, 'Raziana II', *Orientalia*, NS, 5 (1936), pp. 35–56, 358–378. See also Hans Daiber, 'Abū Ḥātim ar-Rāzī (10th Century A.D.) on the Unity and Diversity of Religions', in *Dialogue and Syncretism: An Interdisciplinary Approach*, ed. J. Gort et al. (Grand Rapids, Michigan, 1989), pp. 87–104. Some of the translations in the article (pp. 87–100) need revision.

15 Abū Ḥātim, *A'lām*, pp. 171–177. See also S. M. Stern, 'Abū Ḥātim al-Rāzī on Persian Religion', in his *Studies in Early Ismā'īlism* (Jerusalem–Leiden, 1983), pp. 30–46.

16 See Abū Ḥātim, *A'lām*, pp. 125–127, 131–132, and Walker, *Early Philosophical Shiism*, p. 51.

17 Stephen Gersh, *Middle Platonism and Neoplatonism: The Latin Tradition* (Notre Dame, 1986), vol. 1, pp. 25ff.

18 W. Ivanow's research in the early period of the *da'wa* in Iran reflects this; see his *Studies in Early Persian Ismailism* (Leiden, 1948; 2nd edn, Bombay, 1955). For Abū Ḥātim's 'corrections' of the misinterpretations of a previous *dā'ī*, al-Nasafī, see Walker, *Early Philosophical Shiism*, pp. 52–53.

NINE

An Isma'ili version of the heresiography of the seventy-two erring sects

PAUL E. WALKER

IN ISLAMIC theological disputation, the use of heresiography was a standard weapon of both offence and defence. It was widely practised and practically no individual group failed to compose, at one time or another, a catalogue of its enemies and to set out therein a list of each sect's distinguishing (and erring) features. Of the great number of treatises of this kind known to have been written, however, relatively few have survived and, although examples have been available that provide the viewpoints of the Ḥanafīs, the Ash'arīs and the Mu'tazilīs, for example, and certain types of Shi'is, no true heresiography was, until recently, known for the Isma'ilis. However, there is no intrinsic reason why it should not have existed. A major Isma'ili writer from the early part of the 4th/10th century, Abū Ḥātim al-Rāzī (d. 322/934), left in his *Kitāb al-zīna* a valuable account of words and terms that appear in heresiographical literature.[1] In his explanations and definitions for these terms, he offered what amounts to materials for a more formal heresiography. At the end of the 4th/10th or beginning of the 5th/11th century, Ḥamīd al-Dīn al-Kirmānī, another highly important Isma'ili *dā'ī*, wrote a fairly extensive refutation of various Islamic sects in his *Tanbīh al-hādī wa'l-mustahdī* and that, again, could easily form, in a slightly different context, a heresiography.[2] Beyond these two examples, other Isma'ili works contain explicit references to any number of opposing sectarian tendencies which they castigate and reject. In short, Isma'ili specialists on doctrinal issues were, like Muslim authorities in other groups, fully conversant with the historical elaboration of theological and legal controversies over a complete range of Islamic sectarian developments.

Recently, additional Isma'ili material has come to light in a hitherto all but unknown work by an obscure Khurāsānī *dāʿī* named Abū Tammām who flourished during the 4th/10th century. The work is called *Kitāb al-shajara*, and Part One of this treatise turns out to contain a full and formal heresiography of the seventy-two erring sects, much in the standard tradition of Islamic writings on that subject. While an early impression of the material in this new Ismaʿili heresiography already shows it to be of major importance, a full analysis of it is not yet complete. Nevertheless, it is useful now both to announce this discovery and to contribute some tentative observations about its value for the study of Islamic sects and the heresiographical tradition about them.

Abū Tammām, the author of the *Kitāb al-shajara*, remains rather obscure – a fact that reflects lack of information about him in both common historical accounts and in the records of the later Ismaʿili *daʿwa*. His name appears, for example, in later Ismaʿili works solely in this form without an *ism* or a *nisba*. His Khurāsānī origin is established only from information in his writings which contain references to his being in Khurāsān and to material showing that he was a disciple of the famous Khurāsānī philosopher and *dāʿī*, Muḥammad al-Nasafī (d. 332/943). Further references prove also that he was the author of another work called *Kitāb al-burhān*.[3] The latter treatise was the subject of an adverse judgement by the Fatimid caliph-imam al-Muʿizz (341–365/953–975) and, probably as a consequence, ceased to be preserved by the *daʿwa*. The little information that does exist thus locates him, in the greatest likelihood, as part of the Khurāsānī school of Ismaʿilism that followed al-Nasafī in the second quarter of the 4th/10th century.[4]

Ironically, Abū Tammām's *Shajara* first appeared in print falsely labelled as a work of a 10th/16th century Syrian Nizārī Ismaʿili *dāʿī*, Abū Firās Shihāb al-Dīn al-Maynaqī,[5] and then, in a second version, as that of the 3rd/9th century *dāʿī* ʿAbdān.[6] Those publications, both by ʿĀrif Tāmir, although largely the same, contain only that portion of Abū Tammām's work which once formed, more or less, Part Two of the *Kitāb al-shajara*. Despite these publications of Tāmir, we have no manuscripts of this Part Two nor any information about them. On the other hand, Professor Abbas Hamdani, once alerted to the importance of this text, was able to trace and obtain a copy of Part One of the *Kitāb al-shajara* among the manuscript holdings of his family.[7] His efforts, meanwhile, have convinced him that copies of Part Two are not readily available in the Ismaʿili collections held by the Ṭayyibī Ismaʿilis and that it may not have survived with them at all. It is Part One which offers a largely self-contained heresiography and it can be investigated independently of the many, unresolved but peripheral, questions that relate to the rest of Abū Tammām's original *Shajara*.

The book as a whole is roughly organized around an inquiry into the various kinds of beings: angels, *jinn*, *shayṭān*s, *iblīs*es, and humans, as each in turn exists, first, as a potential (*bi'l-quwwa*) and, second, as an actuality (*bi'l-fi'l*). It is the third section on the *shayṭān*s that provided Abū Tammām an opportunity to insert his heresiography.

Having completed his account of the angels and the *jinn*, he launches into the subject of the *shayāṭīn*. They are, as might be supposed from other Isma'ili sources, the propagators of the *ẓāhir* (exterior) of scripture and relgion without the corresponding *bāṭin* (interior). The *shayāṭīn*, Abū Tammām says, are the *fuqahā' al-qishriyya*, those who cling to the external word, the *qishr* (shell), without comprehending the internal meaning, the *lubb* (kernel).[8] Lest there be any doubt about his Isma'ili viewpoint, he specifically cites in this section for the *ahl al-bāṭin* ('Adherents of the Inner Meaning') the well known 'rope of God' which, according to him in this case, runs as follows: *qalam*, *lawḥ*, *jadd*, *fatḥ*, *khayāl*, *nāṭiq*, *asās*, *imām*, *ḥujja* and *janāḥ*. This is the standard version of the Isma'ili hierarchy as expressed in the distinctive, technical language that is common to members of the Persian *da'wa* in the 4th/10th century.[9] Next, he mentions several *ḥadīth*s concerning dissension in Islam or in other religious communities which has occurred or will occur. Finally, he concludes this thought with the famous *ḥadīth* that claims that the Banū Isrā'īl were divided after Moses into seventy-one sects, all of which are in Hell except one which is in Paradise; that the community of Jesus divided after him into seventy-two, all in Hell save one in Paradise; and finally that after the Prophet his community will divide into seventy-three sects, seventy-two in Hell and one in Paradise.[10] Moreover, says Abū Tammām,

> No doubt exists that for each of these sects there was a chief or a *dā'ī* who called the people to his particular point-of-view and belief. These are the *shayāṭīn* . . . After the Messenger departed from this world, the *ahl al-ẓāhir* ('Adherents of the External Word') split into seventy-two sects, while the *ahl al-bāṭin* remained as they were, no dissension occurring among them nor animosities and doubt as happened among the *ahl al-ẓāhir*, who curse one another and separate into opposing groups.[11]

It is at this point that he announces his intention to

> delineate these *madhāhib* and *firaq*, *madhhab* by *madhhab*, *firqa* by *firqa* and to explain the beliefs of each of them.[12]

From this point in the *Shajara*, Abū Tammām turns away from the general theme of his book to begin a detailed outline of the distinguishing doctrines of the seventy-two sects, which he proceeds now to discuss with reasonable care and thoroughness. In fact, the next 122 folios (or some 244 pages) of the *Shajara* – with the exception of a few short digressions – are taken up with an account of the erring sects, arranged, as he had stated, sect by sect. Only at the end of this does he return once again to the *ahl al-bāṭin* and to the explanation of how this group alone, through the operation of *ta'wīl* (interpretation), which is the cornerstone of their doctrine, allow a reconciliation of the various issues of conflict that have separated those other, diverging Islamic sects, bringing about a single, undifferentiated, enduring truth; one that transcends dissension and contradiction.

Given its overall length and the amount of specific information about each sect, this new heresiography is likely to be of great importance. Moreover, Abū Tammām was far less concerned with refutation than many other Muslim writers of this type of work. Although he is not above expressing disgust at a blatantly unacceptable sectarian doctrine, he generally intends merely to illustrate conscientiously how Muslims who lack proper guidance will inevitably go astray. By holding exclusively to the literal, external teaching of false leaders, people fall into error. His heresiography is a catalogue of such errors. But, by ultimately relying on a grand principle that provides an escape – the ultimate accommodation vouchsafed by interpretative reconciliation – Abū Tammām is able to delineate freely a full account of each sect and its distinguishing features without immediately engaging in partisan rhetoric. Nevertheless, in a few instances, especially at those points where he interjects his own personal observations of sectarian behaviour, as he does with the infamous Mubayyiḍa, Abū Tammām does cross this line to the partisan position one finds in other examples of heresiography. Still, on balance, his effort to understand and explain sectarian differences is admirably thorough and relatively non-partisan.

Unlike any other known work on the sects, Abū Tammām's commences with a division of the whole into three classes according to three different fundamental principles. Each principle groups together exactly twenty-four of the seventy-two sects. These principles are the following: (1) that obedience [to God] is entirely a matter of faith (*al-qawl bi-anna al-ṭā'a kulluhā min al-īmān*); (2) that the laws are not constitutive of faith (*al-qawl bi-anna al-sharā'i' laysat min al-īmān*); and (3) that the imam after the Messenger of God is 'Alī. However, except for this arrangement in divisions of 24 × 24 × 24, the sect list which he presents divides irregularly into eleven *madhhabs* as follows: the Muʿtazila (six sects), the Khawārij (fourteen sects), the Ḥadīthiyya or *aṣḥāb al-ḥadīth* (four sects), the Qadariyya or Mujbira (five sects), the Mushabbiha (thirteen sects), the Murji'a (six sects), the Zaydiyya (five sects), the Kaysāniyya (four sects), the ʿAbbāsiyya (two sects), the Ghāliya (eight sects), and the Imāmiyya (five sects). Later, he will claim that there cannot be seventy-two without a seventy-third or eleven without a twelfth as if these numbers, including especially the eleven *madhāhib*, were necessary and essential to his schema.

For the initial division into twenty-fours, however, there seems to be no logical reason as to why it must be exactly this way, or where such an arrangement might have come from. Moreover, at least in the case of one of the ʿAbbāsiyya sects, the Rāwandiyya, he admits that they believe the imamate to have passed directly from the Prophet to his uncle al-ʿAbbās, not to ʿAlī as stipulated in the general statement of principle.

This raises serious questions about the origin of Abū Tammām's sect list and whether or not it fits his declared purpose. An obvious explanation is that his list was derived from another work, perhaps one that did not share his particular focus and sectarian interests. Further evidence for this conclusion exists in his section on the Mushabbiha where he has inadvertently added a sect that violates the proper numerical order – an order which is otherwise obvious. Abū Tammām simply continues the following entry, as one of his sources must have done, with the original numbering scheme and he thus winds up with two successive sects numbered 'seventh' in that section. He was, moreover, seemingly unaware of this mistake.

Decisive evidence suggesting that Abū Tammām's sect list comes from an outside source is its appearance in virtually identical form in the list provided by al-Khwārazmī in his *Mafātīḥ al-ʿulūm*.[13] This work, written at the Sāmānid court in Khurāsān around 370/980–981 or slightly earlier, offers an exceedingly brief enumeration of the Islamic sects and provides, in nearly all cases, only a name, a principal from whom the sect stems, and for a few of them a sentence about their doctrine. Abū Tammām, on the other hand, gives extensive entries for each, although he does so for the same list of sects with only a rare, apparently minor, exception.[14] Still, the lists of Abū Tammām and al-Khwārazmī possess a striking degree of similarity. But they do contain enough small divergences in details to prove that they both were derived from yet another source – a source about which one can, at present, only speculate.

On the other hand, while it is true that the list itself is of unknown provenance, the actual material contained in Abū Tammām's individual entries – material missing in al-Khwārazmī's brief statements – can in many cases be found elsewhere, often in the *Maqālāt al-Islāmiyyīn* of Abu'l-Ḥasan al-Ashʿarī (d. 324/935–936).[15] Since Abū Tammām included the Ashʿariyya among the sects and mentioned as its founder al-Ashʿarī (fol. 64r), even citing al-Ashʿarī's work *Kitāb al-lumaʿ*, it would be reasonable to expect this link to indicate the lineage of his heresiography. Even admitting the substantial overlap in the material in both works, closer examination reveals, however, that al-Ashʿarī is not Abū Tammām's source. Rather, the individual entries in al-Ashʿarī's text that match Abū Tammām's in some respects, are, almost certainly, parallel versions of a common, earlier source. This is confirmed on the basis of comparisons with another known heresiography, the *Ḥūr al-ʿīn* by Nashwān al-Ḥimyarī (d. 574/1178).[16] Although relatively late, this heresiography is based on much older material. It contains, in several cases, sentences that appear also in the *Shajara*, although not in al-Ashʿarī's text even when all three coincide for the same entry in other respects. Since al-Ḥimyarī cites his source, which is the heresiographical treatise of Abu'l-Qāsim al-Balkhī (d. 319/931), one may presume that al-Balkhī's work lies behind the heresiography of Abū Tammām, as it certainly does also for that of al-Ashʿarī. At any rate, the published portion of al-Balkhī's text – the section on the Muʿtazila[17] – allows an instance for specific textual comparison of the two.

A noteworthy feature of al-Balkhī's account of the Muʿtazila is his statement of what they, as a group, agree upon in general. An almost identical version of the same statement is found at the beginning of Abū Tammām's entry on them. Although there are slight discrepancies between the wording of the two works, there is little doubt that Abū Tammām's section on the Muʿtazila derives from al-Balkhī, including most of the points Abū Tammām enumerates for each of the six individual subsects. But it is also likely that there was an intermediary – not al-Ashʿarī – between al-Balkhī and Abū Tammām. This step is necessary to account for the sect list in the *Shajara*, which cannot have been based on al-Balkhī to judge from the arrangement of his Muʿtazila section as a whole. In addition, the division by three general statements of principle remains unaccounted for. Perhaps such an intermediary was an earlier Ismaʿili authority; one candidate would be Muḥammad al-Nasafī and his work *Kitāb al-maḥṣūl*, which Abū Tammām recommends in the *Shajara*.[18] On the other hand, al-Nasafī, as an Isma'ili, is unlikely to be al-Khwārazmī's source. Another candidate, who might have been available to both Abū Tammām and al-Khwārazmī, is the philosopher Abū Zayd al-Balkhī who is known to have written a work on the sciences called *Kitāb aqsām al-'ulūm* which may have been similar to the later *Mafātīḥ al-'ulūm*.[19] Abū Zayd once worked for the Isma'ili *amīr* al-Marwazī in Khurāsān and was also a good friend of Abu'l-Qāsim al-Balkhī. At one time, he, Muḥammad al-Nasafī, the *amīr* al-Marwazī and quite likely Abū Tammām, were all members of the same circle living in the same city.

Significantly, none of the material in Abū Tammām comes from the earlier *Kitāb al-zīna* of his Isma'ili colleague Abū Ḥātim or, for that matter, from Imāmī Shi'i works like the *firaq* treatises of al-Nawbakhtī and al-Qummī.

Still, the instances where the texts of al-Ḥimyarī, al-Ash'arī, or even al-Balkhī himself, help establish the ultimate source of Abū Tammām for various passages and thus seem to account for such material in the *Shajara*, do not fully explain the whole of what it contains. A number of personal observations exist, for example, that surely belong to Abū Tammām alone. Other, relatively numerous, entries relate to sects that do not appear in the works of either al-Ash'arī or al-Ḥimyarī; many are, in fact, not dealt with in any other *firaq* treatise (excepting that of al-Khwārazmī). Since al-Balkhī's work is, until now, available only for the portion that covers the Mu'tazila, judgements about the rest of its original contents depend at this time solely on the evidence from al-Ash'arī and al-Ḥimyarī. Accordingly, where there is no material on a given sect in these two works, does an entry for that sect by Abū Tammām nevertheless reflect al-Balkhī as its ultimate source? Or were there yet other sources that Abū Tammām or an intermediary utilized besides al-Balkhī?

Abū Tammām's descriptions of as many as eight sects are, for most purposes, unique in the literature of heresiography. Furthermore, his account of several others stands alone even though the basic facts surrounding these sects were known previously from other sources. In several more cases, his entries, although in part a reflection of other material, provide either additional information, or in some instances, versions of al-Balkhī which are slightly at odds with either al-Ash'arī or al-Ḥimyarī. In the absence of al-Balkhī's work, these passages constitute a valuable second or third witness to his original text. All in all, the material that Abū Tammām's heresiography contributes to the study of Islamic sects is more extensive than can readily be summarized here. On this occasion, we can present only a few tentative conclusions and some examples that indicate what may be expected from a full exploration of the new material in the *Shajara*.

In presenting these conclusions and examples, it is useful to group the following remarks into several categories: (A) new versions of al-Balkhī's text; (B) new facts that add to older materials; (C) new accounts of known sects; (D) personal observations that confirm other reports; and (E) descriptions of sects that were previously unknown.

(A) New versions of al-Balkhī

Almost all of the entries in the *Shajara* which appear also in one form or another in al-Ashʿarī and/or al-Ḥimyarī contain variant readings or phrasing. This is also true in regard to al-Balkhī's text where it exists, as in his introduction to the Muʿtazila. Moreover, although it is often possible to find a part of Abū Tammām's description of a particular sect in al-Ashʿarī and the balance in al-Ḥimyarī, not infrequently certain items are missing in both. Thus, for example, in the case of the Bidʿiyya (fols. 35v–37r) of the Khawārij, Abū Tammām provides the name of the principal, Yaḥyā b. Aṣram, and the fact that they accept only three daily prayers and hold that the tradition requiring five is a fake.[20] They also forbid, he reports, eating fish that are not slaughtered.[21] The rest of the entry can be found in either al-Ashʿarī or al-Ḥimyarī. Another example is Abū Tammām's account of the Ḍaḥḥākiyya (fols. 42r–43r) where again he gives the name of the principal and at least one fact about this group not found in the other two works. Al-Ashʿarī and al-Ḥimyarī, on the other hand, both mention a doctrine held in a subsect of the Ḍaḥḥākiyya about the non-rights of non-Khārijī women that Abū Tammām did not include. Yet another example of this type is the whole of Abū Tammām's version of the Ḥadīthiyya (fols. 43r–51v) which goes beyond the limited material that exists in the other two.

(B) New facts that add to older materials

In a number of cases Abū Tammām's entries provide clarification of items in previous accounts that were formerly either incomplete or vague and problematic. One relatively simple example of this type relates to the section on the Zaydiyya and to his discussion of the Dukayniyya[22] (fols. 109v–110v) who were, according to him, disciples of al-Faḍl b. al-Dukayn and Ibrāhīm b. al-Ḥakam. Abū Tammām explicitly reports of this group that in general they upheld the doctrines of the Muʿtazila. Abū Nuʿaym al-Faḍl b. al-Dukayn was a reasonably famous traditionist in Kūfa whose Zaydī tendencies, while not everywhere recognized, were nonetheless clear. That he was the founder of a school was also understood.[23] The second person, Ibrāhīm b. al-Ḥakam, on the other hand, must be the same as the Ḥakam al-Muʿtazilī, vaguely cited in this context by others.[24] Another curious fact comes from Abū Tammām's entry for the Nāʾūsiyya (fols. 140r–141r), a sect in the Imāmiyya *madhhab*. They maintained, says Abū Tammām, that Jaʿfar al-Ṣādiq is not dead but rather is still alive and 'is imprisoned on one of the islands in the Western Sea' – the latter assertion does not appear elsewhere.

(C) New accounts for known sects

The Karrāmiyya offer a good example here. As a sect the Karrāmiyya were more apt to be discussed in later heresiographical literature such as the 5th/11th century *al-Farq bayn al-firaq* of al-Baghdādī. Al-Ashʿarī had included them among the Murjiʾa and had given a brief and rather uninformative description of them.[25] Although it is one of the earliest reports available, his report is hardly adequate. By contrast, Abū Tammām provides a fairly extensive entry on the Karrāmiyya (fols. 64v–66v), which he locates among the Mushabbiha (following in numerical order his account of the Ashʿariyya). Although many of the details in this material conform to facts otherwise known about this sect, the overall presentation is not directly related to that of al-Ashʿarī and, therefore, possibly not to al-Balkhī. A striking new piece of information that Abū Tammām adds, for example, is that the Karrāmiyya,

> maintain that the people will be gathered [at the *ḥashr*] in Jerusalem and that their chief, Muḥammad b. Karrām, had brought about the relocation to Jerusalem from Khurāsān and its vicinity of more than five thousand families. Seeing that humanity will be gathered in it, having removed there at this time, [the *ḥashr*] will be easier for them on the day of resurrection since they will be already closer to it.

That Ibn Karrām moved to Jerusalem at the end of his life and that his followers existed there in large numbers was previously known.[26] Abū Tammām now explains why this happened.

Another section of the *Shajara* covers both the Kullābiyya (fols.

62v–63v) and the Ashʿariyya (fols. 63v–64v), as if the second were closely related to the first. This is an association that is prominent in the discussions of both groups by Ibn al-Nadīm and the Qāḍī ʿAbd al-Jabbār – that is, in accounts produced during the 4th/10th century – but it is not so noticeable in the version of their origin offered by the later Ashʿarīs. For the Kullābiyya, on whom there might have been a passage in al-Balkhī, a new piece of information offered by Abū Tammām is that Muḥammad b. Kullāb was a Christian prior to becoming Muslim. The entry on al-Ashʿarī by itself is curious in that it presupposes recognition of him and his following as a sect at a fairly early date, assuming that Abū Tammām did, in fact, belong to the second quarter of the 4th/10th century as appears likely. Does this citation of the Ashʿariyya also mean that, for example, al-Balkhī too might have included such an entry? Al-Balkhī's death in 319/931, before that of al-Ashʿarī, certainly suggests otherwise. Thus, the Kullābiyya/Ashʿariyya material may belong to a slightly later period.

Another example of this type is Abū Tammām's entry on a sect he calls the Ghamāmiyya (fols. 131v ff.), one of the Ghāliya *madhhab* among the Shiʿa. Al-Khwārazmī knew that this was an unfamiliar sect and he therefore included a line of description about it, namely, that these people believe that God comes down to earth in a cloud (*ghamām*). Abū Tammām, however, goes further and comments that the Ghamāmiyya base this claim on verse II: 210 of the Qur'an which says that God will come to them in the shadow of the clouds (*fī ẓulalin min al-ghamām*) and, in addition, he quotes several lines of a poem by the Kaysānī poet al-Sayyid al-Ḥimyarī in censure of them. Now, although the material in Abū Tammām's account belongs, according to him, to a sect called the Ghamāmiyya, this reference is surely to the same group that al-Ashʿarī lists under the Sabā'iyya and the heresiographer al-Ḥimyarī actually labels 'al-Saḥābiyya', *saḥāb* here being a synonym of *ghamām*.[27]

(D) Personal observations that confirm other reports

The Mubayyiḍa, the 'wearers of white', are a sect that emerged in the wake of the ʿAbbasid revolution but continued independently of it in various parts of Iran long afterward. For the details of their doctrines and activities, Abū Tammām's entry in the *Shajara* (fols. 88r–92r) by and large duplicates information previously known. However, none of the other reports are as direct and succinct as his, nor – especially important in this case – as personal.

They began, he says, as the followers of al-Muqanna' whose name was Hishām b. Ḥakīm al-Marwazī, and they are a part of the Mushabbiha because they believe that God is corporeal. To them each of the messengers was divine; if God wishes to speak to corporeal beings He enters the form of one of them and makes him a messenger-prophet, able to command and prohibit. For this doctrine they cite the Qur'an (LIII: 3–12). The humans so chosen by God were Adam, Abraham, Moses, Jesus, Muḥammad, Abū Muslim and finally al-Muqanna'. Between His manifestation in these persons, God has returned to His throne, and now they – the Mubayyiḍa – await a further reappearance.

The Mubayyiḍa, according to Abū Tammām, consider licit among themselves access to each other's women, as well as carrion, blood, the flesh of pigs, wine and other forbidden things; in the scripture these items signify only the names of men whose leadership God has rejected. At this point Abū Tammām interjects his own presence. He says,

> I have seen a great number of them and disputed with them. None of them have any knowledge of what constitutes the foundations of their faith. We do not know al-Muqanna' nor his times except [only] their [present] deceits.[28]

They are an exclusive sect, he continues, not mixing with others although living interspersed with Muslims.

(E) *New sects*

The following entries in the *Shajara* describe sects for which there is apparently no other information (or almost none).[29]

(i) The Ṣabbāḥiyya (fols. 60r–62r). They are a part of the Qadariyya and stem from a certain Abū Ṣabbāḥ b. Ma'mar (or Mu'ammar). They claim that the most excellent person after the Prophet was 'Umar b. al-Khaṭṭāb. Among their other doctrines is a refusal to accept animals slaughtered by the *ahl al-kitāb* or enter into marriage with their womenfolk. These prohibitions commenced, they insist, with the changing of the *qibla*.[30]

(ii) The B_tāniyya (fols. 73r–75r). As the seventh entry among the Mushabbiha, Abū Tammām names first a sect which could be either al-B_tāniyya or al-T_bāniyya. These people believe that Adam was created in the image of al-Raḥmān (God).

(iii) Aṣḥāb al-Faḍā' (fols. 75r–76r). Next, he describes another sect, also numbered as the seventh of the Mushabbiha, which he calls 'Aṣḥāb al-Faḍā'' (fols. 75r–76r). Al-Khwārazmī, who does not list the former, calls the latter al-Qaḍā'iyya. Abū Tammām is more informative. This group consists of two sections, one stemming from someone named ʿAbd Allāh b. Abī ʿAbd Allāh al-Taymī and the other from Manṣūr b. Bishr al-Umawī. Both say that God is '*al-Faḍā*''.

(iv) The Minhāliyya (fols. 86v–88v). The Minhāliyya stem from al-Minhāl b. al-Maymūn al-ʿIjlī and are one of the Mushabbiha who believe that God is a body with length, breadth, and width and that He is able to change His essence into different, physical forms.

(v) The Ijtihādiyya (fols. 104r–105v). Ijtihādiyya is a name which relates to two different groups: followers respectively of Jaḥdar b. Muḥammad al-Tamīmī and Muḥammad b. Rammād al-Ḥulaybī (?) al-Mukawwaʿ (?). They are a part of the Murji'a and they hold basically that every Muslim who exercises *ijtihād*, viz., every *mujtahid*, is correct and sound in belief, regardless of other details, and that all these will enter Paradise without judgement. Some of them even argue that all who affirm the existence (*aysiyya*) of God will attain Paradise even if they do not recognize the Messenger(s).

(vi) The Khashabiyya (fols. 110v–111v). According to the *Shajara*, they were originally those adherents of al-Mukhtār who used wooden weapons but who were known later in Khurāsān by their leader Ṣurkhāb al-Ṭabarī. Strangely, although the affiliation with al-Mukhtār might place them among the Kaysāniyya, Abū Tammām lists them as a subsect of the Zaydiyya and goes on to explain that for them ʿAlī was not an imam but merely the 'executor' (*waṣī*) of the imamate that the Prophet had deposited with him until he could pass it on to al-Ḥasan. Thereafter the imamate will remain among the descendants of al-Ḥasan and al-Ḥusayn, that is, with the Fatimids. It may reside in any one of them who rises in revolt whether that person is knowledgeable or ignorant, just or tyrannical, and, if two should claim it at the same time, no one should take sides in the struggle between them.

(vii) The Ḥubbiyya (fols. 76v–78v). Perhaps the most curious of the newly revealed sects are these Ḥubbiyya, another of the Mushabbiha. Abū Tammām has little sympathy for them, calling them the partisans of pompous talk and delusions. They were given the name 'Ḥubbiyya' because they maintain that they love God and do not worship Him out of fear of punishment or hope of His reward. God, for them, is a body in the form of a handsome youth. Abū Tammām then relates the following report about their secret activities that he says comes to him from Abu'l-Ḥasan al-Nāshi'. The latter had said that a certain ʿAbd Allāh b.

Muḥammad b. Isḥāq b. Mūsā b. Ja'far reported to him the following ceremony from Yaḥyā b. Mu'ādh al-Rāzī who was himself well known among these people. Al-Rāzī said that he was in Iraq where he attended a ceremony in which a beautiful youth, clothed in the finest garments, was seated on a dais that was raised above the floor. Two hooks were placed above him and a curtain was suspended between him and the audience with a keeper to raise and lower the curtain on command. The people in attendance at the house where this ceremony took place then recited songs of desire and plaintive hymns, mentioning the *ḥūr al-'īn* and Paradise and what God has prepared in it for the saints. These supplicants continued, with increasing fervour, to ask to be permitted a visit and to savour that youth. When we implored, says al-Rāzī, and begged, he ordered the keeper of the curtain to raise it. We persisted relentlessly until the keeper raised it and when it was raised and he appeared on that throne, we fell on our faces. This continued in this fashion until dawn broke at which time we departed and dispersed.

(viii) The Khalafiyya (fols. 111v–114v). The Khalafiyya are a subsect of the Zaydiyya, stemming from a certain Khalaf b. 'Abd al-Ṣamad. They claim that the imam after Zayd was this 'Abd al-Ṣamad, a son of Zayd! Abū Tammām readily admits that the genealogists agree that this man was a client of Zayd, and not his son, and those who make this claim are liars. However, for the Khalafiyya the imamate was passed from 'Abd al-Ṣamad to his own son Khalaf, to the latter's son Muḥammad, and then to Aḥmad, a son of this Muḥammad. Khalaf fled from the Umayyads to the country of the Turks. According to them, there is a descendant of Aḥmad b. Muḥammad b. Khalaf who resides there even now and will rise as the Messiah (*al-Mahdī*). They do not know the names of the imams after Aḥmad, however, but as the knowledge of an imam comes to him by inspiration (*ilhām*), not by acquisition (*iktisāb*), and the imam comprehends all languages, he (and he alone) will be able to explicate the book that Khalaf left behind which he composed in letters of an alphabet unknown to any one else.

The Khalafiyya subscribe to a doctrine of *tawḥīd* which denies that one may describe or characterize God in any way. For example, one may say neither that He is knowing nor that He is *not* knowing (*'ālim wa lā lā 'ālim*). He is not 'powerful' and not *not* 'powerful' (*lā qādir wa lā lā qādir*); He is not a thing and not *not* a thing (*lā shay' wa lā lā shay'*). Such a teaching is almost identical to that of the Isma'ilis, particularly as taught by the *dā'ī* Abū Ya'qūb al-Sijistānī, who was presumably a contemporary of Abū Tammām.

Yet another complex set of doctrines held by these Khalafiyya reflect a form of pentadist (otherwise called in Arabic *al-mukhammisa*) devotion to fives: five primary angels, Mīkhā'īl,[31] Jibrā'īl, 'Izrā'īl, Mīkā'īl and Isrāfīl, for example; and five chosen creatures on earth, namely, Muḥammad, 'Alī, Fāṭima, al-Ḥasan and al-Ḥusayn. They also cite many other examples of fives: five fingers, five pillars of Islam, five senses, five prayer times, five books of scripture, five things leading to salvation and five special months of the year.

With his description of this strange sect, Abū Tammām concludes his account of the Zaydīs by appending a few general remarks on the common characteristics of this *madhhab* as a whole. In this regard, he mentions that the Zaydīs have produced a great number of books on the laws, the *aḥkām* and *fiqh*, among which is the *Kitāb al-mustarshid*, written, reports Abū Tammām, by al-Nāṣir al-'Alawī.[32] It is possible that the author of the *Shajara* may himself have been personally familiar with Zaydī writings such as the one he cites here.

(ix) The Isḥāqiyya (fols. 117r–118v). This group is a part of the Kaysāniyya that derive from someone named Isḥāq (b. 'Amr).[33] They trace the imamate from 'Alī b. Abī Ṭālib to Muḥammad b. al-Ḥanafiyya, then to Abū Hāshim 'Abd Allāh b. Muḥammad b. al-Ḥanafiyya, then to the son of his brother al-Ḥasan b. 'Alī b. Muḥammad b. al-Ḥanafiyya, then to 'Alī the son of al-Ḥusayn (al-Ḥasan),[34] who died without issue. Thereupon, the Isḥāqiyya broke up into two groups, one reverting to the expectation of the reappearance of Muḥammad b. al-Ḥanafiyya himself, and a second holding that the imamate would be confined to the progeny of this Muḥammad. The latter group held that upon the death of 'Alī b. al-Ḥusayn, the imamate reverted to the descendants of Ibn al-Ḥanafiyya and that it resides at the time with one of them who had fled the Umayyads and 'Abbasids by going to the country of the Turks. They maintain that they know his name and place of residence and that the Messiah (*al-Mahdī*) will come from there, i.e., from the direction of the Turks, and that he will explain the Qur'an in Turkish (*bi'l-Turkiyya*), answering all questions in Turkish with a translator as an intermediary.[35] Otherwise, reports Abū Tammām, this group accepts doctrines which conform to those propounded by the Mu'tazila.[36]

NOTES

I gratefully acknowledge the help and guidance of both Abbas Hamdani and Wilferd Madelung in the investigation described in this report.

1 This section of the *Kitāb al-zīna* was edited and published by 'A. S. al-Sāmarrā'ī in his *Al-Ghuluww wa'l-firaq al-ghāliya fi'l-ḥaḍāra al-Islāmiyya* (Baghdad, 1972), pp. 228–312.

2 Ms. Fyzee Collection, Bombay University Library.

3 An *urjūza* that both W. Ivanow (*Ismaili Literature*, Tehran, 1963, p. 68) and I. K. Poonawala (*Biobibliography of Ismā'īlī Literature*, Malibu, Calif., 1977, p. 132) mention in their catalogues of Isma'ili works as belonging to Abū Tammām is, most likely, the product of a Ṭayyibī author as, for certain, is the 'summary' of the *Shajara* found in Isma'ili collections. Manuscripts of both exist in the Institute of Ismaili Studies Library in London.

4 For a complete presentation of the evidence for these conclusions, see my study 'Abū Tammām and his *Kitāb al-Shajara*: A New Ismaili Treatise from Tenth-Century Khurasan', JAOS, 114 (1994), pp. 343–352.

5 *Kitāb al-īḍāḥ*, ed. 'Ārif Tāmir (Beirut, 1965).

6 *Shajarat al-yaqīn*, ed. 'Ārif Tāmir (Beirut, 1982).

7 This manuscript – the only one presently known – contains 236 folios of ten lines per page. It was copied in Shawwāl 1310/May 1893, apparently as Part One (*al-juz' al-awwal*) alone. The copyist says: 'waqa'a al-farāgh min tansīkh hādha al-kitāb al-musammā bi'l-juz' al-awwal min al-shajara li-Abī Tammām', implying that as far as he knew the work itself was known as *Part One of the Shajara*. This seems to mean that Part Two had long since become separated from Part One and quite possibly lost. Significantly, al-Majdū' in his important 12th/18th century catalogue of Isma'ili works, *Fihrist al-kutub wa'l-rasā'il*, ed. 'A. N. Munzavī (Tehran, 1966), did not refer to such a book directly but only as a series of second hand quotations in another, later text. Hereafter, this work is cited as *al-Shajara*.

8 *Al-Shajara*, fol. 13r.

9 They are identical, for example, to those employed by Abū Ya'qūb al-Sijistānī.

10 *Al-Shajara*, fol. 22v.

11 Ibid., fols. 22v–23r.

12 Abū Tammām's use of these two terms is fairly standard although an exact English rendering of both is difficult. A *madhhab* (plural, *madhāhib*) is a broader and more inclusive tendency, perhaps like a 'school' but not quite so academic, and a *firqa* (plural, *firaq*) is a splinter grouping, which is, more properly, a 'sect'. A *madhhab* will most often have divided or splintered into *firqa*s.

13 Abū 'Abd Allāh al-Khwārazmī, *Mafātīḥ al-'ulūm* (Cairo, 1923). On this work see, C. E. Bosworth, 'Al-Ḫwārazmī on Theology and Sects, the Chapter on *Kalām* in the *Mafātīḥ al-'ulūm*', in *Hommage Henri Laoust, Bulletin d'Etudes Orientales*, 29 (1977); pages 88–91 of this article give an English translation of the key passage that contains al-Khwārazmī's version of the sect list.

14 Although al-Khwārazmī did not make this claim, his list covers exactly seventy-two sects plus the conspicuously added al-Ismā'īliyya, which he placed at the end of the Ghāliya. In Bosworth's translation, it appears (p. 91) as if the Mamṭūra are separate whereas, as Abū Tammām makes clear, this is merely a pejorative name of the previously cited al-Wāqifiyya. But he also recognized only seven *madhāhib* and, unlike Abū Tammām, clustered all the Shi'a together as one by enumerating the main divisions as *firaq* and the subdivisions as *aṣnāf* (types).

15 Al-Ash'arī, *Kitāb maqālāt al-Islāmiyyīn*, ed. H. Ritter (Wiesbaden, 1963).

16 Nashwān b. Sa'īd al-Ḥimyarī, *al-Ḥūr al-'īn* (Cairo, 1948).

17 Abu'l-Qāsim al-Balkhī, 'Dhikr al-Muʿtazila', from his *Kitāb al-maqālāt*, in *Faḍl al-iʿtizāl wa-ṭabaqāt al-Muʿtazila*, ed. F. Sayyid (Tunis, 1974), pp. 61–119.

18 *Al-Shajara*, fol. 175r.

19 This possibility was suggested to me by Wilferd Madelung.

20 According to Abū Tammām, the Bidʿiyya maintained that the compulsory prayers were three per day. Most later heresiographers report that, for them, it was only two per day – a doctrine quite obviously heretical. Abū Tammām says explicitly that it was three: *al-fajr*, *al-maghrib*, and *al-ʿatama* and insists that the proof for them is the Qur'an, XI: 114 (And perform the prayer at the two ends of the day and nigh of the night; surely the good deeds will drive away the evil deeds).

21 This fact is substantiated by al-Nāshi' but with a different textual presentation; see J. van Ess, *Frühe muʿtazilitische Häresiographie* (Beirut, 1971), p. 70.

22 It must be observed here, as in several other instances, that the reading of the Hamdani manuscript is corrupt or uncertain and needs to be corrected from other sources, such as those in this instance that give the names of the individuals in question.

23 On this point, see W. Madelung, *Der Imam al-Qāsim ibn Ibrāhīm und die Glaubenslehre der Zaiditen* (Berlin, 1965), p. 73.

24 Ibid.

25 Al-Ashʿarī, *Maqālāt*, p. 141.

26 On the Karrāmiyya in general, about which there are a number of important fairly recent studies, see C. E. Bosworth's article in EI2 and the references given there.

27 Al-Ḥimyarī, *al-Ḥūr*, p. 154, and al-Ashʿarī, *Maqālāt*, p. 16.

28 The manuscript reads apparently *ḥidāqahum*, which I trust is probably *khidaʿahum*.

29 These all will have been known to a degree from al-Khwārazmī, but in these particular cases, not from another earlier, or in most instances, later source.

30 On these Ṣabbāḥiyya, see now J. van Ess, *Theologie und Gesellschaft im 2. und 3. Jahrhundert Hidschra* (Berlin, 1991–), vol. 2, pp. 562–563, and vol. 5, pp. 226–227.

31 This is the chief angel, according to Abū Tammām, but the word is unpointed in the manuscript and, therefore, the reading Mīkhā'īl when there is yet another angel named Mīkā'īl, must be a conjecture.

32 A *Kitāb al-mustarshid* or *Kitāb al-mustarshid fi'l-tawḥīd* by al-Hādī ila'l-Ḥaqq (d. 298/911) is known; see Madelung, *Der Imam*, pp. 166 ff., and C. van Arendonk, *Les débuts de l'Imāmat Zaidite au Yémen*, tr. J. Ryckmans (Leiden, 1960), pp. 283–287. It is not clear why Abū Tammām attributes this work to al-Nāṣir al-ʿAlawī, since that could mean either al-Nāṣir al-Uṭrūsh, al Hādī's contemporary, or perhaps more likely, Aḥmad al-Nāṣir, the son of al-Hādī.

33 The Hamdani manuscript gives only the name Isḥāq with a blank space following. I have completed it from information in al-Khwārazmī.

34 The Hamdani Ms. reads in part 'thumma abūhā Hāshim thumma ʿAbd Allāh b. Muḥammad b. al-Ḥanafiyya', but the manuscript is certainly garbled at this point. Also, the name ʿAlī b. al-Ḥusayn is probably an error for ʿAlī b. al-Ḥasan.

35 Ibn al-Nadīm, *Kitāb al-fihrist*, ed. M. R. Tajaddud (Tehran, 1971), p. 408, mentions an Isḥāq the Turk in his section on the Muslimiyya (Abū Muslimiyya) which may represent a garbled response to Abū Tammām's Isḥāq. If so, Ibn al-Nadīm conflated into one sect Abū Tammām's Khalafiyya (of the Zaydiyya), the Isḥāqiyya, and the supporters of Abū Muslim.

36 Since writing this article, I have discovered an important connection between Abū Tammān and Zurqān, a Muʿtazilī heresiographer of a generation prior to al-Balkhī about whom little is known except quotations from his work by later authors, including especially al-Ashʿarī. It appears, therefore, that Abū Tammām drew on at least this one additional source.

PART II

The Nizārī phase

TEN

Ḥasan-i Ṣabbāḥ and the origins of the Nizārī Isma'ili movement

FARHAD DAFTARY

THIS STUDY is concerned with the background to and the earliest history of the Isma'ili movement that appeared in Persia during the final decade of the 5th/11th century and subsequently became known as the Nizārī Isma'ili movement; and the crucial role of Ḥasan-i Ṣabbāḥ in organizing and leading the opening stage of that movement from his mountain headquarters at the fortress of Alamūt.

There are disagreements among modern scholars regarding the very nature of early Nizārī Isma'ilism. While many Islamists and Isma'ili scholars have generally seen it as a mere schismatic Isma'ili movement that split away from the Fatimid caliphate and the headquarters of the Fatimid Isma'ili *da'wa* in Cairo over the issue of succession to the Isma'ili imamate, others (especially some Iranian scholars) have tended to view it purely as an Iranian revolutionary movement with 'nationalistic' ideals. The reality, as is often the case, seems to have been much more complex. As no Nizārī sources have survived from the time of Ḥasan-i Ṣabbāḥ, it is impossible to know how the earliest Nizārīs themselves perceived their movement some nine centuries ago.

As is known, it was in the very heart of the Iranian world, in the mediaeval region of Daylam in northern Persia, that Nizārī Isma'ilism first appeared on the historical stage as a revolutionary movement in opposition to the Saljuq Turks and their injustices. This movement of the Persian Isma'ilis was actually launched, it may be recalled, even before the Nizārī-Musta'lī schism of 487/1094; and, from early on, Persian was adopted as the religious language of the Persian (Nizārī) Isma'ilis. Indeed, significant aspects of the opposition of the Persian Isma'ilis to the Saljuqs may be traced to antecedents in older traditions of dissent in the Iranian lands. Thus, in order to have a proper understanding of the origins of the Nizārī Ismaʿili movement, it is necessary to review certain earlier religio-political opposition movements and traditions in the Iranian lands, including aspects of Iranian Ismaʿilism. It is only against such a background that the various factors contributing to the genesis of the Nizārī Ismaʿili movement can be correctly identified and evaluated in their historical contexts.

Different religio-political currents of thought and sectarian movements persisted in the Iranian lands through the ʿAbbasid and later times. They were all opposed to the established caliphate, while several of them manifested anti-Arab, anti-Turkish or even anti-Islamic sentiments rooted in various Iranian traditions. In particular, by the early ʿAbbasid times, a number of sectarian groups, designated generically as the Khurramiyya or Khurramdīniyya, had become active in different parts of Persia.[1] In their doctrines, these groups amalgamated Islamic teachings with Iranian religious traditons and sentiments, giving the Khurramī movement its peculiar Irano-Islamic nature. Despite the claims of the Sunni sources hostile towards the Ismaʿilis, Iranian Ismaʿilism should not however be viewed (particularly in the doctrinal field) as the continuation of the Khurramiyya, even though the two movements shared a common enmity toward the ʿAbbasids.

Besides the Khurramiyya, a number of Iranian dynasties contributed significantly to the revival of Iranian 'national' sentiments (if this modern concept may be applied broadly in a mediaeval context). The Ṣaffārids were the first of such major dynasties to appear in the Iranian world. They in effect pioneered the renaissance of a specifically Irano-Islamic culture based on the 'national' sentiments of the Islamicized Iranians who had continued to be consciously aware of their Iranian identity and cultural heritage during the centuries of Arab domination.[2] The revival of Persian culture continued under the Sāmānids, who patronized numerous Persian poets and had religious works translated from Arabic into Persian. And this process continued under the Būyids or Buwayhids, who haled from Daylam in the Caspian region and founded the most powerful of those Iranian dynasties flourishing during what Vladimir Minorsky has called the Daylamī interlude in Iranian history, covering the period between the earlier Arab and the later Turkish dominations.[3]

It was under such circumstances that the Iranian lands lent their support also to certain Islamic movements opposed to the established caliphate, notably Khārijism and Shiʿism. Of the various religio-political opposition movements in Islam, it was, however, Shiʿism that produced the most lasting impact on the Iranian world. By the final decades of the 3rd/9th century, all the major branches of Shiʿism, including the Imāmiyya, the Zaydiyya and the Ismāʿīliyya, had acquired communities of followers in the Iranian world. Imāmī Shiʿism achieved its greatest success in Persia only under the Ṣafawids who adopted it as the official religion of their realm, while the impact of the Zaydiyya, who by contrast to the quiescent Imāmiyya had developed into a revolutionary movement, remained rather marginalized in the Iranian world. Ismaʿilism had greater and more widespread impact on Persia than the Zaydī movement. By the end of the 3rd century/903–913, the Ismaʿili *daʿwa* had become well established in many parts of Persia.[4]

Within Ismaʿilism itself, the Iranian communities from early on acquired features that set them apart from the Ismaʿilis of the Arab lands. Due to the remoteness of the Iranian regions from the central headquarters of the *daʿwa* and the poor communications systems of the time, the chief local *dāʿī*s of the Iranian world enjoyed a large degree of independence and local initiative from early on, which gave Iranian Ismaʿilism one of its distinctive features. This, in turn, permitted the Iranian *dāʿī*s to modify their policies as required by local circumstances. The same spirit of local initiative and autonomy permitted many of the *dāʿī*s of the Iranian lands to break away from the central headquarters of the Ismaʿili *daʿwa* in the aftermath of the schism of 286/899, which divided the early Ismaʿili movement into the loyal Fatimid Ismaʿili and the dissident (Qarmaṭī) factions.[5]

The *daʿwa* activities on behalf of the Fatimid Ismaʿili imams did not cease upon the establishment of the Fatimid *dawla* or state in North Africa. This was presumably because the Fatimids never abandoned the hope of extending their rule over the entire Muslim world. The Fatimid *daʿwa* activities in the Iranian lands reached their peak in the time of al-Mustanṣir (427–487/1036–1094), the eighth Fatimid caliph and the eighteenth Ismaʿili imam. By the early decades of his rule, the eastern Ismaʿili communities had either disintegrated or switched their allegiance to the Fatimid *daʿwa*. It was also during al-Mustanṣir's long reign that the Fatimid state embarked on its rapid political decline.

In the meantime, important changes had taken place in the political topography of the Iranian world. The internal strifes of the later Būyids in western Persia and Iraq, and the collapse of the Sāmānids and other native Iranian dynasties in Khwārazm, Transoxania and Khurāsān by the early decades of the 5th/11th century, had generally permitted the emergence of a number of Turkish dynasties in the Iranian lands. This trend toward the Turkish domination of the region began with the establishment of the Ghaznawid and Qarakhānid dynasties, and soon acquired a major significance under the Saljuqs who had originated as chieftains of the Oghuz Turks in the steppes of Central Asia. When Toghril, the Saljuq leader, proclaimed himself sultan at Nīshāpūr in 429/1038, another alien, now Turkish instead of Arab, age had begun in the Islamic history of the Iranian world.

The establishment of Turkish rule over the Iranian lands checked the rapid resurgence of Persian culture and Iranian 'national' sentiments. It should be noted, however, that the process had become irrevocable by the 5th/11th century, when the conversion of the Iranians to Islam was finally completed. The Isma'ili *dā'ī* and theologian Nāṣir-i Khusraw (d. after 465/1072–1073) now composed all of his works in the Persian language. Niẓām al-Mulk, too, wrote his *Siyāsat-nāma* for Sultan Malik Shāh in the Persian language. Indeed, the Saljuqs themselves soon learned to appreciate the advantages of the Iranian system of statecraft and central administration. Be that as it may, the Turkish Saljuqs were aliens and their rule was intensely detested by the Iranians. The anti-Turkish feeling of the Iranian populace was further aggravated due to the anarchy and depredation caused in towns and villages by the Turkmen, who were continuously attracted in new waves from Central Asia to Persia by the success of the Saljuqs. The Saljuqs with their *iqṭā'* system had also accentuated the socio-economic grievances resulting from the existing stratified social structure in Persia. The insubordination of the Turkish tribes and the unruly behaviour of their soldiery continued throughout the entire period of the Great Saljuq sultanate and beyond.[6] The ground was thus rapidly being paved for the appearance of the anti-Saljuq revolutionary movement that was to be designed and led by Ḥasan-i Ṣabbāḥ.

By around 460/1067, the Persian Isma'ilis in the Saljuq territories had come to own the authority of a single chief *dā'ī* who had his secret headquarters at Iṣfahān, the main Saljuq capital. The chief *dā'ī* in Persia at this time was 'Abd al-Malik b. 'Aṭṭāsh. A highly learned *dā'ī*, Ibn 'Aṭṭāsh seems to have been the first Iranian *dā'ī* to have organized the various Isma'ili communities of the Saljuq territories in Persia, and possibly Iraq, under a central leadership. This new institutional frame was essentially retained in subsequent times and it was utilized effectively by Ḥasan-i Ṣabbāḥ. Ibn 'Aṭṭāsh occupies a particularly important place in the annals of Iranian Isma'ilism and the Nizārī movement for his role in launching the career of Ḥasan-i Ṣabbāḥ.

Little information is available on the early life of Ḥasan-i Ṣabbāḥ whose career as the first lord of Alamūt is better documented. The Persian Nizārīs compiled chronicles recording the detailed history of the Persian Nizārī state and community according to the reigns of the successive lords of Alamūt.[7] This Nizārī tradition of historiography started with a work known as the *Sargudhasht-i Sayyidnā* (*Biography of our Master*), which covered the major events of Ḥasan-i Ṣabbāḥ's rule as the first lord of Alamūt.[8] Copies of this work, as in the case of other Nizārī chronicles, were kept at the famous library in Alamūt, founded by Ḥasan-i Ṣabbāḥ, as well as in other Nizārī fortresses. As is well-known, the bulk of the meagre literature produced by the Persian Nizārīs during the Alamūt period perished in the course of the Mongol destruction of the Nizārī strongholds in Persia in 654/1256. However, the *Sargudhasht-i Sayyidnā* was among the few Nizārī works that in different ways survived into the Īlkhānid times. These Nizārī sources were seen and utilized extensively by a group of Persian historians of the Īlkhānid period, notably Juwaynī (d. 681/1283), Rashīd al-Dīn Faḍl Allāh (d. 718/1318), and Kāshānī (d. ca. 738/1337–1338). These historians compiled detailed accounts of the Persian Nizārī state and community of the Alamūt period, and they have been utilized here as our primary sources for Ḥasan-i Ṣabbāḥ's life and career.[9] Later Persian historians, such as Ḥāfiẓ Abrū (d. 833/1430),[10] who devoted lengthy sections to Ḥasan-i Ṣabbāḥ and the Persian Nizārīs of the Alamūt period, based their accounts almost exclusively on Juwaynī and Rashīd al-Dīn.

Ḥasan-i Ṣabbāḥ was born in the mid-440s/1050s in Qumm, into a Twelver Shiʿi family. His father, ʿAlī b. Muḥammad b. Jaʿfar b. al-Ḥusayn b. Muḥammad b. al-Ṣabbāḥ al-Ḥimyarī, a Kūfan claiming Ḥimyarī Yemenite origins, had migrated from Kūfa to Qumm. Subsequently, the Ṣabbāḥ family moved to the nearby town of Rayy, another important centre of Shiʿi learning in Persia, where the youthful Ḥasan received his early religious education as a Twelver Shiʿi. It was at Rayy, a centre of Ismaʿili activity, that Ḥasan, soon after the age of seventeen, was introduced to Ismaʿili teachings by a certain Amīra Ḍarrāb, one of the several local *dāʿīs*. Later, Ḥasan found out more about the Ismaʿilis from other *dāʿīs* in Rayy, including Abū Naṣr Sarrāj. Soon afterwards, Ḥasan converted to the Ismaʿili faith and the oath of allegiance (*bayʿa*) to the Imam al-Mustanṣir was administered to him by a *dāʿī* called Muʾmin. In Ramaḍān 464/May–June 1072, the newly initiated Ḥasan was brought to the attention of Ibn ʿAṭṭāsh, who was then staying in Rayy. Ibn ʿAṭṭāsh approved of Ḥasan and appointed him to a post in the *daʿwa*, also instructing him to proceed to Cairo to further his Ismaʿili education. In 467/1074–1075, Ibn ʿAṭṭāsh returned from Rayy to Iṣfahān, the *daʿwa* headquarters in Persia, accompanied by Ḥasan-i Ṣabbāḥ.

According to quotations from the *Sargudhasht*, Ḥasan-i Ṣabbāḥ finally set off from Iṣfahān for Cairo in 469/1076–1077, when al-Muʾayyad fiʾl-Dīn al-Shīrāzī (d. 470/1078) was still the *dāʿī al-duʿāt* there. He travelled to Ādharbāyjān and then to Mayyāfāriqīn, from where he was driven out by the town's *qāḍī* for having asserted, in a religious disputation, the exclusive right of the Ismaʿili imam to interpret religion and refuting the authority of the Sunni *ʿulamāʾ*, ideas which he later elaborated in terms of the doctrine of *taʿlīm*. He finally arrived in Cairo in Ṣafar 471/August 1078, the same year in which the Fatimids lost Syria to Tutush, who established a Saljuq principality there. Ḥasan spent some three years in Egypt, first in Cairo and then in Alexandria, a base of opposition to Badr al-Jamālī, the all-powerful Fatimid vizier and 'commander of the armies' (*amīr al-juyūsh*). Badr al-Jamālī had now succeeded al-Muʾayyad also as the *dāʿī al-duʿāt*.

Almost nothing is known about Ḥasan's experiences in Egypt. It is certain, however, that he did not see al-Mustanṣir. According to the later Nizārī sources used by our Persian historians, he also came into conflict with Badr al-Jamālī, evidently because of his support for Nizār, al-Mustanṣir's heir-designate. According to another anachronistic account, cited by Ibn al-Athīr, al-Mustanṣir had personally informed Ḥasan in Cairo that his successor would be Nizār.[11] At any rate, eventually Ḥasan seems to have been banished from Egypt, under obscure circumstances and on Badr al-Jamālī's order. He returned to Iṣfahān in Dhuʾl-Ḥijja 473/June 1081.

Ḥasan must have learned important lessons during his stay in Fatimid Egypt, which were to be taken into account in his subsequent revolutionary designs. By the 460s/1070s, when the Fatimid state was witnessing numerous political, economic, and military crises, the Persian Ismaʿilis must have already become aware of the declining fortunes of the Fatimids. Subsequently in al-Mustanṣir's reign, Badr al-Jamālī did restore peace and some prosperity to Fatimid Egypt, but henceforth the power of the Fatimids remained manifestly inferior to that of the Saljuqs who had firmly established their own hegemony throughout the Near East, to the utter disillusionment of different Shiʿi communities there. Whilst in Egypt, the shrewd Ḥasan-i Ṣabbāḥ had a valuable opportunity to evaluate at close hand the conditions of the Fatimid regime, becoming better aware of the fact that the Persian

Isma'ilis could no longer count on receiving any effective support from the Fatimid state.

In Persia, Ḥasan did not remain at the *da'wa* headquarters in Iṣfahān. Instead, he embarked on an extensive programme of journeys to different localities in the service of the *da'wa* for the next nine years. Doubtless, it was during this period that he formulated his own ideas and revolutionary strategy, also assessing the military strength of Saljuqs in different parts of Persia. By the late 470s/1080s, he had concentrated his efforts on the general region of Daylam, removed from the centres of Saljuq power and also predominantly Shi'i. He was then preparing for a revolt against the Saljuqs, for the implementation of which he was systematically searching for a site to establish his headquarters. At the time, the *da'wa* in Persia was still under the overall leadership of Ibn 'Aṭṭāsh, but Ḥasan had already started to pursue an independent policy. By around 480/1087–1088, Ḥasan seems to have selected the castle of Alamūt, situated in the region of Rūdbār in Daylam, on a high rock in central Alburz mountains, as a suitable site for his headquarters.[12] He then devised a detailed plan for the seizure of Alamūt, which at the time was in the hands of a certain 'Alid called Mahdī who held the castle from the Saljuq sultan. He despatched a number of subordinate *dā'īs* to various districts around Alamūt to convert the local inhabitants. Ḥasan-i Ṣabbāḥ, who was in due course appointed *dā'ī* of Daylam, was now truly reinvigorating the *da'wa* activities in northern Persia, and his efforts were soon brought to the notice of Niẓām al-Mulk, who remained vizier for some thirty years under Toghril's next two successors, Alp Arslān (455–465/1063–1073) and Malik Shāh (465–485/1073–1092). The Saljuq vizier, who nurtured a deep hatred for the Isma'ilis, failed to capture Ḥasan, who in due time arrived in Rūdbār.

Early in 483/1090, Ḥasan arrived in the neighbourhood of Alamūt, where he stayed for some time disguising himself as a school teacher. On the eve of Wednesday 6 Rajab 483/4 September 1090, Ḥasan entered the castle of Alamūt clandestinely calling himself Dihkhudā. He lived there for a while in disguise, teaching the children of the garrison and infiltrating the castle with his own men. With his followers firmly installed in and around Alamūt, Ḥasan finally divulged his true identity. Realizing that his position at Alamūt was no longer tenable, Mahdī now agreed to surrender the castle peacefully. According to quotations from the *Sargudhasht*, Ḥasan voluntarily gave Mahdī a draft for 3,000 gold dinars as the price of the castle. The draft, drawn on Ra'īs Muẓaffar, a secret Isma'ili convert then in the service of the Saljuqs who was to become the commander of the fortress of Girdkūh, was honoured in due time, to Mahdī's amazement.

The seizure of Alamūt signaled the initiation of the Persian Isma'ilis' revolt against the Saljuqs, also marking the effective foundation of what was to become the Nizārī state. It thus ushered in a new, revolutionary phase in the activities of the Persian Isma'ilis who had hitherto operated clandestinely. It is certain that Cairo had played no part in the initiation of this revolt in Persia. Not only there is no evidence suggesting that Ḥasan-i Ṣabbāḥ was receiving instructions from Badr al-Jamālī, then the all-powerful Fatimid vizier and chief *dā'ī* in Cairo, but the sources, as noted, indicate the existence of serious disagreements between the two men from the time of Ḥasan's visit to Egypt. Once installed at Alamūt, Ḥasan embarked on the task of renovating that castle, also improving its fortifications, storage facilities and water supply system. He made Alamūt truly impregnable, enabling it to withstand long sieges. He also improved and extended the cultivation and irrigation systems of the Alamūt valley, making the locality self-sufficient in its food production. Similar policies were later implemented in connection with other major Isma'ili strongholds.

Ḥasan-i Ṣabbāḥ was no ordinary man, and as M. Hodgson has noted, 'his personality may well have offered the other Isma'ilis a crucial rallying-point of unyielding strength'.[13] He was indeed held in great esteem by the Nizārīs who referred to him as Sayyidnā, or 'our master'. An organizer and a political strategist of the highest calibre, he was at the same time a learned theologian who led an ascetic life. Our Persian historians relate that during all the thirty-four years that Ḥasan spent at Alamūt, he never descended from the castle, and only twice left his living quarters in the castle to mount the roof-top. The rest of the time, adds Rashīd al-Dīn, he passed inside his quarters reading books, committing the teachings of the *da'wa* to writing, and administering the affairs of his realm.[14] He was equally strict with friend and foe, and highly uncompromising in his austere life style. It is reported that he observed the *sharī'a* strictly and imposed it on the community. In his time, nobody drank wine openly in the Alamūt valley. At a time of siege, Ḥasan sent his wife and daughters to Girdkūh, where they were to earn a simple living by spinning, like other womenfolk there; and they were never brought back to Alamūt. This evidently set a precedent for the commanders of the Isma'ili fortresses. And he had both his sons executed, one on a charge of murder which later proved false, and the other on suspicion of drinking wine.

Ḥasan-i Ṣabbāḥ seems to have had a complex set of religio-political motives for his revolt against the Saljuqs. As an Isma'ili Shi'i, he clearly could not have supported the ardently Sunni Saljuq Turks. Less conspicuously, but of equal significance, Ḥasan's revolt was also an expression of Iranian 'national' sentiments, which accounts for a major share of the early support extended to this revolt in Persia. It cannot be doubted that Ḥasan truly detested the Turks and their alien rule over Persia. He is reported to have referred to the Saljuq sultan as a mere ignorant Turk;[15] he is also reported to have said that the Turks were *jinn* and not men, descendants of Adam.[16] And it was to the ultimate goal of uprooting the Saljuq Turks that he dedicated himself and organized the Persian Isma'ilis of diverse backgrounds as a revolutionary force. Henceforth, the ordinary Persian Isma'ilis, as was fitting in a revolutionary movement, were to address one another as *rafīq*, comrade. It is also extremely important to note that Ḥasan, obviously as an expression of his Persian awareness and in spite of his Islamic piety, took an unprecedented step and from early on substituted Persian for Arabic as the religious language of the (Nizārī) Isma'ilis of Persia. This was indeed the first time that a major Muslim community had adopted Persian as its religious language. This explains why the literature of the Persian-speaking (Nizārī) Isma'ilis of the Alamūt period and later times was produced entirely in the Persian language.

After firmly establishing himself at Alamūt, Ḥasan-i Ṣabbāḥ concerned himself with extending his influence in the region, by winning more Isma'ili converts and gaining possession of more castles in Rūdbār and adjacent areas in Daylam. Ḥasan took such castles whenever he could and wherever he found a suitable rock he built a castle upon it. This strategy was reminiscent of the insurrectional policy adopted by Bābak Khurramī (d. 223/838), who, from his stronghold at Badhdh and other inaccessible mountain fortresses in Ādharbāyjān, launched the most successful anti-'Abbasid revolt of the Khurramiyya. At any rate, Ḥasan's religio-political message evoked the popular support of the Daylamīs of Rūdbār and its environs, mostly villagers and highlanders who had already been introduced also to Isma'ilism and other forms of Shi'ism. There is evidence suggesting that Ḥasan also attracted the remnants of some of the earlier Khurramīs of Ādharbāyjān who, as an expression of their Persian sentiments, now called themselves Pārsiyān.[17] Soon, Ḥasan's headquarters began to be raided by the forces of the nearest Saljuq *amīr*, who held the district of Alamūt as his *iqṭā'* granted by the sultan. Henceforth, the Saljuqs and the Persian Isma'ilis were drawn into an endless series of military encounters.

In 484/1091–1092, Ḥasan sent Ḥusayn-i Qā'inī, a capable *dāʿī* who had played an important role in the seizure of Alamūt, to his native Quhistān to mobilize support there. In Quhistān, a barren region in southeastern Khurāsān, Ḥusayn met with immediate success. The Quhistānīs, who had already been familiar with Shiʿi traditions, were at the time highly discontented with the oppressive rule of a local Saljuq *amīr*. As a result, the spread of the Ismaʿili *daʿwa* there did not proceed simply in terms of secret conversions and the seizure of castles, but it erupted openly into a popular uprising for acquiring independence from alien, oppressive Saljuq rule. Thus, in many parts of Quhistān the Ismaʿilis rose in open revolt, also seizing control of several major towns, including Tūn, Ṭabas and Qā'in. Quhistān now became another major territory, along with Rūdbār in Daylam, for the activities of the Persian Ismaʿilis. And in both territories, in less than two years after the capture of Alamūt, the Persian Ismaʿilis had effectively asserted their local independence from the Saljuqs. Ḥasan-i Ṣabbāḥ had now actually founded an independent territorial state for the Persian Ismaʿilis in the midst of the Saljuq sultanate.

Early in 485/1092, realizing that local Saljuq forces could not deal with the growing power of the Persian Ismaʿilis, Malik Shāh decided, on the advice of Niẓām al-Mulk, to send armies against the Ismaʿilis of both Rūdbār and Quhistān. These military operations were, however, soon terminated due to the asassination of Niẓām al-Mulk in Ramaḍān 485/October 1092, followed by Malik Shāh's death a few weeks later. On hearing the news of the sultan's death, the Saljuq armies besieging Alamūt and Ismaʿili sites in Quhistān dispersed, as the Saljuq forces traditionally owed their allegiance to the person of the ruler and not to the state.

On Malik Shāh's death, the Saljuq empire was thrown into civil war which lasted more than a decade. Malik Shāh's succession was disputed among his sons, who were supported by different Saljuq *amīr*s. And these *amīr*s, who controlled various provinces, continuously changed their allegiance and aggravated the internal disorders of the Saljuq sultanate. It was under such circumstances that Barkiyāruq, Malik Shāh's eldest son and the most prominent claimant to the Saljuq sultanate, was placed on the throne in Rayy. However, Barkiyāruq (487–498/1094–1105) had to devote much of his energy to fighting his relatives, especially his half-brother Muḥammad Tapar who received effective support from his own full brother Sanjar, the ruler of Khurāsān from 490/1097 onwards. Peace was restored to the Saljuq dominions, especially in western Persia and Iraq, only on Barkiyāruq's death in

498/1105, when Muḥammad Tapar emerged as the undisputed sultan while Sanjar remained at Balkh as his viceroy in the east.

During this period of rivalries among the Saljuqs, Ḥasan-i Ṣabbāḥ found the much needed respite to consolidate and extend his power. The chaos caused by the quarrelling Saljuqs also made the Persians more responsive to Ḥasan's message of resistance against the alien and oppressive rule of the Saljuq Turks. Important Isma'ili strongholds were now acquired in other parts of Persia, outside Daylam and Quhistān. Extending their network of fortresses eastwards from Alamūt in the Alburz range, the Isma'ilis came to possess a number of castles near Dāmghān, capital of the mediaeval province of Qūmis, especially Girdkūh which was situated strategically on a high rock along the main route between western Persia and Khurāsān.[18] They also seized several fortresses near Arrajān in the Zagros mountains, in the border region between the provinces of Fārs and Khūzistān in southwestern Persia, and acquired supporters in many towns throughout the Saljuq domains.

Meanwhile, Ḥasan had strengthened and extended his position in Daylam itself, where the Isma'ilis repelled intermittent Saljuq offensives. His greatest achievement in Daylam during this period was, however, his acquisition of the castle of Lamasar, also called Lanbasar, to the west of Alamūt in 489/1096.[19] Ḥasan-i Ṣabbāḥ entrusted the Lamasar campaign to Kiyā Buzurg-Ummīd and three other commanders who seized the fortress by assault. Ḥasan then appointed Buzurg-Ummīd as the commander of that second most important Isma'ili stronghold in Daylam. Buzurg-Ummīd stayed at Lamasar until he was summoned to Alamūt in 518/1124 to succeed Ḥasan-i Ṣabbāḥ. In order to understand the Iranian connection of the early Nizārī movement it is also important to bear in mind that its key figures, besides Ḥasan himself, were all Iranians who led the movement during its crucial early phase in their native territories: the Daylamī Buzurg-Ummīd in Daylam, the Khurāsānī Ḥusayn-i Qā'inī in Quhistān, the Arrajānī Abū Ḥamza in Arrajān, and Ra'īs Muẓaffar, who had served as a Saljuq officer in Qūmis, was retained at Girdkūh, etc. Furthermore, they were all commanders and capable military strategists well suited to the task at hand, rather than theologians and philosophers like those who produced the classical treatises of the Fatimid period.

The revolt of the Persian Isma'ilis against the Saljuqs soon acquired its distinctive pattern as well as its particular methods of struggle, which were appropriate to the times.[20] After Malik Shāh, and even earlier, there was no longer a single all-powerful sultan to be overthrown by a large army, even if such an army could be mobilized by the Isma'ilis. Political and military power had by then come to be localized in the hands of numerous *amīr*s and commanders of garrisons, individuals who had received *iqṭā'* assignments throughout the Saljuq dominions. In such a regime of many *amīr*s, with no major military targets of conquest, the overthrow of the Saljuqs had to proceed on a piecemeal basis, locality by locality, stronghold by stronghold, and *amīr* by *amīr*. This reality was clearly recognized by Ḥasan-i Ṣabbāḥ who devised an appropriate strategy for the revolt of the Persian Isma'ilis, aiming to subdue the Saljuqs by acquiring a multiplicity of strongholds. Each Isma'ili stronghold, normally a defensible and fortified mountain fortress, could then be used as the base of operations for the activities of the armed Isma'ilis of a particular locality. Such strongholds were also well placed for providing assistance to, or serving as refuge for, the garrisons of other localities in times of need.

The commanders of the major Isma'ili strongholds enjoyed a large degree of scope for local initiative while each Isma'ili territory was under the overall leadership of a regional chief, appointed from Alamūt. The regional chiefs, too, acted independently in the daily affairs of their communities. All this contributed to the dynamism of the revolt. However, all the regional Isma'ili leaders received their main instructions from Alamūt, which served as the central and co-ordinating headquarters of the Nizārī Isma'ili movement. And the multiplicity of Isma'ili strongholds, localities, and territories, formed a single, cohesive community, united in its sense of mission.

The same decentralized structure of existing power and the vastly superior military strength of the Saljuqs suggested to Ḥasan-i Ṣabbāḥ the use of an auxiliary technique for attaining military and political objectives: the technique of assassination. Ḥasan did not invent assassination of religio-political adversaries as a political weapon. Many earlier Muslim communities, such as some of the early Shi'i *ghulāt* and the Khawārij, had resorted to this policy; and at the time of the revolt of the Persian Isma'ilis, when authority was distributed locally and on a personal basis, assassination was commonly resorted to by all factions, including the Saljuqs. But Ḥasan did assign an important political role to this policy, which was used systematically and openly with the commencement of the armed revolt of the Persian Isma'ilis against the much more powerful Saljuqs. This policy was maintained by Ḥasan's successors at Alamūt, though it gradually lost its initial importance. At any rate, this policy became identified in a highly exaggerated manner with the Nizārī Ismaʿilis, so that almost any assassination of any religious, political or military significance in the central Islamic lands during the Alamūt period was attributed to them.

The Nizārī assassinations were carried out by their *fidāʾī*s or *fidāwī*s, the young self-sacrificing devotees of the community who offered themselves for suicidal missions. Few details are known about the recruitment and training of the *fidāʾī*s, who were glorified in the community for their bravery and devotion.[21] Rolls of honour of their names and assassination missions were evidently compiled and retained at Alamūt and probably other fortresses.[22] The *fidāʾī*s do not seem to have received any training in languages and other subjects, as suggested by the elaborate accounts of the occidental chroniclers of the Crusaders and later European writers. In fact, the Crusaders and other westerners were responsible for fabricating and putting into circulation a number of interconnected tales regarding the recruitment and training of the Nizārī Ismaʿili *fidāʾī*s, who personally volunteered to sacrifice their lives, as a matter of conviction, in the service of their religion and community.[23] From early on, the assassinations were countered by the massacres of Ismaʿilis, or of all those in a town suspected, or accused, of being Ismaʿili.[24] The massacres, in turn, provoked assassinations of their instigators, which led to further assassinations.

As the revolt of the Persian Ismaʿilis was unfolding successfully, Ismaʿilism suffered its greatest internal conflict. In Dhu'l-Ḥijja 487/December 1094, the Fatimid caliph-imam Abū Tamīm Maʿadd al-Mustanṣir bi'llāh died in Cairo after an eventful reign of almost sixty years. The dispute over his succession was to split the Ismaʿilis permanently into two separate factions.[25] A few months earlier, Badr al-Jamālī, the real master of the Fatimid state during the last two decades of al-Mustanṣir's reign, had died after arranging for his son al-Afḍal to succeed him as vizier and commander of the armies. Al-Mustanṣir had earlier designated his eldest surviving son Abū Manṣūr Nizār (437–488/1045–1095) as his successor to the caliphate and imamate by the Shiʿi rule of the *naṣṣ*. However, al-Afḍal, aiming to strengthen his own dictatorial position, had other plans. Immediately upon al-Mustanṣir's death and in what amounted to a palace *coup d'état*, al-Afḍal moved swiftly with the support of the army and placed Nizār's much younger half-brother Abu'l-Qāsim Aḥmad (467–495/1074–1101) on the Fatimid throne with the caliphal title of al-Mustaʿlī bi'llāh. Al-Mustaʿlī, al-Mustanṣir's youngest son who was also married to al-Afḍal's sister, was to remain entirely dependent on his powerful vizier. The dispossessed Nizār, who had refused to endorse al-Afḍal's designs, fled to Alexandria where he rose in revolt early in 488/1095 with much local support. There, Nizār was declared caliph with the title of al-Muṣṭafā li-Dīn Allāh and received the allegiance of the inhabitants of Alexandria. The declaration of Nizār as caliph and imam in Alexandria is attested to by numismatic evidence which came to light in 1994. The legends of this newly recovered gold dinar, the first known specimen of its kind, minted in Alexandria in 488 AH at the time of Nizār's rising there, bear the inscriptions *al-Muṣṭafā li-Dīn Allāh* and *daʿā al-Imām Nizār*.[26] Nizār was initially successful and his forces advanced to the vicinity of Cairo, but he was eventually defeated by al-Afḍal. In the event, Nizār surrendered and was taken to Cairo where he was imprisoned and then immured; all of these events took place during the year 488/1095.

The dispute over al-Mustanṣir's succession resulted in a permanent schism, dividing the Fatimid Ismaʿilis into two rival factions. The imamate of al-Mustaʿlī, who had been installed to the Fatimid caliphate, was recognized by the Ismaʿilis of Egypt, who had remained a minority there, and by the whole Ismaʿili community of the Yemen, then dependent on the Fatimid regime. Having been a subsidiary community of the Yemen, the Ismaʿilis of Gujarāt in western India, too, now acknowledged al-Mustaʿlī as their new imam. These Ismaʿilis, who later traced the imamate in al-Mustaʿlī's progeny, became known as Mustaʿliyya or Mustaʿlawiyya and they maintained their relations with the *daʿwa* headquarters in Cairo, which henceforth served as the headquarters of Mustaʿlian Ismaʿilism.

The situation was drastically different in the eastern lands throughout the Saljuq dominions, where the Fatimids no longer exercised any political influence. By 487/1094, Ḥasan-i Ṣabbāḥ had emerged as the undisputed leader of the Persian Ismaʿilis, and, indeed, of the Ismaʿilis of the Saljuq realm. Nothing is known about the final years of Ibn ʿAṭṭāsh, who seems to have been gradually eclipsed by Ḥasan-i Ṣabbāḥ. At any rate, the responsibility in Persia and in the wider Saljuq domains for taking sides in the Nizārī–Mustaʿlī conflict now rested with Ḥasan-i Ṣabbāḥ. He had been following an independent, revolutionary policy already for several years, and now he showed no hesitation in supporting Nizār's cause and severing his ties with the Fatimid regime and the *daʿwa* headquarters in Cairo, which had transferred their own allegiance to al-Mustaʿlī. In this decision, Ḥasan was supported by the entire Persian Ismaʿili community without any dissenting voice. This is another testimony to the successful leadership of Ḥasan and his strong hold over the Persian Isma'ilis, who remained united also in their opposition to the Saljuqs. In fact, the Persian Isma'ilis continued to amaze the quarrelling Saljuqs and the Sunni establishment by their unwavering unity and sense of loyalty.

Ḥasan's decision not to endorse the developments in Fatimid Egypt and the imamate of al-Musta'lī was supported also by the Isma'ilis of Iraq, where his leadership had been recognized. These Isma'ilis, upholding al-Mustanṣir's announced *naṣṣ* in favour of Nizār now recognized the latter as his father's successor to the imamate; they became designated as the Nizāriyya, a term rarely used by the Nizārīs themselves. Nizār's partisans in Egypt were quickly suppressed by al-Afḍal. But the original reaction of the Isma'ilis of Syria to this schism remains unclear. Both factions seem to have been initially present in Syria, where the overall size of the Isma'ili community must have been rather insignificant at that time. As a former Fatimid dominion, however, the bulk of the Syrian Isma'ilis initially seem to have recognized al-Musta'lī's imamate. It was not until the 510s/1120s that, due to the success of the Persian *dā'īs* sent from Alamūt, the Syrian Musta'lians began to be rapidly overshadowed by an expanding Nizārī community which later became the sole Isma'ili community in Syria.

The Nizārī Isma'ilis, who had acknowledged Nizār as their new imam after al-Mustanṣir, soon faced a major difficulty revolving around Nizār's successor to the imamate. Nizār, as noted, had claimed the imamate during his rising. But he was executed about a year after his father's death, and now the nascent Nizāriyya wondered about the identity of their imam after Nizār. Matters must have been particularly complicated as no Nizārid seems to have laid an open claim to the imamate on Nizār's death.

It is an historical fact that Nizār did have male progeny. The sources mention the names of at least two of his sons: Abū 'Abd Allāh al-Ḥusayn and Abū 'Alī al-Ḥasan. It is also known that a line of Nizārids, descendants of Nizār's sons, continued to live in the Maghrib and Egypt until the late Fatimid times. Some of these Nizārids were pretenders to the Fatimid caliphate, and they may also have claimed the Nizārī imamate. For instance, Abū 'Abd Allāh al-Ḥusayn himself launched an abortive revolt against the Fatimid caliph al-Ḥāfiẓ from his base in the Maghrib, but he was captured and executed in 526/1131.[27] The sources relate another abortive attempt, in 543/1148, by a descendant of Nizār to seize power in Cairo.[28] This Nizārid, whose name has not been preserved, was also based in the Maghrib where he had received considerable support from the Kutāma and other Berbers. The last known attempt by the Nizārids based in the Maghrib to overthrow the Fatimid dynasty occurred in the reign of al-ʿĀḍid (555–567/1160–1171), the last Fatimid caliph.[29] In 556/1161, Muḥammad b. al-Ḥusayn b. Nizār, a grandson of Nizār, came to Barqa from his base in the Maghrib. Aiming to seize Cairo, he rose in revolt with much support and adopted the caliphal title of al-Muntaṣir biʾllāh. He was however betrayed by one of his chief allies who had him arrested and sent to Cairo where he was executed.

In the meantime, Nizār's successor had not been named at Alamūt by Ḥasan-i Ṣabbāḥ. It is possible that the eastern Ismaʿilis may not have been informed in time of Nizār's tragic fate in Cairo and that they continued to await his reappearance for some time. The matter remains obscure, especially since no Nizārī sources have been recovered from that early period. However, published numismatic evidence reveals that Nizār's name and caliphal title had continued to be mentioned on the coins struck at Kursī al-Daylam, viz., Alamūt, for some seventy years after his death until the time of Muḥammad b. Buzurg-Ummīd (532–557/1138–1162), Ḥasan-i Ṣabbāḥ's second successor at Alamūt. The latest known specimens of such coins, dinars minted at Alamūt in 553/1158 and 556/1161, bear the legends *ʿAlī walī Allāh/al-Muṣṭafā li-Dīn Allāh, Nizār*, blessing Nizār's progeny anonymously.[30]

Be that as it may, the nascent Nizāriyya were now left without an accessible imam. The Ismaʿilis had once before, during the pre-Fatimid period of their history, experienced a similar situation when the Ismaʿili imams were hidden from the eyes of their followers. Drawing on that earlier antecedent, the Nizārīs, too, were now experiencing a *dawr al-satr*, or period of concealment, when the imams would not be accessible to their followers. According to later Nizārī traditions and as reported by our Persian historians, already in Ḥasan-i Ṣabbāḥ's time many Nizārīs had come to hold the view that a son or grandson of Nizār had in fact been brought secretly from Egypt to Persia, and this Nizārid became the progenitor of the line of the Nizārī imams who emerged later at Alamūt.[31] This Nizārī tradition must have had wide currency by the final years of Ḥasan-i Ṣabbāḥ's life as it is corroborated by an anti-Nizārī polemical epistle issued by the Fatimid chancery in 516/1122. In this epistle, sent to the Mustaʿlian community in Syria, the Fatimid caliph al-Āmir (495–524/1101–1130) ridicules the idea that a descendant of Nizār was then living somewhere in Persia.[32] That in the absence of a manifest imam, Ḥasan himself continued to be obeyed as the supreme leader of the Nizārī movement without any challenges to his authority, is yet another testimony to his achievements and hold over the Nizārī community.

It seems that not long after the schism of 487/1094, Ḥasan was recognized also as the *ḥujja* of the inaccessible imam, reminiscent of another pre-Fatimid Isma'ili tradition. It may be recalled that the central leaders of the early Isma'ili movement, too, had been regarded at least until 286/899 as the *ḥujja*s of the concealed imam whose reappearance was eagerly awaited. On the basis of this tradition, it was held that in the time of the imam's concealment his *ḥujja* would be his chief representative in the community. And Ḥasan-i Ṣabbāḥ acted as the imam's *ḥujja* until such time as the imam himself would appear and take charge of the leadership of his community.[33]

It was under such circumstances that the outsiders from early on acquired the distinct impression that the movement of the Persian (Nizārī) Isma'ilis reflected a new teaching, which was to become known as the 'new preaching' (*al-da'wa al-jadīda*) in contradistinction to the 'old preaching' (*al-da'wa al-qadīma*) of the Fatimid Isma'ilis maintained by the Musta'lian Isma'ilis.[34] The 'new preaching', expressed in the Persian language, also meant the distancing of the Persian Isma'ilis from the earlier Isma'ili literature produced in the Arabic language, a literature which was later partially preserved by the Syrian Nizārīs who used Arabic. The 'new preaching' did not represent any new set of doctrines however; it was essentially the reformulation, in a more rigorous manner, of an old Shi'i doctrine of long standing among the Isma'ilis: the doctrine of *ta'līm*, or authoritative teaching. This doctrine was now restated by Ḥasan in a Persian treatise entitled *Chahār faṣl* (Arabic, *al-Fuṣūl al-arba'a*), or *The Four Chapters*, which has not survived; but the treatise was seen and quoted by our Persian historians,[35] as well as by Ḥasan's contemporary al-Shahrastānī (d. 548/1153), who may have been a crypto-Isma'ili. Extensive extracts of this treatise have been preserved by al-Shahrastānī in his Arabic heresiographical work written around 521/1127, a few years after Ḥasan's death.[36] In a series of four propositions Ḥasan established the inadequacy of human reason in knowing God and argued for the necessity of an authoritative teacher (*mu'allim-i ṣādiq*) for the spiritual guidance of men; a teacher who would be none other than the Isma'ili imam of the time. The doctrine of *ta'līm*, emphasizing the autonomous teaching authority of each imam in his time, became the central doctrine of the early Nizārīs who now became known also as the Ta'līmiyya. The doctrine, thus, stressed loyalty to the imam, and to his full representative who was then leading the movement; it also provided the foundation for all the subsequent Nizārī teachings of the Alamūt period.

Isma'ili fortunes were continuously rising in Persia during Barkiyāruq's reign. In addition to seizing strongholds and consolidating their position in Rūdbār, Qūmis and Quhistān, the Isma'ilis were now directing their attention closer to the seat of Saljuq power, Iṣfahān. In this area, the Isma'ilis through the efforts of Aḥmad b. 'Abd al-Malik b. 'Aṭṭāsh attained a major political success by gaining possession of the fortress of Shāhdiz in 494/1100. Shāhdiz, situated about eight kilometres south of Iṣfahān, had been rebuilt by Malik Shāh as a key fortress guarding the routes to the main Saljuq capital. Soon afterwards, Barkiyāruq in western Persia and Sanjar in Khurāsān agreed to check, in their respective territories, the rising power of the Isma'ilis who were now posing a general threat to the Saljuqs. Despite the Saljuq offensives however, the Isma'ili revolt continued in Persia unabated.

By the time of Barkiyāruq's death in 498/1105, Ḥasan-i Ṣabbāḥ had extended his activities also to Syria, reflecting his wider Isma'ili ambitions.[37] A number of Persian *dā'īs* now arrived in northern Syria, where they concentrated their efforts in Aleppo and in the towns of the Jazr region. As in Persia, Saljuq rule in Syria had caused many problems and was detested by the Syrians who were divided among themselves and unable to repel the Turks. Aiming to organize and lead the small Syrian Nizārī community and win new converts from other Muslim communities in Syria, the Persian *dā'īs* who were despatched from Alamūt used the same methods of struggle as had been adopted in Persia. Although Ḥasan-i Ṣabbāḥ did manage to establish a subsidiary community in Syria, almost half a century of uninterrupted efforts were required before the Nizārī Isma'ilis could finally acquire a network of mountain strongholds in central Syria.

With the accession of Muḥammad Tapar (498–511/1105–1118) to the Saljuq sultanate, marking the end of the dynastic disputes among the Saljuqs, a new phase was initiated in the Saljuq–Isma'ili relations. Barkiyāruq and Sanjar had already checked what could have been a Nizārī sweep through the Saljuq dominions in Persia, but the Nizārīs had managed to maintain or even strengthen their local positions in several territories. Muḥammad Tapar now set out to deal with the Nizārīs more firmly. During his reign, the Nizārīs lost most of their strongholds in the Zagros mountains as well as in Iraq; they also lost their position in northern Syria. But Muḥammad Tapar's chief anti-Nizārī campaign, led by the sultan himself, was directed against Shāhdiz.[38] With the fall of Shāhdiz in 500/1107, the Nizārīs lost their influence in the Iṣfahān region as well.

Sultan Muḥammad Tapar from early on had also concerned himself with the main centre of Nizārī power in Rūdbār, especially Alamūt where Ḥasan-i Ṣabbāḥ himself was staying. After several preliminary campaigns in the region, the reduction of Alamūt was entrusted in 503/1109 to Anūshtegin Shīrgīr, the governor of Sāwa. For eight consecutive years, according to our Persian historians, Shīrgīr beseiged Alamūt and Lamasar, destroying the crops of Rūdbār and engaging in sporadic battles with the Nizārīs.[39] Ḥasan-i Ṣabbāḥ's resistance during this period continued to amaze Shīrgīr, who received regular reinforcements from other Saljuq *amīr*s. Despite their much superior military power and a prolonged war of attrition, the Saljuqs failed to take Alamūt by force, and on receiving the news of Muḥammad Tapar's death in 511/1118 they broke camp hurriedly and left Rūdbār. Ḥasan-i Ṣabbāḥ thus emerged victorious from a dangerous situation which could have resulted in his irrevocable defeat.

On Muḥammad Tapar's death, the Saljuq sultanate entered into another period of internal strife, providing yet another timely respite for the Nizārī Isma'ilis to recover from some of the defeats they had suffered previously. But for all intents and purposes the Nizārī revolt against the Saljuqs had now lost its effectiveness, much in the same way that the Saljuq offensive of Muḥammad Tapar's time against the Nizārīs had failed to achieve its targets. In Hodgson's words,[40] the Saljuq–Isma'ili relations had now entered a new phase of 'stalemate'. For almost three decades since the seizure of Alamūt, the Nizārī Isma'ilis had carried out an open revolt throughout the Saljuq dominions. For a while, they had posed a serious threat to the seat of Saljuq power in Iṣfahān itself. Meanwhile, the Nizārīs themselves had suffered serious setbacks. Not only did the Saljuqs regularly check the growth of their power in various localities, but their partisans in the cities were continuously massacred. Ḥasan-i Ṣabbāḥ had in effect failed to overthrow the Saljuqs, and he could not launch a new revolt from the mountain bases which remained in Nizārī hands, as he had done before. However, his revolt had in fact resulted in regional successes, enabling the Nizārī Isma'ilis of Persia to hold on to important territories in Rūdbār, Qūmis and Quhistān, with their numerous fortresses, villages and towns.

Ḥasan-i Ṣabbāḥ maintained his own dedication to the cause he had set before himself to the very end, never weakening in his resolve or despairing in the face of massacres and military defeats suffered by his partisans. His last act of wisdom unfolded in the careful manner in which he handed down the leadership of the Nizārī Isma'ili community. Feeling the end of his days, Ḥasan summoned his lieutenant at Lamasar, Kiyā Buzurg-Ummīd, and designated him as head of the Nizārī community and state. Buzurg-Ummīd was, however, enjoined to rule in consultation with three Persian Nizārī dignitaries, who had different fields of expertise, until such time as the imam himself would appear. Ḥasan-i Ṣabbāḥ died at Alamūt, after a brief illness, towards the end of Rabīʿ II 518/middle of June 1124; he was buried near the fortress of Alamūt and his mausoleum was regularly visited by the Nizārīs until it, too, was destroyed by the Mongol hordes in 654/1256.

The early Nizārī Ismaʿili movement was, indeed, a multi-dimensional, religio-political movement. Broadly speaking, it was another Irano-Islamic revolutionary movement amalgamating aspects of Iranian 'national' aspirations with Ismaʿili Islam in response to the challenges of the time. As such, some of its roots may be sought in earlier Iranian as well as Ismaʿili traditions of social protest and religio-political opposition to the established order. In the political domain, as noted, it started primarily as an Iranian revolutionary movement, representing Iranian opposition to the alien, oppressive rule of the Saljuq Turks much in the same way as the earlier Khurramiyya movement had represented Iranian opposition to ʿAbbasid-Arab domination. However, in the religious domain, and in the milieu of the 5th/11th century, when the Persians had completely embraced Islam, the movement was conducted in the name of the Ismaʿili imam and upheld the ideals of that branch of Shiʿi Islam; and subsequent to the Nizārī–Mustaʿlī conflict, the movement severed its relations with the Fatimid regime and Cairo. The Persian Ismaʿilis of the Saljuq times also retrieved the revolutionary zeal of the pre-Fatimid Ismaʿilis who were opposed to the unjust rule of the ʿAbbasids supported by the Sunni establishment. Thus, Ḥasan-i Ṣabbāḥ's well-earned contributions need to be rightfully recognized in the contexts of both the history of the Iranian revolutionary movements and among the organizers of major Islamic movements.

NOTES

1 The classical treatment of the Khurramī sects and revolts remains G. H. Sadighi's *Les mouvements religieux Iraniens au IIe et IIIe siècle de l'hégire* (Paris, 1938), pp. 111–286; see also B. Scarcia Amoretti, 'Sects and Heresies', in *The Cambridge History of Iran*: Volume 4, *The Period from the Arab Invasion to the Saljuqs*, ed. R. N. Frye (Cambridge, 1975), pp.

481 ff., 494–519; W. Madelung, *Religious Trends in Early Islamic Iran* (Albany, N.Y., 1988), pp. 1–12, and his 'Khurramiyya', EI2, vol. 5, pp. 63–65.

2 For further details, see B. Spuler, *Iran in früh-islamischer Zeit* (Wiesbaden, 1952), pp. 225 ff.; J. Rypka, *History of Iranian Literature*, ed. K. Jahn (Dordrecht, 1968), pp. 126–171; S. M. Stern, 'Ya'qūb the Coppersmith and Persian National Sentiment', in *Iran and Islam, in Memory of the late Vladimir Minorsky*, ed. C. E. Bosworth (Edinburgh, 1971), pp. 535–555; C. E. Bosworth, 'The Interaction of Arabic and Persian Literature and Culture in the 10th and Early 11th centuries', *al-Abḥāth*, 27 (1978–1979), pp. 59–75, reprinted in his *Medieval Arabic Culture and Administration* (London, 1982), article VIII, and his *The History of the Saffarids of Sistan and the Maliks of Nimruz* (Costa Mesa, Calif., and New York, 1994), pp. 168–180.

3 For an excellent discussion of the resurgence of the Persian 'national' consciousness under the Būyids, see W. Madelung, 'The Assumption of the Title Shāhānshāh by the Būyids and the Reign of the Daylam (*Dawlat al-Daylam*)', *Journal of Near Eastern Studies*, 28 (1969), pp. 84–108, 168–183, reprinted in his *Religious and Ethnic Movements in Medieval Islam* (London, 1992), article VIII. See also V. Minorsky, *La domination des Dailamites* (Paris, 1932), pp. 1–26.

4 See Niẓām al-Mulk, *Siyar al-mulūk* (*Siyāsat-nāma*), ed. H. Darke (2nd edn, Tehran, 1347/1968), pp. 289–295, 297–305; English trans., *The Book of Government or Rules for Kings*, tr. H. Darke (2nd edn, London, 1978), pp. 208–218, 220–226. See also S. M. Stern, 'The Early Ismā'īlī Missionaries in North-West Persia and in Khurāsān and Transoxania', BSOAS, 23 (1960), pp. 56–90, reprinted in his *Studies in Early Ismā'īlism* (Jerusalem–Leiden, 1983), pp. 189–233, and F. Daftary, *The Ismā'īlīs: Their History and Doctrines* (Cambridge, 1990), pp. 120 ff.

5 On the causes of this schism and its implications, see W. Madelung, 'Das Imamat in der frühen ismailitischen Lehre', *Der Islam*, 37 (1961), pp. 65–86; F. Daftary, 'A Major Schism in the Early Ismā'īlī Movement', *Studia Islamica*, 77 (1993), pp. 123–139, and his *The Ismā'īlīs*, pp. 125–134, 611–612.

6 See, for instance, Ibn al-Athīr, *al-Kāmil fi'l-ta'rīkh*, ed. C. J. Tornberg (Leiden, 1851–1876), vol. 9, pp. 266–273, 311–312, 321 ff., 358, 384–385, and elsewhere.

7 For further details, see F. Daftary, 'Persian Historiography of the Early Nizārī Ismā'īlīs', *Iran, Journal of the British Institute of Persian Studies*, 30 (1992), pp. 91–97.

8 Two short manuscripts (Persian 162, and Persian 177), each one entitled *Sargudhasht-i Sayyidnā*, are among the Persian Isma'ili manuscripts of the Institute of Ismaili Studies Library, London. These manuscripts, transcribed in India at the beginning of the present century, are late compilations based on unknown sources. They contain an admixture of highly anachronistic details, such as Ḥasan-i Ṣabbāḥ's meeting with Nāṣir-i Khusraw in Cairo, the tale of the three schoolfellows, etc., as well as some of the events reported by our Persian historians in their extracts from the original *Sargudhasht-i Sayyidnā*.

9 'Alā' al-Dīn 'Aṭā Malik Juwaynī, *Ta'rīkh-i jahān-gushāy*, ed. M. Qazvīnī (Leiden–London, 1912–1937), vol. 3, pp. 186–216; English trans., *The History of the World-Conqueror*, tr. J. A. Boyle (Manchester, 1958), vol. 2, pp. 666–683; Rashīd al-Dīn Faḍl Allāh, *Jāmi' al-tawārīkh; qismat-i Ismā'īliyān va Fāṭimiyān va Nizāriyān va dā'īyān va rafīqān*, ed. M. T. Dānishpazhūh and M. Mudarrisī Zanjānī (Tehran, 1338/1959), pp. 97–137; Abu'l-Qāsim 'Abd Allāh b. 'Alī Kāshānī, *Zubdat al-tawārīkh; bakhsh-i Fāṭimiyān va Nizāriyān*, ed. M. T. Dānishpazhūh (2nd edn, Tehran, 1366/1987), pp. 133–172. Briefer biographical

details on Ḥasan, from a different source, are related in Ibn al-Athīr, *al-Kāmil*, vol. 10, pp. 216, 217, 369–370. In modern times, a few popular accounts of Ḥasan-i Ṣabbāḥ have been produced, including those by Jawad al-Muscati, ʿĀrif Tāmir, and Muṣṭafā Ghālib; Karīm Kishāvarz's *Ḥasan-i Ṣabbāḥ* (Tehran, 1344/1965) is a semi-popular but documented biography. For brief scholarly accounts of Ḥasan-i Ṣabbāḥ and his career, see Marshall G. S. Hodgson, *The Order of Assassins* (The Hague, 1955), pp. 41–98, and his 'The Ismāʿīlī State', in *The Cambridge History of Iran*: Volume 5, *The Saljuq and Mongol Periods*, ed. J. A. Boyle (Cambridge, 1968), pp. 424–449; B. Lewis, *The Assassins* (London, 1967), pp. 38–63, 145–148, and Daftary, *The Ismāʿīlīs*, pp. 324–371, 669–681. The relevant studies of Russian scholars generally suffer from excessive Marxist biases; see, for instance, Ludmila V. Stroeva's *Gosudarstvo ismailitov v Irane v XI–XIII vv.* (Moscow, 1978); Persian trans., *Taʾrīkh-i Ismāʿīliyān dar Īrān*, tr. P. Munzavī (Tehran, 1371/1992).

10 ʿAbd Allāh b. Luṭf ʿAlī al-Bihdādīnī, Ḥāfiẓ Abrū, *Majmaʿ al-tawārīkh al-sulṭāniyya; qismat-i khulafā-i ʿAlawiyya-yi Maghrib va Miṣr va Nizāriyān va rafīqān*, ed. M. Mudarrisī Zanjānī (Tehran, 1364/1985), pp. 191–225.

11 Ibn al-Athīr, *al-Kāmil*, vol. 10, pp. 161–162. See also Rashīd al-Dīn, p. 77; Kāshānī, p. 114, and Taqī al-Dīn Aḥmad b. ʿAlī al-Maqrīzī, *Ittiʿāẓ al-ḥunafāʾ bi-akhbār al-aʾimma al-Fāṭimiyyīn al-khulafāʾ*, ed. Jamāl al-Dīn al-Shayyāl and M. Ḥilmī M. Aḥmad (Cairo, 1967–1973), vol. 2, p. 323, and vol. 3, p. 15.

12 On the castle of Alamūt and its environs, see F. Stark, *The Valleys of the Assassins* (London, 1934), pp. 197–233; W. Ivanow, *Alamut and Lamasar: Two Mediaeval Ismaili Strongholds in Iran* (Tehran, 1960), pp. 1–11, 30–59; P. Willey, *The Castles of the Assassins* (London, 1963), pp. 204–226; M. Sutūda, *Qilāʿ-i Ismāʿīliyya* (Tehran, 1345/1966), pp. 72–108, and B. Hourcade, 'Alamūt', EIR, vol. 1, pp. 797–801.

13 Hodgson, 'Ismāʿīlī State', p. 429.

14 Rashīd al-Dīn, pp. 133–134. See also Juwaynī, vol. 3, pp. 215–216; tr. Boyle, vol. 2, p. 683, and Kāshānī, p. 168.

15 Rashīd al-Dīn, p. 112, and Kāshānī, p. 148.

16 *Haft bāb-i Bābā Sayyidnā*, ed. W. Ivanow, in his *Two Early Ismaili Treatises* (Bombay, 1933), p. 30; English trans., in Hodgson, *Order*, p. 314.

17 See Rashīd al-Dīn, pp. 149–153; Kāshānī, pp. 186–190, and Madelung, *Religious Trends*, pp. 9–12.

18 See Juwaynī, vol. 3, pp. 207–208; tr. Boyle, vol. 2, pp. 678–679; Rashīd al-Dīn, pp. 116–120, and Kāshānī, pp. 151–155.

19 Juwaynī, vol. 3, pp. 208–209; tr. Boyle, vol. 2, p. 679; Rashīd al-Dīn, pp. 115–116, and Kāshānī, pp. 150–151. Juwaynī places the seizure of Lamasar in 495/1102, which seems to be incorrect. See also Ivanow, *Alamut and Lamasar*, pp. 60–74; Willey, *Castles of the Assassins*, pp. 269–279; Sutūda, *Qilāʿ*, pp. 54–71, and C. E. Bosworth, 'Lanbasar', EI2, vol. 5, p. 656.

20 Our discussion here owes much to the pioneering ideas of Marshall Hodgson (1922–1968), who produced the first comprehensive and scholarly history of the Nizārī Ismaʿilis of the Alamūt period; see especially his *Order*, pp. 77–84, 87–89, 110–120; 'Ismāʿīlī State', pp. 439–443, and his monumental *The Venture of Islam: Conscience and History in a World Civilization* (Chicago, 1974), vol. 2, pp. 58–60.

21 See W. Ivanow, 'An Ismaili Poem in Praise of Fidawis', JBBRAS, NS, 14 (1938), pp. 63–72.

22 For the list of some forty-eight such missions conducted in Ḥasan-i Ṣabbāḥ's time, see Rashīd al-Dīn, pp. 134–137, and Kāshānī, pp. 169–172.

23 For further details on the early formation of these tales, rooted in ignorance and imaginative fantasies, see F. Daftary, *The Assassin Legends: Myths of the Isma'ilis* (London, 1994), especially pp. 88–127.

24 See, for instance, Ẓahīr al-Dīn Nīshāpūrī, *Saljūq-nāma* (Tehran, 1332/1953), pp. 40–41; Muḥammad b. 'Alī al-Rāwandī, *Rāḥat al-ṣudūr*, ed. M. Iqbāl (London, 1921), pp. 157–158, and Ḥamd Allāh Mustawfī Qazwīnī, *Ta'rīkh-i guzīda*, ed. 'Abd al-Ḥusayn Navā'ī (Tehran, 1339/1960), pp. 445–446.

25 On al-Mustanṣir's succession dispute and the rising of Nizār, see Juwaynī, vol. 3, pp. 179–181; tr. Boyle, vol. 2, pp. 661–663; Rashīd al-Dīn, pp. 77–79; Kāshānī, pp. 114–115; Ibn al-Qalānisī, *Dhayl ta'rīkh Dimashq*, ed. H. F. Amedroz (Leiden, 1908), p. 128; ed. S. Zakkār (Damascus, 1983), pp. 210–211; Ibn Muyassar, *Akhbār Miṣr*, ed. A. Fu'ād Sayyid (Cairo, 1981), pp. 59–63; Ibn Ẓāfir, *Akhbār al-duwal al-munqaṭi'a*, ed. A. Ferré (Cairo, 1972), pp. 83–85; al-Maqrīzī, *Itti'āẓ*, vol. 3, pp. 11–16, 27; Ibn Taghrībirdī, *al-Nujūm al-ẓāhira fī mulūk Miṣr wa'l-Qāhira* (Cairo, 1348–1391/1929–1972), vol. 5, pp. 142–145; Ibn al-Athīr, *al-Kāmil*, vol. 10, pp. 161–162, and H. A. R. Gibb 'Nizār b. al-Mustanṣir', EI2, vol. 8, p. 83.

26 See Sotheby's *Coins, together with Historical Medals and Banknotes*, Catalogue LN 4229 'Nizar' (London, 1994), pp. 36–37.

27 Ibn Ẓāfir, *Akhbār*, p. 97, naming this Nizārid as Abū 'Abd Allāh al-Ḥasan b. Nizār, and al-Maqrīzī, *Itti'āẓ*, vol. 3, p. 147.

28 Ibn al-Qalānisī, *Dhayl*, ed. Amedroz, p. 302; ed. Zakkār, pp. 469–470; Ibn Muyassar, *Akhbār*, p. 139; al-Maqrīzī, *Itti'āẓ*, vol. 3, p. 186, and Ibn Taghrībirdī, *al-Nujūm*, vol. 5, p. 282. The anonymous *Bustān al-jāmi'*, ed. Claude Cahen, in his 'Une chronique Syrienne du VIe/XIIe siècle: *Le Bustān al-Jāmi'*', *Bulletin d'Etudes Orientales*, 7–8 (1937–1938), p. 127, places this revolt in the year 540/1145–1146.

29 Ibn Ẓāfir, *Akhbār*, p. 111; al-Maqrīzī, *Itti'āẓ*, vol. 3, p. 246, and Ibn Taghrībirdī, *al-Nujūm*, vol. 5, p. 339.

30 See P. Casanova, 'Monnaie des Assassins de Perse', *Revue Numismatique*, 3 série, 11 (1893), pp. 343–352; George C. Miles, 'Coins of the Assassins of Alamūt', *Orientalia Lovaniensia Periodica*, 3 (1972), pp. 155–162, and *Centuries of Gold: The Coinage of Medieval Islam*, Islamic Coins at the Zamana Gallery (London, 1986), p. 46, no. 134.

31 See Juwaynī, vol. 3, pp. 180–181, 231–237; tr. Boyle, vol. 2, pp. 663, 691–695; Rashīd al-Dīn, pp. 79, 166–168, and Kāshānī, pp. 115, 202–204. See also Ibn al-Qalānisī, *Dhayl*, ed. Amedroz, pp. 127–129, citing a passage from the *Ta'rīkh* of Ibn al-Azraq al-Fāriqī; Ibn Muyassar, *Akhbār*, p. 102; Hodgson, *Order*, pp. 160–162, and Daftary, *The Ismā'īlīs*, pp. 350, 391–392.

32 Al-Āmir bi-Aḥkām Allāh, *al-Hidāya al-Āmiriyya*, ed. A. A. A. Fyzee (Bombay, etc., 1933), pp. 23–24, reprinted in *Majmū'at al-wathā'iq al-Fāṭimiyya*, ed. Jamāl al-Dīn al-Shayyāl (Cairo, 1958), pp. 226–227. This epistle and the circumstances surrounding its issue, representing the first official Musta'lian attempt to refute the claims of Nizār and his descendants to the imamate, is fully analyzed in S. M. Stern, 'The Epistle of the Fatimid Caliph al-Āmir (al-Hidāya al-Āmiriyya) – its Date and its Purpose', JRAS (1950), pp. 20–31, reprinted in S. M. Stern, *History and Culture in the Medieval Muslim World* (London, 1984), article X. See also Ibn Muyassar, *Akhbār*, pp. 99–101, 103, and al-Maqrīzī, *Itti'āẓ*, vol. 3, pp. 84–87.

33 See *Haft bāb*, p. 21; tr. Hodgson, in his *Order*, p. 301; this is the earliest extant Nizārī work, written anonymously around 596/1200. In later Nizārī sources, too, Ḥasan-i Ṣabbāḥ is given the title of *ḥujja*; see, for instance, Naṣīr al-Dīn al-Ṭūsī, *Rawḍat al-taslīm*, ed. and tr. W. Ivanow (Leiden, 1950), text p. 148; Abū Isḥāq Quhistānī, *Haft bāb*, ed. and tr. W. Ivanow (Bombay, 1959), text pp. 23, 43, translation pp. 23, 43, and Khayrkhwāh-i Harātī, *Taṣnīfāt*, ed. W. Ivanow (Tehran, 1961), pp. 52, 102.

34 See, for instance, Abu'l-Fatḥ Muḥammad b. ʿAbd al-Karīm al-Shahrastānī, *Kitāb al-milal wa'l-niḥal*, ed. W. Cureton (London, 1842), pp. 147–150; partial English trans., *Muslim Sects and Divisions*, tr. A. K. Kazi and J. G. Flynn (London, 1984), pp. 165, 167; Juwaynī, vol. 3, p. 195; tr. Boyle, vol. 2, p. 671; Rashīd al-Dīn, p. 105, and Kāshānī, p. 142.

35 Juwaynī, vol. 3, pp. 195–199; tr. Boyle, vol. 2, pp. 671–673; Rashīd al-Dīn, pp. 123–124, and Kāshānī, pp. 142–143.

36 Al-Shahrastānī, *al-Milal*, pp. 150–152; tr. Kazi and Flynn, pp. 167–170, also translated into English by Hodgson, in his *Order*, pp. 325–328; French trans., *Livre des religions et des sectes*, tr. D. Gimaret and G. Monnot (Paris, 1986), vol. 1, pp. 560–565. See also Hodgson, *Order*, pp. 51–61, his 'Ismāʿīlī State', pp. 433–437, and Daftary, *The Ismāʿīlīs*, pp. 367 ff.

37 See B. Lewis, 'The Ismāʿīlites and the Assassins', in *A History of the Crusades*, ed. K. M. Setton: Volume I, *The First Hundred Years*, ed. M. W. Baldwin (2nd edn, Madison, Wisconsin, 1969), pp. 99–114, and his *The Assassins*, pp. 97–104.

38 See Rashīd al-Dīn, pp. 120–122, and his *Jāmiʿ al-tawārīkh; ta'rīkh-i āl-i Saljūq*, ed. A. Ateş (Ankara, 1960), pp. 69–74; Kāshānī, pp. 156–157; Ẓahīr al-Dīn Nīshāpūrī, *Saljūq-nāma*, pp. 41–42; al-Rāwandī, *Rāḥat al-ṣudūr*, pp. 155–161; Ibn al-Athīr, *al-Kāmil*, vol. 10, pp. 299–302, and Ibn al-Qalānisī, *Dhayl*, ed. Amedroz, pp. 151–156; ed. Zakkār, pp. 244–250. See also Caro O. Minasian, *Shah Diz of Ismaʿili Fame, its Siege and Destruction* (London, 1971).

39 Juwaynī, vol. 3, pp. 211–213; tr. Boyle, vol. 2, pp. 680–681; Rashīd al-Dīn, pp. 124–132, and Kāshānī, pp. 160–167.

40 Hodgson, *Order*, pp. 99 ff., 145–146, and his 'Ismāʿīlī State', pp. 447–448.

ELEVEN

The power struggle between the Saljuqs and the Isma'ilis of Alamūt, 487–518/1094–1124: The Saljuq perspective

CAROLE HILLENBRAND

THE HISTORY of the Saljuqs' struggle against the Isma'ilis of Alamūt has already been written several times, but there are always new insights to be gleaned from a detailed reading of the primary sources and I hope to supplement, and on occasion, modify, what has already been said by scholars such as Hodgson, Lewis and Daftary.[1] As for the events of this period viewed from the Saljuq side, Sanaullah's lengthy study, covering precisely these crucial years, regrettably does not tackle at all the Saljuqs' relationship with Alamūt.[2] On the other hand, Kafesoğlu's emotional and simplistic condemnation of this period does not stand up to scrutiny:

> With the exception of Sultan Sanjar, the general history of the Seljuk state of Iraq and Khurasan is a chronicle of brave but inept rulers devoid of political sense and unworthy of their ancestors, ambitious and devious state officials, and *bāṭinī* crimes.[3]

His statement does, however, provide a convenient starting point for an analysis of the Saljuqs' activities between 487/1094 and 518/1124.

THE REIGN OF BARKIYĀRUQ, 487–498/1094–1105

The year 485/1092 was a fateful one for the Saljuq state, removing in quick succession its twin pillars, the vizier, Niẓām al-Mulk, and the sultan, Malik Shāh, after a long period of governmental continuity. Almost immediately, Malik Shāh's sons and relations made the traditional bid for power. Although by 488/1095 his eldest son, Barkiyāruq, had achieved overall recognition in the western sultanate of Iraq and western

Iran, his hold on power was always tenuous and, for the remainder of his reign, his energies were almost exclusively directed towards defending his position against all comers.[4] In particular, until 497/1103–1104, Barkiyāruq was locked in a debilitating and expensive power struggle with his half-brother, Muḥammad, who first rose in opposition against him in 492/1099. During Barkiyāruq's rule, only Khurāsān enjoyed some political continuity under his half-brother, Sanjar, whom he appointed as his deputy to rule over the eastern provinces in 490/1097.[5] In general, however, there is no doubt that the population of areas under Saljuq control in this period suffered at the hands of the Saljuq princes and governors: under the year 495/1101–1102, Ibn al-Qalānisī, in distant Damascus, comments on the situation in the Saljuq territories of Khurāsān, Iraq and Syria, singling out 'the protracted discord, enmity, wars, corruption and mutual fear' experienced by the population, as a result of their governors being 'too preoccupied with dispute and fighting to pay attention to them and to keep an eye on their affairs'.[6] As well as misrule, the period of Barkiyāruq's reign is characterized by decentralization, with the various Saljuq princes and Turkman *amīr*s often changing allegiances and jockeying for power, and by increasing fragmentation of the empire into semi-autonomous principalities on its peripheries. Small wonder, therefore, that both the Crusaders and the Isma'ilis were able to make inroads into Saljuq territory with such ease during these years.

As is well known, it was during Barkiyāruq's reign that the Isma'ilis of Alamūt achieved their greatest successes in Saljuq territory, in terms of citadels taken, assassinations of public figures and infiltration of urban and court circles.[7] In 489/1096, the Isma'ilis seized Girdkūh near Dāmghān, a citadel on the route from Khūrāsān to western Iran. They also captured Shāhdiz outside Iṣfahān, which was the key to control of the city, and many other fortresses in different parts of Iran.[8]

Kāshānī's detailed list of the assassinations allegedly carried out by the Isma'ilis and based on material found at the time of the Mongol conquest of Alamūt should not be accepted uncritically, even though he supplies dates and the names of both victims and assassins. Indeed, there are wide discrepancies, for example, between some of his dates and those of Ibn al-Athīr and other chroniclers.[9] It is clear, however, from all accounts that the crucial years in which assassinations occurred in the greatest number form a cluster between 488/1095 and 493/1100, peaking around 490/1097. This timing is very telling – predictably, it is at a moment of extreme disarray and weakness on the Saljuq side. As well as the seizure of citadels and the removal of prominent military and religious figures, there were rumours of the Isma'ili 'contagion' infiltrating the Saljuq army and court circles. This moment of extreme vulnerability will be examined in greater detail below.

Most of the sources are harsh on Barkiyāruq, in spite of the genuine difficulties that any Saljuq ruler would have had to face in establishing himself in an empire, bereft of the towering figure of Niẓām al-Mulk. To be sure, the latter's sons were in plentiful supply and a number of them were to fill important positions in this period. They were not, however, of the calibre of their father and, above all, lacked his ability to stay in office for a very long time.[10] Not only did Barkiyāruq lack good administrative support; he seemed also to have alienated the Niẓāmiyya, the late vizier's crack troops, who defected to the side of Muḥammad and Sanjar.[11] It is as if most of the chroniclers, normally so reticent, are looking in their reflections on this dire period of Saljuq weakness to find a scapegoat. It is not difficult to load blame onto Barkiyāruq. In addition to a doleful tale of successive intrusions from the Crusaders and the dreadful havoc wrought by the Isma'ilis, the chroniclers provide smears and innuendoes. Al-Ḥusaynī describes Barkiyāruq as a drunkard,[12] whilst al-Bundārī speaks of his having a 'bad character', 'associating with youths' and indulging in frivolous music-making.[13] It was also Barkiyāruq's misfortune to be afflicted with smallpox and piles,[14] ailments which scarcely enhanced his public image.

There are no concessions made here to Barkiyāruq's extreme youth and inexperience, although these same two qualities of youth and inexperience in his two half-brothers, Muḥammad and Sanjar, are tacitly condoned. But of course the chroniclers are writing with the benefit of hindsight, and Barkiyāruq's brothers both had indisputably more successful reigns.

The worst smear on the part of the chroniclers of Saljuq history is the insinuation that Barkiyāruq himself had Isma'ili sympathies. To what extent is this true? After all, he himself had been the target of a failed assassination attempt.[15] It is worth looking closely at the evidence provided by Ibn al-Jawzī and Ibn al-Athīr on this matter. Both choose the year 494/1101 – just after the most widespread spate of reported assassinations – in which to reflect more generally on the rise of the Bāṭinīs.[16] The coverage of Barkiyāruq's alleged Isma'ili proclivities is fuller in Ibn al-Athīr's account and will be followed here. This historian mentions that there was considerable resentment in Iṣfahān at the fact that most of the *amīr*s killed in the recent wave of murders, such as

Arghūsh and Surmuz, belonged both to the Niẓāmiyya and to Muḥammad's side. This threw suspicion onto Barkiyāruq. The details given by Ibn al-Athīr indicate that an atmosphere of paranoia and intrigue must have pervaded both the army and the court. The situation deteriorated further when, emboldened by Muḥammad's defeat of Barkiyāruq, the Isma'ilis infiltrated the latter's army and nearly gained the upper hand. Barkiyāruq was then called upon by his close associates, who had taken to wearing chain mail under their clothes, to act before it was too late, especially in view of the fact that he himself had 'Isma'ili leanings'. Barkiyāruq therefore rooted out and killed many suspects, including the alleged leader of the Isma'ili troops, Muḥammad b. Dushmanziyār, from Yazd. He had acted vigorously, if rather belatedly and under pressure. But this does not necessarily imply that he was a secret Isma'ili sympathizer. He was short of troops and money and may well have been ill, weary of warfare and ill-advised. The evidence against him remains opaque and ambivalent.

Also in 494/1101, Sanjar took action against the Isma'ilis, sending an expedition under the leadership of an *amīr* of his, Boz-Qush, to Kūhistān (Arabic, Quhistān). Boz-Qush was persuaded by bribes to lift his siege of the Isma'ili stronghold of Ṭabas Masīnān, thus allowing the Isma'ilis to recoup their losses thereafter.[17] On a second campaign in 497/1104, Boz-Qush granted the inhabitants of Ṭabas safe conduct. Ibn al-Athīr comments that 'many people were angry with Sanjar about this'.[18]

Posterity has perhaps judged Barkiyāruq a little harshly. Certainly, moments of compromise with the Isma'ilis are condoned in his half-brother, Sanjar, but condemned in him. Even Lewis follows the line laid down by mediaeval chronicles, speaking of Barkiyāruq's 'complacency or worse'[19] vis-à-vis the Isma'ili threat. The evidence from the sources suggests that neither Barkiyāruq nor Sanjar nor Muḥammad was strong enough singly to resist the necessity of using whatever troops were available to them, even if they were 'Isma'ili'. All three were accused at some time of using the Isma'ilis to dispose of their enemies. The reality was that none of the three brothers, including Muḥammad, considered the extirpation of 'heretical' Isma'ilis to be a major part of their military strategies. Their youth, inexperience and preoccupation with each other allowed the Isma'ilis to expand during Barkiyāruq's reign. Barkiyāruq's massacre of some eight hundred suspected Isma'ilis in Iṣfahān was his sole decisive measure aimed at stemming their growth and infiltration.

THE REIGN OF MUḤAMMAD TAPAR, 498–511/1105–1118

Muḥammad's reign witnessed not only a diminution in the number of assassinations attributed to Alamūt but also a greater political stability. This was possible both because of the harmonious relationship which he enjoyed with his uterine brother, Sanjar, and because of the continuing support of the Niẓāmiyya for Muḥammad. Although his rule was not without crises, the spectre of the almost uninterrupted wars of Barkiyāruq's reign had gone.

In view of this improved political landscape it might be expected that Muḥammad would be able to turn his attention to the 'enemy within', the Isma'ilis of Alamūt. What measures did he in fact take against them during the thirteen years of his reign? His first move came quickly, as early as 500/1106–1107, when he recaptured the citadel of Shāhdiz which had fallen into Isma'ili hands. This victory is seized upon eagerly by the chroniclers, who were no doubt weary of recounting Saljuq weakness and Isma'ili success. The Damascene historian, Ibn al-Qalānisī, who includes in his city chronicle snippets or longer extracts from other parts of the Islamic world, triumphantly interrupts his narrative for the year 500 AH to provide a lengthy text purporting to be a *fatḥ-nāma* written by Muḥammad's scribe, Abū Naṣr b. 'Umar al-Iṣfahānī, after the reconquest of the citadel of Shāhdiz and intended to be read from the *minbar*s of the empire.[20] Couched in high epistolary prose, this victory proclamation finally affords the Sunni world a pretext to exult at the 'shedding of a river of blood of the heretical Bāṭiniyya'.[21]

Muḥammad thus became the hero of the hour. He had acted early in his reign against the Isma'ilis and he had won. Here begins the process whereby Muḥammad's activities are embellished by the Sunni chroniclers and result in the creation of his image as 'the strong he-camel' of the Saljuqs.[22] Yet it would be stretching historical credibility to attribute Muḥammad's prompt action against Shāhdiz to ideological fervour. In this, the only anti-Isma'ili initiative of his whole reign in which he participated personally, his motives were, in part anyway, more practical. He was forced to deal with the problem of the Isma'ilis in Iṣfahān since this was his power base and the Isma'ilis were well entrenched there, with widespread support. They had even been reaping the benefits of tax revenues from the outlying areas around Iṣfahān. Here, it could be argued, he had no choice but to act. The Saljuq armoury and treasury were there, and the citadel at Shāhdiz held the key to domination of the city.[23] Iṣfahān was the traditional centre of Saljuq rule and Muḥammad's own power and prestige were linked with possessing it. So Muḥammad began with a siege of the citadel of Shāhdiz, an action prolonged by what Ibn al-Athīr presents as delaying ploys by the Ismaʿilis inside. Finally, however, Muḥammad successfully seized and destroyed the citadel and killed the Ismaʿili leaders, Aḥmad Ibn ʿAṭṭāsh and his son. An important, indeed essential, victory had been achieved. The fall of Shāhdiz seems to mark the end of extensive Ismaʿili power in Iṣfahān, although the burning of the Friday mosque in 515/1121–1122 was blamed on the Ismaʿilis – an unlikely deed for them to have perpetrated, since such tactics were not a usual feature of their anti-Sunni strategy.[24] Henceforth, until his death in 511/1118 Muḥammad kept Iṣfahān as the main centre of his power.

The same year Muḥammad moved against his own vizier, Saʿd al-Mulk, seized his possessions and crucified him at the gate of Iṣfahān. Saʿd al-Mulk was accused of treachery against the sultan but four other close associates, suspected of Bāṭinī beliefs, were killed with him. Given that Muḥammad had endured the cost of the lengthy siege of Shāhdiz and that the mulcting or killing of ministers of state often occurred at moments of economic difficulty, Muḥammad's killing of these five could have had a motive much more mundane than zeal against the Ismaʿilis.[25]

The finger of suspicion was pointed at many. When a suspected Ismaʿili, one Surkhān b. Kaykhusraw al-Daylamī, was brought before Muḥammad, Ibn al-Athīr uses the opportunity to point out Muḥammad's impeccable Sunni credentials, putting the following pious words into the sultan's mouth:

> I have made a vow to God that I will not kill a prisoner. (But) if it is established that you are a Bāṭinī, then I will kill you.[26]

The next move initiated by Muḥammad against the Ismaʿilis struck at the heart of their power, Alamūt, to which the sultan sent an army, probably in 503/1109–1110, under the command of his vizier, Aḥmad b. Niẓām al-Mulk.[27] According to Ibn al-Athīr, the siege was eventually lifted because 'winter took them by surprise and they returned without achieving their goal'.[28] The same admission of honest failure is made by Juwaynī.[29] Al-Ḥusaynī, however, obscures this fact by alleging that the Saljuq army had 'inflicted a defeat on the Bāṭinīs'.[30]

The most ambitious anti-Ismaʿili offensive of Muḥammad's reign was conducted by Anūshtegin Shīrgīr against Alamūt in 511/1118.[31] The siege was long, lasting around nine months.[32] It is likely that a familiar device is used by the chroniclers to obscure the unpalatable fact that the siege had failed. Certainly, Juwaynī argues that in the reign of Malik Shāh, the campaign led by Qïzïl Sarïgh into Kūhistān in 485/1092 had failed because of the untimely news of Malik Shāh's death:

> Before he could take the place, however, he received the news of Malik Shāh's death, whereupon he raised the siege and his army dispersed.[33]

An identical argument is used by Juwaynī for the lifting of the siege by Shīrgīr in 511/1118. Pious deception dictates that the sources are unanimous in their assurance that, as al-Ḥusaynī puts it, Shīrgīr 'was on the point of taking Alamūt' when the news of the sultan's death arrived.[34] Thereafter, there was no hope of continuing the siege; the commanders left immediately and their supplies were taken by the inhabitants of Alamūt. Once again, fate had intervened and snatched the victory from the Saljuqs: there is no reference to the tenacity of the Isma'ilis in withstanding the latest siege of their stronghold.

TAILPIECE

After Muḥammad's death, the Isma'ilis were given a respite by the ensuing power struggles of the Saljuqs. Certainly they remained entrenched in Alamūt. In Kūhistān they regained enough strength to force Sanjar to come to terms with them.[35] Sanjar, who had not seen the need to come in person to western Iran during the rule of his brother Muḥammad to join forces against the Isma'ilis and root them out, came in great pomp and with a massive army, in a show of strength in 513/1119–1120 against his nephew, Maḥmūd b. Muḥammad.[36] Well before the death of Ḥasan-i Ṣabbāḥ in 518/1124 Sanjar had become the uncontested leader of the Saljuqs.[37] Yet he does not seem to have felt that this position of responsibility made it incumbent upon him to grapple seriously with the Isma'ili problem.

SOME HISTORIOGRAPHICAL CONSIDERATIONS

The treatment of this period by Ibn al-Athīr is extensive and thorough and raises a number of interesting issues. Periodically in his *Universal History* Ibn al-Athīr breaks with the traditional annalistic format to reflect more generally on an historical topic of significance. Like Ibn al-Jawzī, he accords the emergence of the Isma'ilis of Alamūt a special excursus under the year 494/1101.[38] Individual incidents which involve the Saljuq–Isma'ili encounter are dealt with in their proper chronological place. When recounting the activities of the Isma'ilis in Iṣfahān, Ibn al-Athīr speaks about them with a kind of invective reminiscent of Niẓām al-Mulk or Juwaynī:

> When this affliction became widespread among the people in Iṣfahān, Almighty God allowed their covers to be ripped asunder and vengeance to be exacted from them.[39]

According to Ibn al-Athīr, after Muḥammad's accession there was nothing more pressing for the new sultan's attention than to deal with the Isma'ili threat:

> When Muḥammad became sultan and nobody opposed him any longer, there was no matter more important for him than attacking the Bāṭiniyya, fighting them and exacting justice for the Muslims against their tyranny and oppression.[40]

Ibn al-Athīr also devotes several pages to an obituary of Muḥammad. It is a masterpiece of exaggeration and pious deception. He is described with the usual array of laudable epithets – just, virtuous and courageous. An example of his justice was his removal of illegal taxes and duties (*mukūs* and *ḍarā'ib*) in all his territories. The rest of the obituary is devoted to the sultan's activities against the Bāṭiniyya:

> Amongst the finest of his deeds (*maḥāsin*) was what he did with the Bāṭiniyya, as we shall relate. We have already mentioned what he undertook in the way of besieging their citadels. Here we will mention his increased concern about them, for, when he realized that the well-being of the faithful and the country lay in the wiping out of their traces and the destruction of their fortresses and citadels, he devoted himself indefatigably to attacking them.[41]

High-sounding words indeed. But, as we have seen, it is debatable whether Muḥammad had the eradication of the Isma'ilis as his prime concern. Nor did he ever fight personally against them at Alamūt. His only personal involvement was to recapture his own power base in Iṣfahān, an action that could quite well have been prompted by self-interest. The subsequent evidence in the obituary which Ibn al-Athīr produces for Muḥammad's anti-Isma'ili zeal consists of a detailed account of the siege of Alamūt in 511/1118. Muḥammad delegated the conduct of this enterprise to Anūshtegin Shīrgīr, the governor of Sāwa, and it is to this man's activities rather than those of his ostensible subject, that Ibn al-Athīr devotes the remaining section of his obituary. Historical veracity compels Ibn al-Athīr to admit Saljuq failures in the past. There is a brief but vague reference to unsuccessful attempts by Muḥammad to take Alamūt:

> The sultan sent troops against him (Ḥasan al-Ṣabbāḥ), as we have already mentioned, and they returned without achieving (their) goal.[42]

There then follows an account of the successful siege of Alamūt, lifted on the news of Muḥammad's death. An inadequate obituary, by any standards. So how much does Muḥammad deserve the eulogies given to him by Ibn al-Athīr? How hard did he fight a *jihād* against the 'heretics' and rescue the fortunes of the Saljuq house? It would appear that the image of him created by Ibn al-Athīr and others is a pious figment. The contemporary epigraphic evidence on Muḥammad's titulature is conventional. The undated inscription at Gulpāyagān in his name gives him the following laudatory and quite lengthy epithets: 'the just king (*malik*), the exalted sultan, the most venerated king of kings (*Shāhanshāh*), the client (*mawlā*) of the Arabs and non-Arabs . . . the associate (*qasīm*) of the Commander of the Faithful'.[43] But there is no reference here, as Ibn al-Athīr would wish us to believe, to Muḥammad being a fighter of *jihād* against heretics in general or the Isma'ilis of Alamūt in particular.

The perception of Sultan Muḥammad as a zealous 'smiter of heretics' seems to have accrued to him in the strongly Sunni, *jihād*-pervaded milieu of Zangid and Ayyūbid times, when the achievements of the Turkish military leaders in this sphere were attributed by the chroniclers of that period retrospectively to their Turkish predecessors, the Great Saljuqs. All this goes some way to explaining the attitude of Ibn al-Athīr towards Sultan Muḥammad and his careful but easily overlooked inflating of Muḥammad's role in the Saljuq attacks on the Isma'ilis of Alamūt. His death marked the end of effective Saljuq rule in the western sultanate and his reign signalled a slowing down of Isma'ili successes. He was the last of the line and as such, was a suitable subject for historiographical remoulding.

There is disagreement in the sources on the actual number of Saljuq campaigns against Alamūt. According to Juwaynī and other Persian historians,[44] the Saljuqs sent campaigns against Alamūt for eight successive years, whilst other sources mention only two specific attempts; Ibn al-Athīr hints rather vaguely that there may have been other unsuccessful ventures.[45] On the one hand, the version offered by Juwaynī implies firm Saljuq commitment to the destruction of the Isma'ilis' centre; on the other hand, the account given in the remaining sources suggests a more piecemeal effort on the part of the Saljuqs. What interpretations can be made on the basis of these conflicting views? It could be argued that it is certainly more plausible to give credibility to the latter interpretation, since the main body of sources for this period, and above all, Ibn al-Athīr, are at pains to praise the Saljuqs', and notably Sultan Muḥammad's achievements against the Isma'ilis. Why would they omit to mention such a major fact as eight successive campaigns against Alamūt? This number of campaigns would be a clear sign of commitment to *jihād* and the eradication of 'heresy'. The other line of argument would be that the main body of sources would naturally wish to minimize the fact that the Saljuqs failed in their attempts at destroying the Isma'ilis' centre at Alamūt and therefore did not reveal the true extent of the Saljuqs' unsuccessful efforts against them. Juwaynī's possible desire to exaggerate the number of Saljuq campaigns and to dwell on their failure is also explicable. After all, it was the Mongol destiny to achieve the definitive conquest of Alamūt in the fullness of time:

> Yet when the time was not yet ripe, during the reign of Hasan-i-Sabbah, that same castle of Alamut, whose garrison and resources were then but small, had during a period of 11 years been several times besieged by Muhammad, son of Malik-Shah, son of Alp-Arslan, (as may be read in books of history), and all to no avail.[46]

Thus, Juwaynī may well have had his own reasons for inflating the actual number of failed Saljuq expeditions against the Isma'ilis at Alamūt, and for suggesting that there were eight rather than two. As Morgan rightly argues, it was hardly coincidental that Juwaynī makes the Mongol destruction of Alamūt the climax of his book. Juwaynī 'was able to discern some silver linings in the Mongol clouds'.[47] One such 'silver lining' was indeed Hülegü's virtual extermination of the Isma'ilis of Alamūt. Juwaynī, as befits a public servant of the Mongols, omits all reference to their sack of Baghdad and the Mongols' murder of the last 'Abbasid caliph in 656/1258 but deems it historiographically opportune to exaggerate the number of Saljuq failures at Alamūt in order to pinpoint with greater force the magnificent achievement of the Mongols in ridding the Sunni world of its longstanding enemy.

In his obituary notice of Muḥammad, Ibn al-Athīr mentions, in passing, an interesting point. He writes that when the Bāṭiniyya were suffering extremes of hardship, the news reached them of the death of Sultan Muḥammad. At this point, the morale of the Bāṭiniyya rose. He then adds the following little detail:

The news reached the troops besieging them [the Bāṭiniyya] a day after they [the Bāṭiniyya] learned of it.[48]

This cryptic detail remains unexplained. One may wonder how this occurred and why Ibn al-Athīr mentions it. Unwittingly, however, Ibn al-Athīr points to the more effective communications system of the beleaguered Isma'ilis who heard this important piece of news before the Saljuq troops did. This detail is supported by the archaeological evidence which reveals the intervisibility of the network of Isma'ili fortresses in Daylam and which would permit fire, light or smoke signals to be exchanged, to say nothing of messages by carrier pigeons. It is known from archaeological evidence, for example, that Ghutinar had intervisibility with Alamūt, Lamasar and Maymūndiz.[49]

Did Ḥasan-i Ṣabbāḥ and other prominent Isma'ili figures in this period have some kind of standing army or irregular troops on which they themselves could draw or which could even be hired out to other military leaders? There are some tantalizingly brief but revealing references in the sources which support the latter hypothesis. As early as 493/1100, some five thousand 'Bāṭinī foot soldiers' are mentioned as being part of the troops of Amīrdād Ḥabashī, the lord of the stronghold of Girdkūh, in a battle against Barkiyāruq. These foot soldiers apparently belonged to Ismā'īl al-Kalkalī, the lord of Ṭabas.[50] Al-Ḥusaynī has Sanjar fighting on Barkiyāruq's side in this battle,[51] but according to Ibn al-Athīr, Sanjar fought with Ḥabashī's troops.[52] For the year 497/1103–1104 Ibn al-Athīr mentions a great gathering of Isma'ilis from the area of Bayhaq who were on the rampage; this was caused, he adds, by the neglect of the three sultans.[53] In 501/1107–1108, Ṣadaqa gathered twenty thousand horsemen of the 'scattered bands of Kurds, Turks, Daylamīs and Arabs'.[54] Of course, Daylamīs were not necessarily synonymous with Isma'ilis. Under the year 513/1119–1120, Ibn al-Athīr mentions the name of Ghuzzoğlu as being the leader of the 'Isma'ili Turks'.[55] As for Sanjar's mighty army which accompanied him in 513/1119–1120 across Khurāsān to Rayy to terrify his nephew, Maḥmūd, into submission, this included five kings and 'thousands of Bāṭiniyya and infidels'.[56]

It is unclear who these troops were or what their status was in the Saljuq armies, but it is likely that they were hired for specific engagements and could appear on either side of an inter-Saljuq power struggle. Clearly, however, ideological questions played little part in all this, although the Isma'ili presence is deemed worthy of mention by the chroniclers. Their involvement in Saljuq military activities suggests that, even in Ḥasan's lifetime, the Ismaʿili policy of the assassination of major figures was giving way to the strategies and survival tactics of other small territorial leaders involved in the power struggles of the day. By 518/1124 the Ismaʿilis were one group among many, vying for power in localized contexts. The references to their military participation in different power struggles of the time suggest that their presence was more tolerated in the Iranian context than later mediaeval chroniclers, with their stylized anti-Ismaʿili diatribes, would have us believe.

CONCLUSIONS

It is apparent from the preceding discussion that there are still new insights to be gleaned from a subject which might be regarded as almost too familiar in scholarly writings, especially when those scholars who have worked on this topic are of a high calibre and write persuasively. Yet there are still unanswered questions, both about individual episodes and the grander sweep of events. It is all too easy to accept at face value what mediaeval chroniclers say. Much more work needs to be done on the historiographical jigsaw on which the general history of the Saljuq–Ismaʿili struggle has been based.

The Sunni sources of the 6th/12th and 7th/13th centuries generally try to inflate the Saljuq achievement against the Ismaʿilis of Alamūt. This is especially the case with Sultan Muḥammad. Juwaynī, who draws on material found at Alamūt, suggests greater activity on the part of the Saljuqs at certain stages against the Ismaʿilis and a larger number of actual campaigns against Alamūt. There may well be propaganda motives behind this – namely to glorify the Mongol conquest of Alamūt.

The combined forces of Muḥammad and Sanjar might have been able to remove the Ismaʿilis from Alamūt and thus to eradicate their major military centre. The threat of undercover Ismaʿili operations, aimed at conversion and subversion, at court and in the major cities of the Saljuq empire, would have remained. This more 'pernicious contagion' would be more difficult to isolate and contain. It is, however, difficult to prove its existence definitively from the primary sources, which resort to hysterical and far-fetched stories.

Muḥammad, Barkiyāruq and Sanjar never formed a united front against the Ismaʿilis of Alamūt in the period of Ismaʿili growth in Iran, 485–498/1092–1105. Muḥammad and Sanjar could, on occasion, unite against Barkiyāruq but never in the latter's reign did all three brothers attack their common enemy within. This lack of solidarity and common cause was scarcely surprising: all three had expectations of patrimonial inheritance and would not cede their share without military struggle. Three chunks of patrimonial inheritance were to be seized and retained from the Great Saljuq empire ruled by Malik Shāh. Sanjar was relatively secure in the east. But the western territories (western Iran and Iraq) were the scene of a grim and protracted struggle between Barkiyāruq and Muḥammad which lasted almost until Barkiyāruq's death in 498/1105 and which weakened both sides. Five battles between Barkiyāruq and Muḥammad must have demanded large resources and depleted their finances. To continue to be able to pay their troops was the prime task. Any concerted offensive against the Isma'ilis was, therefore, not a priority or even a major objective for either brother at this point. Could Muḥammad and Sanjar together have defeated the Isma'ilis at Alamūt? This is a difficult question to answer. Numerically, they would or could have been large but they lacked the aura of invincibility of the Mongols when they finally came to Alamūt and the weapon of terror that such invincibility instilled in the future victims.

Later on, after 498/1105, when Muḥammad was uncontested ruler in the western sultanate, he must have had severe financial problems, at least for parts of his reign. There were other demands on his treasury, such as financing campaigns against the Crusaders, as he was later pressurized to do. There was clearly a limit to the amount of time and financial resources he could afford to invest in military campaigns and sieges against Alamūt and other Isma'ili centres. After all, he had to take steps to keep himself in power and there were also other calls on his attention between 498/1105 and 511/1118.

However many campaigns were sent to Alamūt, it is telling that Sultan Muḥammad never went there in person to attack the enemy. He always delegated this task, either to one of the sons of Niẓām al-Mulk (who had good reasons for hating the Isma'ilis), or to a competent military commander, notably Shīrgīr. This stance by Sultan Muḥammad, during the thirteen-year period of his reign, suggests, at the very least, that he did not make the extirpation of the Isma'ili threat his top priority. The sources do not, however, indicate that there *were* more pressing needs than this threat posed by the 'heretical' enemy from within. It is clear that the Crusaders, who were actively consolidating their position in Syria and the Holy Land, and who might have constituted an alternative and valid outlet for Muḥammad's energies, were only peripheral to his activities. So, the most that can be said of Sultan

Muḥammad's efforts against the Ismaʿilis is that they were piecemeal and delegated to his associates. Their efficacy was limited.

Certain facts can be summarized at the end of this discussion. The Saljuqs did not eradicate the overall Ismaʿili threat but they did remove the major threat of Ismaʿili power at Iṣfahān. It is clear that they devoted some, but not all, of their energies to attacks on the Ismaʿilis. Much of the 'blame' for the Saljuqs' failure to wipe out the Ismaʿilis within their own territories lies with them and is not to be attributed to Ismaʿili dynamism alone.

The possibility remains that the combined forces of Muḥammad and Sanjar could have definitively wiped out the Ismaʿilis at Alamūt in the way that Hülegü's troops eventually did. The factors which contributed to the Saljuqs' failure to do this include the atomization of Saljuq power, the lack of concerted Saljuq military activity, the problem of financial resources – even under Sultan Muḥammad – and the probability, barely addressed in Saljuq sources, that the new Ismaʿili preaching was not confined to known Ismaʿili strongholds but that it had infiltrated much more deeply into many areas of Iran, both urban and rural, both in the Saljuq armies and at court. As such, it was much more difficult to stamp out. Altogether, then, at this dynamic stage of Ismaʿili propaganda, under the leadership of Ḥasan-i Ṣabbāḥ, there was a lack of real concerted will or effort in the Saljuq empire to deal with the Ismaʿilis.

NOTES

1 See M. Hodgson, *The Order of Assassins* (The Hague, 1955), pp. 73–99; B. Lewis, *The Assassins* (London, 1967), pp. 43–63, and F. Daftary, *The Ismāʿīlīs* (Cambridge, 1990), pp. 351–371.

2 M. F. Sanaullah, *The Decline of the Saljuqid Empire* (Calcutta, 1938).

3 G. Leiser, *A History of the Seljuks: Ibrahim Kafesoğlu's Interpretation and the Resulting Controversy* (Carbondale and Edwardsville, 1988), p. 56.

4 Ṣadr al-Dīn ʿAlī al-Ḥusaynī, *Akhbār al-dawla al-Saljūqiyya*, ed. M. Iqbāl (Lahore, 1933), p. 76; Ibn al-Qalānisī, *Dhayl taʾrīkh Dimashq*, ed. H. F. Amedroz (Leiden, 1908), pp. 137, 139–140, and Abu'l-Qāsim Kāshānī, *Zubdat al-tawārīkh; bakhsh-i Fāṭimiyān va Nizāriyān*, ed. M. T. Dānishpazhūh (2nd edn., Tehran, 1366/1987), p. 115.

5 Ibn Khallikān, *Wafayāt al-aʿyān*, ed. I. ʿAbbās (Beirut, 1968–1972), vol. 2, p. 428.

6 Ibn al-Qalānisī, *Dhayl*, p. 140.

7 See Hodgson, *Order*, pp. 75–77. Kāshānī (*Zubdat al-tawārīkh*, pp. 115–116) comments, for example, that the Crusaders were able to take advantage of the strife between the Saljuq princes of Syria, Riḍwān and Duqāq.

8 See the names of citadels provided by Ibn al-Athīr, *al-Kāmil fiʾl-taʾrīkh*, ed. C. J. Tornberg (Leiden, 1851–1876), vol. 10, pp. 215–218.

9 Kāshānī, *Zubdat al-tawārīkh*, pp. 154–157. The death of Aḥmadīl, for example, is

recorded by Kāshānī for the year 493/1100, whereas for Ibn al-Athīr (vol. 10, p. 361), who is usually accurate with his chronology, it occurs as late as 510/1116–1117.

10 See, for instance, the list given in C. L. Klausner, *The Seljuk Vezirate: A Study of Civil Administration, 1055–1194* (Cambridge, Mass., 1973), p. 106.

11 Ibn al-Athīr, vol. 10, p. 220.

12 Al-Ḥusaynī, *Akhbār*, p. 78.

13 Al-Fatḥ b. 'Alī al-Bundārī, *Zubdat al-nuṣra*, ed. M. Th. Houtsma (Leiden, 1889), p. 84. Not all the chroniclers, however, indulge in this vilification of Barkiyāruq. Al-Rāwandī, for example, praises him in conventionally glowing terms, as befits a scholar who wishes to gain favour at Konya with the Saljuqs of Rūm; see al-Rāwandī, *Rāḥat al-ṣudūr*, ed. M. Iqbāl (London, 1921), p. 138. For an as yet unknown reason, moreover, the artist of the Edinburgh manuscript of Rashīd al-Dīn honours Barkiyāruq alone among the Saljuq sultans with a hanging crown; see D. Talbot Rice, *The Illustrations to the 'World History' of Rashīd al-Dīn* (Edinburgh, 1976), p. 171.

14 Al-Bundārī, *Zubdat al-nuṣra*, p. 89, and Sibṭ Ibn al-Jawzī, *Mir'āt al-zamān* (Hyderabad, 1951), vol. 8, p. 13.

15 Ibn al-Jawzī, *al-Muntaẓam*, ed. M. and M. 'Aṭā (Beirut, 1992), vol. 17, p. 488.

16 Ibn al-Athīr, vol. 10, pp. 213–220, and Ibn al-Jawzī, *al-Muntaẓam*, vol. 17, pp. 62–65. It should be recalled that the great propaganda war against the Isma'ilis was being waged in Baghdad during his reign. Al-Ghazālī was commissioned by the caliph al-Mustaẓhir to write a systematic refutation of Isma'ili doctrines and a defence of 'Abbasid legitimacy; see al-Ghazālī, *Faḍā'iḥ al-Bāṭiniyya*, ed. 'Abd al-Raḥmān Badawī (Cairo, 1964). However, it is doubtful whether al-Ghazālī's polemical skills had any impact on Saljuq power struggles.

17 Ibn al-Athīr, vol. 10, p. 221.

18 Ibid., vol. 10, p. 253.

19 Lewis, *The Assassins*, p. 52.

20 Ibn al-Qalānisī, *Dhayl*, pp. 152–156. The *fatḥ-nāma* is also quoted by Sibṭ Ibn al-Jawzī, *Mir'āt*, vol. 8, p. 20.

21 Ibn al-Qalānisī, *Dhayl*, p. 155.

22 Al-Bundārī, *Zubdat al-nuṣra*, p. 118.

23 For the siege of Shāhdiz, see al-Rāwandī, *Rāḥat al-ṣudūr*, p. 161; al-Ḥusaynī, *Akhbār*, p. 79; Ibn al-Athīr, vol. 10, pp. 299 ff.; Ibn al-Jawzī, *al-Muntaẓam*, vol. 17, p. 102; Sibṭ Ibn al-Jawzī, *Mir'āt*, vol. 8, p. 20, and al-Bundārī, *Zubdat al-nuṣra*, pp. 90–91.

24 Ibn al-Athīr, vol. 10, p. 420.

25 Al-Bundārī, *Zubdat al-nuṣra*, p. 90.

26 Ibn al-Athīr, vol. 10, p. 313.

27 Al-Ḥusaynī, *Akhbār*, p. 81; Ibn al-Athīr, vol. 10, p. 335; Juwaynī, *The History of the World-Conqueror*, tr. J. A. Boyle (Manchester, 1958), vol. 2, p. 680.

28 Ibn al-Athīr, vol. 10, p. 335.

29 Juwaynī, tr. Boyle, vol. 2, p. 680.

30 Al-Ḥusaynī, *Akhbār*, p. 81.

31 Al-Ḥusaynī, *Akhbār*, pp. 79, 82; al-Bundārī, *Zubdat al-nurṣra*, p. 117, and Ibn al-Athīr, vol. 10, pp. 369–370.

32 Juwaynī, tr. Boyle, vol. 2, p. 681.

33 Ibid., vol. 2, pp. 675–676.

34 Al-Ḥusaynī, *Akhbār*, p. 79.
35 Juwaynī, tr. Boyle, vol. 2, p. 682.
36 Sibṭ Ibn al-Jawzī, *Mirʾāt*, vol. 8, p. 77.
37 Ibn Khallikān, *Wafayāt*, vol. 2, p. 428.
38 Ibn al-Athīr, vol. 10, pp. 213 ff.
39 Ibid., vol. 10, p. 214.
40 Ibid., vol. 10, p. 299.
41 Ibid., vol. 10, p. 369.
42 Ibid.
43 E. Herzfeld, *Matériaux pour un corpus inscriptionum arabicarum* (Cairo, 1955), vol. 1, pp. 118–119. The numismatic evidence that survives is sparse but confirms the titulature found on architectural monuments. Inevitably, the confined space on coins does not allow for the full panoply of epithets often found on buildings; see, for instance, G. Hennequin, 'Monnaies Salǧuqides inédites ou peu courantes', *Annales Islamologiques*, 19 (1983), pp. 76–92. It is, perhaps, significant too that Ibn Khallikān (*Wafayāt*, vol. 5, p. 72) who uses many of the same sources as Ibn al-Athīr and shares many of the latter's attitudes towards the Saljuq period, devotes a long obituary to Sultan Muḥammad but says little of Muḥammad's fight against the Ismaʿilis of Alamūt, commenting only that Muḥammad fought against the 'heretical party'.
44 Juwaynī, tr. Boyle, vol. 2, p. 681, and Kāshānī, *Zubdat al-tawārīkh*, p. 166; see also Rashīd al-Dīn, *Jāmiʿ al-tawārīkh; qismat-i Ismāʿīliyān*, ed. M. T. Dānishpazhūh and M. Mudarrisī Zanjānī (Tehran, 1338/1959), p. 131.
45 Ibn al-Athīr, vol. 10, p. 369.
46 Juwaynī, tr. Boyle, vol. 2, p. 637.
47 D. Morgan, *The Mongols* (Oxford, 1990), pp. 17–18.
48 Ibn al-Athīr, vol. 10, p. 370.
49 W. Kleiss, 'Assassin Castles in Iran', in *The Art of the Saljūqs in Iran and Anatolia*, ed. R. Hillenbrand (Costa Mesa, Calif., 1994), p. 316. Kleiss regards the identification of Ghutinar as an Ismaʿili castle as probable but not proven.
50 Al-Ḥusaynī, *Akhbār*, p. 87; Ibn al-Athīr, vol. 10, p. 201, and al-Bundārī, *Zubdat al-nuṣra*, pp. 259–260.
51 Al-Ḥusaynī, *Akhbār*, p. 87.
52 Ibn al-Athīr, vol. 10, p. 201.
53 Ibn al-Athīr, vol. 10, p. 270.
54 Al-Ḥusaynī, *Akhbār*, p. 55.
55 Ibn al-Athīr, vol. 10, p. 393.
56 Sibṭ Ibn al-Jawzī, *Mirʾāt*, vol. 8, p. 77.

TWELVE

The Isma'ilis of Quhistān and the Maliks of Nīmrūz or Sīstān

C. EDMUND BOSWORTH

THE EASTERN Persian region of Quhistān ('mountainous country'), at present adjacent to Persia's eastern frontier with Afghanistan, was regarded by mediaeval Islamic historians and geographers as one of a somewhat indeterminate nature, forming the southern part of the more clearly-defined province of Khurāsān but without any very distinct personality of its own. Nor did it contain any great cities comparable to those on its peripheries, such as Nīshāpūr, Ṭūs, Herat, and Zarang, and its economy was a localized one, of agriculture based entirely on irrigation from *qanāt*s or from wells (for the region has no perennial rivers) and of artisanal production of carpets and textiles (some of which, however, achieved a more than local fame, such as the *qūhī* cloths and silks mentioned by the geographers as amongst the products of Quhistān).[1] The sparse reports of the mediaeval Islamic historians show that, at various times, the modest towns and the fortresses of Quhistān had their own local rulers or governors although, on the whole, the region was subsumed administratively within the larger unit of Khurāsān or, as in the Īlkhānid and Tīmūrid periods, for instance, within that centred on Herat and western Afghanistan.

Quhistān's mountainous topography and its lack of prominence in eastern Islamic history favoured a role for it as a region where older religious beliefs and social customs or 'heterodox' Islamic ones could linger on, comparatively unmolested by the 'orthodox' Sunni authorities of the Khurāsānian cities. In the earliest Islamic times, it long remained a refuge area for Zoroastrianism; in the early 'Abbasid period, it was strongly affected, like virtually all of Khurāsān and also Sīstān, by the dynamic Khārijī movement of Ḥamza b. Ādharak (d. 213/828); and with the advent of the Great Saljuqs, a Nizārī Isma'ili *da'wa* was implanted there after Ḥasan-i Ṣabbāḥ in 484/1091 sent his partisan Ḥusayn-i Qā'inī back to his native Quhistān in order to spread this form of Shi'ism.[2]

Taking advantage of local discontents against an oppressive Saljuq administration and conceivably drawing on a persistent local strain of Islamic 'heterodoxy', Isma'ilism became firmly rooted in Quhistān, so that the Isma'ili populations of such centres as Ṭabas Masīnān, Qā'in, Mu'minābād, Turshīz, Tūn and Dara – the peoples described in the Sunni historical sources as *al-malāḥida al-qūhiyya* – became a factor in the internal history of Khurāsān during the Great Saljuq, Ghūrid and Khwārazmshāhī periods. But here, as elsewhere in the Persian lands, the Mongol invasions of the 7th/13th century were to place a severe check on external military and political activity by the Quhistān Isma'ilis, and the community was to survive on a much more restricted (though still intellectually active and flourishing, as the scholars and literary men produced by the community show) basis in the post-Mongol age.[3]

It is not our task here to trace the course of the Nizārī *da'wa* in Quhistān. This can be followed in such standard works on the development and history of Isma'ilism as those of Marshall G. S. Hodgson[4] and Farhad Daftary,[5] although a fully detailed, connected study of this movement is a desideratum. An elucidation of the historical geography and demography of Quhistān at this time is likewise important, for, in addition to the urban Isma'ili groups, power was in large measure exercised by them, as in Daylam and in Syria, from a series of fortresses (numbered by the contemporary Ghūrid historian Minhāj-i Sirāj Jūzjānī at seventy in the early decades of the 7th/13th century);[6] some of these are named specifically in the sources, and remains of certain fortresses have survived to this day.[7] For the older period, J. H. Kramers' (updated) *Encyclopaedia of Islam* article 'Ḳūhistān, Ḳuhistān' remains useful. An especially valuable review of the historical and sectarian geography of the region has been given for Tīmūrid times, viz., for the later 8th/14th and 9th/15th centuries, by Jean Aubin.[8] Admittedly, this covers the period after Isma'ilism's greatest florescence in Quhistān, but much of its information is valid and significant for earlier times. Thus Aubin notes that, in the 9th/15th century, districts like those of Tūn, Nahārjān and Mu'minābād had Nizārī communities, and that financial contributions were reputedly forwarded by the faithful of these groups to their imams.[9] By now, however, the greater part of Quhistān was probably Sunni in its religious allegiance. The hold of Isma'ilism in Quhistān had always been patchy, with many towns and rural areas not wavering in their allegiance to Sunnism. Thus the town of Zawzan remained generally Sunni,[10] and the great mosque-*madrasa* complex of Zawzan was probably being built in 615–616/1218–1219 at a time when the local Isma'ilis were particularly active, testifying to the enduring strength and influence of Sunnism at that moment.[11]

To the south-southeast of Quhistān, and contiguous with it, lay the province of Sīstān or, as it was often called from the 5th/11th century onwards, Nīmrūz 'the midday, viz., southern, land'. Sīstān differed from Quhistān in that it had a distinct identity and cohesiveness of its own, with an ancient historical tradition supposedly stretching back into legendary Iranian epic times.[12] Under indigenous dynasties like the Ṣaffārids and then the Naṣrid Maliks of Nīmrūz, a certain feeling of local solidarity had grown up which had made the Sagzīs or Sīstānīs resentful of outside control, such as that of the Arab governors of the 'Abbasids and Ṭāhirids and, in the early 5th/11th century, of the governors of the Turkish Ghaznawids; this feeling, whilst something less definite than a proto-nationalism, comes out well in the two local histories of Sīstān, the anonymous *Ta'rīkh-i Sīstān* and the *Iḥyā' al-mulūk* of Malik Shāh Ḥusayn. From the religious point of view, earlier 'heterodoxy' in the shape of Khārijism had disappeared from Sīstān by the 5th/11th century, and the attempt by a Fatimid *dā'ī*, Abū Ya'qūb Isḥāq b. Aḥmad al-Sijistānī, to introduce Isma'ilism into Sīstān from Transoxania (after the failure of Isma'ilism to secure a hold in the realm of the Sāmānid Naṣr b. Aḥmad) was scotched by the Ṣaffārid Amīr Khalaf b. Aḥmad's execution, at some unknown date and in unspecified circumstances, of al-Sijistānī.[13] Thus Sunnism was dominant in the Sīstān of the Naṣrid Maliks, who gave a loose allegiance to the Great Saljuqs (in practice, the Maliks were left largely alone, beyond the occasional requirement of sending troop contingents to the army of Sultan Sanjar for certain specific military campaigns).[14]

Close connections at many points of their respective histories followed naturally from their geographical proximity. A road ran northwards from the capital of Sīstān, Zarang, through Juwayn, situated to the north of the Hāmūn basin, to Dara and then to Ṭabas Masīnān and Bīrjand, and Quhistān could also be reached by travelling westwards to the frontier town of Nih and then turning northwards to Bīrjand. It was occasionally to Quhistān that defeated commanders or pretenders to the throne of Sīstān in Zarang retired in times of difficulty, and in the last years of the 7th/13th century, Quhistān was for a while the appanage of a prince of the ruling dynasty in Sīstān of the Mihrabānid Maliks.

The establishment of a dynamic Isma'ili *da'wa* in Quhistān at the end of the 5th/11th century, necessarily at odds with the Sunni milieux surrounding it, brough a new factor into relations between the two regions. The Isma'ilis of Quhistān soon came under attack from armies of the Great Saljuq sultans, from Malik Shāh's time onwards to the reign in Khurāsān of Sanjar, and the Turkish *amīr*s who inherited the Saljuq position in Khurāsān after Sanjar's death in 552/1157 also led attacks on Quhistān; none of these expeditions succeeded in dislodging the Isma'ilis.[15] The Isma'ili community in Quhistān felt firmly enough rooted there to take the offensive and to attempt to spread their religious message beyond the region's borders; and Sīstān, whose Maliks depended almost wholly on their own military resources, despite their theoretical subservience to the distant Great Saljuqs, mentioned above, presented an attractive target for the Isma'ilis.

The raids began early. In 487/1094, only two years after the punitive expedition into Quhistān of Malik Shāh's former commander Qïzïl Sarïgh, an Isma'ili force marched from Quhistān almost to the gates of Nih before it was halted. This provoked a counter-attack two years later from the Naṣrid Malik Bahā' al-Dawla Khalaf b. Abi'l-Faḍl Naṣr, when the army of Sīstān defeated the Isma'ilis at a place near Nih, whose location is unknown, called (?) Mukhtārān (489/1096). According to the local historian of Sīstān, 1,400 of the Qarāmiṭa, as the author here anachronistically terms the enemy, were killed.[16] Nevertheless, this reverse did not deter the Isma'ilis, for in 495/1101 they penetrated into Sīstān proper, as far as Daraq near Juwayn,[17] and killed the local *qāḍī*, presumably because he was regarded as the official representative there of the Sunni establishment.[18] It may have been in connection with these depredations that, in 496/1103, Sanjar's commander-in-chief Boz-Qush came to Zarang and made an agreement with Malik Bahā' al-Dawla Khalaf and his son, the future Malik Tāj al-Dīn (II) Abu'l-Faḍl Naṣr. This must have been for mutual aid and support operations, since in 494/1101 Boz-Qush had led an expedition into Quhistān and had besieged the Isma'ilis in Ṭabas Masīnān, and in 497/1104 he was to return there, with a force of regular troops plus *jihād*-motivated volunteers, and to capture and devastate Ṭabas.[19]

Isma'ili raids on Sīstān – another one by the *malāḥida* is recorded for 523/1129[20] – doubtless helped aggravate the disturbed state of the Sīstān countryside at this time, with its towns and villages suffering from Turkmen incursions, local magnates jockeying for power there and several sharp famines, as the narrative of the *Ta'rīkh-i Sīstān* shows.[21]

Isma'ili attacks are not, however, mentioned for the middle decades of the 6th/12th century, although this may merely reflect the thinness of our sources for the history of Sīstān at this time, with the continuation of the anonymous local history becoming very sparse for the period from the later 5th/11th century to the early 8th/14th century, after which Malik Shāh Ḥusayn's *Iḥyā' al-mulūk* begins to provide us with a very detailed account of the later Mihrabānids.[22] But then in 590/1194, during the reign of Malik Tāj al-Dīn (III) Ḥarb b. 'Izz al-Mulūk Muḥammad, the Isma'ilis raided a village in Sīstān named Khūraq or Jūraq. A counter-attack by the forces of Sīstān was repulsed, and a fresh Isma'ili incursion was launched in 591/1195 which captured a village called (?) R-y-ḥ-n and its fortress and carried off two local *qāḍīs*. The event was of sufficient gravity to bring about a second counter-attack by the combined troops of Naṣrid Sīstān, of Ghūrid Afghanistan and of Khurāsān (these last being either forces of local Turkish *amīrs* in post-Saljuq Khurāsān or of the Khwārazmian prince and claimant to the Khwārazmshāhī throne, Sulṭān Shāh b. Īl Arslān).[23]

Probably linked with all these events was a large-scale Ghūrid attack on Quhistān, or Mulḥidistān as Jūzjānī opprobriously terms it, in 597/1200–1201 (Ibn al-Athīr) or 601/1204–1205 (Jūzjānī), when Sultan Ghiyāth al-Dīn Muḥammad and his brother Mu'izz al-Dīn or Shihāb al-Dīn Muḥammad b. Bahā' al-Dīn Sām were mounting an offensive against Khwārazm. Either Mu'izz al-Dīn (Ibn al-Athīr) or his cousin 'Alā' al-Dīn Muḥammad b. Shujā' al-Dīn 'Alī (Jūzjānī) led an army to Qā'in and then to Gunābād (whose population is described as being totally Isma'ili), captured it and had the public worship there performed according to Sunni practice. Ibn al-Athīr's account has a further, complicating strand, in that he relates how the head of the Isma'ilis there (the *ṣāḥib Quhistān*, presumably the *muḥtasham*) protested to the supreme Ghūrid sultan, Ghiyāth al-Dīn Muḥammad, about Mu'izz al-Dīn's aggressive operations against various Isma'ili centres in the region, adducing an agreement (*'ahd*) which existed between the sultan and the Nizārī community; but nothing is known of such an arrangement, if indeed it existed.[24]

One of the last Naṣrid Maliks in Nīmrūz was Yamīn al-Dīn Bahrām Shāh b. Tāj al-Dīn (III) Ḥarb (reigned 610–618/1213–1221), and he continued his father's policy of keeping the Isma'ilis from harrying the frontiers of Sīstān by displays of military force. He led two expeditions against them, which included, according to the Persian literary anthologist and biographer Muḥammad 'Awfī, the conquest of their centre of

Turshīz and the slaughter of 100,000 (*sic*) of the 'heretics'. ʿAwfī and Jūzjānī quote from a panegyric by one Sharaf al-Dīn Aḥmad Farāhī on the Malik's exploits as a *ghāzī* in Quhistān.[25] However, Yamīn al-Dīn Bahrām Shāh's attempt to recover a fortress called Shāhanshāhī (identified by Tate with the ruined citadel now called Shāhdiz on an isolated hill outside Nih), which his cousin ʿUthmān Shāh b. Nāṣir al-Dīn ʿUthmān had for some undescribed reason sold to the Ismaʿilis, led the latter group to despatch a band of *fidāʾī*s to Zarang, and these killed Yamīn al-Dīn Bahrām Shāh when he was on his way to the mosque for the Friday worship on 5 Rabīʿ II 618/29 May 1221.[26]

The line of Naṣrid Maliks in Sīstān came to an end in 622/1225, after Sīstān had suffered the shock of an invasion by the Mongols in 619/1223: the Mongols devastated Zarang and killed Tāj al-Dīn Nuṣrat b. Yamīn al-Dīn Bahrām Shāh.[27] Out of the ensuing period of chaos in Sīstān, a former Ghūrid and Khwārazmshāhī commander, Tāj al-Dīn Inaltegin Khwārazmī, seized power there in 622/1225, retaining this power for almost a decade. At the outset, Inaltegin had good relations with the Ismaʿilis of Quhistān, continuing the pacific policy of the last Naṣrid successors of Yamīn al-Dīn Bahrām Shāh. Jūzjānī was himself sent in 621/1224 on an embassy via Qāʾin to the *muḥtasham* Abu'l-Fatḥ Shihāb al-Dīn Manṣūr. He praises him lavishly in his history for his wisdom and knowledge and for his kindness to visitors, poor travellers and refugees fleeing before the Mongols, so that his *majālis* were splendid concourses of the illustrious scholars of Khurāsān. It was this eirenic spirit and his lavish hospitality, says Jūzjānī, which caused the central head of the Ismaʿili community in Alamūt – presumably ʿAlāʾ al-Dīn Muḥammad III, successor to Jalāl al-Dīn Ḥasan III, who died in 618/1221[28] – to become fearful lest the resources of the Nizārī community in Quhistān be dissipated and, accordingly, he sent out a new *muḥtasham*, Shams al-Dīn Ḥusayn-i Ikhtiyār, whom Jūzjānī characterizes as a soldier (*mardī lashkarī*) rather than a scholar. Jūzjānī was in Quhistān again on a second embassy in 622/1225 from Ghūr to Ṭabas Masīnān, Mu'minābād and Qāʾin, where he met the new *muḥtasham*, Shams al-Dīn; the motive behind this mission is stated to have been a desire on the part of the Ghūrids for the opening up of caravan routes between Ghūr and Quhistān.[29]

But after this pacific beginning, relations between the Ismaʿilis of Quhistān and the new master of Zarang, Inaltegin, speedily deteriorated, the *casus belli* being once more the border fortress of Shāhanshāhī near Nih. Inaltegin led an army against the Ismaʿilis there, but was defeated and had to fall back on Farāh. He wanted to send Jūzjānī once more on a peace-making mission to Quhistān, although the historian, having set his heart on journeying to India, on this occasion refused (and was imprisoned by Inaltegin for six weeks on account of his refractoriness).[30]

During the period of the Mongol invasions, Quhistān suffered like Sīstān and other parts of the eastern Islamic world, and in 651/1253 and 654/1256 the Īlkhān Hülegü's commanders devastated Isma'ili centres there, including Turshīz and Tūn.[31] The faith survived there, albeit on a reduced scale, and during the early Īlkhānid decades, Quhistān came administratively within the principality of the Īlkhānids' vassals, the Kart Maliks of Herat, until towards the end of the 7th/13th century the Mihrabānid Malik of Sīstān, Naṣīr al-Dīn Muḥammad b. Mubāriz al-Dīn Abi'l-Fatḥ (reigned 653–718/1255–1318), conquered Quhistān temporarily and gave it as an appanage for his son Shams al-Dīn 'Alī.[32] In any case, the Isma'ili community of Quhistān ceased to have any military importance for Sīstān, and no Isma'ili attacks are mentioned in the *Ta'rīkh-i Sīstān* after the one on Zarang in 619/1223.

NOTES

1 R. B. Serjeant, *Islamic Textiles: Material for a History up to the Mongol Conquest* (Beirut, 1972), pp. 95–96.

2 See on the beginnings of the Quhistān *da'wa*, Farhad Daftary, *The Ismā'īlīs: Their History and Doctrines* (Cambridge, 1990), p. 341; hereafter cited as Daftary.

3 See M. G. S. Hodgson, *The Order of Assassins: The Struggle of the Early Nizārī Ismā'īlīs Against the Islamic World* (The Hague, 1955), p. 275; hereafter cited as Hodgson, and Daftary, pp. 439, 445–446.

4 Hodgson, pp. 74–75, 77, 88, 102, 115–116, 146, 215.

5 Daftary, pp. 341–342, 354, 356, 372, 381–382, 385, 391, 413–414.

6 Jūzjānī, *Ṭabaqāt-i Nāṣirī*, ed. 'Abd al-Ḥayy Ḥabībī (2nd edn, Kabul, 1342–1343/1963–1964), vol. 2, p. 186, English trans., *The Ṭabaḳāt-i-Nāṣiri: A General History of the Muhammadan Dynasties of Asia*, tr. H. G. Raverty, (London, 1881–1899), vol. 2, p. 1205; hereafter cited as Jūzjānī.

7 See P. R. E. Willey, 'The Assassins in Quhistan', *Journal of the Royal Central Asian Society*, 55 (1968), pp. 180–183. This preliminary reconnaissance indicated that the number of surviving sites and ruins may be considerable.

8 J. Aubin, 'Un santon Quhistānī de l'époque Timouride', *Revue des Etudes Islamiques*, 35 (1967), pp. 185–204.

9 Ibid., p. 201.

10 The episode when a local governor of Zawzan was accused of Isma'ili sympathies and killed by the representative in Quhistān of the Khwārazmshāh 'Alā' al-Dīn

Muḥammad (see Hodgson, p. 215, quoting al-Nasawī) seems to indicate that Zawzan was generally controlled by Sunni notables.

11 This remarkable building, first brought to the notice of the scholarly world by André Godard, in *Athār-é Īrān*, 4 (1949), pp. 117–125, is now being surveyed and evaluated, in the hope of future repair and reconstruction, by Dr Chahriyar Adle of the C.N.R.S., Paris.

12 See C. E. Bosworth, *The History of the Saffarids of Sistan and the Maliks of Nimruz (247/861 to 949/1542–3)*, Columbia Lectures on Iranian Studies no. 7 (Costa Mesa, Calif. and New York, 1994), pp. 30 ff.; hereafter cited as Bosworth.

13 See S. M. Stern, 'The Early Ismāʿīlī Missionaries in North-West Persia and in Khurāsān and Transoxania', BSOAS, 23 (1960), pp. 80–81, 84, 86.

14 See Bosworth, pp. 394–395.

15 See Daftary, pp. 341, 354, 356, 361, 372, 385, 391.

16 *Taʾrīkh-i Sīstān*, ed. Malik al-Shuʿarāʾ Bahār (Tehran, 1314/1935), p. 388, English trans., *The Tārikh-e Sistān*, tr. M. Gold (Rome, 1976), p. 317.

17 Possibly to be identified with the ancient site of Dārg a few miles to the south of Juwayn and on the lower reaches of the Farāh Rūd, which empties (when there is enough water in it) into the Hāmūn basin; the site and its modern village are mentioned by G. P. Tate in his topographical survey of the region, see his *Sistan, a Memoir on the History, Topography, Ruins, and People of the Country* (Calcutta, 1910–1912), pp. 118, 121, 188–190.

18 *Taʾrīkh-i Sīstān*, text p. 389, tr. p. 318.

19 Ibn al-Athīr, *al-Kāmil fiʾl-taʾrīkh* (Beirut, 1385–1387/1965–1967), vol. 10, pp. 324, 378–379.

20 *Taʾrīkh-i Sīstān*, text p. 391, tr. p. 319.

21 See Bosworth, pp. 389–393.

22 The original, anonymous author of the *Taʾrīkh-i Sīstān* ended his detailed narrative in mid-sentence whilst recording the events of 448/1056, and his history was thereafter continued by another, equally unknown hand, in a much more sketchy form; see Bosworth, pp. 23–24.

23 *Taʾrīkh-i Sīstān*, text p. 392, tr. p. 320.

24 Jūzjānī, text vol. 1, p. 380, tr. vol. 1, p. 394; see also text vol. 1, p. 407, tr. vol. 1, p. 491, where the capture of Gunābād is listed amongst Muʿizz al-Dīn's many victories, and also translation vol. 1, p. 381, n. 5, and Ibn al-Athīr, vol. 12, pp. 166–167. In Bosworth, p. 400, the account of these operations is perhaps over-simplified; the exposition of these events in the present article should for preference be followed.

25 ʿAwfī, *Lubāb al-albāb*, ed. S. Nafīsī (Tehran, 1335/1956), p. 50 (who attributes this expedition to Yamīn al-Dīn Bahrām Shāh's brother Nāṣir al-Dīn ʿUthmān), and Jūzjānī, text vol. 1, p. 282, tr. vol. 1, pp. 195–196.

26 *Taʾrīkh-i Sīstān*, text p. 393, tr. p. 321, and Jūzjānī, text vol. 1, p. 282, tr. vol. 1, p. 196.

27 *Taʾrīkh-i Sīstān*, text p. 394, tr. p. 322, and Jūzjānī, text vol. 1, pp. 283–284, tr. vol. 1, p. 198.

28 Hodgson, pp. 256–258, and Daftary, pp. 412–413.

29 Jūzjānī, text vol. 1, p. 285, vol. 2, pp. 135, 182–184, 186–187, tr. vol. 1, p. 201, and vol. 2, pp. 1061–1062, 1197–1203, 1212–1213.

30 *Taʾrīkh-i Sīstān*, text p. 395, tr. p. 322, and Jūzjānī, text vol. 2, pp. 184–185, tr. vol.

2, pp. 1203–1205. See in general on this period of Sīstān-Quhistān relations, Hodgson, pp. 244–246, and Daftary, pp. 413–414.

31 Juwaynī, *Taʾrīkh-i jahān-gushāy*, ed. M. Qazvīnī (Leiden–London, 1912–1937), vol. 3, pp. 102–103, English trans., *The History of the World-Conqueror*, tr. J. A. Boyle (Manchester, 1958), vol. 2, pp. 615–616; see also Daftary, pp. 421–422.

32 Bosworth, p. 436.

THIRTEEN

The philosopher/vizier: Khwāja Naṣīr al-Dīn al-Ṭūsī and the Isma'ilis

HAMID DABASHI

KHWĀJA NAṢĪR AL-DĪN AL-ṬŪSĪ (597–672/1201–1274) was still in Nīshāpūr, completing his course of studies, when the Mongols invaded Khurāsān. Sultan Muḥammad Khwārazmshāh's escape left the rich northeastern region of Iran defenceless at the mercy of the Mongol invaders. In 617/1220, when Khwāja Naṣīr was a twenty-year-old student in Nīshāpūr, Chingiz Khan conquered Transoxania, while the last Khwārazmshāh sultan, Jalāl al-Dīn Mingburnu (617–628/1220–1231), had begun to spend the rest of his life in heroic but futile attempts to save his kingdom. The Mongol invasion of Iran left the country in ruins. For centuries afterwards, no historian ever tired of relating the atrocious savageries perpetrated by the Mongols. A debilitating sense of fear and helplessness may still be detected in various historical narratives left from that time.[1]

No part of Khurāsān was immune to the onslaught of Mongol conquest except a few well-built Isma'ili fortresses. In the area of Quhistān, these fortresses provided safe havens for those who could not altogether leave Khurāsān. The local Isma'ili chief in Quhistān was a certain Nāṣir al-Dīn 'Abd al-Raḥīm b. Abī Manṣūr (d. 655/1257), who on behalf of the contemporary Nizārī Isma'ili imam 'Alā' al-Dīn Muḥammad III (618–653/1221–1255) presided over the affairs of the Nizārī community there. Nāṣir al-Dīn is remembered as a particularly benevolent and learned prince at whose safe court many men of knowledge, Isma'ili or otherwise, gathered and pursued their intellectual interests.[2]

The protective prince and the philosopher fearful for his safety were naturally drawn to each other and very soon, sometime between 619/1222 and 632/1234, Khwāja Naṣīr, already an accomplished scholar, found a safe haven with Nāṣir al-Dīn ʿAbd al-Raḥīm.[3] After spending some time with Nāṣir al-Dīn, Khwāja Naṣīr was summoned to the court of the Ismaʿili imam, ʿAlāʾ al-Dīn Muḥammad III, to the fortresses of Alamūt and Maymūndiz in Daylam. He was with the last lord of Alamūt, Rukn al-Dīn Khurshāh, when the Nizārīs finally surrendered to the Mongols in 654/1256.

The period of his Ismaʿili connection, lasting some thirty years until 654/1256, was particularly productive for Khwāja Naṣīr. Among the works commissioned to him by Nāṣir al-Dīn ʿAbd al-Raḥīm is a translation into Persian of ʿAyn al-Quḍāt al-Hamadhānī's *Zubdat al-ḥaqāʾiq*.[4] Sometime between 630/1232 and 632/1234, Nāṣir al-Dīn ʿAbd al-Raḥīm had also asked Khwāja Naṣīr to translate into Persian, with additional passages and commentaries, Abū ʿAlī Aḥmad Miskawayh al-Rāzī's *Kitāb al-ṭahāra*, also known as *Tahdhīb al-akhlāq*.[5] This treatise, partially based on Miskawayh's work, has come down to us as the *Akhlāq-i Nāṣirī*.[6]

The productivity of Khwāja Naṣīr in this period is characterized by a remarkable diversity of genres and discourses. Other than the *Akhlāq-i Nāṣirī* and the *Akhlāq-i Muḥtashamī*, which he wrote for and in the name of his chief patron Nāṣir al-Dīn ʿAbd al-Raḥīm, he also produced his main treatise in logic, *Asās al-iqtibās*, and his famous commentary on Avicenna's *al-Ishārāt waʾl-tanbīhāt*, called *Sharḥ al-ishārāt*. While in the service of the Ismaʿilis, Khwāja Naṣīr also wrote the *Risāla-yi Muʿīniyya* in astronomy for Nāṣir al-Dīn ʿAbd al-Raḥīm's son Muʿīn al-Dīn with a Persian commentary on it.

During the time he spent with the Ismaʿilis, Khwāja Naṣīr also wrote a number of treatises with Ismaʿili imprints to their theological teachings. Among these mention may be made of his spiritual autobiography *Sayr va sulūk*, the *Āghāz va anjām*, and the *Awṣāf al-ashrāf*. The attribution of certain other Ismaʿili writings to Khwāja Naṣīr has been the subject of much controversy – accepted by some,[7] and questioned by others[8] – even though his authorship of the *Rawḍat al-taslīm*, a major Ismaʿili treatise of the late Alamūt period, has been accepted by the modern scholars in Ismaʿili studies.

After Chingiz Khan's death, much of western Asia slipped from the Mongol control. While Khwāja Naṣīr was in the service of the Ismaʿilis, the supreme Mongol warlord, Mengü (649–658/1251–1259) despatched his brother Hülegü to defeat the Ismaʿilis, capture Baghdad, and perhaps advance even beyond. Early in Dhuʾl-Ḥijja 653/January 1256, Hülegü crossed the Oxus and the major onslaught of the Mongol reconquest had begun. By late 654/1256, the Isma'ilis of northern Persia were defeated, and soon after in 656/1258 the last 'Abbasid caliph, al-Musta'ṣim, was captured and killed. Eventually, Hülegü's army was defeated in 658/1260 by the Mamlūks at 'Ayn Jālūt in Palestine. Ruling over Persia, Iraq, the Caucasus and Anatolia, Hülegü now established the Īlkhānid dynasty, which remained in power from 654/1256 to 754/1353, when it withered away into local dynasties, waiting for Tīmūr to inaugurate the next major empire of the Tīmūrids in Iran and adjacent lands.

Khwāja Naṣīr was instrumental in facilitating the surrender of Rukn al-Dīn Khurshāh (653–654/1255–1256), the last Isma'ili ruler at Alamūt. Thus, in 654/1256, at the age of fifty-seven, Khwāja Naṣīr entered the services of Hülegü. He accompanied the Mongol leader in his conquest of Baghdad and the destruction of the 'Abbasid caliphate.[9] Upon his return from Baghdad, Khwāja Naṣīr established the famous observatory in Marāgha, an institution of higher learning which was one of the greatest intellectual achievements in mediaeval Persia.[10] After the death of Hülegü, Khwāja Naṣīr entered the services of Abaqa (663–680/1265–1282) and continued with his scientific and philosophical research. Having also served as vizier under the Īlkhānids, Khwāja Naṣīr al-Dīn al-Ṭūsī died in Baghdad on 18 Dhu'l-Ḥijja 672/25 June 1274, and was buried there.

The presence of Khwāja Naṣīr at the court of the Isma'ili prince has been the subject of some considerable controversy. Twelver Imāmī Shi'i scholars are adamant that he was kept in Quhistān against his will, and insist that he was also forced to go to Alamūt and was kept there against his wishes.[11] The pious Twelver sources are, indeed, hagiographical in their celebration of Khwāja Naṣīr's championing of the Imāmī Shi'i cause.[12] Scholars more sympathetic to the Isma'ilis, however, go so far as suggesting that Khwāja Naṣīr and his family were in fact all Isma'ilis.[13] A number of more objective scholars have suggested the possibility of Khwāja Naṣīr's transitory Isma'ili conversion.[14] Some scholars have even condemned Khwāja Naṣīr and questioned his moral principles. Edward G. Browne goes so far as to say 'what irony that this double-dyed traitor should be the author of one of the best-known works on Ethics written in Persian!'[15] Slightly more charitable than Browne, Wickens suggests that 'to contrast his life in practice with his elaboration of an ethical system of this kind is little more valid an exercise than to contrast a mathematician's overdraft with his writings on harmonic functions!'[16] Others have come to Khwāja Naṣīr's defence and offered his contemporary political circumstances as compelling reasons for his change of loyalty.

On a few occasions, Khwāja Naṣīr himself complains of hardships that some modern scholars have interpreted to mean that he had been kept at Alamūt against his will. At the conclusion of his famous commentary on Avicenna's *al-Ishārāt waʾl-tanbīhāt*, for example, he complains that:

> I wrote most of it [*Sharḥ al-ishārāt*] under most difficult circumstances, no more difficult circumstance than which is possible. I composed most of it at a time of emotional anxiety, no more anxious an emotional condition than which is to be found – a time every portion of which was a container for unbearable sadness, suffering, remorse, and sorrow . . . No instance went by without my sorrow increasing, my calamities and sadness multiplying. Yes indeed as the poet says in Persian:
>
> So far as I can see all around me
> Calamity is a ring and I am a bezel to it.[17]

In the same passage, probably added years after the original composition of the *Sharḥ al-ishārāt*, Khwāja Naṣīr has a more sweeping generalization about his emotional conditions in life:

> There has never been a moment in my life which has not been filled with events conducive to constant remorse, perpetual sorrow. The course of my life has always been interrupted by an army of sadness, soldiers of discomfort. God Almighty! For the sake of Thy Chosen Messenger, and the sake of his Righteous Successor [ʿAlī], God's Benedictions be upon them and upon their household, rescue me from the injuries of the waves of calamities, the surges of hostilities, and save me from things which are injurious to me. I have none other than Thee, and Thou art the Most Benevolent of all benevolents.[18]

A modern Twelver Shiʿi biographer of al-Ṭūsī has concluded from such passages that 'Khwāja was in pain and suffering while in the Ismaʿili fortresses. He did not live there voluntarily. On the contrary, he stayed there involuntarily and out of necessity. In fact, he was a prisoner there. That is why he is asking God to save him from that condition as soon as possible, and rescue him from the Ismaʿili incarceration.'[19]

There are enough historical indications, however, to suspect at least a temporary acquiescence or conversion to the Ismaʿili cause and doctrines.[20] As Daftary has observed:

> There is no evidence suggesting that these outside scholars [such as Khwāja Naṣīr] were detained in the [Ismaʿili] community against their will or that they were forced to embrace Ismāʿīlism during their stay

> amongst the Nizārīs, although at the time of the Mongol invasion, al-Ṭūsī and a few other similarly situated scholars claimed otherwise. On the contrary, it seems that these learned guests partook of the hospitality of the Nizārīs willingly, and were free, in the time of *satr*, to maintain their previous religious convictions.[21]

The relation of power between a prince and his court philosopher, however, cannot be underestimated. With the proverbial dictum of 'people follow the religion of their kings'[22] in his mind, Khwāja Naṣīr could not have remained totally indifferent to the royal presence of his patron. The religious affiliation of a powerful patron/prince in whose fortress one is engaged in matters of theology, philosophy, and other fields of learning cannot be considered as totally irrelevant and immaterial.

After reviewing a number of historical sources, Mudarris Raḍavī has concluded that:

> Perhaps in the beginning Khwāja went to Quhistān and Alamūt voluntarily, following an invitation by Nāṣir al-Dīn and 'Alā' al-Dīn [Muḥammad III]. Because of the anarchical situation in Iranian urban centres, and the violent behaviour of the Mongol conquerors, the prejudices of the Sunni *'ulamā'*, their persecution of the Shi'is, and thinking that perhaps in Quhistān and Alamūt he would find comfort and peace of mind and thus could pursue his research and writing agenda, he voluntarily decided to reside with the Isma'ilis.[23]

The last two comments by Daftary and Mudarris Raḍavī seem to be the most moderate assessments that we can make of Khwāja Naṣīr's time spent with the Isma'ilis, if we confine ourselves to the dominant themes of sectarian hostilities among the Sunnis, the Twelver Shi'is, and the Isma'ili Shi'is. However, I wish to shift the discourse on Khwāja Naṣīr's character and political disposition to a different level. I believe too much emphasis on the sectarian affiliations of political and intellectual figures in mediaeval Persia (or Islam in general) distorts the complexity of their characters and blinds our understanding of the specific moral and political choices they had to make. Application of abstract ethical principles equally ignores the particular historical exigencies under which moral and political decisions are made and executed.

Whether cited in Khwāja Naṣīr's defence or against him, the assumption of ethical positions based entirely on sectarian or abstract moral principles neglects a fundamental aspect of his character as a Persian philosopher/vizier, fully present and active in the social and political context of his time. Elsewhere, I have already dealt extensively with the theoretical proposition of considering the category of the 'philosopher/vizier' as an important element in Persian political culture.[24] It is in the context of that theoretical proposition that I would like to consider Khwāja Naṣīr's political character in general and his connection with the Isma'ilis in particular. Khwāja Naṣīr al-Dīn al-Ṭūsī can be understood neither as an Imāmī Shi'i (who may or may not have been obliged to convert to Isma'ilism) nor as an individual who lacked stable moral principles. Rather, he should be understood primarily as a philosopher/vizier, simultaneously concerned with matters of power and knowledge, politics and philosophy. The impressive body of scientific treatises he has left behind, his monumental achievement in the establishment of the Marāgha Observatory, and his indiscriminate association with men of knowledge from every religious, ethnic, and epistemic origin and affiliation leaves the impression that Khwāja Naṣīr saw himself in a category distinctly above and beyond sectarian divisions. His friends and colleagues included Chinese, Turkish, Arab and Persian jurists, philosophers, theologians, mystics, mathematicians, astronomers, etc., with diverse religious persuasions.[25] A consideration of the relation of power conducive to any production of knowledge, as well as dominant in any legitimate production of morality, should lead us to a mode of understanding Khwāja Naṣīr's Isma'ili connection beyond the stale sectarian arguments of pro-Twelvers versus pro-Isma'ilis.

Khwāja Naṣīr served an Isma'ili prince (and two Isma'ili Imams) and two Mongol pagans with equal administrative and intellectual competence. There are reasons to believe that prior to seeking a safe haven with the Isma'ilis at Quhistān, he even tried, in vain, to seek refuge with the (Sunni) 'Abbasid caliph al-Musta'ṣim.[26] However, the presumption that this attempt was made through Ibn al-'Alqamī, a vizier to al-Musta'ṣim, is untenable. Ibn al-'Alqamī came to power in Baghdad in 642/1244, long after Khwāja Naṣīr had already joined the Isma'ilis – sometime between 619/1222, the year of Khwāja Naṣīr's *ijāza* from Sālim b. Badrān, and 633/1235, the year of the *Akhlāq-i Nāṣirī*'s completion. Be that as it may, the fact that Khwāja Naṣīr tried to join al-Musta'ṣim's court is a solid indication that in his moral universe there was nothing particularly wrong about joining a Sunni, an Isma'ili, a Twelver, or even a pagan ruler. Khwāja Naṣīr's actual associations with diverse rulers provide clear indications that it is primarily as a philosopher/vizier, and not as an exclusively Twelver Imāmī or Isma'ili Muslim, that he ought to be recognized and characterized.

What are the exact terms of this characterization as a 'philosopher/vizier'?

The close relationship reported between Nāṣir al-Dīn ʿAbd al-Raḥīm and Khwāja Naṣīr al-Dīn al-Ṭūsī is strikingly reminiscent of the classical legand of Anūshīrwān and Buzurgmihr, a paradigm that since the pre-Islamic times has been a recurring motif in Persian political culture. On that model, the 'philosopher/king' relationship reported between Khwāja Naṣīr and Nāṣir al-Dīn was extended from a mere political necessity, often present in such relationships, to collaborative works on ethics and political philosophy. Khwāja Naṣīr's two major works in these fields, the *Akhlāq-i Nāṣirī* and the *Akhlāq-i Muḥtashamī* were not just dedicated to the Nizārī prince, they were in effect collaborative works. The structural design and original work on the *Akhlāq-i Muḥtashamī* were the ideas of Nāṣir al-Dīn ʿAbd al-Raḥīm himself. However, his administrative responsibilities prevented him from completing this project, and he thus left proper instructions for Khwāja Naṣīr to proceed with his plan and finish the book accordingly. Such episodes are particularly conducive to legendary reminiscences about Anūshīrwān/Buzurgmihr paradigm which is a uniquely Persian version of the Platonic idea of the philosopher/king.[27] The interchangeable characters of Anūshīrwān and Buzurgmihr, as particularly evident in Firdawsī's *Shāhnāma*, has had a powerful and enduring effect on many subsequent pairing of kings and philosophers in Iranian history. Khwāja Naṣīr himsefl, as noted, served not only Nāṣir al-Dīn ʿAbd al-Raḥīm, Muḥammad III and his son and successor Rukn al-Dīn Khurshāh, but he later joined Hülegü and his successor Abaqa as their court philosopher/vizier/physician/astronomer/chronographer. Generations earlier, the same pattern had been repeated by the Saljuq monarch Malik Shāh (465–485/1072–1092) and his vizier Khwāja Niẓām al-Mulk, or by ʿAlāʾ al-Dawla Muḥammad b. Dushmanziyār (398–433/1008–1041) and Avicenna. It is precisely the same model which is later filled by the Ṣafawid monarch Shāh ʿAbbās I (995–1038/1587–1629) and the collectivity of Mīr Dāmād/Mīr Findiriskī/Shaykh Bahāʾī, or even by Nāṣir al-Dīn Shāh (1264–1313/1848–1896) and Amīr Kabīr during the Qājār period, the last monarchy in the pre-modern mould of Persian political culture.

The production of the *Akhlāq-i Nāṣirī* in Persian is a crucial fact for understanding the nature of Khwāja Naṣīr's political disposition as a philosopher/vizier. The original version of Khwāja Naṣīr's introduction to this text testifies to his outright devotion to his Ismaʿili prince, Nāṣir al-Dīn ʿAbd al-Raḥīm. The *Akhlāq-i Nāṣirī*, completed in 633/1235, is an edited translation, with some additional sections, of Miskawayh's *Kitāb al-ṭahāra*. Miskawayh (d. 421/1030) was a Persian Zoroastrian who had converted to Islam. The Zoroastrian connection is particularly significant in detecting a non-Islamic line of ethical discourse which constituted a powerful alternative language of legitimacy for the prototype of philosopher/vizier.

A key clue to the metamorphic characters of the philosopher and the prince is the customary designation of the ethical treatises that Khwāja Naṣīr wrote in the name of his patron, Nāṣir al-Dīn ʿAbd al-Raḥīm, the *muḥtasham* or leader of the Nizārīs in Quhistān. The *Akhlāq-i Nāṣirī* and the *Akhlāq-i Muḥtashamī*, as their titles indicate, are both known by the name of the patron prince for whom they were written. This is a crucial symbolic indication that in the context of Persian political culture the idea of the philosopher/king is divided into the two metamorphic characters of a philosopher (Khwāja Naṣīr) and a king (Nāṣir al-Dīn ʿAbd al-Raḥīm), in the larger sense of the term. The metamorphic characters of the philosopher and the king are evident not only in cases where the king assumes philosophical positions of authoring a text but also in the philosopher's assumption of a kingly position, such as Khwāja Naṣīr's negotiations for the terms of the Ismaʿilis' surrender to the Mongols, or, later and even more emphatically, by leading a flank of the Mongol army in the conquest of Baghdad.

The productive relationship between the philosopher and his Ismaʿili patron/prince was not to last however. Ultimately, the advancing Mongol army found its way to the Ismaʿili fortresses and the Nizārī Ismaʿilis of Persia faced the prospect of a catastrophe. Khwāja Naṣīr now left his Nizārī patrons and joined Hülegü to engage in precisely the same metamorphic relation of power and knowledge. He wrote an astronomical treatise in the name of the reigning Mongol warlord and called it *Zīj-i Īlkhānī*. This treatise and the *Akhlāq-i Nāṣirī* are written with the same spirit, a spirit that reflects in the production of knowledge what the negotiations on behalf of the Ismaʿilis with Hülegü and the commanding of a flank of Hülegü's army against al-Mustaʿṣim, reflect in the context of power. What, more than anything else, characterizes Khwāja Naṣīr is not his Twelver Imāmī or Ismaʿili Shiʿi affiliation. His most historically relevant characterization rests on that metamorphic construction of power-and-knowledge that puts a sword in his hand to fight on behalf of a prince or a warlord with the same felicity that it puts a pen in the same hand and has him write a treatise on ethics or astronomy in the name of that same ruler.

By mastering all the diverse fields of Islamic learning, from theology to philosophy and mysticism, and then by effectively equating their respective significance with such scientific disciplines as astronomy, mathematics, music and logic, Khwāja Naṣīr challenged the exclusive claim of any 'Islamic' branch of knowledge to political power. In both religious and non-religious disciplines of systematic learning – from jurisprudence to astronomy – men of knowledge were in effect men of power. Theology for theologians, jurisprudence for jurists, philosophy for philosophers, mysticism for mystics, and of course astronomy for astronomers created and sustained institutionalized disciplines of knowledge/power. Khwāja Naṣīr mastered most of these disciplines, and produced seminal texts in virtually all of them. The consequence of this mastery was that in the classical tradition of the Persian philosopher/vizier he recreated and consolidated an authority for the office and institution of vizierate. All the rest of the established institutions of authority – those of the theologians, jurists, philosophers, mystics, astronomers, etc. – had to submit to his superior position of knowledge/power, supported by whichever patron/prince happened to be in power and was in need of the philosopher/vizier's help.

The centrality of the position of vizier in Persian political culture in general and in the Saljuq period in particular has been noted and examined extensively by a number of scholars.[28] Klausner, in particular, pays well-deserved attention to the education and training of the vizier and his religious and cultural background.[29] However, the significance of an encyclopaedic knowledge of both 'rational' (*'aqlī*) and 'transmitted' (*naqlī*) sciences (*'ulūm*), which elevates the position of the Persian vizier to that of the philosopher/vizier, has not yet been examined in any detail. While in his treatment of the protective position of the 'Grosswesirs', safeguarding the charismatic status of the Persian kings or Muslim caliphs, Max Weber failed to recognize this aspect of the Persian viziers,[30] in his treatment of the Chinese literati he came very close to such a conception when he stipulated the concept of 'Bildung' as the defining factor of this Chinese stratum.[31] In his definition of the Chinese literati, Weber observes that: '[i]t has been of immeasurable importance for the way in which Chinese culture has developed that this leading stratum of intellectuals [i.e., the Chinese literati] has never had the character of the clerics of Christianity or of Islam, or of Jewish rabbis, or Indian Brahmans, or Ancient Egyptian priests, or Egyptian or Indian scribes.'[32] Weber considered that position, erroneously (in view of what I am now suggesting about the Persian philosopher/vizier), as something peculiar to the Chinese literati and specifically distinguished it from Christian, Islamic, Indian and Egyptian models. He also failed to note any similarity between the function of the Chinese literati in relation to the Emperor and the Platonic conception of the philosopher/king. That failure is particularly surprising in view of the fact that he *did* note the two critical pieces of data that he needed: That '[a]ccording to the *Annals*, the Emperor addressed the literati, and them alone, as "My lords" ', and that the literati were called *puo che*, that is, 'living libraries'. The nominal separation/conjunction of the figure of the philosopher/king into a 'philosopher' and a 'king' prevented Weber from noticing their metamorphic characters.

That metamorphosis is strikingly evident in the Persian case.[33] In the Persian version of the philosopher/king, the prince and the philosopher have a mutually metamorphic character whereby the encyclopaedic *knowledge* of the vizier is publicly performed, through court-sponsored 'publication' of treatises, in the name of the prince, while the omnipotent *power* of the prince is publicly staged through the intermediary of the vizier. That is why, I suggest, that the literary, scientific, and philosophical treatises written by the Persian vizierate stratum carry the name of their princely patrons: *Akhlāq-i Nāṣirī*, *Akhlāq-i Muḥtashamī*, etc. At stake here is the political function of the philosopher/vizier as a particularly Persian version of the Platonic philosopher/king, whereby the metamorphic character of the philosopher/king is politically translated into the administrative power/knowledge of the philosopher/vizier, leaving the charismatic position of the king symbolically immune to political failures. Weber realized this much of the protective position of the Persian vizier very well when he observed that 'the position of the Grand Vizier . . . protect[s] the Shah and his charisma'.[34] By elevating the office of the philosopher/vizier above and beyond the sectarian and scholastic divisions endemic to Islamic political culture, both that office and by extension the office of the charismatic king become symbolically immune to the volatile world of doctrinal and epistemic disputes. The translation of the Platonic philosopher/king into the Persian philosopher/vizier is thus politically advantageous while it still leaves and legitimizes a royal space wherein the charismatic authority of the king remains immune to any serious rupture.

The possibility of considering Khwāja Naṣīr al-Dīn al-Ṭūsī as a philosopher/vizier rests on the theoretical proposition of considering the Persian court as a self-legitimizing institution founded on its distinct prerogatives of authority. All instruments of power – symbols and ceremonies, characters and cultures, functional necessities and structural self-referentialities – are historically present and legitimate in that court.

The ideal type of the philospher/vizier, exemplified in the figure of Khwāja Naṣīr and his affiliation with the Isma'ilis and others, facilitates the formulation of an ethical discourse for that court. The production of treatises on ethics, in particular, became the self-legitimizing discourse of the Persian court in contradistinction to Islamic law and theology.

Whether delivered in the narrative form of ethics, *akhlāq* proper, or in that of the mirrors of princes, *naṣīḥat al-mulūk*, the ethical discourse is distanced from Islamic law by a number of significant symbolics: First and foremost, it is delivered in the non-canonical Persian language; secondly, its constituent narrative examples are drawn as much from non-Islamic traditions as from the Islamic sources; thirdly, the agency of its delivery, the vizierate, is a patently non-clerical class which stands in institutional distinction to the Muslim clergy; and, fourthly, its institutional basis is located inside the court and is quite distinct from the *madrasa* and the mosque.

Our understanding of such Persian texts on ethics as the *Akhlāq-i Nāṣirī* and the *Akhlāq-i Muḥtashamī* should rest on recognition of their having been written in Persian in the context of a literary and philosophical culture pervasively Arabic in its sacred linguistic primacy. The cultural production of a political and intellectual authority for Khwāja Naṣīr, beyond his sectarian identity, rests precisely on the adoption of Persian as a space of ethical discourse. The hermeneutic density of Persian texts such as the *Akhlāq-i Nāṣirī* contains the combined intellectual weight of pre-Islamic Arabic and non-Islamic Greek, Persian and Indian sources, and yet it stands in a narrative space beyond any one of these constituent forces.

Here, I wish to argue that the textual production of an ethical treatise in the Persian language leads to the moral production of a political space outside but adjacent to the Islamic sacred territory. Khwāja Naṣīr's use of the Persian language *ipso facto* distances the world of the text from any visible reference to the Islamic sacred imagination. But even beyond the linguistic aspect of the ethical discourse, treatises such as the *Akhlāq-i Nāṣirī* rely heavily on non-Islamic and Islamic sources for particular ethical injunctions. As the author of a Persian text on ethics that rests as much on the Qur'anic and *ḥadīth* references as on non-Islamic Greek, Persian and Indian traditions, Khwāja Naṣīr is fully in control, and the political beneficiary, of the moral and political space thus assayed in the *Akhlāq-i Nāṣirī* and the *Akhlāq-i Muḥtashamī*.

The production of that moral and political space, and its reliance on Persian as a legitimizing ethical narrative, is rooted in the institutional autonomy of the Persian court. Throughout mediaeval times, the Persian court was consistent in producing self-legitimizing texts. The text of the *Chahār maqāla* (also known as *Majmaʿ al-nawādir*) of Aḥmad b. ʿUmar Niẓāmī ʿArūḍī, composed around 550/1155, is one crucial example, among many others (such as Niẓām al-Mulk's *Siyāsat-nāma*, produced in 479/1086, or Qābūs b. Vushmgīr's *Qābūs-nāma*, written in 475/1082) in support of the autonomous functioning of the Persian court as a self-legitimizing institution. Niẓāmī ʿArūḍī composed his *Chahār maqāla* for Abu'l-Ḥasan Ḥisām al-Dīn ʿAlī, the son of the Ghūrid Fakhr al-Dīn Masʿūd (540–558/1145–1163) who ruled over Bāmiyān and Ṭukhāristān. Prince Ḥisām al-Dīn ʿAlī never became a Ghūrid monarch however; it was his brother, Shams al-Dīn Muḥammad (558–588/1163–1192) who succeeded their father. Nevertheless, Niẓāmī ʿArūḍī dedicated his *Chahār maqāla* to prince Ḥisām al-Dīn ʿAlī, referring to him as '*pādishāh*' and '*pādishāh-zāda*'.[35] The relationship between Niẓāmī ʿArūḍī and prince Ḥisām al-Dīn ʿAlī is, in fact, precisely on the same model as that of Malik Shāh/Niẓām al-Mulk or Nāṣir al-Dīn/Khwāja Naṣīr.

In the *Chahār maqāla*, which in effect became a manual of kingship and royal administration in mediaeval Persia, Niẓāmī ʿArūḍī defines the Persian monarch and the Persian court as autonomous figures and institutions of royal authority.[36] More specifically, he proceeds to (1) produce a Persian text of proper courtly functions and decorum, (2) substantiate it with stories and anecdotes of non-Qur'anic origin, (3) effectively constitute himself as a legitimate and legitimizing agency for issuing such a manual, and then (4) deliver it at the institutional base of prince Ḥisām al-Dīn ʿAlī's court. The combination of these four factors are constitutional to the establishment of the Persian court as a self-legitimizing institution with its relevant discourses as well as figures and symbols of authority. It is in this context that the intellectual/political functioning of the Persian philosopher/vizier is to be understood. And it is as a Persian philosopher/vizier, and not as an exclusively Twelver Shiʿi or Ismaʿili Shiʿi, that the figure of Khwāja Naṣīr – particularly in his relation to the Ismaʿili prince Nāṣir al-Dīn ʿAbd al-Raḥīm and Mongol warlords Hülegü and Abaqa – should be considered.

Further immunizing the court to the institutional power of the religious authorities (Sunni, Twelver Shiʿi or Ismaʿili), and thus safeguarding a 'secular' space for the political functioning of the philosopher/vizier, was the balancing presence of a number of religions in both the Mongol and Īlkhānid courts. The Mongols gradually gave more or less equal protection to their Christian, Muslim, Buddhist and Confucian subjects. This religious ecumenicalism prevented any specific religion, and Islam in particular, from assuming a dominant institutional authority. The conversion of Maḥmūd Ghāzān Khan (694–703/1295–1304) to Islam did not in any significant way alter the normative codes of accepted behaviour, especially in matters related to the political administration of the empire.

Whether in the liberal Isma'ili court, which was a relatively safe haven for scientists and philosophers of all religious persuations, or in the religiously multifarious court of the Īlkhānid warlords, Khwāja Naṣīr's writings in the Persian language, his works on the self-legitimizing narrative of ethics, his authoritative scientific enquiries, and ultimately his diverse students and colleagues from all religious and ethnic origins should lead us to locate him on a plane of identity beyond generic sectarian or abstract moral categories. The ideal-typical position of the Persian philosopher/vizier offers an historically nuanced angle on the moral and social universe of Khwāja Naṣīr al-Dīn al-Ṭūsī's time and imagination, his political character and culture, his relationship with the Isma'ilis and the Mongols, and then beyond those specific cases onto the entire stratum of the Persian vizierate.

NOTES

1 See, for instance, Shihāb al-Dīn Muḥammad al-Nasawī, *Sīrat-i Jalāl al-Dīn Mingburnu*, ed. M. Mīnuvī (Tehran, 1344/1965), pp. 110–130; 'Alā' al-Dīn 'Aṭā Malik Juwaynī, *Ta'rīkh-i jahān-gushāy*, ed. M. Qazvīnī (Leiden–London, 1912–1937), vol. 1, pp. 103–149; English translation, *The History of the World-Conqueror*, tr. J. A. Boyle (Manchester, 1958), vol. 1, pp. 130–190, and Rashīd al-Dīn Faḍl Allāh, *Jāmi' al-tawārīkh*, ed. B. Karīmī (Tehran, 1338/1959), vol. 1, pp. 213–340.

2 See M. Mīnuvī, 'Bāṭiniyya Ismā'īliyya', in his *Ta'rīkh va farhang* (Tehran, 1352/1973), pp. 170–225; M. T. Mudarris Raḍavī, *Aḥvāl va āthār-i Khwāja Naṣīr al-Dīn Ṭūsī* (Tehran, 1354/1975), pp. 136–138; 'A. Muqallid, *Niẓām al-ḥukm fī'l-Islām: Aw al-nubuwwa wa'l-imāma 'ind Naṣīr al-Dīn al-Ṭūsī* (Beirut, 1406/1986), p. 243; Ivanow's introductory remarks in his edition of Naṣīr al-Dīn al-Ṭūsī, *Rawḍat al-taslīm*, ed. and tr. W. Ivanow (Leiden, 1950), p. 24, and F. Daftary, *The Ismā'īlīs: Their History and Doctrines* (Cambridge, 1990), pp. 407–410.

3 Mudarris Raḍavī, *Aḥvāl*, p. 8, and Daftary, *The Ismā'īlīs*, p. 408.

4 Al-Qāḍī Nūr Allāh al-Shūshtarī, *Majālis al-mu'minīn* (Tehran, 1365/1986), vol. 2, p. 207.

5 Mudarris Raḍavī, *Aḥvāl*, pp. 8–9, and Muqallid, *Niẓām*, p. 245.

6 See Khwāja Naṣīr al-Dīn al-Ṭūsī, *Akhlāq-i Nāṣirī*, ed. M. Mīnuvī and 'A. Ḥaydarī (Tehran, 1356/1977), introduction pp. 1–32; Jalāl al-Dīn Humā'ī, 'Muqaddima-yi qadīm-i Akhlāq-i Nāṣirī', *Majalla-yi Dānishkada-yi Adabiyyāt*, 3 (1335/1956), pp. 17–25, and W. Madelung, 'Naṣīr ad-Dīn Ṭūsī's Ethics Between Philosophy, Shi'ism,

and Sufism', in *Ethics in Islam*, ed. R. G. Hovannisian (Malibu, Calif., 1985), pp. 85 ff.

7 Ivanow's remarks in al-Ṭūsī, *Rawḍat al-taslīm*, introduction pp. 17–23, and W. Ivanow, *Ismaili Literature: A Bibliographical Survey* (Tehran, 1963), p. 135; I. K. Poonawala, *Biobibliography of Ismāʿīlī Literature* (Malibu, Calif., 1977), p. 262, and Muqallid, *Niẓām*, pp. 211–227.

8 M. T. Dānishpazhūh, 'Guftārī az Khwāja-yi Ṭūsī bih ravish-i- Bāṭiniyya', *Majalla-yi Dānishkada-yi Adabiyyāt*, 3 (1335/1956), p. 82.

9 See Khwāja Naṣīr's own description of his participation in the conquest of Baghdad in Juwaynī, *Ta'rīkh*, vol. 3, pp. 280–292.

10 See E. S. Kennedy, 'The Exact Sciences in Iran under the Saljuqs and Mongols', in *The Cambridge History of Iran*: Volume 5, *The Saljuq and Mongol Periods*, ed. J. A. Boyle (Cambridge, 1968), pp. 659–679, and G. Saliba, 'The Role of Maraghah in the Development of Islamic Astronomy: A Scientific Revolution before the Renaissance', *Revue de Synthèse*, 4 série, 3–4 (1987), pp. 361–373.

11 Mudarris Raḍavī, *Aḥvāl*, pp. 10–16, and M. Mudarrisī Zanjānī, *Sargudhasht va 'aqā'id-i falsafī-yi Khwāja Naṣīr al-Dīn Ṭūsī* (Tehran, 1363/1984), pp. 49–51.

12 See al-Shūshtarī, *Majālis*, vol. 2, pp. 201–202; Muḥammad Bāqir al-Khwānsārī, *Rawḍat al-jannāt* (Tehran, 1360/1981), vol. 6, pp. 221–222, and Mīrzā Muḥammad Tunikābunī, *Qiṣaṣ al-ʿulamā'* (Tehran, 1364/1985), p. 367.

13 See Ivanow's comments in al-Ṭūsī, *Rawḍat al-taslīm*, introduction p. 25.

14 Mīnuvī and Ḥaydarī in al-Ṭūsī, *Akhlāq-i Nāṣirī*, pp. 14–32; M. T. Dānishpazhūh's introductory remarks in his edition of al-Ṭūsī's *Akhlāq-i Muḥtashamī* (Tehran, 1361/1982), pp. 10–14, and Daftary, *The Ismāʿīlīs*, pp. 408–411.

15 Edward G. Browne, *A Literary History of Persia* (Cambridge, 1928), vol. 2, p. 457. See also Jan Rypka, *History of Iranian Literature*, ed. K. Jahn (Dordrecht, 1968), pp. 313–314.

16 See G. M. Wickens' introductory remarks in his translation of Naṣīr al-Dīn al-Ṭūsī's *Akhlāq-i Nāṣirī* into English under the title of *The Nasirean Ethics* (London, 1964), p. 13.

17 Al-Ṭūsī, *Sharḥ al-ishārāt* (Qumm, 1404/1983), vol. 2, p. 145.

18 Ibid., vol. 2, p. 145.

19 Mudarris Raḍavī, *Aḥvāl*, p. 13.

20 See al-Shūshtarī, *Majālis*, vol. 2, pp. 202–208; *Dabistān-i madhāhib*, ed. R. Riḍāzāda Malik (Tehran, 1362/1983), vol. 1, p. 258; Humā'ī, 'Muqaddima', p. 17; Mudarris Raḍavī, *Aḥvāl*, pp. 14–16; Mudarrisī Zanjānī, *Sargudhasht*, pp. 24–26; Dānishpazhūh in al-Ṭūsī, *Akhlāq-i Muḥtashamī*, pp. 10–14, and Daftary, *The Ismāʿīlīs*, pp. 408–411, 423–424, 693–694.

21 Daftary, *The Ismāʿīlīs*, p. 408.

22 Badīʿ al-Zamān Furūzānfar, *Aḥādīth-i Mathnawī* (Tehran, 1361/1982), p. 28.

23 Mudarris Raḍavī, *Aḥvāl*, p. 12.

24 See H. Dabashi, 'Farhang-i siyāsī-yi Shāhnāma: Andīsha-yi siyāsī-yi fīlsūf/pādishāh dar salṭanat-i Khusraw Anūshīrwān' [The Political Culture of the Shāhnāmah: The Concept of the 'Philosopher King' in the Reign of Anūshīrwān], *Iranshenasi*, 2 (1990), pp. 321–341.

25 See M. Mīnuvī, 'Tarjuma-yi 'ulūm-i Chīnī bih Fārsī dar qarn-i hashtum-i Hijrī', *Majalla-yi Dānishkada-yi Adabiyyāt*, 3 (1334/1955), pp. 1–26.

26 Mudarris Raḍavī, *Aḥvāl*, pp. 9–10, and Tunikābunī, *Qiṣaṣ*, p. 378.

27 For further discussion of this argument, see Dabashi, 'Farhang-i siyāsī', pp. 327–337.
28 See, for instance, ʿAbbās Iqbāl, *Vizārat dar ʿahd-i salāṭīn-i buzurg-i Saljūqī* (Tehran, 1338/1959); D. Sourdel, *Le Vizirat ʿAbbaside de 749 à 946* (Damascus, 1960); Carla L. Klausner, *The Seljuk Vezirate: A Study of Civil Administration, 1055–1194* (Cambridge, Mass., 1973); and the following works by Ann K. S. Lambton: *Theory and Practice in Medieval Persian Government* (London, 1980); *State and Government in Medieval Islam* (Oxford, 1981), and *Continuity and Change in Medieval Persia* (Albany, N.Y., 1988).
29 Klausner, *Seljuk Vezirate*, pp. 62–75.
30 Max Weber, *Economy and Society: An Outline of Interpretive Sociology*, ed. G. Roth and C. Wittich (Berkeley, 1978), vol. 2, p. 1147.
31 Max Weber, *From Max Weber: Essays in Sociology*, ed. and tr. H. H. Gerth and C. Wright Mills (New York, 1946), pp. 416–444.
32 Ibid., pp. 416–417.
33 See Dabashi, 'Farhang-i siyāsī', pp. 327 ff.
34 Weber, *Economy and Society*, vol. 2, p. 1147.
35 See Niẓāmī ʿArūḍī's *Chahār maqāla*, ed. M. Qazvīnī (Leiden, 1909), p. 2.
36 Ibid., p. 3.

FOURTEEN

'Sometimes by the sword, sometimes by the dagger': The role of the Isma'ilis in Mamlūk–Mongol relations in the 8th/14th century

CHARLES MELVILLE

FOLLOWING THE surrender of their stronghold at Girdkūh on 29 Rabī' II 670/4 December 1271 and their failure to regain Alamūt in 674/1275, the Nizārī Isma'ilis, who had already largely withdrawn from the historical stage, ceased to pose any political threat to the new Mongol dynasty in Persia.[1] At much the same time, the new Mamlūk regime in Egypt was in the process of destroying the independence of the western branch of the Isma'ilis. With the surrender of Kahf, the last Isma'ili castle, on 22 Dhu'l-Ḥijja 671/10 July 1273 and the elimination of their power in Syria, Baybars I completed what Hülegü Khan had begun in Persia in 654/1256.[2]

The Isma'ilis still had their uses, however, and even while reducing them to his obedience, Baybars was not slow to employ them against whoever opposed him, both far and near.[3] Since his enemies were also former foes of the Isma'ilis, they probably needed little persuasion to co-operate, particularly if it helped them to win Baybars' favour.

Among the sultan's targets, the Frankish Crusaders were the nearest to hand.[4] They themselves were not averse to employing assassins, for Bohemond VI of Antioch and Tripoli seems to have been behind a plot to murder Baybars in 669/1271. The sultan threatened to return the compliment and warned Bohemond not to rely on support from the Mongol Īlkhān Abaqa.[5]

Another of Baybars' intended victims at this period was Bartholomew, the ruler of Maraclea. In Rabī' I 670/October 1271, Baybars informed his *amīrs* that he had sent some *fidāwīs* in pursuit of the lord of Maraclea (Marqiyya), who had fled to the Mongols. One of the *fidāwīs* returned to report that they had attacked and killed him. This is given as an example of how power could be consolidated, 'sometimes by the sword, sometimes by the dagger'.[6] In fact, Bartholomew made his escape to the Mongol court and later returned to defend his castle against Qalāwūn,[7] but Baybars' murderous intentions are clear enough.

The ground rules for Mamlūk policy were thus laid out, in this respect as in so many others, by Baybars, the first effective Mamlūk sultan. At the same time, flight to the Mongol court remained an attractive option to many (like Bohemond and Bartholomew) opposed to the Mamlūk regime in Egypt. Compared with the Crusaders, who were expelled from the Holy Land in 690/1291, the more distant Īlkhāns posed the greater threat to the Mamlūks, as was clearly perceived by Baybars and his successors. Their enmity persisted into the 8th/14th century and reached a late peak in the time of al-Nāṣir Muḥammad (third reign, 709–741/1310–1341), when improving relations were complicated by the celebrated defection of the Mamlūk *amīr* Shams al-Dīn Qarāsunqur al-Manṣūrī. His flight to Persia in 712/1312 revived the contest with both sword and dagger, though ultimately these struggles proved to be the catalyst for a negotiated peace treaty between the two powers.

My intention in this essay is to focus on al-Nāṣir Muḥammad's various attempts to have Qarāsunqur (and others) assassinated, within the wider context of Mamlūk–Mongol relations during his reign. The fact that the Isma'ili communities in Syria managed to maintain their identity and reputation so long after their formal absorption into the Mamlūk state is not the least interesting aspect of the story. However, space does not permit me to go into this matter here, nor to discuss the evidence of their activities during the final quarter of the 7th/13th century.[8]

The survival of the Isma'ilis in the mountains west of Ḥamā is attested not only by the details of their missions into Persia, but also by the traveller Ibn Baṭṭūṭa, who visited some of their castles in 726/1326 and found that the sect maintained its exclusive character. He calls them the 'arrows of al-Malik al-Nāṣir', sent in pursuit of anyone fleeing to Iraq or elsewhere. Ibn Baṭṭūṭa observes, however, that they were not always successful, and goes on to recount the story of Qarāsunqur.[9] The latter, a former Mamlūk governor of Aleppo, supported al-Nāṣir Muḥammad's restoration to the sultanate in 709/1310 and was rewarded with the governorship of Damascus. However, the two men remained wary of each other, particularly since Qarāsunqur had been involved in the assassination of al-Nāṣir's brother, al-Ashraf Khalīl, in 693/1293.

The evidence for Qarāsunqur's career has been analyzed by Donald Little, who also discusses what might be called the conceptual aspects of

Mamlūk–Mongol hostility in the light of Qarāsunqur's defection and the way this is treated in the sources.[10] The biographers recount about half a dozen separate attacks on Qarāsunqur, stating that many more were undertaken and that some 100 Isma'ilis perished in the attempt on his life.[11] On the whole, the annalists contain different material about Qarāsunqur and the Isma'ilis, but it is often possible to recognize independent versions of the same event. Al-'Aynī's chronicle is particularly useful in locating most of the anecdotes narrated out of context by Mufaḍḍal and al-Maqrīzī back in their chronological framework.[12] On the other hand, the material provided by al-Ṣafadī is not so easy to place. There are inevitably certain similarities between the incidents described, and it is possible that the same basic stock of stories is simply being retold with variations, exaggerations and inaccuracies. Nevertheless, most of the anecdotes are compatible with the known facts of the political and diplomatic history of the period, and can be accommodated within the sequence of events reported in the chronicles.

Qarāsunqur, justifiably suspicious of al-Malik al-Nāṣir's intentions towards him, fled to members of the Āl Faḍl tribe in the Syrian desert in Dhu'l-Ḥijja 711/April–May 1312. He eventually took refuge with Öljeitü Khan in Rabī' I 712/July 1312. He was accompanied by Āqqūsh al-Afram, like Qarāsunqur a former governor of Damascus, together with al-Afram's father-in-law, Aidemür al-Zamr al-Zardkāsh, Balabān al-Dimashqī and a number of *mamlūk*s. They were well received by Öljeitü, who assigned Marāgha to Qarāsunqur and Hamadān to al-Afram.[13] They soon encouraged the Īlkhān to launch an attack on Mamlūk territory, and accompanied the Mongol army that laid siege to Raḥba on the Euphrates during most of Ramaḍān 712/January 1313. Öljeitü then abandoned the siege, which proved to be the last major conflict in Syria between the two powers, and retired to Baghdad.[14]

Isma'ili missions to assassinate the defectors started almost immediately. According to al-'Aynī, Qarāsunqur, seeing the crowds gathered to greet them in Tabrīz, anticipated a *fidāwī* attack and advised his companions to wear chain mail under their clothing. Some time later, a *fidāwī* attacked and wounded al-Afram, who was saved by his protective mail. After a fight the *fidāwī* was overpowered and killed. Chūpān ordered an investigation and all foreigners in Tabrīz were rounded up and put to the question. Al-Afram suggested an identity parade, on the grounds that he knew all the *fidāwī*s and secret agents thanks to his former position as governor of Syria. This was arranged, but the suspects were all deemed to be regular merchants and were released. It later transpired that the agent responsible for orchestrating the assault, named as [ʿAlāʾ al-Dīn] ʿAlī b. al-Muʿallim from Ḥadītha, had resourcefully evaded recognition and was able to leave in the company of the merchants from Salmās with whom he had arrived, together with a second *fidāwī*, who had failed to carry out his part of the plan to attack Qarāsunqur.[15]

Despite differences in detail, this story is similar enough to one recounted by other sources to indicate that the same incident is being described. The attack was commissioned by al-Nāṣir Muḥammad, who wrote asking the ruler of Maṣyāf to supply the two *fidāwī*s; their mission was organized by the governor of Raḥba, Badr al-Dīn al-Azkashī.[16] Al-Afram was treated for his wounds and recovered. Several further attempts are said to have been made on him, without success;[17] he died of natural causes on 13 Muḥarram 716/7 April 1316.[18]

Al-ʿAynī puts this whole episode in 711 AH, but the plan was only hatched after news of the Mamlūks' flight to Persia reached al-Nāṣir Muḥammad. Although there is no other evidence that Öljeitü was in Ūjān when they arrived, this is perfectly plausible, as is the information that he rode to Tabrīz on hearing news of the attack, which reassured him that the Mamlūks were genuine refugees and not part of some treacherous plan. He then received the defectors in Shām-i Ghāzān outside the city. The attack should be dated sometime between the Mamlūks' arrival on 3 Rabīʿ I/9 July and Chūpān's departure for the Raḥba campaign in Jumādā II 712/October 1312. During this period, further efforts were made to round up suspected *fidāwī*s, with some success, though it proved difficult to wring any information out of those who fell into the hands of the authorities.[19]

Shortly after the *ordu* arrived in Baghdad from Raḥba, another Ismaʿili attack occurred. Several people were knifed in Baghdad by 'Syrian *fidāwī*s' on 30 Dhuʾl-Qaʿda 712/29 March 1313. Qarāsunqur is not said to have been the target; the only casualty named is the leader of the *fidāwī*s, Saʿd al-Dīn ʿAlī Jakbīn.[20] Saʿd al-Dīn's death is confirmed by further reports from Baghdad, brought by his brother Jamāl al-Dīn ʿUbayda. A number of Muslim (i.e. Mamlūk) agents were arrested. They had been exposed by the *mamlūk*s of al-Zardkāsh, who had arrived with Qarāsunqur.[21]

It is not certain that Saʿd al-Dīn was actually an Ismaʿili. He had returned to Cairo in 711 AH, after operating for five months in Baghdad on an unspecified mission.[22] His presence in Baghdad cannot have been connected originally with Qarāsunqur and the defectors, who were still in Mamlūk territory in 711 AH; more probably he was part of a long-term programme of espionage.[23] The Isma'ili *fidāwīs*, who now did not form a special corps and who were in all probability ordinary sectarians chosen and sent on such missions forcibly, were usually commissioned for specific tasks, in the course of which they came under the operational control of the regular agents. Perhaps it was to oversee such a mission that Sa'd al-Dīn had returned to Baghdad sometime in 712 AH, only to have his cover exposed by al-Zardkāsh's *mamlūks* and find himself associated with the Isma'ilis under his care.

Evidently not all the Isma'ilis were captured, however, for a fortnight later, on Friday 15 Dhu'l-Ḥijja 712/13 April 1313, a further assassination was carried out 'on the orders of Nāṣir of Egypt' by Isma'ili *fidāwīs*. The victim was a certain Ītqulī.[24] Shortly afterwards, Öljeitü set off back to Sulṭāniyya.

These attacks can probably be equated with al-Maqrīzī's report of the murder of the governor of Baghdad, following his oppressive treatment of a merchant purchasing *mamlūks* for al-Malik al-Nāṣir. The assailant escaped to Maṣyāf.[25] This news caused further concern to Qarāsunqur, Chūpān and the Īlkhānid vizier, 'Alī Shāh, who redoubled their efforts. They identified and arrested four men, one of whom provided information under torture.[26]

The first actual attack reported on Qarāsunqur occurred on Monday 17 Rabī' I 714/1 July 1314, when he was knifed.[27] A Mamlūk agent brought the news that two men had attacked and wounded the *amīr* in Sulṭāniyya. One of the assailants was killed and the other escaped. As a result of the assault, a large number of Arabs and Mozarabs [*must'araba*] had been killed in Tabrīz. Further news arrived that the wound was in Qarāsunqur's leg, but it had been treated successfully and he was able to ride again.[28] This seems to have been the only occasion on which the *fidāwīs* succeeded in wounding Qarāsunqur.[29]

Al-Nāṣir Muḥammad's neurotic hounding of Qarāsunqur might have laid behind the Mamlūk attack on Malaṭya in Muḥarram 715/April 1315. According to al-Maqrīzī, al-Nāṣir ordered this expedition because he had sent a group of *fidāwīs* from Maṣyāf to kill Qarāsunqur, but they had been exposed by a certain Kurd named Mandūh, who had then been sent to Malaṭya to collect taxes on behalf of Chūpān. The governor of Malaṭya, named Mīzamīr, was afraid Mandūh would replace him as governor and entered into a conspiracy with the Mamlūk sultan to hand over the city. On the arrival of the Mamlūk army, Malaṭya was surrendered and Mandūh arrested, but he later escaped.[30] The city was sacked, but was quickly recovered by Chūpān at the head of a Mongol force.[31] Al-Maqrīzī's explanation for the raid might be as good as any other,[32] and if correct is further evidence of the effect of Qarāsunqur's defection on worsening Mamlūk–Mongol relations. The campaign was initiated in late Dhu'l-Qa'da 714/February 1315, so it seems more *fidāwī*s had been sent against Qarāsunqur earlier in the year.

Qarāsunqur spent the following winter in Baghdad, while Öljeitü was in Mūghān. Sometime between Ramaḍān 715 and Muḥarram 716/ December 1315–March 1316, Qarāsunqur was again attacked, but was unscathed.[33] Al-Nāṣir's dissatisfaction at the failure of efforts to assassinate Qarāsunqur is perhaps revealed by the decree he issued in 715/1315, that the Isma'ili community of Maṣyāf should no longer enjoy exemptions from the various dues to which the other people of the Ḥamā region were liable.[34]

Öljeitü's reign closed on a sour note with antagonisms coming to a head in the Ḥijāz. The accession of Abū Sa'īd and the increased power of his viceregent, Chūpān, brought more conciliatory attitudes in the Īlkhānate.[35] Qarāsunqur's presence in Persia and al-Nāṣir Muḥammad's continuing efforts to remove him, however, worked in a contrary direction. It is clear from various stories that several attempts were made on Qarāsunqur during Abū Sa'īd's reign (717–736/1317–1335), and they had an important impact on the peace negotiations between the two powers. A leading figure here is Majd al-Dīn al-Sallāmī.[36] He was closely involved in the negotiations, on one hand, and in the *fidāwī* missions on the other; many of the anecdotes concerning the *fidāwī*s are either based on reports deriving from al-Sallāmī himself, or mention his part in events, making it difficult sometimes to distinguish episodes that all bear a strong family resemblance.

Al-Sallāmī had struck up a warm relationship with Abū Sa'īd's vizier, 'Alī Shāh, and fostered friendly contacts between 'Alī Shāh and the Mamlūk *nāẓir al-khāṣṣ*, Karīm al-Dīn al-Kabīr. Anyone coming to Persia from Cairo was received as a guest by al-Sallāmī. In the course of 719/1319–1320, al-Nāṣir Muḥammad sent a message to the governor of Maṣyāf requesting some *fidāwī*s. Thirty men were despatched to Cairo, where they were kept on generous allowances. When a messenger arrived from al-Sallāmī, probably early in 720 AH, the *fidāwī*s were sent with him back to Persia, but one of their number betrayed them to Qarāsunqur, who began to round them up one by one.[37] Nevertheless, one of them was able to attack Qarāsunqur, though perishing in the attempt. Qarāsunqur now raised the alarm, and it was rumoured that *fidāwī*s had been sent to kill not only him, but Abū Sa'īd, Chūpān and 'Alī

Shāh as well. This caused great consternation among the Mongols, and Abū Sa'īd was so afraid that he refused to leave his tent for eleven days. The Mongol authorities' response was to round up and torture many suspects in Tabrīz. By his own good fortune, al-Sallāmī was away on business at this time, but he was summoned to court by Chūpān.[38]

In the meantime, Qarāsunqur was attacked again, while out hunting. A *fidāwī* jumped onto Qarāsunqur's horse while he was crossing a river, but the horse reared up and the *amīr* was able to escape, while his *mamlūk*s killed the would-be assassin.[39]

On his arrival at the *ordu*, al-Sallāmī was accused by Chūpān of coming with gifts and messages of peace from al-Nāṣir Muḥammad, while secretly he was sending *fidāwī*s to sow discord and confusion. Al-Sallāmī protested his innocence of any knowledge of the *fidāwī*s, pointed out his absence from the scene at the time of the attacks, and said that he could not be held responsible for what the Mamlūk sultan did in secret. 'Alī Shāh intervened on his behalf. However, news then arrived from Baghdad of another attack there, aimed at the governor. He had escaped injury, but the blow had fallen on one of the Mongol *amīr*s in his company. The *fidāwī* fled, but when he saw that his capture was inevitable, he killed himself.

This information fuelled Chūpān's anxieties; he agreed with 'Alī Shāh to send an embassy to al-Malik al-Nāṣir to find out whether the Mamlūk sultan was indeed as anxious to pursue peace as his messages suggested, and what was his purpose in sending *fidāwī*s into Mongol territory. Al-Sallāmī was given the task of heading this mission.[40]

Al-Sallāmī arrived in Ḥamā on 9 Dhu'l-Ḥijja 720/10 January 1321 and was in Damascus at the end of the month; he was received in Cairo in Muḥarram 721/February 1321.[41] He reported the Mongols' desire for peace and outlined the conditions proposed by Abū Sa'īd. These reveal the extent to which Qarāsunqur and the missions sent to kill him dominated Mamlūk–Mongol relations at this time. Of the six conditions mentioned, half concerned this issue:

1. Al-Nāṣir Muḥammad would end the *fidāwī*s' presence in Mongol territory and ensure that none of them entered it.

2. The Mamlūks would not seek the return of anyone fleeing to Persia, and nor should anyone be sent back from Egypt against his will.

3. The Mamlūk sultan would not seek the return of Qarāsunqur, about whom there should be no further discussion, because he was residing in Mongol territory and was entitled to respect (as their guest).

Finally, the Mongols asked al-Nāṣir to send a reliable envoy with a document from the sultan, whereupon Abū Saʿīd and Chūpān would swear to maintain peace between them, and the two countries would become as one.[42]

After some hesitation, the sultan decided to accept these proposals and added some of his own. He might have been influenced by the discovery in Cairo of a group of *fidāwī*s sent by Qarāsunqur to murder him. He was obliged to take precautions to safeguard his person when out riding in the streets.[43]

Al-Sallāmī was sent back to Persia at the end of Rajab 721/August 1321, with lavish presents for the Īlkhān.[44] However, this was far from being the end of the question of Qarāsunqur and the *fidāwī*s. Although the treaty was finally ratified in 723 AH, there continued to be a conflict between the terms outlined in principle and what actually happened.

On his arrival in Cairo with the treaty proposal from Abū Saʿīd, al-Sallāmī had been recruited by the sultan to be an 'eye' (*ʿayn*) in the Mongol court and to supervise the missions of the *fidāwī*s.[45] Returning to Persia in 721/1321, al-Sallāmī took advantage of the position of trust that he already enjoyed and maintained a correspondence with the sultan, who then sent a number of *fidāwī*s. By chance, three were captured but the one carrying the sultan's (incriminating) letter to al-Sallāmī escaped to Maṣyāf. Al-Sallāmī continued to foster peace between the two kingdoms.[46]

On 26 Rabīʿ I 722/14 April 1322, a large embassy from Abū Saʿīd arrived in Egypt, wanting to conclude the peace treaty. After pointing out that the Īlkhānate was now a fully Muslim state, the envoys reiterated their request for an oath that no further *fidāwī*s would be sent from Egypt. There seems, however, to have been a change of heart over the question of the return of defectors, Abū Saʿīd now proposing that anyone who came to either country should return home. Al-Nāṣir Muḥammad was opposed to this – perhaps existing defectors such as Qarāsunqur were excluded – but otherwise responded favourably, agreeing to all of Abū Saʿīd's proposals, to which he added some of his own. The most important of these was that al-Nāṣir's name should be mentioned in the *khuṭba* alongside Abū Saʿīd's, and that al-Sallāmī should be established in the Mongol *ordu* as the sultan's official merchant, to purchase *mamlūk*s and slaves. Al-Nāṣir Muḥammad then appointed Aitamish to lead the return embassy to negotiate the final terms.[47]

In the course of his mission, Chūpān told Aitamish that they accepted all the sultan's proposals, but as for Qarāsunqur (whom al-Nāṣir

Muḥammad had not actually mentioned), he was an old man and a stranger who had come to Persia in fear of the sultan, and it was fitting that he should be their guest. He apologized for him, and asked on his part for the sultan to confirm that he would adhere to the condition already proposed, not to send any more *fidāwī*s.[48]

On Monday 14 Jumādā II 723/20 June 1323, Abū Saʿīd's envoys arrived in Cairo, informing the sultan of his compliance with the terms of the treaty, which was now formally ratified in Cairo. The embassy departed on 22 Jumādā II/28 June. Karīm al-Dīn summoned al-Sallāmī to Egypt for private discussion with the sultan.[49]

Abū Saʿīd's envoys had also raised the matter of the *fidāwī*s, and referred to yet another attack having taken place, despite the assurances in the document brought by Aitamish and only shortly after the latter's departure. The attack is said only to have been directed against 'a foreigner in our midst' – probably Qarāsunqur – who survived, but the *fidāwī* killed one of the great *amīr*s and *nā'ib*s. As this violated one of the first conditions of the treaty, the envoys demanded an explanation. After some delay, the sultan denied all knowledge of the matter. 'These people are in your country because I have expelled them from mine.' Once peace had been agreed no more *fidāwī*s had been sent, nor was he going to resume their missions. Al-Nāṣir ended by swearing by God that he knew nothing about them.[50]

The same source makes no attempt to hide al-Nāṣir's perfidy over this matter, however, for when al-Sallāmī arrived in Cairo in response to Karīm al-Dīn's summons, the sultan informed him that he was to return to Persia with a *fidāwī*. The latter had been sent by the governor of Maṣyāf and ʿUllayqa, and concealed by Karīm al-Dīn in Cairo for thirty-four days.[51] Al-Sallāmī protested that this violated the treaty that had just been concluded, and that if the Mongols discovered his involvement, not only would he meet a violent end, but the sultan's interests in Persia would be compromised. These protests were ignored by al-Nāṣir Muḥammad, who told al-Sallāmī that Qarāsunqur and the others were now feeling secure because of the treaty. He was despatched to Persia with the *fidāwī*, who was installed at the house of one of the sultan's agents.[52]

The *fidāwī* remained concealed until the *ʿīd al-fiṭr* (1 Shawwāl [723]/3 October 1323), when Qarāsunqur and others were at the *ordu* offering their congratulations first to Abū Saʿīd and Chūpān, then to the vizier ʿAlī Shāh.[53] Al-Sallāmī was present at ʿAlī Shāh's *majlis* and sent his agent to get the *fidāwī*. The agent gave the *fidāwī* the knife assigned for the mission, described his target, and gave a signal when Qarāsunqur was about to leave. The governor of Rūm, Temürtash son of Chūpān, was also present at the *majlis* and got up to leave soon after Qarāsunqur; he had a fine head of grey hair and, like Qarāsunqur, was wearing a red robe of honour bestowed by Abū Sa'īd.[54] By chance, 'Alī Shāh called Qarāsunqur back for a few words, so that Temürtash actually left first. Supposing him to be Qarāsunqur, the *fidāwī* attacked Temürtash by mistake. The commotion was heard by Qarāsunqur, who realized the attack had been intended for him.[55]

Al-Sallāmī was in a dangerous predicament, for the *fidāwī*, who was immediately arrested, was recognized as having come with him to Persia. Chūpān summoned him and after accusing both him and al-Nāṣir Muḥammad of bad faith, started to torture him. Al-Sallāmī thought himself doomed, but continued to swear his innocence. 'Alī Shāh intervened to say he was sure that the sultan would not go back on an oath sworn on the Qur'an. Thereupon, it was decided instead to wring a confession from the poor *fidāwī*, who suffered mutilation in silence while al-Sallāmī prayed God to give him endurance and conceal their association. Chūpān then produced a savage black dog. The terrified *fidāwī* let out a horrible cry; a ball was stuffed in his mouth and the dog was released. It tore him to pieces and began to eat him. Al-Sallāmī was saved.[56]

Another story, told on the authority of al-Sallāmī, might be a garbled version of the same incident, for it also took place on the *'īd* in an undated year and involved a son of Chūpān, but there are sufficient differences for it to refer perhaps to another occasion. In the *majlis*, Qarāsunqur happened to be sitting on the hem of Dimashq Khwāja's clothing. When a *fidāwī* leapt forward, Dimashq Khwāja saw the knife flash and rose in flight, so pulling his garment out from under Qarāsunqur, who toppled over. The blow therefore fell harmlessly on thin air. The *fidāwī* was chopped to pieces by Qarāsunqur's *mamlūk*s, and the latter turned to al-Sallāmī and accused him of having concealed the *fidāwī*. They went before Abū Sa'īd, and Qarāsunqur demanded reassurance: 'even the birds can rely on branches of thorns to protect them from the heat and cold'. Abū Sa'īd asked al-Sallāmī how long he was going to go on harbouring *fidāwī*s while he remained among them. Al-Sallāmī denied having sheltered him; but he had often heard al-Nāṣir say that Qarāsunqur was his *mamlūk* and his brother [al-Ashraf Khalīl]'s and his father [Qalāwūn]'s *mamlūk*. Qarāsunqur had murdered the sultan's brother and he would not cease trying to avenge him even if he emptied the treasuries of Egypt. Al-Sallāmī also said that the *fidāwī* had been in the country before the peace treaty, and was therefore not covered by it. Chūpān is supposed to have seen the truth of this; he had no wish to come between the sultan and the *mamlūk* who had killed his brother, and closed the matter.[57]

A similar argument is advanced on another occasion by Aitamish, in the course of his second diplomatic mission to the Īlkhānate.[58] If this story does indeed concern a separate incident from the one mentioned above, the *fidāwī* must have been in hiding for about three years, for the treaty was finally concluded in 723 AH, as a result of Aitamish's first embassy; his second mission was in Persia in the mid-summer of 726/1326.[59]

The last documented attempt on Qarāsunqur's life must have occurred later in 726 AH. According to Aitamish's *mamlūk*s, Quṭayba and Kurumās, who had arrived in the *ordu* three days before the feast of the sacrifice (10 Dhu'l-Ḥijja/7 November 1326), Qarāsunqur was attacked on the day of the *'īd* as he left Abū Sa'īd's tent together with other Mongol *amīr*s. On seeing his assailant, Qarāsunqur threw himself to the ground, but the *fidāwī* jumped on him and stabbed him. However, Qarāsunqur twisted to one side and the knife stuck in the ground. The *fidāwī* was killed while still sitting on Qarāsunqur's chest. He arose, shaken and terrified, having lost his turban and torn his clothing.

The uproar brought Abū Sa'īd from his tent. The two *mamlūk*s were brought before Chūpān, who threatened to tear them to bits and wreck the peace treaty with al-Nāṣir Muḥammad. It seems from their own testimony, however, that (unlike al-Sallāmī) they were innocent of any knowledge of the *fidāwī*, and it was Qarāsunqur who came to their rescue. He had frequently seen his assailant, in the guise of a merchant, and had always tried to keep clear of him. When he saw him come out of the crowd, he threw himself down, and it was through God's decree that he turned the way he did as the knife fell. The *mamlūk*s knew nothing about him. The vizier blessed him for this intervention, and Chūpān turned to the *mamlūk*s with the comment, 'you have a second life'.[60]

Quṭayba and Kurumās' mission is not well documented, but they must have been sent to Persia after Aitamish's return in July 1326. Kurumās is reported to have returned to Cairo in the first half of 727 AH, where the information he brought helped the *amīr* Ḥusām al-Dīn Ḥusayn b. Kharbandā make up his mind to return to the Īlkhānate. He had fled to Egypt two years earlier, and been made an '*Amīr* of Forty'. He left Cairo on 5 Jumādā I 727/29 March 1327.[61]

Interestingly, the Mongols had been pressing for the return of Ḥusām al-Dīn because of the peace treaty, in which they had modified their first proposal and suggested that refugees should return home. But al-Nāṣir Muḥammad had preferred the original condition that refugees should not be sent back against their will. Temürtash's flight to Egypt after the downfall and death of his father Chūpān in Muḥarram 728/November 1327, produced a diplomatic crisis, with similar though more intense pressure from Abū Sa'īd for the return of the refugee. The Temürtash affair is tangential to the question of the Isma'ilis, which comes to a full circle at this point. Although al-Nāṣir Muḥammad resisted requests for the extradition of Temürtash, he inclined to a Mongol proposal to send Qarāsunqur's head in exchange for Temürtash's. Temürtash was executed by al-Nāṣir and his head was sent with Aitamish to the Mongol court, but Qarāsunqur died in Marāgha before Abū Sa'īd could carry out his side of the bargain. In Ibn Baṭṭūṭa's colourful version of the story, Qarāsunqur is said to have poisoned himself.[62]

With the death of Qarāsunqur, the main target of the Mamlūk attacks in Persia was removed. No further incidents are reported in the chronicles, although the legend that the *fidāwī*s remained a potential source of threat proved durable.[63]

Thus we have seen that for a period of about 15 years, from 712/1312 to 726/1326, a series of *fidāwī* attacks were launched into Persia from Mamlūk Egypt, directed particularly but not exclusively against Qarāsunqur. Through his vigilance and good fortune, Qarāsunqur survived and did not give al-Nāṣir Muḥammad the satisfaction of killing him.[64] Although it is an assumption that all these attacks were carried out by Isma'ilis, whenever their origin is mentioned the assassins are reported to have come from the Isma'ili castles in Syria, usually Maṣyāf. It is unlikely that they remained as devoted to such missions as these reports suggest, and no doubt the sources reveal the persistence of the distorted image of the Isma'ilis and hostile rumours surrounding their community.[65] Nevertheless, evidence of their involvement seems reasonably clear. These attacks not only encouraged the Mongols to negotiate for peace with al-Nāṣir Muḥammad in an attempt to bring them to an end, but nearly compromised the treaty of 723/1323 when they continued unabated. Despite the alarm they caused in Persia, the Mongols probably came to accept that the *fidāwī* missions were directed only against Qarāsunqur and not against the Īlkhānid state. The last few years of Abū Sa'īd's reign saw a gradual reduction in the tension between the two powers.

NOTES

I am grateful to David Morgan for reading and commenting on the final draft of this essay.

1 Rashīd al-Dīn, *Jāmi' al-tawārīkh*, vol. 3, ed. A. A. Alizade (Baku, 1957), p. 140, and Ḥamd Allāh Mustawfī, *Ta'rīkh-i guzīda*, ed. 'A. Navā'ī (Tehran, 1339/1960), p. 592. See also M. G. S. Hodgson, *The Order of Assassins* (The Hague, 1955), pp. 258–270, 275.

2 A. A. Khowaiter, *Baibars the First: His Endeavours and Achievements* (London, 1978), pp. 118–126, and P. Thorau, *The Lion of Egypt, Sultan Baybars I and the Near East in the Thirteenth Century*, tr. P. M. Holt (London, 1992), pp. 147, 176, 201–203.

3 Ibn Shaddād, *Ta'rīkh al-Malik al-Ẓāhir*, ed. A. Hutait (Wiesbaden, 1983), p. 313.

4 Thorau, *Lion*, pp. 204, 222 (for 18 May *read* 18 June).

5 Ibn 'Abd al-Ẓāhir, *al-Rawḍ al-zāhir fī sīrat al-Malik al-Ẓāhir*, ed. A. A. Khowaiter (Riyadh, 1976), pp. 376–377; C. Defrémery, 'Nouvelles recherches sur les Ismaéliens ou Bathiniens de Syrie', *Journal Asiatique*, 5 série, 5 (1855), pp. 65–66, citing the continuator of al-Makīn (= Mufaḍḍal b. Abi'l-Faḍā'il, *al-Nahj al-sadīd*, ed. E. Blochet, in *Patrologia Orientalis*, 12 (1919), pp. 191–195 [pp. 533–537]); see also Ibn al-Dawādārī, *Kanz al-durar*, vol. 8, ed. U. Haarmann (Cairo, 1971), pp. 157–160. Bohemond sought Abaqa's help in vain.

6 Ibn 'Abd al-Ẓāhir, *al-Rawḍ*, p. 395; al-Maqrīzī, *Kitāb al-sulūk li-ma'rifat duwal al-mulūk*, ed. M. M. Ziyāda and S. 'A. F. 'Āshūr (Cairo, 1936–1958), vol. 1, pp. 599–600, hereafter cited as al-Maqrīzī; Defrémery, 'Nouvelles', p. 66, and Thorau, *Lion*, p. 208.

7 Ibn 'Abd al-Ẓāhir, *Tashrīf al-ayyām*, ed. M. Kāmil (Cairo, 1961), p. 87; R. Irwin, 'The Mamlūk Conquest of the County of Tripoli', in *Crusade and Settlement*, ed. P. W. Edbury (Cardiff, 1985), p. 248.

8 See provisionally Defrémery, 'Nouvelles', pp. 68–70.

9 Ibn Baṭṭūṭa, *The travels of Ibn Baṭṭūṭa*, tr. H. A. R. Gibb (Cambridge, 1958), vol. 1, p. 106; he went on to Damascus, which he left in Shawwāl 726/September 1326 with the Syrian pilgrim convoy, led this year by Sayf al-Dīn al-Jūbān, see Ibn Kathīr, *al-Bidāya wa'l-nihāya* (Cairo, n.d.), vol. 14, p. 124. Ibn Faḍl Allāh al-'Umarī, *Masālik al-abṣār*, ed. A. F. Sayyid (Cairo, 1985), pp. 77, 132–133, confirms the survival of the Isma'ili communities (under the jurisdiction of Tripoli); their chief in his time (some twenty years later) was Mubārak b. Alwān. See E. Quatremère, 'Notice historique sur les Ismaëliens', *Fundgruben des Orients*, 4 (1814), p. 368, al-Qalqashandī, *Ṣubḥ al-a'shā* (Cairo, n.d.), vol. 4, pp. 146, 202, and vol. 13, p. 245.

10 D. P. Little, *An Introduction to Mamlūk Historiography* (Wiesbaden, 1970), pp. 100–135; see also G. Wiet, 'Un réfugié Mamlouk à la cour Mongole de Perse', in *Mélanges Henri Massé* (Tehran, 1963), pp. 388–404.

11 Al-Ṣafadī, *al-Wāfī bi'l-wafayāt*, Arab League Institute of Arabic Manuscripts, Ms. 565 *ta'rīkh*, fol. 103r, says 80; Mufaḍḍal, *al-Nahj al-sadīd*, ed. S. Kortantamer (Freiburg, 1973), p. 112 and al-Maqrīzī, vol. 2, p. 554, say 124. It is unlikely that al-Maqrīzī is borrowing directly from Mufaḍḍal, for he inserts too much material not found in the earlier work. Both are probably derived from a third source, seemingly sympathetic to Qarāsunqur. Al-Maqrīzī's text is translated in Quatremère, 'Notice', pp. 369–373. Ibn Baṭṭūṭa (tr. Gibb, vol. 1, p. 109) also mentions that several Isma'ilis perished, as well as stating that Qarāsunqur always slept in a house made of wood and iron!

12 Al-'Aynī, *'Iqd al-jumān fī ta'rīkh ahl al-zamān*, Topkapi Library, Istanbul, Ms. Ahmed

III, 2912/4. He relies heavily on al-Yūsufī (see D. P. Little, 'The Recovery of a Lost Source for Baḥrī Mamlūk History: al-Yūsufī's *Nuzhat al-nāẓir fī sīrat al-Malik al-Nāṣir*', JAOS, 94 (1974), pp. 42–54), who cannot be the sole original source for Mufaḍḍal and al-Maqrīzī. His testimony is very detailed and appears to be reliable.

13 Abu'l-Fidā, *The Memoirs of a Syrian Prince*, tr. P. M. Holt (Wiesbaden, 1983), pp. 57–59; Abu'l-Qāsim Kāshānī, *Ta'rīkh-i Uljaytū*, ed. M. Hambly (Tehran, 1348/1969), pp. 136–142; hereafter cited as Kāshānī.

14 See al-ʿAynī, fols. 296v ff., on the siege of Raḥba; and C. Melville, 'The Itineraries of Sultan Öljeitü, 1304–16', *Iran*, 28 (1990), p. 65, for the chronology.

15 Al-ʿAynī, fols. 293r–294r.

16 Mufaḍḍal ed. Kortantamer, pp. 108–109; similar in al-Maqrīzī, vol. 2, pp. 554–555, who says the sultan dealt kindly with the ruler of Maṣyāf and sent a lot of money, suggesting the Ismaʿili chief enjoyed a certain independence of action. In these accounts the merchant is called Yūnus; they also say al-Afram was lightly wounded in the forearm (or hand). Neither author dates the event. In view of al-Azkashī's role in planning the mission, mentioned only by al-ʿAynī, it is not surprising that he was unwilling to hand over Raḥba to his former comrade al-Afram.

17 Al-Ṣafadī, *al-Wāfī*, vol. 9, ed. J. van Ess (Wiesbaden, 1974), p. 334. He says he died in Hamadān after 720 AH, but see next note.

18 Mufaḍḍal, ed. Blochet, p. 771 [III, 265], al-ʿAynī, fol. 316r; al-Maqrīzī, vol. 2, p. 167, has 23 Muḥarram.

19 Al-Maqrīzī, vol. 2, p. 555; the search was assisted by the fact that one of Qarāsunqur's servants was from the Ismaʿili castle of ʿUllayqa, and was able to reveal the identity of *fidāwī*s sent to kill him. The same story, but without this information, appears in Mufaḍḍal, ed. Kortantamer, p. 109.

20 Kāshānī, p. 144.

21 Mufaḍḍal, ed. Blochet, pp. 719–720 [III, 213–214]. Though placed in 711 AH, the fact that the agents were betrayed by al-Zardkāsh's *mamlūk*s again points to 712 AH. Ibn Kathīr, p. 63 (also under 711 AH), names two men, Ibn al-ʿIqāb [?] and Ibn al-Badr among the victims, and confirms ʿUbayda's flight.

22 Mufaḍḍal, ed. Blochet, p. 718 [III, 212].

23 For background, see R. Amitai, 'Mamlūk Espionage among Mongols and Franks', *Asian and African Studies*, 22 (1988), pp. 173–181.

24 Kāshānī, p. 146; the Ītqulī mentioned by Rashīd al-Dīn, *Jāmiʿ*, vol. 3, p. 244, is perhaps the same, and he might have become governor of Baghdad.

25 Al-Maqrīzī, vol. 2, p. 555. The sultan was kept informed of these events by his agents. This association is made on the assumption of some chronological order in al-Maqrīzī's account. Attacks in Baghdad are also reported in 715 and 720 AH (see below). Mufaḍḍal, ed. Blochet, p. 745 [III, 239], reports the death of the governor of Maṣyāf, Jamāl al-Dīn Āqqūsh al-Kanjī, in 713/1313.

26 Mufaḍḍal, ed. Kortantamer, p. 109, without mentioning Baghdad. Since four men are said to have been arrested, we might equate this story with the one provided by al-Ṣafadī, fols. 103v–104r, concerning the arrest of four *fidāwī*s in a company of merchants as they approached Marāgha. This anecdote is recounted on the authority of an agent called ʿAlā' al-Dīn ʿAlī al-ʿĀdil, who is perhaps to be identified with the ʿAlī b. al-Muʿallim mentioned earlier.

27 Kāshānī, p. 166.

28 Mufaḍḍal, ed. Blochet, pp. 747–748 [III, 241–242]; Wiet, 'Un réfugié', p. 400. The agent arrived on 20 Rabīʿ II 714/3 August 1314.

29 Al-Ṣafadī, fol. 103r, says he was only hurt once, at the entrance to the khan's palace, and received a minor graze in the leg.

30 Al-Maqrīzī, vol. 2, p. 143.

31 Kāshānī, pp. 171–172.

32 See Abu'l-Fidā, *Memoirs*, pp. 67–68; Mufaḍḍal, ed. Blochet, pp. 749, 751–754 [III, 243, 245–248], and Ibn Kathīr, vol. 14, p. 73: none mention Qarāsunqur. Other accounts differ; see, for instance, Ibn al-Dawādārī, *Kanz*, vol. 9, ed. H. R. Roemer (Cairo, 1960), pp. 284–285, and al-ʿAynī, fols. 309r–v (under 714 AH).

33 The *fidāwī* was killed. Abu'l-Fidā, *Memoirs*, p. 69, and Ibn Kathīr, vol. 14, p. 74. The same winter, al-Nāṣir tried to lure Qarāsunqur into Mamlūk territory, by spreading false rumours that he had been succeeded as Mamlūk sultan by Qarāsunqur's son. Öljeitü prevented him by force from crossing the Euphrates; see Kāshānī, p. 220.

34 Abu'l-Fidā, *Memoirs*, p. 68.

35 C. Melville, 'The Year of the Elephant. Mamluk–Mongol Rivalry in the Hejaz in the Reign of Abū Saʿīd (1317–1335)', *Studia Iranica*, 21 (1992), pp. 197–214.

36 Al-Ṣafadī, vol. 9, pp. 220–221, and al-Shujāʿī, *Ta'rīkh al-Malik al-Nāṣir*, ed. B. Schäfer (Wiesbaden, 1977), p. 251.

37 Al-ʿAynī, fols. 329v–330r. This is rather similar to the earlier story of Qarāsunqur's servant from ʿUllayqa; see note 19 above.

38 Ibid., fol. 330r (under 720 AH).

39 Ibid., fol. 330r; also in al-Maqrīzī, vol. 2, p. 207.

40 Al-ʿAynī, fol. 330r; much briefer in al-Maqrīzī, vol. 2, pp. 207–208. Both historians almost certainly base this account on the chronicle of al-Yūsufī, cited by al-ʿAynī on fol. 328v.

41 Abu'l-Fidā, *Memoirs*, p. 81, and Ibn Kathīr, vol. 14, p. 97. Gifts from ʿAlī Shāh, which had been intercepted by members of the Āl Muhannā bedouin, caught up with al-Sallāmī in Cairo on 29 Muḥarram; see al-Nuwayrī, *Nihāyat al-arab*, Leiden Ms. 19-B, fol. 3v; Ibn Kathīr, vol. 14, p. 98; Mufaḍḍal, ed. Kortantamer, pp. 11–12; al-ʿAynī, fols. 328v, 333r, and al-Maqrīzī, vol. 2, p. 209. Bektāsh al-Fākhirī, in *Beiträge zur Geschichte der Mamlūkensultane*, ed. K. V. Zettersteen (Leiden, 1919), p. 171, says al-Sallāmī arrived on 29 Dhu'l-Ḥijja 720.

42 Al-ʿAynī, fol. 328v; less detail in al-Maqrīzī, vol. 2, pp. 209–210. The other conditions were that merchants should come and go freely, that Arab and Turkman raids should cease, and that the sultan should provide a banner for the Iraqi pilgrimage, see Melville, 'Year of the Elephant', p. 204.

43 Al-ʿAynī, fol. 330v; less detail in al-Maqrīzī, vol. 2, pp. 208–209.

44 Mufaḍḍal, ed. Kortantamer, p. 15, and Ibn Kathīr, vol. 14, p. 99.

45 Mufaḍḍal, ed. Kortantamer, p. 109, and al-Maqrīzī, vol. 2, p. 556. Al-Sallāmī saw the sultan together with Karīm al-Dīn al-Kabīr; see al-Maqrīzī, vol. 2, p. 209, and al-ʿAynī, fol. 328v. This is the first time al-Sallāmī's arrival in Cairo is mentioned. Earlier in 720 AH, he had sent an envoy requesting a *sanjaq* for the Iraqī pilgrim caravan that year (al-ʿAynī, fol. 327v), and the envoy had returned to Persia with the 30 *fidāwīs* mentioned above. The order in which al-ʿAynī places these events resolves the chronological problem to which I have drawn attention elsewhere; see 'Year of the Elephant', p. 204, n. 31.

46 Al-Maqrīzī, vol. 2, p. 556, adding that one of the conditions was that no *fidāwī*s should be sent; less detail in Mufaḍḍal, ed. Kortantamer, p. 109. Both authors next relate the story of the attack on Qarāsunqur while out hunting, which I have placed earlier, *before* al-Sallāmī's mission to Egypt; see note 39 above.

47 Bektāsh al-Fākhirī, p. 172 (for the date); al-ʿAynī, fol. 339v, citing al-Yūsufī. See also D. Ayalon, 'The Great Yasa of Chingiz Khān: A Re-examination (Part C1)', *Studia Islamica*, 36 (1972), pp. 140–141.

48 Al-ʿAynī, fol. 345v. Abū Saʿīd and the Mongol *amīr*s solemnly swore to the treaty soon afterwards, and the sultan's name was mentioned in the *khuṭba* in the Friday mosque in Tabrīz.

49 Ibid., fols. 343v–344r; dates in Bektāsh al-Fākhirī, p. 173; see also al-Nuwayrī, fols. 29v–31r. Ibn al-Dawādārī, *Kanz*, vol. 9, pp. 312–313, says the peace was to last ten years and ten days.

50 Al-ʿAynī, fol. 344r. The date of Aitamish's departure from Tabrīz is not recorded. The death of a prominent *amīr* and *nā'ib* suggests the attack on Temürtash, although this seems to have happened later, and was not (in fact) fatal. See note 55 below.

51 Ibid., fols. 344r–v; he quotes an oral source for a description of the *fidāwī* (fair skinned, with long moustaches and broad shoulders). Al-Maqrīzī, vol. 2, p. 557, says the sultan wrote to the ruler of Maṣyāf complaining at the delay in Qarāsunqur's assassination and describes the lavish diet on which Karīm al-Dīn kept the *fidāwī* in Cairo.

52 Al-ʿAynī, fol. 344v, and al-Maqrīzī, vol. 2, p. 557. Al-Sallāmī travelled with fine gifts for the Mongols and a private business commission from Karīm al-Dīn.

53 The year must have been 723 AH, for ʿAlī Shāh was dead by the *ʿīd al-fiṭr* in 724; see Mustawfī, p. 616; furthermore, Temürtash was at court at this time. From this point the story is taken up by Mufaḍḍal, ed. Kortantamer, pp. 110–111. Another story involving an *ʿīd* does not feature al-Sallāmī (see below).

54 On his arrival in the Īlkhānate, Qarāsunqur was called Āqsunqur because of his grey hair.

55 Mufaḍḍal, ed. Kortantamer, p. 110, and al-Maqrīzī, vol. 2, pp. 557–558. The fact that Temürtash was said to have been killed calls into question the veracity of this story, and by implication of the narrator.

56 Mufaḍḍal, ed. Kortantamer, pp. 110–111. Al-Maqrīzī, vol. 2, p. 558, omits all these gruesome details, which Mufaḍḍal evidently received either first hand, or at one remove, from al-Sallāmī himself and recounts with great immediacy.

57 Al-Ṣafadī (d. 764/1363), fols. 103r–v, on the testimony of al-Sallāmī (d. 743/1342), who contradicts himself, for he had previously said the *fidāwī* had only recently arrived. Chūpān was probably no great supporter of Qarāsunqur, who might have appeared more trouble than he was worth, see Little, *Introduction*, especially p. 120. ʿAlī Shāh had said from the start that al-Nāṣir's hostility was directed only at Qarāsunqur, not at the leading figures in the Īlkhānid state; see al-ʿAynī, fol. 330r (under 712 AH).

58 Al-Maqrīzī, vol. 2, pp. 557–558, where it precedes the *ʿīd al-fiṭr* anecdote, not found in Mufaḍḍal's comparable narrative. It is tempting to equate al-Maqrīzī's Aitamish story with al-Ṣafadī's al-Sallāmī story.

59 D. P. Little, 'Notes on Aitamiš, a Mongol Mamlūk', in *Die islamischen Welt zwischen Mittelalter und Neuzeit*, ed. U. Haarmann and P. Bachmann (Wiesbaden, 1979), pp. 396–397. It is also possible that the incident should be associated with Aitamish's first embassy, in 722 AH (see above).

60 Mufaḍḍal, ed. Kortantamer, pp. 111–112; less detail in al-Maqrīzī, vol. 2, p. 558.

61 Al-Nuwayrī, fol. 119r. Al-Maqrīzī, vol. 2, p. 282, mentions his arrival in Syria a fortnight later. A less probable alternative would be to place this attack in 724 AH, when Quṭayba was sent to Persia to bring back al-Sallāmī for questioning in connection with the fall of Karīm al-Dīn al-Kabīr; see al-ʿAynī, fol. 355r.

62 Al-Nuwayrī, fol. 136v, followed by al-Muqrī, *Nathr al-jumān*, Chester Beatty Library, Ms. Ar. 4113, part 2, fol. 232r, suggests the exchange was proposed by Abū Saʿīd's envoy, and al-Nāṣir hesitated over whether to seek official confirmation of the deal. See also Ibn Baṭṭūṭa, *Travels*, p. 109; al-Ṣafadī, *al-Wāfī*, vol. 10, ed. A. Amara and J. Sublet (Wiesbaden, 1980), p. 403; al-Maqrīzī, vol. 2, p. 299, and al-ʿAynī, fols. 380v and 381r, the latter citing Aitamish. Qarāsunqur died on 27 Shawwāl 728/4 September 1328, three weeks after Temürtash.

63 Mufaḍḍal, ed. Kortantamer, p. 107, and al-Shujāʿī, pp. 123, 263. See also, Quatremère, 'Notice', p. 373.

64 See Mufaḍḍal, ed. Kortantamer, pp. 113–114, and al-Maqrīzī, vol. 2, p. 554, who say he died of diarrhoea. Al-Ṣafadī, *al-Wāfī*, fol. 104r, thinks he must have had spies in Damascus and Cairo to inform him of imminent attacks. In 722/1322, the sultan had ordered the detention of the governor of Kahf, Faraj b. al-Ṣābūnī, because of his correspondence with Qarāsunqur; see al-ʿAynī, *Ta'rīkh al-Badr*, British Library, Ms. Or. 22360, fol. 12v.

65 Bernard Lewis, *The Assassins* (London, 1967), p. 123, regards the stories repeated by Ibn Baṭṭūṭa as 'probably the offspring of legend and suspicion', and notes that after the 7th/13th century there are no further 'authenticated murders by Syrian Assassins acting for the sect'. While it is clear that al-Yūsufī too liked a good story, the evidence assembled here does suggest that the Ismaʿilis were still active at this later period, though not of course employed in their own cause. Their missions on behalf of the Mamlūk sultan are recounted not with aversion, but with approval and even admiration.

FIFTEEN

The Isma'ili *ginān*s: Reflections on authority and authorship

ALI S. ASANI

AMONG THE literary genres associated with the Isma'ili tradition, the *ginān*s of the Khoja communities of South Asia are unique.[1] Composed in several Indic languages and dialects, these hymn-like poems have been strongly influenced by North Indian traditions of folk poetry and piety.[2] They thus represent a distinctive regional strand within a larger corpus of Isma'ili literature that is mostly in Arabic and Persian. Not surprisingly, the *ginān*s are markedly different in their style and ethos from the more scholarly Arabic and Persian Isma'ili treatises that have usually attracted the attention of researchers.

The apparently 'syncretistic' manner in which the *ginān*s employ Indian or Hindu mythological and theological concepts to present religious ideas has raised questions about their 'Islamic' character.[3] For example, a prominent scholar of South Asian Islam, the late Aziz Ahmad, felt that the *ginān*s possessed a 'literary personality' that is 'un-Islamic', presumably on account of their vernacular and 'syncretistic' characteristics.[4] Such judgements have, in turn, provoked debate within the community concerning the validity of using externals of culture such as language and idiom as yardsticks for measuring Islamic identity.[5] Ironically, in earlier times, when the religious identity of the Khoja community was the subject of intense dispute, the courts of colonial British India drew on evidence from these very hymns to determine that the Khojas were indeed Muslims of the Nizārī Isma'ili persuasion.[6]

For historians of religion, the *ginān*s are of particular interest for the prominent role they play in the religious life of Isma'ili Khoja communities in the Indian subcontinent and elsewhere.[7] Like many genres of Indian devotional poetry, they are intended to be sung in designated *rāga*s or melodies. The singing of *ginān*s constitutes a prominent item during prayer meetings held every morning and evening in the *jamāʿat-khāna*s (halls of congregation). As Tazim Kassam points out, to sing a *ginān* in the context of the Khoja religious practice is to pray. The singing of *ginān*s constitutes ritualized worship, a phenomenon generally characteristic of the Indian religious landscape.[8] Participation in *ginān* singing, especially in a large congregation, can have a powerful emotional and sensual impact on individuals, even those who may not fully understand the meanings and significance of the words they sing. During a particularly melodious *ginān* recitation, it is not uncommon to observe individuals being moved sometimes to the point of tears. An oft-repeated story within the community concerns the penitence and redemption of Ismail Ganji, a not exactly pious Ismaʿili of Junagadh, after he was reduced to tears one evening while he was sitting in the *jamāʿat-khāna* listening to the recitation of a *ginān*.[9]

Beyond their role in worship, the *ginān*s permeate communal and individual life in many ways. At a communal level, functions or meetings, be they religious or secular, frequently begin with a short Qurʾan recitation followed by one from the *ginān*s. Verses from the *ginān*s are often cited as proof-texts during sermons, religious discussions, and in religious education materials. Certain *ginān*s have even been interpreted as predicting modern scientific and political developments such as the atom bomb or the rise of Communism.[10] Occasionally, for both entertainment and religious edification, special concerts or *ginān meḥfil/mushāʿiro* are organized, during which professional and amateur singers recite *ginān*s to musical accompaniment.[11] Again, outside the context of formal worship or liturgy, community institutions responsible for religious education may sponsor *ginān* competitions in which participants are judged on their ability to sing and properly enunciate *ginān* texts. Such competitions are a popular method among religious educators to encourage the learning of *ginān*s among young students and adults.

At a personal and family level, too, *ginān*s are used in many different contexts: individual verses can be quoted as proverbs; verses can be recited in homes to bring *baraka*, spiritual and material blessing; housewives, in a usage that stresses the links between the *ginān*s and the folk tradition, often recite them while working or as lullabies; audio-cassettes with *ginān*s sung by popular singers or recordings of *ginān meḥfil*s can be found in many an Ismaʿili home and even in automobiles!

As I have discussed in a previous article,[12] the *ginān*s enjoy a scriptural status in the Khoja community, for they are commonly perceived as being 'holy' or 'sacred'. Some members of the community declare them to be a 'divine literary corpus',[13] a viewpoint to which not all could comfortably subscribe. The *ginān*s have been described as 'an unbounded and immeasurable sea of knowledge, a unique storehouse of wisdom and guidelines for every day life'.[14] They contain instruction on a broad range of themes, including the religious obligations of the believer, ethics and morals, eschatology, the mystical life and the spiritual quest of the soul. Indeed their function as vehicles for imparting religious teachings and precepts is reflected in their very name which is derived from the Sanskrit word *jñāna*, meaning 'knowledge' or 'sacred wisdom'.

In the community's traditional self-image, the *ginān*s originated in mediaeval times, approximately around the 5th/11th or 6th/12th centuries, when they were first composed by Iranian preacher-saints, called *pīr*s. The *pīr*s were sent to North India by Isma'ili imams from Iran on missions to convert Hindus to Isma'ili Islam and to provide spiritual guidance for the newly-created convert communities. These preacher-saints, tradition asserts, in order to overcome cultural and linguistic barriers facing potential converts, composed *ginān*s to explain the gist of the Qur'an and Isma'ili Islam to Indian populations in their native languages and idioms. According to one community publication, these poetic compositions provided the faithful with an understanding of the 'true meaning' of the Qur'an as well as the true meaning of religion.[15] Another explains that they are living commentaries on the Qur'an,[16] serving to penetrate its 'inner (*bāṭin*) signification'.[17] The *ginān*s were, in effect, 'secondary' texts generated in the vernacular to transmit the teachings of a 'primary' scripture – the Qur'an – to non-Arabic speaking peoples.[18]

The authority of the *ginān*s and the veneration accorded to them is entirely due to their being perceived as substantiations of the truth of the faith as taught by the *pīr*s. For those who revere them, the *ginān*s are sacred since they were uttered by the *pīr*s. These preachers were no ordinary missionaries and evangelists; in the community's understanding, they were spiritually enlightened individuals whose religious and spiritual authority the Isma'ili imams had formally endorsed by bestowing on them the title of *pīr*.[19] The *ginān*s extol the virtues of love for and unquestioning obedience to the *pīr* and his teachings, for he is the true guide (*sat guru*) who can guide the faithful on the path to salvation.[20] Since the imams resided in Iran, the *pīr*s became tangible symbols of the imams' authority in South Asia with total control over the community and its members. W. Ivanow describes their theological position as being the 'link between God and man, really the "door", *bāb*, of the imam, without whose guidance and instruction all efforts of the individual may remain futile and useless'.[21] Not surprisingly, the *pīr*s stand out in the tradition's history as figures of dominating importance, next only to the imam.[22] In fact, in many contexts the *ginān*s do not always distinguish between the *pīr* and the *imām*, both being merged in doublets such as *gur-nar* and *pīr-shāh*, meaning 'guide and lord'.[23]

The most vexing question confronting scholars of the *ginān*s concerns their provenance and authorship. As is the case with many of the poet-saints of mediaeval India, we possess remarkably little accurate historical information about the reputed authors of the *ginān*s and their activities. What we do have, however, are hagiographic and legendary accounts, some of which are incorporated in the *ginān*s themselves. Notwithstanding the admirable attempts made by Azim Nanji to analyze this 'mythic' material, the historical personalities of the *pīr*s remain 'dim and obscure'.[24] In the case of many *pīr*s, we do not possess even basic biographic information such as birth and death dates. In fact, doubts have been cast on the historical existence of Pīr Satgur Nūr, the *pīr* claimed in traditional accounts to have been the first to be sent to India as early as the 4th/10th or 5th/11th century.[25] According to Azim Nanji, this *pīr* remains at best a symbolic and archetypal figure.[26] We are on slightly firmer ground with his successors, Pīrs Shams, Ṣadr al-Dīn and Ḥasan Kabīr al-Dīn, but only just. In addition to a host of problems associated with their biographies, there is much confusion about the exact identities of the first two.[27] A fourth figure, Imām Shāh (d. 919/1513), about whom we possess somewhat more reliable information, was allegedly the founder of a 'schismatic' movement that resulted in the formation of the Imām-Shāhī subsect.[28] Consequently, the Isma'ili Khoja tradition only accords him the status of '*sayyid*', a rank inferior to that of *pīr*. To these four personalities, who reportedly lived between the 6th/12th and 9th/15th centuries, are attributed the vast majority of *ginān*s.

The *ginān*s contain very little evidence to corroborate religious claims that they were composed during the historical period traditionally associated with these early *pīr*s. On the contrary, the linguistic and grammatical features of the *ginān*s, as well as their idioms and style, point to later origins. W. Ivanow, though afraid of offending the sentiments of his Isma'ili friends, declares that in his opinion *ginān*s attributed to a certain *pīr* seem to be more *about* him than *by* him and that there was no doubt about their being composed much later.[29] Christopher Shackle and Zawahir Moir, in their recent study, remark:

No realistic discussion of the ginans is possible without first facing the realization that they are, at least in their present form, of quite recent origin. The linguistic evidence, which reveals a notable lack of discernibly archaic features, is itself a quite sufficient demonstration of the truth of this assertion.[30]

They go on to state quite confidently that many, perhaps most, of those *ginān*s which are attributed to the early *pīr*s are in fact compositions from a later period in the community's history, the so-called 'age of the *sayyids*', which extended from 1500 to 1850 AD.[31] A growing number of studies on works ascribed to individual *pīr*s arrive at similar conclusions concerning authorship. Tazim Kassam's analysis of the *Brahma Prakāśa*, a work attributed to Pīr Shams, points to a much later date of composition than that of the period identified with the *pīr*.[32] My own study of the *Būjh Nirañjan*, attributed to Pīr Ṣadr al-Dīn, demonstrates with a massive array of evidence that this *ginān* was not composed by him but rather by an anonymous individual affiliated with the Qādirī Sufi order.[33] Similarly, evidence from Pyarali Keshwani's study of the *ginān Sī Ḥarfī* suggests a possible Sufi origin for that work as well.[34] Clearly, we are treading here on delicate ground where the results of scholarly research are in open conflict with the truth claims of religious tradition.

The situation become even more complex when one discovers in manuscripts and printed texts that the same *ginān*s are attributed to two or more authors. The *Sī Ḥarfī*, for example, has been variously attributed to Aḥmad Shāh, Nar Muḥammad Shāh and Imām Shāh.[35] Then again the *ginān Allāh ek khasam subuka* has two *pīr*s as authors, Pīr Ṣadr al-Dīn and Pīr Ḥasan Kabīr al-Dīn, raising the possibility of either a joint authorship or perhaps one *pīr* (Ḥasan Kabīr al-Dīn) transmitting the work of an earlier predecessor (Ṣadr al-Dīn).[36] A few *ginān*s have as their authors individuals whose names are associated with Hindu mythological figures such as Sahadeva, the youngest of the five Pandava brothers, and Harishchandra, a king known for his legendary generosity.[37] In several compositions the author's name simply consists of an honorific title, such as *sat gur brahmā* (the divine guide), or *bār gur* (the guide of the twelve), or a compound of terms like Pīr Satgur Nūr, 'the True Guide of Light'. The identity of authors also becomes obscure on account of similar sounding names such as Pīr Indra Imāmdīn, Imām Dīn, and Sayyid Imām Shāh. Tradition believes these names to refer to the same individual, but on the basis of poetic style we may in fact be dealing with three different persons.

Finally, there are a few anonymous *ginān*s, not attributed to any particular *pīr*. The obvious example in this category is the ever popular *Kalām-i Mawlā*, claimed to be an anonymous translation into Hindustani of an Arabic or Persian work allegedly written by the first Shiʿi imam, ʿAlī b. Abī Ṭālib (d. 40/661).[38]

What are we to make of this terribly confused state of affairs? The tradition's claims of authorship of *ginān*s by *pīr*s rest on the fact that in almost every composition there occurs a *bhaṇitā* or 'signature-verse'. This verse, which normally occurs towards the end of the *ginān*, customarily contains the name of a *pīr*. When the *pīr*'s name is mentioned during recitation, members of the congregation demonstrate their respect and devotion to his spiritual authority by bowing their heads slightly and touching with their forefinger the lips and/or the bridge of the nose and the forehead in a bipartite or tripartite gesture.

The *bhaṇitā* is not a poetic feature unique to the *ginān*s. It is in fact an essential element of many genres of South Asian religious poetry including the *pada*, the most popular form of devotional verse in North India. As in the *ginān*s, the *bhaṇitā* containing the name of the poet occurs in the last one or two verses of mediaeval devotional poems as an oral signature. And as is also the case with the *ginān*s, these signatures have been generally interpreted as indications of authorship.

In a ground-breaking study on the role of the *bhaṇitā* in North Indian devotional poetry, John Hawley convincingly demonstrates that this verse signifies authorship in other ways than simply 'writer', as we commonly use the term.[39] Citing definitions of the word 'author' from the *Oxford English Dictionary* – 'a person on whose authority a statement is made . . .', and 'a person who has authority over others . . .' – he argues that the occurrence of a poet's name in a poem points in the direction of authority rather than strictly authorship.[40] For example, in the hymns of the *Guru Grañth Ṣāḥib*, the sacred scripture of the Sikhs, one hears only the name of Guru Nānak, the first *guru* of the community, even in verses known to have been composed by other *guru*s. Guru Nānak's name clearly serves as a symbol of authority rather than personal identity. When the *guru*s after him composed poetry, they did so in his name, invoking his authority.[41]

In support of his contention, Hawley analyzes the *bhaṇitā* in the poetry attributed to prominent poet-saints of the North Indian *bhakti* tradition such as Ravidās, Sūrdās and Mīrābāī. In every case, he shows the many ways in which the authority of the poet in the signature-verse is more significant than the actual fact of composition:

> In devotional Hindi poetry, to give an author's name is not so much to denote who said what as to indicate the proper force of an utterance and the context in which it is to be appreciated. The author's name is no mere footnote. It anchors a poem to life, a personality, even a divinity that gives the poem its proper weight and tone; and it connects it to a network of associations that makes the poem not just a fleeting flash of truth – not just new and lovely – but something that has been heard before and respected, something familiar and beloved.[42]

The *bhaṇitā* serves as a means of 'anchoring' the poem by invoking a poet-saint's authority. In this connection, Hawley also points out that the *bhaṇitā* may also be called *chāp*, 'stamp or seal', a term that indicates its function authoritatively; that what has been said is true and bears listening to.[43] It functions, in a way, as an authoritative seal of approval for the poem.

Several of Hawley's other observations on the *bhaṇitā* are relevant to our discussion on authorship of the *ginān*s. A cursory examination of signature-verses in the *ginān*s shows that the name of the relevant *pīr* is invariably associated with verbs which mean to speak, to say, to utter, to instruct, or to teach. It is on account of phrases such as '*pīr* so-and-so says' that those who revere these hymns and use them in worship, as well as those who study them, have assumed that these signatures signify the simple fact of a *ginān*'s authorship. Significantly, a substantial proportion of *bhaṇitā*s in Hindi devotional poetry, too, either explicitly contain the verb 'to say' or some variant of it or imply it in context. But this should not mislead us. In order to better understand this apparently confusing situation, we need to first examine the relationship of the poetic signature to the rest of the verse and, second, the relationship of the *bhaṇitā* itself to the rest of the poem.

We observe in the diction surrounding the *bhaṇitā*s of the *ginān*s that there is frequently a break in syntax between the name mentioned in the signature and the remainder of the verse. A similar situation exists in Hindi devotional poetry, where this 'grammatical hiatus' in the *bhaṇitā* transfers the responsibility for forming the grammatical connection between the signature and the verse to the listener.[44] Since verbs of actual 'authoring' rarely occur in the *bhaṇitā*s of the *ginān*s or any other mediaeval Indian devotional verse, the interpretation of these verses is fraught with ambiguity. This ambiguity is further compounded by the telegraphic style of poetry so greatly favoured by poets in the tradition. In this regard, Hawley remarks that the 'relation between the signature and the line of which it is a part can be an intricate matter indeed – not at all so simple as the linear "Sūrdās says" or "Ravidās says" would suggest'.[45]

As regards the relationship of the *bhaṇitā* to the entire poem, we can usually notice a subtle change in the direction of the poem when the poet's signature is revealed. The purpose of this shift, Hawley suggests in the examples of poetry he examines, is to convey not only 'authorship' but also to highlight authority.[46] Such a reorientation is characteristic of many *ginān*s where it is marked by dramatic changes in the narrative perspective of the *bhaṇitā*, frequently from the first or third person.[47] Sometimes there will be a prayer or petition:

> Pir Sadruddin says: 'O Master, it is to You that we owe all that we have eaten. If You are merciful, the soul will be delivered.'[48]
>
> Pir Indr Imamuddin, with hope on his lips, has entreatingly said: 'Master, forgive the sins of your community!'[49]

But often the verse will consist of a command, an injunction, or a proverbial religious truth directly addressed to the listener:

> Pir Tajuddin says: 'Magnify the Lord! Only true believers will be rewarded, o brother.'[50]
>
> 'O brother', Pir Imam Shah has said, 'Listen, o brother believers. Let those who would wake remain awake, for the Light has been revealed.'[51]
>
> 'Assemble, o congregations, and perform your devotions', says Pir Sadruddin.[52]
>
> Pir Sadruddin has said: 'If anyone would make his mind understand, then what comes of washing clothes? Discovery comes through cleansing the heart.'[53]

The point to note here is that the *bhaṇitā*, whether it contains an intercessory petition, a command, or a statement of religious truth, invokes in some manner the authority of the *pīr*.

If we now re-evaluate and re-examine the signature-verses of the *ginān*s as being invocations of authority, then some of the confusion on the 'authorship' issue begins to dissipate: the disproportionately large number of compositions attributed to the three or four *pīr*s who, in the community's self-image, played a central or seminal role in the development of the tradition; the inconsistencies of style in works supposedly written by the same author; and the anachronisms of content. All of these points can now be better comprehended. Considering the *bhaṇitā* from this perspective makes it possible to understand that disciples of individual *pīr*s, like those of the *bhakti* poet-saints, could compose poems in the names of their spiritual guides as a way of expressing their spiritual affiliation, as well as their devotion and veneration to their mentors.[54] Furthermore, the *pīr*s' names served to 'anchor' the poems giving them validity and weight, confirming that the teachings contained within them were in conformity with those preached by the great masters. Significantly, the *ginān*s themselves contain some supporting evidence. An obvious example occurs in a popular *ginān*, *Āe raḥem raḥemān*, by the only known female composer Sayyida Imām Begum (d. 1283/1866?). In the *bhaṇitā* of this composition, Imām Begum invokes the name of her *pīr*, Ḥasan Shāh, to validate her teachings, since she herself was not regarded as a *pīr*.[55] Similarly, the *ginān Muṛbañdhjo achoṛo* contains a reference to the effect that it is being recorded by Vimras, a disciple of Pīr Shams. Elsewhere, the *pīr* asks the same disciple to recite *ginān*s to new converts, presumably in his name.[56] In several other cases, some verses specifically indicate that *ginān*s, attributed to Pīr Shams, were uttered by his devotees.[57]

That the name of the *pīr* in the *bhaṇitā* was conceived as a way of 'anchoring' a composition to the Isma'ili *pīr* tradition is also illustrated by the case of the *Būjh Nirañjan*. In my study of this text, I have shown that textual and linguistic evidence overwhelmingly indicates that this *ginān* was composed outside the Khoja tradition, specifically in the Qādirī Sufi order.[58] As a mystical poem, outlining the various stages and experiences on the spiritual path, its general tenor has strong affinity to Isma'ili mystical ideas. Historically, Isma'ili and Sufi relationships, in the Iranian and Indian contexts, have been so intimate that there even developed a style of discourse in Persian that Ivanow has appropriately termed 'Sufico-Ismaili', since works composed in it could be interpreted within both the Sufi and the Isma'ili perspectives.[59] Keeping in mind both the close Sufi–Isma'ili links and the 'authorizing' role of the *bhaṇitā*, we may suggest that the name of Pīr Ṣadr al-Dīn, perhaps the most important personality in the Khoja *pīr* tradition, was added to the *Būjh Nirañjan* not as a way of establishing 'authorship' but as a way of validating its teachings and stating that they were in consonance with the *pīr*'s precepts. It is significant that the signature-verse, which is rather unusual in its phraseology, says: 'Know the path of Pīr Ṣadr al-Dīn which is eternally accepted.' The verse makes no claim of the *pīr* writing the poem; it simply endorses his path and thus his authority.[60] His name serves as a 'stamp of approval', making the work legitimate for his disciples. With it, Isma'ili audiences could interpret the mysticism and esotericism of the *Būjh Nirañjan* within a meaningful Isma'ili context. To view the insertion of the *pīr*'s name as an act of plagiarism or forgery is to miss the point. As Hawley points out, 'the meaning of authorship in devotional India is not what we have come to expect in Europe and America since the Renaissance'.[61]

One more issue pertains to the subject of the origins and authorship of *ginān*s. Khoja tradition itself, as well as scholars who have studied the *ginān*s, concur that these religious poems began as oral literature and for a considerable period in their history were transmitted orally before being recorded in writing in Khojkī, a script peculiar to the community.[62] Though at present very few *ginān* manuscripts date earlier than the 12th/18th century (the earliest recorded manuscript dates to 1149/1736[63]), A. Nanji postulates that the tradition of written transcription may have begun around the 10th/16th century.[64] While no scholar to date has examined the corpus of *ginān*s from the perspective of its oral origins, we have little reason to doubt this theory, especially when we bear in mind parallel traditions of religious literatures in South Asia, such as the *sañt*, the *bhakti*, and the Sufi ones. Shackle and Moir consider a long period of oral transmission very plausible in light of the fact that some older members of the community today can still recite a repertoire of two hundred or more *ginān*s by heart.[65] Nanji, citing evidence concerning the bardic role of the Bhatias of Sind, a caste from which many Khojas seem to have originated, speculates that the teachings of the *pīr*s may have been put to music and sung for adherents by professional bards.[66] My own examination of the role of the *ginān*s in the community's religious life indicates that even today, notwithstanding the existence of printed texts, the *ginān*s function primarily as scripture in their oral/aural dimension.[67]

If the *ginān*s did indeed originate as oral literature and were orally transmitted in their early history, then, from this perspective too, we need to re-evaluate the way in which we have been approaching the issue of their authorship. My late colleague Albert Lord argued that it is a myth to assume that in the oral tradition there are fixed texts which are transmitted unchanged from one generation to another, through an analysis of which one can trace 'original authors'.[68] Songs that are transmitted orally are both synchronically and historically 'fluid' in the sense that performers may change outward forms such as wording, which they consider 'inessential'. Only the basic idea or combination of ideas forming the core of the song remains fairly stable. In other words, Lord observes that:

> His [the singer's] idea of stability, to which he is deeply devoted, does not include wording, which to him has never been fixed, nor the inessential parts of the story. He builds his performance . . . on the stable skeleton of narrative.[69]

Consequently, in the oral tradition, concepts such as 'author' and 'original' have no meaning at all, or they may have a meaning quite different from the one usually assigned to them.[70] The fluidity of the song makes it virtually impossible to retrace the song through the generations of singers to the moment when the first singer performed it; each performance is in a sense an original.[71] It is only with the onset of the written tradition that the 'correct' text is fixed, sounding the death knell for the oral traditional process; singers become reproducers rather than recreators.[72]

Albert Lord's remarks may explain the tremendous variations in *ginān* texts as they are recorded in manuscripts and the 'great latitude' that seems to have existed in the rendering of the originals.[73] But more importantly, they serve as words of caution for societies permeated by the written tradition, societies who feel that for every text there must be an 'original' which can be scientifically attributed to a certain author. If, during part of their history, the *ginān*s did indeed exist as an oral tradition, before they were reduced to writing, then by searching for evidence of 'original authors' in them, we may be asking questions that are illogical and inappropriate. 'Once we know the facts of oral composition', Albert Lord writes, 'we must cease trying to find an original of any traditional song.'[74]

This essay suggests the need for new approaches to the issue of the authorship of the *ginān*s. It argues on several grounds for the need to redefine the manner in which 'authorship' as it applies to these religious poems has been usually viewed. Although the implications of its arguments may seem to challenge traditional religious claims, the essay does not deny that the central core of the *ginān* literary tradition may have in fact been originally initiated by the *pīr*s. Its intent is only to point out that, on account of factors intrinsic to the very nature of these poems, the search for evidence within the *ginān*s themselves to resolve questions of their 'authorship' (as we normally understand this term), will be a frustrating exercise that will only leave us dissatisfied. The application of conventional canons of textual criticism involving the tracing of transmission lines to an ideal archetype or autograph is futile and inappropriate. Between the actual composition of the *ginān*s and their first reduction to a written form lie several generations of singers, reciters and devoted redactors who have left their impress on most of these poems.[75] The more interesting and fruitful questions we need to ask about the *ginān*s concern their 'relational, contextual or functional' qualities.[76] By this we mean the interaction of these religious poems with the people who memorize, recite and listen to them. In the final analysis, texts are 'sacred' only when a religious community can discover religious meaning and truth within them. The ability of the Khoja community to draw inspiration from the *ginān*s, to interpret them, validate them and ultimately invest them with power brings us to the subject of communal authority, a discussion of which we must postpone for another forum.[77]

NOTES

The author is grateful to Sultaan Ali Asani, Michael Currier and Tazim Kassam for their comments on various drafts of this essay.

1 The term Khoja is used in this essay to refer to Nizārī Isma'ilis originating in Sind, Punjab or Gujarāt who hold Aga Khan IV to be their religious leader or imam. Believed to be a popularization of the Persian word *khwāja*, meaning lord or master, the title Khoja was bestowed on Hindu converts to Isma'ili Islam in mediaeval times, apparently to replace the original term *ṭhākur* or *ṭhākkar* (also meaning 'lord, master') used by the Hindu Lohāṇās. Between the mid-nineteenth and early twentieth centuries, various secessionist movements within the larger community resulted in the formation of small Sunni and Ithnā'asharī (Twelver) Shi'i Khoja groups as well. See W. Ivanow, 'Khodja', SEI, pp. 256–257, and W. Madelung, 'Khōdja', EI2, vol. 5, pp. 25–27.

2 For a brief summary of the principal features of the *ginān*s see Ali S. Asani, 'The Ginān Literature of the Ismailis of Indo-Pakistan: Its Origins, Characteristics and Themes', in *Devotion Divine: Bhakti Traditions from the Regions of India*, ed. D. Eck and F. Mallison (Gröningen–Paris, 1991), pp. 1–18, and Christopher Shackle and Zawahir Moir, *Ismaili Hymns from South Asia: An Introduction to the Ginans* (London, 1992).

3 The most dramatic instance of this controversial 'mixing' of traditions occurs in *ginān*s, such as the 'classic' *Dasa Avatāra*, which through a process of mythopoesis, seek to create an ostensible correspondence between the Vaiṣṇava Hindu concept of *avatāra* and the Isma'ili concept of the *imām*. The tenth *avatāra* of the Hindu deity Viśṇu, renamed in the *ginān* tradition as Nakalankī, 'the stainless one', was identified with 'Alī, the first Shi'i imam. Other basic Hindu deities were redirected to significant Islamic personalities: Brahma, for example, was identified with the Prophet Muḥammad while the Prophet's daughter, Fāṭima, was identified with Śaktī and Sarasvatī. See Azim Nanji, *The Nizārī Ismā'īlī Tradition in the Indo-Pakistan Subcontinent* (Delmar, N.Y., 1978), pp. 110–120.

4 Aziz Ahmad, *An Intellectual History of Islam in India* (Edinburgh, 1969), p. 126. As a reaction to such perceptions, recent editions of *ginān*s published by the Isma'ili community have purged terms that could be perceived as 'non-Islamic' or 'Hinduistic',

replacing them with those considered more in consonance with the Islamic tradition.

5 One angry tract on this subject asks: 'Do we think that Islam can be preached and understood only through the medium of Arabic and Persian languages and the same teaching presented in any other [Indic] language should be regarded as a Hindu element?' See 'Observations and Comments on our Modern Ginanic Literature', Paper presented by His Highness the Aga Khan Shia Imami Ismailia Association for Canada at the Ismailia Association International Review Meeting, Nairobi, Kenya, 1980, p. 30.

6 See, for example, the famous Khoja Case of 1866, presided over by the Bombay High Court Judge Sir Joseph Arnould, described in Asaf A. A. Fyzee, *Cases in the Muhammadan Law of India and Pakistan* (London, 1965), pp. 504–549. Evidence from the *ginān*s was also presented before Justice Russell of the Bombay High Court in the Ḥājjī Bībī Case of 1908.

7 Due to a combination of social, economic and political factors, the Khoja community has, since the early twentieth century, established itself in East Africa, Southeast Asia, Western Europe and North America.

8 Tazim R. Kassam, 'Songs of Wisdom and Circles of Dance: An Anthology of Hymns by the Satpanth Ismāʿīlī Saint, Pīr Shams' (Ph.D. thesis, McGill University, 1992), p. 10.

9 *The Great Ismaili Heroes* (Karachi, 1973), pp. 98–99.

10 To cite one example of this trend: a lecture at a communal function in Toronto on 29 January 1982 was entitled, 'Gināns: Prophesies and Science in Gināns'. The use of scriptures as 'scientific proof-texts' is a common phenomenon in the history of religions.

11 In deference to the reluctance among many Muslims to permit the use of musical instruments in explicitly religious contexts, such concerts are not usually held within the premises of *jamāʿat-khāna*s.

12 Ali S. Asani, 'The Ismaili *Ginān*s as Devotional Literature', in *Devotional Literature in South Asia*, ed. R. S. McGregor (Cambridge, 1992), pp. 101–112.

13 His Highness the Aga Khan Shia Imami Ismailia Association for Canada, 'A Suggestive Guide to the Islamic Interpretation and Refutation of the Hindu Elements in our Holy Ginans', Paper presented at the Ismailia Associations International Conference, Nairobi, Kenya, 1979, p. 11.

14 Comments made during a speech by a prominent preacher in Pakistan. See 'The Ismaili Tariqah Board: Two Special Evenings', *Ismaili Mirror* (August, 1987), p. 33.

15 'Observations and Comments on our Modern Ginanic Literature', p. 26.

16 'A Suggestive Guide', p. 20.

17 Ibid., p. 10.

18 Viewed from this perspective, the 'mediating' role of the *ginān*s has its parallels with other works of Islamic literature in the vernacular, such as Mawlānā Jalāl al-Dīn Rūmī's *Mathnawī* (popularly called 'the Qur'an in Persian') or the Sindhi poet Shāh 'Abd al-Laṭīf's *Risālo*, the collection of mystical poetry so sacred to Sindhi-speaking Muslims.

19 '*Pīr*s are appointed by the Imam of the Time, and only such persons can claim to call themselves *Pīr*s. The son, brother or a relative of a *Pīr* cannot on his own accord become a *Pīr* [through inheritance], unless he has been so designated by the Imam of the Time.' See *Collection of Ginans Composed by the Great Ismaili Saint Pir Sadruddin* (Bombay, 1952), foreword p. 3.

20 Shackle and Moir, *Ismaili Hymns*, p. 21.

21 W. Ivanow, 'Satpanth', in *Collectanea*: Vol. 1, ed. W. Ivanow (Leiden, 1948), p. 31.
22 Aziz Esmail, 'Satpanth Ismailism and Modern Changes Within it with Special Reference to East Africa' (Ph.D. thesis, University of Edinburgh, 1971), p. 14.
23 Shackle and Moir, *Ismaili Hymns*, p. 22.
24 Nanji, *Nizārī Ismā'īlī Tradition*, p. 69.
25 Shackle and Moir, *Ismaili Hymns*, p. 7.
26 Nanji, *Nizārī Ismā'īlī Tradition*, p. 61.
27 See Nanji, *Nizārī Ismā'īlī Tradition*, pp. 50–83, and Kassam, 'Songs of Wisdom', ch. 5: Pīr Shams: Problems of Historical Identity, pp. 143–205.
28 See W. Ivanow, 'The Sect of Imam Shah in Gujrat', JBBRAS, NS, 12 (1936), pp. 19–70.
29 Ivanow, 'Satpanth', p. 41.
30 Shackle and Moir, *Ismaili Hymns*, p. 15.
31 Ibid., p. 8.
32 T. R. Kassam, 'Syncretism on the Model of Figure-Ground: A Study of Pir Shams' Brahma Prakāśa', in *Hermeneutical Paths to the Sacred Worlds of India*, ed. Katherine K. Young (Atlanta, 1994), pp. 231–241, as quoted in her thesis 'Songs of Wisdom', p. 9.
33 Ali S. Asani, *The Būjh Nirañjan: An Ismaili Mystical Poem* (Cambridge, Mass., 1991).
34 P. Keshwani, *Sī Ḥarfī: A Ginanic Treatise, Text and Context* (unpublished paper); see especially ch. 2: The Authorship of *Sī Ḥarfī.*
35 Ibid., pp. 105–106.
36 See the text in *Sau ginānjī ćopaḍī ćogaḍīevārī* (Bombay, 1903), pp. 48–50.
37 Tradition claims these Hindu mythological names are epithets of the great Pīr Ṣadr al-Dīn. See Shackle and Moir, *Ismaili Hymns*, pp. 154, 191.
38 See *Kalāme Maulā* (8th edn, Bombay, 1963).
39 John S. Hawley, 'Author and Authority in the *Bhakti* Poetry of North India', *Journal of Asian Studies*, 47 (1988), pp. 269–290.
40 Ibid., p. 270.
41 Ibid., p. 273.
42 Ibid., p. 287.
43 Ibid., pp. 285–286.
44 Ibid., p. 278.
45 Ibid.
46 Ibid., pp. 282–285.
47 Shackle and Moir, too, remark on the directness of speech that characterizes the signature-verses of *ginān*s, where it is a regular commonplace; see their *Ismaili Hymns*, p. 27.
48 Shackle and Moir, *Ismaili Hymns*, *ginān* number 32.
49 Ibid., *ginān* number 11.
50 Ibid., *ginān* number 8.
51 Ibid., *ginān* number 16.
52 Ibid., *ginān* number 30.
53 Ibid., *ginān* number 12.
54 A similar situation is found in the poetry of Mawlānā Jalāl al-Dīn Rūmī (d. 672/1273), the greatest mystical poet of the Persian language, who uses the name of his mentor Shams-i Tabrīz as his own poetic name or *nom de plume*.
55 See *Sau ginānjī ćopaḍī ćālu ginān āgal na ćhapāelā bhāg trījo* (1st edn, Bombay, 1903), p. 108.
56 Nanji, *Nizārī Ismā'īlī Tradition*, p. 13.

57 See *ginān*s number 13, verse 8, and number 37, verse 12, in Shackle and Moir, *Ismaili Hymns*, pp. 86, 132; and *ginān* 68, verses 11–12, in Kassam, 'Songs of Wisdom', p. 319. Dr Kassam translates the word *ginān* here as 'wisdom'.
58 See Asani, *Būjh Nirañjan*, ch. 1, pp. 19–46.
59 W. Ivanow, *Ismaili Literature: A Bibliographical Survey* (Tehran, 1963), pp. 10 ff., 130–131, and 'Sufism and Ismailism: The Chirāgh-Nāma', *Revue Iranienne d'Anthropologie*, 3 (1959), pp. 13–17. See also Azim Nanji's comments: 'The Nizārī *da'wa*, when it entered the Subcontinent, already carried within its repertoire a strain of mysticism rooted in Ismā'īlism but tinged with the Ṣūfic terminology of the time', in his *Nizārī Ismā'īlī Tradition*, p. 126.
60 For a detailed contextual analysis of this *bhaṇitā*, see Asani, *Būjh Nirañjan*, pp. 24–25.
61 Hawley, 'Author and Authority', p. 287.
62 For a fuller description of this script see Ali S. Asani, 'The Khojkī Script: A Legacy of Ismā'īlī Islam in the Indo-Pakistan Subcontinent', JAOS, 107 (1987), pp. 439–449.
63 See Zawahir Noorally [Moir], *Catalogue of Khojki Manuscripts in the Collection of the Ismailia Association for Pakistan* (Unpublished, Karachi, 1971), Ms. 25. See also Ali S. Asani, *The Harvard Collection of Ismaili Literature in Indic Languages: A Descriptive Catalog and Finding Aid* (Boston, 1992).
64 Nanji, *Nizārī Ismā'īlī Tradition*, p. 12. A Gujarātī history of the community, *Khojā Vṛttānt* by S. Nanjiani (Ahmadabad, 1892), pp. 240–250, also notes that Pīr Dādū (d. 1593) was supposedly instructed by the imam to collect the teachings of the earlier *pīr*s and produce a written record.
65 Shackle and Moir, *Ismaili Hymns*, p. 15.
66 Nanji, *Nizārī Ismā'īlī Tradition*, p. 13.
67 Asani, 'The Ismaili *Ginān*s as Devotional Literature', pp. 104–106.
68 Albert Lord, *Singer of Tales* (Cambridge, Mass., 1968), p. 9.
69 Ibid., p. 99.
70 Ibid., p. 101.
71 Ibid., p. 100.
72 Ibid., p. 137.
73 Ivanow, 'Satpanth', p. 41.
74 Lord, *Singer of Tales*, p. 100.
75 I am aware that this statement may appear puzzling to some readers in light of my previous work on the *Būjh Nirañjan*, in which I do consider questions of its provenance. That *ginān*, however, represents a rather unusual case for which there exists a written attestation from independent sources. The presence of a reasonably developed manuscript tradition justifies my approach in this particular case. At present, the only other work in the *ginān* tradition for which we have a manuscript existing outside the community is the *Sī Ḥarfī*. See Keshwani, *Sī Ḥarfī*, ch. 2.
76 I borrow this term from William A. Graham's study of sacred texts, *Beyond the Written Word: Oral Aspects of Scripture in the History of Religion* (Cambridge, 1987).
77 As testimony to the strength of communal authority, we note here that popular compositions attributed to individuals who technically did not have the 'official' status of *pīr*, namely the so-called 'unauthorized *pīr*s', are nevertheless accepted as part of the *ginān* literature. Examples of 'unauthorized' *pīr*s include Imām Shāh (d. 919/1513) and his son Nar Muḥammad Shāh (d. ca. 940/1534), the pivotal figures of a 10th/16th century schismatic group, the Imām-Shāhīs, and the so-called Sayyids who

disseminated religious teaching within the Isma'ili communities in the 12th/18th and 13th/19th centuries. For all intents and purposes, most members of the community do not differentiate in status between these 'unofficial' *ginān*s and those by 'authorized' *pīr*s. Audience appeal is clearly more important than considerations of religious history.

SIXTEEN

The Nuqṭawī movement of Maḥmūd Pisīkhānī and his Persian cycle of mystical-materialism

ABBAS AMANAT

IN THE year 1002 of the Islamic era (1593–1594 AD), at the height of the Ṣafawid persecution of the Nuqṭawī heresy, a certain Darwīsh Kūchak, a *qalandar* from Qazwīn, committed suicide by consuming a large dose of opium. Sought by the Ṣafawid henchmen for his heretical beliefs, just before his death the Nuqṭawī leader told his fellow guards: 'We leave until we return in another cycle' (*raftīm tā dawr-i dīgar biyāʾīm*) and then covered his head with his robe.[1] Darwīsh Kūchak's confidence in his personal reincarnation, if that is what he had in mind, may or may not have proved warranted. The spirit of millenarian renewal, however, which motivated him and many others like him, persisted as it had endured for many centuries in the Persian heterodox milieu. In that respect there was a symbolic truth in Darwīsh Kūchak's word.

The destruction of the Alamūt castle and other Nizārī Ismaʿili strongholds at the hands of the Mongol armies and the dispersal of the Nizārī communities after 654/1256 marked a turning point in Islamic history no less significant than the simultaneous demise of the ʿAbbasid caliphate in Baghdad. The deep-rooted tradition of dissent that for centuries was kept alive by various Ismaʿili trends had now lost its organizational core and its confined fortress community. Pockets of Nizārī resistance in Iran were forced to adopt a cryptic existence often in the garb of Sufi orders. Our knowledge of the post-Alamūt Nizārī Ismaʿilis and their communal endurance in Iran remains scanty, but enough is known to believe that in most cases Nizārī activism was turned into a parochial acquiescence typical of all sectarian religions in their post-revolutionary phase. Not before the end of the 12th/18th century was there a noticeable change in this pattern.

The dynamics of dissent inherent in Ismaʿilism could not have remained dormant infinitely, however. The 8th/14th and 9th/15th centuries witnessed one of the most intense, yet diffuse, phases of 'heterodox' resurgence in the Iranian world with doctrinal features and political consequences akin to Nizārī Ismaʿilism. Ranging from Niʿmat Allāhī and Nūrbakhshī Sufi orders to Ḥurūfī and Nuqṭawī heresies, these movements shared a doctrinal pattern founded on the ideas of cyclical renewal of the sacred time, anticipation for a messianic advent, and hermeneutical (*bāṭinī*) interpretation of the text. The Ṣafawid movement in part owed its making to this vibrant messianic milieu. The Ṣafawid state (907–1135/1501–1722) on the other hand ultimately suppressed and discarded the same messianic spirit in favour of a normative Shiʿism presided over by the Twelver Shiʿi *ʿulamā'*. Official Ṣafawid repression helped the diffusion of these movements into the religiously more receptive environments of Mughal India and Ottoman Anatolia and beyond.

The Nuqṭawī movement was one important, and largely overlooked, product of this dynamic fermentation. By resorting to a nascent materialism with its roots in ancient Greco-Persian beliefs, Nuqṭawism represented a rare example of a conscious departure from Islam. Moreover, an incipient sense of Persian 'national' awareness complemented the Nuqṭawī doctrinal departure. The former characteristic may be seen as a culmination of Qarmaṭī Ismaʿili (and certain Shiʿi *ghulāt*) aspirations to extend the cyclical renewal beyond Islam. The latter characteristic, on the other hand, anticipated the Ṣafawid movement and its Perso-Shiʿi particularism, which was destined to constitute the core of Iran's national ethos. With a religious latitude that was missing in the state-sponsored Shiʿism of the Ṣafawid era, Nuqṭawism, similar to its parent Ḥurūfī movement, provided a crucial link between the religious dissent of the classical Islamic era and its development in the age of Muslim empires in the early modern period.

EARLY HISTORY

That precious little that is known about the early history of Nuqṭawism and the life of its founder, Maḥmūd Pisīkhānī, is based on the evidence recorded almost two centuries later. Like other post-Islamic movements of the Iranian world, the history of Nuqṭawism is largely lost to posterity and may never be recovered. Until such time that new Nuqṭawī texts in the Iranian and Indian collections (if extant) come to light we are bound to rely for the large part on literary and historical accounts by non-Nuqṭawīs.

By piecing together the meagre evidence and applying a critical treatment we can retrieve a hazy picture of the movement's early history and its founder, just enough to highlight the need for further research.[2]

Born in the village of Pisīkhān in the vicinity of Rasht in the Gīlān province (on the southern shores of the Caspian Sea) in the second half of the 8th/14th century, Maḥmūd Pisīkhānī, as he came to be known, began advocating his new religion around 800/1397–1398. We know that the village of Pisīkhān, Maḥmūd's birth place, was the battle ground between the two feuding regions of the Biya-pīsh, dominated by the warlords of eastern Gīlān (based in Lāhījān and Langarūd), and their western Gīlānī rivals of the Biya-pas (based in Fūman and Rasht).[3] A border situation such as this may have had some effect on Maḥmūd's attitude toward political power and its temporality.

It is not clear to what extent, if at all, Maḥmūd's movement was a conscious effort to break away from his contemporary and presumably his mentor, Faḍl Allāh Astarābādī, the founder of the Ḥurūfī movement. To be sure Maḥmūd seems to have owed to Faḍl Allāh much of his cabbalistic symbology and hermeneutics. It is possible that after Faḍl Allāh's execution in 804/1401–1402 at the hands of the Tīmūrid prince Mīrānshāh, Maḥmūd was involved in a power struggle with other leaders of the movement. He may have tried to introduce into Ḥurūfism, then popular throughout northern Iran, the Caucasus and Anatolia, a new chiliastic impetus.[4] Maḥmūd's messianic pronouncements at the turn of the ninth Islamic century were not accidental. Similar to those of Faḍl Allāh, Maḥmūd's call may have been inspired by a popular prophecy attributed to the Prophet Muḥammad which anticipated the advent of an Islamic renewer at the outset of every century (*mujaddid ra's mā'a*). In a pattern familiar to many messianic trends in Islam, Maḥmūd seems to have set out to advocate a message more radical in substance than the existing antinomian movement of Ḥurūfism. Such a dramatic move away from its parent movement may have been the reason why a Ḥurūfī source labelled him as the 'excommunicated Maḥmūd' (*Maḥmūd-i maṭrūd*) for his presumed egocentricity (*anāniyat*). This disparaging title may convey more than personal ambition however given the fact that according to another Ḥurūfī source Maḥmūd was one of the four closest companions of Faḍl Allāh.[5]

Maḥmūd's motives for rupture with Ḥurūfism are indeed evident in his cabbalistic doctrine. In contrast to Ḥurūfism, which emphasized the secrets of the letters, Maḥmūd elaborated a system based on points. As one source puts it, 'he created a system based on a point' (*az nuqṭa kārkhānih pardākht*). In his sixteen books and reportedly his thousand and one treatises he expounded the centrality of the point (*nuqṭa*), an effort which in spite of its popularity among the Nuqṭawī adepts (*umanā'*) was viewed by a pro-Ḥurūfī author as 'embellishments' (*zakhārif*) worthy of eternal damnation.[6] The title of Maḥmūd's most important work, *Mīzān* (*Balance*), which so far has remained lost, also implies a clear cabbalistic connotation. We may surmise that he saw his book as the apocalyptical balance by which the good and the evil are reckoned on the Day of Resurrection, a concept similar to the *furqān* (distinguisher), one of the names of the Qur'an denoting its eschatological property. It is possible that in the *Mīzān* the reckoning for salvation or damnation was determined by means of *jafr* (the science of occult prognostication), a practice common to all Shi'i movements.

Our information about Maḥmūd's reclusive retirement on an unspecified locale on the bank of the Aras River on the frontier of Ādharbāyjān and Arrān (the Caucasus), where he died around 831/1427–1428, is meagre. One may surmise that Maḥmūd's departure from his home province was due to the fact that his guide, Faḍl Allāh, was residing in the Shīrwān region on the northwestern Caspian coast not far from the banks of the Aras River. Maḥmūd's residence was also in the general vicinity of Ardabīl, the convent of the celebrated Shaykh Ṣafī al-Dīn Ardabīlī (d. 735/1334), the founder of the Ṣafawī order which during the course of the 9th/15th century became openly Shi'i. Throughout the Īlkhānid period the capital city of Tabrīz in northwestern Iran was one of the largest metropolises of the Muslim world. Through its commercial outlets to the Black Sea, such as the Byzantine port of Trabzon, it thrived from trade with the principalities of Anatolia, the Armenian and Georgian centres in the Caucasus, and with the venturing Mediterranean city states such as Venice. The impact of this diverse and bustling environment may also be seen in the departure of the Gīlānī 'prophet' from Muslim norms. He practised celibacy and regarded it as the highest status in the hierarchy of his religion, an act of asceticism reminiscent of the Byzantine monastic tradition. Yet reincarnation themes in the Nuqṭawī doctrine along with celibacy may point to an eastern Buddhist (or even Manichaean) influence rampant under the religiously tolerant Mongols.[7]

DOCTRINE AND WORLDVIEW

The idea of cyclical renewal of prophetic revelations was an ancient Zoroastrian legacy present in Islamic Persia and particularly prominent in Isma'ilism. With Nuqṭawism, however, it took a dramatic turn essential for the understanding of Persian religious thought in the Tīmūrid era and beyond. Loyal to the basic theory of cyclical renewal, Nuqṭawism viewed human history as a series of consecutive prophetic cycles each running its course before being superseded by the advent of a new one. The cycles followed an identical pattern in their commencement, duration and termination but this did not mean, at least in its Nuqṭawī rendition, that their renewal was devoid of a forward progression in time.

For Nuqṭawism, however, the doctrine of renewal did not imply an Islamic messianic manifestation in the conventional sense. The advent of the Islamic Mahdi, who often was expected to consolidate the quivering pillars of the faith rather than to dislodge them, was not what Maḥmūd had in mind. Rather, the advent of the new prophet in the Nuqṭawī scheme was to bring to an end the Islamic cycle (*dawr*) altogether and replace it with a new cycle initiated by Maḥmūd himself. Such a departure from one of Islam's most fundamental creeds, namely the eternal nature of the Prophet Muḥammad's divine mission and his status as the 'seal of the prophets' (*khātam al-nabiyyīn*), should be seen as a rare phenomenon in Muslim history. The early Isma'ilis, for instance, came to see their messiah as inaugurating a complementary phase within the Islamic cycle rather than a new era beyond it.

More significantly, this break from Islam was explicitly linked in the Nuqṭwaī writings with the ethnic origin of the new prophet and his teachings. The end of the 'Arab cycle' which was initiated by the Arabian Muḥammad was superseded in the new religion by the 'Persian cycle' (*dawr-i 'ajam*) of Maḥmūd Pisīkhānī who was the 'Persian soul' (*nafs-i 'ajamī*) and the 'unique person' (*shakhṣ-i wāḥid*) of the new cycle. This aspiration to divorce the Arabian religion is traceable, for example, in a verse by an anonymous Nuqṭawī poet who seemed to be stirring the Shu'ūbī sentiments of the bygone times:

> Now is the turn for the fortunate sceptics (*rindān-i 'āqibat maḥmūd*),
> The time is now gone for the Arabs to scold the Persians.[8]

The Persian cycle was the latest phase of a broad cosmological process. According to the Indo-Persian author of the *Dabistān-i madhāhib*, who in the 11th/17th century provided the most succinct exposition of the Nuqṭawī doctrine, Maḥmūd viewed the entire lifetime of the world in terms of four super cycles of 16,000 years each, covering the era between the creation of the world and its termination. Mankind was now still in the first of these super cycles which itself consisted of two successive shorter cycles: the first eight thousand years, Maḥmūd believed, was the Arab cycle which began with Adam, continued with six other prophets, and ended with Muḥammad. The second eight thousand years of the Nuqṭawī cosmology, the Persian cycle, on the other hand, begins with Maḥmūd and would continue after him with seven consecutive manifestations, identified as explicators (*mubayyin*). The first cycle of eight thousand years he defined as super-terrestrial (*fawq-i tharā*), apparently because it was divine in origin and inspiration and thus above the physical world. The Persian cycle on the other hand, was regarded as a sub-terrestrial (*taḥt-i tharā*) cycle, presumably because it was originated in the earth and conceived of human substance. 'When the Persian cycle prevails', declares the *Dabistān*, 'people will discover the truth and worship man and hold the human essence to be the truth'.[9] This contrast between the super-terrestrial and sub-terrestrial may be traced back to Zoroastrian doctrines.

The dichotomy between Muḥammad's and Maḥmūd's respective cycles was further highlighted in the Nuqṭawī sources by celestial symbolism, also akin to Zoroastrian metaphors. Muḥammad is the full moon (*badr*) in the prophetic heavens, but he is also viewed as a herald for the advent of Maḥmūd who is defined as the prophetic sun. The celestial contrast between the lunar chaos and the solar cosmos has long been employed in Iranian belief systems to explain the state of the human microcosm. In the Nuqṭawī belief this metaphor was also tied to the difference between the Arabian/Islamic lunar calendar and the Iranian solar calendar or the 'ancient zodiac' (*burj-i qadīm*), as a Nuqṭawī source recognizes it. Muḥammad's lunar calendar, asserts Maḥmūd, is inferior to the Persian solar calendar. Because the latter is based on twelve fixed months, it is 'accurate and unchangeable and is not like lunar months which are based on full moon, half-moon and crescent'.[10] Whereas Muḥammad is the 'lord of the twenty eight', the cycle of a lunar month, Maḥmūd is the 'lord of the twelve' (*ṣāḥib-i ithnāʿashar*) solar months, an idea which at the same time hints at a veiled affinity with the twelve imams of Ithnāʿasharī Shiʿism. Not only was the rotation of the zodiacal cosmos to be measured by the solar calendar, but Maḥmūd also sought to restore the navel centre of his religious universe. The Nuqṭawīs' special prayer was to be set in the direction of the sun as opposed to the Islamic *qibla*, an act of worship clearly pointing to the Zoroastrian veneration of *mihr*.

Needless to say that emphasis on time reckoning went far beyond its practical function. Adoption of the Persian calendar denoted the end of the Islamic era and the beginning of Iranian times. The alternating lunar calendar indeed provided Maḥmūd with a chance to extend his criticism to other aspects of Islamic religion with the aim of accentuating the superiority of his own. In the same celestial vein the contrast between the two prophets found other allegorical dimensions familiar to the Persian worldview. Whereas Muḥammad is the night, like the dark hair of the beloved, Maḥmūd is the day, like the beloved's countenance (*wajh*). While Muḥammad is created (*jadīd*) as a 'centennial prince' (*mīr-i ṣad*) and a herald (*mukhbir*), Maḥmūd is uncreated (*qadīm*) and is precursor to the 'millennial king' (*pādishāh-i hazār*). Maḥmūd's mission is to be an explicator (*mubayyin*) of the mystery of creation.[11] The nocturnal temporality of Islam, like the dark entangled hair of the divine beloved, shall end in the dawn of her face. The mystical allegorism of Maḥmūd hints unmistakably at the 8th/14th-century poetry of Ḥāfiẓ, a contemporary of his who had the same fascination with Zoroastrianism.

The most dramatic aspect of Nuqṭawī doctrine, however, was its materialist cosmogony and the way it interpreted the course of man's intellectual evolution. In the view of the Persian prophet, all existence primarily originated in the earth (*khāk*, literally, soil), which according to Nuqṭawīs was the source of the other three essential elements. The earth, in Nuqṭawī thought, was the origin of an evolutionary process which occurs over the course of successive cycles. In spite of its seemingly modern attributes, Nuqṭawism shared this pantheistic outlook with Sufism of the Persian school. From the earthly matter (*jamād*), so Maḥmūd advocated, emerged the plants, and from the plants came the animals and from the animals grew the human beings. But in contrast to mainstream Sufism, the Nuqṭawī eschatology viewed man as an earthly being retractable to his earthly origin. 'Once a human being dies and is buried, his bodily organs will revert to material and vegetational modes. Then vegetation is consumed by animals or human beings to appear [once again] in human guise.' Yet the essence of human existence is not all lost. 'All dispersed elemental parts of the body which are worthy of knowledge (*'ilm*) and action (*'amal*) will come back together and will not decompose, whether in the material (non-organic), vegetational, animalistic, or humanly states, even if their composition is broken up.' It is difficult to determine the origin of this reincarnatory eschatology. It may very well be the outcome of a later Indian environment when Nuqṭawism interacted in the Mughal period with Hinduism and Janism.

The Nuqṭawī emphasis on earth as the elemental origin of all beings is significant because it corresponds to the status of man as the earth's ultimate objective and outcome. It may be argued that such a view of man's elemental endurance was forged in order to resolve the problem of corporeal resurrection in Islam. In obvious contrast to the monotheistic religions of the time, which held mankind as a unique creation of God, Nuqṭawism considered man as purely earth bound though still created by God. The statement attributed to Maḥmūd: 'I am the manifest composite' (*anā murakkab al-mubīn*) has an agnostic tone typical of his mystical materialism. Man is no more than an earthly composite (*murakkab*), endowed with a manifest (*mubīn*) mission, a concept reminiscent of a famous verse by his contemporary Ḥāfiẓ:

> Last night I dreamed the angels knocked on the tavern's door,
> Mixing man's clay and casting it out in a cup.

The idea of man's earthly origins is further reinforced by a sense of self-reliance which is epitomized in the Nuqṭawī motto 'Seek help in yourself for there is no god but he' (*istaʿīn bi-nafsik al-ladhī lā ilāh illā hū*). The enigmatic pronoun *hū* (or *huwa*) in the Nuqṭawī context seems to point to man's divine status at the centre of the creation. Nuqṭawī anthropocentric materialism, thus, seems to depart from the sceptic outlook latent in Persian fatalism (*dahriyya*) and is closer in substance to the modern notion of man. Emphasis on knowledge and action, reliance on the self (*nafs*), and belief in an earthly evolution that culminates in man while believing in his composite perishability, point in that direction.

The Nuqṭawīs shared messianic yearnings with other 'extremist' movements, but for them speculation with the letters (*ḥurūf*) took a peculiar essentialist turn. Unlike the Ḥurūfīs, they were not so much concerned with the magical values of the letters and thus, so far as we know, were alien to the *abjad* numerological calculations. Instead, following earlier cabbalistic trends in Sufism (as in Jewish mysticism), Maḥmūd emphasized the significance of the point (*nuqṭa*) as the building block of his symbological system from which first alphabetical letters and then words were constructed. Thus is the conscious recognition of his new religion as *Nuqṭawiyya* (Pointism), his cabbalistic speculations as the 'science of the point' (*ʿilm-i nuqṭa*), and his followers as the People of the Point' (*ahl-i nuqṭa*).[12]

The symbolic adoption of the *nuqṭa* to signify the four essential elements: earth, water, air and fire seem to be unique to Nuqṭawism. The quadrangular compound, represented by four dots as (::) in the Nuqṭawī texts, was at the basis of Maḥmūd's cosmology. Identified as the 'quadrangular essence' (*dhāt-i murabbaʿ*), this cosmology only acquired a structural completion in the Nuqṭawī cycle when the 'fourth essence' (*dhāt-i rābiʿ*), which is the earth element, gained its primal place. Devoid of the 'fourth essence' the remaining 'triangular bond' (*ʿiqd-i thālith*), represented with three dots (.˙.), epitomizes the Muḥammadan cycle. The Muḥammadan versus Maḥmūdian binary is thus played out in full and much to the benefit of the latter. The essential quadrangle (: :) once perfected in its human form, represented by four vertical dots (⁞), denoting the original man, Adam, who is constituted of the four elements and is the fourth and final stage of creation above things, plants and animals. In its most perfect form, however, the original man appears in Maḥmūd himself. He stands in contrast to Muḥammad who is the embodiment of the 'triangular bond' and, therefore, represented in the Nuqṭawī symbology with three vertical dots (⁝). The disparity of one point between the two figures translates in the Nuqṭawī doctrine to a whole range of other differences, which again corresponds to its author's evolutionary view of prophethood.[13]

Beyond an encounter with the 'fourth essence' (*dhāt-i rābiʿ*), which in Maḥmūd's thought is tantamount to an earthly manifestation of a cyclical resurrection, however, the Nuqṭawī doctrine denies the conventional eschatology of Islam, including Paradise and Hell as conventionally understood. The Nuqṭawī anthropocentric Resurrection is tied closely with the progression of man in the course of time and is geared toward understanding his own earthly essence, an association which turns Resurrection into a this-worldly event within the grasp of humanity. Resurrection is an event brought about by man's own deeds in his own lifetime rather than an event beyond his control which will only occur after his death. Likewise, the residents of Paradise are none but the 'People of the Point', who earn their sublime recompense in this world not because they followed the *sharīʿa* but because they recognized the truth of Maḥmūd's religion. In contrast, Maḥmūd's opponents were relegated to the abyss of a this-worldly Hell because they ignored the advent of the new prophet. Emphasis on virtue rather than observation of the dogma (as in Christian Protestantism) was dormant in Nuqṭawism. The fulfilment of the earthly Paradise was also bound up with a certain persistence on the Persian cultural identity.

NUQṬAWISM UNDER THE ṢAFAWIDS AND THE MUGHALS OF INDIA

Beyond the internal evidence of Nuqṭawī catechisms, whatever external evidence is available on Maḥmūd and the early history of Nuqṭawism comes from the Ṣafawid and Mughal sources written almost two centuries after the movement's inception. The noticeable absence of the Nuqṭawīs from the late Tīmūrid and post-Tīmūrid accounts implies that prior to the early decades of the 10th/16th century they were viewed as offshoots of Ḥurūfism or had failed to attract any attention. During the reign of Ismāʿīl I (907–930/1501–1524) and Ṭahmāsp I (930–984/1524–1576), however, for the first time references are made to Nuqṭawism as a heresy harassed and persecuted by the Ṣafawid state. Only after Ṭahmāsp's death, during an interregnum of political instability and conflict prior to ʿAbbās I's accession to the throne in 996/1588, do we witness a revival of Nuqṭawism as a widespread movement with a millenarian message. It is not unlikely that this revival benefited from the policy of religious tolerance of Ismāʿīl II (984–985/1576–1578).

One of the earliest known references to the resurfacing of the Nuqṭawīs is found in the late 10th/16th century *Taʾrīkh-i alfī* (literally, 'the millennial history', for it chronicled the events at the turn of the first Islamic millennium). Under the year 983/1575–1576, it records a revolt by the followers of Maḥmūd (whom the author misidentifies as Maḥmūd Fasākhānī) in the villages surrounding the city of Kāshān. Interestingly, this revolt occurred in conjunction with an uprising in the Ismaʿili village of Anjudān in the Malāyir region led by a certain Murād, a young Nizārī imam with followers in Sind and Makrān. The Nuqṭawī revolt was put down by the Qizilbāsh governor of Hamadān, Amīr Khan Mawṣil-lū, who acted on Shāh Ṭahmāsp's order.[14] The coincidence between the two revolts, which carried over to the period after Ṭahmāsp's death, is not accidental. Although Tatawī is vague about the connection between the two revolts – even though his father directly took part in suppressing the Kāshān revolt – he seems to be suggesting that the followers of Maḥmūd were collaborating with the Ismaʿilis of Anjudān. It is not unreasonable to assume that a revival of Nuqṭawism 'one hundred and fifty years after the death of Maḥmūd', as Tatawī points out, was part of a millenarian awakening that grew upon a network of Ismaʿili and other older religious communities in central and northern Iran.

The Nuqṭawī aspirations persisted, however, after the accession of the greatest of the Ṣafawid kings, ʿAbbās I (996–1038/1588–1629), four years before the end of the Islamic millennium. Nuqṭawī activism is often played down by the pro-Ṣafawid chronicles, yet it must have been acute enough to attract the young ʿAbbās' attention at the shaky start of his reign when he was still grappling with the Qizilbāsh hegemony.

Evidently fascinated by Nuqṭawism and its potential to counterbalance the Shiʿi 'orthodoxy', on several occasions he visited in disguise the convent (*tikkiya*) of a prominent Nuqṭawī leader, Darwīsh Khusraw Qazwīnī. The shāh's favourable leaning toward the Nuqṭawīs, whether out of curiosity or expediency, reflects the growth of the movement among certain segments of the Persian urban population.

Around the year 1000 AH (1591–1592 AD) the movement seems to have reached the height of its popularity. Darwīsh Khusraw, a leading Nuqṭawī, whose views had previously brought him into trouble with the *ʿulamāʾ* and who repeatedly was the subject of inquisitorial examinations and harassments, is blamed by Iskandar Beg Munshī, the author of the *ʿĀlam-ārā-yi ʿAbbāsī*, for luring to his convent the 'low-minded commoners' (*kūtah-khiradān-i ʿawāmm*) and the 'penniless villains among the Turkmen and the Persians (*Turk va Tājik*)'. Yet it is as though he reserves some secret praise not only for Khusraw's taste for the good life, his 'well-kept gardens' and his taste for 'colourful dishes' prepared in the convent's kitchen, but also for the facility with which he had long negotiated his way through theological and juristic ambushes laid for him by the ever-anxious *ʿulamāʾ*. A Ḥāfiẓian *rind*, perhaps, he knew how to sit with the prince and the pauper at the same table. Many nights he entertained ʿAbbās in his convent during the shāh's nocturnal outings around the capital. Yet in spite of his accomplishments and apparent popularity, it was the need for 'implementing the rites of the luminous *sharīʿa*', as Iskandar Beg puts it, that finally obliged the shāh to pay back Khusraw's hospitality by ordering his arrest together with his followers. Conveniently, 'wine jars' were found in his convent and the *ʿulamāʾ* lost no time to discover that Khusraw's 'open-mindedness and ill-beliefs (*wusʿat-i mashrab va bad-iʿtiqādī*) had reached such a level that he is not observing the obligations of the *sharīʿa*'. Condemned to death by the shāh, who now was convinced of Khusraw's Nuqṭawī adherence, he was tied by the neck to a camel's saddle and dragged along the streets of Qazwīn.[15] Earlier on in Fārs a certain Abu'l-Qāsim Amrī, a Sufi poet with Nuqṭawī tendencies who had already been blinded by the order of Ṭahmāsp for his heretical beliefs, was lynched in 990/1582 after the *ʿulamāʾ* pressed against him charges of 'major sedition and rebellion'.[16] But it was Khusraw's murder and the events related to the shāh's temporary abdication which set off in earnest the 'hereticide' (*mulḥid-kushī*) of 1002/1593–1594.

In a seemingly bizarre move in the year 1000/1591–1592, upon the occurrence of an ominous celestial conjunction at the turn of the millennium, ʿAbbās I abdicated in favour of a Nuqṭawī adept, Ustād Yūsufī[-yi] Tarkish-dūz, a master quiver-maker as his name implies. Only three days later the shāh was restored on his throne and Ustād Yūsufī was killed by royal executioners. This temporary investiture was apparently patterned after an ancient Persian annual rite of Spring renewal known as *Mīr-i Nawrūzī*, whereby on the occurrence of the Spring equinox a carnival king presided over the symbolic shift from the chaos to cosmos. In reality, however, the episode was symptomatic of ʿAbbās' concern with the Nuqṭawī millenarian prophecies. It aimed at preventing celestial misfortunes from falling on the real shāh, a pre-emptive measure against a millennial calamity propagated by the Nuqṭawīs and awaited by the public. Even through the pro-Ṣafawid accounts of Iskandar Beg Munshī and Mullā Jalāl Munajjim Yazdī, the royal astrologer and the chief instigator of the anti-Nuqṭawī campaign who oversaw the shāh's temporary sidestep, it is possible to see flashes of Nuqṭawī popularity among the urban guilds and the dervishes. 'It became apparent', writes Iskandar Beg, 'that in the guarded realms [of Iran] the number of these people who strive for heedlessness has greatly increased.'

In the ensuing wave of persecution and mass killing that was championed by the shāh and blessed by the *ʿulamāʾ*, a large number of the leading Nuqṭawīs were slain and communities of the Nuqṭawīs in Kāshān (particularly in Naṣrābād), Iṣfahān, Iṣṭahbānāt (in Fārs) and Qazwīn were massacred. Darwīsh Yūsufī himself, as Iskandar Beg euphemistically puts it, 'was stripped from the garb of life and fell from the throne onto the mortuary board'. The fate of another prominent Nuqṭawī, Mawlānā Sulaymān Sāwujī, a physician from Sāwa who was 'the most learned' of the Nuqṭawīs, was referred to the *ʿulamāʾ*. Fearful of the 'backlash of the heedless ruffians', no doubt a reference to his supporters among the city inhabitants, the *ʿulamāʾ* opted for his temporary detention but the '*sharīʿa*-nurturing' shāh who regarded his elimination equal to a *ḥajj* pilgrimage insisted on his death. Likewise, Mīr Sayyid Aḥmad Kāshānī, another Nuqṭawī leader, captured in the village of Naṣrābād in the vicinity of Kāshān, was cut in half on the spot by the shāh's own sword.[17]

Driven away from the 'guarded domains' of the Ṣafawid empire many Nuqṭawīs immigrated to the neighbouring Mughal (Indo-Tīmūrid) empire even before the massacre of 1002/1593–1594. There, they found a refuge in the court of emperor Akbar (963–1014/1556–1605) and an enthusiastic listener in the person of his celebrated adviser Abu'l-Faḍl

ʿAllāmī, the author of *Akbar-nāma*. The Nuqṭawī revolt in Iran was crushed in its inception but its intellectual residue endured and contributed to the court culture of Mughal India. The Persian Nuqṭawīs and their Indian sympathizers found the great emperor a more plausible candidate for the 'millennial king' and his court became a venue for debates among representatives of different religious traditions (including the Zoroastrian Pārsīs and the Portuguese Jesuit missionaries) and inter-confessional innovation. ʿAbd al-Qādir Badā'ūnī, the chief chronicler of Akbar's era and himself a staunch Sunni, holds the Nuqṭawīs in Akbar's court responsible for the dissemination of millenarian prophecies. The emperor was so influenced by Nuqṭawī views, Badā'ūnī implies, to declare himself the prophet of what came to be known as the 'divine religion' (*dīn-i ilāhī*) and advocate the doctrine of 'universal conciliation' (*ṣulḥ-i kull*). Indeed, a prominent Nuqṭawī scholar and a refugee to the Mughal court, Mīr Sharīf Āmulī, seems to have been a source of intellectual inspiration for Akbar and his minister Abu'l-Faḍl ʿAllāmī, the architect of 'universal conciliation'. Āmulī and other Nuqṭawīs in Akbar's court drew upon Maḥmūd Pisīkhānī's prophecies to speculate on the advent of a 'remover of falsehood' in the year 990/1582 which, as they saw it, implied the abrogation of Islam by Akbar at the end of the millennium. Khwāja Mawlānā Shīrāzī, a Nuqṭawī specializing in *jafr*, offered to Akbar a *Risāla* presumably from the *sharīf*s of Mecca which, on the bases of the Islamic *ḥadīth*, predicted the impending doomsday and the advent of the Mahdi at the end of the seventh millennium from the time of Adam. Corresponding to Maḥmūd's super-cycles, the idea of seven millennial cycles was long popular among Ismaʿilis and other Shiʿi communities. Similarly, among other 'Shiʿi superstitions', so Badā'ūnī puts it, the Nuqṭawīs relied on a chiliastic quadrant attributed to the Ismaʿili poet and philosopher Nāṣir-i Khusraw:

> In the year nine hundred and ninety by the ordinance of the fate,
> Gather all the stars in one place.
> In the year Leo, month Leo, day Leo,
> Walks out from behind the curtain the God's lion.

Badā'ūnī believed that it was such insinuations that persuaded Akbar 'to claim prophethood (*nubuwwa*) in all respects but name', for he was the 'lord of the age' (*ṣāḥib al-zamān*) and 'God's lion' (*asad Allāh*) who, as Nuqṭawīs insisted, removed the communal barrier between the seventy-two nations (*haftād-u du millat*) of Muslim and Hindu persuasions.[18]

After Akbar, the court patronage of Nuqṭawism gradually subsided before finally turning into open hostility under Awrangzīb in the middle of the 11th/17th Century. Sarmad Kāshānī, a Persian Sufi poet of Jewish origin who later seems to have adopted Janist views and practices in India, is the last important Nuqṭawī known to us. A protege and companion of the celebrated Mughal prince and scholar, Dārā Shukōh, son of Shāh Jahān, he was executed when the *'ulamā'* issued a *fatwā* condemning him to death soon after the prince's defeat by his half-brother Awrangzīb and his subsequent murder in 1069/1659. This marked the end of the Nuqṭawīs' unhampered activities in India for close to a century. It was also an end to a remarkable age of religious innovation and communal tolerance under the early Mughal emperors.[19]

The diffused Nuqṭawī impact on the Perso-Indian environment was not depleted altogether. In the middle of the 11th/17th century, the author of the *Dabistān-i madhāhib*, himself presumably a Pārsī priest (*mu'bad*) and a product of the confessional syncretism of Mughal India, could still meet Perso-Indian Nuqṭawī writers and poets in the North Indian intellectual capital, Lahore, and record a summary account of their beliefs as a distinct 'sectarian' creed. Even as late as the middle of the 13th/19th century from time to time the wandering dervishes of Jalālī and Khāksār affiliations with eclectic *qalandarī* tendencies uttered views reminiscent of Nuqṭawīsm. No reference to their hierarchical or communal existence however has come to light.

The Nuqṭawī texts may have also continued to be read in the mystical and 'heterodox' circles up to the 13th/19th century. The striking resemblance between the ideas of Sayyid 'Alī Muḥammad Shīrāzī, the Bāb (1236–1266/1821–1850), the founder of the Bābī movement, and the beliefs and practices of Nuqṭawism is too explicit to be attributed solely to the diffuse esotericism (*bāṭinī*) of the Persian 'heterodox' milieux.[20] Nor could such an affinity be solely assigned to the Shaykhī school whose founder, Shaykh Aḥmad Aḥsā'ī (d. 1241/1825), was indirectly influenced by Isma'ili-related themes, as was his successor, Sayyid Kāẓim Rashtī (d. 1259/1844).

During the 10th/16th and 11th/17th centuries, some poets and literary figures of the 'Indian' school were inspired by Nuqṭawī themes even at the risk of harassment by the *'ulamā'*. Their lives and works deserve an independent examination but even as early as the late-Tīmūrid era traces of Nuqṭawī themes may be detected in the poetry of Iran and in no less a prominent contemporary of Maḥmūd Pisīkhānī than Ḥāfiẓ of Shīrāz (d. ca. 792/1390). Ḥāfiẓ's allusions may indeed be counted among the earliest evidence of the popularity of Nuqṭawī themes. The author of the *Dabistān* recognizes Ḥāfiẓ as a Nuqṭawī sympathizer. For this claim he relies on the word of an anonymous Nuqṭawī, possibly a Shīrāzī friend of the author in Lahore. To buttress his claim he also quotes a famous, and indeed enigmatic, verse from the poet:

> O, zephyr (*ṣabā*)! When passing by the banks of River Aras,
> Kiss the soil (*khāk*) of the plain and sweeten your breath.[21]

Whether this is an allusion to Maḥmūd who was residing on the bank of Aras in northern Ādharbāyjān, so that Ḥāfiẓ symbolically salutes Maḥmūd's veneration of the earth, is a matter of interpretation. There are enough references in Ḥāfiẓ's poetry to *nuqṭa*, the change of cycle (*dawr*), man's earthly creation and resurrection, and enough scepticism about the Islamic hereafter to merit a separate study.

The paucity of data makes it difficult to determine the connections between Nuqṭawism and Isma'ilism. What evidence remains is circumstantial. Nuqṭawism, one may conjecture, absorbed certain values dormant in later Isma'ilism: millenarian aspirations based on cyclical renewal, preoccupation with occult sciences, and symbolic explanation of Resurrection. Hierarchical grading and missionary appeal to the non-elite urban and rural populace as well as to the intelligentsia were also common between the two. Geographical distribution of Nuqṭawism may also have matched the pattern of the crypto-Isma'ili centres in post-Mongol Iran. Yet there are fundamental differences. Nuqṭawism did not conceive the inward–outward (*bāṭin–ẓāhir*) dichotomy in the same fashion as Isma'ilism, which never departed from the boundaries of Shi'i Islam. This can be explained by the Nuqṭawī movement's aspirations to bring about in this world a millenarian utopia free from the concealment of the *bāṭin* or the auspices of a hidden or revealed imam. To achieve it, the Nuqṭawīs seem to have favoured a benevolent ruler who could merge political and religious legitimations. In this context Nuqṭawism anticipated the incipient Ṣafawid Shi'ism.

The time-honoured cord that tied the twin siblings, the 'just ruler' and the 'good religion', and keystone of social order in the Perso-Islamic system, was too strong to be ruptured with the Nuqṭawīs' millenarian agnosticism. What seemed in another time and place, for instance Europe of the Enlightenment, a plausible proposition for reshaping human thoughts and societies, was destined to be labelled a heresy in its own world and witness suppression while the religious conservatives of the Ṣafawid and late Mughal eras closed their ranks.

NOTES

1 Iskandar Beg Munshī, *Ta'rīkh-i 'ālam-ārā-yi 'Abbāsī*, ed. Ī. Afshār (Tehran, 1334–1335/1955–1956), vol. 2, pp. 475–476. Iskandar Beg eulogizes Darwīsh Kūchak's death with a sarcastic hemistich: 'He has gone and gone and gone and gone and is still going.'

2 Beyond Ṣādiq Kiyā's pioneering work, *Nuqṭawiyān yā Pisīkhāniyān* (Tehran, 1320/1941), there is no critical treatment of the history and doctrines of Nuqṭawism. Kiyā's collection of primary material is superseded neither by A. Bausani's entry in EI2 nor by the ideologically coloured rehash of 'A. Mīrfiṭrūs, *Junbish-i Ḥurūfiyya va nihḍat-i Pisīkhāniyān 'Nuqṭawiyān'* (Tehran, 1356/1976). Paucity of primary sources and lack of access to the surviving Nuqṭawī manuscripts have obliged most scholars to rely on Kiyā's gleanings from historical sources, biographical dictionaries and selections of the Nuqṭawī writings, the only fragments so far published.

3 Mīrfiṭrūs, *Junbish*, p. 60.

4 For the Ḥurūfī movement, see H. Ritter, 'Studien zur Geschichte der islamischen Frömmigkeit, II: Die Anfänge der Ḥurūfīsekte', *Oriens*, 7 (1954), pp. 1–54; Persian trans. by Ḥ. Mu'ayyad as 'Āghāz-i firqa-yi Ḥurūfiyya', in *Farhang-i Īrānzamīn*, 10 (1341/1962), pp. 319–393; E. G. Browne, 'Some Notes on the Literature and Doctrines of the Ḥurūfī Sect', JRAS (1898), pp. 61–94, and his 'Further Notes on the Literature of the Hurufis and their Connection with the Bektashi Order of Dervishes', JRAS (1907), pp. 533–581; *Textes Persans relatifs à la secte des Ḥouroūfīs*, ed. C. Huart (London, 1909); Ṣ. Kiyā, *Vāzhih-nāma-yi Gurgānī* (Tehran, 1330/1951), and A. Bausani 'Ḥurūfiyya', EI2, vol. 3, pp. 600–601.

5 Kiyā, *Vāzhih-nāmā*, p. 26, and Ritter (Persian trans.), pp. 328, 367, 375.

6 Taqī al-Dīn Awḥadī Baliyānī, *'Arafāt-i 'āshiqīn*, MS. Malik Library, cited in Kiyā, *Nuqṭawiyān*, p. 58.

7 Scanty reference to Maḥmūd's life appears primarily in the anonymous *Dabistān-i madhāhib*, ed. R. Riḍāzāda Malik (Tehran, 1362/1983), pp. 273–278; English trans., *The Dabistān, or School of Manners*, tr. D. Shea and A. Troyer (London, 1901), pp. 337–344. The *Dabistān* is the only source which refers to the Nuqṭawīs as *Wāḥidiyya* (Unitarians). In addition to the nomenclature *Nuqṭawiyya*, most hostile Ṣafawid and Mughal accounts identify them with the generic term *mulḥid* (heretic), and occasionally as followers of Pisīkhānī (Pisīkhāniyān). Nuqṭawism is occasionally identified as 'Maḥmūd's religion' (*dīn-i Maḥmūd*). See Kiyā, *Nuqṭawiyān*, p. 5, for further sources on Maḥmūd's life.

8 *Rasīd nawbat-i rindān-i 'āqibat maḥmūd/gudhasht ānkih 'Arab ṭa'na bar 'ajam mīzad* (*Dabistān*, p. 276). Both *rind* and *maḥmūd* are intentional puns with obvious Nuqṭawī connotation.

9 *Dabistān*, p. 275.

10 Nuqṭawī catechism, cited in Kiyā, *Nuqṭawiyān*, p. 84. Identified by Kiyā as 'a Nuqṭawī work' (*niwishtih-yi Nuqṭawī*), this catechism is apparently authored by a certain Abu'l-Maryam in 820/1417–1418 and at the time of Kiyā's writing was in private hands. The original manuscript consist of 188 folios but Kiyā only cites excerpts in the appendix.

11 Catechism, Kiyā, *Nuqṭawiyān*, p. 76.

12 Catechism, Kiyā, *Nuqṭawiyān*, pp. 102, 120–121.

13 Ibid., pp. 84–86.

14 Aḥmad b. Naṣr Allāh Qāḍīzāda Tatawī, MS. Malik Library, cited in Kiyā, *Nuqṭawiyān*, no. 13, p. 36. The same Isma'ili revolt is cited in Qāḍī Mīr Aḥmad Munshī Qummī's *Khulāṣat al-tawārīkh*, ed. I. Ishrāqī (Tehran, 1359/1980), vol. 1, pp. 582–584, under the year 981/1573–1574 but with no explicit reference to the Nuqṭawīs.

15 Iskandar Beg, *'Ālam-ārā*, vol. 2, p. 476.

16 Awḥadī Baliyānī, *'Arafāt-i 'āshiqīn*, in Kiyā, *Nuqṭawiyān*, pp. 59–60.

17 Iskandar Beg, *'Ālam-ārā*, vol. 2, p. 476. Darwīsh Yūsuf's story was a source of inspiration for another antinomian of later times. Mīrzā Fatḥ 'Alī Ākhūndzāda's Persian play *Sitārihgān-i farīb khurdih yā ḥikāyat-i Yūsuf Shāh Sarrāj* [Betrayed Stars or the Story of Yūsuf Shāh, the Saddler], first published in Tiflīs (Tbilisi) in 1857 is a sympathetic dramatization of Yūsuf's ephemeral reign and the Nuqṭawī massacre of 1593.

18 'Abd al-Qādir Badā'ūnī, *Muntakhab al-tawārīkh* (Calcutta, 1865–1869), vol. 2, pp. 286–288.

19 For Sarmad, see Jalālī Nā'īnī's introduction to Dārā Shukōh's Persian translation of the *Upanishads* entitled *Sir-i akbar*, ed. Ḥ. Jalālī Nā'īnī (Tehran, 1340/1961), pp. 129–130, 246.

20 The points of affinity between the Nuqṭawī and the Bābī doctrines have been alluded (beyond Kiyā's brief reference in his *Nuqṭawiyān*, p. 15n) in A. Amanat, *Resurrection and Renewal: The Making of the Babi Movement in Iran, 1844–1850* (Ithaca, 1989), pp. 13–14, 144–145, 333.

21 *Dabistān*, p. 277.

Bibliography

The bibliography includes some basic works of reference and a selection of the published sources cited in the notes to the individual chapters. The abbreviations used in the bibliography are the same as those used in the notes. For a list of these abbreviations see page xiii.

WORKS OF REFERENCE

Asani, Ali S. *The Harvard Collection of Ismaili Literature in Indic Languages: A Descriptive Catalog and Finding Aid*. Boston, 1992.

Bacharach, Jere L. *A Middle East Studies Handbook*. Cambridge, 1984.

Behn, Wolfgang H. *Index Islamicus, 1665–1905*. Millersville, Pa., 1989.

Berthels, Andrei E. and Baqoev, M. *Alphabetic Catalogue of Manuscripts found by 1959–1963 Expedition in Gorno-Badakhshan Autonomous Region*, ed. B. G. Gafurov and A. M. Mirzoev. Moscow, 1967.

Bosworth, C. Edmund. *The Islamic Dynasties: A Chronological and Genealogical Handbook*. Revised edn, Edinburgh, 1980.

Brockelmann, Carl. *Geschichte der arabischen Litteratur*. 2nd edn, Leiden, 1943–1949.

Geschichte der arabischen Litteratur. Supplementbände. Leiden, 1937–1942.

Dā'irat al-ma'ārif-i buzurg-i Islāmī [*The Great Islamic Encyclopaedia*], ed. K. Musavi Bojnurdi. Tehran, 1367– /1989–

Encyclopaedia Iranica, ed. E. Yarshater. London, 1982–

The Encyclopaedia of Islam, ed. M. Th. Houtsma et al. 1st edn, Leiden–London, 1913–1942; reprinted, Leiden, 1987.

The Encyclopaedia of Islam, ed. H. A. R. Gibb et al. New edn, Leiden–London, 1960–

The Encyclopedia of Religion, ed. M. Eliade. London–New York, 1987.

Freeman-Grenville, G. S. P. *The Muslim and Christian Calendars*. 2nd edn, London, 1977.

Gacek, Adam. *Catalogue of Arabic Manuscripts in the Library of the Institute of Ismaili Studies*. London, 1984–1985.

Goriawala, Muʿizz. *A Descriptive Catalogue of the Fyzee Collection of Ismaili Manuscripts*. Bombay, 1965.

The Great Ismaili Heroes, ed. A. R. Kanji. Karachi, 1973.

Handbook of Oriental History, ed. C. H. Philips. London, 1951.

Handwörterbuch des Islam, ed. A. J. Wensinck and J. H. Kramers. Leiden, 1941.

Ivanow, Wladimir. *A Guide to Ismaili Literature*. London, 1933.

Ismaili Literature: A Bibliographical Survey. Tehran, 1963.

Lane-Poole, Stanley. *The Mohammadan Dynasties*. London, 1894.

Modarressi Tabātabā'i, Hossein. *An Introduction to Shīʿī Law: A Bibliographical Study*. London, 1984.

Netton, Ian R. *A Popular Dictionary of Islam*. London, 1992.

Pearson, James D. *Index Islamicus, 1906–1955*. Cambridge, 1958.

Index Islamicus, Supplement. Cambridge–London, 1962–

Poonawala, Ismail K. *Biobibliography of Ismāʿīlī Literature*. Malibu, Calif., 1977.

Sauvaget, Jean. *Introduction to the History of the Muslim East: A Bibliographical Guide*, English translation based on the second edition as recast by Claude Cahen. Berkeley, 1965.

Sezgin, Fuat. *Geschichte des arabischen Schrifttums*. Leiden, 1967–

Shorter Encyclopaedia of Islam, ed. H. A. R. Gibb and J. H. Kramers. Leiden, 1953.

Storey, Charles A. *Persian Literature: A Bio-bibliographical Survey*. London, 1927– . Revised Russian trans., *Persidskaya literatura: Bio-bibliograficheskii obzor*, ed. and tr. Yu. E. Bregel. Moscow, 1972. Persian trans., based on the Russian version, *Adabiyyāt-i Fārsī*, tr. Y. Āriyanpūr et al. Tehran, 1362– /1983–

Tajdin, Nagib. *A Bibliography of Ismailism*. Delmar, N.Y., 1985.

Zambaur, E. de. *Manuel de généalogie et de chronologie pour l'histoire de l'Islam*. Hanover, 1927.

PRIMARY SOURCES: TEXTS AND TRANSLATIONS

ʿAbd al-Jabbār b. Aḥmad al-Hamadhānī. *Tathbīt Dalāʾil al-nubuwwa*, ed. ʿA. ʿUthmān. Beirut, 1966–1968.

Abu'l-Fidā, al-Malik al-Mu'ayyad ʿImād al-Dīn Ismāʿīl b. ʿAlī. *The Memoirs of a Syrian Prince*, tr. P. M. Holt. Wiesbaden, 1983.

Abū Firās, Shihāb al-Dīn al-Maynaqī. *Risālat maṭāliʿ al-shumūs*, ed. ʿĀ. Tāmir, in his *Arbaʿ rasāʾil Ismāʿīliyya*. Salamiyya, 1952, pp. 27–57.

Akhbār al-Qarāmiṭa, ed. S. Zakkār. Damascus, 1400/1980.

al-Āmir bi-Aḥkām Allāh, Abū ʿAlī al-Manṣūr. *al-Hidāya al-Āmiriyya*, ed. A. A. A. Fyzee. Bombay, etc., 1933, reprinted in *Majmūʿat al-wathāʾiq al-Fāṭimiyya*, ed. J. al-Shayyāl. Cairo, 1958, pp. 203–230.

al-Anṭākī, Yaḥyā b. Saʿīd. *Taʾrīkh*, ed. L. Cheikho et al. Paris–Beirut, 1909; partial ed. and French trans. I. Kratchkovsky and A. A. Vasiliev, *Histoire de Yahya-Ibn-Saʿïd d'Antioche*, in *Patrologia Orientalis*, 18 (1924), pp.

699–833, and 23 (1932), pp. 347–520.
ʿArīb b. Saʿd al-Qurṭubī. *Ṣilat taʾrīkh al-Ṭabarī*, ed. M. J. de Goeje. Leiden, 1897.
al-Ashʿarī, Abu'l-Ḥasan ʿAlī b. Ismāʿīl. *Kitāb maqālāt al-Islāmiyyīn*, ed. H. Ritter. Istanbul, 1929–1930; reprinted, Wiesbaden, 1963.
al-Baghdādī, Abū Manṣūr ʿAbd al-Qāhir b. Ṭāhir. *al-Farq bayn al-firaq*, ed. M. Z. al-Kawtharī. Cairo, 1948. English trans. under the title *Moslem Schisms and Sects*, part I, tr. K. C. Seelye. New York, 1919; part II, tr. A. S. Halkin. Tel Aviv, 1935.
al-Bīrūnī, Abu'l-Rayḥān Muḥammad b. Aḥmad. *al-Āthār al-bāqiya*, ed. C. E. Sachau. Leipzig, 1878. English trans. C. E. Sachau, *The Chronology of the Ancient Nations*. London, 1879.
al-Bundārī, al-Fatḥ b. ʿAlī. *Zubdat al-nuṣra wa-nukhbat al-ʿuṣra*, ed. M. Th. Houtsma. Leiden, 1889.
Commentaire de la Qasida Ismaélienne d'Abu'l-Haitham Jorjani, attributed to Muḥammad b. Surkh al-Nīsābūrī, ed. H. Corbin and M. Muʿīn. Tehran–Paris, 1955.
Dabistān-i madhāhib, ed. R. Riḍāzāda Malik. Tehran, 1362/1983. English trans. D. Shea and A. Troyer, *The Dabistān, or School of Manners*. London, 1901.
al-Daylamī, Muḥammad b. al-Ḥasan. *Bayān madhhab al-Bāṭiniyya wa-buṭlānuhu*, ed. R. Strothmann. Istanbul, 1939.
Eutychii Patriarchae Alexandrini Annales, anonymous continuation of Eutychius (Saʿīd b. Biṭrīq), ed. L. Cheikho et al. Paris, 1909.
al-Ghazālī, Abū Ḥāmid Muḥammad. *Faḍāʾiḥ al-Bāṭiniyya*, ed. ʿAbd al-Raḥmān Badawī. Cairo, 1964. Abbreviated edition with commentary, in I. Goldziher, *Streitschrift des Ġazālī gegen die Bāṭinijja-Sekte*. Leiden, 1916.
Ḥāfiẓ Abrū, ʿAbd Allāh b. Luṭf ʿAlī al-Bihdādīnī. *Majmaʿ al-tawārīkh al-sulṭāniyya; qismat-i khulafā-i ʿAlawiyya-yi Maghrib va Miṣr va Nizāriyān va rafīqān*, ed. M. Mudarrisī Zanjānī. Tehran, 1364/1985.
Haft bāb-i Bābā Sayyidnā, ed. W. Ivanow, in his *Two Early Ismaili Treatises*. Bombay, 1933, pp. 4–44. English trans. M. Hodgson, in his *Order of Assassins*, pp. 279–324.
Ḥamd Allāh Mustawfī Qazwīnī. *Taʾrīkh-i guzīda*, ed. ʿA. Navāʾī. Tehran, 1339/1960.
al-Ḥimyarī, Nashwān b. Saʿīd. *al-Ḥūr al-ʿīn*, ed. K. Muṣṭafā. Cairo, 1948.
Ḥudūd al-ʿālam, ed. M. Sutūda. Tehran, 1340/1961. English trans. V. Minorsky, *Ḥudūd al-ʿĀlam, the Regions of the World*. 2nd edn, London, 1970.
al-Ḥusaynī, Ṣadr al-Dīn Abu'l-Ḥasan ʿAlī b. Nāṣir. *Akhbār al-dawla al-Saljūqiyya*, ed. M. Iqbāl. Lahore, 1933.
Ibn ʿAbd al-Ẓāhir, Muḥyi'l-Dīn Abu'l-Faḍl ʿAbd Allāh. *al-Rawḍ al-zāhir fī sīrat al-Malik al-Ẓāhir*, ed. A. A. Khowaiter. Riyadh, 1976.
Ibn al-Athīr, ʿIzz al-Dīn Abu'l-Ḥasan ʿAlī b. Muḥammad. *al-Kāmil fi'l-taʾrīkh*, ed. C. J. Tornberg. Leiden, 1851–1876.
Ibn Baṭṭūṭa, Shams al-Dīn Abū ʿAbd Allāh Muḥammad b. ʿAbd Allāh al-Ṭanjī.

Riḥla, tr. H. A. R. Gibb and C. F. Beckingham under the title *The Travels of Ibn Baṭṭūṭa*. Cambridge, 1958–1994.

Ibn al-Dawādārī, Abū Bakr b. ʿAbd Allāh. *Kanz al-durar*, vols. 6–9, ed. Ṣ. al-Munajjid et al. Cairo, 1961–1971.

Ibn Faḍl Allāh al-ʿUmarī, Shihāb al-Dīn Aḥmad b. Yaḥyā. *Masālik al-abṣār fī mamālik al-amṣār*, ed. A. Fu'ād Sayyid. Cairo, 1985.

Ibn Ḥammād, Abū ʿAbd Allāh Muḥammad b. ʿAlī. *Akhbār mulūk Banī ʿUbayd*, ed. and tr. M. Vonderheyden. Algiers–Paris, 1927.

Ibn Ḥawqal, Abu'l-Qāsim b. ʿAlī al-Naṣībī. *Kitāb ṣūrat al-arḍ*, ed. J. H. Kramers. 2nd edn, Leiden, 1938–1939. French trans. J. H. Kramers and G. Wiet, *Configuration de la terre*. Paris, 1964.

Ibn Ḥawshab, Abu'l-Qāsim al-Ḥasan b. Faraj Manṣūr al-Yaman. *Kitāb al-rushd wa'l-hidāya*, ed. M. Kāmil Ḥusayn, in *Collectanea*: Vol. 1, ed. W. Ivanow. Leiden, 1948, pp. 185–213. English trans. W. Ivanow, 'The Book of Righteousness and True Guidance', in his *Studies in Early Persian Ismailism*, pp. 29–59.

Ibn Ḥazm, Abū Muḥammad ʿAlī b. Aḥmad. *Kitāb al-fiṣal fi'l-milal*. Cairo, 1317–1321/1899–1903.

Ibn ʿIdhārī al-Marrākushī, Abu'l-ʿAbbās Aḥmad b. Muḥammad. *al-Bayān al-mughrib*, ed. G. S. Colin and E. Lévi-Provençal. New edn, Leiden, 1948–1951.

Ibn al-Jawzī, Abu'l-Faraj ʿAbd al-Raḥmān b. ʿAlī al-Ḥanbalī. *al-Muntaẓam fī ta'rīkh al-mulūk wa'l-umam*, ed. F. Krenkow. Hyderabad, 1357–1362/1938–1943; ed. M. and M. ʿAṭā. Beirut, 1992.

Ibn Kathīr, ʿImād al-Dīn Ismāʿīl b. ʿUmar. *al-Bidāya wa'l-nihāya fi'l-ta'rīkh*. Cairo, 1351–1358/1932–1939.

Ibn Khaldūn, Walī al-Dīn Abū Zayd ʿAbd al-Raḥmān b. Muḥammad. *Kitāb al-ʿibar*. Cairo, 1289/1872.

Ibn Khallikān, Abu'l-ʿAbbās Aḥmad b. Muḥammad al-Irbilī. *Wafayāt al-aʿyān wa-anbā' abnā' al-zamān*, ed. I. ʿAbbās. Beirut, 1968–1972. English trans. W. MacGuckin de Slane, *Ibn Khallikan's Biographical Dictionary*. Paris, 1842–1871.

Ibn Mālik al-Yamānī, Abū ʿAbd Allāh Muḥammad. *Kashf asrār al-Bāṭiniyya wa-akhbār al-Qarāmiṭa*, ed. M. Z. al-Kawtharī. Cairo, 1357/1939.

Ibn Miskawayh, see Miskawayh, Abū ʿAlī Aḥmad b. Muḥammad.

Ibn Muyassar, Tāj al-Dīn Muḥammad b. ʿAlī. *Akhbār Miṣr*, ed. A. Fu'ād Sayyid. Cairo, 1981.

Ibn al-Nadīm, Abu'l-Faraj Muḥammad b. Isḥāq al-Warrāq. *Kitāb al-fihrist*. Cairo, 1348/1929–1930; ed. M. R. Tajaddud. Tehran, 1971. English trans. B. Dodge, *The Fihrist of al-Nadīm*. New York, 1970.

Ibn al-Qalānisī, Abū Yaʿlā Ḥamza b. Asad. *Dhayl ta'rīkh Dimashq*, ed. H. F. Amedroz. Leiden, 1908; ed. S. Zakkār. Damascus, 1983. Partial English trans. H. A. R. Gibb, *The Damascus Chronicle of the Crusades*. London, 1932.

French trans. Roger Le Tourneau, *Damas de 1075 à 1154*. Damascus, 1952.
Ibn Taghrībirdī, Jamāl al-Dīn Abu'l-Maḥāsin Yūsuf. *al-Nujūm al-zāhira fī mulūk Miṣr wa'l-Qāhira*. Cairo, 1348–1391/1929–1972; ed. T. G. J. Juynboll and B. F. Matthes. Leiden, 1855–1861.
Ibn al-Ṭuwayr, Abū Muḥammad al-Murtaḍā. *Nuzhat al-muqlatayn fī akhbār al-dawlatayn*, ed. A. Fu'ād Sayyid. Beirut, 1992.
Ibn Ẓāfir, Jamāl al-Dīn ʿAlī b. Abī Manṣūr al-Azdī. *Akhbār al-duwal al-munqaṭiʿa*, ed. A. Ferré. Cairo, 1972.
Idrīs ʿImād al-Dīn b. al-Ḥasan. *Taʾrīkh al-khulafāʾ al-Fāṭimiyyīn biʾl-Maghrib* (= *ʿUyūn al-akhbār*, vol. 5 and part of vol. 6), ed. M. al-Yaʿlāwī. Beirut, 1985.
ʿUyūn al-akhbār wa-funūn al-āthār, vols. 4–6, ed. M. Ghālib. Beirut, 1973–1984.
Iskandar Beg Munshī. *Taʾrīkh-i ʿālam-ārā-yi ʿAbbāsī*, ed. Ī. Afshār. Tehran, 1334–1335/1955–1956. English trans. R. M. Savory, *History of Shah ʿAbbas the Great*. Boulder, Col., 1978–1986.
Jaʿfar b. Manṣūr al-Yaman, Abu'l-Qāsim. *Kitāb al-kashf*, ed. R. Strothmann. London, etc., 1952; ed. M. Ghālib. Beirut, 1984.
al-Jawdharī, Abū ʿAlī Manṣūr al-ʿAzīzī. *Sīrat al-ustādh Jawdhar*, ed. M. Kāmil Ḥusayn and M. ʿA. Shaʿīra. Cairo, 1954. French trans. M. Canard, *Vie de l'ustadh Jaudhar*. Algiers, 1958.
Juwaynī, ʿAlāʾ al-Dīn ʿAṭā Malik b. Muḥammad. *Taʾrīkh-i jahān-gushāy*, ed. M. Qazvīnī. Leiden–London, 1912–1937. English trans. John A. Boyle, *The History of the World-Conqueror*. Manchester, 1958.
Jūzjānī, Minhāj al-Dīn Abū ʿAmr ʿUthmān b. Sirāj al-Dīn Muḥammad. *Ṭabaqāt-i Nāṣirī*, ed. ʿAbd al-Ḥayy Ḥabībī. 2nd edn, Kabul, 1342–1343/1963–1964. English trans. Henry G. Raverty, *The Ṭabakāt-i-Nāṣirī: A General History of the Muhammadan Dynasties of Asia*. London, 1881–1899.
Kāshānī, Abu'l-Qāsim ʿAbd Allāh b. ʿAlī. *Taʾrīkh-i Uljaytū*, ed. M. Hambly. Tehran, 1348/1969.
Zubdat al-tawārīkh; bakhsh-i Fāṭimiyān va Nizāriyān, ed. M. T. Dānishpazhūh. 2nd edn, Tehran, 1366/1987.
Khams rasāʾil Ismāʿīliyya, ed. ʿĀrif Tāmir. Salamiyya, 1956.
al-Khushanī, Abū ʿAbd Allāh Muḥammad b. Ḥārith. *Kitāb ṭabaqāt ʿulamāʾ Ifrīqiya*, ed. M. Ben Cheneb. Paris, 1915–1920.
al-Khwārazmī, Abū ʿAbd Allāh Muḥammad b. Aḥmad. *Mafātīḥ al-ʿulūm*. Cairo, 1923.
al-Kindī, Abū ʿUmar Muḥammad b. Yūsuf. *Kitāb al-wulāt wa-kitāb al-quḍāt*, ed. R. Guest under the title *The Governors and Judges of Egypt*. Leiden–London, 1912.
al-Kirmānī, Ḥamīd al-Dīn Aḥmad b. ʿAbd Allāh. *Kitāb al-riyāḍ*, ed. ʿĀ. Tāmir. Beirut, 1960.
Kitāb al-ʿālim waʾl-ghulām, ed. M. Ghālib, in his *Arbaʿ kutub ḥaqqāniyya*. Beirut, 1983, pp. 13–75. Abridged English trans. W. Ivanow, 'The Book of the Teacher and the Pupil', in his *Studies in Early Persian Ismailism*, pp. 61–86.

al-Kulaynī, Abū Jaʿfar Muḥammad b. Yaʿqūb. *al-Uṣūl min al-Kāfī*, ed. ʿA. A. al-Ghaffārī. Tehran, 1388/1968.

al-Majdūʿ, Ismāʿīl b. ʿAbd al-Rasūl. *Fihrist al-kutub waʾl-rasāʾil*, ed. ʿA. N. Munzavī. Tehran, 1966.

al-Maqrīzī, Taqī al-Dīn Aḥmad b. ʿAlī. *Ittiʿāẓ al-ḥunafāʾ bi-akhbār al-aʾimma al-Fāṭimiyyīn al-khulafāʾ*, ed. J. al-Shayyāl and M. Ḥ. M. Aḥmad. Cairo, 1967–1973; partial edition of volume one by H. Bunz. Leipzig, 1909.

Kitāb al-mawāʿiẓ waʾl-iʿtibār bi-dhikr al-khiṭaṭ waʾl-āthār. Būlāq, 1270/1853–1854.

Kitāb al-muqaffā al-kabīr, ed. M. al-Yaʿlāwī. Beirut, 1987.

Kitāb al-sulūk li-maʿrifat duwal al-mulūk, vols. 1–2, ed. M. M. Ziyāda and S. ʿA. F. ʿĀshūr. Cairo, 1936–1958. Partial English trans. Ronald J. C. Broadhurst, *A History of the Ayyūbid Sultans of Egypt*. Boston, 1980.

al-Masʿūdī, Abuʾl-Ḥasan ʿAlī b. al-Ḥusayn. *Kitāb al-tanbīh waʾl-ishrāf*, ed. M. J. de Goeje. Leiden, 1894. French trans. B. Carra de Vaux, *Le livre de l'avertissement et de la revision*. Paris, 1896.

Miskawayh, Abū ʿAlī Aḥmad b. Muḥammad. *Tajārib al-umam*, ed. and tr. H. F. Amedroz and D. S. Margoliouth under the title *The Eclipse of the ʿAbbasid Caliphate*. Oxford, 1920–1921.

al-Muʾayyad fiʾl-Dīn al-Shīrāzī, Abū Naṣr Hibat Allāh b. Abī ʿImrān Mūsā. *Dīwān*, ed. M. Kāmil Ḥusayn. Cairo, 1949.

al-Majālis al-Muʾayyadiyya, vols. 1 and 3, ed. M. Ghālib. Beirut, 1974–1984.

Sīrat al-Muʾayyad fīʾl-Dīn dāʿī al-duʿāt, ed. M. Kāmil Ḥusayn. Cairo, 1949.

Mufaḍḍal b. Abiʾl-Faḍāʾil. *al-Nahj al-sadīd*, ed. and tr. E. Blochet under the title *Histoire des sultans Mamlouks*, in *Patrologia Orientalis*, 12 (1919), pp. 345–550, 14 (1920), pp. 375–672, and 20 (1929), pp. 3–270; ed. S. Kortantamer. Freiburg, 1973.

al-Muqaddasī (al-Maqdisī), Shams al-Dīn Abū ʿAbd Allāh Muḥammad b. Aḥmad. *Aḥsan al-taqāsīm fī maʿrifat al-aqālīm*, ed. M. J. de Goeje. 2nd edn, Leiden, 1906.

al-Musabbiḥī, ʿIzz al-Mulk Abū ʿAbd Allāh Muḥammad b. ʿUbayd Allāh. *Akhbār Miṣr*, ed. A. Fuʾād Sayyid et al. Cairo, 1978–1984.

al-Nahrawālī (al-Nahrawānī), Quṭb al-Dīn Muḥammad b. Aḥmad. *al-Iʿlām bi-aʿlām balad Allāh al-ḥaram*, ed. F. Wüstenfeld, in his *Die Chroniken der Stadt Mekka*, vol. 3. Leipzig, 1857.

Nāṣir-i Khusraw. *Jāmiʿ al-ḥikmatayn*, ed. H. Corbin and M. Muʿīn. Tehran–Paris, 1953. French trans. I. de Gastines, *Le livre réunissant les deux sagesses*. Paris, 1990.

Khwān al-ikhwān, ed. Y. al-Khashshāb. Cairo, 1940.

Safar-nāma. Berlin, 1341/1922; ed. M. Dabīr Siyāqī. 5th edn, Tehran, 1356/1977. English trans. W. M. Thackston, Jr., *Nāṣer-e Khosraw's Book of Travels*. Albany, N.Y., 1986.

al-Nawbakhtī, Abū Muḥammad al-Ḥasan b. Mūsā. *Firaq al-Shīʿa*, ed. H. Ritter. Istanbul, 1931.

Niẓām al-Mulk, Abū ʿAlī al-Ḥasan b. ʿAlī al-Ṭūsī. *Siyar al-mulūk* (*Siyāsat-nāma*),

ed. ʿA. Iqbāl. Tehran, 1320/1941; ed. H. Darke. 2nd edn, Tehran, 1347/1968. English trans. H. Darke, *The Book of Government or Rules for Kings*. 2nd edn, London, 1978.
al-Nuʿmān b. Muḥammad, al-Qāḍī Abū Ḥanīfa. *Asās al-taʾwīl*, ed. ʿĀ. Tāmir. Beirut, 1960.
Daʿāʾim al-Islām, ed. Asaf A. A. Fyzee. Various editions, Cairo, 1951–1969. Partial English trans. Asaf A. A. Fyzee, *The Book of Faith*. Bombay, 1974.
Iftitāḥ al-daʿwa, ed. W. al-Qāḍī. Beirut, 1970; ed. F. al-Dashrāwī. Tunis, 1975.
Kitāb al-himma fī ādāb atbāʿ al-aʾimma, ed. M. Kāmil Ḥusayn. Cairo, n.d. [1948].
Kitāb ikhtilāf uṣūl al-madhāhib, ed. S. T. Lokhandwalla. Simla, 1972.
Kitāb al-iqtiṣār, ed. M. W. Mirza. Damascus, 1957.
Kitāb al-majālis waʾl-musāyarāt, ed. al-Ḥabīb al-Faqī et al. Tunis, 1978.
Sharḥ al-akhbār, ed. S. M. al-Ḥusaynī al-Jalālī. Qumm, 1409–1412/1988–1992.
Taʾwīl al-daʿāʾim, ed. M. Ḥ. al-Aʿẓamī. Cairo, 1967–1972.
al-Nuwayrī, Shihāb al-Dīn Aḥmad b. ʿAbd al-Wahhāb. *Nihāyat al-arab fī funūn al-adab*, vol. 25, ed. M. J. ʿA. al-Ḥīnī et al. Cairo, 1984.
al-Qalqashandī, Shihāb al-Dīn Abuʾl-ʿAbbās Aḥmad b. ʿAlī. *Ṣubḥ al-aʿshā fī ṣināʿat al-inshāʾ*. Cairo, 1331–1338/1913–1920.
al-Qummī, Saʿd b. ʿAbd Allāh al-Ashʿarī. *Kitāb al-maqālāt waʾl-firaq*, ed. M. J. Mashkūr. Tehran, 1963.
Rasāʾil Ikhwān al-Ṣafāʾ. Beirut, 1957.
Rashīd al-Dīn Ṭabīb, Faḍl Allāh b. ʿImād al-Dawla Abiʾl-Khayr. *Jāmiʿ al-tawārīkh*, vol. 3, ed. A. A. Alizade. Baku, 1957.
Jāmiʿ al-tawārīkh; qismat-i Ismāʿīliyān va Fāṭimiyān va Nizāriyān va dāʿīyān va rafīqān, ed. M. T. Dānishpazhūh and M. Mudarrisī Zanjānī. Tehran, 1338/1959.
al-Rāwandī, Muḥammad b. ʿAlī. *Rāḥat al-ṣudūr wa-āyat al-surūr*, ed. M. Iqbāl. London, 1921.
al-Rāzī, Abū Ḥātim Aḥmad b. Ḥamdān. *Aʿlām al-nubuwwa*, ed. Ṣ. al-Ṣāwī and G. R. Aʿvānī. Tehran, 1977. Extracts in P. Kraus, 'Raziana II', *Orientalia*, NS, 5 (1936), pp. 35–56, 358–378.
Kitāb al-zīna, vols. 1–2, ed. Ḥ. F. al-Hamdānī. Cairo, 1957–1958; vol. 3, ed. ʿAbd Allāh S. al-Sāmarrāʾī, in his *al-Ghuluww waʾl-firaq al-ghāliya*. Baghdad, 1972, pp. 245–312.
al-Shahrastānī, Abuʾl-Fatḥ Muḥammad b. ʿAbd al-Karīm. *Kitāb al-milal waʾl-niḥal*, ed. W. Cureton. London, 1842. Partial English trans. A. K. Kazi and J. G. Flynn, *Muslim Sects and Divisions*. London, 1984. French trans. D. Gimaret and G. Monnot, *Livre des religions et des sectes*. Paris, 1986.
al-Shūshtarī, al-Qāḍī Nūr Allāh. *Majālis al-muʾminīn*. Tehran, 1365/1986.
Sibṭ Ibn al-Jawzī. *Mirʾāt al-zamān*. Hyderabad, 1951.
al-Sijistānī, Abū Yaʿqūb Isḥāq b. Aḥmad. *Kashf al-maḥjūb*, ed. H. Corbin. Tehran–Paris, 1949. French trans. H. Corbin, *Le dévoilement des choses cachées*. Lagrasse, 1988.

Kitāb al-yanābī', ed. and partial French tr. Henry Corbin, in his *Trilogie Ismaélienne*. Tehran–Paris, 1961, text pp. 1–97, translation pp. 1–127. English trans. Paul E. Walker, in his *The Wellsprings of Wisdom*. Salt Lake City, 1994, pp. 37–111.

al-Ṭabarī, Abū Ja'far Muḥammad b. Jarīr. *Ta'rīkh al-rusul wa'l-mulūk*, ed. M. J. de Goeje et al., 3 series. Leiden, 1879–1901. English trans. by various scholars, *The History of al-Ṭabarī*. Albany, N.Y., 1985–

Ta'rīkh-i Sīstān, ed. Malik al-Shu'arā' Bahār. Tehran, 1314/1935. English trans. M. Gold, *The Tārikh-e Sistān*. Rome, 1976.

al-Ṭūsī, Khwāja Naṣīr al-Dīn Muḥammad b. Muḥammad. *Akhlāq-i Muḥtashamī*, ed. M. T. Dānishpazhūh. Tehran, 1361/1982.

Akhlāq-i Nāṣirī, ed. M. Mīnuvī and 'A. Ḥaydarī. Tehran, 1356/1977. English trans. G. M. Wickens, *The Nasirean Ethics*. London, 1964.

Rawḍat al-taslīm, ed. and tr. W. Ivanow. Leiden, 1950.

Umm al-kitāb, ed. W. Ivanow, in *Der Islam*, 23 (1936), pp. 1–132. Italian trans. P. Filippani-Ronconi, *Ummu'l-Kitāb*. Naples, 1966.

Yāqūt, Abū 'Abd Allāh Ya'qūb b. 'Abd Allāh al-Ḥamawī al-Rūmī. *Mu'jam al-buldān*, ed. F. Wüstenfeld. Leipzig, 1866–1873. Partial French trans. C. Barbier de Meynard, *Dictionnaire géographique, historique et littéraire de la Perse*. Paris, 1861.

Ẓahīr al-Dīn Nīshāpūrī. *Saljūq-nāma*. Tehran, 1332/1953.

SECONDARY WORKS

Arendonk, C. van. *Les débuts de l'Imāmat Zaidite au Yémen*, tr. J. Ryckmans. Leiden, 1960.

Asani, Ali S. 'The Khojkī Script: A Legacy of Ismā'īlī Islam in the Indo-Pakistan Subcontinent', JAOS, 107 (1987), pp. 439–449.

The Būjh Nirañjan: An Ismaili Mystical Poem. Cambridge, Mass., 1991.

'The Ginān Literature of the Ismailis of Indo-Pakistan: Its Origins, Characteristics and Themes', in *Devotion Divine: Bhakti Traditions from the Regions of India*, ed. D. Eck and F. Mallison. Gröningen–Paris, 1991, pp. 1–18.

'The Ismaili *Ginān*s as Devotional Literature', in *Devotional Literature in South Asia*, ed. R. S. McGregor. Cambridge, 1992, pp. 101–112.

Barthold, Vasiliĭ V. *Turkestan down to the Mongol Invasion*, ed. C. E. Bosworth. 3rd edn, London, 1968.

Bausani, Alessandro. 'Scientific Elements in Ismā'īlī Thought: The Epistles of the Brethren of Purity (*Ikhwān al-Ṣafā'*)', in *Ismā'īlī Contributions to Islamic Culture*, pp. 121–140.

Becker, Carl H. *Beiträge zur Geschichte Ägyptens unter dem Islam*. Strassburg, 1902–1903.

'Badr al-Djamālī', EI2, vol. 1, pp. 869–870.

Bianquis, Thierry. 'La prise de pouvoir par les Fatimides en Egypte

(357–363/968–974)', *Annales Islamologiques*, 11 (1972), pp. 49–108.
Damas et la Syrie sous la domination Fatimide, 359–468/969–1076. Damascus, 1986–1989.
Bosworth, C. Edmund. 'The Political and Dynastic History of the Iranian World (A.D. 1000–1217)', in *The Cambridge History of Iran*: Volume 5, pp. 1–202, 683–689.
Sīstān under the Arabs, from the Islamic Conquest to the Rise of the Ṣaffārids (30–250/651–864). Rome, 1968.
The Medieval History of Iran, Afghanistan and Central Asia. London, 1977.
'The Interaction of Arabic and Persian Literature and Culture in the 10th and early 11th Centuries', *al-Abḥāth*, 27 (1978–1979), pp. 59–75, reprinted in his *Medieval Arabic Culture and Administration.* London, 1982, article VIII.
The History of the Saffarids of Sistan and the Maliks of Nimruz (247/861 to 949/1542–3). Costa Mesa, Calif., and New York, 1994.
''Abbasid Caliphate in Iran', EIR, vol. 1, pp. 89–95.
Bowen, Harold. *The Life and Times of 'Alī Ibn 'Īsā 'The Good Vizier'.* Cambridge, 1928.
Browne, Edward G. *A Literary History of Persia.* Cambridge, 1928.
Bruijn, J. T. P. de. 'al-Kirmānī', EI2, vol. 5, pp. 166–167.
Brunschvig, Robert. 'Fiqh Fatimide et histoire de l'Ifriqiya', in *Mélanges d'histoire et d'archéologie de l'occident Musulman, Hommages à G. Marçais.* Algiers, 1957, vol. 2, pp. 13–20.
The Cambridge History of Iran: Volume 4, *The Period from the Arab Invasion to the Saljuqs*, ed. R. N. Frye. Cambridge, 1975.
The Cambridge History of Iran: Volume 5, *The Saljuq and Mongol Periods*, ed. J. A. Boyle. Cambridge, 1968.
Canard, Marius. 'L'impérialisme des Fatimides et leur propagande', *Annales de l'Institut d'Etudes Orientales*, 6 (1942–1947), pp. 156–193, reprinted in his *Miscellanea Orientalia.* London, 1973, article II.
'Da'wa', EI2, vol. 2, pp. 168–170.
'Fāṭimids', EI2, vol. 2, pp. 850–862.
Casanova, Paul. 'Monnaie des Assassins de Perse', *Revue Numismatique*, 3 série, 11 (1893), pp. 343–352.
'Notice sur un manuscrit de la secte des Assassins', *Journal Asiatique*, 9 série, 11 (1898), pp. 151–159.
'Une date astronomique dans les Epîtres des Ikhwān aṣ-Ṣafā', *Journal Asiatique*, 11 série, 5 (1915), pp. 5–17.
'La doctrine secrète des Fatimides d'Egypte', BIFAO, 18 (1921), pp. 121–165.
Corbin, Henry. *Etude préliminaire pour le 'Livre réunissant les deux sagesses' de Nasir-e Khosraw.* Tehran–Paris, 1953.
'L'initiation Ismaélienne ou l'ésotérisme et le Verbe', *Eranos Jahrbuch*, 39 (1970), pp. 41–142, reprinted in his *L'Homme et son ange.* Paris, 1983, pp. 81–205.

'Nāṣir-i Khusrau and Iranian Ismā'īlism', in *The Cambridge History of Iran*: Volume 4, pp. 520–542, 689–690.

'Un roman initiatique Ismaélien', *Cahiers de Civilisation Médiévale*, 15 (1972), pp. 1–25, 121–142.

Cyclical Time and Ismaili Gnosis, tr. R. Manheim and J. W. Morris. London, 1983.

Dabashi, Hamid. 'Farhang-i siyāsī-yi Shāhnāma: Andīsha-yi siyāsī-yi fīlsūf/pādishāh dar salṭanat-i Khusraw Anūshīrwān', *Iranshenasi*, 2 (1990), pp. 321–341.

Dachraoui, Farhat. *Le Califat Fatimide au Maghreb, 296–365 H./909–975 Jc.* Tunis, 1981.

'al-Mahdī 'Ubayd Allāh', EI2, vol. 5, pp. 1242–1244.

'al-Nu'mān', EI2, vol. 8, pp. 117–118.

Daftary, Farhad. *The Ismā'īlīs: Their History and Doctrines*. Cambridge, 1990.

'The Earliest Ismā'īlīs', *Arabica*, 38 (1991), pp. 214–245.

'Persian Historiography of the Early Nizārī Ismā'īlīs', *Iran, Journal of the British Institute of Persian Studies*, 30 (1992), pp. 91–97.

'A Major Schism in the Early Ismā'īlī Movement', *Studia Islamica*, 77 (1993), pp. 123–139.

The Assassin Legends: Myths of the Isma'ilis. London, 1994.

'Carmatians', EIR, vol. 4, pp. 823–832.

'Dā'ī', EIR, vol. 6, pp. 590–593.

'Rāshid al-Dīn Sinān', EI2, vol. 8, pp. 442–443.

Daiber, Hans. 'Abū Ḥātim ar-Rāzī (10th Century A.D.) on the Unity and Diversity of Religions', in *Dialogue and Syncretism: An Interdisciplinary Approach*, ed. J. Gort et al. Grand Rapids, Michigan, 1989, pp. 87–104.

Defrémery, Charles F. 'Nouvelles recherches sur les Ismaéliens ou Bathiniens de Syrie', *Journal Asiatique*, 5 série, 3 (1854), pp. 373–421, and 5 (1855), pp. 5–76.

van Ess, Josef. *Frühe mu'tazilitische Häresiographie*. Beirut, 1971.

Chiliastische Erwartungen und die Versuchung der Göttlichkeit. Der Kalif al-Ḥākim (386–411 H.). Heidelberg, 1977.

Filippani-Ronconi, Pio. *Ismaeliti ed 'Assassini'*. Milan, 1973.

Fyzee, Asaf A. A. 'Qadi an-Nu'man: The Fatimid Jurist and Author', JRAS (1934), pp. 1–32.

'Shī'ī Legal Theories', in *Law in the Middle East*: Vol. 1, *Origins and Development of Islamic Law*, ed. M. Khadduri and H. Liebesny. Washington D.C., 1955, pp. 113–131.

Compendium of Fatimid Law. Simla, 1969.

'Aspects of Fatimid Law', *Studia Islamica*, 31 (1970), pp. 81–91.

Outlines of Muhammadan Law. 4th edn, Delhi, 1974.

'al-Nu'mān', EI, vol. 3, pp. 953–954.

Gibb, Hamilton A. R. and Kraus, P. 'al-Mustanṣir', EI2, vol. 7, pp. 729–732.

Goeje, Michael Jan de. *Mémoire sur les Carmathes du Bahraïn et les Fatimides*. 2nd

edn, Leiden, 1886.
'La fin de l'empire des Carmathes du Bahraïn', *Journal Asiatique*, 9 série, 5 (1895), pp. 5–30.
Guyard, Stanislas. *Fragments relatifs à la doctrine des Ismaélîs*. Paris, 1874.
Halm, Heinz. *Kosmologie und Heilslehre der frühen Ismāʿīlīya: Eine Studie zur islamischen Gnosis*. Wiesbaden, 1978.
'Die Söhne Zikrawaihs und das erste fatimidische Kalifat (290/903)', WO, 10 (1979), pp. 30–53.
Die islamische Gnosis: Die extreme Schia und die ʿAlawiten. Zürich–Munich, 1982.
'Der Treuhänder Gottes: Die Edikte des Kalifen al-Ḥākim', *Der Islam*, 63 (1986), pp. 11–72.
Shiism, tr. J. Watson. Edinburgh, 1991.
Das Reich des Mahdi: Der Aufstieg der Fatimiden (875–973). Munich, 1991.
'Die Fatimiden', in *Geschichte der arabischen Welt*, ed. U. Haarmann. Munich, 1991, pp. 166–199, 605–606, 637–638.
'Abū Ḥātem Rāzī', EIR, vol. 1, p. 315.
'Bāṭenīya', EIR, vol. 3, pp. 861–863.
Hamdani, Abbas. 'Evolution of the Organisational Structure of the Fāṭimī Daʿwah', *Arabian Studies*, 3 (1976), pp. 85–114.
'Abū Ḥayyān al-Tawḥīdī and the Brethren of Purity', IJMES, 9 (1978), pp. 345–353.
'An Early Fāṭimid Source on the Time and Authorship of the *Rasāʾil Iḫwān al-Ṣafāʾ*', *Arabica*, 26 (1979), pp. 62–75.
'Shades of Shīʿism in the Tracts of the Brethren of Purity', in *Traditions in Contact and Change*, ed. P. Slater and D. Wiebe. Waterloo, Ont., 1983, pp. 447–460, 726–728.
'The Arrangement of the *Rasāʾil Ikhwān al-Ṣafāʾ* and the Problem of Interpolations', *Journal of Semitic Studies*, 29 (1984), pp. 97–110.
'Faṭimid History and Historians', in *The Cambridge History of Arabic Literature: Religion, Learning and Science in the ʿAbbasid Period*, ed. M. J. L. Young et al. Cambridge, 1990, pp. 234–247, 535–536.
al-Hamdānī, Ḥusain F. 'Rasāʾil Ikhwān aṣ-Ṣafā in the Literature of the Ismāʿīlī Ṭaiyibī Daʿwat', *Der Islam*, 20 (1932), pp. 281–300.
Ḥasan, Ḥasan Ibrāhīm. *Taʾrīkh al-dawla al-Fāṭimiyya*. 3rd edn, Cairo, 1964.
Ḥasan, Ḥasan I. and Sharaf, Ṭāhā A. *al-Muʿizz li-Dīn Allāh*. Cairo, 1367/1948.
ʿUbayd Allāh al-Mahdī. Cairo, 1947.
Hawley, John S. 'Author and Authority in the *Bhakti* Poetry of North India', *Journal of Asian Studies*, 47 (1988), pp. 269–290.
Hodgson, Marshall G. S. *The Order of Assassins: The Struggle of the Early Nizārī Ismāʿīlīs against the Islamic World*. The Hague, 1955.
'The Ismāʿīlī State', in *The Cambridge History of Iran*: Volume 5, pp. 422–482.
'Bāṭiniyya', EI2, vol. 1, pp. 1098–1100.
'Ḥasan-i Ṣabbāḥ', EI2, vol. 3, pp. 253–254.

Hourcade, Bernard. 'Alamūt', EIR, vol. 1, pp. 797–801.
Humā'ī, Jalāl al-Dīn. 'Muqaddima-yi qadīm-i Akhlāq-i Nāṣirī', *Majalla-yi Dānishkada-yi Adabiyyāt, Dānishgāh-i Tehran*, 3 (1335/1956), pp. 17–25.
al-Imad, Leila S. *The Fatimid Vizierate, 969–1172*. Berlin, 1990.
Ismā'īlī Contributions to Islamic Culture, ed. S. H. Nasr. Tehran, 1977.
Ivanow, Wladimir [Vladimir Alekseevich]. 'Notes sur l'Ummu'l-Kitab des Ismaëliens de l'Asie Centrale', *Revue des Etudes Islamiques*, 6 (1932), pp. 419–481.
'Some Ismaili Strongholds in Persia', *Islamic Culture*, 12 (1938), pp. 383–396.
'An Ismaili Poem in Praise of Fidawis', JBBRAS, NS, 14 (1938), pp. 63–72.
'The Organization of the Fatimid Propaganda', JBBRAS, NS, 15 (1939), pp. 1–35.
'Ismailis and Qarmatians', JBBRAS, NS, 16 (1940), pp. 43–85.
Ismaili Tradition Concerning the Rise of the Fatimids. London, etc., 1942.
The Alleged Founder of Ismailism. Bombay, 1946.
Nasir-i Khusraw and Ismailism. Bombay, 1948.
'Satpanth', in *Collectanea*: Vol. 1, ed. W. Ivanow. Leiden, 1948, pp. 1–54.
Brief Survey of the Evolution of Ismailism. Leiden, 1952.
Studies in Early Persian Ismailism. 2nd edn, Bombay, 1955.
Ibn al-Qaddah (The Alleged Founder of Ismailism). 2nd revised edn, Bombay, 1957.
Alamut and Lamasar: Two Mediaeval Ismaili Strongholds in Iran. Tehran, 1960.
'Ismā'īlīya', EI, Supplement, pp. 98–102, reprinted in SEI, pp. 179–183.
Jambet, Christian. *La grande résurrection d'Alamût*. Lagrasse, 1990.
Kassam, Tazim R. 'Syncretism on the Model of Figure-Ground: A Study of Pir Shams' Brahma Prakāśa', in *Hermeneutical Paths to the Sacred Worlds of India*, ed. K. K. Young. Atlanta, 1994, pp. 231–241.
Kiyā, Ṣādiq. *Nuqṭawiyān yā Pisīkhāniyān*. Tehran, 1320/1941.
Klausner, Carla L. *The Seljuk Vezirate: A Study of Civil Administration, 1055–1194*. Cambridge, Mass., 1973.
Kleiss, Wolfram. 'Assassin Castles in Iran', in *The Art of the Saljūqs in Iran and Anatolia*, ed. R. Hillenbrand. Costa Mesa, Calif., 1994, pp. 315–319.
Klemm, Verena. *Die Mission des fāṭimidischen Agenten al-Mu'ayyad fī d-dīn in Šīrāz*. Frankfurt, etc., 1989.
Lambton, Ann K. S. *Continuity and Change in Medieval Persia*. Albany, N.Y., 1988.
Lev, Yaacov. *State and Society in Fatimid Egypt*. Leiden, 1991.
Lewis, Bernard. *The Origins of Ismā'īlism: A Study of the Historical Background of the Fāṭimid Caliphate*. Cambridge, 1940.
'Ismā'īlī Notes', BSOAS, 12 (1947–1948), pp. 597–600.
'The Sources for the History of the Syrian Assassins', *Speculum*, 27 (1952), pp. 475–489, reprinted in his *Studies in Classical and Ottoman Islam (7th–16th Centuries)*. London, 1976, article VIII.
'The Ismā'īlites and the Assassins', in *A History of the Crusades*, ed. K. M. Setton: Volume I, *The First Hundred Years*, ed. M. W. Baldwin. 2nd edn,

Madison, Wisconsin, 1969, pp. 99–132.
The Assassins: A Radical Sect in Islam. London, 1967.
'Ibn 'Aṭṭāsh', EI2, vol. 3, p. 725.
Little, Donald P. *An Introduction to Mamlūk Historiography*. Wiesbaden, 1970.
Madelung, Wilferd. 'Fatimiden und Baḥrainqarmaṭen', *Der Islam*, 34 (1959), pp. 34–88.
'Das Imamat in der frühen ismailitischen Lehre', *Der Islam*, 37 (1961), pp. 43–135.
Der Imam al-Qāsim ibn Ibrāhīm und die Glaubenslehre der Zaiditen. Berlin, 1965.
'The Assumption of the Title Shāhānshāh by the Būyids and the Reign of the Daylam (*Dawlat al-Daylam*)', *Journal of Near Eastern Studies*, 28 (1969), pp. 84–108, 168–183, reprinted in his *Religious and Ethnic Movements in Medieval Islam*. London, 1992, article VIII.
'The Sources of Ismā'īlī Law', *Journal of Near Eastern Studies*, 35 (1976), pp. 29–40, reprinted in his *Religious Schools and Sects*, article XVIII.
'Aspects of Ismā'īlī Theology: The Prophetic Chain and the God Beyond Being', in *Ismā'īlī Contributions to Islamic Culture*, pp. 51–65, reprinted in his *Religious Schools and Sects*, article XVII.
Religious Schools and Sects in Medieval Islam. London, 1985.
'Naṣīr ad-Dīn Ṭūsī's Ethics between Philosophy, Shi'ism, and Sufism', in *Ethics in Islam*, ed. R. G. Hovannisian. Malibu, Calif., 1985, pp. 85–101.
Religious Trends in Early Islamic Iran. Albany, N.Y., 1988.
'Abū Ya'qūb al-Sijistānī and Metempsychosis', in *Iranica Varia: Papers in Honor of Professor Ehsan Yarshater*. Leiden, 1990, pp. 131–143.
'Cosmogony and Cosmology: vi. In Isma'ilism', EIR, vol. 6, pp. 322–326.
'Ismā'īliyya', EI2, vol. 4, pp. 198–206.
'Ḳarmaṭī', EI2, vol. 4, pp. 660–665.
'Khōdja', EI2, vol. 5, pp. 25–27.
'Shiism: Ismā'īlīyah', in *The Encyclopedia of Religion*, vol. 13, pp. 247–260.
Marquet, Yves. *La Philosophie des Iḫwān al-Ṣafā'*. Algiers, 1975.
'Ikhwān al-Ṣafā'', EI2, vol. 3, pp. 1071–1076.
Massignon, Louis. 'Esquisse d'une bibliographie Qarmaṭe', in *A Volume of Oriental Studies Presented to Edward G. Browne*, ed. T. W. Arnold and R. A. Nicholson. Cambridge, 1922, pp. 329–338.
'Ḳarmaṭians', EI, vol. 2, pp. 767–772.
Melville, Charles. 'The Itineraries of Sultan Öljeitü, 1304–16', *Iran, Journal of the British Institute of Persian Studies*, 28 (1990), pp. 55–70.
'The Year of the Elephant: Mamluk–Mongol Rivalry in the Hejaz in the Reign of Abū Sa'īd (1317–1335)', *Studia Iranica*, 21 (1992), pp. 197–214.
Miles, George C. 'Coins of the Assassins of Alamūt', *Orientalia Lovaniensia Periodica*, 3 (1972), pp. 155–162.
Minasian, Caro O. *Shah Diz of Isma'ili Fame, its Siege and Destruction*. London, 1971.
Mudarris Raḍavī, Muḥammad Taqī. *Aḥvāl va āthār-i Khwāja Naṣīr al-Dīn Ṭūsī*.

Tehran, 1354/1975.

Mudarrisī Zanjānī, Muḥammad. *Sargudhasht va ʿaqāʾid-i falsafī-yi Khwāja Naṣīr al-Dīn Ṭūsī.* Tehran, 1363/1984.

Muqallid, ʿAlī. *Niẓām al-ḥukm fiʾl-Islām: Aw al-nubuwwa waʾl-imāma ʿind Naṣīr al-Dīn al-Ṭūsī.* Beirut, 1406/1986.

Nanji, Azim. 'An Ismāʿīlī Theory of *Walāyah* in the *Daʿāʾim al-Islām* of Qāḍī al-Nuʿmān', in *Essays on Islamic Civilization Presented to Niyazi Berkes*, ed. D. P. Little. Leiden, 1976, pp. 260–273.

The Nizārī Ismāʿīlī Tradition in the Indo-Pakistan Subcontinent. Delmar, N.Y., 1978.

'Ismāʿīlism', in *Islamic Spirituality: Foundations*, ed. S. H. Nasr. London, 1987, pp. 179–198, 432–433.

'Nāṣir-i Khusraw', EI2, vol. 7, pp. 1006–1007.

Nasr, S. Hossein. *An Introduction to Islamic Cosmological Doctrines.* 2nd edn, Albany, N.Y., 1993.

Netton, Ian R. *Muslim Neoplatonists: An Introduction to the Thought of the Brethren of Purity (Ikhwān al-Ṣafāʾ).* London, 1982.

Poonawala, Ismail K. 'Al-Qāḍī al-Nuʿmān's Works and the Sources', BSOAS, 36 (1973), pp. 109–115.

'A Reconsideration of al-Qāḍī al-Nuʿmān's *Madhhab*', BSOAS, 37 (1974), pp. 572–579.

'Al-Sijistānī and his *Kitāb al-Maqālīd*', in *Essays on Islamic Civilization Presented to Niyazi Berkes*, ed. D. P. Little. Leiden, 1976, pp. 274–283.

'Ismāʿīlī *taʾwīl* of the Qurʾān', in *Approaches to the History of the Interpretation of the Qurʾān*, ed. A. Rippin. Oxford, 1988, pp. 199–222.

'al-Muʾayyad fiʾl-Dīn', EI2, vol. 7, pp. 270–271.

'al-Nasafī', EI2, vol. 7, p. 968.

al-Qāḍī, Wadād. 'An Early Fāṭimid Political Document', *Studia Islamica*, 48 (1978), pp. 71–108.

Quatremère, Etienne M. 'Notice historique sur les Ismaëliens', *Fundgruben des Orients*, 4 (1814), pp. 339–376.

Rypka, Jan. *History of Iranian Literature*, ed. K. Jahn. Dordrecht, 1968.

Sayyid, Ayman Fuʾād. 'Lumières nouvelles sur quelques sources de l'histoire Fatimide en Egypte', *Annales Islamologiques*, 13 (1977), pp. 1–41.

al-Dawla al-Fāṭimiyya fī Miṣr. Cairo, 1992.

Scarcia Amoretti, B. 'Sects and Heresies', in *The Cambridge History of Iran*: Volume 4, pp. 481–519, 688–689.

Schacht, Joseph. *The Origins of Muhammadan Jurisprudence.* Oxford, 1950.

Shackle, Christopher and Moir, Zawahir. *Ismaili Hymns from South Asia: An Introduction to the Ginans.* London, 1992.

Silvestre de Sacy, Antoine I. *Chrestomathie Arabe.* 2nd edn, Paris, 1826–1827.

Exposé de la religion des Druzes. Paris, 1838.

Stern, Samuel M. 'The Authorship of the Epistles of the Ikhwān-aṣ-Ṣafāʾ', *Islamic Culture*, 20 (1946), pp. 367–372, and 21 (1947), pp. 403–404.

'The Epistle of the Fatimid Caliph al-Āmir (al-Hidāya al-Āmiriyya) – its Date and its Purpose', JRAS (1950), pp. 20–31, reprinted in his *History and Culture in the Medieval Muslim World*. London, 1984, article X.
'Heterodox Ismāʿīlism at the Time of al-Muʿizz', BSOAS, 17 (1955), pp. 10–33.
'The Early Ismāʿīlī Missionaries in North-West Persia and in Khurāsān and Transoxania', BSOAS, 23 (1960), pp. 56–90.
'Ismāʿīlīs and Qarmaṭians', in *L'Elaboration de l'Islam*, Colloque de Strasbourg. Paris, 1961, pp. 99–108.
'New Information about the Authors of the Epistles of the Sincere Brethren', *Islamic Studies*, 3 (1964), pp. 405–428.
'Cairo as the Centre of the Ismāʿīlī Movement', in *Colloque international sur l'histoire du Caire*. Cairo, 1972, pp. 437–450.
'The Earliest Cosmological Doctrines of Ismāʿīlism', in his *Studies in Early Ismāʿīlism*, pp. 3–29.
Studies in Early Ismāʿīlism. Jerusalem–Leiden, 1983.
Strothmann, Rudolf. 'Recht der Ismailiten', *Der Islam*, 31 (1954), pp. 131–146.
'al-Ṭūsī, Naṣīr al-Dīn', EI, vol. 4, pp. 980–981.
Sutūda, Manūchihr. *Qilāʿ-i Ismāʿīliyya*. Tehran, 1345/1966.
Walker, Paul E. 'An Ismāʿīlī Answer to the Problem of Worshipping the Unknowable, Neoplatonic God', *American Journal of Arabic Studies*, 2 (1974), pp. 7–21.
'The Ismaili Vocabulary of Creation', *Studia Islamica*, 40 (1974), pp. 75–85.
'The Doctrine of Metempsychosis in Islam', in *Islamic Studies Presented to Charles J. Adams*, ed. W. B. Hallaq and D. P. Little. Leiden, 1991, pp. 219–238.
'The Universal Soul and the Particular Soul in Ismāʿīlī Neoplatonism', in *Neoplatonism and Islamic Thought*, ed. P. Morewedge. Albany, N.Y., 1992, pp. 149–166.
Early Philosophical Shiism: The Ismaili Neoplatonism of Abū Yaʿqūb al-Sijistānī. Cambridge, 1993.
'The Ismaili Daʿwa in the Reign of the Fatimid Caliph al-Ḥākim', *Journal of the American Research Center in Egypt*, 30 (1993), pp. 161–182.
'Abū Tammām and his *Kitāb al-Shajara*: A New Ismaili Treatise from Tenth-Century Khurasan', JAOS, 114 (1994), pp. 343–352.
'Abū Yaʿqūb Sejestānī', EIR, vol. 1, pp. 396–398.
Willey, Peter. *The Castles of the Assassins*. London, 1963.
'The Assassins in Quhistan', *Journal of the Royal Central Asian Society*, 55 (1968), pp. 180–183.
Wüstenfeld, Ferdinand. *Die Statthalter von Ägypten zur Zeit der Chalifen*. Göttingen, 1875–1876.
Geschichte der Faṭimiden-Chalifen. Göttingen, 1881.
Zāhid ʿAlī. *Taʾrīkh-i Fāṭimiyyīn-i Miṣr*. Hyderabad, 1367/1948.
Hamārē Ismāʿīlī madhhab kī ḥaqīqat awr us kā niẓām. Hyderabad, 1373/1954.

Index

Main entries are arranged alphabetically; their sub-headings are arranged thematically. The Arabic definite article 'al-' is ignored for the purposes of alphabetization. In the alphabetization no distinction is made between different Arabic letters which are represented by the same letter in transliteration. The abbreviation 'b.' for *ibn* ('son of') is alphabetized as written. The letter 'n.' ('note') following a page reference indicates the number of a chapter endnote on that page (e.g. 55n.27), and '*passim*' indicates scattered references to the subject, not necessarily on consecutive pages.

ʿAqarqūf, in Iraq, 48
al-ʿaql (intellect, reason), 77, 85, 86, 125, 126
al-ʿaql al-kullī (universal intellect), 13, 75, 85, 86, 87–8
Āqqūsh al-Afram, Mamlūk *amīr*, *see* al-Afram
Arabia, 2
Arabic language, 7, 12, 78, 82, 182, 189, 197, 265, 270
Arabs, 31, 32, 34, 47–51 *passim*, 148, 153, 213, 215, 236, 251, 285
Aras, river, 284, 295
Ardabīl, in Ādharbāyjān, 284
ʿArīb b. Saʿd al-Qurṭubī, historian, 29, 30, 32, 50
Armenia, Armenians, 110, 284
Arrajān, fortresses and town, in Khūzistān, 191
Arrān, 284
see also Caucasus
al-Aʿṣam, *see* al-Ḥasan al-Aʿṣam
Asani, Ali S., 16, 17, 265
asās, 163
al-Ashʿarī, Abu'l-Ḥasan ʿAlī b. Ismāʿīl, Sunni theologian and heresiographer, 166, 167, 168, 169, 170
Ashʿariyya, 161, 166, 169, 170
al-Ashraf Khalīl, Mamlūk, 248, 256
Asia, 8, 232
see also South Asia
Asia Minor, *see* Anatolia
ʿAskar Mukram, in Khūzistān, 83
Assassin legends, *see* Assassins
assassination, 9, 10, 16, 24, 25, 27, 42, 192–3, 206, 207, 209, 248–53 *passim*
Assassins, 9–10, 75
see also assassination; *fidāʾīs*; Nizārīs
astrology, 14, 48, 49, 69n.254, 71n.263, 145–50 *passim*, 291
see also Capricorn; Sagittarius; Scorpio; zodiac, signs of
Aubin, Jean, 222
Avicenna, *see* Ibn Sīnā
ʿAwfī, Muḥammad, biographer, 225, 226
awliyāʾ, *see walī*
Awrangzīb, Mughal emperor, 294
Awṣāf al-ashrāf, of Khwāja Naṣīr al-Dīn al-Ṭūsī, 232
awṣiyāʾ, *see waṣī*
ʿAwwā, ʿĀdil, 145
ʿAyn Jālūt, in Palestine, 233
ʿAyn al-Quḍāt al-Hamadhānī, 232
al-ʿAynī, Abū Muḥammad, historian, 249, 250
Ayyūbids, 7, 213
ʿAzāziʾīl, angel, 82
al-Azhar, mosque and university, Cairo, 3, 102, 103, 108
al-ʿAzīz, Fatimid caliph, 24, 40, 93, 97, 102–9 *passim*, 124, 131
Azodi, Azizeh, 21, 83, 112

Bāb, ʿAlī Muḥammad Shīrāzī, 294
Bābak Khurramī, Khurramī leader, 189
Badakhshān, 7
Badāʾūnī, ʿAbd al-Qādir, historian, 293
Badr al-Dīn al-Azkashī, 250
Badr al-Jamālī, Fatimid vizier, 110, 186, 188, 193
Baghdad, 4, 21, 30, 31–7 *passim*, 41, 48, 50, 51, 148, 149, 214, 232–8 *passim*, 249, 250, 251, 252, 253, 281
al-Baghdādī, ʿAbd al-Qāhir b. Ṭāhir, Sunni jurist and heresiographer, 43–9 *passim*, 70n.255, 97, 148, 169
Bahāʾ al-Dawla Khalaf b. Abiʾ l-Faḍl Naṣr, Naṣrid *malik*, 224
Bahāʾī, Shaykh, 237
Baḥrayn, 2, 13, 21, 22, 23, 25, 33, 36, 37, 41–50 *passim*
balāgh (initiation), 43
al-Balāgh al-akbar, anonymous anti-Ismaʿili treatise, 44, 66n.217, 67n.219
Balkh, 191
al-Balkhī, Abuʾ l-Qāsim, 166, 167, 168, 169, 170, 177n.36
Bāmiyān, 242
Banū, followed by the name of the eponymous ancestor of a tribe, *see under the name of that ancestor*
al-Bāqillānī, Abū Bakr Muḥammad, al-Qāḍī, 22, 44
Baqliyya, 49, 50, 51
Barkiyāruq, Saljuq sultan, 190–191, 198, 205, 206, 207–8, 215, 216, 217
Barqa, 30, 31, 33, 34, 196
Bartholomew, ruler of Maraclea, 247–8
al-Basāsīrī, Arslān, Turkish general, 148
Baṣra, in Iraq, 29, 30–7 *passim*, 49, 75, 83
bāṭin, *bāṭinī* (hidden, esoteric meaning), 2, 17, 26, 91, 93, 95, 100, 101, 120, 129, 132, 163, 267, 282, 294, 295
Bāṭinīs, Bāṭiniyya, 22, 23, 29, 43, 45–6, 67n.217, 209–15 *passim*
Bausani, Alessandro, 146, 160n.11
bayʿa, 93, 94, 107, 185
Baybars I, Mamlūk sultan, 247, 248
Bayhaq, in Khurāsān, 215
bayt al-māl, 103
Becker, Carl H., 45
Berbers, 31, 92, 99, 100, 118, 196
see also individual tribes
bhakti, religious literary tradition in South Asia, 270, 272, 274
bhaṇitā (signature-verse), 17, 270–3 *passim*
al-Bharūchī, Ḥasan b. Nūḥ, Ṭayyibī author, 93
Bibliothèque Iranienne, of Henry Corbin, 12

ginān(s), 8, 265, 266
arrangement in written sources, 269, 275–6
authority of, 267, 271, 272, 273, 279n.77
authorship of, 16–17, 268, 269–75 *passim*
form and themes of, 266, 267
scriptural status, 266–7
transmission of, 8, 269, 274
Girdkūh, fortress, in northern Persia, 188, 191, 206, 215, 247
Goodman, Lenn E., 146
Gnosis, *see* gnosticism
gnosticism, 80–1, 83
in doctrine of Isma'ilis, 2, 3, 14, 82
Goeje, Michael Jan de, orientalist, 11, 13, 22–5 *passim*, 29, 30–1, 33, 34, 35–6, 37–8, 39, 40–9 *passim*, 51, 147
Gospels, the, 96
Great Saljuqs, *see* Saljuqs
Greek philosophy, 75, 241
see also Neoplatonism
A Guide to Ismaili Literature, of W. Ivanow, 76
Gujarāt, 8, 194
Gulpāyagān, in Persia, 213
Gunābād, in Khurāsān, 225
Guru Nānak, 270
Guyard, Stanislas, orientalist, 75, 146

ḥadīth, 121, 122, 123, 126, 128, 129, 130, 163, 241, 293
Ḥadīthiyya, 165, 168
al-Ḥāfiẓ, Fatimid caliph, 195
Ḥāfiẓ, Shams al-Dīn Muḥammad, poet, 287, 288, 294–5
Ḥāfiẓ Abrū, historian, 185
Ḥāfiẓīs, Ḥāfiẓiyya, branch of Musta'lians, 4
see also Musta'lians
Hajar, in eastern Arabia, 39, 48
al-ḥajar al-aswad, *see* Black Stone of the Ka'ba
ḥajj (pilgrimage to Mecca), 95, 96, 119, 127, 292
Ḥājjī Khalīfa, 145
al-Ḥākim, Fatimid caliph, 93, 97, 102–9 *passim*, 124
Halm, Heinz, 13, 57n.55, 91
Ḥamā, in Syria, 248, 252
Hamadān, in Persia, 249, 290
Ḥamdān Qarmaṭ, Qarmaṭī leader in Iraq, 22, 23, 24, 25, 27–8, 42, 48, 49, 91, 103
Hamdani, Abbas, 14, 145, 162, 174
al-Hamdānī, 'Abd Allāh b. 'Umar, Zaydī historian, 77
al-Hamdānī, Ḥusayn F., 12, 146
Ḥamdānids, of Iraq and Syria, 34
Ḥāmid b. al-'Abbās, 'Abbasid vizier, 32
Ḥamīd al-Dīn al-Kirmānī, *see* al-Kirmānī, Ḥamīd al-Dīn
Hammer-Purgstall, Joseph von, orientalist, 11, 12
Ḥamza b. Ādharak, Khārijī leader, 221
Ḥamza b. 'Alī b. Aḥmad, Druze leader, 106, 107
Ḥanafī, branch of 'Alids, *see* Ḥanafids
Ḥanafī Sunnism, 109, 132n.2, 161
Ḥanafids, branch of 'Alids, 23, 25, 26, 27
ḥaqīqa, *ḥaqā'iq* (unchangeable truths), 2, 22
ḥaqq (truth), 85
ḥarf, *see* *ḥurūf*
al-Ḥasā, *see* al-Aḥsā
Ḥasan, Ḥasan Ibrāhīm, 23, 30–1, 34, 48, 66n.204
Ḥasan III, Nizārī imam, *see* Jalāl al-Dīn Ḥasan III
al-Ḥasan al-A'ṣam, Qarmaṭī commander, 23, 35, 39, 40, 42, 51–3, 61n.143
al-Ḥasan b. 'Alī b. Abī Ṭālib, Shi'i imam, 117, 172, 174
al-Ḥasan b. 'Alī al-Ṭūsī, *see* Niẓām al-Mulk
al-Ḥasan b. al-Ṣabbāḥ, *see* Ḥasan-i Ṣabbāḥ
al-Ḥasan b. Sanbar, 46, 69n.245
al-Ḥasan b. Ṭughj, 34
al-Ḥasan b. 'Ubayd Allāh b. Ṭughj, Ikhshīdid governor of Syria, 35, 39
Ḥasan Kabīr al-Dīn, *pīr*, 268, 269, 273
Ḥasan-i Ṣabbāḥ, Nizārī leader and founder of Nizārī state, 5, 6, 7, 15, 181, 184, 191, 196, 199–200, 211–18 *passim*, 222
biographies of, 185
early career, 185–6, 187, 188, 190
in Egypt, 186–7
established at Alamūt, 187–8
and Nizārī-Musta'lī schism, 4, 194
and Saljuqs, 5, 187, 188–9, 192
as head of Nizārī movement, 194–5, 198
recognized as *ḥujja* of the imam, 196–7
and doctrine of *ta'līm*, 197–8
and Turks, 189, 200
hashish, 10
Hawley, John, 270–1, 272, 274
ḥayāt (life), 85
Hell, 95, 96, 157, 163, 289
see also eschatology; *qiyāma; Paradise; soteriology*
Herat, 221, 227
heresiography, 14, 154, 161, 162, 164, 166, 168, 197
and Isma'ilis, 9, 13, 23, 43
heretics, *see* *mulḥid*
ḥikma (wisdom), 82, 98–9, 104
Hillenbrand, Carole, 15, 205
al-Ḥimyarī, Nashwān b. Sa'īd, see Nashwān b. Sa'īd al-Ḥimyarī
Hindi language, 271
Hindus, Hinduism, 8, 17, 265–9 *passim*, 287, 293

ʿImād al-Dīn b. Kathīr, *see* Ibn Kathīr
imam, 3, 5, 7, 8, 9, 22, 23, 26, 29, 41, 50, 78, 93, 95, 99, 110, 118, 121, 124–32 *passim*, 146, 149, 163, 186, 197, 267, 268
Imām Begum, Sayyida, 273
Imām Shāh, Imām al-Dīn ʿAbd al-Raḥīm, eponym of Imām-Shāhīs, 268, 269, 272
imamate, 2, 3, 17, 23, 24–9 *passim*, 41, 42, 50, 76, 124, 125–6, 127, 129, 165, 172, 181, 194–5
Imāmīs, Imāmiyya, Shiʿi community, 1, 121, 125, 127, 128, 130, 165, 169, 183, 236
Imām-Shāhīs, 268
India, Indians 5, 7, 8, 11, 17, 98, 131, 132, 149, 153, 194, 239, 265–74 *passim*, 282, 287, 293, 294
Indian subcontinent, *see* India
Indic languages, 8, 265
inheritance, 117, 119
Institute of Ismaili Studies, London, 12, 175n.3
intellect, *see al-ʿaql*
ʿIqdāniyya, council, in the Qarmaṭī state of Baḥrayn, 36, 38
iqṭāʿ, 184, 189, 192
Iran, Iranians, 15, 170, 181, 182–3, 206, 211, 216–23 *passim*, 231, 233, 267, 273, 281, 283, 290, 293, 294
  see also Persia
Iranian national sentiments, 7, 181, 182, 184, 189, 200, 282
Irano-Islamic, 182, 200
Iraq, 2, 33, 48, 51, 80, 81, 82, 97, 103, 173, 183, 184, 190, 195, 198, 205, 206, 217, 233, 248
ʿĪsā (Jesus), 2, 5, 26, 46, 48, 86, 171
ʿĪsā b. Mūsā, Qarmaṭī *dāʿī*, 51, 55n.27
Iṣfahān, in central Persia, 46, 184, 186, 187, 198, 199, 206–12 *passim*, 218, 292
Isfarāʾinī, Abu ʾl-Muẓaffar, 44
Isḥāqiyya, 174
al-Ishārāt waʾl-tanbīhāt, of Ibn Sīnā, 232, 234
Iskandar Beg Munshī, historian, 291, 292
Islam, 5, 9, 10, 21, 48, 49, 80, 82, 92, 126, 127, 153–63 *passim*, 174, 182, 238, 239, 282, 293
Islamic Research Association, Bombay, 11
Ismāʿīl I, founder of the Ṣafawid dynasty of Persia, 290
Ismāʿīl II, Ṣafawid shāh, 290
Ismāʿīl b. Jaʿfar al-Ṣādiq, Ismaʿili imam, 44, 47, 56n.52
Ismaili Heritage Series, 12
Ismaili Society, Bombay, 11, 12
Ismaʿili studies, 1, 8, 11–13
Ismailia Association, Pakistan, 12
Ismaʿilis, Ismāʿīliyya, 1, 2, 3, 4, 17, 50, 75, 82, 99, 130, 182, 183, 189, 208, 222, 236, 295
  early (pre-Fatimid) doctrine, 2, 3, 26, 76, 77, 78–80, 82, 173
  daʿwa, *see al-daʿwa*
  hostilities towards, 1, 8–9, 42–3
  initiation into, 8, 13, 43, 91–2, 98
  jurisprudence, *see* under *fiqh*
  literary heritage, *see under* literature
  and the 'other', 14, 153, 154
  see further Nizārīs; Mustaʿlians; Ḥāfiẓīs; Ṭayyibīs; Dāʾūdīs; Sulaymānīs; Bohras; Khojas
  see also Fatimid caliphate; Fatimids; Qarmaṭīs
isnād (chain of transmitters of *ḥadīth*), 121, 122, 123, 128, 130
Isrāfīl (Seraphiel), angel, 80, 174
Isrāʾīl, Banū, 163
Iṣṭahbānāt, in Fārs, 292
istidlāl, 125, 126
al-Istiftāḥ, 77
istiḥsān, 124, 125, 126
istiṣlāḥ, 125, 126
Istitār al-imām, of Aḥmad b. Muḥammad al-Nīsābūrī, 24
Ithnāʿashariyya, *see* Twelvers
Ittiʿāẓ al-ḥunafāʾ, of al-Maqrīzī, 94
Ivanow, Wladimir, 76, 140n.60, 160n.18, 175n.3, 267–8, 273
  and modern Ismaʿili studies, 11–12
  and Qarmaṭīs, 23, 25, 28–9, 54n.12, 69n.252
  and Ismaʿili *ʿahd*, 98
  and Anjudān revival, 8
  and the Nuqṭawiyya, 17
ʿIzrāʾīl, 174

al-Jadd, 77, 80, 163
Jaʿfar b. Falāḥ, Fatimid general, 35, 40
Jaʿfar b. Manṣūr al-Yaman, Ismaʿili author, 55n.27, 79, 92, 132n.2
Jaʿfar b. Muḥammad al-Ṣādiq, *see* Jaʿfar al-Ṣādiq
Jaʿfar al-Ṣādiq, Shiʿi imam, 1, 121, 124, 127, 128, 130, 139n.48, 158, 169
jafr, 293
Jahannam, *see* Hell
jāhiliyya, *jāhilī*, 153, 156
Jalāl al-Dīn Ḥasan III, Nizārī imam, 6, 226
Jalāl al-Dīn Khwārazmshāh, 231
Jalāl al-Dīn Mingburnu, Khwārazmshāh, *see* Jalāl al-Dīn Khwārazmshāh
jamāʿat (community), 8
jamāʿat-khāna (house of congregation), 266
Jamāl al-Dīn ʿUbayda, 250
Jāmiʿ al-ḥikmatayn, of Nāṣir-i Khusraw, 86–7, 89n.11
janāḥ, 163
al-Jannābī, Abū Saʿīd, founder of the Qarmaṭī state of Baḥrayn, 22, 23, 24, 25, 27–37 *passim*, 39, 42, 51, 52–3

Malūsa, Banū, 100
*mamlūk*s (slaves), 96, 105, 249, 250, 251, 254, 256, 257
Mamlūks, of Egypt and Syria, 7, 16, 233, 247, 248, 250, 252, 253, 258
Mandaeans, 80–1, 82
Mangū Khan, *see* Mengü
Mani, 83
Manichaeism, 14, 80–1, 82, 284
al-Manṣūr, Fatimid caliph, 37, 38, 39, 44, 45, 101, 119–23 *passim*,
Manṣūr al-Yaman, *see* Ibn Ḥawshab
Manṣūriyya, Fatimid capital in Ifrīqiya, 79, 101, 120, 131
Maqālāt al-Islāmiyyīn, of Abu 'l-Ḥasan al-Ash'arī, 166
al-Maqarrī, historian, 145
al-Maqrīzī, Taqī al-Dīn Aḥmad, historian, 45, 61n.143, 63n.156, 94, 98, 102, 111, 118, 131, 249, 251, 252
Maraclea (Marqiyya), 247
Marāgha, in Ādharbāyjān, 233, 249, 258
Marāgha Observatory, 233, 236
Marāqiya, 31
Marco Polo, traveller, 10
Marquet, Yves, 76, 146
Mars, planet, 71n.263
al-Marwazī, *amīr*, *see* al-Ḥusayn b. 'Alī al-Marwazī
al-Marwazī, Muḥammad b. 'Umar b. Yaḥyā, Fatimid *qāḍī*, 117, 118, 133n.3
Mary, *see* Maryam
Maryam (Mary), the mother of 'Īsā, 48
Maṣāla b. Ḥabūs, Fatimid general, 31
Masrūr b. Sulaymān b. Kāfī, Fatimid general, 33
Massignon, Louis, 3, 43
al-Mas'ūdī, 'Alī b. al-Ḥusayn, historian, 30, 32, 41, 46, 47, 49, 60n.116, 63n.156, 97
Maṣyāf, in Syria, 75, 250, 251, 252, 254, 255, 258
Maymūn al-Qaddāḥ, 23, 29, 148
Maymūndiz, fortress, in northern Persia, 215, 232
Mayyāfāriqīn, 186
maẓālim, 78, 120, 131
Mecca (Makka), 2, 21, 33, 34, 35, 37, 49, 293
Medina (Madīna), 125
mehfil, 266
Melville, Charles, 16, 247
Memoir on the Dynasty of the Assassins, of Silvestre de Sacy, 10
Mengü (Möngke), Great Khan, 232
Mesopotamia, 21, 33, 81, 82
 see also Iraq
messiah, 25, 87, 173, 174
Michael, *see* Mīkā'īl
Mihrabānid Maliks, of Sīstān, 223, 225, 227
Mīkā'īl (Michael), angel, 80, 174
Mīkhā'īl, 174
Minhāj-i Sirāj Jūzjānī, *see* Jūzjānī, Minhāj al-Dīn
al-Minhāl b. al-Maymūn al-'Ijlī, eponym of the Minhāliyya, 172
Minhāliyya, 172
Minorsky, Vladimir, 182
Mīr Dāmād, 237
Mīr Findiriskī, 237
Mīrābāī, poet-saint, 270
Mīrānshāh, Tīmūrid, 283
Miskawayh, Abū 'Alī Aḥmad, historian and philosopher, 29, 32, 232, 237–8
Miṣr, *see* Fusṭāṭ (Old Cairo)
mīthāq (oath of allegiance), 91, 94
 see also 'ahd; bay'a
Mīzān, of Maḥmūd Pisīkhānī, 284
Mohammed, the Prophet, *see* Muḥammad, the Prophet
Moir, Zawahir, 268–9, 274
Möngke, *see* Mengü
Mongols, 214, 216, 217, 222, 226, 227, 231–8 *passim*, 242, 243, 284,
 and Nizārīs, 5, 6, 7, 185, 206, 232, 281
 and Mamlūks, 16, 247, 248, 249, 252, 253, 254, 255, 258
Morgan, David, 214, 259
Moses, *see* Mūsā
Mozarabs, 251
al-Mu'ayyad bi'llāh Aḥmad b. al-Ḥusayn b. Hārūn al-Buṭhānī, Zaydī imam, 44
Mu'ayyad al-Dīn Muẓaffar b. Aḥmad, *see* Ra'īs Muẓaffar
al-Mu'ayyad fi'l-Dīn al-Shīrāzī, Abū Naṣr Hibat Allāh, Isma'ili *dā'ī* and author, 4, 108–9, 110, 186
Mubayyiḍa, 69n.254, 164, 170–1
Mudarris Raḍavī, Muḥammad Taqī, 235
Mufaḍḍal b. Abi'l-Faḍā'il, historian, 249, 260n.16
Mughal empire, 17, 282, 289–90, 292, 295
Muḥammad, the Prophet, 2, 22, 25, 27, 46, 47, 48, 86, 95, 117, 123, 126–30 *passim*, 147, 156, 163, 165, 171, 172, 174, 283–9 *passim*
Muḥammad I, Saljuq sultan, *see* Muḥammad Tapar
Muḥammad III, Nizārī imam, *see* 'Alā' al-Dīn Muḥammad III
Muḥammad b. 'Alī b. al-Ḥusayn, Akhū Muḥsin, anti-Isma'ili polemicist, 24, 25, 28, 32, 40, 42, 43–4, 45, 49, 51, 52, 55n.22, 73n.310, 94, 97, 98
Muḥammad b. Buzurg-Ummīd, head of Nizārī state, 196
Muḥammad b. Dushmanziyār, 208

nāṭiq, nuṭaqā' (speaking, or law-announcing prophets), 2, 163
Nā'ūsiyya, Imāmī sect, 169
al-Nawbakhtī, al-Ḥasan b. Mūsā, Imāmī scholar and heresiographer, 28, 71n.269, 167
naẓar (reason), 125, 126
see also al-'aql
Near East, 9, 186
Neoplatonism, 4, 13, 75, 76, 77, 88, 146, 158
see also Greek philosophy
Netton, Ian R., 146, 155, 156
Nih, in Sīstān, 223, 224, 226
Nihāyat al-arab, of al-Nuwayrī, 94
Ni'mat Allāhī, Sufi order, 282
Nīmrūz, in eastern Persia, 15, 221, 223, 225
see also Sīstān
al-Nīsābūrī, Aḥmad b. Muḥammad, *see* Aḥmad b. Muḥammad al-Nīsābūrī
Nīshāpūr (Nīsābūr), in Khurāsān, 184, 221, 231
Niẓām al-Mulk, Saljuq vizier, 44, 63n.164, 97, 184, 187, 190, 205, 207, 212, 217, 237, 242
Niẓāmī 'Arūḍī, Aḥmad b. 'Umar, 242
Niẓāmiyya, party, 207, 208, 209
Nizār b. al-Mustanṣir, Nizārī imam, 4, 186, 193–4, 195, 196
Nizārids, descendants of Nizār b. al-Mustanṣir, 195
revolts of, 195–6
Nizārī-Musta'lī schism, 4, 5, 97, 181, 193–4, 200
Nizārīs, Nizāriyya, 15, 98, 182, 195, 200, 221, 231, 235, 265, 281
literature, *see* under literature
historiography, 6, 185
origins, 4, 5, 181, 195
and Ḥasan-i Ṣabbāḥ, 181, 188, 194
Nizārī methods of struggle, 191–3, 198
and Saljuqs, 5, 188, 190, 198, 199, 210–11, 213, 216–18, 224
succession of imams, 193, 194, 195, 196
numismatic evidence, 194, 196
doctrine, 6, 197–8
and the Mongols, 5, 6, 7, 185, 247
da'wa, see under *al-da'wa*
of named areas, see Daylam; India; Khurāsān; Iran (Persia); Quhistān; Rūdbār; Syria; etc.
see also Assassins; *fidā'īs*; Khojas
Noah, *see* Nūḥ,
North Africa, 2, 3, 22, 24, 30, 33, 36, 37, 41, 79, 100, 119, 125, 129, 131, 145, 183
North America, 8, 274
Nūḥ (Noah), 25, 86
al-Nu'mān b. Muḥammad, al-Qāḍī Abū Ḥanīfa, Isma'ili jurist and author, 44, 76, 78, 98–104 *passim*, 108, 109, 110, 117, 118, 119–21, 124–7 *passim*, 129, 130, 131, 132
and sources of law, 124, 127–8, 129
and Isma'ili system of *fiqh*, 4, 14, 120–1, 122, 123
numismatic evidence, 194, 196, 220n.43
nuqṭa (point), 283–4, 288, 295
Nuqṭawīs, Nuqṭawiyya, 17, 281
origins of, 282–3
and cyclical renewal, 284–5, 293, 295
doctrines of, 282, 283, 284–9, 293
and Shāh 'Abbās I, 291, 292
in India, 290
Nūrbakhshī, Sufi order, 282
Nuṣayrīs, Nuṣayriyya, Shi'i community, 44, 75, 82
al-Nuwayrī, Aḥmad b. 'Abd al-Wahhāb, historian, 42, 63n.156, 94, 97, 98

oath of allegiance, *see 'ahd*; *mīthāq*; *bay'a*
occultation, *see ghayba*
Oghuz Turks, 184
Old Man of the Mountain, 9, 10, 98
Öljeitü (Uljaytū), Īlkhānid, 249, 250, 251, 252
ordu (royal Mongol encampment), 250, 253, 254, 255, 257
Orientalism, 10, 11
Ottomans, 282
Oxford, 145
Oxus (Āmū Daryā), river, 232

Pakistan, 132
Palestine, 3, 233
Pamir, in Central Asia, 82
Paradise, 6, 95, 96, 163, 172, 173, 289
see also eschatology; *qiyāma*; Hell; soteriology
Paris, 12
Pārsiyān, 189
Pasīkhānī, Maḥmūd, *see* Maḥmūd Pisīkhānī
pilgrimage to Mecca, *see ḥajj*
Persia, Persians, 2–7 *passim*, 15, 16, 17, 46, 47, 48, 51, 148, 163, 181–7 *passim*, 190, 191, 194, 221, 222, 232–40 *passim*, 247, 248, 250, 252–8 *passim*, 285, 289, 291
see also Iran, Iranians
Persian language, 7, 12, 82, 181–9 *passim*, 197, 241, 243, 265, 270
Persian sentiments, *see* Iranian national sentiments
Pingree, David, 147
pīr (spiritual guide), 7, 17, 267, 268, 269, 270–4 *passim*,
see also murshid
Pir Sadruddin, *see* Ṣadr al-Dīn, *pīr*
Pir Shams al-Dīn, *see* Shams al-Dīn, *pīr*
Pisīkhānī, Maḥmūd, *see* Maḥmūd Pisīkhānī
Plato, 158, 240
Polo, Marco, *see* Marco Polo

Silsilat Makhṭūṭāt al-Fāṭimiyyīn, of M. Kāmil Ḥusayn, 12
Silvestre de Sacy, Antoine Isaac, orientalist, 10–11, 98
Simon Magus, 83
Sinān, Rāshid al-Dīn, *see* Rāshid al-Dīn Sinān
Sind, 8, 274, 290
Sīra, of Abū 'Abd Allāh al-Shī'ī, 99
Sīrat al-Imām al-Mahdī, biography of the Fatimid al-Mahdī, 100
Sīstān, in eastern Persia, 15, 221, 223–7 *passim*
see also Nīmrūz
Siyāsat-nāma, of Niẓām al-Mulk, 184, 242
Socrates, 156
soteriology, 81, 156
see also eschatology; *qiyāma*
soul, *see al-nafs*
South Asia, 265, 267, 270, 274
Spain, 145
Spiritual Beings, *see rūḥāniyya*
Stern, Samuel M., 1, 77, 78, 97, 108, 110, 146, 203n.32
Strothmann, Rudolf, 129
Sufis, Sufism, 7, 86, 146, 269, 273, 274, 281, 287, 288, 291
see also Ni'mat Allāhī; Nūrbakhshī; Qādirī; *pīr*; *murshid*
Sulaym, Banū, 34
Sulaymānīs, branch of Ṭayyibīs, 5
Sultan Muḥammad Khwārazmshāh, *see* 'Alā' al-Dīn Muḥammad, Khwārazmshāh
Sulṭān Muḥammad Shāh, Aga Khan III, see Aga Khan III
Sulṭān Shāh b. Īl Arslān, 225
Sulṭāniyya, in Persia, 251
sunna, (custom), 93, 95, 124–30 *passim*
Sunnis, Sunnism, 2, 6, 8, 10, 13, 42, 51, 75, 106–12 *passim*, 119, 123, 125, 128, 130, 132, 146, 154, 195, 209, 222, 223, 224, 235
Sūrdās, poet-saint, 270, 272
Ṣurkhāb al-Ṭabarī, 172
Surt, 30
surūr (joy), 85
Syria, 5–9 *passim*, 16, 24, 25, 34–9 *passim*, 40, 43, 49, 75, 82, 83, 97, 98, 109, 186, 195–8 *passim*, 206, 217, 222, 247, 248, 249, 258

al-Ṭabarī, Abū Ja'far Muḥammad b. Jarīr, historian, 24, 25, 26–7, 55n.22
Ṭabas, in Quhistān (southern Khurāsān), 190, 208, 215, 222, 223, 224, 226
Ṭabas Masīnān, *see* Ṭabas
Tabrīz, in Ādharbāyjān, 249, 250, 251, 253, 284
ṭahāra (ritual purity), 123, 127, 131
Tahdhīb al-akhlāq, of Miskawayh, see *Kitāb al-ṭahāra*
Ṭāhirids, 223
Ṭahmāsp I, Ṣafawid shāh, 290, 291
Tāj al-Dīn II, Abu 'l-Faḍl Naṣr, Naṣrid *malik*, 224
Tāj al-Dīn III, Ḥarb b. 'Izz al-Mulūk Muḥammad, Naṣrid *malik*, 225
Tāj al-Dīn Inaltegin Khwārazmī, 226–7
Tāj al-Dīn Nuṣrat b. Yamīn al-Dīn Bahrām Shāh, Naṣrid *malik*, 226
ṭalāq (divorce), 96, 117, 119
al-tālī (the following one), 77
see also al-nafs
ta'līm (authoritative teaching), 6, 186, 197–8
Ta'līmiyya, 197
see also Bāṭinīs; Nizārīs
Ṭāliqān, in Persia, 23
al-Tamīmī, Yemenite poet, 76–7
Tāmir, 'Ārif, 162
Tanbīh al-hādī wa', l-mustahdī, of Ḥamīd al-Dīn al-Kirmānī, 161
al-Tanūkhī, Abū 'Alī al-Muḥassin, 45, 68n.237
tarāwīḥ, 106, 117
Ta'rīkh-i alfī, anonymous history, 290
Ta'rīkh-i Sīstān, anonymous history of Sīstān, 223, 224, 227
ṭarīqa, 7
taṣawwuf, *see* Sufis, Sufism
Tatawī, Aḥmad b. Naṣr Allāh, historian, 290
Tate, G.P., 226
tawḥīd (unity of God), 94, 158, 173
al-Tawḥīdī, Abū Ḥayyān, *see* Abū Ḥayyān al-Tawḥīdī
ta'wīl (esoteric interpretation), 3, 6, 25, 76, 107, 164
Ta'wīl al-da'ā'im, of al-Qāḍī al-Nu'mān, 110
al-Tawrāt, 96
Ṭayyibīs, Ṭayyibiyya, branch of Musta'lians, 4, 5, 75, 129, 131, 132, 146, 162
see also Musta'lians; Dā'ūdīs; Sulaymānīs
Tehran, 12
temporary marriage, *see mut'a*
Temürtash b. Chūpān, governor of Rūm, 256, 258
Thābit b. Sinān, historian, 37, 41, 42, 52, 68n.244
theology, *see kalām*
Tibawi, A.L., 146
Tīmūr (Temür), founder of the Tīmūrid dynasty, 233
Tīmūrids, of Persia and Transoxania, 221, 222, 233, 283, 285, 290, 294
Toghril I, Saljuq sultan, 184, 187
Torah, *see* al-Tawrāt
Transoxania (Mā warā' al-Nahr), 4, 88, 183, 223, 231
see also Central Asia